THE
WHOLESALE-
BY-MAIL
CATALOG®
1996

THE WHOLESALE-BY-MAIL Catalog® 1996

BY THE PRINT PROJECT

Lowell Miller, Executive Producer
Prudence McCullough, Executive Editor

HarperPerennial
A Division of HarperCollinsPublishers

THE WHOLESALE-BY-MAIL CATALOG® 1996. Copyright © 1995 by Lowell Miller and Prudence McCullough. All rights reserved. Printed in the United States of America. No part of this book may be used or reproduced in any manner whatsoever without written permission except in the case of brief quotations embodied in critical articles and reviews. For information address Harper-Collins Publishers, Inc., 10 East 53rd Street, New York, NY 10022.

HarperCollins books may be purchased for educational, business, or sales promotional use. For information please write to: Special Markets Department, HarperCollins Publishers, Inc., 10 East 53rd Street, New York, NY 10022.

FIRST HARPERPERENNIAL EDITION

ISSN 1049-0116
ISBN 0-06-273311-7

95 96 97 ◆/RRD 5 4 3 2 1

CONTENTS

INTRODUCTION

Welcome to *The Wholesale-by-Mail Catalog® 1996*, in its 18th year as the most popular guide to mail-order values. In this book, "wholesale" denotes the savings required as one of the qualifications for a listing—30% or more on list or comparable retail on some of a firm's products or services. While WBMC isn't a directory of wholesalers, some of the firms will sell to crafters, small businesses, and others on a wholesale basis. Those firms are denoted with a symbol in the icon line in their listings. For details, see "Buying at Wholesale," page 588.

There are other icons that will help you get the most from the information, so before sending for a catalog or placing an order, please read the key to the symbols in "The Listing Code" (from p. xi). For more detailed information on mail-order shopping, see "The Complete Guide to Buying by Mail," beginning on page 583.

Enjoy *The Wholesale-by-Mail Catalog® 1996*, and please report on your experiences with these firms—see "Feedback," page 619, for address information.

Prudence McCullough, Executive Editor

USING THIS BOOK

The *Wholesale-by-Mail Catalog® 1996* is written to help consumers get good values when buying by mail—or phone, fax, or modem. Following is a guide to several of this book's features that will help you make the best use of the material.

"FIND IT FAST"

This list, right after the introduction and before the listings (in most of the chapters), is an at-a-glance guide to different types of products offered by firms listed in that section. For example, if you're looking for companies selling contact lenses and eyeglasses, check the "Find It Fast" roster in the "Medicine" chapter instead of reading through all of the listings. "Find It Fast" supplements the Product Index and the "See Also" section (see below) at the end of each chapter.

"SEE ALSO"

Each firm is listed in the chapter that best reflects its business focus, and *cross-referenced* in the "See Also" sections at the end of other chapters, as appropriate. For example, Gohn Bros. is listed in the "Clothing" chapter, because that's its strong suit. Because Gohn also sells horse blankets, you'll find it cited in the "See Also" section at the end of the "Animal Supplies" chapter. See "Find It Fast," above, for another aid to locating what you need.

PATIENCE

Since companies are constantly revising their catalogs and printing new ones, please allow *six to eight weeks* for delivery, unless the listing indicates potential for a longer delay. If the catalog doesn't arrive within the designated period, write or call the company. Please remember that some products, such as flower bulbs and highly perishable foods, can be ordered only at certain times of the year, and catalogs may be mailed during shipping season only.

PRICE QUOTES

Some firms don't issue catalogs at all. Most of these operate under a price-quote system: You tell them the exact make and model number of the item you want, and they give you the price and shipping cost. Price quotes are given by mail, phone, and fax. Businesses that operate this way are clearly indicated in the listings. (Be sure to check the "Special Factors" notes at the end of each listing as well as the core information.) Price-quote firms often have the lowest prices on such goods as appliances, audio and TV components, and furniture; they usually sell well below both the standard manufacturers' suggested list prices and the less-formal minimum prices that some manufacturers try to enforce. Before writing or calling for a price quote or making a purchase in this way, remember to read the "Price Quotes" section of "The Complete Guide to Buying by Mail."

MINIMUM ORDERS

In a few cases, the best buys are available from firms that require a minimum order in dollars or goods. Minimum requirements are usually flexible, and most firms will accept orders below the minimum, although an extra "handling fee" is often imposed. If you want something that's a real bargain, you may have friends who'll want it as well.

BEFORE SENDING MONEY

If you're unsure of any company, or want to double-check a firm before placing a large order, contact the Better Business Bureau nearest the company. You can locate it by phone, through directory assistance (the firm's area code-555-1212), or by looking it up in the current list of member Bureaus, available free by sending a stamped, self-addressed envelope to Council of Better Business Bureaus, 4200 Wilson Blvd., Suite 800, Arlington, VA 22203. If you call, you may be given a report over the phone, or you may be asked to write instead.

A CAVEAT

The Wholesale-by-Mail Catalog® 1996 is compiled as a resource for consumers, to help you to find good values available by mail. Never order goods directly from this book, even if prices are given in the listing. Always contact the company first to get a catalog or a current price quote, and follow specific ordering and payment instructions. *Don't request extra discounts or wholesale prices, unless the listing states they are available. Attempting to bargain with these firms makes the vendors quite unhappy.* All of the information in this book is based on research and fact-checking as of press time, and is subject to change.

THE LISTING CODE

Some of the information in the listings is presented in a simple coded form at the head of each entry, formatted as follows:

1. Company name, mailing address, and phone numbers, including 800, fax, e-mail, and TDD lines
2. Literature form (catalog, brochure, flyer, leaflet, price list, etc.); the price, followed by "refundable" or "deductible" if you can redeem the price by placing an order; *SASE:* send a long (business-sized), self-addressed envelope with a first-class stamp (unless more postage is requested); "Information": price quote or information is given over the phone and/or by letter (when there is no catalog)
3. **Save:** the percentage of savings possible on the "suggested list" or "comparable retail" prices of the goods and/or services. The percentage is often an average and usually applies to some, but not all, goods. *Don't deduct this percentage from the order total* unless so instructed in the listing text
4. **Pay:** methods of payment accepted for orders (catalog fees should be paid by check or money order unless the listing states otherwise), listed in order of frequency accepted:

    - check: personal check
    - MO: bank or postal money order
    - MC: MasterCard credit card
    - V: VISA credit card
    - AE: American Express credit card
    - DC: Diners Club credit card
    - Discover: Discover credit card

5. **Sells:** general type of goods sold
6. **Store:** location(s), hours, and/or phone number(s) of the firm's retail site or other outlets, if applicable

THE MAPLE LEAF

This symbol means the firm will ship goods to Canada. Canadian shoppers should check current import restrictions and tariffs before placing an order, and request shipping charges or an estimate before finalizing the order. *Please note:* U.S. firms generally request payment for goods and catalogs in U.S. funds.

🏳 THE FLAG

A small "Old Glory" on the symbol line means the firm will ship goods to APO and FPO (U.S. military) addresses. For more information, see "Shipments Abroad," page 600.

⊕ THE WORLD

A small globe on the symbol line means the firm will ship goods worldwide (this was previously noted in the "Special Factors" section of each listing). Readers ordering from or having goods delivered abroad should read the listing before sending for a catalog; check with local authorities to make sure products can be imported, what restrictions may apply, and what tariffs may be charged. For more information, see "Shipments Abroad," page 600.

¡Si! SPANISH SPOKEN HERE

This icon means that the firm has Spanish-speaking sales representatives on staff. Before calling a company so indicated, read the listing and the "Special Factors" notes, since the person's availability may be limited to certain hours or days.

🖥 THE TERMINAL SYMBOL

A computer on the icon line means the firm is online with America Online, CompuServe, Delphi, GEnie, Prodigy, or another computer-based service. See the "Special Factors" section of the listing for the name of the service; subscription kits are sold at a discount by some of the firms listed in "Office: Computing," page 493.

𝒞 THE TDD SYMBOL

This symbol indicates that the firm can communicate with a TDD (telecommunication device for the deaf). In most cases, the firm uses a separate phone line for the equipment; sometimes, it's combined with a fax line. Read the listing, and if a separate phone line or other information isn't noted, send for the catalog.

★ THE "WHOLESALE" STAR

Firms so marked will sell at wholesale rates to *qualified individuals or other firms.* To sell to you at genuine wholesale, most firms require proof that you're running a company—a business card, letterhead, resale number, or all three—and may impose different minimum orders and sell under terms different from those that apply to retail purchases. Please note that, unless specified, all information in these listings applies to consumer transactions only. For more information, see "Buying at Wholesale," page 588.

✓ SPECIAL TO READERS OF THIS BOOK

If a check mark appears in the icon line, the firm is giving a special discount or offer to readers of *The Wholesale-by-Mail Catalog® 1996.* For more information, see "WBMC Reader Offers," page 588.

THE COMPLETE GUIDE TO BUYING BY MAIL

This primer on mail-order shopping, which begins on page 583, can help you with questions on everything from sending for catalogs to interpreting warranties. If a problem arises with a mail-order transaction, look here for help in resolving it. You'll find additional consumer information in the chapter introductions.

THE WHOLESALE-BY-MAIL CATALOG® 1996

ANIMAL SUPPLIES

Livestock and pet supplies and equipment,

veterinary instruments and biologicals,

live-animal referrals, and services

It's now accepted as fact that owning an animal, particularly a cat or a dog, has therapeutic benefits for people suffering from a range of maladies. Pets are supposed to help prolong life, lower high blood pressure and cholesterol, and reduce incidence of backaches, headaches, and colds. In fact, pets are now widely used in programs for nursing-home patients, hospitalized children, and psychiatric patients. All this, and companionship, too!

If you're thinking about getting a pet, make sure you're picking the best companion for your needs and lifestyle. "The Veterinarian's Way of Selecting a Proper Pet" asks a series of questions that will help you to define your criteria for the ideal animal. The brochure is available on request; send a long, stamped, self-addressed envelope with your request to the American Veterinary Medical Association, Suite 100, 1931 N. Meacham Rd., Schaumburg, IL 60173-4360. Once you've decided on the kind of animal you want, don't rush to the pet store: Seek out pet shelters and orphanages, where you can save an animal from a questionable fate *and* save money. Even purebreds can be acquired inexpensively, when a "purebred rescue" group takes in an animal no longer wanted by its owner and holds it for adoption. If your local animal shelter doesn't have information on groups that perform this service, write to Project Breed Inc., 18707 Curry Powder Lane, Germantown, MD 20874; include a long, stamped, self-addressed envelope. If the dog of your dreams happens to be a greyhound, you may be able to adopt a former racetrack star. For information on the greyhound rescue group nearest you, write to the National Greyhound Adoption Network, c/o Palo Alto Humane Society, P.O. Box 60715, Palo Alto, CA 94306.

Most of us are unaware of the long-term price of ownership: The average cat will cost its owner an estimated $8,600 over its lifetime; the average dog, over $11,500. Pet products make up a $15 billion business that serves the 53 million homes in this country that harbor some kind of animal. Fortunately, there's now an alternative to buying pet needs from the grocery store, pet boutique, or from the vet—superstores. Modeled on the successful office and home-improvement models, they offer varying savings on food, grooming products, cages, supplies, and a wide range of pet needs. Petco, Petstuff, and Petsmart are the major contenders, and if there's one near you, check the prices on food and litter against the discounts a local pet store may give on case purchases, and see if they'll deliver. The companies listed here won't give you great deals on heavy cans of food and bags of litter—the costs of shipping will usually offset the savings. But check the prices of collars and leashes, cages and carriers, feeding dishes and devices, grooming tools, beds, and medications. These firms carry products for a wide range of animals—from hamsters and ferrets to horses and barnyard animals— and all can save you money.

Mastering the basics of pet care can save you considerable sums in a variety of ways—in salon costs, the price of obedience school, and sometimes even on vet fees. The brochures "Caring for Your Dog" and "Caring for Your Cat," from The Humane Society, deal with pet health, feeding, grooming, and selecting pets. The organization also publishes a booklet on spaying and neutering animals. Request the "Cat Care" or "Dog Care" brochures ($1 each) or "Just One Litter" ($3.25) from The Humane Society of the United States, 2100 L St. NW, Washington, DC 20037. There's no lack of books and magazines on the topic: *The Common Sense Book of Kitten and Cat Care* and *The Common Sense Book of Puppy and Dog Care* (Bantam Books), by Harry Miller, are excellent reference works. The advice of the late Barbara Woodhouse is especially valuable to owners of uncooperative canines, and can be found in *Encyclopedia of Dogs and Puppies* and *Dog Training My Way* (Berkley Books), as well as *No Bad Dogs* (Summit Books, 1982). *Teach Your Dog to Behave: Simple Solutions to Over 300 Common Dog Behavior Problems from A to Z*, by Bashkim Dibra (E.P. Dutton), adds more to the literature on canine discipline. Also helpful is *101 Questions Your Cat Would Ask Its Vet if Your Cat Could Talk*, by a British vet, Dr. Bruce Fogle (Carroll & Graf Publishers). And to prepare for their twilight years, see *Caring for Older Cats and Dogs*, by Dr. Robert Anderson (Williamson Publishing, 800-234-8791). There are scores of guides to the care of fish, birds, reptiles, and more exotic creatures; the Simon &

Schuster Guides (Fireside), on cats, fish, dogs, birds, horses, and other animals, are especially helpful and easy to use. Consult your local library or bookstore for available titles. And the Massachusetts Society for the Prevention of Cruelty to Animals (MSPCA) publishes *Animals,* a terrific magazine that features articles on both household pets and wildlife. Proceeds from the magazine benefit the MSPCA's human-education work, and the organization is offering WBMC a year's subscription (six issues) for $14.98, a 25% savings on the regular rate of $19.94. Send payment, or write for a free sample copy, to *Animals* Magazine, Dept. W, 350 S. Huntington Ave., Boston, MA 02130.

If you're among the owners of this country's 50 million pet birds, tell your vet about the Avian Referral Service, which helps vets get advice on bird problems. Your vet should write to AAHA, Avian Referral Service, P.O. Box 15899, Denver, CO 80215, for more information.

Several of the firms listed in this chapter retain veterinarians who can answer questions on products and use, but they're not allowed to give specific medical advice. If your pet is ailing, consult a vet, and *always* seek professional guidance if you plan to administer any vaccines or medications to your animal yourself. There are other ways to safeguard your pet's well-being: Keep the number of a local 24-hour service that handles medical emergencies posted near the phone, and become familiar with symptoms and the first-aid measures you may have to take in order to transport the animal to the clinic.

FIND IT FAST

FISH • **Aquatic Supply, Daleco, Jeffers, Mail Order Pet Shop, Pet Warehouse, That Fish Place**

HORSES • **Dairy Association, Discount Master Animal, Jeffers, Kennel Vet, State Line Tack, UPCO**

LIVESTOCK • **Dairy Association, Jeffers, Kansas City, Omaha Vaccine**

PETS (DOGS AND CATS) • **Discount Master Animal, Drs. Foster & Smith, Dog's Outfitter, Jeffers Vet, Kennel Vet, Mail Order Pet Shop, Pet Warehouse, R.C. Steele**

TRAPS • **Tomahawk Live Trap**

VET, KENNEL, AND GROOMER • **Discount Master Animal, Drs. Foster & Smith, Dog's Outfitter, J-B Wholesale, Kennel Vet, Omaha Vaccine, R.C. Steele, UPCO, Wholesale Veterinary**

AQUATIC SUPPLY HOUSE

42 HAYES ST.
ELMSFORD, NY 10523
800-777-7387
914-592-3620
FAX: 914-592-8658

Catalog: $2.50
Save: up to 40%
Pay: check, MO, MC, V, AE, Discover
Sells: freshwater and saltwater fish supplies
Store: same address; Monday, Tuesday, Saturday 10–6, Wednesday, Thursday, Friday 10–7, Sunday 11–5; also Wappinger Falls, NY

Aquatic Supply House, established in 1975, specializes in products for tropical and saltwater fish. The catalog features a complete line of aquarium supplies and equipment, including air pumps, filters, water pumps, heaters, pond equipment, lighting, tank novelties, chemicals, plants, and fish food and medication. The manufacturers represented here include Aquanetics, Aquarium Pharmaceuticals, Aquarium Products, Coralife Products, Eheim, Hagen, Jungle, Mardell, Marineland, Penn-Plax, Perfecto, Sea Chem, Second Nature, Tetra (including Tetra Press books), Vortex, and Wardley, among others. Prices run up to 50% off list, and the catalog has a "tropical fish problem solver chart," with advice on troubleshooting fish difficulties.

Special Factors: Authorized returns are accepted (a 15% restocking fee is charged) within 30 days for exchange, refund, or credit; minimum order is $20 with credit cards.

DAIRY ASSOCIATION CO., INC.

DEPT. WBMC
P.O. BOX 145
LYNDONVILLE, VT
  05851-0145
802-626-3610
FAX: 802-626-3433

Brochure and Price List: free
Save: up to 35%
Pay: check or MO
Sells: livestock treatments and leather balm
Store: mail order only

Generations of herd farmers know Dairy Association Co., Inc., for its Bag Balm ointment. This unguent, formulated to soothe the chapped, sunburned udders of cows, is also recommended by horse trainers for cracked heels, galls, cuts, hobble burns, and other ailments—and is "great as a sweat" as well. Bag Balm can be used on sheep, goats, dogs, and cats, and is touted as a softener for weather-beaten, chapped hands. A ten-ounce can costs $5.15 here; a 4-1/2-pound pail costs $34.90. (The one-ounce size, great for travel, is $3.50.) Green Mt. Horse Products, a division of Dairy Association, produces Hoof Softener—made of petrolatum, lanolin, and vegetable oils, it helps keep hoofs pliable and sound ($5.50 per pint). And Tackmaster—a one-step, all-around conditioner, cleaner, and preservative for leather—is cheaper than similar products at $2.45 for four ounces.

Dairy Association has been in business since 1899, and provides product literature free on request.

Canadian readers, please note: Contact Dr. A.D. Daniels Co. Ltd., N. Rock Island, Quebec, for prices and ordering information.

Special Factors: Phone orders are accepted for C.O.D. payment.

DALECO MASTER BREEDER PRODUCTS

3556 N. 400 EAST
WARSAW, IN 46580-7999
800-987-1120
FAX: 219-269-6302

Catalog: $6, refundable (see text)
Save: up to 40%
Pay: check, MO, MC, V
Sells: tropical fish supplies and aquarium specialties
Store: mail order only

Daleco, in business since 1966, publishes the "Aquarists Supply Manual," a catalog/reference book that's packed with information useful to owners of fresh- and saltwater fish. The catalog costs $6, but $4 of the price is refundable with a $50 order. Daleco discounts tank filters, aquarium heaters, lights, tank stands, air and water pumps, foods, water test kits, UV water sterilizers, water conditioners, reef trickle filter systems, and related goods. The brands include Aquanetics, Aquarium Products, Aquarium Systems, Eugene Danner, Dupla, Ebo-Jager, Energy Savers, Hagen, Hawaiian Marine, Hikari, Jungle Laboratories, Kordon, Little Giant, Lustar, Mardel, Marineland, Perfecto, Sanders, Sandpoint, Tetra, Vortex, and WISA. The catalog is geared to serious hobbyists and breeders, who should find the catalog's "Fish Problem Solver" and "Fish Disease" charts helpful; savings run up to 40%.

Canadian readers, please note: the Manual costs $6 (in U.S. funds) via surface mail, $9 via airmail.

Special Factors: Shipping included on orders over $30 sent in the contiguous United States; C.O.D. orders are accepted; authorized returns are accepted.

DISCOUNT MASTER ANIMAL CARE

P.O. BOX 3333
MOUNTAINTOP, PA
18707-0333
800-346-0749
FAX: 717-384-2550

Catalog: free
Save: up to 50%
Pay: check, MO, MC, V, Discover
Sells: dog and cat supplies and biologicals
Store: Humboldt Outlet, I Maplewood Dr., Hazleton, PA; Tuesday to Saturday, 10–4:30

 ¡Si!

Discount Master Animal Care specializes in dog and cat health supplies, sold at highly competitive prices through the 104-page catalog, which includes helpful information on health care and vaccinating procedures, and includes products for both cats and dogs. You'll find grooming tools, a range of cages, feeding devices, training aids, leashes and leads, and related goods here, at prices up to 50% below list. Vet supplies—such as vaccines, biologicals, and medications—are also available. Discount Master Animal Care offers the latest innovations in pet products, such as airline-approved cages in designer colors, timer-operated feeding dishes that keep two meals fresh, natural and biodegradable cleaners and disinfectants, pet car seats and harnesses, and hot-oil skin treatments for dogs and cats. But it's also a good place to save on pet beds and cartons of rawhide bones—and pet-theme gifts and crafts kits.

Special Factors: Satisfaction is guaranteed; returns are accepted for exchange, refund, or credit.

DRS. FOSTER & SMITH INC.

2253 AIR PARK RD.
P.O. BOX 100
RHINELANDER, WI
54501-0100
800-323-4208
FAX: 715-369-2821

Catalog: free
Save: up to 30%
Pay: check, MO, MC, V, AE, Discover
Sells: dog, cat, and horse supplies
Store: mail order only

As "The Company Owned and Operated by Practicing Veterinarians," Doctors Foster & Smith (the actual people) provide owners of cats, dogs, and horses quality products for health, nutrition, and fun.

The 132-page color catalog shows beds and mats, cat perches and scratching posts, nutritional supplements and biologicals, grooming tools and products, lots of toys and rawhide bones and treats, leashes and collars (including a "no-pull humane anti-tug system" that won't choke your dog, and a cat muzzle), feeding dishes, cages and carriers, and much more. The catalog is clearly written, with complete product descriptions and helpful sidebars on topics of interest (the role of ash in the diet, heat strokes, how the doctors selected their rawhide bones, how to measure pets for collars, traveling with your pet, etc.). Doctors Foster & Smith also sells books, videos, and training audiotapes, and if that's not enough, on Thursdays you can speak to a staff vet on general pet issues and health care. The special vet hotline number is in the current issue of the catalog.

Special Factors: Satisfaction is guaranteed; returns are accepted.

THE DOG'S OUTFITTER

DEPT. 30
P.O. BOX 2010
HAZLETON, PA 18201
800-367-3647
717-384-5555
FAX: 717-384-2550

Catalog: $5, refundable
Save: up to 50%
Pay: check, MO, MC, V, AE, Discover
Sells: vet, kennel, groomer, and pet supplies
Store: Humboldt Outlet, 1 Maplewood Dr., Hazleton, PA; Tuesday to Saturday, 10–4:30

  ¡Si!

Although The Dog's Outfitter catalog is geared to professionals, it has one of the best selections of products for pet owners around. The firm has been in business since 1969, and is exclusive in name only—the 104-page catalog is full of things for cats, and there's even a section devoted to the needs of ferrets. The Dog's Outfitter offers a full range of pet products, including grooming tools, shampoo, flea and tick collars and insecticides, cages, gates and doors, training aids, feeding and watering equipment, nutritional supplements, collars and leads, pet beds, carriers, toys and bones, and even books and gifts. The brands include Andis, Bio-Groom, 8-1, Farnum, General Cage, Gimborn, Hava-hart, Lambert Kay, Oster, Penn Plex, Resco, Ring 5, Speedy, André Tis-scrand (shears), Twinco, and Zodiac.

There are a number of items pet owners might appreciate: molting combs for dogs and cats, no-tears pet shampoo, herbal flea collars, pet doors to fit screen doors, a variety of yard scoops, all types of feeding bowls and crocks, "small animal" nurser kits, reflective collars and leads, dog parkas, bulk rawhide bones, and toys in boxes of 50. There are gifts, pet jewelry (for owners), note cards, and books (Arco, Howell, T.F.H.); grooming videos from Oster, and Animal Academy training tapes. The Dog's Outfitter has its own warehouse and does not drop ship, paying for shipping on most items.

Canadian readers, please note: Shipments are not made to Canada.

Special Factors: Satisfaction is guaranteed; shipping is not charged on most items; authorized returns of new and unused goods are accepted within ten days for exchange, refund, or credit; minimum order is $50; C.O.D. orders are accepted.

J-B WHOLESALE PET SUPPLIES, INC.

5 RARITAN RD., DEPT. WB
OAKLAND, NJ 07436
201-405-1111
FAX: 201-405-1706

Catalog: free
Save: up to 50%
Pay: check, MO, MC, V, AE, Discover
Sells: vet, kennel, and pet supplies
Store: 289 Wagaraw Rd., Hawthorne, NJ;
Monday to Wednesday 9–6, Thursday and
Friday 9–8, Saturday 10–5, Sunday 11–4

J-B Wholesale Pet Supplies, in business since 1981, stocks "over 8,500 different items for showing, grooming, training, breeding," and other animal-related functions. J-B is staffed by professional animal handlers who've kennel-tested all of the products the company sells.

The 88-page catalog features a wide range of goods for cats and dogs, with the emphasis on canines: vaccines, remedies for common health problems, vitamins and nutritional supplements, repellents and deodorizers, shampoos and grooming products, beds and mats, flea and tick control products, cages, kennels, pet doors, grooming tables and dryers, leashes and leads, feeding devices, rawhide bones, and rubber toys. Every major manufacturer is represented, and J-B's own line of grooming aids—shampoo and coat conditioners and tints—is also featured. Send for the catalog, or call for prices and availability on specific name-brand items.

Special Factors: Satisfaction is guaranteed; C.O.D. orders are accepted; returns are accepted within seven days for exchange, refund, or credit; minimum order is $25.

JEFFERS VET SUPPLY

P.O. BOX 100
DOTHAN, AL 36302-0100
800-JEFFERS
FAX: 334-793-5179

Catalog: free
Save: up to 50%
Pay: check, MO, MC, V, Discover
Sells: animal health supplies
Store: 353 West Inez Rd., Dothan, AL; also
Old Airport Rd., West Plains, MO; every day
6 A.M.–10 P.M., both locations

   ¡Si!

Jeffers Vet Supply, in business since 1976, publishes a 160-page quarterly catalog of supplies for livestock farmers and anyone who keeps a horse, as well as goods for cats, dogs, fish, and even rabbits, iguanas, and ferrets. Livestock farmers who raise cattle (including dairy), swine, sheep, goats, and poultry should see the catalog for antibiotics and sulfa drugs, biologicals, wormers, milking equipment, incubators, and other necessities. A large part of the catalog is devoted to equine supplies—biologicals and nutritional supplements, wormers, grooming tools and products, farrier supplies, stable equipment, and tack—including several pages of saddles. Equine videotapes by Al Dunning and John Lyons are also available. The line of goods for dogs and cats is also extensive—everything from the newest flea and tick products to collars, cages, clippers, toys, and grooming and feeding supplies are available.

Special Factors: Satisfaction is guaranteed; quantity discounts are available; returns are accepted for exchange, refund, or credit; C.O.D. orders are accepted.

KENNEL VET CORP.

DEPT. WBMC
P.O. BOX 835
BELLMORE, NY
  11710-0835
800-782-0627 (CT, NJ, NY,
  PA)
516-783-5400
FAX: 516-783-7516

Catalog: $1 (see text)
Save: up to 70%
Pay: check, MO, MC, V, AE, Discover
Sells: vet, kennel, cattery, and pet supplies
Store: 1811 Newbridge Rd., Bellmore, NY;
Monday to Friday 9–6, Saturday 10–4

If you own or raise dogs or cats, you'll find Kennel Vet's compact, 80-page catalog great reading. This firm is price-competitive on products for horses, as well as house pets, and has been in business since 1971.

Kennel Vet offers vaccines and biologicals, remedies for common health problems, vitamins and nutritional supplements, repellents and deodorizers, and other professional products. Kennel Vet also sells droppings composters, shampoos and grooming products, flea and tick control products, cages/crates, pet doors, dog and cat beds, grooming tables, dryers, leashes, leads, feeding devices, rawhide bones and rubber toys, and other goods. The brands represented include Adams, Classic, Doskocil (carriers), Eight-in-One, Gem-Line, Holiday, Johnson, Lambert Kay, Lawrence (brushes), Mid-West, Mycodex, Natra-Pet, Norden, Oster, Pervival, Pet Tabs, Redi, Rich Health, Ring 5, Sulfodene, 3M,

Vet-Kem, and others. Kennel Vet also sells Eukanuba, Iams, and Science Diet pet food by mail, as well as in the store. The book department includes veterinary manuals, books on dog breeds, and a selection on cats, birds, and horses—all at a discount.

Kennel Vet is offering readers a $2 discount on orders from the first catalog they receive. Identify yourself as a WBMC reader when you send for the catalog, and deduct the discount from the cost of the applicable goods only. This WBMC reader discount expires February 1, 1997.

Special Factors: Authorized returns are accepted; shipping is not charged on orders of $75 or more (with some exceptions—see the catalog); vaccines and biologicals are sent where ordinances permit.

MAIL ORDER PET SHOP

1338 NORTH MARKET
 BLVD.
SACRAMENTO, CA 95834
800-3266-6677
916-928-0215

Catalog: free
Save: up to 30%
Pay: check, MO, MC, V, AE, Discover
Sells: fish and pet supplies
Store: mail order only
E-mail: AOL: mopet shop @aol.com

Mail Order Pet Shop has been in business for over 17 years, serving the needs of pet owners coast to coast. Two-thirds of the 94-page catalog is devoted to fish—aquarium equipment, foods, medications, coral, plants, water conditioners, and many other goods are available, as well as products for ponds. The brands include Coralife Products, Eheim, Hagen, Jungle, Mardell, Marineland, Penn-Plax, Perfecto, Sea Chem, Tetra (including Tetra Press books), T.F.H., and Wardley, among others. The "dog and cat" section includes beds and cushions, collars and leashes, feeding dishes, grooming tools and supplies, nutritional supplements, carriers, dog houses, toys, bones, and books. Mail Order Pet Shop also publishes a separate "bird and reptile" catalog for birds, reptiles, hamsters, ferrets, rabbits, and other small animals. Prices run up to 30% below pet-shop rates, and Mail Order Pet Shop has shipping facilities in New York and California, to get your order to you as fast as possible.

Special Factors: Satisfaction is guaranteed; authorized, resalable returns are accepted within 10 days for exchange, refund, or credit; online with America Online.

OMAHA VACCINE COMPANY, INC.

3030 L ST.
OMAHA, NE 68107
800-367-4444
402-731-9600
FAX: 402-731-9829

Catalog: free
Save: up to 50%
Pay: check, MO, MC, V, Discover
Sells: dog, cat, bird, horse, and livestock supplies
Store: same address; Monday to Friday 7–7, Saturday 8–5, Sunday 11–5

Omaha Vaccine Company's 284-page "Master Catalog," published yearly, offers products for livestock, horses, and household pets. Established in 1965, Omaha Vaccine does much of its business with livestock producers, breeders, and veterinarians, but has branched into the consumer market. The Master Catalog features vaccines and biologicals, medications, surgical instruments, grooming tools, wormers, nutritional supplements, flea and tick products cages and carriers, leads and collars, bird products, and horse tack, among other goods. Omaha also publishes three specialty catalogs: "Best Care," for owners of dogs and cats, "Professional Producer," for livestock care; and "First Place," for horse and rider. The last should be useful to the noncommercial owner, since it offers a comprehensive selection of tack, saddles, vet manuals, and other supplies. Whether you're looking for flea treatments for your dog or opening a llama farm, you'll appreciate Omaha's 20,000 products and wholesale pricing.

Omaha Vaccine Company is offering readers who are first-time purchasers free shipping on their first order if it's under $50, or $5 off orders over $65. Be sure to identify yourself as a WBMC reader when you order. This WBMC reader discount expires February 1, 1997.

Special Factors: Some pharmaceutical products are available by prescription only (shipment is subject to local ordinances); C.O.D. orders are accepted.

PET WAREHOUSE

DEPT. BMC
P.O. BOX 310
XENIA, OH 45385
800-443-1160
FAX: 513-374-2524

Catalogs: free (see text)
Save: up to 60%
Pay: check, MO, MC, V, AE, Discover
Sells: pet supplies
Store: mail order only

The color catalogs from Pet Warehouse are among the best around for the typical pet owner, who probably doesn't need a wall-sized aquarium, but wants good prices on basics and neat pet stuff. The firm has been in business since 1986, selling supplies for cats, dogs, birds, and fish, and even goodies for "small animals"—hamsters, gerbils, and mice—as well as rabbits and reptiles. The inventory has been split into two catalogs—one for fish and reptiles (or the "aquatic and herpetological enthusiast"), and the second for dogs, cats, birds, and small animals; please specify which you want.

Whether you have a freshwater or marine aquarium, or even a pond, Pet Warehouse can supply you with filters, air pumps, heaters, feeders, lighting, maintenance equipment and water conditioners, tank decorations and plants, fish medication, food, and other fish goods—but no tanks. The brands include Aquarium Pharmaceuticals, Eheim, Hagen, Marineland, Perfecto, Rainbow Lifeguard, and Tetra, among others. Bird owners can choose from Hagen and Prevue Hendryx cages, Acrobird perches and play structures, cage accessories and bird toys, nests, feeders, bird food from Fiesta, Kaytee, and other firms, and dietary supplements and medication. For dogs and cats, there are beds, collars and leashes, Regal kibbles, feeding devices, grooming supplies and implements, flea and tick repellents, nutritional supplements, cages and carriers, pet doors, litter boxes and scoopers, and toys. And there are rabbit hutches, supplies for reptiles (from supplements to habitats), small animals, and even hermit crabs. If you want to read up on pet care or breeds, Pet Warehouse can provide Barrons and T.F.H. titles on a wide range of topics.

Special Factors: Specify catalog (aquatic or cats and dogs); online with CompuServe.

STATE LINE TACK, INC.

RTE. 125, DEPT. HS013
P.O. BOX 1217
PLAISTOW, NH
03865-0428
800-228-9208
603-382-6008 (STORE)
FAX: 603-382-8471

Catalog: free
Save: up to 40%
Pay: check, MO, MC, V, Discover
Sells: saddles and tack, grooming supplies,
medicine, apparel, etc.
Store: Rte. 121, Plaistow, NH; Monday to
Saturday 9–6, Thursday and Friday 9–9, Sunday 10–6

¡Si!

State Line Tack covers the needs of horse and rider with comprehensive catalogs of saddles, tack, stable gear, rider clothing, grooming and medical tools and preparations, and much more. State Line's regular prices are discounted up to 25% routinely, and the coupon catalogs further the savings to 40% plus. State Line publishes a "Western" catalog with clothing and tack for Western riders, a separate catalog for hunt-seat riders, and The National Bridle Shop catalog for saddle seats. When you request the catalog, state your riding preference—pleasure, roping, Western show, cutting, barrel racing, or English.

Special Factors: Satisfaction is guaranteed; returns are accepted.

R.C. STEELE CO.

DEPT. WC
P.O. BOX 910
1989 TRANSIT WAY
BROCKPORT, NY
14420-0910
800-872-3773
FAX: 716-637-8902
TDD: 800-468-8776

Catalog: free
Save: up to 50%
Pay: check, MO, MC, V
Sells: cat, dog, and aquarium supplies
Store: 1989 Transit Way, Brockport, NY;
Monday to Friday 9–8:30, Saturday 9–6, Sunday 11–6

R.C. Steele Co. was founded in 1959 and is the wholesale division of Sporting Dog Specialties, well known as a source for products for both companion and hunting dogs. R.C. Steele's prices are excellent—sometimes as much as 50% less than comparable retail—and the only drawback is the $50 minimum order. The 72-page color catalog features products and equipment for canines—cages, pet doors, insecticides, feeding equipment, droppings composters, training dummies and jumps, leashes and leads, grooming supplies and tools, and manuals. There are great buys on rawhide bones, which are sold in case lots at a fraction of full retail, and all types of pet beds, at about half the going rate. The catalog features an extensive list of books and tapes from the American Kennel Club (breed shows), Arco, Denlinger, Doral, Howell, Oster, T.F.H., and Volhard (obedience). There are eight pages of products for cats, and 32 pages of aquarium supplies. Customers receive supplemental price lists with new offerings—books, videos, bird supplies, cages, toys, parts, and accessories.

Special Factors: C.O.D. orders are accepted; authorized returns are accepted; minimum order is $50.

THAT FISH PLACE

237 CENTERVILLE RD.
LANCASTER, PA 17603
800-733-3829
FAX: 800-786-3829

Catalog Supplement: free (see text)
Save: up to 70%
Pay: check, MO, MC, V, AE, Discover
Sells: supplies for aquariums, reptiles, birds, dogs, cats
Store: same address; Monday to Saturday 10–9, Sunday 12–5

That Fish Place, also known as "That Pet Place," has been selling aquarium supplies since 1973, and stocks the works. The 56-page color Fish Catalog Supplement is packed with everything from aquariums and filters to ornaments and plastic plants. The manufacturers represented are well-known—Energy Savers, Mardel, Marineland, Supreme, and Tetra, to name just a few. The catalog supplement also features several pages of items for ponds—filters, fountains, liners, etc.—as well as supplies for invertebrates and reptiles. (You'll receive the supplement on request; place an order, and you'll get the 168-page master fish catalog.) Scores of books on fish species and care are available, and the catalog includes several pages of charts and information that can help you determine what might be ailing your fish or aquarium. The discounts are excellent—up to 50% on list prices—and the quarterly sales brochures will save you even more.

That Fish Place has also launched a 72-page color "Dog & Cat Catalog," with hundreds of supplies for both species—leashes, collars, beds, treats, grooming tools, toys, and more—from Booda, Dogloo, Diskocil, Midwest, and other familiar names. And a catalog devoted to the needs of birds, reptiles, and small animals by 1996.

Please note: Request the "fish" catalog or the "pet" catalog—and be sure to mention WBMC.

Special Factors: Authorized, unused returns are accepted (a 15% restocking fee may be charged); minimum order is $15 for dry goods, $25 for live plants.

TOMAHAWK LIVE TRAP COMPANY

P.O. BOX 323-WBMC
TOMAHAWK, WI 54487
800-27-A-TRAP
715-453-3550
FAX: 715-453-4326

Brochure: free (see text)
Save: up to 50%
Pay: check, MO, MC, V
Sells: humane animal traps
Store: Tomahawk, WI; Monday to Friday 8–5; also Coburn Company, Whitewater, WI; and Plow & Hearth, Orange, VA

Tomahawk's box traps are used by the U.S. Army Medical Corps, state and federal conservation departments, dog wardens, universities, and others who want to catch a critter without endangering its pelt or its life. It's somewhat ironical that the founders of this firm once operated a fur farm, and developed the traps to cope with their own runaways. The success of the traps put an end to the farm, a conclusion that should please animal-rights activists.

Tomahawk, which was established in 1930, makes traps for 58 different animals, from mice (about $13) to large dogs (about $173), as well fish and turtles, birds, beavers, grackles, raccoons, skunks, bobcats, jackrabbits, and cats. There are rigid and collapsible styles, transfer cages, station wagon and carrying cages, several with sliding doors (for shipping animals), and special sizes can be made to order. Tomahawk also sells animal control poles in several sizes, "repeating" (multiple-catch) rodent traps, cat graspers, snake tongs, and leather protection gloves.

If you're familiar with Tomahawk's traps, *send a self-addressed, stamped envelope for the free brochure and price list.* Or you can order the comprehensive, 56-page book, "Trapped the Humane Way"; it includes tips on trapping animals, a list of common foods that can be used to lure over 20 species, and trap dimensions and specifications.

The book is $3.95 (regularly $4.95) if you identify yourself as a WBMC reader when you order.

Special Factors: Quantity discounts of 50% are available on orders of six or more of the same trap.

UNITED PHARMACAL COMPANY, INC.

P.O. BOX 969, DEPT.
WBM96
ST. JOSEPH, MO
64502-0969
800-254-8726
FAX: 816-233-9696

Catalog: free
Save: up to 50%
Pay: check, MO, MC, V, AE, Discover
Sells: vet, kennel, and pet supplies
Store: 3705 Pear St., St. Joseph, MO; Monday to Friday 7:30–6, Saturday 7:30–5

United Pharmacal Company, known as UPCO, offers thousands of products for dogs, cats, birds, and horses in a 178-page catalog that runs from hayracks to catnip-filled fur fish. UPCO's veterinary line includes antibiotics, wormers, medical instruments, nutritional supplements, skin treatments, insecticides, grooming aids, and related goods. Horse owners should check the dozen pages of medications and supplements, farrier supplies, and tack. Dog and cat owners will appreciate the savings on leashes and leads, collars, feeders, books, toys, feeding dishes and stations, pet doors, and other goods. Professional groomers should note the 42 pages of grooming products for show dogs. UPCO also has a selection of bird cages and supplies and products for hamsters, gerbils, guinea pigs, ferrets, and rabbits. The manufacturers include Absorbine, Borden, Dubl Duck, Farnam, Happy Jack, Lambert Kay, Nylabone, Oster, St. Aubrey, and Zema, to note a few. And UPCO offers hundreds of books and manuals that cover the care and breeding of a wide range of animals.

Canadian readers, please note: Payment must be made in U.S. funds, and vaccines are not shipped to Canada.

Special Factors: Quantity discounts are available; C.O.D. orders are accepted; returns are accepted within 20 days; minimum order is $10; C.O.D. orders are accepted.

SEE ALSO

Cabela's Inc. • *dog beds; hunting dog training equipment* • **SPORTS**
Defender Industries, Inc. • *pet life preservers* • **AUTO**
Gander Mountain, Inc. • *hunting and fishing gear* • **SPORTS**
Gohn Bros. • *horse blankets* • **CLOTHING**
Mellinger's Inc. • *live pest controls, fly traps, bird feeders, etc.* • **FARM**
Sharp Bros. Seed Co. • *forage and fodder seed* • **FARM**
Weston Bowl Mill • *bird feeders and bird calls* • **GENERAL MERCHANDISE**

APPLIANCES, AUDIO, TV, AND VIDEO

Major, small, and personal-care appliances;

sewing machines and vacuum cleaners;

audio components and personal stereo;

TV and video equipment

The companies listed here offer the full range of electronic devices, including white goods (washers, dryers, refrigerators, and ranges), brown goods (TVs, air conditioners, etc.), small kitchen and personal-care appliances, pocket calculators, phones and phone machines (auto-dialers, answerers, line switchers, etc.), sewing machines, vacuum cleaners, and floor machines. Some also sell blank audiotapes and videotapes, luggage, cameras, typewriters, computers, pens, and video games. Thanks to stiff price competition across the country, discounts often run from 15% to 40%—more on extremely popular brands, and less on high-end audio and video components.

Price is important, but it's just one purchase consideration. One of the best product information resources is *Consumer Reports,* which features monthly reviews of name-brand goods and services; it's supplemented by the annual *Buying Guide,* which summarizes scores of the reviews. In addition to dispassionate assessments of product performance and guides to features, the reviews often include both suggested list and "benchmark" retail selling prices. *Consumer Reports* also publishes news on product recalls, deceptive selling practices, health issues, money management, and related consumer interests. The corporate parent, Consumers Union, also publishes books that treat current concerns in depth: chemotherapy, choosing baby products, mutual funds, home maintenance, income taxes, etc. The "Consumer Reports New Car Price Service" and "Used Car Price Service" are available, as are individual reports, which can be sent by fax. See the "Auto" introduction for more on the car-buying data services. For information on the other services and subscription rates, see the current issue or write to Consumers Union, 256 Washington St., Mount Vernon, NY 10553.

Most appliance and electronics manufacturers will send brochures on specific models upon request. You can often find the manufacturers' address on product packaging, and the consumer contacts and addresses of hundreds of major corporations are listed in *Consumer's Resource Handbook,* which is available from the Consumer Information Center (see the listing in "Books").

Planning to purchase a refrigerator, freezer, or air conditioner? The Association of Home Appliance Manufacturers (AHAM) publishes guides to the features and specifications of refrigerators and freezers in the *Consumer Selection Guide for Refrigerators and Freezers.* Air conditioners are examined in *Consumer Selection Guide for Room Air Conditioners,* which includes the "Cooling Load Estimate Form." This work sheet will help you determine how many BTUs your home or room requires, something you should find out *before* you decide on the model you want. Send a check or money order for $1.50 for each title requested to AHAM, Public and Consumer Relations Dept., 20 N. Wacker Dr., Chicago, IL 60606.

Since even small appliances and light bulbs can consume large amounts of energy over time, determining how much power you're using when you flip the switch will help you figure out wise use of the appliances you own—and help you make energy-efficient purchases in the future. To compute the hourly cost of an appliance, find its *wattage* and divide that figure by 1,000 to find the *kilowattage,* which you can multiply by the price of a *kilowatt hour* (kWh) charged by your utility company. (The wattage of an appliance can usually be found in the same place as its model and serial number, or can be obtained from the manufacturer.) For example, a 600-watt vacuum cleaner has a kilowattage of 0.6 (600 divided by 1,000). Run in New York City, where the price per kilowatt hour is 14.204¢, the operating cost per hour is 8.52¢. If you have cheaper rates at night, reserve as much high-consumption use (ironing, running the dishwasher and dryer, self-cleaning the oven) for evening hours.

In addition to price and energy consumption, try to find out as much as possible about a product's repair record before you buy. *Consumer Reports* surveys repair shops periodically, and reveals which brands seem to be turning up most frequently. Unfortunately, models in the same line can vary widely in performance, so undifferentiated reviews of brands may not accurately predict how an individual model will behave. You can conduct your own interviews, too, asking your local appliance repair center about lemons and troublesome brands. And don't overlook your friends, who are probably happy to share both their horror stories and the triumphs of their best buys.

The next-best thing to keeping something out of the shop is having it repaired under warranty. The electronics boom of the mid-1980s helped to popularize service contracts (erroneously termed "extended warranties"), which kick in when the manufacturers' warranties expire. Extended warranties are often pushed on big-ticket items at the point of sale on in-store purchases, but they're also sold by mail-order vendors. (Some credit-card companies provide similar protections, free of charge, for products purchased with their cards. Check the fine print of your card's policy before assuming it provides comprehensive coverage.) Extended warranties are honored by the seller, not the manufacturer, at the seller's repair center. Are they worth the money? According to one analyst who examined the warranties, service contracts, and repair records of color TVs, air conditioners, refrigerators, washers, and ranges in the course of a National Science Foundation/MIT study, the answer is no. In many cases, the *probable* repair bill is lower than the cost of the service contract. But if you've had a post-warranty appliance breakdown, you may feel that a contract is worthwhile insurance. If you decide to buy one, get answers to these questions:

- Does the service contract duplicate the manufacturer's warranty coverage?
- Does the service contract cover parts and labor?
- Is the company selling the contract stable, and is its service department reputable? (Contact the local Better Business Bureau for information on its record.)
- Could you troubleshoot or repair the appliance yourself? Contact the manufacturer (many have 800 lines staffed by technicians who can provide advice on making repairs) or your local repair center before bringing in a malfunctioning product—it may be something you could fix at home.
- What's your *own* history of appliance and electronics failure? If machines seem to enjoy long and healthy lives in your care, you may not need the insurance.

Good maintenance and care will help extend a product's performance. VCRs, which appear susceptible to breakdown, will work better longer if you keep the heads clean, ease wear and tear by using a rewinder, and follow the manufacturers' use and care instructions carefully. If you find the manuals overly technical or opaque, you'll appreciate "How to Install, Connect, and Expand TVs, VCRs, Telephones,

Audio Systems, and Other Consumer Electronic Products," a 52-page brochure that shows you how. To receive a copy, send 78¢ in postage on a long, self-addressed envelope, to Electronic Industries Association, Installation Products, P.O. Box 19100, Washington, DC 20036. Audio components also reward good treatment, and you'll find a battery of cleaning solutions and devices for LPs and CDs available from Lyle Cartridges and several other firms in this chapter.

If you run into trouble with a *major appliance* and can't get it resolved, you may be able to get help from the Major Appliance Consumer Action Panel (MACAP). MACAP, which is sponsored by AHAM (see above), can request action from a manufacturer and make recommendations for resolution of the complaint. (The panel's advice is not binding, but it resolves over 80% of the cases it handles.) You can turn to MACAP with problems about dishwashers, ranges, microwave ovens, washers, dryers, refrigerators, freezers, garbage disposals, trash compactors, air conditioners, water heaters, and dehumidifiers. If your complaint concerns one of these appliances, and your attempts to get the problem resolved with the seller and the manufacturer have been futile, write to Major Appliance Consumer Action Panel, 20 N. Wacker Dr., Chicago, IL 60606. Your letter should include the manufacturer's name, model number of the appliance, and date purchased, as well as *copies* of relevant receipts and correspondence. (Call 800-621-0477 for more information.)

For listings of additional firms selling appliances and electronics, see "General Merchandise," "Office and Business" (including the "Computing" subchapter), and "Tools." For recorded audiotapes and videotapes, see the "Recordings" section of "Books."

FIND IT FAST

APPLIANCES • **Bernie's, Cole's, Dial-a-Brand, Discount Appliance Centers, EBA, LVT, Percy's**

AUDIO • **Audio Concepts, Bernie's, Crutchfield, EBA, J & R, Lyle Cartridges, S & S Sound City, Wholesale Tape**

OFFICE MACHINES AND PHONES • **Crutchfield, EBA, J & R, LVT, Percy's, S & S Sound City**

SEWING MACHINES • **Derry's, Discount Appliance Centers, EBA, LVT, Sewin' in Vermont, Sew Vac City, Suburban Sew 'N Sweep**

TV AND VIDEO • **Bernie's, Cole's, Crutchfield, Dial-a-Brand, EBA, J & R, LVT, S & S Sound City, Westcoast Discount**

VACUUM CLEANERS • **AAA-Vacuum, ABC Vacuum Cleaner, Bernie's, Derry's, Discount Appliance Centers, EBA, LVT, Midamerica, Sew Vac City**

AAA-VACUUM CLEANER SERVICE CENTER

1230 N. 3RD.
ABILENE, TX 79601
915-677-1311

Flyer: $2, refundable
Save: up to 50%
Pay: check, MO, MC, V, AE, Discover
Sells: vacuum cleaners, floor shampooers and polishers
Store: same address; Monday to Friday 8:30–5

You can save on some of the best names in the cleaning business at AAA-Vacuum Cleaner, which offers discounts of up to 50% on list prices. Canister, upright, convertible, and mini vacuum models are available, by Bissell, Dirt Devil, Eureka, Hoover, Oreck, Panasonic, Regina, Royal, Sanitaire, Sharp, Tri-Star, and other firms. Both home and commercial lines of vacuum cleaners, floor buffers, and rug shampooers are stocked, and AAA-Vacuum Cleaner also sells reconditioned Kirby and Rainbow machines. AAA-Vacuum Cleaner has been in business since 1975 and sells supplies and accessories as well as floor machines.

Canadian readers, please note: Only U.S. funds are accepted.

Special Factors: Satisfaction is guaranteed; layaway plan is available; C.O.D. orders are accepted; returns are accepted within 10 days.

ABC VACUUM CLEANER WAREHOUSE

6720 BURNET RD., WM96
AUSTIN, TX 78757
512-459-7643
FAX: 512-451-2352

Price List: free
Save: up to 50%
Pay: check, MO, MC, V, AE, Discover
Sells: vacuum cleaners
Store: same address; Monday to Friday 9–6, Saturday 9–5

 (see text)

ABC purchases from suppliers who are overstocked or going out of business, and passes the savings—up to 50% on the suggested retail or usual selling price—on to you. ABC has been in business since 1977, and sells machines by Electrolux, Filter Queen, Kirby, Oreck, Panasonic, Riccar, Royal, Sanitaire, Sanyo, Sharp, Thermax, and Tri-Star. The Rainbow, by Rexair, is sold at a discount, as well as all of its accessories and parts. (Rebuilt Rainbows are sold at lower prices.) Built-in (central) cleaning systems are also available. See the price list for bags, filters, and accessories and attachments for selected models. ABC also offers repair services by mail—call for information if you're having trouble getting your machine repaired locally.

Canadian readers, please note: Shipments are not made to Canada.

Special Factors: Satisfaction is guaranteed; returns are accepted within 30 days for exchange, refund, or credit; C.O.D. orders are accepted.

AUDIO CONCEPTS, INC.

901 S. 4TH ST.
LA CROSSE, WI 54601
608-784-4579
FAX: 608-784-6367

Catalog: free
Save: up to 40% (see text)
Pay: check, MO, MC, V
Sells: ACI speakers
Store: mail order only
E-mail: CS: 74652,3400@compuserve.com

If you'd like to assemble a good audio system but don't think you can afford it, here's one way to save on the thing that seems to cost the most: the speakers. Audio Concepts, Inc. (ACI) has been manufacturing and selling speakers factory direct since 1977, and invites you to save up to 40% over the cost of comparable speakers. ACI's models are sold in pairs and individually, or you can buy a home theater package for extra savings. ACI sells everything from satellites to three-ways, from in-wall speakers to subwoofers and center channels to rear speakers. All of the cabinets are made with furniture-grade wood veneers, and a number of finish options are available. Prices begin at $139 per pair for wall speakers and run to around $3,500 for the top-of-the-line home theater system. The 16-page catalog shows the speakers and a range of accessories—stands, cables, wall brackets, etc. Most models are also available in kit form for do-it-yourselfers (plans are included). ACI has put the most technical specs, as well as graphs and sidebars, into the separate "TAGS" guide. Ask for both when you request literature.

Special Factors: Satisfaction is guaranteed; authorized returns are accepted in new condition in original packaging within 15 days for exchange, refund, or credit.

BERNIE'S DISCOUNT CENTER, INC.

821 SIXTH AVE., D-6
NEW YORK, NY
  10001-6305
212-564-8758, 8582, 9431
FAX: 212-564-3894

Catalog: $1, refundable (see text)
Save: 30% average
Pay: check, MO, MC, V, AE (see text)
Sells: appliances, TV and audio components, office machines
Store: same address; Monday to Friday 9–5:30, Saturday (except July and August) 11–3:30

 ¡Si! ![maple leaf] (see text)

Bernie's has been in business since 1947, and sells "pluggables"—everything from electric brooms to fax machines—at 10% to 15% above dealers' cost, or an average of 30% off list. The catalog is available for $1 (refundable with a purchase), but it shows just a smattering of the stock at Bernie's, and you're better off calling for a price quote. One of the city's best sources for discounted electronics and appliances, Bernie's tries to carry the top-rated goods listed in popular buying guides, and Bernie's does not handle gray-market goods.

Bernie's sells electronics (audio, TV, and video equipment) by Aiwa, AT&T, Brother, Canon, Fisher, JVC, Mitsubishi, Panasonic, Quasar, RCA, Sharp, Sony, and Toshiba. White goods (shipped in the New York City area only) are available from Amana, Caloric, G.E., Jenn-Air, Magic Chef, Maytag, KitchenAid, RCA, Tappan, Whirlpool, White-Westinghouse, and other manufacturers. Bernie's is one of the best sources in the metropolitan area for air conditioners (Airtemp, Carrier, Emerson, Friedrich, G.E., Gibson, Panasonic, etc.), fans by Holmes and Lakewood, heaters by Black & Decker, Holmes, and Pelonis, and air cleaners and ionizers by Bionaire and Envirocare. Small and personal-care appliances from Black & Decker, Braun, Britta, Clairol, Eureka, Farberware, Hamilton Beach, Hitachi, Hoover, Interplak, KitchenAid, Krups, Norelco, Oster, Panasonic, Presto, Remington, Sanyo, Simac, Sunbeam, Teledyne (Water Pik and Instapure), Toastmaster, Wearever, West Bend, and other brands are available as well.

Please note: Purchases charged to American Express/Optima cards are shipped to billing addresses only, and MasterCard and VISA are accepted for *in-store* purchases only.

Canadian readers, please note: Orders are shipped to Canada via UPS only.

Special Factors: Store is closed Saturdays in July and August.

COLE'S APPLIANCE & FURNITURE CO.

4026 LINCOLN AVE.
CHICAGO, IL 60618-3097
312-525-1797

Information: see text
Save: up to 50%
Pay: check, MO, MC, V, Discover
Sells: appliances and home furnishings
Store: same address; Monday and Thursday
9:30–9, Tuesday, Friday, and Saturday
9:30–5:30 (closed Wednesdays and Sundays)

Cole's, founded in 1957, sells electronics (TV and video), appliances, and home furnishings and bedding at discounts of up to 50%. If you're pricing something from Admiral, Amana, Brown, Caloric, Dacor, G.E., Gibson, Hitachi, Hotpoint, Insinkerator, KitchenAid, Magic Chef, Maytag, Panasonic, Pioneer, Premier, Speed Queen, Sub-Zero, Whirlpool, Zenith, or any other major manufacturer, call Cole's for a price quote.

Special Factors: Price quote by phone or letter.

CRUTCHFIELD CORPORATION

ONE CRUTCHFIELD PARK,
DEPT. WH
CHARLOTTESVILLE, VA
22906-6020
800-955-9009
804-973-1811
FAX: 804-973-1862

Catalog: free (see text)
Save: 10% to 55%
Pay: check, MO, MC, V, AE, DC, Discover,
Crutchfield charge card
Sells: audio and video components, car stereo, phone equipment, and home and car alarms
Store: 1784 Rio Hill Center, Charlottesville, and Market Square East Shopping Center, Harrisonburg, VA; Monday to Saturday 9–7, Sunday 12–5, both locations

Crutchfield publishes an informative, 100-plus-page catalog of home and car stereo components, video equipment, telephones, and car security equipment. The catalog is loaded with buying tips and product specifications on featured goods, which are priced from 10% to 55% below list price. Good prices are just one of the pluses here—you may find the Crutchfield catalog more helpful when you're comparing product features than the articles in industry magazines. And Crutchfield backs everything it sells with a guarantee of satisfaction, and the staff can provide extensive support: Installation walk-throughs over the phone, car stereo kits for genuinely customized installation, and informative consumer service manuals are among the available benefits. Crutchfield, which was established in 1974, is a factory-authorized repair station for most of the brands it sells, and does not sell gray-market goods.

Crutchfield's car stereo components line, which includes equipment for pickup trucks and hatchbacks, features goods by Advent, Alphasonik, Blaupunkt, Cerwin-Vega, Clarion, Infinity, JBL, Jensen, JVC, Kenwood, Kicker, Pioneer, Polk Audio, Profile, Pyle, Sanyo, Sherwood, and Sony. Crutchfield also sells radar detectors by BEL and Whistler, as well as dozens of types of car antennas, and Crimestopper and Prestige alarm systems to protect your investment.

The home audio portion of the catalog includes pages of features comparisons of current models of receivers, CD players, cassette decks, speakers, and shelf systems, and shows amps, portable and personal audio, headphones, remote controls, CD cabinets, and other accessories. The brands include Advent, Atlantic Technology, Bose, Carver, Cerwin-Vega, Infinity, JVC, Kenwood, NHT, Pioneer, Polk Audio, Sony, and Yamaha. You'll also find camcorders, laser disc players, and TVs and VCRs from JVC, Mitsubishi, Pioneer, and Sony offered here.

Please note: The catalog is free to readers of this book, but be sure to identify yourself as a WBMC reader when you request your copy.

Special Factors: Satisfaction is guaranteed; returns are accepted within 30 days; online with CompuServe.

DERRY'S SEWING CENTER

**430 ST. FERDINAND
FLORISSANT, MO 63031
314-837-6103**

Brochure: see text
Save: up to 30%
Pay: MO, MC, V
Sells: sewing machines and vacuum cleaners
Store: same address; Monday to Friday 10–7, Saturday 10–4

Upgrading your sewing machine may cost less at Derry's, which carries models (sewing and overlock) by Necchi, Singer, Viking, and White. Savings run up to 40%, and parts for new and older machines are available, as well as supplies—needles, belts, bobbins, etc. Derry's has been in business since 1979, and provides in-warranty service on the Necchi, Simplicity, and Singer sewing machines. Panasonic vacuum cleaners and bags are also available. You can request the brochure (send a $1 bill and a long, stamped, self-addressed envelope), but if you know the model you want, it's easier to call for a price quote.

Special Factors: Price quote by phone or letter (see above).

DIAL-A-BRAND, INC.

57 S. MAIN ST.
FREEPORT, NY 11520
516-378-9694
FAX: 516-867-3447

Information: price quote
Save: 30% average
Pay: check, MO, MC, V, Discover
Sells: appliances, TVs, and video equipment
Store: same address; Monday to Saturday 9–6

¡Si!

Dial-a-Brand, which was founded in 1967, has earned the kudos of institutions and individuals with its wide range of appliances and popular electronics. Dial-a-Brand offers discounts averaging 30%, and does not sell gray-market goods. Call or write for prices on air conditioners, TVs, video equipment, microwave ovens, and large appliances. Dial-a-Brand ships chiefly within the New York/New Jersey/Connecticut area, but deliveries (via UPS) are made nationwide. Freight charges may offset savings on outsized or heavy items shipped long distances, so be sure to get a firm quote or estimate before you place your order. Please note: You *must* call with the manufacturer's name and model number to receive a price quote.

Special Factors: Returns are accepted for exchange if goods are defective or damaged in transit; minimum order is $100.

DISCOUNT APPLIANCE CENTERS

8426 20TH AVE., SUITE 100
ADELPHIA, MD 20783
301-559-8932
FAX: 301-559-1335

Information: price quote
Save: up to 60%
Pay: check, MO, MC, V, AE
Sells: vacuum cleaners and sewing machines
Store: mail order only

Discount Appliance Centers offers sewing machines, vacuum cleaners, and accessories and supplies for both at good discounts. The firm has been in business since 1965, and doesn't have a catalog—please *write* for prices and availability information, since quotes are given over the phone as staff time permits.

Discount Appliance Centers offers the latest models in vacuum cleaners by Airway, Electrolux, Eureka, Filter Queen, Hoover, Kirby, Mastercraft, Oreck, Panasonic, Royal, Sanitaire, and Tri-Star, as well as bags, belts, and attachments. Write for prices on sewing machines by Bernina, Consew, Elna, Juki, Necchi, New Home, Pfaff, Riccar, Singer, and Viking.

Special Factors: Price quote by letter only with SASE; minimum order is $49.

EBA WHOLESALE

2361 NOSTRAND AVE.
BROOKLYN, NY 11210
800-380-2378
718-252-3400

Flyer: free
Save: up to 40%
Pay: check, MO, MC, V
Sells: appliances, audio, video, etc.
Store: same address; Monday to Friday 9–8, Tuesday, Wednesday, Saturday 9–6, Sunday 11–5

Bargains abound at this Brooklyn discount house, which sets prices based on its cost plus 5% to 10%—the savings run from 10% to 40% on list or suggested selling prices. You'll find everything from Maytag washers and Amana refrigerators to AT&T phones and Canon copiers, including lines from Caloric, G.E., Hotpoint, Jenn-Air, KitchenAid, Magic Chef, Magnavox, Panasonic, RCA, Sanyo, Sony, Sylvania, Whirlpool,

White-Westinghouse, and Zenith, among others. The flyer features some of the current specials, which are also given in the voicemail system; you can order from those, or call for a price quote on another model.

Special Factors: Satisfaction is guaranteed; price quote by phone or letter.

J & R MUSIC WORLD

DEPT. WL096
59-50 QUEENS-MIDTOWN
  EXPRESSWAY
MASPETH, NY 11378
800-221-8180
718-417-3737
212-238-9000
FAX: 718-497-1791

Catalog: free
Save: up to 50%
Pay: check, MO, MC, V, AE, Discover
Sells: audio, video, computers, music, small appliances, etc.
Store: Park Row, New York, NY; Monday to Saturday 9–6:30, Sunday 10–6

J & R enjoys top billing among New York City electronics and computer discounters for its depth of saving and selection, especially in the audio, video, and computer departments. You can call for the 200-page catalog, or to get price quotes on current lines of TVs, VCRs and video equipment, audio components and equipment, computers and peripherals, phones, fax machines, radar detectors, cameras, and personal appliances. J & R also sells tapes, CDs, and software, as well as exercise equipment, vacuum cleaners and microwave ovens, and even pens and watches. All major brand names, from Acoustic Research to Yamaha, are represented here, and everything sold by J & R is guaranteed to be brand new and factory fresh.

Special Factors: Satisfaction is guaranteed; minimum order is $25; online with Bloomberg.

LVT PRICE QUOTE HOTLINE, INC.

BOX 444-W96
COMMACK, NY
11725-0444
516-234-8884
FAX: 516-234-8808

Brochure: free
Save: up to 30%
Pay: check or MO
Sells: major appliances, TVs, vacuum cleaners, electronics, office machines, etc.
Store: (phone hours) Monday to Saturday 9–6
E-mail: AOL: CALL LVT; CS: 75132,1640; Prodigy: KKES99A; Net: calllvt@aol.com

LVT, established in 1976, gives you instant access to over 4,000 products from over 75 manufacturers, at savings of up to 30% on suggested list or full retail prices. The brochure includes a roster of available brands, and price quotes are given on individual items. LVT does not sell gray-market goods. For information, read LVT's brochure for the sales and shipping policies, then call with the manufacturer's name and exact model number for a price quote on major appliances, bread-making machines, microwave ovens, air conditioners, vacuum cleaners, washers and dryers, TVs, video equipment, phones and phone machines, calculators, typewriters, scanners, radar detectors, copiers, fax machines, and word processors.

The brands available include Adcom, Admiral, Airtemp, Aiwa, Amana, AT&T, Bearcat, Bell Atlantic, Braun, Brother, Bunn, Caloric, Canon, Carrier, Casio, Champion, Cobra, Code-A-Phone, Denon, Eagle, Emerson, Eureka, Fedders, Fisher, Franke, Freedom Phone, Friedrich, Frigidaire, G.E., Harmon Kardon, Hewlett-Packard, Hitachi, Hoover, Hotpoint, Jenn-Air, JVC, Kelvinator, Kenwood, KitchenAid, Magic Chef, Maxon, Maytag, Mitsubishi, Modern Maid, Mont Blanc, Murata, Olympus, Onkyo, Panasonic, Phone-Mate, Pioneer, Quasar, Rangaire, RCA, Ricoh, Rolodex, Roper, Royal, Samsung, Sanyo, Sharp, Sherwood, Singer, Smith Corona, Sony, Southwestern Bell, Speed Queen, Sub-Zero, Tappan, Teac, Technics, Texas Instruments, Thermador, Toshiba, Uniden, Victor, Viking, Welbilt, Whirlpool, Whistler, White-Westinghouse, Wolf, Xerox, Yamaha, and Zenith—see the brands list for others.

Special Factors: Shipping (UPS), handling, and insurance charges are included in quotes; all sales are final; all goods are sold with manufacturers' warranties; minimum order is $25; C.O.D. orders are accepted.

LYLE CARTRIDGES

DEPT. WBMC
115 SO. CORONA AVE.
VALLEY STREAM, NY
11582
800-221-0906
516-599-1112
FAX: 516-599-2027

Catalog: free with self-addressed, stamped envelope
Save: up to 60%
Pay: check, MO, MC, V, AE, Discover
Sells: phono cartridges, replacement styli, and accessories
Store: same address; Monday to Friday 9–5

Lyle Cartridges has been in business since 1952 and is a great source for the cartridges and replacement styli (factory original) that bring your music to life. If you're sticking by your LPs despite CDs, you'll really appreciate this reliable, well-informed source. As the proprietors put it, "We specialize in phono-related products, and have the largest stock of 78RPM replacement styli in the country. As LPs have become harder to find, so too have our products and services."

Lyle sells phono cartridges and replacement styli by Audioquest, Audio-Technica, Bang & Olufsen, Dynavector, Grado/Signature, Ortofon, Pickering, Shure, Signet, Stanton, and Sumiko. Record-care products by Discwasher, LAST, and VPI are stocked, as well as Tweek's contact enhancer. Lyle also sells Grado headphones, Rotel three-speed turntables, and VPI turntables. This is the first source to consult if you have to replace arm parts, since you may be able to save on both labor and material costs—parts prices are up to 60% less than list or comparable retail.

Special Factors: Authorized returns are accepted; defective goods are replaced; minimum order is $15, $25 with credit cards.

MIDAMERICA VACUUM CLEANER SUPPLY CO.

666 UNIVERSITY AVE.
ST. PAUL, MN 55104-4896
612-222-0763
FAX: 612-224-2674

Information: price quote
Save: 25% plus
Pay: check, MO, MC, V, AE, Discover
Sells: vacuum cleaners, floor machines, and appliance parts
Store: same address; Monday to Friday 9–5:30, Saturday 9–3; other locations in Hopkins, Minnetonka, and Richfield

Midamerica sells vacuum cleaners and related parts and supplies, as well as floor machines and appliance parts, by and for Beam, Bissell, Eureka, Hoover, MagNuM, Mastercraft, Optimus, Oreck, Panasonic, Progress Mercedes, Royal, Sanitaire, Sharp, Shop Vac, and Simplicity. In addition, Midamerica offers discounts on related products, such as bags, belts, hoses, brushes, and cleaning chemicals. Price quotes on the vacuum cleaners, parts, and supplies are given by phone or letter.

Special Factors: Quantity discounts are available; minimum order is $15.

PERCY'S, INC.

GOLD STAR BLVD.
WORCESTER, MA 01605
508-755-5269
FAX: 508-797-5578

Information: price quote
Save: up to 40%
Pay: MO, MC, V, Discover
Sells: large appliances, audio and TV components, video, computers, etc.
Store: same address; Monday to Friday 10–9, Saturday 10–5

Percy's has been selling appliances of all types since 1926, at prices 3% above wholesale cost, or up to 40% below list. Percy's sells no gray-market goods.

You can call or write for a price quote on washers, dryers, dishwashers, refrigerators, freezers, ranges, standard and microwave ovens, TVs, video equipment and tapes, audio components, computers, radar detectors, dehumidifiers, disposals, and other appliances. The brands available at Percy's include Bose, Caloric, Fisher, Frigidaire, G.E., Hotpoint,

Jenn-Air, JVC, KitchenAid, Magic Chef, Maytag, Mitsubishi, Pioneer, Quasar, RCA, Sharp, Sony, Sub-Zero, Thermador, Toshiba, Whirlpool, White-Westinghouse, and Zenith. Please note that Percy's *does not sell small appliances,* and *does not publish a catalog.*

Special Factors: Price quote by phone or letter.

S & S SOUND CITY

58 W. 45TH ST., DEPT. WBMC
NEW YORK, NY
10036-4280
212-575-0210
FAX: 212-221-7907

Brochure: free (see text)
Save: up to 50%
Pay: check, MO, MC, V, AE, Discover
Sells: audio and video, optics, phones, office machines, etc.
Store: same address; Monday to Friday 9–7, Saturday 9–6

S & S Sound City has been in business since 1975, selling TVs and video equipment, audio components, radios, telephones, microwave ovens, air conditioners, and closed-caption decoders. The inventory includes goods from AT&T, G.E., Harman Kardon, JBL, JVC, Minolta, Mitsubishi, NAD, Onkyo, Panasonic, Quasar, RCA, Sharp, Sony, and Southwestern Bell. S & S operates a photo department that offers cameras and accessories, binoculars, telescopes, and related goods. A seasonal brochure that showcases popular gift selections is available, but call or write for a price quote if you're shopping out of season or don't see the item you want.

Special Factors: Returns are accepted within seven days; special orders are accepted.

SEW VAC CITY

DEPT. WBMC
1667 TEXAS AVE.
COLLEGE STATION, TX
  77840
800-338-5672
FAX: 409-696-9262

Brochure: $3 (see text)
Save: 40% average
Pay: MO, MC, V, Discover
Sells: sewing machines, sergers, and vacuum cleaners
Store: same address; Monday to Thursday 10–8, Friday and Saturday 10–5; also Pittsburg Sewing Machine Warehouse, 602 N. Broadway, Pittsburg, KS; Sewing Machine Warehouse, Willowbrook Ct., 17776 Tomball Pkwy., Houston; Sewing Machine Warehouse, 9602A FM 1960 Bypass, Humble; and Sew Vac City, Town West Center, Waco, TX

Sew Vac City, in business since 1976, sells sewing machines, sergers, and vacuum cleaners. Call for a price quote on sewing machines by Singer and other manufacturers, or Panasonic, Sharp, and other vacuum cleaners. All of the machines sold here are new, and layaways are accepted—inquire for information.

Special Factors: Layaway plan is available; minimum order is $30; C.O.D. orders are accepted.

SEWIN' IN VERMONT

84 CONCORD AVE.
ST. JOHNSBURY, VT
  05819-2095
800-451-5124
802-748-3803

Catalog: $3
Save: 35% average
Pay: check, MO, MC, V, Discover
Sells: sewing machines and accessories
Store: same address; Monday to Friday 9:30–5, Saturday 9:30–1

If you're shopping for sewing supplies or a sewing machine or serger, see the catalog from Sewin' in Vermont. The firm carries several of the best American and European brands: Jaguar, New Home, Singer, and Viking sewing machines, as well as sergers from these and other manufacturers. Professional-quality irons and presses by Rowenta, Singer, and

Sussman are also carried. The 112-page color catalog is a well-organized treat that features a wide range of sewing aids—from pins and needles to pressing hams—as well as Singer dress forms, Johnson ruffling machines, cabinets and carrying cases, sewing-room furniture, rubber stamps, supplies, books, videos, and more. The retail and discount prices are given for each item, and the product mix is suited to serious home sewers and small crafts businesses.

Sewin' in Vermont has been in business since 1960, and the knowledgeable sales staff can help you choose the right equipment for your needs; call the 800 number for information and price quotes.

Special Factors: Price quote by phone or letter; C.O.D. orders are accepted.

SUBURBAN SEW 'N SWEEP, INC.

8814 OGDEN AVE.
BROOKFIELD, IL 60513
800-642-4056
708-485-2834
FAX: 708-387-0500

Information: inquire
Save: up to 50%
Pay: check, MO, MC, V, AE, Discover
Sells: sewing machines and vacuum cleaners
Store: same address; Monday to Saturday 9–5

Suburban Sew 'N Sweep has been selling sewing machines since 1975, and although a brochure is available, you can call for a price quote on sewing and overlock machines by New Home, Singer, White, and other top brands. Discounts vary, but run up to 50%. Suburban Sew 'N Sweep is an authorized dealer for several major sewing machine manufacturers and also sells Oreck vacuum cleaners.

Special Factors: Price quote by phone; C.O.D. orders are accepted.

WESTCOAST DISCOUNT VIDEO

Catalog: $5
Save: up to 35%
Pay: check, MO, MC, V, AE, Discover
Sells: camcorders and accessories
Store: mail order only

5201 EASTERN AVE.

BALTIMORE, MD 21224

800-344-7123

410-633-0508

FAX: 410-633-7888

Westcoast Discount Video is a specialty firm that sells camcorders, attachments, and accessories—for both 8mm and VHS formats. Discounts run up to 35% on models by Canon, G.E., Hitachi, JVC, Magnavox, Panasonic, Quasar, RCA, Sharp, Sony, and Zenith. This is also a good source for auxillary lenses and filters, lighting equipment, power packs, rewinders, microphones, tripods, cases, movie and slide converters, and other equipment. The 48-page catalog includes specs on every model Westcoast sells, a list of the optional accessories, and a separate price list. If you don't know much about video equipment, you'll appreciate the three-page glossary of terms and abbreviations in the back of the catalog, and it's nice to know that everything Westcoast Discount Video sells is sent in factory-sealed cartons with the full U.S. manufacturer's warranty.

Special Factors: Price quote by phone; shipping is not charged on orders over $75; C.O.D. orders are accepted.

WHOLESALE TAPE AND SUPPLY COMPANY

P.O. BOX 8277,
  DEPT. WBM
CHATTANOOGA, TN
  37414
800-251-7228
615-894-9427
FAX: 615-894-7281

Catalog: free
Save: up to 50%
Pay: check, MO, MC, V, AE, Discover
Sells: audio and video tapes, duplicating services, etc.
Store: 2841 Hickory Valley Rd., Chattanooga, TN

Wholesale Tape, which has been selling audio/visual supplies and services worldwide since 1977, publishes a catalog featuring blank audio and video cassettes, reel-to-reel tapes in all configurations, duplication equipment, services, and accessories. Wholesale Tape produces audiotapes for professional duplication; six types of tape are available, in clear, white, and black shells (housing) and standard tape lengths (12 to 122 minutes); custom tape lengths can be provided. Wholesale Tape also sells its own videotape, as well as professional-quality audio and video tape from Ampex, Fuji, and Maxell.

If you need an audiotape or videotape copied but don't have the necessary equipment, consider Wholesale Tape's duplicating services. Custom labels and shell imprinting can be produced, and cassette boxes, albums, shipping envelopes, and storage units are also sold.

Special Factors: Satisfaction is guaranteed; quantity discounts are offered; C.O.D. orders are accepted; minimum order is $25.

SEE ALSO

Atlanta Thread & Supply • commercial sewing machines, sergers, and irons • **CRAFTS**
CISCO • garbage disposals, spas, whirlpools, etc. • **HOME: IMPROVEMENT**
Defender Industries, Inc. • marine electronics • **AUTO**
E & B Marine Supply, Inc. • marine electronics • **AUTO**
Ewald-Clark • video cameras • **CAMERAS**
Fivenson Food Equipment, Inc. • commercial restaurant equipment • **HOME: KITCHEN**

Goldberg's Marine Distributors • marine electronics • **AUTO**

Kaplan Bros. Blue Flame Corp. • commercial restaurant appliances • **HOME: KITCHEN**

LIBW • bathroom fixtures, whirlpools, and other hardware • **HOME: IMPROVEMENT**

Main Lamp/Lamp Warehouse • lamps and ceiling fans • **HOME: DECOR: LIGHTING**

Park Slope Sewing Center • sewing machines • **CRAFTS: TEXTILE ARTS**

Peerless Restaurant Supplies • commercial restaurant fixtures, appliances, and supplies • **HOME: KITCHEN**

Solo Slide Fasteners, Inc. • professional pressing and sewing equipment • **CRAFTS: TEXTILE ARTS**

Thread Discount Sales • sergers, overlock machines, etc. • **CRAFTS: TEXTILE ARTS**

West Marine • marine electronics • **AUTO**

ART, ANTIQUES, AND COLLECTIBLES

Fine art, limited editions, antiques, and collectibles

The firms listed here offer everything from Victoriana to fruit crate labels, bronze "art" furniture to vintage advertising ephemera, limited-edition porcelain figures and plates, and contemporary movie posters. Although buying from "dealer" sources means you're usually getting the piece at a lower price than you'd pay at retail, don't buy with the expectation of reselling at a profit, unless you're sure of what you're doing. And be sure to buy antiques from firms that have liberal return policies.

Getting to know the market is one of the pleasures of collecting, and there are hundreds of reference books and guides available to give you the necessary grounding. The guides to prevailing market prices for antiques and collectibles are especially helpful in determining whether you're overpaying—or getting a real buy. Ralph and Terry Kovel have been publishing price indexes and collectors' guides for decades, and are best known for the annual *Kovels' Antiques and Collectibles Price List*. The Kovels also help you get the best price on what you buy—or sell—with *Kovels' Guide to Selling, Buying and Fixing Your Antiques and Collectibles* (both titles from Crown). And you can hear from them through their monthly newsletter, *Kovels on Antiques and Collectibles*. Write to Kovels on Antiques, Box 22900, Beachwood, OH 44122 for current rates. But there's no substitute for old-fashioned legwork when it comes to learning about your field of interest. Visit flea markets, antique shops, art galleries, museums, and auction previews, and don't just look—*ask questions*. Dealers enjoy an appreciative customer, and will usually share valuable tips on what to look for if you demonstrate interest in their wares.

A collection of any merit usually requires the protection of archival quality materials. University Products, Inc. (in the "Small Business" section of "Office") is an excellent source for display binders, albums, boxes, and restoration materials for art works, books, manuscripts, photographs, textiles, posters, and postcards. The firm's archival products catalog includes goods for mounting, display, and storage.

FIND IT FAST

ANTIQUES • **Antique Imports**
ART BRONZES • **Excalibur**
FRUIT CRATE LABELS • **Original Paper Collectibles**
NOSTALGIC ITEMS (REPRODUCTION) • **Desperate Enterprises**
POSTERS • **Cinema City, Miscellaneous Man, Rick's Movie Graphics**

ANTIQUE IMPORTS UNLIMITED

P.O. BOX 2978-WBMC
COVINGTON, LA
70434-2978
504-892-0014
FAX: 504-898-0785

Catalog: $3 (see text)
Save: up to 60%
Pay: check, MO, MC, V
Sells: antiques and collectibles
Store: mail order only

Antique Imports, in business since 1981, markets antique jewelry and ephemera through its catalogs, which are published several times a year. The firm sells at "dealer" prices—up to 60% below what's being charged for comparable goods in antique shops. The catalog features old jewelry, charms, watches, glassware, china, metalware, and related miscellany. A sample copy costs $3, a year's subscription of 10 to 12 issues, $30. A recent edition included a Victorian 10K gold ring, set with a cameo ($208), a gold-filled Wahl fountain pen ($80), a 1912 Limoges dessert set ($60), and a Victorian gold and agate stickpin. Please note that the catalog has just a few illustrations, but Antique Imports accepts returns within two days of receipt.

Special Factors: All goods are one-of-a-kind items, subject to prior sale; listing second choices is recommended; UPS is *not* used; returns are accepted within two days for exchange, refund, or credit; minimum order is $110.

CINEMA CITY

P.O. BOX 1012-HK
MUSKEGON, MI 49443
616-722-7760
FAX: 616-722-4537

Catalog: $3, refundable
Save: 30% average
Pay: check, MO, MC, V
Sells: movie posters and ephemera
Store: mail order only

Movie posters circa 1975 and later are the specialty at Cinema City, which has been selling to collectors and dealers since 1976. Thousands of movies are listed in the 64-page catalog, from *A Bridge Too Far* ($15 for a set of 12 stills) to *Ziggy Stardust* (27" by 41" poster, $25). Press kits, scripts, and lobby cards are available for some of the titles. The catalog is arranged alphabetically by movie title and includes a glossary of terms and guide to the poster sizes. (Posters are sent rolled if Cinema City received them "flat," but folded materials are stiffened to minimize damage and shipped that way.) Cinema City adds to its gigantic inventory with each new movie release, and once you're on the mailing list, you'll receive periodic updates—including offerings of autographed posters and photos. Cinema City also handles materials for foreign films and limited-release items. You can send inquiries about these, as well as queries about films made before 1975, but include a self-addressed, stamped envelope if you want to receive a reply.

Canadian readers, please note: Only U.S. funds are accepted.

Special Factors: Orders are shipped worldwide.

DESPERATE ENTER-PRISES INC.

620 E. SMITH RD., #E-8
MEDINA, OH 44256
216-725-1897
FAX: 216-725-0150

Catalog: free
Save: up to 50%
Pay: check, MO, MC, V
Sells: tin advertising and vintage poster reproductions
Store: mail order only

Desperate Enterprises takes its name from an observation made by Thoreau, not from the nature of its industry. The firm began business in 1987, selling two reproductions of tin advertising signs, which has expanded to a line of over 500 different images. Desperate Enterprises uses two production processes—four-color photolithography and silk-screen printing—to approximate the detail and depth of color in the originals. Most of the examples are from the late 1800s through the 1920s, chiefly ads for seeds and vegetables, drinks, baseball-related advertising, food, endorsements by famous people, ammunition, fishing, tobacco, transportation, highway, liquor, and African-American images. The ads, which average 11" by 16", begin at $12 and go down to $4.24 each depending on how many you buy. Miniatures of 60 of the ads are offered as refrigerator magnets ($14 to $7.75 per set of six). Sepia-toned photo assortments in broad categories (movies and westerns, sports, motorcycle, etc.) are sold for $54 per hundred, 20" by 30" posters, and T-shirts are also available.

Special Factors: Satisfaction is guaranteed; C.O.D. orders are accepted.

EXCALIBUR BRONZE SCULPTURE FOUNDRY

Catalog: $10, refundable (see text)
Save: 25% average
Pay: check, MO, MC, V
Sells: art bronze sculptures and furniture
Store: same address

85 ADAMS ST.
BROOKLYN, NY 11201
718-522-3330
FAX: 718-522-0812

Excalibur Bronze Sculpture Foundry has been casting the works of sculptors and artists across the country since 1967. (Services include mold making, precision sand and ceramic shell casting, enlarging, chasing, patinating, etc.) But the firm is listed here because of its bronze reproductions of renowned sculptures, and its delightful furniture.

The $10 fee brings you three catalogs. *The Excalibur Collection*, includes replicas of works by Rodin, Antoine-Louis Barye, Emile Bourdelle, and other artists. Scores of reproductions of Remingtons, Art Noveau and Art Deco figures, lamps, vases, and mirrors are shown in *The Decorative Arts Collection*, at prices beginning at under $200. And the *Hommage à Diego Collection* shows scores of the type of "art" lamps and cocktail tables featured prominently in shelter magazines—wrought metal bases embellished with birds, leaves, hoofs, turtles, and other playful touches, topped with thick slabs of glass—inspired by the work of Diego Giacometti. Please note that the $10 catalog/portfolio fee is refundable only with a purchase, but you can call or write directly about specific pieces or custom work.

Special Factors: Orders are shipped worldwide.

MISCELLANEOUS MAN

P.O. BOX 1776-W4
NEW FREEDOM, PA 17349
717-235-4766
FAX: 717-235-2853

Catalog: $5
Save: up to 75%
Pay: check, MO, MC, V
Sells: rare and vintage posters and labels
Store: mail order only

George Theofiles, ephemerologist extraordinaire, is the moving force behind Miscellaneous Man. He founded his firm in 1970, trading in vintage posters, handbills, graphics, labels, brochures, and other memorabilia, all of which are original—he sells no reproductions or reprints.

Each Miscellaneous Man catalog offers an average of about a thousand items, including posters, theater and movie publicity materials, collections of colorful product labels, and broadsides. Posters are the strong suit, representing everything from aviation to weaponry: patriotic themes (including both World Wars, other conflicts, and related topics), sports of all sorts, wines and spirits, food advertising, labor, publishing, fashion, African-Americana, the performing arts, and travel, among other subjects. Some of the posters are offered mounted on linen or conservation paper, and Mr. Theofiles can provide references for other firms that can mount your poster after purchase (proper backing helps to preserve the poster, and doesn't detract from its value). Collections of unused broom handle labels, luggage stickers, cigar box labels, and other such ephemera have appeared in previous catalogs. Size and condition are noted in the catalog entries, and photos of many of the offerings are shown; larger shots of individual items may be purchased for $2.

Miscellaneous Man's prices are usually at least 30% below the going rate, and regular customers receive sale catalogs with further reductions. If you're in the market for a vintage poster, give Miscellaneous Man a call before you buy elsewhere. Although his prices are sometimes comparable (especially on scarce or rare posters), Miscellaneous Man can and has charged 30% to 75% less than New York City sources—and his selection is invariably better.

Special Factors: Layaways are accepted; returns are accepted within three days; minimum order is $50 with credit cards.

ORIGINAL PAPER COLLECTIBLES

700-W CLIPPER GAP RD.
AUBURN, CA 95603

Brochure, Sample Label: free with *long*, self-addressed, stamped envelope (see text)
Save: up to 75%
Pay: check or MO
Sells: original, vintage labels
Store: mail order only

  ¡Si!

William Wauters began his business in 1970, when fruit crate labels were among the hot collectibles in antique and curio shops nationwide. Original Paper Collectibles has thrived over the years, attesting to the enduring appeal of the label designs. At this writing, Mr. Wauters offers labels originally intended for brooms, soda pop, canned fruits and vegetables, and produce—apples, pears, lettuce, oranges, asparagus, lemons, and other fruits and vegetables. And collectors of African-Americana will find a selection of ten labels depicting black characters.

The collections offer the best per-label prices, and Mr. Wauters says that dealers routinely double his prices when they resell. The price list describes the most popular collection of fruit crate labels that include orange, apple, asparagus, lemon, pear, lettuce, cherry, grape, and carrot varieties—150 for $25, postpaid. (A vintage poster gallery in New York City charges that much for a *single* label.) Sliding discounts of 10% to 35% are given on orders of $100, $250, and $500. If you're searching for a specific label, you may find it among the listings of individual labels, which are grouped by size and type. And if you're looking for something out of the ordinary to cover the walls, ask here—the labels can be used as wall treatments. One Detroit pizza parlor even used them in a decoupage treatment on the tabletops!

Please note: Payment for orders should be made to William Wauters, *not* Original Paper Collectibles, and requests for catalogs *must* include the long, stamped, self-addressed envelope.

Canadian and non-U.S.-based readers, please note: Send a self-addressed envelope with an International Reply Coupon, available at your local post office (do not include a stamp, unless it's U.S. postage).

Special Factors: Satisfaction is guaranteed; price quote by letter with SASE; quantity discounts are available.

RICK'S MOVIE GRAPHICS, INC.

**P.O. BOX 23709-WM
GAINESVILLE, FL
32602-3709
904-373-7202
FAX: 904-373-2589**

Catalog: $3
Save: up to 60%
Pay: check, MO, MC, V
Sells: current and vintage movie posters
Store: mail order only

Today's collectibles can become tomorrow's investments, and although the possibilities of appreciation attract some of the people who buy movie posters, most of us just want mementos of favorite flicks. Rick's Movie Graphics has been serving both interests since 1985 and publishes a 64-plus-page catalog packed with current releases and "vintage" posters dating back to the 1950s. The listings are coded to indicate whether the posters have been rolled or folded. At an average price of $15 (10% to 30% below the going rate), the new releases deliver a lot of visual bang for the buck. Prices of vintage posters are higher here, but dealers usually charge so much more that the savings through Rick's can reach 30% to 65% in this category.

Recent catalogs have offered original releases of *Star Wars* and *Star Trek* in their infinite variety, the original Spanish poster for *Casablanca,* and new and advance releases—*Pulp Fiction, Forrest Gump, Stargate, Interview with a Vampire,* lots of *Three Stooges,* Marilyn Monroe, and *James Bond* titles, and much more. The catalog shows just a fraction of the inventory, and new titles and collections are constantly added to stock. If you don't see what you're looking for, send your requests with a long, self-addressed, stamped envelope.

Please note: Only U.S. funds are accepted.

Special Factors: Returns are accepted within five days for exchange, refund, or credit.

SEE ALSO

Barrons • *Goebel and Royal Doulton collectibles* • **HOME: TABLE SETTINGS**
Beverly Bremer Silver Shop • *heirloom and estate silver pieces* • **HOME: TABLE SETTINGS**
Caprilands Herb Farm • *collectors' dolls* • **FARM**

China-Silver-Crystal • David Winter cottages and Belleek, Hummel, and Lladró collectibles • *HOME: TABLE SETTINGS*
Editions • first editions and rare books • *BOOKS*
Elderly Instruments • vintage fretted instruments • *MUSIC*
Charles W. Jacobsen, Inc. • new and antique Oriental rugs • *HOME: DECOR: RUGS, CARPETING, AND FLOORING*
Mandolin Brothers, Ltd. • vintage fretted instruments • *MUSIC*
Record-Rama Sound Archives • vintage LPs and 45's • *BOOKS: RECORDINGS*
Rogers & Rosenthal, Inc. • figurines and collectibles • *HOME: TABLE SETTINGS*
The Scholar's Bookshelf • remaindered university-press art books • *BOOKS*
Strand Book Store, Inc. • books on the fine and applied arts • *BOOKS*
University Products, Inc. • archival-quality collection storage, mounting, and display materials • *OFFICE: SMALL BUSINESS*

ART MATERIALS

Materials, tools, equipment, and supplies for the fine and applied arts

You don't *have* to starve to be an artist, but the cost of good tools and supplies almost guarantees it—unless you can buy them at discount. Small art stores usually sell at list, and seldom knock off more than 10%, except on quantity purchases. But discount mail-order firms routinely offer savings of at least twice that. The firms listed here sell supplies and materials for fine arts and some crafts: pigments, paper, brushes, canvas, frames, stretchers, pads, studio furniture, vehicles and solvents, silk-screening supplies, carving tools, and much more—at great discounts.

Since different materials can have a profound effect on the quality and direction of your work, familiarize yourself with what's on the market through catalogs and artists' magazines. The catalog from Daniel Smith, listed in this chapter, provides a wealth of information. For a comprehensive assessment of the properties and uses of almost every medium available today, see *The Artists' Handbook of Materials and Techniques* (Viking Press), which can be found in libraries and is available from several firms in this chapter.

Concern about the safety of art materials has led to the Art Materials Labeling Act of 1988, and Congress has also asked the Consumer Products Safety Commission to create standards for the art materials industry, and banned the use of hazardous materials by children in the sixth grade or younger. This is important legislation, since the list of substances found in widely used materials has included toluene, asbestos, chloroform, xylene, n-hexane, carbolic acid, trichlorethylene, and benzene, to note just a few. Even with reformulation and warnings, art materials can still pose some hazards. Good studio protocol can minimize much of the exposure:

- Select the least toxic and hazardous products available.
- If your work creates dust or fumes, use a quality, OSHA-approved respirator suitable to the task—there are masks to filter organic vapors, ammonia, asbestos, toxic dusts, mists and fumes, and paint spray.
- Use other protective gear as applicable: gloves to reduce the absorption of chemicals through the skin, earplugs to protect against hearing damage from loud machinery, and safety goggles to avoid eye damage from accidents.
- A good window-exhaust system is essential to reducing inhaled vapors. Create a real airflow when working with fume-producing materials—the breeze from an open window isn't enough.
- Keep children and animals out of the work place since chemicals reach higher levels of concentration in their systems.
- Don't eat, drink, or smoke in the work area, or before cleaning up.
- Keep appropriate safety equipment on hand to deal with emergencies: an eyewash station if caustics are being used, a first-aid kit, a fire extinguisher if combustible materials are present, etc.
- Ask your school board to make sure the least toxic and hazardous products are used in the classroom.

For further reading, consult *Artist Beware: The Hazards and Precautions in Working with Art and Craft Materials,* by Michael McCann (Watson-Guptill Publications, 1979). *Health Hazards Manual for Artists* (Nick Lyons Books, 1985), a smaller book by Mr. McCann, includes specifics on materials commonly used by children. Both are sold by Ceramic Supply of New York & New Jersey (listed in this chapter). Mr. McCann, who is a chemist and an industrial hygienist, also founded the Center for Safety in the Arts. The organization deals with art-safety issues in *Art Hazards News,* a four-page newsletter published ten times a year. For current subscription rates and more information write to Center for Safety in the Arts at 5 Beekman St., Suite 1030, New York, NY 10038, or call 212-227-6220.

For firms that sell related products, see "Crafts and Hobbies" and "General Merchandise."

FIND IT FAST

CERAMICS AND POTTERY • Ceramic Supply
CHILDREN'S AND EDUCATIONAL ART SUPPLIES • Dick Blick, Sax

FINE ARTS • **Art Express, Cheap Joe's, Italian Art Store, Jerry's Artarama, Ott's, Pearl Paint, Daniel Smith, Utrecht**
FRAMES • **American Frame, Frame Fit, Graphik Dimensions, Daniel Smith, Stu-Art, Utrecht**
GRAPHIC DESIGN • **A.I. Friedman, Utrecht**
MAILING TUBES • **Yazoo**
PAPER AND PRINTMAKING • **Daniel Smith**
SILKSCREENING • **Crown Art**

AMERICAN FRAME CORPORATION

400 TOMAHAWK DR.
MAUMEE, OH 43537-1695
800-537-0944
FAX: 419-893-3553

Catalog: free
Save: up to 50%
Pay: check, MO, MC, V, AE, Discover
Sells: sectional frames, mat board, acrylic picture glass
Store: same address; Monday to Friday 9–4

American Frame, in business since 1973, sells *wood* sectional frames—a great way to get the look of a custom framing job, at do-it-yourself prices—as well as *metal* sectional frames in a wonderful selection of colors. American Frame's prices are 35% to 50% lower than those charged by other art-supply firms.

The 33-page catalog features frame sections in basswood, maple, poplar, mahogany, oak, and cherry, in a variety of stains, some with gilding. The profiles and dimensions of the sections are shown in detail, and each wood frame (two pairs of sections) is sent with corner insets for assembling the sections, spring clips to hold the mounted art work securely in place, and wall protectors. (Assembly requires attaching one end of the spring clips to the frame with screws, which are provided, and gluing the joints. No clamps are required, and instructions are given in the catalog.) The metal frames are offered in a choice of 11 profiles, to accommodate ordinary flat work and standard and extra-deep canvases. Seventeen metallic and 24 enameled colors are available, including French blue, graphite, rosewine, bronze, fern, and sapphire, among others.

Crescent board—acid-free mat, perfect-mount, and foam core—is sold in groups of ten or more sheets, depending on the item. The mat board is offered in over 100 colors in the 32" by 40" size; foam core and perfect-mount boards are cut to order in dimensions up to 24" by 30".

Rolls of polyester film are available, as well as acid-free acrylic picture "glass" (cut to order in dimensions up to 24" by 30").

Special Factors: Measure carefully before ordering; phone hours are 8:30 A.M. to 7 P.M., ET.

ART EXPRESS

DEPT. C
P.O. BOX 21662
COLUMBIA, SC 29212
800-535-5908
FAX: 803-750-1492

Catalog: $3.50
Save: up to 60%
Pay: check, MO, MC, V, AE, Discover
Sells: art supplies and equipment
Store: mail order only

Art Express publishes a 80-page catalog featuring a well-chosen selection of art tools and equipment at discounts averaging 40%. The inventory includes papers and board, canvas, brushes, mediums and solvents, pens, portfolios, paint (including casein), Art Bin artists' cases, folding stools, art racks, inks, pastels, pencils, airbrushing equipment, easels by Anco, Julian, Mabef, Stanrite, and Trident; light boxes, Logan mat cutters, and Artograph and Seerite opaque projectors. Among the other names represented are Arches, Berol, Bienfang, Canson, Da Vinci, Fabriano, Fredrix, Golden, Grumbacher, Holbein, Isabey, Le Franc & Bourgeois, Liquitex, Luma, Raphaël, Rembrandt, Rives, Bob Ross, Rowney, Schmincke, Sennelier, Shiva, Speedball, Strathmore, Studio RTA, Talens, and Winsor & Newton. Several pages list available books and videotapes on art technique, history, and related topics. If you don't see what you're looking for, write or fax Art Express with product information—the item might be in stock.

Special Factors: Quantity discounts are available; institutional accounts are available; minimum order is $25 on stock paper.

DICK BLICK CO.

P.O. BOX 1267-WM96
GALESBURG, IL 61401
309-343-6181
FAX: 309-343-5785

Catalog: $4
Save: up to 30%
Pay: check, MO, MC, V, AE, Discover
Sells: art and crafts supplies
Store: 38 locations in CT, GA, IA, IL, IN, KS, MI, MO, MN, NE, NV, OH, and PA
(addresses are listed in the catalog)

Dick Blick, an arts-and-crafts supplier geared to schools, publishes seasonal 52-page sale catalogs, but also lists tens of thousands of items in the big catalog, a 480-page compendium of supplies and equipment. Blick was established in 1911 and has everything in general art and craft supplies: Liquitex paints, Shiva pigments, Crayola crayons and finger paints, drawing tables and other art furniture, paint brushes, kraft paper, canvas, scissors, and adhesives. The catalog includes silk-screening materials, display lighting, printmaking equipment, wood-carving tools, molding materials, kilns, glazes, copper enamels, decoupage supplies, leather-working kits, dyes, macramé materials, weaving tools and equipment, blackboards, and much more. Over 20 pages are devoted to films, slides, videotapes, manuals, and books on arts and crafts.

Special Factors: Satisfaction is guaranteed; price quote by phone or letter on quantity orders; quantity discounts are available; returns are accepted within 30 days for exchange, refund, or credit; minimum order is $10 with credit cards.

CERAMIC SUPPLY OF NEW YORK & NEW JERSEY, INC.

7 RTE. 46 W.
LODI, NJ 07644
201-340-3005
FAX: 201-340-0089

Catalog: $4
Save: up to 40%
Pay: check, MO, MC, V
Sells: sculpture, pottery, glazing, and crafts supplies and equipment
Store: same address; Monday to Friday 9–5, Saturday 9–1; also 534 La Guardia Pl., New York, NY; Monday to Saturday 9–5

  ¡Si!

Ceramic Supply of New York & New Jersey serves both its name states with free delivery (in many areas) on orders of $100 or more. The company has been doing business since 1981, and offers good values on glazes, brushes, and a wide range of lightweight ceramics supplies that can be shipped worldwide at nominal expense. The 212-page catalog devotes most of its space to ceramics supplies and equipment: gas and electric kilns (including some that run on household current), raku and fiber kilns, glazes, resists, mediums, brushes, airbrushing tools, slip-casting equipment, potters' wheels, armatures, grinders, and related goods. The manufacturers include Alpine, Amaco, Brent, Kemper, Kimple, North Star, Shimpo, and Skutt, among others. The catalog includes color charts of glazes, underglazes, and other finishes by Duncan and Mayco, glazed and bisqued tiles of varying sizes and shapes, and dozens of types of clay, from white Grolleg porcelain to "economy" clay made of odds and ends of other clays. And there are lots of other modeling materials—FIMO plastic, Sculpey, Van Aken Plastelene, wax, and water-based clay.

Even if you're not a potter or sculptor, the catalog may interest you: music box parts and movements in scores of tunes, lights and accessories for ceramic Christmas trees, hard-to-find lamp parts, clock movements and parts, jewelry findings, studio furniture, and safety equipment are all available. Don't overlook the reference section, which features books on sculpture, ceramics, art hazards, and related topics, and videotapes and filmstrips.

Special Factors: Returns are accepted within ten days (a restocking fee may be charged).

CHEAP JOE'S ART STUFF

300A INDUSTRIAL PARK RD.
BOONE, NC 28607
800-227-2788
CUSTOMER SERVICE:
  800-227-5562
FAX: 800-257-0874

Catalog: free
Save: up to 50%
Pay: check, MO, MC, V, Discover
Sells: art supplies and equipment
Store: Boone Drug Co., 617 W. King St., Boone, NC

There *is* a Joe here at Cheap Joe's, and he expresses his persona throughout the 72-page, full color catalog in pithy product descriptions and tips on how to make the most of your tools and materials. Cheap Joe's dream of keeping his company small may be confounded by his great prices—savings of 30% are routine, and quantity pricing deepens the discounts to 70% on at least a few items.

The catalog features papers by Arches, Bockingford, Canson, Fabriano, Lana, and Waterford, paint from Da Vinci, Daler Rowney, Holbein, Rembrandt, Sennelier, and Winsor & Newton, paintbrushes from Jack Richeson, Robert Simmons, and Winsor & Newton, as well as Cheap Joe's own line. You'll also find easels, shrink-wrap systems, Logan mat cutters, adhesives, foam core, Artograph projection equipment, Fredrix canvas, print racks, and books and videotapes on painting and art theory. Cheap Joe set up shop in 1986, and he wants to keep his company from getting too big so he can stay in touch with his artist customers. He's a serious watercolorist, and welcomes your questions and suggestions about materials and equipment.

Special Factors: Satisfaction is guaranteed; shipping is not charged on brushes; institutional accounts are available.

CROWN ART PRODUCTS CO., INC.

90 DAYTON AVE.
PASSAIC, NJ 07055
201-777-6010
FAX: 201-777-3088

Catalog: free
Save: up to 50%
Pay: check, MO, MC, V, AE, Discover
Sells: silk-screening supplies and materials
Store: same address; Monday to Friday
9–4:30, Saturday 11:30–6

Crown Art has been making and selling silk-screening supplies and equipment since 1974, under the direction of a silk-screen artist who's developed several products for the craft. The 16-page catalog features Crown's products: simple silk-screening kits for textiles and paper ($35), water-based "3-D" paints, Voilà squeeze fabric dyes (nontoxic and air-cured), Crown Aqua and Crown Opaque textile inks, Supertex airbrush ink, Posterelle ink for paper, and even "puffy" and metallic inks. Ready-to-print customized silk screens, screen printing stretcher strips, squeegees, and photo emulsion chemicals are available. Prices are reasonable, and if you're an art teacher, printer, or dealer, contact Crown for information on the special discount program. If you're within commuting distance of the store in New Jersey, you may be interested in taking a silk-screening workshop or lessons at Crown.

Special Factors: Price quote by phone or letter on special sizes and volume orders; minimum order is $25 with credit cards.

FRAME FIT CO.

DEPT. WBMC
P.O. BOX 8926
PHILADELPHIA, PA 19135
800-523-3693
215-332-0683
FAX: 215-335-1772

Brochure and Price List: free
Save: up to 50%
Pay: check, MO, MC, V
Sells: aluminum and wood sectional frames
Store: mail order only

Frame Fit sells aluminum sectional frames in four profiles, for both stretched canvas and other works of art. The colors include anodized metallics in polished and satin finishes, and enamel in 21 colors (the canvas profile is available in five metallics only). The stock sizes run from 8" to 40", but larger sizes are available, and since any frame can be cut to a fractional measurement, they can be made as small as you like. All of the sections are sold in pairs, and include corner assembly hardware (springs, screw hangers, and picture wire are sold separately). Wood sectional frames are available in four profiles and six wood finishes.

Frame Fit has been in business since 1977, and although the selection here is not as extensive as those offered by many other frame specialists, the prices are better than those on *discounted* frames sold elsewhere by 20% and more. If you can use 50 pairs of the same color, size, and profile, you can save from 15% to 25% on top of that, depending on the color you choose. And if your order totals $300 or more, shipping is free (except on bulk chop goods).

Special Factors: Shipping is not charged on orders over $300 sent within the continental U.S.; C.O.D. orders are accepted.

A.I. FRIEDMAN

ATTN: WBMC SALES
   MANAGER
44 W. 18TH ST.
NEW YORK, NY 10011
212-243-9000
FAX: 212-242-1238

Catalog: $5 (see text)
Save: up to 40% (see text)
Pay: check, MO, MC, V, AE
Sells: graphic arts supplies and tools
Store: same address; and 25 W. 45th St., New York, NY; Monday to Friday 9–6, both locations; also Caldor Plaza, Port Chester, NY; open daily

If you're a professional graphic designer or artist, you'll want to add A.I. Friedman to your short list of suppliers. The firm, which has been in business since 1929, serves the creative community with the best in tools and equipment. You can send $5 for the well-organized loose-leaf catalog, but it's free to design professionals requesting it on letterhead.

The catalog itself is an object lesson in good design, making it easy to find what you want amid the equipment for computer graphics, presentation materials, studio furniture, drawing instruments, markers, paint, brushes, paper and board, airbrushing supplies, audio/visual equipment, frames, and reference books. Friedman offers goods not found in every art supply catalog: light boxes, dry-mounting presses, the *complete* Pantone line, precision drawing and drafting tools, a large selection of templates, and complete photostat systems. Among the manufacturers represented are Agfa Gevaert, Bainbridge, Canson, Chartpak, D'Arches, Dr. Ph. Martin's, Grumbacher, Iris, Iwata, Koh-I-Noor, Kolinsky, Lamy, LeRoy, Letraset, Liquitex, Luxo (lamps), Mont Blanc, Mutoh, Osmiroid, Paasche, Pelikan, Stacor, Staedler-Mars, Strathmore, 3M, and Winsor & Newton. The catalog prices are not discounted, but if your order totals $50 or more, discounts of 20% to 40% are given. (Some items aren't discounted, including the Agfa products.) Call or write for a quote on specific items.

Special Factors: Institutional accounts are available; minimum order is $50 (see text).

GRAPHIK DIMENSIONS LTD.

▬▬▬▬▬

2103 BRENTWOOD ST.
HIGH POINT, NC 27263
800-221-0262
910-887-3700
FAX: 910-887-3773

Catalog: free
Save: up to 60%
Pay: check, MO, MC, V, Discover
Sells: sectional and custom-made frames and accessories
Store: same address

  ⊕

You can get the frame you want with frame sections from Graphik Dimensions—or you can have it custom-made by the firm's expert crafters. Graphik Dimensions is run by an artist and photographer who have firsthand experience in selecting the right frame for the piece, and finding the best price. Their 36-page color catalog offers the "classic" metal sectional frames often sold in art-supply stores, in both standard depths, for use with glass, and "canvas" depth, for oil paintings, in metallics and enamels. The selection also includes wooden gallery frames in plain, gilded, embossed, rustic, and natural finishes. Graphik Dimensions' custom line features wood moldings, some of which include linen liners at no extra charge. If the whole prospect of putting a frame together seems too much, there's help: Graphic Dimensions also sells preassembled and custom-made assembled frames in several different styles.

Framing kits are available in your choice of wood frames, and include the glass (or acrylic), backing board, retainer clips, hanging screws, and wire—no tools necessary. Before you order a frame, order the sample set of corners. These are actual pieces of the frame that show color, depth, and corner joinery style. The cost of the sample sets ($5 to $30, depending on the line) is repaid in the trouble you save if the frame wasn't right for the work. (Individual pieces are available free on request.) And all wood frames come with hangers, retainer clips, and wire.

Special Factors: Quantity discounts are available; authorized returns (except custom frames) are accepted (a 15% restocking fee may be charged); C.O.D. orders are accepted.

THE ITALIAN ART STORE

84 MAPLE AVE.
MORRISTOWN, NJ 07960
800-643-6440
201-644-2717
FAX: 201-644-5074

Catalog: free
Save: up to 75%
Pay: check, MO, MC, V, Discover
Sells: fine art supplies
Store: same address; Monday to Friday 9–5

The Italian Art Store began business as a homage to the epicenter of the Renaissance, by selling *only* Italian art supplies. Consider Raphaël watercolor brushes, Maimeri Restoration Colors, Fabriano papers, and Sennelier pastels—all among the finest of their type. But the patrons of The Italian Art Store petitioned the owner for a more cosmopolitan selection, and he obliged, with Blockx and Sennelier oils, Golden acrylics, Fredrix canvas, Holbein, Rowney, and Winsor & Newton watercolors and mediums, Rembrandt and Aquarelle pencils, Schmincke gouache, Gamblin oil mediums, Brera paints, Isabey brushes, and easels by Julian and Mabef. The Italian Art Store's own line of goods includes pigments, brushes, canvas, and easels.

Discounts average 50% on list prices, but specials and closeouts run up to 75% off. In the past The Italian Art Store has offered a year of free shipping to customers in the United States and Canada, who placed an order of at least $100 in goods. Check for details in the catalog you receive (the offer may be extended or revived).

Special Factors: Check the catalog for free shipping program.

JERRY'S ARTARAMA, INC.

**P.O. BOX 1105-WBMC
NEW HYDE PARK, NY
11040
516-328-6633
FAX: 516-328-6752**

Catalog: $2
Save: 33% average
Pay: check, MO, MC, V, AE, Discover
Sells: art supplies, picture frames, etc.
Store: 1109 New Britain Ave., West Hartford, CT (203-232-0073); 248-12 Union Tpk., Bellerose, NY (718-343-0777); and 270 S. Federal Hwy. (U.S. 1), Deerfield Beach, FL (305-427-6264)

Jerry's Artarama publishes a 102-page compendium of materials, tools, and equipment for commercial and fine arts that includes both basics and specialty goods that are seldom discounted elsewhere. Jerry's was established in 1968, and carries over 12,000 different items.

The catalog offers pigments, brushes, vehicles and solvents, airbrushes and compressors, studio furniture, lighting, visual equipment, canvas and framing supplies, papers, and other goods, with an extensive section of oil, watercolor, and acrylic painting supplies. Jerry's also sells supplies for drawing, graphic arts, drafting, calligraphy, printmaking, sumi-e, airbrushing, fabric painting, marbleizing, and professional framing. There are some "generic" brands, but most are familiar names: Alvin, Badger, Blockx, Conté, Deka, D'Arches, Fabriano, Fredrix, Grumbacher, Holbein, Isabey, Iwata, Koh-I-Noor, Langnickel, Mayline, Paasche, Bob Ross, Robert Simmons, Stabilo, Strathmore, Winsor & Newton, and X-Acto are among the many represented. Don't miss the dozen pages of publications, including technique manuals, color guides, and workshop videotapes—all of which are discounted.

Special Factors: Satisfaction is unconditionally guaranteed; color charts and product specifications are available on request; quantity discounts are available; minimum order is $20, $50 with phone orders.

OTT'S DISCOUNT ART SUPPLY, INC.

DEPT. WBMC
102 HUNGATE DR.
GREENVILLE, NC
  27858-8045
800-356-3289
919-756-9565
FAX: 919-756-2397

Catalog: free
Save: up to 75%
Pay: check, MO, MC, V
Sells: art, graphics, and crafts supplies
Store: mail order only

Painters, sculptors, and artists of all types can get great prices on all of their needs from Ott's, a family-run firm that also serves schools and institutions. The 60-page catalog runs from Academy watercolors to Zec Quick Dryer from Grumbacher. The brands include Amaco (clay and kilns), Amsterdam, Arches, Badger, Bemis-Jason, Berol, Bienfang, Canson, Dixon, Faber Castell, General Pencil, Grumbacher, Hunt, Koh-I-Noor, Liquitex, Loew-Cornell, Morilla, Paasche, Prang, Rembrandt, Bob Ross, Sakura, Strathmore, Tara-Fredrix, Van Gogh, Winsor & Newton, and X-Acto, among others. You'll find oils and tempera paints, stretchers, canvas, pencils and charcoal, paper, airbrush and silkscreening equipment, easels, projection equipment, craft paints, clay and kilns, styrofoam, candle-making and wood-burning supplies, adhesives, craft knives and brushes, and more. There's a good selection of instructional materials, including guides from North Light Books, and great rainy-day projects like the Deluxe Volcano and Solar System Kits.

Quantity discounts are available, and if you're looking for something not shown in the catalog, just call—Ott's may be able to get it.

Special Factors: Satisfaction is guaranteed; quantity discounts are available; returns are accepted within 30 days for exchange, refund, or credit; institutional orders are accepted; orders under $30 are charged $2 shipping and $5 handling.

PEARL PAINT CO., INC.

ATTN: CATALOG DEPT.
308 CANAL ST.
NEW YORK, NY
10013-2572
800-221-6845
212-431-7932
FAX: 212-274-8290

Catalog: $1
Save: up to 70%
Pay: check, MO, MC, V, AE, Discover
Sells: art, craft, and graphics supplies, studio furniture, etc.
Store: same address; also 42 Lispenard St., New York, NY (architectural furniture showroom); open daily; also Altamonte Springs, Ft. Lauderdale, Miami, and Tampa, FL; Atlanta, GA; Chicago, IL; Cambridge, MA; Rockville, MD; Cherry Hill, Paramus, and Woodbridge, NJ; East Meadow, NY; Houston, TX; and Alexandria, VA

Gotham artists have been flocking to Pearl Paint since 1933 for good prices on fine paints, tools, and supplies, and since then Pearl has opened stores in nine other states as well (locations are listed in the catalog). Since the catalog represents a fraction of the available stock (fine art materials), call, fax, or write if you're looking for something that's not listed. In addition to tools and supplies for the fine arts, Pearl sells materials and equipment for all kinds of crafts: pigments, brushes, vehicles and solvents, stretchers, papers, canvas, manuals, studio furniture, and much more. The brands include Bainbridge, Canson-Talens, Caran D'Ache, Deka, DeVilbiss, Fabriano, Grumbacher, Holbein, Iwata, Koh-I-Noor, Lascaux, Letraset, Liquitex, Paasche, Pantone, Pebeo, Pelikan, Sculpture House, Sennelier, Robert Simmons, Staedtler, and Winsor & Newton, among others. Pearl also stocks fine writing instruments, house paint, frames and framing supplies, gilding and "faux" finishing supplies.

Special Factors: Quantity discounts are available; weekly specials are run on selected items; minimum order is $50.

SAX ARTS & CRAFTS

DEPT. 96WBMC
2405 S. CALHOUN RD.
NEW BERLIN, WI 53151
414-784-6880
FAX: 414-785-8410

Catalog: $5, refundable
Save: up to 50%
Pay: check, MO, MC, V, AE, Discover
Sells: arts and crafts supplies
Store: mail order only

Sax Arts & Crafts publishes a "resource of art and craft materials and equipment for the classroom and studio," a color catalog ($5) of over 500 pages that serves both educator and professional artist. Sax is notable for the range of supplies it offers—everything from craft sticks to kilns—and identifies products that have been certified "safe" or non-toxic by the Art and Craft Materials Institute, a helpful feature if you're buying products for children.

Sax has been in business since 1945, and sells tools and materials for paper lithography, "friendly" plastic for making jewelry, airbrushing, drawing, paper collage and tissue craft, paper sculpture, papermaking, etching, framing and matting, drafting, calligraphy, scratch art, ceramics, copper enameling, engraving, weaving, rug making, bead work, basketry, fabric painting, mosaics, and wood burning. Among the names represented are Amaco, Bockingford, Canson, Chromacryl, Cra-Pas, Crayola, Crescent, D'Arches, Deka, Fabriano, Fimo, Fredrix, Liquitex, Paasche, Pelikan, Pentel, Prang, Prismacolor, Shiva, Speedball, Strathmore, Whatman, and Winsor & Newton. The catalog features a number of unusual items: fluorescent modeling clay, erasable felt-tip pens, balsa foam (cuts with a toothpick, prints like a woodblock), silhouette paper, and Venetian glass tile, among others. And there are 40 pages of books, manuals, videotapes, and cards on art-related topics. Prices are competitive, but the real savings are on quantity purchases.

Special Factors: Satisfaction is guaranteed; authorized returns are accepted for exchange, refund, or credit; institutional accounts are available; minimum order is $10.

DANIEL SMITH

P.O. BOX 84268
SEATTLE, WA 98124-5568
800-426-6740 (U.S. AND
CANADA)
206-223-9599
FAX: 800-238-4065

Catalog: free
Save: 30% average
Pay: check, MO, MC, V, AE
Sells: fine-arts supplies and equipment
Store: 4150 First Ave. South, Seattle, WA;
Monday, Tuesday, Thursday, Friday, Saturday
9–6, Wednesday 9–8, Sunday 10–6

Daniel Smith's catalogs are designed by artists, for artists, and are appreciated as much for their book reviews, technical discussions, and visual appeal as for their offerings. Daniel Smith has been recommended by artists impressed by the company's line of materials and responsive service department; the firm features competitive pricing and regular sales.

The annual Reference Catalog presents an extensive collection of paper from Arches, Canson, Fabriano, Lana, Magnani, Rising, Strathmore, and other makers, for watercolors, printmaking, drawing, bookmaking, and other applications. This catalog also features uncommon specialty papers, including banana paper from the Philippines, Mexican bark paper, genuine papyrus, and Japanese "fantasy" paper embedded with maple leaves.

Daniel Smith has been manufacturing etching inks and artists' paints for more than 18 years, and features the Daniel Smith Original Oils, Autograph Series Oils and the newly created Daniel Smith Extra-Fine line of artists' watercolors—paints notable for their quality, rich formulation, and unique color range—including luminescent and metallic colors. Daniel Smith sells acrylics, oils, watercolors, egg tempera, and gouache from such companies as Golden, Lascaux, Rowney, Schmincke, Talens, and Winsor & Newton. The brush line covers all painting media, and includes Daniel Smith's own line, as well as brushes from Isabey, Strathmore, and Winsor & Newton. Canvas, Nielsen sectional metal frames, wood frames, airbrush equipment, solvents, pastels, colored pencils, calligraphy pens, printmaking materials, and other tools and supplies available, rounded out by a fine collection of studio furniture, portfolios, easels, and reference books.

Canadian readers, please note: Only U.S. funds are accepted.

Special Factors: Satisfaction is guaranteed; authorized returns are accepted for exchange, refund, or credit; minimum order of paper is ten sheets.

STU-ART SUPPLIES

2045 GRAND AVE.,
DEPT. WBMC
BALDWIN, NY
11510-2999
516-546-5151
FAX: 516-377-3512

Catalog: $5, refundable
Save: up to 50%
Pay: check, MO, MC, V, AE, Discover
Sells: arts and crafts supplies
Store: mail order only

Stu-Art sells sectional frames and framing materials—everything you'll need to do a professional job. The firm has been supplying galleries and institutions since 1970, and it offers the best materials, a range of sizes, and savings of up to 50% on list prices.

Nielsen metal frames are offered in nine profiles, for flat, stretched canvas and dimensional art (deep) mounting, in a stunning array of brushed metallic finishes, soft pastels, and deep decorator colors. Sectional wood frames are also available, in eight different profiles and a variety of finishes. Acid-free single and double mats are sold in rectangles and ovals. The catalog includes precise specifications of the frames, and samples of the mats. Stu-Art also sells nonglare and clear plastic (which can be used in place of picture glass), and shrink film and dispensers. If you have to get work framed, see the catalog before handing it over to a professional—you may decide you can do the job yourself.

Special Factors: Shipping is not charged on UPS-delivered orders over $300 net; authorized returns are accepted (a restocking fee may be charged); minimum order is $15 on sectional frames, $25 on other goods; C.O.D. orders are accepted.

UTRECHT ART AND DRAFTING SUPPLY

33 35TH ST.
BROOKLYN, NY 11232
800-223-9132
718-768-2525
FAX: 718-499-8815

Catalog: free
Save: up to 70%
Pay: check, MO, MC, V
Sells: art supplies
Store: 111 Fourth Ave, New York, NY; Monday to Saturday 9–6; also Berkeley and San Francisco, CA; Washington, DC; Chicago, IL; Boston, MA; Detroit, MI; and Philadelphia, PA

 ¡Si!

Utrecht has been selling supplies and equipment for painting, sculpture, and printmaking since 1949, and manufactures some of the best-priced oil and acrylic paints on the market. The 48-page catalog describes the manufacturing process and quality controls used to produce Utrecht's paint, and features Utrecht acrylics, oils, watercolors, gesso, and other mediums and solvents. The firm also sells a full line of professional artists' materials and equipment, including canvas, stretchers, frames, pads, paper, brushes, books, easels, flat files, taborets, pencils, drafting tools, and much more. In addition to the Utrecht label, goods by Arches, Bainbridge, Bienfang, Canson, Chartpak, Claessens, D'Arches, Deka, Eberhard Faber, Grumbacher, Koh-I-Noor, Kolinsky, Liquitex, Niji, Pentel, Rembrandt, Speedball, Strathmore, Vermeer, Winsor & Newton, and other manufacturers are available. Utrecht's prices are competitive, and the best buys are on the house brand and quantity purchases.

Special Factors: Institutional accounts are available; quantity discounts are available; minimum order is $40.

YAZOO MILLS, INC.

COMMERCE ST.
P.O. BOX 369
NEW OXFORD, PA 17350
717-624-8993
FAX: 717-624-4420

Price List: free
Save: 50% plus
Pay: check, MO, MC, V, AE
Sells: shipping tubes
Store: mail order only

Yazoo Mills takes its name from the Mississippi town where it was founded in 1902, but since moving to Pennsylvania in 1936, Yazoo has run the plant from New Oxford. The firm manufactures paper tubes for shipping and industry—carpet "cores," cable reels, fax paper tubes, even heavy blast casings for the mining industry—Yazoo makes them all. Yazoo also offers shipping tubes in the sizes most popular among artists: lengths from 12" to 85", in diameters of 2" to 12" (the larger sizes are "heavy duty" or "extra heavy duty"). The tubes are sold by the case—48 in a carton of 2" by 12" tubes, to one of the 12" by 85"—with plastic plug inserts for the ends. The prices, which include shipping, are so low that even if all you need are two mid-sized tubes, it's probably worth buying from Yazoo—they're priced up to 80% below art-supply houses!

The tubes can be used for storage as well as shipping art and other objects; although they're made of recycled paperboard, they're not acid-free. Yazoo does much of its manufacturing to job specifications, and can give you quotes on custom sizes or colors.

Special Factors: Shipping is not charged; minimum order is one carton of stock tubes; C.O.D. orders are accepted.

SEE ALSO

Dharma Trading Co. • *tools and materials for fabric painting and dyeing* • **CRAFTS: TEXTILE ARTS**
Plexi-Craft Quality Products Corp. • *acrylic display pedestals* • **HOME: FURNISHINGS**
The Potters Shop Inc. • *books on pottery and ceramics* • **BOOKS**
Print's Graphic Design Book Stores • *books and manuals on the graphic arts* • **BOOKS**
Thai Silks • *silk fabrics for fabric painting* • **CRAFTS: TEXTILE ARTS**
Utex Trading Enterprises • *silk fabric for fabric painting* • **CRAFTS: TEXTILE ARTS**

AUTO, MARINE, AND AVIATION EQUIPMENT

Parts, supplies, maintenance products,

and services

You'll find a range of parts and supplies for cars, motorcycles, RVs, trucks, and vans in this chapter—mufflers, shocks, tires, batteries, and much more. Some companies stock products for vintage cars, and one offers products for the "general pilot." You can even buy salvaged parts through several of the firms listed here, priced as much as 70% below the same parts if new. You can also buy cars, trucks, and vans, through services offered by American Auto Brokers. Here are some additional information sources to help you make the best selection when buying a car:

- *Consumer Reports* publishes reliable vehicle ratings each year and offers price comparisons and reliability ratings of new and used cars. The "Consumer Reports Auto Price Service" provides a computer printout showing both list price and dealer's cost for the model you specify, information on rebates and recommended options, and guidelines for negotiating the lowest possible price. At this writing, one report costs $11; two are $20; three, $27; and each additional report thereafter, $5. See the current *Consumer Reports* for information, or write to Consumer Reports Auto Price Service, Box 8005, Novi, MI 48376. The "Consumer Reports Used Car Price Service" gives current prices on models as far back as 1986. To get a price, you answer questions about a specific model—condition, mileage, age, options, etc.—to which the computer adds other facts, and calculates a price. The service is terrific for someone who wants to negotiate a better deal on a used car, or set a price when they sell. (See the current issue of *Consumer Reports* for the 900 number and per-minute charges (touch-tone required).

- Another benchmark pricing service, *IntelliChoice,* provides two types of reports: "Just the Facts," which gives you data on *one* car, for all models within that line—factory and dealer prices, taxes and surcharges, nationwide rebate programs, standard and available options, etc. The "Arm-Chair Compare" report ($19.95) compares two different models in a line; you provide IntelliChoice with a list of all the options and finishes you want on *each* model. Call IntelliChoice at 800-227-2665 for current rates and to order a report (have the car information ready when you call).

- More car-buying tips and traps are detailed in W. James Bragg's *In the Driver's Seat: The New Car Negotiating Bible* (Random House), and Burke Leon's *The Insider's Guide to Buying a New or Used Car* (Betterway Books, 800-289-0963).

- *The Car Book,* by Jack Gillis (HarperCollins), rates current domestic and imported models on crash-test performance, as well as fuel economy, preventive-maintenance costs, repair costs, and insurance rates. The book also includes valuable information on evaluating warranties, service contracts, insurance, tires, children's car seats, and used cars. The comprehensive, easy-to-understand "Complaint" chapter should help you resolve difficulties, and the "Checklist" at the back of the book will help you ask the right questions. *The Car Book* is available in bookstores or from The Center for Auto Safety, 2001 S St., N.W., Suite 410, Washington, DC 20009. (Send a long, self-addressed, stamped envelope for the publications list and ordering information.)

- *The National Highway Administration Auto Safety Hotline* can help you check safety factors when you're shopping for a new or used car, or buying tires. In addition to crash test reports, tire quality grading results, and guidelines to buying a safer car, the hotline has recall information on autos and auto-related goods, such as infants' car seats. And you can *report* safety problems here, too. Call 800-424-9393 for more information.

- The Better Business Bureau publishes guides to buying cars and tires, as well as other consumer goods. Send a self-addressed, stamped envelope to the Council of Better Business Bureaus, Inc., 4200 Wilson Blvd., Suite 800, Arlington, VA 22203, Attn.: Publications Dept., and request the list of available brochures and ordering information.

You can save hundreds or even thousands of dollars when buying your car, only to squander as much thanks to bad driving habits. The following tips will conserve funds and fuel, keeping your wallet fatter and the air cleaner:

- Drive at 55 miles per hour or less, whenever possible. You'll go about 20% farther on the same tank than you do when traveling at 70 mph.
- Don't burn fuel you don't have to: Don't leave the car in idle for more than a minute (turn it off), don't use air conditioning unless it's really necessary, and keep the car free of excess weight.
- Have the wheels aligned at least once a year, and switch to radials, which maximize mileage.
- Check your tire pressure monthly, using a gauge (the old pencil style is inexpensive and reliable, and stows easily in the glove compartment). If you're driving on underinflated tires, you're using more gas than necessary—as much as 2% of your bill at the pump could be waste. Take the reading when the tires are cold, using guidelines provided by the car manufacturer.
- Follow other care instructions outlined in your car manual, including scheduling tune-ups and changing oil and filters.

Preventive maintenance notwithstanding, your car will need some kind of repair eventually. Mark Eskeldon, a car mechanic himself, tells all in *What Auto Mechanics Don't Want You to Know* ($14.95 postpaid; 800-247-6553). It will help you identify good repair shops and to recognize deceptive trade practices. Last, the monthly *Nutz & Boltz®* provides regular reading on a wide range of automotive topics; write to Box 123, Butler, MD 21023 for current subscription information.

Fear of getting stranded far from home with a disabled car leads many drivers to join auto clubs. Service and survival are great benefits, but most of the organizations provide far more than emergency towing. The best-known club, the American Automobile Association (AAA), boasts about 30 million members among its affiliates and offers a wide range of membership benefits. The AAA of New York, for example, provides travel-planning services, discounts on lodging and car and rentals, fee-free travelers' checks, special services for travel abroad, personal accident insurance, assistance in solving license problems, home-equity loans, discount eyeglass prescriptions, a newsletter, and other benefits. The package of services varies from affiliate to affiliate; to find the AAA club nearest you, call 800-336-4357. Other clubs worth contacting for rates and services are Amoco Motor Club (800-782-7887) and Exxon Travel Club (800-833-9966).

If you find you're stuck with a lemon, you have help—consumer advocates uncovered the auto industry's "secret warranties" several years ago, and Consumer Reports Books has produced the guide to making them work for you: *Get Your Car Fixed Free*, by Mort Schultz. For other sources of assistance *after* you've worked your way through the service manager, dealer, and the manufacturer (check your sales agreement and warranty for procedures), first, contact The Center for Auto Safety, 2001 S St. NW, Washington, DC 20009; the staff can often suggest agencies you can contact. If you exhaust other remedies, you may proceed to *mediation*; car manufacturers have arrangements with groups that mediate and arbitrate consumer disputes. For the name of the group handling problems with your car's manufacturer, call the National Automobile Dealers Association, Autocap, at 703-821-7000. The names of many of the mediators, as well as government agencies, are listed in *The Consumers Resource Handbook*, available free of charge from the Consumer Information Center (see the listing in "Books" for more information).

If your interest is boating, you already know about the expenses— insurance, dock fees, upkeep, and new equipment. You can save 30% *routinely* on the cost of maintenance products, gear, and electronics by buying from the marine suppliers listed here, who sell every type of coating, tool, and device you'll need to keep your vessel afloat. You'll find exhaustive selections of electronics, hardware, and instruments, as well as galley accoutrements and foul-weather clothing. Even landlubbers should see these catalogs for the well-designed slickers and oiled sweaters. And the reference sections of the biggest catalogs have a full range of books and videos on boat maintenance and other marine topics.

If you're a private pilot who'd like to save on some of the gear and electronics you need while flying high, see the listings of Aircraft Spruce and San-Val, aviation discounters. Like the marine suppliers, these firms also sells goods of interest to those on terra firma, at savings of up to 50%. For great leads on good buys in used aircraft, try *Trade-A-Plane*, a tabloid packed with ads for planes and aviation equipment. For current rates, write to Trade-A-Plane, P.O. Box 509, Crossville, TN 38557-9909.

FIND IT FAST

AVIATION • *Aircraft Spruce, San-Val*
BOATING SUPPLIES AND EQUIPMENT • *Defender, E & B, Goldbergs', M&E Marine, West Marine*
CAR PARTS AND ACCESSORIES • *Car Racks Direct, Cherry Auto, Clark's*

Corvair, IMPCO, Mill Supply, ProAm
CARS, TRUCKS, JEEPS • American Automobile Brokers
FARM EQUIPMENT PARTS • Central Michigan
MOTORCYCLE PARTS • Capital Cycle
RACING EQUIPMENT • ProAm, Racer Wholesale
TIRES • Euro-Tire, Teletire

AIRCRAFT SPRUCE & SPECIALTY CO.

P.O. BOX 424

201 W. TRUSLOW AVE.

FULLERTON, CA 92632

714-870-7551

FAX: 714-871-7289

Catalog: $5, refundable (see text)
Save: up to 35%
Pay: check, MO, MC, V, AE, Discover
Sells: small aircraft and pilot equipment
Store: 201 W. Truslow Ave. and Aircraft Spruce Avionics, 240 N. Dale Pl., Fullerton, CA; Monday to Friday 6–6, Saturday 7–3:30

Aircraft Spruce & Specialty Co. has been selling aircraft parts and equipment since 1965 and is the source to call for aircraft plywood, flight seats, tubing and sheeting, cable, wire, circuit breakers, AN-MS hardware, headsets, and all kinds of avionics. The brands represented include Arnav, Bendix/King, B.F. Goodrich, Champion, David Clark, Flybuddy, ICOM, Magellan, Pelican, Randolph, S-Tec, Sony, Telex, Terra, TKM, Trimble, and Whelen (lighting), among others. In addition to an exhaustive inventory of supplies, equipment, and electronics for plane and pilot, there are neat things for the nonflyer: Dahon folding bicycles, propeller wall clocks, and a ceiling fan that's an authentic replica of the P-40 Warhawk World War II fighter, complete with shark mouth ($269). Savings are comparable to those offered by other major aircraft supply discounters, and the firm has a "lowest price" policy. Call for a quote if you know what you want, or send $5 for the 448-page catalog ($20 for overseas orders, U.S. funds only); it's refundable with a $50 purchase.

Special Factors: Satisfaction is guaranteed; minimum order is $10.

AMERICAN AUTO-MOBILE BROKERS, INC.

24001 SOUTHFIELD RD.,
SUITE 110
SOUTHFIELD, MI 48075
810-569-5900
FAX: 810-569-2022

Information: see text
Save: see text
Pay: check or MO (see text)
Sells: new vehicles
Store: same address

 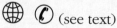 (see text)

When it comes to buying a new vehicle, one option is purchasing from American Automobile Brokers, which has been in business since 1972. Prices include dealer prep, all factory rebates, and delivery directly from the factory to a dealership near you by train or truck (for domestic vehicles), and savings depend on the prices in your area.

If you're shopping for a domestic model, you can buy vehicles by General Motors, Ford/Lincoln-Mercury, and Chrysler/Jeep/Eagle. The foreign makes include Alfa Romeo, BMW, Honda, Isuzu, Mercedes, Mitsubishi, Porsche, Saab, Toyota, and others. (American Automobile Brokers doesn't sell imports to residents of California.) The procedure is simple: Call or write with complete details about the vehicle and options desired, or send a self-addressed, stamped envelope for American Automobile Brokers' price-quote form. You get *one free quote;* extra quotes cost $5 each. Send a self-addressed, stamped envelope both when requesting the form and when sending it back for the quote. You can shop your local dealers, then get a quote here and see what you'll save by buying through American Automobile Brokers.

TDD callers: American Automobile Brokers has worked with operators who assisted incoming calls on TDD equipment, and has successfully completed transactions—but the firm doesn't have its own TDD.

Special Factors: Price quote by phone, letter, or American Automobile Brokers quote form with SASE; checks and money orders are accepted for deposit only, balance payable by certified check, cashier's check, or wire transfer.

CAPITAL CYCLE CORPORATION/CAPITAL EUROSPORT

21580 BEAUMEADE CIRCLE, #170
ASHBURN, VA 22011
800-642-5100
703-729-7900
FAX: 703-729-7908

Catalog: free
Save: up to 65%
Pay: check, MO, MC, V, AE
Sells: BMW and European aftermarket motorcycle parts and accessories
Store: 21580 Beaumeade Circle, #170, Ashburn, VA; Monday to Friday 8:30–6, Saturday 9–5

Capital Cycle is the nation's definitive source for replacement parts for BMW motorcycles, with an inventory of over 10,000 genuine, original parts, which are priced up to 65% below what the dealers are charging. Capital Cycle, which has been in business since 1972, publishes a 54-page catalog featuring specials and much-requested items.

Capital offers genuine BMW motorcycle parts, manufactured from 1955 through the current year. The catalog includes only a fraction of the enormous inventory, including engine parts and electronics, carburetors, fuel tanks, mufflers, pipes, clutches, gears, steering bearings, shocks, springs, handlebars, mirrors, brakes, tires, rims, forks, fenders, fairings, locks and keys, paint, seats, switches and relays, tachometers, voltmeters, lights, tools, and decals. Parts books and factory repair manuals for BMW cycles are offered, as well as original BMW tools and a selection of BMW car parts. Capital Cycle's European division, Capital Eurosport, offers premium aftermarket parts and accessories from top manufacturers in Europe. Items include luggage, panniers, gloves, covers, and exhausts, among others.

Canadian readers, please note: Only U.S. funds are accepted.

Special Factors: Quantity discounts are available; UPS ground shipping is not charged; repair services are available by mail; authorized returns are accepted within 30 days (a 15% restocking fee may be charged); minimum order is $20.

CAR RACKS DIRECT

82 DANBURY RD.
WILTON, CT 06837
800-722-5734
FAX: 203-761-0812

Catalog: free
Save: see text
Pay: check, MO, MC, V, AE
Sells: vehicle racks
Store: mail order only

Car Racks Direct sells just that—Thule and Yakima car racks, to secure bicycles, kayaks, canoes, skis, surfboards, and less playful items like lumber and furniture. In addition to basic racks, Car Racks Direct carries security cables, locks, straps, crossbars, fairings, brackets, and even cases and boxes engineered to fit the racking systems. Discounts vary on individual items, generally running from 12% to 18% off suggested retail—not deep, but better than paying list. Car Racks Direct has been in business since 1987, and will send you the Thule and Yakima catalogs on request, or give you a price quote over the phone.
Special Factors: Authorized returns are accepted.

CENTRAL MICHIGAN TRACTOR & PARTS

2713 N. U.S. 27
ST. JOHNS, MI 48879
800-248-9263
517-224-6802
FAX: 517-224-6682

Catalog: free
Save: up to 50%
Pay: check, MO, MC, V
Sells: used, new, and rebuilt tractor parts
Store: mail order only

Central Michigan can save you up to 50% on parts for tractors and combines. The company stocks new, used, reconditioned, and rebuilt parts, all of which are backed by a 30-day guarantee. Through the 220-page catalog, you can buy everything from starters to cylinder blocks for machines made by almost every major manufacturer—Allis, Case, Chalmers, John Deere, Massey Ferguson, Ford, International, Moline, White/Oliver, and others. The rebuilt parts are overhauled completely, so they should function as well and for as long as new ones. Central Michigan, one of 13 firms that make up the "Parts Express Network,"

maintains customers' want lists for parts not in stock. Call between 8 and 5:30, Monday to Friday, or 8 and 3:00 on Saturdays for information.

Special Factors: Price quote by phone or letter.

CHERRY AUTO PARTS

5650 N. DETROIT AVE.
TOLEDO, OH 43612
419-476-7222
FAX: 419-470-6388

Information: price quote
Save: up to 70%
Pay: check, MO, MC, V
Sells: used and rebuilt imported-car parts
Store: same address; Monday to Friday 8:30–5, Saturday 8:30–12; also 25425 John Rd., Madison Heights, MI (Detroit area); Monday to Friday 8:30–5

Why pay top dollar for new car parts if you can get perfectly good ones, used, for up to 70% less? Cherry Auto Parts, "The Midwest's Leading Imported Car Dismantler," can supply you with used and rebuilt imported-car components at sizable savings. Cherry Auto has 45 years of experience in the business, and keeps rebuilt cylinder heads, engines, starters, steering gears, alternators, drive axles, turbos, and other vital parts on hand. If you drive an Acura, Alfa Romeo, Audi, BMW, Chrysler Import (Champ, Colt, Conquest, Raider Vista), Nissan, Eagle, GEO, Honda, Isuzu, Jaguar, Mazda, Mercedes, Merkur, MG, Mitsubishi, Peugeot, Porsche, Renault, Saab, Spectrum, Sprint, Subaru, Toyota, Triumph, Volkswagen, Volvo, or other imported car, you may save up to 70% on your parts bills by getting them here. Cherry can access two nationwide computerized parts-locating networks to trace hard-to-find parts.

Special Factors: Price quote by phone (preferred) or letter; "All parts are guaranteed in stock at the time of quotation, guaranteed to be the correct part, and in good condition as described"; minimum order is $20.

CLARK'S CORVAIR PARTS, INC.

400 MOHAWK TRAIL,
DEPT. WC
SHELBURNE FALLS, MA
01370
413-625-9776
FAX: 413-625-8498

Catalog: $5
Save: up to 40%
Pay: check, MO, MC, V, Discover
Sells: Corvair parts
Store: mail order only

Clark's, in business since 1973, is an indispensable source for the Corvair owner since it stocks parts available nowhere else. Clark's can save you up to 40% on original and replacement General Motors parts, reproductions, and goods by Champion, Chevrolet, Clevite, Delco, Gabriel, Loctite, Michigan Bearings, Moog, Permatex, Sealed Power, TRW, and hundreds of other suppliers. The exhaustive inventory includes brakes, cables, lights, air filters, body parts and panels, carburetor and engine parts, gauges, gas tanks, manuals, pistons, points, seals, rims, specialty tools, paint, reproduction upholstery, trim, carpets, and many other parts and supplies. Every other year, Clark's Corvair Parts publishes an inventory of over 10,000 new Corvair parts in an indexed, 400-page catalog, supplemented by a second, 120-page catalog of used car parts, NOS parts, and high-performance parts—all for $5 to U.S. addresses. If you're looking for a specific part, you can call for a quote—but the catalogs are valuable reference tools and well worth the $5 to any do-it-yourself Corvair owner.

Special Factors: Price quote by phone or letter; returns are accepted; C.O.D. orders are accepted; minimum order is $10.

DEFENDER INDUSTRIES, INC.

255 MAIN ST.
P.O. BOX 820
NEW ROCHELLE, NY
10802-0820
914-632-3001
FAX (U.S. AND CANADA):
800-654-1616
FAX: 914-632-6544

Catalog: free
Save: up to 60%
Pay: check, MO, MC, V, Discover
Sells: marine supplies, gear, equipment, and clothing
Store: The Marine Discount Supermarket, 321 Main St., New Rochelle, NY; Monday to Friday 9–5:45, Thursday 9–8:45, Saturday 9–4:45 (call for hours, October–February)
E-mail: defenderus@aol.com, defender@sailnet.com

Defender has been selling marine hardware and equipment since 1938, and backs its claim of "the largest selection in the USA at the very lowest prices" with a 404-page catalog that runs from anchors to winches. It features page after page of boat maintenance supplies, resins and coatings, winches, windlasses, cordage, communications devices, foul-weather gear, books, tools and hardware, optics, galley fittings, navigation equipment, and electronics. You'll find sailboat hardware from Harken, Schaefer, and Lewmar, Evinrude, Nissan, and Tohatsu outboard engines, and lines of marine electronics from Apelco, Autohelm, Humminbird, ICOM, Impulse, Lowrance, Micrologic, Motorola, Navico, Northstar, and Raytheon. Also available: Shakespeare antennae, Pioneer and Sony radios, optics from Fujinon, Minolta, and Steiner, inflatable boats and life rafts by Avon, Achilles, and over a dozen other lines; Compaq and other computers and software, Henri Lloyd, Musto, and Douglas Gill boating wear, Sebago and Timberland shoes, Force 10 cookers, and Hurricane boat tops and covers—among other items. In addition to equipment, Defender is a national leader in boat-building supplies: fiberglass, xynole, epoxy and polyester resins, and other boat construction and maintenance materials are stocked in depth. Defender also offers a range of custom services, such as life raft repacking and repair, rigging services, and canvas goods to order (seat covers, pool covers, car covers, etc.).

Defender's wholesale affiliate, Atlantic Main Corp., specializes in small boat marine hardware and safety gear. Atlantic Main is also the U.S. agent for Holt Allen sailboat hardware, Blake heads, Dynous inflatable boats, and Scanstrut radar mounts. For details, contact Atlantic Main at 319 Main St., New Rochelle, NY 10801.

Special Factors: Price quote by phone, fax, or letter; returns are accepted within 20 days (a restocking fee may be charged); minimum order is $25.

E & B MARINE SUPPLY, INC.

DEPT. WBMC
201 MEADOW RD.
EDISON, NJ 08818
800-533-5007
FAX: 908-819-9222

Catalog: free
Save: up to 60%
Pay: check, MO, MC, V, AE, Discover
Sells: marine supplies, gear, and equipment
Store: 52 outlets in AL, CT, FL, GA, MA, MD, MI, MS, NJ, NY, PA, RI, and VA (locations are listed in the catalog)

  ¡Si! ★

E & B Marine, founded in 1946, has a lowest-price policy that assures you great savings on a full range of products for power boating and sailing, boat maintenance and repair, safety, communications, and navigation. The brands include Apelco, Aqua Meter, Boatlife, Bow t' Stern, Chelsea, Eagle, Humminbird, Icom, Igloo, Interlux, Kidde, Micrologic, Pettit, Ray Jeff, Raytheon, Ritchie, SeaFit, SeaRanger, Standard, and Stearns, among others. Water skis and Bombard inflatables are stocked, as well as boating apparel and sportswear. New products are featured in every catalog, and many items are useful on land as well—clothing, safety equipment, and hardware. Savings vary, but are typically 10% to 25%, and up to 60% on sale items and specials.

Special Factors: Authorized returns are accepted; minimum order is $15, $25 on phone orders.

EURO-TIRE, INC.

80 LITTLE FALLS RD.
FAIRFIELD, NJ 07004
800-631-0080
201-575-0080
FAX: 201-575-6800

Brochure: free
Save: up to 35%
Pay: check, MO, MC, V, AE
Sells: auto tires, wheels, and shocks
Store: 500 Rte. 46 East, Fairfield, NJ; also East 290, Rte. 4, Paramus, NJ; and 393 West Ave., Stamford, CT

Euro-Tire has been selling tires since 1974, and currently offers Armstrong, Avon, Bridgestone, Continental, Dunlop, Goodyear, Michelin, Pirelli, Toyo, and Yokohama. The firm's specialty is imported tires and auto components, but domestic lines are also available. Shock absorbers by Bilstein, Boge, and Koni are priced an average of 34% below list, and the brochure lists light alloy wheels by BBS, Centra, MSW, and Ronal. Euro-Tire's concise brochure gives complete details on its sales and warranty policies, as well as services offered at its facilities in Connecticut and New Jersey.

Special Factors: No seconds or retreads are sold; returns are accepted within 30 days (see the catalog for details); minimum order is $25.

FREEPORT MARINE

47 WEST MERRICK RD.
FREEPORT, NY 11520
516-379-2610
FAX: 516-379-2909

Catalog: free
Save: up to 60%
Pay: check, MO, MC, V, AE, Discover
Sells: boating and marine supplies and equipment
Store: same address; Monday to Saturday 8:30–6 (Friday till 9 April till Labor Day)

Freeport Marine has been in business, owned by the same family, since 1939, and publishes a 256-page catalog of marine hardware, maintenance products, and electronics for sailboats and powerboats. The stock includes epoxies and finishes, rope, anchors, windlasses, buoys, horns, seacocks, winches, VHF radios, global positioning systems, navigation instruments, safety equipment, radar, marine optics, inflatable boats, and a complete line of marine hardwear. Among the manufacturers represented are Apelco, Avon, Barr, Garelick, Icom, Interlux, ITT, Jabsco, Magellan, Marinco, Perko, Raritan, Raytheon, Sitex, Standard, Stearns, Steiner, and Teleflex. Savings run up to 60%, and if you don't see what you're looking for, call and ask.

Special Factors: Satisfaction is guaranteed; minimum order is $25 with credit cards.

GOLDBERGS' MARINE DISTRIBUTORS

DEPT. WBMC
201 MEADOW RD.
EDISON, NJ 08818
800-262-8464
FAX: 908-819-9222

Catalog: free
Save: up to 60%
Pay: check, MO, MC, V, AE, Discover
Sells: marine supplies, gear, and equipment
Store: 12 W. 37th St., New York, NY

 ¡Si!

Goldbergs' has been a marine supplier since 1946, and offers thousands of products at discounts of up to 60%, and even better savings in the sales catalogs. Goldbergs' sells everything from anchors to zinc collars, including rope, bilge pumps, fishing tackle, rigging, knives, lifeboats, life preservers, navigation equipment, boat covers, winches, and even kitchen (galley) sinks. The brands are the best in boating—SeaRanger electronics, Taylor Made buoys, PowerWinch windlasses and winches, motors, and Stearns life preservers are but a few. The emphasis is on pleasure-boat equipment, but much of the sailing apparel—heavy sweaters, sunglasses, boots, Sperry boating shoes, and slickers—has landlubber appeal. A selection of stylish galley gear, teak bulkhead racks, and other yacht accessories rounds out the catalog.

Special Factors: Authorized returns are accepted (policy is stated in the catalog); minimum order is $10.

IMPCO, INC.

DEPT. WBMC
5300 GLENMONT DR.
HOUSTON, TX 77081-2002
800-243-1220
713-661-0900
FAX: 800-243-8893

Catalog: free
Save: 30% average
Pay: check, MO, MC, V, AE, Discover
Sells: OEM Mercedes-Benz auto parts, 1973
to current year
Store: same address; Monday to Friday 8–7,
Saturday 9–2

IMPCO has been in business since 1984 and sells only first-quality parts through the 55-page catalog. Whether you're overhauling your engine, or just want to replace the wiper blades, IMPCO provides everything from front fender moldings to trunk seals, as well as electrical parts and supplies, bulbs, cooling and heating system components, upholstery materials, filters, brake parts, suspension and drive-line parts, exhaust systems, window switches, accessories, tools, and Owner's Workshop manuals. If you're overhauling your car, check out IMPCO's engine rebuilding kits. IMPCO also sells Lexol leather cleaner and conditioner, and fuel and engine additives by Lubro Moly. IMPCO's unlimited two-year warranty on all parts should give you peace of mind, and if you're looking for a part or Mercedes-Benz product not listed or have any questions, just call.

Special Factors: Satisfaction is guaranteed; authorized, unused returns (except tools and manuals) are accepted within 30 days for exchange, refund, or credit; C.O.D. orders are accepted.

M&E MARINE SUPPLY COMPANY, INC.

P.O. BOX 601
CAMDEN, NJ 08101
800-541-6501
FAX: 609-757-9175

Catalog: $2
Save: up to 60%
Pay: check, MO, MC, V, Discover
Sells: boating supplies and equipment
Store: Glasgow, DE; and Collingswood,
Northfield, and Trenton, NJ

M&E has been serving boaters since 1946 with good prices on everything needed to set sail and stay afloat. The 330-page catalog gives you access to over 30,000 products from anchors to zippers, from well-known manufacturers like Apelco, Aqua Meter, Barient, Harken, Magellan, Maxxima, Schaefer, Signet, Si-Tex, Tasco, and Weems & Plath. If you have a boat or enjoy sailing, you'll appreciate the savings, which average 25% but can reach 80%. A recent sale catalog included navigation equipment, lighting, pumps, electronics, safety equipment, hull repair compounds and finishes, ladders, rope, inflatables (dinghies), horns, bells, and other equipment and supplies. There are lots of products useful on land, like the Sperry Top-Siders, teak boat accessories, acrylic glassware, watches, fishing equipment, and flags. Both list and M & E's discount prices are given, and everything is covered by the blanket guarantee of satisfaction.

Special Factors: Satisfaction is guaranteed; returns are accepted within 30 days for exchange, refund, or credit; minimum order is $15 with credit cards; C.O.D. orders are accepted.

MILL SUPPLY, INC.

DEPT. WBMC
3241 SUPERIOR AVE.
CLEVELAND, OH 44114
800-888-5072
216-241-5072
FAX: 216-241-0425

Catalog: $4
Save: up to 40%
Pay: check, MO, MC, V, Discover
Sells: replacement auto panels and hardware
Store: same address; Monday to Friday 8–5

Whether you're a car buff or you own a body shop, you'll want Mill Supply's 192-page catalog on your shelf. Mill Supply has been selling car parts since 1944, and specializes in replacement panels and supplies for collision and rust repairs for American and foreign vehicles. The index runs from Alfa Romeo to Volvo, with all the hardware, tools, finishes, and other shop equipment you need to do installations. You have to have the know-how to do certain types of jobs, but even driveway mechanics can install rubber mud flaps and replacement side mirrors, or use the professional brushes and car-washing equipment.

Canadian readers, please note: Only U.S. funds are accepted, paid by postal money order only.

Special Factors: Quantity discounts are available; authorized returns are accepted (a 10% restocking fee is charged) within 60 days for exchange, refund, or credit.

PROAM SEAT WAREHOUSE

6125 RICHMOND AVE.
HOUSTON, TX 77057
713-781-7755
FAX: 713-781-8207

Information: inquire
Save: up to 30%
Pay: check, MO, MC, V, AE
Sells: performance driving equipment and accessories
Store: same address; Monday to Friday 9:30–6, Saturday 9:30–4

ProAm sells all kinds of accessories to enhance the looks and comfort of high-performance cars—Acuras, Nissans, Porsches, Jaguars, BMWs, etc. You can upgrade the driver's seat with one from the line of Recaro seats with full recline and full lumbar support, enjoy an anatomically designed steering wheel from ProAm's collection, and replace the stick shift in your car with one made of a rare wood. ProAm also carries shocks by Bilstein, Koni, Kyb, and Tokico, replacement dashboard covers, wheels by ARE, ATEV, BBS, MOMO, and Ronal, and aerodynamically designed panels, spoilers, rear aprons, air dams, skirts, and other products by BBS, Kamei, Kaminari, Mitcom, Pacific, and Zender. (In addition to adding a sporty edge to the looks of the car, these accessories can improve handling and performance.)

ProAm has been in business since 1984, and although the firm serves both amateur and professional drivers with racing suits and helmets by Simpson and pit stop accessories, the average car driver will enjoy the good buys on Wolf car covers, sunglasses by Carrera and Porsche Designs, radars, steering wheel locks, alarms, floor mats, and tire gauges.

Please note: Identify yourself as a WBMC reader when you call or write.

Special Factors: C.O.D. orders are accepted.

RACER WHOLESALE

**DEPT. WBM
1020 SUN VALLEY DR.
ROSWELL, GA 30076
404-998-7777
FAX: 404-993-4417**

Catalog: free
Save: up to 70%
Pay: check, MO, MC, V, Discover
Sells: auto racing safety equipment
Store: same address; Monday to Friday 9–6

Racer Wholesale has been serving the serious amateur and professional auto racing markets since 1985, offering safety equipment and accessories at savings of up to 70% on list prices. The 96-page catalog shows professional driving suits from AutoPro, Pyrotect, Racequip, Simpson, and other manufacturers, as well as gloves, boots, helmets, belts, harnesses, window nets, arm restraints, Cobra and Ultrashield racing seats, fire extinguishers, and other safety products. Auto equipment is also available, including K & N filters and accessories, Supertrapp mufflers, Oberg filters and heavy-duty oil, coolers, Aeroquip hoses and connections, fueling accessories, canopies, towing equipment, Wink wide-view mirrors, battery cutoff switches, rod ends, and related goods. Racer Wholesale has a policy of "guaranteed lowest prices"—see the catalog for details.

Special Factors: Authorized, unused returns (except special orders) are accepted within 15 days for exchange, refund, or credit (a restocking fee may be charged); C.O.D. orders are accepted.

SAN-VAL DISCOUNT, INC.

**7444 VALJEAN AVE.
VAN NUYS, CA 91406
800-423-3281
IN CA: 800-924-9658
CUSTOMER SERVICE:
 818-786-8274
FAX: 818-786-9072**

Information: price quote
Save: up to 35%
Pay: check, MO, MC, V, AE, Discover
Sells: aircraft parts and pilot supplies
Store: same address; Monday to Friday 7:30–6, Saturday 8–5

San-Val guarantees "lowest prices" on a huge inventory of parts, supplies, and electronics for small aircraft and pilots. Call for a price quote on headsets, gyros, magnetos, scanners, compasses, batteries, fuel pumps, or anything else you need for your craft. Flight cases, kneeboards, flight seats, training aids, textbooks and study manuals, log books, charts, and other pilot gear is sold as well. Shipping is not charged on certain items, and San-Val is committed to your satisfaction; ask for terms of the sales and return policy before ordering.

Special Factors: Satisfaction is guaranteed; authorized returns of defective items are accepted (subject to restocking fee) within 30 days for exchange, refund, or credit; minimum order is $10; C.O.D. orders are accepted on some items.

TELETIRE

17662 ARMSTRONG AVE.
IRVINE, CA 92714
800-835-8473
714-250-9141
FAX: 714-250-1977

Brochure: free
Save: 30% average
Pay: check, MO, MC, V, Discover
Sells: tires and wheels
Store: mail order only

Past brochures from Teletire have addresseed issues that befuddle many car owners, such as tire rotation, inflation, Plus-1, and the secret meaning of speed ratings. In addition to giving you an education, Teletire offers a great selection of tires and wheels for passenger cars, trucks, vans, and RVs, from Armstrong, Bridgestone, Firestone, BF Goodrich, Goodyear, Michelin, Pirelli, and Yokohama. If what you want isn't listed in the brochure, call or write for a price quote. Teletire, which began doing business in 1969, is affiliated with Telepro (see the listing in "Sports").

Special Factors: Unused, undamaged returns are accepted within 30 days (a restocking fee may be charged).

WAG-AERO GROUP OF AIRCRAFT SERVICES

P.O. BOX 181
1216 NORTH RD.
LYONS, WI 53148
800-558-6868
414-763-9586
FAX: 414-763-7595

Catalog: free
Save: up to 30%
Pay: check, MO, MC, V, Discover
Sells: aircraft parts, supplies, and aviation accessories
Store: same address; Monday to Friday 8:30–4:30

Wag-Aero is so attuned to the needs of small-aircraft pilots that the catalog includes directions for "fly-in" customers! The firm has been in business for over 30 years, and carries everything from spark plugs and propellers to aircraft decals, aviators' jackets, and manuals. The 148-page catalog features a full range of piloting instruments, windshields, lorans, lighting, spinners, engine mounts, wheels, and much more, by some major names—Aeronca, Cessna, Grumman, etc. And there are many value-priced products sold under Wag-Aero's own label. Specials and sale items show up in the seasonal tabloid catalogs as well. Whether you're a dedicated pilot maintaining and aircraft of just dream of taking to the wild blue yonder, you'll find much of interest here.

Special Factors: Satisfaction is guaranteed; authorized returns are accepted within 90 days for exchange, refund, or credit; C.O.D. orders are accepted.

WEST MARINE

500 WESTRIDGE DR.
WATSONVILLE, CA 95076
800-538-0775
WHOLESALE, U.S.:
 800-621-6885
408-728-2700
FAX: 408-728-4360

Catalog: free
Save: up to 50% off list
Pay: check, MO, MC, V, AE, Discover
Sells: marine supplies and equipment
Store: 45 outlets nationwide

  ¡Si! ★

West Marine publishes a 864-page color compendium of marine electronics, hardware, and maintenance products for sailboats and power-boats, as well as related goods, such as foul-weather clothing and plumbing supplies. The comprehensive selection of gear and materials includes epoxies and finishes, rope, anchors, windlasses, buoys, horns, seacocks, winches, VHF radios, global positioning systems, navigation instruments, safety equipment, hardware, kerosene lamps, marine optics, inflatable boats, and a complete line of galley gear. There are scores of manufacturers represented, including Apelco, Barient, Harken, Interphase, Lewmar, Magellan, Marinco, Navico, Patagonia, Ritchie, Schaefer, Stearns, Steiner, Taylor Made, and Weems & Plath, as well as the firm's private label. West Marine also offers rope-splicing services at "a reasonable fee." Savings run up to 50%, and West Marine has over 18,000 items in stock, so call and ask if you don't see what you're looking for.

Spanish-speaking readers, please note: West Marine has operators who speak Spanish on *some,* but not *all,* shifts.

Special Factors: Satisfaction is guaranteed; special orders are accepted.

SEE ALSO

Arctic Sheepskin Outlet • *sheepskin cover steering wheel and seat covers* • **CLOTHING**
Bart's Watersports • *boat mounts and hardware for water-skiing equipment* • **SPORTS**
Bennett Brothers, Inc. • *infants' car seats* • **GENERAL MERCHANDISE**

BRE Lumber, Inc./Rare Earth Hardwoods • *lumber and flooring for marine use* • **HOME: IMPROVEMENT**

Cabela's Inc. • *boat seats, covers, electronics, etc.* • **SPORTS**

Camelot Enterprises • *automotive tools* • **TOOLS**

Campmor • *inflatable boats* • **SPORTS**

Crutchfield Corporation • *auto audio and security devices* • **APPLIANCES**

Deerskin Trading Post, Inc. • *shearling car seat covers* • **CLOTHING**

Gander Mountain, Inc. • *boat seats, covers, electronics, motors, etc.* • **SPORTS**

The Kennel Vet Corp. • *dog seat belts* • **ANIMAL**

LVT Price Quote Hotline, Inc. • *radar detectors, scanners, CBs, etc.* • **APPLIANCES**

Manufacturer's Supply • *parts for motorcycles, snowmobiles, ATVs, etc.* • **TOOLS**

Mardiron Optics • *marine optics* • **CAMERAS**

Northern Hydraulics, Inc. • *wheels and parts for ATVs, minibikes, etc.; auto tools* • **TOOLS**

Overton's Sports Center, Inc. • *marine equipment and electronics* • **SPORTS**

Percy's Inc. • *radar detectors* • **APPLIANCES**

Red Hill Corporation • *auto-body refinishing products* • **TOOLS**

Sailboard Warehouse, Inc. • *sailboard car racks* • **SPORTS**

R.C. Steele Co. • *life preservers and auto safety harnesses for pets* • **ANIMAL**

BOOKS AND PERIODICALS

Print publications and educational materials

Why pay list prices for books or full rates for magazine subscriptions, when you can get them by mail at discounts of up to 90%? The firms in this chapter can save you hundreds of dollars a year on your own reading and entertainment buys, as well the titles on your gift lists. Many of them also sells videos and CDs, but you'll find companies that specialize in magnetic/vinyl media (except software) in "Recordings," immediately following this chapter. Looking for stationery, cards, and gift wrapping and ribbon? They're offered by a few booksellers, but see "Cards, Stationery, Labels, and Check-Printing Services," the section following "General," for the main listings.

Caring for books properly is a concern that can obsess serious collectors, whose investments require proper storage and display. University Products (listed in the "Small Business" section of "Office") offers a wide range of conservation supplies, including acid-free book-jacket covers, manuscript cases and folders, rare-book boxes, record sleeves, interleaving sheets, and archival-quality repair materials. With the company's quantity discounts, you can afford to take care of your whole library.

Don't overlook the "See Also's" at the end of this chapter, especially if you're looking for a how-to or self-help publication. You'll find gardening guides among the firms in "Farm and Garden," cookbooks offered by firms selling gourmet ingredients, books on color theory sold by art-supply houses, and so on. Many of the firms listed throughout this book also offer videotapes on their specialties, usually at competitive prices. And if you're looking for software and CD-ROM titles, see the "Computing" section of "Office."

FIND IT FAST

ART AND CRAFTS • **Dover, Potters Shop, Print's Graphic Design**
AUDIO AND VIDEO MEDIA • **Astronomical Society, Barnes & Noble, Daedalus, Dover, Potters Shop, Print's Graphic Design, Scholar's Bookshelf**
ASTRONOMY • **Astronomical Society**
CARDS AND STATIONERY • **Dover**
CHILDREN'S • **Barnes & Noble, Daedalus, Dover**
COOKBOOKS • **Barnes & Noble, Daedalus, Editions, Hamilton, Jessica's Biscuit, Strand**
GOVERNMENT PUBLICATIONS • **Consumer Information Center, Superintendent of Documents**
MAGAZINE SUBSCRIPTIONS • **American Family, Delta, Publishers Clearing House**
PAPERBACKS • **Hamilton, Olde Methuen**
UNIVERSITY PRESSES • **Daedalus, Scholar's Bookshelf**
USED BOOKS • **Editions, Olde Methuen, Strand, Tartan**

AMERICAN FAMILY PUBLISHERS

P.O. BOX 62000
TAMPA, FL 33662-2000
800-237-2400

Information: inquire
Save: up to 70%
Pay: check or MO
Sells: magazine subscriptions
Store: mail order only

American Family Publishers is a magazine clearinghouse that offers subscriptions to dozens of popular periodicals at rates that are usually much better than those offered by the publishers themselves. In addition to savings, every time you order you'll be entered into the current sweepstakes, which doesn't happen when you buy your magazines at the newsstand. A recent American Family mailing included offers for *Vacations, Life, People, Golf Digest, TV Guide, Catholic Digest, Time, PC Magazine, Soap Opera Digest,* and *Field & Stream.* Periodically, American Family features books—*The Columbia University Complete Home Medical Guide,* Rodale's home-improvement series, cookbooks, and other popular reference works have appeared in past mailings, all offered on the company's buying program that allows you to spread payments over four months.

Special Factors: Satisfaction is guaranteed; inquire for information.

THE ASTRONOMICAL SOCIETY OF THE PACIFIC

390 ASHTON AVE.
SAN FRANCISCO, CA
94112
415-337-1100
FAX: 415-337-5205

Catalog: free
Save: up to 50%
Pay: check, MO, MC, V, Discover
Sells: astronomy resources and gifts
Store: mail order only
E-mail: asp@stars.sfsu.edu

The Astronomical Society of the Pacific is a not-for-profit organization that was founded in 1889 to support astronomical research and improve the public's appreciation of science, especially astronomy. To further this end, ASP publishes a variety of materials: videotapes, books, charts and maps of the heavens, slides, observing tools, educational items, and astronomy-related gifts. The 32-page color catalog features an intriguing collection that includes a series of videotapes from NOVA, Carl Sagan's award-winning *Cosmos* series, the *Starship Earth* 16" celestial globe, and the comprehensive *Norton's 2000.0 Star Atlas and Reference Handbook*. There are breathtaking posters of the planets, a moon phase calendar for the whole year, astronomical CD-ROMs, computer programs that simulate travel through the galaxy, and a number of slide sets covering nebulas and galaxies, the solar system, images of Venus from the voyage of the *Magellan*, and new Hubble Space Telescope images.

ASP's prices are reasonable but don't seem particularly low ($29.95 for videotapes and $8.95 for posters), until you check the catalogs of supplies for educators selling similar publications. There are school sources charging an astonishing $300-plus for a *single* videotape. So even if you're not in the market for ASP's publications yourself, let your school board or PTA know about this source. Proceeds are used to advance the Society's education programs.

Canadian readers, please note: Only U.S. funds are accepted.

Special Factors: Satisfaction is guaranteed; returns in "as-new" condition are accepted for exchange, refund, or credit; institutional accounts are available.

BARNES & NOBLE BOOKSTORES, INC.

126 FIFTH AVE.,
DEPT. 861F
NEW YORK, NY 10011
201-767-7079

Catalog: free
Save: up to 80%
Pay: check, MO, MC, V, AE
Sells: books, tapes, CDs, gifts, etc.
Store: same address; other locations in AZ, CA, CO, CT, FL, IL, MA, MD, MI, MN, NC, NH, NJ, NV, NY, and OH

  (see text)

Barnes & Noble, founded in 1873, considers itself "America's #1 book sale catalog," with prices up to 80% off published rates. In addition, the catalogs feature audiotapes, CDs, videotapes, calendars, and other gifts, also at a discount. The typical Barnes & Noble catalog is 48 to 72 pages of best-sellers, reference works, publishers' overstock, and the firm's own reprints. The areas of interest include history, mystery, the arts science, literature, film, medicine, satire, juvenilia, current fiction, linguistics, religion, reference, crafts, and photography. The catalogs also offer a selection of audiotapes and CDs (classical music, jazz, drama, and language tapes), and videotapes. Stunning art books, calendars, lighted globes, beechwood bookshelves, book embossers, statuary, cassette cases and cabinets, and book lights have all appeared in past catalogs.

Canadian and APO/FPO readers, please note: Inquire for shipping charges, and allow extra time for order processing.

Special Factors: Satisfaction is guaranteed; returns are accepted; minimum order is $15 with credit cards.

CONSUMER INFORMATION CENTER

P.O. BOX 100
PUEBLO, CO 81009

Catalog: free
Save: see text
Pay: check, MO, MC, V
Sells: consumer publications
Store: over 1,300 Federal Depository Libraries nationwide (see text)

 ¡Si! (see text)

The government's Consumer Information Center was established in 1970 "to help federal agencies promote and distribute useful consumer information." Many of the pamphlets and manuals in the Center's 16-

page quarterly catalog are free, like the *U.S. Government TDD Directory*. The topics include careers and education, child care, federal benefits and laws, food handling and nutrition, health, home building and buying, energy conservation, appliances and electronics, home improvement and safety, travel, hobbies, and money management. You can subscribe to *FDA Consumer* through the Consumer Information Center's catalog, and order pamphlets that help you to learn about ultrasound, find out about Social Security, get tips on buying a mobile home, and obtain government records under the Freedom of Information Act, among other things.

You can also request the *Consumer's Resource Handbook*, a guide to effective complaint procedures, from the Department of Consumer Affairs. It lists the best sources of help if you have a problem as a consumer: contact names, addresses, and phone numbers of customer relations departments of hundreds of major corporations, Better Business Bureau offices worldwide, trade associations, consumer protection offices, and federal agencies. There are over 90 pages of valuable information in the *Handbook*, at the best possible price—free.

If you'd like to see the literature before buying, you can visit one of the over 1,380 Federal Depository Libraries around the country; they don't do *sales,* but they have copies of nearly every Federal Government publication (in print or microfilm) that's designated for use by the general public. Your local library should be able to help you locate one, or you can write to Federal Depository Library Program, Office of the Public Printer, Washington, DC 20401. To locate a U.S. Government Bookstore, see the listing for "Superintendent of Documents" in this chapter.

Please note: A Spanish-language catalog of dozens of federal consumer guides in Spanish is also available.

Special Factors: A handling fee is charged on all orders.

DAEDALUS BOOKS, INC.

P.O. BOX 9132 (WBM)
HYATTSVILLE, MD
20781-0932
800-395-2665
FAX: 800-866-5578

Catalog: free
Save: up to 90%
Pay: check, MO, MC, V, AE, Discover
Sells: new and remaindered literary publications, classical CDs
Store: mail order only
E-mail: db.books@ix.netcom.com

Daedalus, founded in 1980, offers fine books from trade publishers and university presses at 50% to 90% off publishers' prices. These remainders have been culled from thousands to appeal to literary readers looking for culture on the cheap. Daedalus isn't *just* remainders, though—about half the catalog is devoted to current titles that are discounted about 20%. And the witty, clearheaded descriptions of each book are reading pleasures in themselves.

The categories include literature and general interest, visual and performing arts, philosophy, history, feminism, politics, children's books, travel, cookery, and the social sciences. Daedalus is also offering a distinguished selection of CDs, also at a discount. A gift certificate from Daedalus, presented with the latest edition of the catalog, should delight a reader with wide-ranging interests.

Canadian readers, please note: Payment must be made by credit card, a money order drawn in U.S. funds, or a check drawn on a U.S. bank.

Wholesale customers, call 301-779-5618 for more information.

Special Factors: Institutional accounts are available; returns are accepted within 30 days; minimum order is $10 with credit cards.

DELTA PUBLISHING GROUP/MAGAZINE WAREHOUSE

1243 48TH ST.
BROOKLYN, NY 11219
800-SEND-LIST
718-972-0900
FAX: 718-972-4695

Price List: free
Save: up to 75%
Pay: check, MO, MC, V, AE, Discover
Sells: magazine subscriptions
Store: mail order only
E-mail: CS: 76550,3363@compuserve.com

Delta Publishing Group, aka Magazine Warehouse, is the subscription wholesaler we've all been looking for, with over 800 titles at the absolute lowest prices anywhere. It's *shocking* to see magazine after magazine here at prices that beat the ones offered by the sweepstakes operations by 40% or so. You don't get the chance at $10 million and you can't split the payments over three or four months, but at these prices and with a selection that runs from *Accent on Living* to *Zoo Books,* you won't miss the perks.

Delta/Magazine Warehouse, founded in 1991, is a major supplier of wholesale subscriptions to corporation and doctors' offices, and extends similar "courtesy" rates to readers of this book. The firm offers many of the titles in subscriptions of up to three years, so you can lock in the rate of a favorite. (All of the terms are for *full* years.) Delta offers free tracking service on subscriptions bought from other sources, so you can have your renewals picked up seamlessly. And check the price list you receive for specials—bonus subscriptions and free magazine racks have been offered in the past.

Please note that a score of titles require a "trade" address that includes a business name, and a handful ask for a business card or letterhead; the magazines will be mailed to that address only. Be sure to mention WBMC when you call (800-SEND-LIST) or write for the price list.

Special Factors: Lowest subscription rates are guaranteed.

DOVER
PUBLICATIONS, INC.

DEPT. MC
31 EAST 2ND ST.
MINEOLA, NY 11501-3582
516-294-7000

Catalog: free
Save: up to 50% (see text)
Pay: check or MO
Sells: Dover publications
Store: same address; Monday to Friday 8–4; also 180 Varick St., 9th Floor, New York, NY; Monday to Friday 9–4:30

Many of the firms listed in this book sell selections of Dover books, but if you deal with the publisher directly you can buy any in-print Dover publication. In over half a century of publishing, Dover has built a reputation for books as notable for their quality construction as they are for their content. Dover's catalogs feature paperbacks on crafts and hobbies, Americana, mathematics and physics, American Indian arts, architecture, cooking, games, travel, music, and many other topics. Dover's "Pictorial Archives," featuring designs and graphics, typography, banners and scrolls, borders, etc., and the "Clip-Art Series" are copyright-free art that can be used in newsletters, ads, menus, and the like. Dover's postcard sets run from NASA shots to Tiffany windows, and there are stickers, coloring books, posters, and even gift wrap.

Dover's facsimiles and reprints of rare and valuable texts include a reproduction of an 1864 illustrated catalog of Civil War military goods and the earliest known cookbook, *Cookery and Dining in Imperial Rome,* by Apicius, to cite two. Dover's reprint of the catalog of Gustav Stickley's Mission furniture designs is a standard among antiques dealers, and is probably more widely read now than it was when originally published.

Dover also publishes "Listen & Learn" language tapes, as well as bird song tapes and musical scores by Scriabin, Liszt, Scott Joplin, Couperin, Ravel, Bizet, Brahms, and other greats. The prices are easily up to 50% less than those charged for comparable publications, and there are children's books and literary classics for just $1.

Canadian readers, please note: The shipping surcharge on orders sent to Canada is 20%.

Special Factors: Satisfaction is guaranteed; returns are accepted within ten days for refund.

EDITIONS

DESK WM
BOICEVILLE, NY 12412
914-657-7000
FAX: 914-657-8849

Catalog: $2
Save: up to 40%
Pay: check, MO, MC, V
Sells: old, used, and rare books
Store: 2740 Rte. 28, Ashokan, NY; daily
10–5

Editions is a great source for used and out-of-print books, which are often priced 30% to 50% less here than elsewhere. Editions has been selling by mail since 1948, and operates a sprawling store that's stocked with a separate book inventory—55,000 at last count—worth a stop if you're in the area.

The 64-page monthly catalogs include *partial* listings from a range of categories. For example, the January catalog may list poetry titles from Eliot to Neruda, and February's issue will run from Powys to Wyse. Each catalog lists about 10,000 titles, most priced under $20, from categories that include fiction, literature, history, the social sciences, natural history, travel, the law, women, soldiers and war, the Irish, Americana, British history, theater, philosophy and religion, food, labor, espionage, sports, antiques, gardening, animals, publishing, and Judaica. And it's always interesting to see what ends up in the "Miscellaneous Subjects & Nonsense" section. The original hardcover titles, in fine condition, are often cheaper here than the paperback editions. Collectors and researchers may wish to see the catalogs for the first editions and books from the Heritage Press and Lakeside Press, as well as the occasional listings of regimental histories, genealogies, and books on local history.

Special Factors: Inquiries by letter only; returns are accepted within three days.

EDWARD R. HAMILTON, BOOKSELLER

Catalog: free
Save: up to 80%
Pay: check or MO
Sells: closeout and remaindered books
Store: mail order only

BOX 15-66
FALLS VILLAGE, CT
06031-500

Hamilton's monthly catalog lists *thousands* of bargain books in every conceivable category, at savings that average of 50% to 70% off the publishers' prices. The tabloid catalog appeals to the bargain-hunting bookworm who likes to explore old bookstores—it's the literary equivalent of shelves and stacks of volumes—art, humor, poetry, fiction, literature, photography, self-help, reference, business, crafts, psychology, history, film, science, cooking, sports, and biography are all featured. Hamilton's offerings are all new, remainders, closeouts, or publishers' overstock. Past best-sellers show up here frequently, as well as imports and other books no other remainder source seems to have. Hamilton was founded in 1968 and has proven a personal favorite; orders are shipped promptly, and refund checks for out-of-stock titles often arrive before the order itself!

Special Factors: Satisfaction is guaranteed; returns are accepted; prepaid institutional orders are accepted; shipments to U.S. addresses only.

JESSICA'S BISCUIT

Store: mail order only
Catalog: free
Save: up to 80% (see text)
Pay: check, MO, MC, V
Sells: cookbooks and food reference

THE COOKBOOK PEOPLE
P.O. BOX 301
NEWTONVILLE, MA 02160
800-878-4264
617-965-0530
FAX: 617-527-0113

Jessica's Biscuit is so discreet about sweetening its luscious catalog with sale books that you might overlook them at first. But they're here—scores of them throughout the 72 color pages of over 800 books on cooking, food service, and domestic arts. Jessica's Biscuit is the preeminent catalog for in-print specialty cookbooks and updates on the culinary commandments of the taste dictators. In addition to national cuisines, Jessica's Biscuit offers books with recipes for vegetarian, macrobiotic, microwave, diabetic, gluten-free, low-salt, sugar-free, low-cholesterol, wheat-free, fiber-rich, kosher, and low-cost dishes. There are regional books for everything from soul food to Amish fare, as well as volumes devoted to herbs, muffins, tofu, pizza, biscuits, corn, mushrooms, barbecuing, cheesecake, beans, children's food, chili, garlic, and potatoes. Related topics include professional food service, canning and preserving, outfitting a working kitchen, buffets, wines, and entertaining in style, among others. Savings on the sale titles average 45% and run as high as 80%. And if you don't see what you're looking for in the catalog, call; Jessica's Biscuit has thousands of other titles in the warehouse!

Special Factors: Satisfaction is guaranteed; returns are accepted.

OLDE METHUEN BOOKSHOPPE

250 BROADWAY
P.O. BOX 545
METHUEN, MA 01844
508-682-9972

Catalog: $1 each (see text)
Save: up to 50% (see text)
Pay: check, MO, MC, V, AE, Discover
Sells: new and used paperbacks
Store: same address; Monday to Saturday 10–5, Thursday 10–8

If you like popular fiction but balk at paying $5 for a slim paperback, Olde Methuen Bookshoppe has the answer. This firm's affiliate, Book News, publishes the *Book News* catalog ($1) of historical novels, mysteries and suspense, science fiction, westerns, novels for young adults, romances (including the Harlequin and Silhouette lines), thrillers, and general "contemporary" novels. (Any title in print that's not listed can be special-ordered.) The books are listed at publishers' prices, but you get 10% off when you buy one to nine books, 20% off for orders of ten or more, and 25% on 25 or more books.

You'll save the most, though, with Olde Methuen Bookshoppe, which offers the same range of titles in *used condition,* at prices that run from $1.25 to $6 each, with most books commanding $2 or less. Each of the seven categories has its own catalog ($1), so specify your interest and send proper payment: Used Books—Mystery/Thrillers, Used Books—Romance (Historical and Series), Used Books—Fiction, Used Books—

Science Fiction, Used Books—Classics, Used Books—Romance (Regency), and Used Books—Children's titles. To keep prices down, Book News accepts returns under very limited conditions (see below) but will reimburse you for the return postage.

Special Factors: Quantity discounts are available; returns of shipping-damaged, defective, or incorrectly shipped books are accepted for replacement; institutional orders are accepted; minimum order is $15 with credit cards.

THE POTTERS SHOP INC.

31 THORPE RD.

NEEDHAM HEIGHTS, MA

02194

617-449-7687

FAX: 617-449-9098

Catalog: free

Save: up to 75%

Pay: check or MO

Sells: books and videotapes on ceramics and pottery, ceramics tools

Store: same address; Monday to Thursday 9:30–5:30, Friday 9:30–1:30

The Potters Shop, established in 1977, sells books and videotapes on ceramics and pottery at discounts of at least 15%, and as much as 75% on sale titles. The brochure lists hundreds of books and tapes, many of them obscure or hard-to-find imports. You'll find works on pottery technique, historical surveys, profiles of individual potters, ceramics of the East, health and business for the production potter, and even a selection of books for children. Among the videotapes (all VHS) are workshops on raku, form, and technique, and The Potters Shop also sells bamboo and Dolan tools. The firm will search for books, maintains want lists, and buys used books on the pottery and related topics. If you find yourself in Needham Heights, stop in at the shop: The books are there, as well as a pottery school and workshop, where you can both see member potters at their craft, and buy their work.

Special Factors: Orders are shipped worldwide.

PRINT'S GRAPHIC DESIGN BOOK STORE

3200 TOWER OAKS BLVD.
ROCKVILLE, MD
 20852-4216
301-770-2900
FAX: 301-984-3203

Catalog: free
Save: up to 50% (see text)
Pay: check, MO, MC, V, AE
Sells: books on the graphic arts
Store: mail order only

Print Magazine, which serves the graphic-design community, runs a mail-order bookstore that offers well-chosen manuals, color charts, and other aids and reference materials on a range of design-related topics. All of the books are discounted, typically 20%, but some are tagged at 30% and 50% below their published prices. The 16-page color catalog offers annuals, clip-art collections, and books on advertising, graphic design, trademarks and logos, computer-based graphics and desktop publishing, illustration, studio protocol, photography, color, and Pantone color manuals and fanfold color guides. You can also subscribe to *Print Magazine* through the catalog.

Canadian readers, please note: Only U.S. funds are accepted.

Special Factors: Satisfaction is guaranteed; undamaged returns are accepted within 15 days for exchange, refund, or credit; institutional accounts are available.

PUBLISHERS CLEARING HOUSE

101 WINNERS CIRCLE
PORT WASHINGTON, NY
 11050
800-645-9242
516-883-5432

Information: inquire
Save: up to 50%
Pay: check or MO
Sells: magazine subscriptions, books, gifts, etc.
Store: mail order only

Publishers Clearing House primarily acts as an agent for magazine publishers, offering subscriptions to popular and special-interest magazines at savings of up to 50% on regular rates. PCH guarantees lowest to-the-public prices, and a recent mailing featured over 100 periodicals, including *House Beautiful, Reader's Digest, Consumer Reports, Organic Gardening, Changing Times, Money, TV Guide, Time,* and *People.* The mailings usually include bonuses, premiums, and sweepstakes, and you can spread payments for your magazines over four months.

Special Factors: Satisfaction is guaranteed; inquire for information; installment plan is available.

PURCHASE FOR LESS

231 FLORESTA WBM
PORTOLA VALLEY, CA
   94028-7536

Catalog: $2
Save: up to 35%
Pay: check or MO
Sells: books on sewing and quilting
Store: mail order only

Home sewers, and more particularly quilters, will appreciate the collection of pattern books, historical surveys, general reference works, and related titles sold through the 20-page catalog from Purchase for Less. The company's name is based on its other distinguishing feature—discounts of 30% to 35% on publishers' prices. Each book sold here is chosen for its value to the craftsperson who's looking for new designs, techniques, and fresh interpretations of the classics. There are dozens of books on general sewing and serging techniques, fitting clothing, sewing for the home, creating wearable art, sewing fashion accessories, and related topics. Whether you're just mastering the basics or are highly experienced in sewing and design, you'll find something of interest here.

Special Factors: Satisfaction is guaranteed.

THE SCHOLAR'S BOOKSHELF

110 MELRICH RD.
CRANBURY, NJ 08512
609-395-6933
FAX: 609-395-0755

Catalog: free
Save: up to 75%
Pay: check, MO, MC, V
Sells: scholarly and university press books
Store: mail order only

University presses still produce highbrow texts for scholars, but many are of interest—and accessible—to nonprofessionals as well. These books sometimes suffer the same fate as their commercial counterparts—remaindering. The Scholar's Bookshelf, in business since 1974, turns publishing misfortune into intellectual excitement 18 times a year with a wide variety of university press and scholarly imprint remainders, and a selection of videos. The books are sold at an average of 30% below published prices, although savings can run up to 75%.

The 80-page general sale catalog is packed with concise descriptions of volumes on literature and drama, music, the Civil War, architecture and urban planning, archaeology, art history (ancient to modern), photography, world history and politics, psychology, philosophy, religion, Judaica, and the sciences. Past issues have included *Jane's* reference works on military ships and aircraft, Page Smith's eight-volume history of the United States, the *Atlas of Medieval Europe,* and other illuminated manuscripts (reproductions) and special editions. History is the strong suit at The Scholar's Bookshelf, and throughout the year the firm produces separate catalogs devoted to world history and militaria, as well as collections of fine art books, and literature.

Special Factors: Returns are accepted within 30 days for exchange, refund, or credit; minimum order is $10, $45 with credit cards.

STOREY COMMUNI-CATIONS, INC.

SCHOOLHOUSE RD.
P.O. BOX 445
POWNAL, VT 05261
800-441-5700
FAX: 413-664-4066

Catalog: free
Save: up to 30% (see text)
Pay: check, MO, MC, V, AE, Discover
Sells: Country Wisdom Bulletins and books
Store: mail order only

Storey features "books for country living," guides to gardening, cooking, preserving, raising animals, nature appreciation, homesteading, and related topics. Storey can help you learn all about hive management, blacksmithing, composting, organic pest control in the garden, trout fishing, developing a home water supply, raising your own flock of ducks, and outwitting squirrels. The catalog features the Country Wisdom Bulletins, a collection of over 110 manuals that include "all the how-to information you need to easily master dozens of country living skills in 30 minutes or less." The titles illustrate the possibilities of self-reliance: "Building a Solar-Headed Pit Greenhouse," "Drought Gardening," and "Creating a Wildflower Meadow" are examples. The Bulletins are a good buy even at $2.95 each (they're often sold for as little as $1), especially for the person who needs to know the basics, but doesn't have to become an authority on the topic. And even if you're the consummate urbanite, you may find some of the Bulletins of interest, as well as other items—home workshop videos, cookbooks, houseplant guides, and sewing manuals.

Canadian readers, please note: Only U.S. funds are accepted.

Special Factors: Satisfaction is guaranteed; returns are accepted within one year for exchange, refund, or credit.

STRAND BOOK STORE, INC.

828 BROADWAY
NEW YORK, NY
10003-4805
212-473-1452
FAX: 212-473-2591

Catalog: free
Save: up to 80%
Pay: check, MO, MC, V, AE, Discover
Sells: new, used, remaindered, and rare books
Store: main store, same address; Monday to Saturday 9:30–9:30, Sunday 11–9:30; also Strand at the Seaport, 159 John St., New York, NY; Monday to Saturday 10–9, Sunday 10–8

   ¡Si!

The Strand Book Store is the largest used book store in the world. Legendary in stature, the Strand boasts over 2.5 million volumes on eight miles of shelves. Founded in 1929, Strand publishes a number of catalogs of used, rare, and discounted reviewers' copies at 50% off list price. In addition, a huge selection of quality remainders is available.

Call, write, or fax for any of these catalogs: The "Specials" catalog, published several times a year, lists thousands of works that run from William Vollmann's *Fathers and Crows* (list price $30, Strand's price $6.95) and H.W. Janson's *History of Art* (fifth edition; list price $60, Strand's price $44.95), to the three-volume *The Gallery of Maps in the Vatican* (list price $500, Strand's price $395.95). This catalog includes books on art, architecture, philosophy, critique and commentary, biographies, philosophy, literature, politics, food, drama, and other fields of interest. The "Review" catalog, available to institutional accounts, lists new releases at 50% off the publishers' prices. (Request this catalog on your institution's letterhead.) And, in the tradition of British used booksellers, Strand can supply books by the foot for decorators, TV studios, and hotels.

You have to visit the store to do justice to the Strand; if you do, don't miss the Rare Books Department, which has first, fine, and scarce editions, as well as signed and inscribed books.

Special Factors: Satisfaction is guaranteed; want lists are maintained; appraisals are available; returns are accepted.

SUPERINTENDENT OF DOCUMENTS

**U.S. GOVERNMENT
PRINTING OFFICE
WASHINGTON, DC
20402-9325
202-783-3238**

Catalog: free
Save: up to 30% (see text)
Pay: check, MO, MC, V
Sells: Federal government publications
Store: same address; also U.S. Government bookstores in AL, CA, CO, FL, GA, IL, MA, MD, MI, MO, NY, OH, OR, PA, TX, WA, and WI (see the catalog for locations)

This is probably the only book catalog in the country that could run a subscription offer to *Special Warfare* right before the *1987 Folklife Annual,* followed by *Building a Better America,* George Bush's address to Congress at the beginning of his presidency. These are among past hits from the Superintendent of Documents, whose 48-page catalog offers everything from *Walnut Notes,* a manual for the walnut farmer, to the 54-page *Narcotics Identification Manual.* Back in print is the government's "all time best-seller," *Infant Care,* in an updated edition that costs $4. *The Complete Guide to Home Canning* ($11), *A Citizen's Guide to Radon* ($1), *Health Information for the International Traveler* ($5), and the three-volume *Back-Yard Mechanic* ($7), give you an idea of the government's backlist.

Uncle Sam has taken the time to put together "Making Bag Lunches, Snacks and Desserts," compile *Letters of Delegates to Congress, 1774–1789,* and help you realize the American dream with the 54-page *Starting and Managing a Business from Your Home* ($1.75). None of the books or pamphlets is free, but many cost under $10 and are real treasure troves of useful information. (Quantity discounts of 25% on orders of 100 of the same title—with some exceptions—are available.) Subscriptions to consumer magazines published by the government can be ordered through the catalog, and there are calendars and a number of posters of American artists' work as well as space shots and maps.

Special Factors: Quantity discounts are available; authorized returns due to Government error are accepted within six months for exchange or credit; institutional accounts are available.

TARTAN BOOK SALES

Catalog and Brochure: free
Save: up to 75%
Pay: check, MO, MC, V
Sells: used books
Store: same address (Brodart Outlet Bookstore); Monday to Friday 10–6, Saturday 10–4

500 ARCH ST., DEPT. N14
WILLIAMSPORT, PA 17705
800-233-8467, EXT. 461
IN CANADA 800-666-9162,
*   EXT. 461*
FAX: 800-999-6799

Tartan Book Sales, a direct-mail division of Brodart Co., sells recent hardcover titles, including best-sellers, at discounts of up to 75% on the published prices. All of Tartan's books have seen limited circulation in libraries across the country, and are thoroughly inspected prior to shipping.

Hardcover titles by such popular authors as Stephen King, Tom Clancy, Danielle Steele, Dick Francis, Steve Allen, and Kitty Kelly are listed in the current catalog, which also features biographies, books on business and finance, crime, sports and entertainment, health and self-help, politics, current affairs, mysteries, romance novels, books in large print, and much more. Tartan has been in business since 1960, and provides a great way to get hardcovers for little more than you'd pay for the paperback editions!

Special Factors: Quantity discounts are available; institutional and retail accounts are available.

Recordings

Audiotapes, LPs, CDs, videotapes, and films

Whether you want to hear original bluegrass, listen to the gurus of the self-actualization movement, or see a John Wayne favorite anytime you feel like it, you've reached the right place. The firms listed here specialize in recordings—chiefly audiotapes, CDs, and videotapes, and there are some that sell vinyl, some DAT. The savings vary with the offerings, and often compare fairly to record megastores and the big discount chains. Use both kinds of sources—store and catalog—to maximize selection and savings.

If you tape movies or dupe the occasional cassette, you need blank tapes. The choices are confusing—Types I, II, or III, chrome or high bias, high-grade vs. ultra, standard or extended play—the labels themselves don't make the differences clear. For help in figuring out what tape best suits your purposes (and which one was judged best of the batch), see the clarifying November 1994 (video) and January 1993 (audio) articles in *Consumer Reports*. J & R and Wholesale Tape, both listed in "Appliances," have good prices on both blank audio- and videotapes, but you'll save even more by being picky about what you tape in the first place, and that's much easier done with a good movie reference at hand. *VideoHound's Golden Movie Retriever* (Visible Ink/Gale Press, 1995) is one such book, with 22,000 film reviews, cross indexes (including one for laser disk and CD-I recordings), and distributor listings packing over 1,500 pages. It tells you what's in release (so you know what you *have* to record if you want a copy), and you'll avoid critical embarrassments, like recording the wrong version of *A Star Is Born*.

FIND IT FAST

RECORDS, TAPES, CDS • *Adventures in Cassettes, Audio House, Berkshire, Harvard Square, Record-Rama*
VIDEOTAPES • *Adventures in Cassettes, Critics' Choice, Harvard Square*

ADVENTURES IN CASSETTES

A DIVISION OF
   METACOM, INC.
DEPT. WO96
5353 NATHAN LANE
PLYMOUTH, MN 55442
800-328-0108
FAX: 612-553-0424

Catalog: free
Save: up to 30%
Pay: check, MO, MC, V, AE, Discover
Sells: audiotapes and CDs
Store: mail order only

Adventures in Cassettes offers hundreds of audiotapes featuring vintage radio classics, including such comedy greats as Amos and Andy, Abbott and Costello, Baby Snooks, The Great Gildersleeve, The Bickersons, Fibber McGee and Molly, Burns and Allen, Jack Benny, Fred Allen, and Our Miss Brooks. If mysteries, thrillers, and adventure are more your line, see the selection of Sherlock Holmes, Arch Oboler's "Lights Out Everybody," Sam Spade, Bold Venture, The Green Hornet, X-Minus One, and other favorites. And the Western classics are here as well— Hopalong Cassidy, The Lone Ranger, Have Gun Will Travel, and Tales of the Texas Rangers.

Adventures in Cassettes has been in business since 1970, and has moved from folk and rock compilations to more soothing fare. The music choices include classical and "Nature's Magic," as well as meditative medleys. And there's a selection of self-help and motivational tapes that can help you stop smoking, lose weight, or achieve other goals. Prices of the tapes are comparable to those charged by other discount houses, generally running from $4.99 to $9.98 each.

Adventures in Cassettes is offering readers a discount of 25% on their first order from the "Old Time Radio" line only. Be sure to identify yourself as a WBMC reader when you order, and deduct the discount from the cost of the goods only. This WBMC reader discount expires February 1, 1997.

Special Factors: Satisfaction is guaranteed; returns are accepted within 30 days for exchange, refund, or credit.

AUDIO HOUSE

4304-G BRAYAN DR.
SWARTZ CREEK, MI
48473-8823
313-655-8639

Catalog: $2, refundable (see text)
Save: up to 50% (see text)
Pay: check, MO, MC, V, AE
Sells: used CDs
Store: mail order only

  ✓

Audio House has been brokering used CDs to individuals since 1983 and provides you with a great market and great prices—whether you're buying or selling. Audio House publishes a master catalog of CD listings every two months, and releases a ten-page supplement in the off months. A sample costs $2 (refundable with purchase), and a year's subscription is $10 ($12 to Canada). Be sure to request the "$10 in credits" (available only to WBMC readers) when you order the subscription, so you can recoup the whole subscription cost when you buy—one dollar of credit for each CD ordered. And order you will, because a catalog that opens with *10CC's Greatest Hits* and concludes with Zemlinsky's "Diesejungfrau" has something for everyone. Audio House offers its stock of 15,000 titles through the catalog only—there is no membership fee. A number of the selections are on more obscure labels, which are generally hard to find anyway. But finding them at an average of about $8 each, guaranteed to play like new, is even better. If you want to cull your own collection, see the catalog for details on selling your used CDs to Audio House.

Canadian readers, please note: Only U.S. funds are accepted, or payment should be made by credit card.

Special Factors: Satisfaction is guaranteed; returns are accepted within 30 days for exchange, refund, or credit.

BERKSHIRE RECORD OUTLET, INC.

RR 1, RTE. 102 PLEASANT ST.
LEE, MA 01238-9804
413-243-4080
FAX: 413-243-4340

Catalog: $2
Save: 33% plus
Pay: check, MO, MC, V
Sells: classical recordings
Store: same address; Saturday 10–5:30
E-mail: AOL: BerkRecOut@aol.com

If you're an LP holdout who loves classical music, Berkshire has what you've been looking for. The 188-page catalog lists thousands of classical overstocked and remaindered recordings—LPs, tapes, and compact discs—at savings of 33%-plus on the release prices. It's organized alphabetically by label—from Abbey to Xenophone—and within that, by price groups. Each entry is coded to indicate whether the recording is available in stereo, mono, quadraphonic, or reprocessed stereo (or in digital or analog CD), and the country of origin is noted if the recording is an import. Berkshire has been in business since 1974, and the catalog is a gold mine for lovers of classical music, although sound tracks, ethnic music, folk songs, and poetry readings also appear. Several pages of remaindered books on classical music and musicians round out the collection.

Special Factors: Minimum order is $15 with credit cards.

CRITICS' CHOICE VIDEO

Catalog: free
Save: up to 50% (see text)
Pay: check, MO, MC, V, AE, Discover
Sells: videotapes and laser discs
Store: mail order only

DEPT. 30058
800 WEST THORNDALE
AVE.
ITASCA, IL 60143
800-367-7765
FAX: 708-437-7298
TDD: 800-272-2900

 ¡Si! ℂ

You don't go to every movie that's released, so why weed through listings of every video in existence just to find what you want? Critics' Choice Video turns something burdensome to your benefit, with a 124-page catalog of over 2,200 titles, culled from tens of thousands. Critics' Choice Video has developed a good mix of hits, cult favorites, and lesser-known gems, in the categories of movie classics, musicals, drama, foreign films, comedy, family films, action/adventures, great performances, suspense, science fiction, and westerns. Most of the movies cost under $20, and overstock and sale titles are priced under $10. Critics' Choice also sells music videos, travel videos, music and dance instruction tapes, classical music and opera performances, fitness tapes, and videos on science, philosophy, language, and even business skills. The comprehensive catalog index helps you to find exactly what you want. Some of the titles are offered on 8mm video and laser disc as well as VHS video.

Special Factors: Satisfaction is guaranteed; returns are accepted within 30 days for exchange, refund, or credit; Spanish-speaking representatives/TDD service available Monday to Friday 7–7, CST.

HARVARD SQUARE RECORDS, INC.

P.O. BOX 381975-W6
CAMBRIDGE, MA 02238
617-868-3385
FAX: 617-547-2838

Catalog: $2 (see text)
Save: up to 40%
Pay: check, MO, MC, V
Sells: out-of-print LPs, audiotapes, and videos
Store: mail order only

Harvard Square's specialty is sealed, out-of-print LPs, of which it has a large selection of imports and cutouts. (Cutouts are discontinued records, equivalent to remaindered books; they're often so marked by notching or cutting out a small piece of the corner of the jacket, or cover—hence the name.) Harvard Square's current catalog runs from 10,000 Maniacs to The Zummos, and many of the LPs cost just $4 to $6. Compilations are listed separately, along with EPs (12" singles), soundtracks, original cast albums, picture LPs, and a handful of videos. Separate catalogs feature comparatively extensive inventories of audiotapes, imported and cutout.

Because of the volume of the listings, Harvard Square divides them into separate catalogs. When you send your $2 catalog fee, you must specify LPs or audiotapes (cassettes), and you'll receive the appropriate catalog. Please note that stock cannot be held, so order promptly; if the item is sold out, you'll receive a refund check or a merchandise credit—you can indicate which you'd prefer on the order form.

Special Factors: Returns of defective (unplayable) goods are accepted within 14 days for replacement or merchandise credit; minimum order is $30 with credit cards only.

RECORD-RAMA®
SOUND ARCHIVES

4981 MCKNIGHT RD.
PITTSBURGH, PA
15237-0595
412-367-7330 (SEE TEXT)
FAX: 412-367-7388

Information: price quote
Save: up to 30%
Pay: check, MO, MC, V, AE, Discover
Sells: vintage 45's, LPs, and CDs
Store: same address; Tuesday to Saturday
10–6, closed Sunday and Monday

When word reached the Library of Congress that a retired paper goods salesman was claiming to have the country's largest known collection of 45s, a curator was sent over to check it out. Sure enough: Record-Rama Sound Archives, which shares a building with the local Post Office, holds the record with 1.5 *million* oldies on 45s, plus a million LPs. Paul C. Mawhinney's collection began with his youthful purchase of Frankie Lane's "Jezebel," and an obsession was born.

Mr. Mawhinney isn't sitting on this national treasure; he's created the *MusicMaster®: The 45 RPM Singles Directory,* the ultimate reference on 45s produced from 1947 to 1982. The *MusicMaster,* organized by artist and title, is now the most-used reference in the New York Public Library, and a must-have for any library or serious collector. Record-Rama offers the MusicMaster® Database, and other directories—the *CD-5 Singles Directory and The 45 RPM Christmas Singles Directory,* both by artist/title. (Call for current directory prices.)

Mr. Mawhinney is pragmatic about the changes in the recording industry, and is snapping up CDs with the same dedication he once reserved for 45s. He's already amassed 112,000, and does a tidy business in used CDs. If you're looking for a title, he probably has it—just call and ask, or use his WORLDSEARCH LP and CD locating service.

Please note: Calls are not accepted on the weekends.

Record-Rama is offering readers a discount of 10% on all CDs costing $13.99 or more, except boxed and multiple disks. Be sure to identify yourself as a WBMC reader when you order, and deduct the discount from the cost of the goods only. This WBMC reader discount expires February 1, 1997.

Special Factors: Price quote by phone or letter; calls are not accepted on Saturdays.

VIEWER'S EDGE

P.O. BOX 3925
MILFORD, CT 06460
800-847-6753
203-876-9864
FAX: 203-876-8234

Catalog: free
Save: up to 50%
Pay: check, MO, MC, V, AE, Discover
Sells: videotapes
Store: mail order only

If you love old movies and classics, you'll love Viewer's Edge, where videos of everything from *The Birth of a Nation* to *Amadeus* are offered, at prices that average $9.95. The most recent 40-page catalog offered comedy, war classics, intrigue, Westerns, TV series, musicals, fitness, travel, computer instruction, and holiday music tapes, as well as collections of the work of Hitchcock, Cary Grant, Elizabeth Taylor, John Wayne, and Audrey Hepburn, and series (*Star Trek, The Terminator, The Godfather, Indiana Jones*, etc.). There's a selection of entertainment and educational tapes for kids, history, and documentaries, all sold at discount prices. Also, Viewer's Edge offers a "best price guarantee" on every sale and will even track down titles not listed in the catalog (if they're available) through the Special Order Department. See the current catalog for details.

Special Factors: Satisfaction is guaranteed; returns are accepted.

SEE ALSO

American Musical Supply • books, manuals, and videos on rock & roll technique • **MUSIC**
The American Stationery Co., Inc. • custom-printed stationery, wedding invitations • **GENERAL: CARDS**
Aquatic Supply House • Tetra books on fish topics • **ANIMAL**
Art Express • art-related books, manuals, and videotapes • **ART MATERIALS**
Sam Ash Music Corp. • sheet music • **MUSIC**
The Astronomical Society of the Pacific • astronomy-related videos, slides, etc. • **BOOKS**
Astronomics/Christophers, Ltd. • star charts and manuals on astronomy • **CAMERAS**
Atlanta Thread & Supply • books and manuals on sewing and serging techniques • **CRAFTS**
Bailey's, Inc. • books on logging, chain saw use and maintenance, etc. • **TOOLS**

Baron/Barclay Bridge Supplies • books, cards, and teaching aids for bridge • **TOYS**

Bike Nashbar • manuals on bicycle repair • **SPORTS**

Dick Blick Co. • films, slides, videotapes; arts and crafts manuals • **ART MATERIALS**

Bruce Medical Supply • books on vitamins, health care, and medical topics • **MEDICINE: SPECIAL NEEDS**

Butterbrooke Farm Seed Co-Op • booklets on gardening topics • **FARM**

Campmor • field guides, survival and outdoor guides • **SPORTS**

The Caning Shop • books on seat weaving, upholstery, basketry • **CRAFTS**

Capital Cycle Corporation • factory-repair manuals for BMW cycles • **AUTO**

Caprilands Herb Farm • books on herbs and gardening, making wreaths, and cooking • **FARM**

Ceramic Supply of New York & New Jersey, Inc. • art-related manuals and books on crafts • **ART MATERIALS**

Cheap Joe's Art Stuff • art-related books, manuals, and videotapes • **ART MATERIALS**

Cheap Shot Inc. • reloading manuals • **SPORTS**

Cherry Tree Toys, Inc. • manuals on wood projects and toy making • **CRAFTS: WOODCRAFTS**

Clark's Corvair Parts, Inc. • Corvair manuals • **AUTO**

The CMC Company • cookbooks on Mexican, Asia, Mid-East and other cuisines • **FOOD: BEVERAGES AND FLAVORINGS**

Daleco Master Breeder Products • books on fish and saltwater fish care and breeding • **ANIMAL**

Deer Shack • deer-hunting books and videos • **SPORTS**

Defender Industries, Inc. • manuals and videotapes on boating topics • **AUTO**

Dharma Trading Co. • books on textile dyeing, painting, batiking, etc. • **CRAFTS: TEXTILE ARTS**

Discount Master Animal Care • veterinary handbooks • **ANIMAL**

The Dog's Outfitter • books and videotapes on dogs, cats, horses, etc. • **ANIMAL**

EduCALC Corporation • computer books and programs • **OFFICE: COMPUTING**

Elderly Instruments • folk, rock, and esoteric recordings, songbooks, history, and manuals • **MUSIC**

The Fiber Studio • books on knitting, spinning, dyeing, and weaving • **CRAFTS: TEXTILE ARTS**

Frank's Cane and Rush Supply • books on basketry, seat weaving, upholstery, etc. • **CRAFTS**

A.I. Friedman • art-related books, manuals, and videotapes • **ART MATERIALS**

Gander Mountain, Inc. • videotapes on hunting and fishing topics • **SPORTS**

Giardinelli Band Instrument Co., Inc. • records and books on music • **MUSIC**

Gohn Bros. • Amish and country cookbooks, quilting books • **CLOTHING**

Goldberg's Marine Distributors • manuals and videotapes on boating topics • **AUTO**

Golfsmith International, Inc. • texts on golf club making and repair, golfing, etc. • **SPORTS**

Great Northern Weaving • books on shirring, rug weaving, and rug braiding • **CRAFTS: TEXTILE ARTS**

H & R Company • reference books on computing and technical topics • **TOOLS**

IMPCO, Inc. • Mercedes-Benz car maintenance manuals • **AUTO**

Jerry's Artarama, Inc. • art-related books, manuals, and videotapes • **ART MATERIALS**

The Kennel Vet Corp. • manuals and books on dogs, cats, and horses • **ANIMAL**

E.C. Kraus Wine & Beermaking Supplies • books on wine- and beer-making • **FOOD: BEVERAGES AND FLAVORINGS**

Lixx Labelz • custom-designed bookplates • **GENERAL: CARDS**

Lone Star Percussion • books on drumming and percussion recordings • **MUSIC**

M&E Marine Supply Company, Inc. • books and manuals on boating • **AUTO**

Mail Order Pet Shop • books and videotapes on fish, dogs, cats, etc. • **ANIMAL**

Mandolin Brothers, Ltd. • music books, audiotapes, videotapes, and sheet music • **MUSIC**

Mass. Army & Navy Store • survival manuals and outdoor guides • **CLOTHING**

Mellinger's Inc. • books on gardening, farming, landscaping, food preservation, etc. • **FARM**

Metropolitan Music Co. • manuals and plans for making and repairing stringed instruments • **MUSIC**

Model Expo, Inc. • books on ship models, naval history, maritime topics • **CRAFTS**

National Educational Music Co., Ltd. • music software • **MUSIC**

New England Cheesemaking Supply Company, Inc. • publications on making cheese • **HOME: KITCHEN**

Newark Dressmaker Supply, Inc. • patterns, books, and guides on needlework and other crafts • **CRAFTS: TEXTILE ARTS**

Omaha Vaccine Co., Inc. • books on care and breeding of horses, livestock, dogs, and cats • **ANIMAL**

Orion Telescope Center • star charts and manuals on astronomy • **CAMERAS**

Overton's Sports Center, Inc. • windsurfing books and videotapes • **SPORTS**

Patti Music Company • sheet music • **MUSIC**

Pet Warehouse • books and manuals on dogs, cats, birds, and fish • **ANIMAL**

Porter's Camera Store, Inc. • books and videos on photography • **CAMERAS**

ProAm Seat Warehouse • car manuals • **AUTO**

Professional Cutlery Direct • commercial cookbooks • **HOME: KITCHEN**

Rafal Spice Company • cookbooks • **FOOD: BEVERAGES AND FLAVOR-INGS**

Retired Persons Services, Inc. • health-care manuals • **MEDICINE**

Rick's Movie Graphics • movie posters and ephemera • **ART & ANTIQUES**

Sailboard Warehouse, Inc. • windsurfing books and videotapes • **SPORTS**

Sax Arts & Crafts • art-related books, manuals, and videotapes • **ART MATE-RIALS**

Scope City Inc. • star charts, books, manuals • **CAMERAS**

Shar Products Company • sheet music, classical music videotapes, and audio cassettes • **MUSIC**

Solar Cine Products, Inc. • books on photography • **CAMERAS**

R.C. Steele Co. • AKC dog show videotapes, manuals for pet professionals • **ANIMAL**

Sultan's Delight, Inc. • cookbooks featuring Middle Eastern and Greek cuisine • **FOOD**

That Fish Place • books on aquariums, fish, and related topics • **ANIMAL**

Think Ink • guides to Print GOCCO printers • **CRAFTS**

Tool Crib of the North • shop manuals, woodworking guides, and videos • **TOOLS**

Tools on Sale™ • woodworking and construction books, manuals, and videos • **TOOLS**

Turnbaugh Printers Supply Co. • texts on printing • **OFFICE**

Turner Greenhouses • books on gardening • **FARM**

United Pharmacal Company, Inc. • manuals and tapes on animal training and breeds • **ANIMAL**

University Products, Inc. • preservation supplies for book collections, references (books and videos) on archival conservation • **OFFICE: SMALL BUSINESS**

Wag-Aero Group of Aircraft Services • aviation manuals • **AUTO**

Walnut Acres Organic Farms • natural foods and vegetarian cookbooks • **FOOD**

Warner-Crivellaro Stained Glass Supplies, Inc. • books and manuals on stained glass • **CRAFTS**

Weinkrantz Musical Supply Co., Inc. • student music books and cassettes • **MUSIC**

West Manor Music • small selection of music manuals • **MUSIC**

Wholesale Tool Co., Inc. • shop manuals • **TOOLS**

World Wide Aquatics • books on swimming, aquatic fitness, and triathloning • **SPORTS**

CAMERAS, PHOTOGRAPHIC AND DARKROOM EQUIPMENT, OPTICS, FILM, AND SERVICES

Equipment, supplies, and services

In the highly competitive camera market, even major electronics outlets with small camera departments can usually offer good discounts on list price. In addition to cameras, bulbs, and film, large camera houses carry video equipment, lighting equipment, screens, film editors, splicers, batteries, projection tables, lenses, filters, adapters, cases, darkroom outfits and chemicals, and custom photofinishing services—at discounts averaging 40%. Even if you don't need custom work done, you can have your film processed, enlargements made, slides duplicated, and other services done by a discount mail-order lab for half the price often charged by a drugstore or retail outlet.

Take care of your pictures: Keep them out of "magnetic" photo albums, which are made with polyvinyl-film that gives off vinyl chloride gas, and cardboard pages that exude peroxide vapors. Both can cause deterioration of slides and prints. (Photographs should be kept in temperate, relatively dry areas, out of light as much as possible.) To preserve your pictures, use archival-quality materials—acid-free albums and storage boxes, Mylar sheet protectors, "safe" slide sheets, etc. These and other conservation materials are available from University Products, listed in the "Small Business" section of "Office."

THE GRAY MARKET

Some years ago, the camera market was plagued with problems caused by gray-market goods—products intended for sale in other countries.

They're usually imported outside manufacturer-approved distribution channels, without authorization of the U.S. trademark owner. Gray-market goods are usually less expensive than their "authorized" counterparts, and although they may be just as good, they may again be produced under different quality-control standards, contain ingredients not approved for such use in the United States, or have a warranty that is not honored in the United States.

Gray-market activity has abated, but another form has appeared— "diversions" of goods from the authorized path, often by a wholesaler or mass merchant. In this case, the product was intended for the domestic market, but not for the store in which it's sold. Often, the consumer benefits, as when major department stores buy enormous inventory (to get the lowest possible price), and resell the surplus "out the back door" to other stores and discounters. If it's a product that should be used at the direction of a professional, the manufacturer may assume no liability for poor performance unless the product is sold by an authorized dealer. This may not matter much when the product is shampoo, but it does if it's a carburetor.

Gray-marketers who sell goods not intended for the U.S. market are not knowingly listed in this edition of WBMC. Because companies can change selling policies, though, if you want to be sure a firm is an authorized distributor of a product, call the manufacturer. Ask the mail-order company whether the warranty is honored by the service centers of the *U.S. manufacturer,* and make your purchase by credit card, which gives you certain protections under the Fair Credit Billing Act. See page 617 for more information.

FIND IT FAST

BINOCULARS • *Astronomics/Christophers, Mardiron, Orion, Scope City*
CAMERAS • *Ewald-Clark, Porter's, Solar Cine, Westside Camera*
PHOTO PROCESSING • *Ewald-Clark, Owl Photo, Skyline, Solar Cine*
TELESCOPES • *Astronomics/Christophers, Mardiron, Orion, Scope City*

ASTRONOMICS/ CHRISTOPHERS, LTD.

2401 TEE CIRCLE,
   SUITE 106-W96
NORMAN, OK 73069
800-422-7876 (TELE-
   SCOPES)
800-356-6603 (BINOCU-
   LARS AND SPOTTING
   SCOPES)
FAX: 405-447-3337

Catalogs: $1 and SASE
Save: up to 50%
Pay: check, MO, MC, V, AE, Discover
Sells: telescopes and optics
Store: same address; Monday to Friday
9:30–5, Saturday by appointment

Astronomics/Christophers sells top names in telescopes and birding equipment, including CCD cameras for astronomical photography, at up to 50% below list. The firm's information-packed birding and astronomical catalogs are sent free if you specify which one you want, and send $1 and a self-addressed, business-sized envelope. Astronomics/Christophers was established in 1970, and sells no gray-market goods.

Astronomics sells optics and accessories by Astromedia, Bausch & Lomb, Bushnell, Celestron, DayStar, Dover, Edmund, Fujinon, Kowa, Leica (Leitz), Lumicon, Meade, MotoFocus, Nikon, Optolyth, Pentax, Questar, SBIG, Sky Publishing, Steiner, Swarovski, Swift, TeleVue, Vernonscope, and Zeiss. If you're looking for a telescope, choose from catadioptric, refractor and reflector models, as well as such accessories as eyepieces, tripods, photo adapters, visual and photographic filters, equatorial mounts and wedges, spotting scopes for bird watching, and many other items. Astronomical and bird-watching binoculars are also offered, and Astronomics/Christophers offers a great collection of books and star charts, manuals, maps, atlases, and other reference tools.

Special Factors: Shipping is not charged on prepaid orders delivered within the continental United States; minimum order is $25.

CLARK COLOR LABS

P.O. BOX 96300
WASHINGTON, DC 20090
301-595-5300

Mailers: free
Save: up to 65% (see text)
Pay: check or MO
Sells: film-processing and enlargement services
Store: mail order only

Clark Color Labs is a prominent mail-order film processor that develops 110, 126, 127, 620, disc, 35mm, and single-use cameras, as well as slides and movies. You can also order reprints and enlargements (wallet size to 20" by 30") from negatives and slides, have copy negatives made from prints (color and black-and-white), and buy fresh film (Agfa and Kodak). Clark Color Labs uses the Colorwatch system, which means the paper, chemicals, and quality-control standards are all from Kodak. Clark's prices are much lower than those charged by minilabs, averaging 15¢ for one processed print compared to 40¢ for the same print from a typical minilab. Clark Color Lab has a dozen locations around the country to expedite your order, issues credit for unprintable negatives, and will give you a refund or credit if you're not completely satisfied with your pictures.

Special Factors: Returns are accepted for exchange, refund, or credit.

EWALD-CLARK

17 W. CHURCH AVE.
ROANOKE, VA 24011
800-835-0736
703-342-1829
FAX: 703-345-9943

Information: price quote only
Save: 30% average
Pay: check, MO, MC, V, AE
Sells: cameras, darkroom equipment, optics, services
Store: same address; Monday to Friday 8:30–5:30; also 2140 Colonial Ave., Roanoke, and 213 Draper Rd., Blacksburg, VA

  (see text)

Ewald-Clark is a full-service photography center that's been in business since 1949, but *does not publish a catalog—call or write for a price quote on specific models.* In addition to cameras, lenses, darkroom equipment, and finishing services, Ewald-Clark sells binoculars and video cameras, all at discounts of 2% to 40%, or an average of 30% off list prices.

Among the available brands are Amphoto, Beseler, Bogen, Bronica, Canon, Fuji, Gitzo, Gossen, Gralab, Ilford, Kodak, Logan, LowePro, Lumedyne, Mamiya, Minolta, Nikon, Novatron, Pelican, Pentax, Phillips CDI, Polaroid, Quantum, Ricoh, Samyang, Tamrac, Tamron, Tiffen, Varta, and Vivitar. You can also inquire for rate and specifications on custom photofinishing services.

Please note: Shipments to non-U.S. destinations are subject to hazardous materials regulations.

Special Factors: Price quote by phone or letter with SASE.

MARDIRON OPTICS

THE BINOCULAR PLACE
4 SPARTAN CIRCLE, DEPT.
  WBMC
STONEHAM, MA 02180
617-938-8339

Brochures and Price Lists: Require two first-class stamps
Save: up to 45%
Pay: check or MO
Sells: binoculars, telescopes, microscopes, opera glasses, etc.
Store: mail order only

Mardiron, in business since 1983, sells binoculars, spotting scopes, astronomical telescopes, theater glasses, microscopes, rifle scopes, and Russian night-vision binoculars and scopes at savings of up to 45% on list prices. (Overstocked or recently superceded binocular models that are still available are further discounted; request a price quote by model number.) Mardiron features goods from Aus Jena, Bausch & Lomb, Binolux, Bushnell, Jason, Kowa, Leica, Minolta, Monolux, Pentax, Selsi, Sigma, Swift, and the Steiner military, hunting, and fully integrated compass marine binoculars. The new Brunton binoculars developed especially for people who wear eyeglasses are also available. To receive the price lists and brochures, send two first-class stamps, or a SASE, and mention the type of item that interests you.

Special Factors: Price quote by phone or letter with SASE; shipping is not charged.

MYSTIC COLOR LAB

MASON'S ISLAND RD.
P.O. BOX 144
MYSTIC, CT 06355-9987
800-367-6061

Mailers: free
Save: up to 30% (see text)
Pay: check, MO, MC, V, Discover
Sells: film-processing and enlargement services
Store: mail order only

Mail-order film labs abound, but Mystic is one that's gotten good marks in quality comparisons with other labs. Mystic has been in business since 1969, and offers free shipping in postpaid mailers with no handling charges. Mystic Color Lab's prices on processing film, with one set of standard-size prints, are up to 30% below those of other mail-order labs—and considerably less than the one-hour minilabs. But the firm does its best to come close to the minilab turnaround time, by pledging to get your processed film and prints in the mail to you within 24 hours of receipt.

Mystic not only develops 110 and 35mm color and black-and-white film, but it also makes enlargements (to 20" by 30" posters) and slides, and sells its own brand of film: 200 ASA three-packs, 24 exposures each roll, cost $7.95 at this writing. If you're looking for the reusable "panoramic" camera, it's here—for just $9.95, including case and a roll of film. Others charge $19.95, plus $2 for the case, plus....

Special Factors: Shipping is not charged.

ORION TELESCOPE CENTER

DEPT. WBM
P.O. BOX 1158
SANTA CRUZ, CA
  95061-1158
408-464-5710
FAX: 408-464-0466

Catalog: free
Save: up to 40%
Pay: check, MO, MC, V, Discover
Sells: telescopes, binoculars, and accessories
Store: 2450 17th Ave., Santa Cruz, CA (408-464-0465); also 10555 S. De Anza Blvd., Cupertino (408-255-8770), and 3609 Buchanan St., San Francisco (415-931-9966), CA
E-mail: sales@oriontel.com

 (see text)

Orion brings you stellar savings on top-quality telescopes and accessories through an informative, 100-page catalog that includes sidebars on telescope selection and sky watching, as well as complete product descriptions. Orion, in business since 1975, stocks astronomical and terrestrial telescopes, including spotting, reflector, refractor, guide, finder, and "deep sky" scopes by Celestron, Orion, and TeleVue. If you visit Orion's stores, you'll also find goods by Bausch & Lomb, Bushnell, Fujinon, Nikon, Pentax, Swift, and Zeiss. Camera adapters, filters, lenses, optical tubes, tripods, eyepieces, star charts, books, and other accessories are available. Orion is also well known for the firm's comprehensive selection of binoculars—deep-sky, sport, folding, waterproof, and armored models—as well as spotting scopes for sport and nature enthusiasts.

Please note: Orion ships only to the United States and Canada.

Special Factors: Satisfaction is guaranteed; price quote by phone or letter for institutional orders.

OWL PHOTO CORP.

701 E. MAIN ST.
WEATHERFORD, OK 73096
405-772-3353
FAX: 405-772-5809

Mailers: free
Save: up to 40%
Pay: check, MO, MC, V
Sells: film processing and reprinting services
Store: same address; Monday to Friday 7:30–5, Saturday 9–1

Owl Photo offers reasonably priced film processing services by mail, and will send you self-mailers on request. Owl will develop your color and black-and-white film at prices that are competitive with discount drug store processing, and you can also order reprints and fresh film—a price list comes with the mailer. Disc, 110, 120, 126, 127, 135, 616 color (C-41), and 620 film is processed, and reprint sizes run up to 11" by 14". Owl uses Kodak paper and chemicals, and guarantees your satisfaction or your processing costs and postage will be refunded.

Owl Photo Corp. is offering readers a 10% discount on all orders. Be sure to identify yourself as a WBMC reader at the time you order to get the savings—write "10% WBMC Discount" on the film mailer. This WBMC reader discount expires February 1, 1997.

Special Factors: Satisfaction is guaranteed; returns are accepted for refund or credit.

PORTER'S CAMERA STORE, INC.

P.O. BOX 628
CEDAR FALLS, IA 50613
319-268-0104
FAX: 800-221-5329

Catalog: free (see text)
Save: 35% average
Pay: check, MO, MC, V, Discover
Sells: photographic and darkroom equipment and supplies
Store: 323 Viking Rd., Cedar Falls, IA; Monday to Saturday 9:30–5:30

Porter's has been selling photographic and darkroom equipment since 1914, and publishes a 128-page tabloid catalog packed with an enormous range of photographic products, at prices up to 67% below list. Both amateurs and professionals will appreciate the buys on cameras and lenses, filters, darkroom equipment, film, bags and cases, batteries, studio equipment, chemicals, paper, and much more. The brands run from Agfa to Vivitar, the sales policy is clearly detailed in the catalog, and Porter's has deputized one of its staff to answer your questions about equipment. A separate video catalog is also available. If you're in Cedar Falls, drop by the warehouse outlet store where you'll find everything tagged at catalog prices—a welcome departure from the two-tier policies prevailing at most discount stores.

Canadian readers, please note: The catalog costs $3 in *Canadian funds,* but orders must be paid in U.S. funds. The catalog describes purchasing procedures and includes a shipping rate chart.

Please note: The catalog costs $10 in U.S. funds if sent to an address without a U.S. or Canadian postal code.

Special Factors: Price quote by phone or letter; authorized returns are accepted; institutional accounts are available; orders are shipped worldwide, subject to a $100 minimum order.

SCOPE CITY INC.

**679 EASY ST.
SIMI VALLEY, CA 93065
805-522-6646
FAX: 805-582-0292**

Catalogs: $7, refundable (see text)
Save: up to 45%
Pay: check, MO, MC, V, AE, Discover
Sells: telescopes, binoculars, microscopes, and other optics
Store: same address; Monday to Friday 9–6, Saturday 10–6; also Costa Mesa, San Diego, and Sherman Oaks, CA

Scope City has been selling telescopes, binoculars, spotting scopes, and other optics since 1976. Telescopes and accessories by Celestron, Edmund, Meade, Parks, Questar, and TeleVue are available, as well as field and specialty binoculars by Bausch & Lomb, Dr. Optics, Fujinon, Leica, Parks, Zeiss, and other manufacturers. Scope City also offers lenses, eyepieces, adapters, mirrors, star charts, manuals, and other reference tools. Most of the prices are discounted, and savings of up to 45% are possible on selected items. If you know the model you want, you can call for a price quote, or send $7 for the catalog package, which is deductible from your first purchase.

Special Factors: Satisfaction is guaranteed; returns are accepted within 15 days for exchange, refund, or credit.

SKRUDLAND PHOTO

5311 FLEMING CT.
AUSTIN, TX 78744
512-444-0958

Mailers: free
Save: up to 50%
Pay: check or MO
Sells: film processing and reprinting services
Store: mail order only

Skrudland Photo has performed well in tests of mail-order film processors, and offers low prices—as little as $2 a roll—for color film processing (with one set of prints, glossy or matte). In addition to developing 110, 126, Disc, and 35mm film, Skrudland can make prints and enlargements from your negatives, and develop your slides and Super 8 movies. The film mailers (available on request) include prices and the standard liability disclaimer used by most mail-order film processors.

Special Factors: Satisfaction is guaranteed; returns are accepted for credit.

SKYLINE COLOR LAB

9016 PRINCE WILLIAM ST.,
   DEPT. WBMC
MANASSAS, VA 22110
703-631-2216
FAX: 703-631-8064

Catalog: free
Save: up to 30%
Pay: check, MO, MC, V, AE
Sells: film processing
Store: same address; Monday to Friday 9–6, Saturday 8–2

 (see text)

Skyline Color Lab, whose parent firm has been in business since 1945, is a full-service professional and commercial mail-order lab that offers film and slide processing, negative duplication and slide copying, prints, and photographic packages (portraits and weddings) at competitive prices. Skyline's 24-page catalog lists the available services and prices, includes directions for cropping, and features a helpful glossary of terms like "internegative," "dodging," and "push/pull processing." Skyline will process your color or black-and-white film (roll or sheet), produce contact sheets, make prints and enlargements (from 3-1/2" by 5" to 48" by 144"), and create murals and photographic displays (from 40" square to 48" by 96"; larger sizes are available on a custom basis). Custom services are offered, including "push" processing to compensate for underexposed film, glass mounts for slides, slide remounting, duplicate negatives and negatives made from slides or transparencies (internegatives), a choice of finishes for enlargements (canvas, pebble, matte, or luster), dry mounting of prints (on art board, foam core, or "gator" foam), mounting on canvas panels or canvas stretchers, and printing for backlit display. Skyline has also put together economical print packages, including a "relative's special"—one 8" by 10", two 5" by 7", and 24 wallet-sized prints—perfect for sending to friends and family—as well as wedding album packages. Complete details of the firm's sales policy and guarantees are given in the catalog.

Special Factors: Liability for damaged or lost film is limited to replacement with unexposed film; minimum order is $25; C.O.D. orders are accepted (for delivery within the continental United States).

SOLAR CINE PRODUCTS, INC.

4247 SOUTH KEDZIE AVE.
CHICAGO, IL 60632
800-621-8796
312-254-8310
FAX: 312-254-4124

Catalog: free
Save: up to 30%
Pay: check, MO, MC, V, AE, DC, Discover
Sells: photo equipment, supplies, and services
Store: same address; Monday to Friday 8:30–5, Saturday 9–1

 ¡Si!

Solar Cine's 24-page catalog gives a sample of the thousands of items carried by the company—a full range of photographic equipment and accessories from a large number of manufacturers. Solar Cine has been supplying professionals and serious amateurs since 1937, and stocks a full range of still and movie equipment, including videotapes and video batteries. Range Finder cameras, lenses, studio lights, light meters, tripods, and darkroom materials are available from Canon, Kalt/Brandess, Kodak, Minolta, Pentax, Polaroid, and Vivitar, among others. Scores of books on photography for beginners and professionals are available, as well as electronics and processing services (movies, slides, reprints, and prints). The services are described in the catalog; for more information on cameras and equipment, call or write for a price quote.

Special Factors: Returns (except defective goods) are subject to a restocking fee.

SEE ALSO

Berry Scuba Co. • *underwater cameras* • **SPORTS**
Cabela's Inc. • *binoculars and spotting scopes* • **SPORTS**
Central Skindivers • *underwater cameras* • **SPORTS**
Defender Industries, Inc. • *binoculars and marine optics* • **AUTO**
S & S Sound City • *cameras, accessories, binoculars, telescopes, etc.* •
APPLIANCES
20th Century Plastics, Inc. • *photo storage sheets and albums* • **OFFICE**
University Products, Inc. • *archival-quality storage materials for photographs,
slides, film, negatives, microfiche, etc.* • **OFFICE: SMALL BUSINESS**
Wiley Outdoor Sports, Inc. • *binoculars, spotting scopes, etc.* • **SPORTS**

CLOTHING, FURS, AND ACCESSORIES

Clothing, furs, and accessories for men, women, and children

The firms listed here sell a wide range of clothing for men, women, and children—Amish clothing from Indiana, lingerie from New York City's Lower East Side, executive suiting, custom-made deerskin coats and jackets, and much more—at savings of up to 90%.

Finding discount sources for bridal attire isn't easy (see Discount Bridal Service in this chapter), and anyone facing the challenge of planning a wedding today will find *Bridal Bargains: Secrets to Throwing a Fantastic Wedding on a Realistic Budget* an absolute necessity. Written by the intrepid Alan and Denise Fields, the book describes the mechanics of the entire industry, and gives the best strategies for everything from booking the site, buying the dress, ordering food and flowers, hiring the photographer, and covering all of the details—without getting burned. The Fields are so confident that you'll benefit from their research that they offer a complete refund on the cost of the book if it doesn't save you at least $500 on your wedding expenses. To order a copy, call 800-888-0385, or write to Windsor Peak Press, 1223 Peakview Circle, Suite 7000, Boulder, CO 80302.

Clothing that's made in the U.S.A. must bear labels that provide specific information on cleaning and care. The Federal Trade Commission has compiled "What's New About Care Labels," a booklet defining the terms used in the labeling that answers a number of typical consumer questions. For a copy, request it by title from the Federal Trade Commission, Public Reference Office, Washington, DC 20580. If you want to make the best of what you own, you'll appreciate *Taking Care of Clothes,* by Mablen Jones (St. Martin's Press, 1982). It can help you evaluate clothing before purchase, and give tips on stain removal, laundering, dry cleaning, ironing and pressing, storage, and caring for leather, fur, and other special materials. You can also get it from the horse's mouth: The Neighborhood Cleaners' Association (NCA) publishes the "Consumer Guide to Clothing Care," a brochure of tips on the care and cleaning of different fabrics and trims. Send a long, self-addressed, stamped envelope to NCA, 116 E. 27th St., New York, NY 10016, for the pamphlet.

Last, your very best deals on clothing are usually found in *stores,* where very limited inventory, drastic markdowns, closeouts, and irregulars—all of which pose fulfillment problems if sold by mail—can be snatched up at big savings. Thrifts shops are another resource prized by people building a wardrobe on a shoestring. They're also one of the best places to learn about clothing's quality points, since they tell the story of how the fabric, weave, tailoring, and style have performed over the years. The better you train your eye to identify the kind of wool that pills, the soft sheen of good silk, collars that have survived fads, and countless other clothing details, the better you'll be at imagining how something in a catalog actually looks, and will wear.

FIND IT FAST

BRIDAL ATTIRE • **Discount Bridal Servie**
DANCEWEAR • **Dance Distributors**
HATS • **Manny's Millinery**
MEN'S CLOTHING • **Jos. A Bank, Byron & Poole, Deerskin Trading Post, Paul Fredrick, Huntington, Mass. Army, Quinn's Shirt Shop**
SHEEPSKIN, DEERSKIN, AND FUR • **Arctic Sheepskin, Deerskin Place, Deerskin Trading Post**
SPORTSWEAR • **L'eggs Catalog, No Nonsense Direct, Sportswear Clearinghouse**
UNDERWEAR AND HOSIERY • **Asiatic Hosiery, Chock, L'eggs Catalog, National Wholesale, No Nonsense Direct**
UNIFORMS • **Mass. Army, Tafford**
WOMEN'S CLOTHING • **Jos. A Bank, L'eggs Catalog, No Nonsense Direct, One 212, Ultimate Outlet, Willow Ridge**
WORK CLOTHING • **Cahall's, Gohn, Todd, WearGuard**

ARCTIC SHEEPSKIN OUTLET

565 CO. RD. T, BOX WB
HAMMOND, WI 54015
800-428-9276
800-362-9276
  (EAU CLAIRE)
715-796-2292
FAX: 715-796-2295

Brochure: $2, refundable
Save: up to 50%
Pay: check, MO, MC, V, Discover
Sells: sheepskin clothing and accessories
Store: 30 miles east of St. Paul on I-94 at the Hammond exit; also 3015 E. Hamilton Ave., Eau Claire, WI; Monday to Thursday 8–8, Friday 8–5, Saturday 9–5

Arctic Sheepskin Outlet was founded in 1987 by the energetic Joseph Bacon, who's been quite successful with mail-order skylights and insulated glass panels (see the listing of Arctic Glass & Window Outlet in the "Improvement and Maintenance" section of "Home"). His Arctic Sheepskin Outlet features sheepskin favorites—slippers, mittens, hats, car seat covers, rugs, etc.—from the largest sheepskin tannery in the world. Savings vary from item to item; rubber-soled sheepskin moccasins sell here and elsewhere at $49.95, but the car seat covers are real buys at $35 (two for $65), as are mittens for $15.95, kids' slippers for $12.95, and deep-pile sheepskin rugs from $49.95—about half the going rate. There are also hats with earflaps, sheepskin headbands, steering wheel covers, and bicycle seat covers. All purchases are covered by Arctic's "money-back guarantee."

Special Factors: Satisfaction is guaranteed; returns are accepted for exchange, refund, or credit; minimum order is $5.

ASIATIC HOSIERY CO.

P.O. BOX 31
LITTLE FALLS, NJ
  07424-0031
201-872-2111, EXT. 1000

Catalog: free
Save: up to 75%
Pay: check or MO
Sells: hosiery for men, women, and children
Store: mail order only

If you're willing to buy a dozen of the same color, size, and style of hosiery, Asiatic Hosiery will reward you with amazing savings on a full selection of socks, panty hose, and other legwear for the whole family.

The prices range from women's sheer knee-highs at $4 per dozen ($6, queen), to pantyhose from under 84¢ a pair to $1.67 for a sheer support style in seven colors and sizes to 2X. A *gross* of nylon "shoe try-ons," which can be used as footlets, cost just $6. In addition, Asiatic Hosiery sells opaque tights, knee-high and over-the-knee socks, anklets, slouch socks, and athletic socks for both women and girls, and dress and athletic socks for men and boys.

The price list from Asiatic has no pictures or color charts, so you have to correlate the descriptions to products you're familiar with. There are no brand names, so order on the generous side (if you're a "D" in premium pantyhose, take a Q or 1X here). Some color selections will include "assortments," which will be the company's choice. You're really buying at wholesale here, so place a small order to begin with to make sure you'll be happy.

Special Factors: Minimum order is 1 dozen.

JOS. A. BANK CLOTHIERS, INC.

<hr style="width:30%" />

500 HANOVER PIKE,
 DEPT. WBMC
HAMPSTEAD, MD 21074
800-285-BANK
FAX: 410-239-5911

Catalog: $1
Save: up to 30%
Pay: check, MO, MC, V, AE
Sells: men's and women's career clothing and sportswear
Store: 50 stores in 29 states (locations are listed in the catalog)

Bank's business is executive suiting, which it serves with separate catalogs for men and women. Fine tailoring details and prices up to 30% below comparable goods—but not "discount"—distinguish the company's offerings. The men's catalog features suits, jackets, pants, shirts, ties, accessories, weekend separates, and underwear. The suits are handsomely executed in fine wool worsteds, in pin and chalkline stripes, glen plaids, and herringbones. Chesterfield and cashmere topcoats, tuxedos and formal wear, blazers, tweed jackets, and complementing pants and shirts are among the standards, and swatches are available for the suits and sports coats. Braces, silk ties, shoes, and pajamas are sold as well.

The offerings in the women's catalog include fine business ensembles in the "relaxed traditional" style—softly colored suits, double-breasted coatdresses, and Chanel-style jackets are a few examples from past catalogs. Some of the women's clothing is offered in petites and talls, as well as regular sizes. Scarves, belts, jewelry, bags, and coordinated weekend separates are also available. Bank's garments often compare well to similar garments sold elsewhere for more, but note that Bank is recommended more for quality and selection than for prices, and *do not ask for discounts*.

Special Factors: Satisfaction is guaranteed; returns are accepted for exchange, refund, or credit.

BYRON & POOLE

588 BROADWAY, SUITE 1111
NEW YORK, NY 10012
800-542-9766
212-343-9205
FAX: 212-343-9208

Catalog and Swatches: free
Save: up to 40%
Pay: check, MO, MC, V, AE
Sells: men's dress shirts and ties
Store: mail order only

Bespoke shirts in blue pinpoint and white Sea Island broadcloth are not unaffordable, even with a choice of collar styles and in sizes up to 18-1/2 neck and 37" sleeve. The shirts are cut traditionally and beautifully tailored, with single-needle stitching, button sleeve plackets, a mitered split yoke, hand-sewn pockets, removable collar stays, and other custom touches; the prices begin at $29.50 for white Egyptian broadcloth shirt in any of three collar styles. If you want a certain combination of details—shorter sleeves, a different collar or French cuffs, no pocket, a tapered fit, or extra-large or extra-tall—there's a $9 surcharge for each shirt (minimum order four shirts). Handsewn silk neckties ($37.50) are shown with the shirts in the small color catalog/portfolio, which includes sets of shirt fabric swatches. Monogramming (left cuff or pocket) is also available.

Special Factors: Satisfaction is guaranteed.

CAHALL'S BROWN DUCK CATALOG

**P.O. BOX 450-WM
MOUNT ORAB, OH 45154
513-444-2094**

Catalog: $1
Save: up to 40%
Pay: check, MO, MC, V, Discover
Sells: working clothing and footwear
Store: Cahall's Work Wear Store; 112 S. High St., Mount Orab, OH; Monday to Saturday 9–6; also Cahall's Work Wear Store, 35 N. South St., Wilmington, OH; Monday to Saturday 9–5:30

The Cahall family opened its department store in 1946, and took the leap into mail order nearly 30 years later with the 40-page "Brown Duck Catalog" of heavy-duty apparel and footwear. You'll find your favorites—jeans, shirts, jackets, and overalls—at savings of up to 30% on suggested list or retail prices. Popular lines from Carhartt, Hanes, Key, Levi, OshKosh, Wolverine, and other well-known manufacturers are available. Cahall's also offers an excellent selection of work shoes and boots for men and women from LaCrosse, Wolverine, and other names, in hard-to-find sizes. Hush Puppies and Rocky Boot sport boots are also stocked, as well as heavy-duty socks, work gloves, bandannas, T-shirts, hats, and even nail aprons. If you don't see the style or model of a garment or footwear you're looking for in the catalog, call—it may be available.

Special Factors: Satisfaction is guaranteed; returns are accepted for exchange, refund, or credit.

CHOCK CATALOG CORP.

74 ORCHARD ST.,
 DEPT. WBMC
NEW YORK, NY
 10002-4594
212-473-1929
FAX: 212-473-6273

Catalog: $2, refundable
Save: up to 35%
Pay: check, MO, MC, V, Discover
Sells: hosiery, underwear, sleepwear, and infants' clothing
Store: same address; Sunday to Thursday 9–5, Friday 9–1
E-mail: ftp@worldshop.com

Chock, known to generations of New Yorkers as Louis Chock, is a family operation that's been selling unmentionables since 1921. Chock's 66-page catalog is packed with good values on name-brand underthings for men, women, children, and infants. The women's department features underpants by Carter's, Hanes Her Way, Jockey for Her, Calvin Klein, Lollipop, and Vanity Fair; hosiery by Berkshire, Hanes, Calvin Klein, Mayer, and PrimaSport; well-priced dusters, smocks, aprons, slips, pajamas, and nightgowns. (For those with special needs, there are two pages of dusters, nightgowns, and slips that snap up the back.) Men are offered underwear by BVD, Chock's private label, Duofold, Hanes, Jockey, Calvin Klein, Manshape, and Munsingwear; socks by Burlington, Chock's own line, Doré Doré, and Wigwam; pajamas and robes from Knothe, Munsingwear, and Oscar de la Renta; and slippers by Jiffies. Men's sizes run up to XXXL (58 to 60).

Chock's has a good choice of basics for babies and children, running from cloth diapers and complete layettes by Carters and Gerber, creepers and sleepers, underwear and sleepwear for boys and girls by Carters and Hanes, socks by Tic-Tac-Toe and Trimfit, to toys by Montgomery Schoolhouse, bathing accessories, sheets, blankets, and more.

Chock's catalogs usually offer well-priced accessories that make great gifts—typically gloves and Totes umbrellas. How wonderful to find a choice of Caswell-Massey soaps and creams, at nifty discounts of about 25%!

Special Factors: Satisfaction is guaranteed; unopened returns with manufacturer's packaging intact are accepted within 30 days.

DANCE DISTRIBUTORS

DEPT. WBMC
P.O. BOX 11440
HARRISBURG, PA 17108
800-333-2623
FAX: 717-234-1465

Catalog: free
Save: 25% average (see text)
Pay: check, MO, MC, V, AE, Discover
Sells: dance wear and accessories
Store: mail order only

Professional dancers can trim at least 25% from the cost of their next pair of toe shoes, leotards, or tights by buying from Dance Distributors. Nearly half of the current 18-page catalog lists Capezio—shoes for ballet and pointe, jazz and tap, character roles, and modern and folk dance are featured, for men, women, and children, as well as Capezio's classic leotards, dance skirts, tights, and trunks. Footwear and clothing from Baryshnikov, Bloch, Body Wrappers, Chacott, Danskin, Freed, Grishko, K.D.dids, Mirella, and Sansha are also offered, and Dance Distributors sells its own line of leotards, tights, and legwarmers as well. Prices are generally 25% below list, but sale offerings can double the discounts. Special orders are accepted on items not listed in the catalog, but please note that they can't be returned. The catalog has helpful size conversion charts for street shoes to ballet and for Continental sizing to inches.

Special Factors: Satisfaction is guaranteed; returns (except special orders) are accepted within 30 days for exchange, refund, or credit.

THE DEERSKIN PLACE

283 AKRON RD.
EPHRATA, PA 17522
717-733-7624

Brochure and Price List: $1, refundable (see text)
Save: up to 50%
Pay: check, MO, MC, V
Sells: deerskin clothing and accessories
Store: same address; Monday to Saturday 9–9, Sunday (January–December) 12–5

The Deerskin Place, in business since 1969, features clothing and accessories made of deerskin, cowhide, and sheepskin, at prices up to 50% less than those charged elsewhere for comparable goods. Among the offerings are fingertip-length shearling jackets for $399, fringed buck-skin-suede jackets at $179, bomber and motorcycle jackets, and sporty deerskin handbags for about $70. The Deerskin Place offers moccasins and casual shoes, knee-high suede boots, and crepe-soled slip-ons for men and women (from $17), deerskin wallets, clutches, coin purses, and keycases (from about $6), mittens and gloves for the whole family, beaded belts (under $6), and many other accessories.

The Deerskin Place is offering readers of this book a 10% discount on orders of $150 or more. Be sure to identify yourself as a reader when you order, and deduct the discount from the goods total only. This WBMC reader discount expires July 1, 1997.

Special Factors: Satisfaction is guaranteed; inquire before ordering if unsure of color, size, etc.; returns are accepted; C.O.D. orders are accepted.

DEERSKIN TRADING POST, INC.

**119 FOSTER
PEABODY, MA 01961-6008
508-532-4040
FAX: 508-531-7729**

Catalog: $1
Save: up to 30%
Pay: check, MO, MC, V, AE, DC, Discover
Sells: leather clothing and accessories
Store: Rte. 1 South, Danvers, MA

Deerskin Trading Post has been selling leather clothing and accessories since 1944, and offers garments made of lambskin, shearling, and cowhide, as well as deerskin. The 72-page color catalog has up-to-date styles in leatherwear for men and women, and somewhat conservatively styled footwear—walkers, chukka boots, loafers, moccasins, bucks, slippers, boots, scuffs, etc.—for men and women. You'll find all kinds of coat and jacket styles, including bombers, a belted fingertip-length model with shearling collar for men, sport coats, blazers, blouson jackets for women, baseball styles, washable pigskin suede "jeans" jackets, swing coats for women, car coats, and much more. There are leather pants and skirts, fur hats, shearling car accessories, and good buys on things like deerskin gloves. Deerskin Trading Post features extra-large sizes, running to 10 in women's shoes and 20 dress size, and up to 48 long for men.

Special Factors: Satisfaction is guaranteed; returns of unaltered, unused goods are accepted for exchange, refund, or credit; minimum order is $25 with credit cards.

DISCOUNT BRIDAL SERVICE, INC.

14415 NORTH 73RD ST.,
 SUITE 115
SCOTTSDALE, AZ 85260
800-874-8794
FAX: 602-998-3092

Information: call for referral (see text)
Save: up to 40%
Pay: check, MO, MC, V
Sells: bridal attire
Store: see text

How would you like to carve 20% to 40% off one of the biggest single expenses of your wedding—The Dress? Discount Bridal Service (DBS), a network of hundreds of bridal specialists, can refer you to the representative nearest you. You'll work with her directly, ordering your gown at savings that average 20% to 40%, and you can also order the dresses and accessories for the bridesmaids, mother of the bride, the flower girl, and others at similar savings. There's no catalog—simply choose the gown of your dreams from the advertising and editorial in *Bride's, Modern Bride, For the Bride, Elegant Bride, Bridal Guide, Wedding Day Magazine*—or any other source showing current bridal styles. All of the merchandise is first-quality—no seconds or copies are sold. DBS deals with the same manufacturers and resources as do conventional bridal retailers. You'll be responsible for alterations (if they're needed), and if you don't know a good seamstress who specializes in bridal fittings, the DBS rep can give you local references. In addition to savings hundreds of dollars on the gown (and possibly thousands if you outfit the bridal party through DBS), the rep can often recommend well-priced sources for invitations, catering services, and other bridal-related services.

Unfortunately, DBS performs miracles for your wedding budget, but it can't change time: It's still going to take at least ten weeks, or as many as six months, from the time your order is submitted to when you receive your gown. (The differences depend on the manufacturer and the complexity of the dress; your rep will tell you the time frame for your choice.) And note that you'll have to prepay the entire cost of the gown when you place the order. Even with savings, that requires confidence in your rep, but DBS couldn't have survived in this highly competitive business since 1985 unless it had a great reputation and thoroughly reliable salespeople.

Special Factors: Consult with your DBS rep for terms of the sales policy.

PAUL FREDRICK

DEPT. WM96
223 W. POPLAR ST.
FLEETWOOD, PA
   19522-9989
610-944-0909
FAX: 610-944-6452

Catalog: $1
Save: up to 50%
Pay: check, MO, MC, V, AE, DC, Discover
Sells: men's dress and casual shirts, neckties, and accessories
Store: mail order only

How can men buy $70 dress shirts for around $32? Paul Fredrick is the source. Paul Fredrick offers consumers the same shirts it manufactures under private label for fine men's stores across the country, at savings of 35% to 50% on department store retail prices. The selection is show-cased in a 60-page color catalog: a dozen different shirt collar styles, including button-down, tab, spread, traditional, contemporary, or Euro-pean straight versions; cuff options include French or button styles. The fabrics range from such tried-and-true classics as broadcloth and pin-point Oxford cotton, to two-ply Egyptian cotton broadcloth. All of Paul Fredrick's dress shirts—the solids, stripes, contrasting collars and cuffs, and tone-on-tones—as well as the casual shirts, from linens and plaids to denim chambrays, are made in the firm's U.S. workrooms.

If you're in the market for fine silk neckties to complement your shirts, look no further. Paul Fredrick creates stunning ties from Lake Como silk; the styles range from traditional to contemporary, in every-thing from subtle jacquards to conversation-launching designs. Cuff links, stud sets, tie bars, leather belts, monogrammed jewelry, and socks complete the line. Should you find yourself daunted by the choices, just call—trained fashion consultants are available around the clock to assist you.

Special Factors: Satisfaction is guaranteed; returns are accepted; online with CompuServe and Prodigy.

GOHN BROS.

---

105 S. MAIN
P.O. BOX 111
MIDDLEBURY, IN
  46540-0111
219-825-2400

Catalog: $1
Save: up to 40%
Pay: check or MO
Sells: general merchandise and Amish spe-
cialties
Store: same address; Monday to Saturday
8–5:30

Other firms add fax machines and 800 lines, but Gohn Bros. remains firmly rooted in a world where bonnet board and work coats were stock items in the general store. Gohn has been in business since 1904, and sells practical goods at prices up to 40% below comparable retail.

Home sewers appreciate Gohn for yard goods staples and notions, such as the all-cotton Sanforized blue denim ($5.98), muslin (as low as $1.39), cotton oxford shirting ($2.98), quilting thread ($1.29), cotton percale and quilting prints, pillow tubing, all-cotton sheeting, tailor's canvas, haircloth, mosquito netting, Coats & Clark embroidery floss (25¢ per skein), and wool overcoating (under $13 per yard, in navy, black, and "Confederate gray").

At least half of Gohn's closely printed 12-page stock lists are devoted to work-tailored, sturdy Amish clothing, including men's cotton chambray work shirts ($16.98), cotton denim broadfall pants ($14.98), men's underwear, rubber galoshes and footwear by LaCrosse and Tingley, work gloves, felt hats, and handkerchiefs. Much of the clothing is available in large sizes, and many of the items in the men's department are also offered in boys' sizes. If you're assembling a layette, see the catalog for good buys on the basics—diapers, receiving blankets, sleepers, pacifiers, baby pants, and other goods by Curity and Gerber. Nursing bras are available, and women's underwear and hosiery are offered at low prices. And the "book and game" department has some interesting Amish and Mennonite titles.

Special Factors: Satisfaction is guaranteed; C.O.D. orders are accepted.

HUNTINGTON CLOTHIERS

1285 ALUM CREEK DR.
COLUMBUS, OH
43209-2797
800-848-6203
614-252-4422
FAX: 614-252-3855

Catalog: free
Save: up to 50% (see text)
Pay: check, MO, MC, V, AE, DC
Sells: traditional menswear
Store: same address; Monday to Friday 10–6, Saturday 10–5, Sunday 12–5

The 84-page catalog from Huntington Clothiers illustrates all the basics of a conservative wardrobe, from pinstriped suits to pima boxer shorts, with more fashion-forward accessories and casual attire. Huntington's prices are competitive with those of old-line haberdashers; some items cost up to twice as much elsewhere.

Huntington's own line of shirts are offered in Oxford cloth, pima cotton solids, Sea Island cotton, Egyptian cotton broadcloth, and cotton/poly blends. (Monogramming is available for $5.) Huntington also sells neckwear—foulards, silk regimental stripes, and linen solids and paisley ties—at similar savings, and executive suits that run the gamut from gray chalk stripes and gabardines to poplin and seersucker summer suits to tuxedos. Jackets and blazers are shown, as well as trousers, sportswear separates, walking shorts, lisle cotton polo shirts, cotton and wool sweaters, belts, suspenders, underwear, and even shoes. Huntington has been in business since 1978, and has added photos to the color illustrations that have been one of the catalog's trademarks.

Special Factors: Satisfaction is guaranteed; returns (except monogrammed goods) are accepted for exchange, refund, or credit.

L'EGGS HANES BALI PLAYTEX OUTLET CATALOG

L'EGGS BRANDS, INC.
P.O. BOX 843
RURAL HALL, NC
  27098-0843
910-744-1170
FAX: 910-744-1485
TDD: 910-744-5300

Catalog: free
Save: up to 60%
Pay: check, MO, MC, V, Discover
Sells: first-quality and "slightly imperfect" women's hosiery and underwear
Store: mail order only

 (see text)

The 56-page color L'eggs Hanes Bali Playtex Outlet Catalog brings you savings of up to 60% on your favorite panty hose, activewear, and lingerie from Bali, Hanes, Isotoner, L'eggs, Playtex, and Underalls. The best buys are on the "slightly imperfect" irregulars, and the whole range of L'eggs is available, in control-top styles, queen sizes, and a wide range of colors. (Just My Size and Sheer Energy Maternity panty hose are offered, also at savings of up to 60%.) Hanes hosiery—Silk Reflections, Hanes Too!, Hanes Alive, Ultra Silk, etc.—is sold, as well as a wide selection of Bali and Playtex bras and slips, and Hanes socks, underwear, T-shirts, and sweats for the whole family. See the detailed sizing guide in the catalog to be sure you get the best fit.

Special Factors: Satisfaction is guaranteed; "slightly imperfect" goods are clearly identified; returns are accepted; TDD service is available Monday to Friday, 8 A.M. to midnight.

MANNY'S MILLINERY SUPPLY CENTER

26 W. 38TH ST.
NEW YORK, NY 10018
212-840-2253
FAX: 212-944-0178

Catalog: $3
Save: 33% average
Pay: check, MO, MC, V, AE
Sells: hats, millinery supplies, gloves, bridal trimmings
Store: same address; Monday to Friday 9–5:30, Saturday 10–4:30

   ¡Sí!

Manny's is nestled among the shops in New York City's "trimmings" district, which has more sequins, tassels, and decorative add-ons per square foot than a Las Vegas floor show. Manny's offers some of that glitter, but the company's specialty is women's hats, millinery supplies, and bridal accessories.

About half of Manny's 48-page catalog is devoted to headpieces, many of which are trimmed. Hundreds of styles are shown, in parisial, milanette, genuine Milan straw, felt, and fabric. Scores of "frames," or fabric-covered hat forms, are offered. The satin frames are suitable for bridal outfits, and the buckram frames provide a base for limitless flights of fancy. Stunning bridal headpieces, which can be used to decorate the hats and headpieces, are shown in the catalog, as well as fans, satin and velvet gloves, and edged veils. In addition, Manny's offers over a dozen jeweled or beaded hat pins, pearl and sequin trims, bugle-bead appliqués and trims, fringe, fabric flowers, rhinestone buttons, and even feathers—loose and in boas. Professional millinery supplies and equipment are available, including horsehair braid, hat stretchers, display heads and racks, hat boxes and travel cases, netting, and cleaning products. Savings vary from item to item, but average 33% below regular retail.

Please note: If you're buying hats only, the minimum order is three; if you buy one or two hats, you must also buy $15 in assorted items (frames, trims, etc.); if you're buying assorted items only, the minimum order is $25.

Special Factors: Price quote by phone; minimum order on certain items (see text).

MASS. ARMY & NAVY STORE

DEPT. WBMC
15 FORDHAM RD.
BOSTON, MA 02134
617-783-1250
FAX: 617-254-6607

Catalog: free
Save: 25% average
Pay: check, MO, MC, V, AE, Discover
Sells: government surplus apparel and accessories
Store: 895 Boylston St., Boston; Monday to Saturday 9:30–6:30, Sunday 12–6; also 1436 Massachusetts Ave., Cambridge, MA; Monday to Saturday 10–9, Sunday 12–8

Mass. Army & Navy offers both reproduction and genuine government surplus, presented as a fashion statement. The 64-page color catalog features camouflage clothing, Australian outback coats, U.S. and European battle dress uniforms, field and flight jackets, East German guards' boots, U.S. Air Force sunglasses, survival manuals, Yukon hats, and similar surplus. Mass. Army & Navy also offers casual footwear, bandannas, gloves, Levi's jeans, Dockers, bomber jackets, pea coats, knapsacks, sleeping bags, air mattresses, backpacks, duffel bags, tents, mess kits, security products, and insignias and patches, among other useful items.

Special Factors: Satisfaction is guaranteed; returns are accepted for exchange, refund, or credit.

NATIONAL WHOLE-SALE CO., INC.

400 NATIONAL BLVD.,
DEPT. WK
LEXINGTON, NC 27294
704-249-0211

Catalog: free
Save: up to 50%
Pay: check, MO, MC, V, AE, Discover
Sells: women's hosiery, underwear, and apparel
Store: mail order only

National Wholesale's 96-page catalog features a good selection of hosiery in a wide range of sizes—for heights to six feet, and hip sizes to 60". In addition to hosiery, National Wholesale sells bras, girdles, and body shapers by Exquisite Form, Glamorise, and Playtex, slips by Figurfit® and Shadowline®, Models Coat® dusters by Swirl, nightgowns and pajamas, cotton-knit vests, briefs, long-leg underpants, thermal underwear, pants liners, slippers, dickeys, and aprons. And half the catalog is devoted to a nice selection of blouses, skirts, sweaters, coats, and jackets that are perfect wardrobe staples, and well priced—suit jackets at under $50 and denim skirts for $29 are two examples.

Special Factors: Satisfaction is guaranteed; returns are accepted.

NO NONSENSE DIRECT

P.O. BOX 26095
GREENSBORO, NC
  27420-6095
800-677-5995
FAX: 910-275-9329

Catalog: free
Save: up to 60%
Pay: check, MO, MC, V, AE, Discover
Sells: hosiery
Store: mail order only

¡Sí!

If you wear "No nonsense," Burlington, or Easy Spirit legwear, you can save up to 60% on the price of your favorite styles through No Nonsense Direct. This mail-order factory outlet of Kayser Roth has been delivering great buys on panty hose and socks and other items since 1985. You'll save the most on 12 pairs or more of "Practically Perfect" No nonsense, Burlington, and Easy Spirit panty hose, including Sheer & Silky, Control Top, Light Support, Regular, Custom Full Figure, A Touch of Silk, and other lines. The "Practically Perfect" goods have "minor, virtually undetectable imperfections that do not affect looks or wear," and are covered by the No Nonsense Direct guarantee of satisfaction. In addition to saving you money, you get a full choice of sizes and colors when you buy from the catalog—and that means that unless you're under 4' 11", 85 lb., or over 6', 280 lb., you should find a good fit.

Please note: Most items are sold in minimum quantities of three.

Special Factors: Satisfaction is guaranteed; quantity discounts are available; returns are accepted for exchange, refund, or credit.

ONE 212

**11 AVERY ROW
ROANOKE, VA 24012-8569
800-216-2221
703-977-7750**

Catalog: $12 per year (6 issues)
Save: up to 30%
Pay: check, MO, MC, V, AE, Discover
Sells: women's fashion clothing
Store: mail order only

The name of this company—the area code for Manhattan—refers to the sensibility of clothing sold here. It's epitomized in the slightly gamin, young New Yorker wearing short skirts and lots of black, punctuated by dusky winter tones or spring brights. She sports patent leather Oxfords or India red court shoes, jackets over sweaters that both reach mid-thigh, loose velvet pants or skinny leggings, tasseled belts and amulets with river pebbles, and a chenille cloche. If this youthful take on urban chic appeals to you, see the 64-page catalog from One 212. Many of the clothes and accessories are discounted from their boutique prices up to 30%, and both "designer" and selling prices are listed. And One 212 offers a wonderful service for indecisive shoppers: free returns!

Special Factors: Satisfaction is guaranteed; returns are accepted within 6 months for exchange, refund, or credit.

QUINN'S SHIRT SHOP

**RTE. 12
P.O. BOX 131
N. GROSVENORDALE,
   CT 06255
508-943-7183**

Price List: $2 and self-addressed, stamped envelope (see text)
Save: up to 50%
Pay: check or MO
Sells: Arrow shirts
Store: 245 W. Main St., Dudley, MA; Monday to Saturday 10–5

Quinn's, a factory outlet for the Arrow Shirt company, offers slightly irregular shirts at up to 60% below the price of first-quality goods. The firm has been in business since 1956, and will send you a price list for $2 and a stamped, self-addressed envelope (the $2 charge is refundable with your first order). You can also call or write for a price quote on your favorite Arrow shirt (Bradstreet, Dover B.D., Kent Collection, Fairfield, etc.—you must have the style name or line). Quinn's carries in regular, big, and tall sizes, 14-1/2 " to 20" neck, 31" to 38" sleeve. When you order, note whether you want short sleeves or long, and specify the length if long. The shirts may be exchanged if the flaws are too apparent.

Special Factors: Satisfaction is guaranteed; price quote by phone or letter with SASE; returns are accepted for exchange; minimum is 4 shirts per order; only C.O.D. orders are accepted.

SPORTSWEAR CLEARINGHOUSE

P.O. BOX 317746-96
CINCINNATI, OH
45231-7746
513-522-3511

Brochure: free with SASE
Save: up to 70%
Pay: check, MO, MC, V, Discover
Sells: preprinted sportswear overruns
Store: mail order only

Forget about dayglo cycling shorts and $200 court shoes—you won't find these at Sportswear Clearinghouse. The fare is sportswear basics—T-shirts in sizes from youth XS to adult XXXL, golf shirts, sweats, shorts, night shirts, and hats, already printed with corporate or institutional logos. If you succumb to the brochure, you can wind up wearing a T-shirt printed for the American Embassy at Sanaa, Yemen, Notre Dame running shorts, and a hat emblazoned with an advertising message from a local welding shop. The Clearinghouse, which has been in business since 1976, also offers T-shirts bearing the names of universities, running themes, sports themes, and slogans in foreign languages. Prices are hard to beat; T-shirts and shorts cost a few dollars each, and hats and visors are priced under $2 apiece. Most of these items are sold at retail in lots of three, six, or ten or more, and the Clearinghouse selects the colors, logos, and slogans. First-quality unprinted athletic socks and baseball hats embroidered with the replica logos of major league baseball teams and other pro sports, as well as colleges of your choice, are also available.

Special Factors: Satisfaction is guaranteed; unused returns are accepted within 30 days for exchange, refund, or credit; C.O.D. orders are accepted (UPS delivery only).

TAFFORD MANU-FACTURING, INC.

104 PARK DR.
P.O. BOX 1006
MONTGOMERYVILLE, PA
18936
215-643-9666
FAX: 215-643-4922

Catalog: free
Save: up to 30%
Pay: check, MO, MC, V, AE, Discover
Sells: nurses' uniforms and accessories
Store: mail order only

Compared to the average catalog of uniforms for health-care profession-als, Tafford has the best fashion buys for the dollar around. The firm manufactures its own uniforms, which means you beat at least one markup, and the size selection is great—XS to XXXXXXL for women, and S to XXXL for men. The 48-page color catalog shows mostly women's clothing, although there are two pages of men's separates in teal, navy, and white. Some of the women's outfits are quite chic, and there are uniforms to suit every figure type, including a maternity style. The catalog also shows cardigans, jackets, shoes, emblem pins, and nursing equipment—stethoscopes, blood pressure kits, scissors, oto-scopes, etc. Both the retail and the discount prices of the clothing are given, so you see how much you're saving—usually 20% or 30% on the regular retail. Consult your colleagues before ordering, because if you buy as part of a group, Tafford also offers special services such as swatches and samples, volume discounts, additional sizes if required, and embroidery and silkscreening.

Special Factors: Satisfaction is guaranteed; unworn, undamaged, unwashed returns are accepted within 30 days for exchange, refund, or credit.

TODD UNIFORM, INC.

**3668 SOUTH GEYER RD.
ST. LOUIS, MO 63127-1244
314-984-0365
FAX: 314-984-5736**

Catalog: free
Save: up to 30%
Pay: check, MO, MC, V, AE, Discover
Sells: work clothing and uniforms
Store: Service Centers in St. Louis, MO and Louisville, KY; Monday to Friday 8–5; also Outlet Store, Ripley, TN; Monday to Saturday 9–5:30

Todd has been manufacturing and selling uniforms and work apparel since 1881, and offers factory-direct prices—up to 30% below the competition. The clothing runs from the classic work shirt for men and women, which is offered in a range of colors, to jumpsuits, pants, jeans, jackets, T-shirts, polo shirts, aprons, rainwear, and caps. Your logo or slogan can be embroidered on the garments or on emblems, and the order form is designed to make it easy to specify even complicated orders.

Special Factors: Satisfaction is guaranteed; minimum order requirements apply to custom work; institutional accounts are available.

THE ULTIMATE OUTLET

**A SPIEGEL COMPANY
P.O. BOX 182557
COLUMBUS, OH
43218-2557
800-332-6000
FAX: 800-422-6697**

Catalog: $2
Save: up to 60%
Pay: check, MO, MC, V, AE, Optima, FCNB Preferred Charge
Sells: clothing, housewares, etc.
Store: three stores in Chicago area; also Sunrise, FL; Dalton, GA; Gurnee, IL; Edinburgh, IN; Birch Run, MI; Woodbury, MN; Jeffersonville, OH; Lancaster and Philadelphia, PA; and Prince William, VA

¡Sí! 🏳 (see text)

The Ultimate Outlet from Spiegel offers consumers solid values on name-brand fashion apparel and home furnishings. With an emphasis on women's fashions and home textiles, The Ultimate Outlet stands out by emphasizing a high level of style and quality at competitive prices.

Please note: Deliveries to Alaska, Hawaii, and APO/FPO addresses are made by the postal service, *not* UPS.

Special Factors: Satisfaction is guaranteed; returns are accepted for refund or credit.

WEARGUARD CORP.
■■■■■■■■

LONGWATER DR.
NORWELL, MA 02061
617-871-4100
FAX: 617-871-6239

Catalog: free
Save: up to 30%
Pay: check, MO, MC, V, AE, Discover, Optima
Sells: work clothing, rugged casual wear, and accessories
Store: 30 outlets in CT, DE, MA, ME, MI, NH, NJ, NY, PA, and RI

WearGuard, which was founded in 1952, supplies more than a million U.S. companies and consumers with work clothing. Prices run up to 30% below comparable retail, and WearGuard's selection of work shirts is one of the best in the country—23 colors and patterns, in long or short sleeves, sized XS to XXXXXL, from under $19. All-cotton chamois shirts are under $23. There are well-priced jackets (parka, bomber, barn, stadium, windbreaker, and other styles), T-shirts, polo shirts, chambray shirts, turtlenecks, Western and flannel shirts, jeans, gloves, baseball caps, thermal underwear and union suits, jumpsuits, and coveralls. In addition to WearGuard's own label, WearGuard's footwear includes Timberland and Wolverine boots and work shoes. A few jackets and boots are offered in women's styles.

WearGuard's custom department can provide designs on patches, emblems, T-shirts, and work shirts; stock logos and lettering are also available. The screen printing and direct embroidery are done "in house," which means WearGuard should be able to get your custom-embroidered job to you faster.

Special Factors: Satisfaction is guaranteed; returns are accepted; quantity discounts are available; C.O.D. orders are accepted.

WILLOW RIDGE

421 LANDMARK DR.
WILMINGTON, NC 28410
800-388-2012
FAX: 910-343-6859

Catalog: free
Save: up to 60%
Pay: check, MO, MC, V, AE, Discover
Sells: business and casual women's wear
Store: mail order only

Finally—a source for attractive business and weekend wear for misses *and* petites—at cash-conserving prices. Willow Ridge does it with great jackets, shirts, pants, sweaters, dresses, suits, loungewear, and other pieces, in 4 to 16 in petites, and 6 to 20 (with some 4s) in misses sizing. The Willow Ridge look is classy but not stuffy, strong on good, flattering color choices and washable fabrics. The prices will please your budget, with linen-look skirts at $20, pretty drop-waisted floral summer dresses for $36, poly cap-sleeve shells for $10, and linen-blend jackets for under $60. The sizing guide in every catalog helps ensure a proper fit (be sure to double-check your measurements against it), and everything is covered by an assurance of satisfaction.

Special Factors: Satisfaction is guaranteed; returns are accepted for exchange, refund, or credit.

SEE ALSO

Austad's Golf • golf apparel and shoes • **SPORTS**
Bailey's, Inc. • outdoor apparel and footwear • **TOOLS**
Bailey's Wholesale Floral Supply • bridal accessories and floral supplies • **CRAFTS**
Bart's Watersports • water-skiing vests, T-shirts, swim trunks, and wet suits • **SPORTS**
Bike Nashbar • bicycling and sports apparel, and sunglasses • **SPORTS**
Bowhunters Warehouse, Inc. • camouflage clothing • **SPORTS**
Bruce Medical Supply • dressing aids for the disabled, stoma scarves, incontinence products • **MEDICINE: SPECIAL NEEDS**
The Button Shop • replacement zippers for jeans, garment shoulder pads • **CRAFTS: TEXTILE ARTS**
Cabela's Inc. • hunting and fishing wear, outdoor clothing and footwear • **SPORTS**
Campmor • outdoor clothing and accessories • **SPORTS**
Clothcrafters, Inc. • aprons, garment bags, and tote bags • **GENERAL MERCHANDISE**

Defender Industries, Inc. • *foul-weather wear* • **AUTO**

Dharma Trading Co. • *cotton clothing and silk scarves for fabric painting, etc.* • **CRAFTS: TEXTILE ARTS**

E & B Marine Supply, Inc. • *foul-weather wear* • **AUTO**

Gander Mountain, Inc. • *hunting and fishing clothing, outdoor wear* • **SPORTS**

Gettinger Feather Corp. • *feather marabous and boas, loose feathers* • **CRAFTS**

Goldberg's Marine Distributors • *foul-weather wear* • **AUTO**

Golfsmith International, Inc. • *golf clothing and footwear* • **SPORTS**

Leather Unlimited Corp. • *sheepskin mittens, hats, and bags* • **LEATHER**

M&E Marine Supply Company, Inc. • *foul-weather wear* • **AUTO**

New England Leather Accessories, Inc. • *leather handbags and accessories* • **LEATHER**

Northern Hydraulics, Inc. • *work clothing and rugged footwear* • **TOOLS**

Omaha Vaccine Company, Inc. • *Wells Lamont work gloves, Red Ball boots* • **ANIMAL**

Overton's Sports Center, Inc. • *boating and windsurfing apparel* • **SPORTS**

Performance Bicycle Shop • *cycling clothing, footwear, and helmets* • **SPORTS**

Pet Warehouse • *dog costumes* • **ANIMAL**

ProAm Seat Warehouse • *sunglasses, car racing suits and helmets* • **AUTO**

Racer Wholesale • *auto racing suits and accessories* • **AUTO**

Retired Persons Services, Inc. • *support hosiery, slippers, socks, etc.* • **MEDICINE**

Ruvel & Company, Inc. • *government surplus clothing and outdoor wear* • **TOOLS**

Sailboard Warehouse, Inc. • *windsurfing apparel* • **SPORTS**

Senior's Needs, Inc. • *adaptive clothing and extra-large men's and women's underwear* • **MEDICINE: SPECIAL NEEDS**

Sierra Trading Post • *outdoor clothing and accessories* • **SPORTS**

Solo Slide Fasteners, Inc. • *clothing care and cleaning products* • **CRAFTS: TEXTILE ARTS**

Sport Shop • *camouflage clothing* • **SPORTS**

Sunglasses U.S.A., Inc. • *Ray-Ban sunglasses* • **HEALTH**

Support Plus • *support hosiery, comfort-styled shoes, therapeutic apparel* • **MEDICINE: SPECIAL NEEDS**

Thai Silks • *silk ties, scarves, handkerchiefs, lingerie, and blouses* • **CRAFTS: TEXTILE ARTS**

Tool Crib of the North • *work clothing* • **TOOLS**

Utex Trading Enterprises • *silk scarves and ties* • **CRAFTS: TEXTILE ARTS**

Wag-Aero Group of Aircraft Services • *aviator clothing and headwear* • **AUTO**

Wasserman Uniform Company, Inc. • *postal uniforms, footwear, etc.* • **CLOTHING: FOOTWEAR**

West Marine • *foul-weather wear* • **AUTO**

Wiley Outdoor Sports, Inc. • *hunting (camouflage) clothing and accessories* • **SPORTS**

Footwear

Shoes, boots, and slippers for men, women, and children

These firms attempt to solve the problems that befall many of us when we shop for shoes. They offer selection—they sell everything from arctic boots to moccasins to nurses' shoes. The prices are right—you'll find savings of up to 40%. But there's still the problem of fit, unless you're ordering more of the the same model you've worn before. Here are some tips to improve the odds, and to make returns as easy as possible, if they're necessary:

- Have your feet measured at least once a year, and order your true size. (Feet continue to grow and change as you age.)
- Buy from firms with liberal return policies, preferably an unconditional guarantee of satisfaction with a 30-day return period.
- Buy styles and shapes that have fit in the past.
- If the shoes you're buying are also available in a local store, try on a pair before ordering them.
- When the shoes arrive, unwrap them carefully and save the packaging.
- Try them on in the late afternoon, when your feet have swollen slightly.
- Walk around in a carpeted area to avoid scratching the soles.
- Leave the shoes on for at least half an hour, checking for rubbing and pinching after 20 minutes.
- If they fit, consider ordering a second pair *now,* while they're still in stock.
- If the shoes don't fit, return them according to the firm's instructions, indicating whether you want another size or a refund or credit.

A brochure with fitting guidelines and information on foot problems is available from the American Orthopedic Foot and Ankle Society. Send a long, stamped, self-addressed envelope to AOFAS, 701 16th Ave., Seattle, WA 98122; request the "shoe fit/foot problems" brochure.

Good maintenance is critical in preserving the looks and longevity of your shoes and boots. For helpful tips on caring for all types of footwear, see *The Butler's Guide* (Fireside/Simon & Schuster, 1980), by Stanley Ager and Fiona St. Aubyn. Some of the firms listed in "Leather" sell leather care products, as do a number of companies listed in the "See Also's" of that chapter. If your shoes and boots need professional help and you don't have a good repair service nearby, contact the Houston Shoe Hospital, 5215 Kirby Dr., Houston, TX 77098; 713-528-6268. This firm overhauls worn footwear, and handles mail-order repairs.

FIND IT FAST

ATHLETIC FOOTWEAR • **Okun Bros.**
BOOTS • **Knapp Shoes, Okun Bros., Wasserman**
DRESS SHOES • **Okun Bros.**
NURSING SHOES • **Okun Bros.**
WORK SHOES AND BOOTS • **Knapp Shoes, Okun Bros., Wasserman**

GENE'S SHOES DISCOUNT CATALOG

126 N. MAIN ST.
ST. CHARLES, MO 63301
314-946-0804

Catalog: $1
Save: up to 30% (see text)
Pay: check, MO, MC, V, Discover
Sells: women's dress and casual shoes
Store: same address

Gene's Discount "specialty size" catalog offers women's footwear by Nurse Mates, Selby, Soft Spots, and Gene's own brand, GENO's of St. Charles. The shoes are discounted about 20%, but savings run to over 30% on some styles. And you're in luck if you're hard to fit; Gene's offers most of the shoes in AAAA to EEE widths, sizes 3 to 13. The catalog costs $1 and subscriptions (two seasonal issues and notices of interim sales) cost $3 per year.

Please note: The prices in the catalog are good on mail orders only, not on in-store purchases.

Special Factors: Satisfaction is guaranteed; unworn, salable returns are accepted within 30 days for exchange, refund, or credit.

JUSTIN DISCOUNT BOOTS & COWBOY OUTFITTERS

P.O. BOX 67
JUSTIN, TX 76247
800-677-BOOT
FAX: 817-648-3282

Catalog: free
Save: 35% average
Pay: check, MO, MC, V
Sells: Western boots and clothing
Store: 101 W. Hwy. 156, Justin, TX; Monday to Saturday 9–6

This firm, although not owned by the Justin Boot Co., sells a number of the Justin boot lines in men's and women's styles. The footwear choices run from work boots and "ropers," comparatively plain, thick-soled boots with Western vamps that rise to mid-calf (about $90), to artful creations in exotic skins—ostrich, lizard, bull hide, and alligator. The 48-page color catalog shows dozens of women's styles, including lizard Western boots, and "fashion" ropers in a range of colors. Children can get their Justin Juniors in red, navy, brown, and other colors, for under $50 a pair. Coordinating belts are available, and the custom embroidery department will embellish your boots with two initials for $6.50 per letter. Justin Discount Boots, in business since 1978, also sells Stetson Western hats, German silver buckles and belt tips, leather-care products, and Wrangler shirts and jeans for men, women, and boys.

Special Factors: Satisfaction is guaranteed; unworn, unscuffed, unaltered returns are accepted for exchange, refund, or credit; C.O.D. orders are accepted.

KNAPP SHOES INC.

ONE KNAPP CENTRE
BROCKTON, MA 02401
508-588-9009

Catalog: free
Save: up to 25% (see text)
Pay: check, MO, MC, V
Sells: work shoes for men and women
Store: same address; 28 other stores in CA, GA, IL, MD, ME, MI, NC, NJ, NY, OH, and PA; locations are given in the catalog

Knapp has been keeping America in shoes since 1921, and although the company's discounts don't quite reach 30% (most are between 18% and 25%), there are shoes in the Knapp catalog that aren't easy to find at a discount. The 48-page color catalog shows work shoes and boots for men by Clarino, Knapp, New Generation, Red Label, Rocky, Timberland, and Wrangler; dress shoes and loafers by Dexter and Eagle Rock; casuals by Hush Puppies and Pine Cones; walking shoes by Street Cars; and even slippers. Women can choose from athletic-style service shoes, wedge-sole Oxfords, low-heel pumps, loafers, and slip-ons, all of which are priced under $50 a pair at this writing. If you live near one of the 29 Knapp stores, drop by and try them on; otherwise, anything you buy by mail that doesn't fit can be returned, unworn, for an exchange or refund.

Special Factors: Satisfaction is guaranteed; returns of unworn or defective shoes are accepted for exchange, refund, or credit; C.O.D. orders are accepted.

OKUN BROS. SHOES

356 E. SOUTH ST.-WBM
KALAMAZOO, MI 49007
800-433-6344
FAX: 616-383-3401

Catalog: free
Save: 18% average (see text)
Pay: check, MO, MC, V, Discover
Sells: dress, casual, and work shoes
Store: same address; Monday to Friday 8:30 A.M.–9 P.M., Saturday 8:30–7

Okun Bros. has been serving the footwear needs of Kalamazoo since 1920, and brings its shoe store to the rest of world through a 48-page catalog. Okun has the largest stock of men's work and safety shoes available in Michigan, sold at a typical discount of 18%; heavy boots for sub-zero conditions have been sold here at up to 44% off, and specials in the sales flyers further the savings to 50%. Note the *$5 new customer coupon* in your catalog, and the $10-off-3-pairs offer (neither valid on Easy Spirit).

Casual shoes, plain pumps, athletic shoes for several sports, men's dress shoes, sandals, loafers and moccasins, deck shoes, nurses' shoes, bikers' boots, and work shoes and boots are all available through Okun. The brands and lines offered here number over 200, including some of the most popular: Stacy Adams, Adidas, Asics, Auditions, Avia, Bass, Bates, H.H. Brown, Carolina Shoe Co., Clarks, Converse, Dexter, Dingo, Double H, Dr. Martens, Drew, Eastland, Easy Spirit, Allen-Edmonds, Etonic, Extra Depth, Fila, Florsheim, Foot-Joy, Daniel Green, Hi-Tec, Hush Puppies, K-Swiss, L.A. Gear, La Crosse, Life Stride, Minnetonka, New Balance, Nike, Nunn Bush, Nurse Mates, Propet, Red Ball, Red Bird, Reebok, Rockport, Rocky, Saucony, Sebago, Skechers, Soft Spots, Sorel, Sperry Top-Sider, Sporto, Timberland, Tingley, Toe Warmers, Tru-Stitch, and Wolverine. Thor-Lo "padded" specialty sport socks and Spenco insoles are also sold.

Because only a fraction of the stock can be shown in the catalog, inquire about brands and styles not shown—they may be available.

Special Factors: Satisfaction is guaranteed; price quote by phone or letter with SASE.

WASSERMAN UNIFORM COMPANY, INC.

1082 W. MOUND ST.
COLUMBUS, OH
  43223-2296
614-464-2964
FAX: 614-464-0416

Catalog: free
Save: up to 30%
Pay: check, MO, MC, V, AE
Sells: postal uniforms, walking shoes, gifts, etc.
Store: mail order only

¡Si! (see text)

Wasserman is a family-run enterprise that was founded in 1970 to serve the needs of postal employees. (All uniformed personnel receive an allotment for clothing and footwear, which can be used at a certified vendor, like Wasserman.) Since carriers and clerks spend so much time on their feet, they need well-fitting, supportive shoes. Wasserman is so confident in its selection of shoes and boots that it covers every purchase with a "Style-Size-Fit-Comfort" guarantee of satisfaction.

Styles for men and women are shown, from Bates, Carolina Shoe, Cedar Crest, Clinic, Hush Puppies, Lehigh, Munro, New Balance, Ranger, Rocky Boots, and Thorogood. Most are Oxford or athletic-shoe style, with some high tops and work boots, and everything is offered in regulation black. The stock sizes run up to men's 14EEEE in some models, and ladies' to 12EEE (size 13 and larger are offered at a $2 surcharge). Selected styles are discounted to 30%, and closeouts and "Super Savers" can bring the prices to 45% below regular retail.

The catalog has other items of interest to the general public, such as scale model, die-cast USPS trucks, planes, and delivery vehicles that double as banks (save up for the next rate increase!), and mugs, T-shirts, key rings, watches, and other memorabilia celebrating the LOVE stamps—all great gifts for the collector.

Spanish-speaking readers: Please ask for Helen when you call.

Special Factors: Satisfaction is guaranteed; returns are accepted.

SEE ALSO

Austad's Golf • golf apparel and shoes • **SPORTS**

Jos. A. Bank Clothiers, Inc. • men's shoes • **CLOTHING**

Bike Nashbar • bicycling footwear • **SPORTS**

Cabela's Inc. • hunting and fishing wear, outdoor clothing and footwear • **SPORTS**

Cahall's Brown Duck Catalog • rugged footwear for men and women • **CLOTHING**

Campmor • outdoor footwear • **SPORTS**

Dance Distributors • professional footwear for classic and jazz dance, gymnastics, etc. • **CLOTHING**

The Deerskin Place • suede boots, moccasins, etc. • **CLOTHING**

Deerskin Trading Post, Inc. • deerskin and shearling footwear • **CLOTHING**

Defender Industries, Inc. • boating shoes • **AUTO**

Gander Mountain, Inc. • rugged boots and footwear • **SPORTS**

Gohn Bros. • work shoes and boots for men and women • **CLOTHING**

Goldberg's Marine Distributors • boating shoes • **AUTO**

Golf Haus • golf shoes • **SPORTS**

Golfsmith International, Inc. • golf clothing and footwear • **SPORTS**

Holabird Sports • shoes for sports activities • **SPORTS**

Huntington Clothiers • small selection of men's shoes • **CLOTHING**

M&E Marine Supply Company, Inc. • boating shoes • **AUTO**

National Wholesale Co., Inc. • small selection of women's footwear • **CLOTHING**

Northern Hydraulics, Inc. • *rugged footwear* • **TOOLS**

Omaha Vaccine Company, Inc. • *Red Ball boots* • **ANIMAL**

Performance Bicycle Shop • *cycling clothing, footwear, and helmets* • **SPORTS**

Sierra Trading Post • *outdoor shoes* • **SPORTS**

Support Plus • *support hosiery, comfort-styled footwear, therapeutic apparel* • **MEDICINE: SPECIAL NEEDS**

Tafford Manufacturing, Inc. • *nurses' shoes* • **CLOTHING**

Wiley Outdoor Sports, Inc. • *hunting and outdoor footwear* • **SPORTS**

Mother and Child

Clothing and accessories for babies, children, and expectant and nursing mothers; and related goods

The firms in this section sell clothing for babies, children, and expectant and nursing mothers—all at savings of up to 60%. In addition, a number of the firms listed elsewhere in this book sell similar products. *Chock Catalog Corp.* ("Clothing") features Carter's receiving blankets and crib sets, Curity diapers, and underwear and nightwear for newborn through toddler sizes. *Gohn Bros.* ("Clothing") sells Curity diapers and Gerber bibs, baby sleepers, waterproof pants, and shirts. *Campmor* ("Sports") offers baby buntings, Snuglis, and a diaper-changer backpack for the intrepid parent.

One of the best all-around sources for discount baby supplies and buying strategies is *Baby Bargains: Secrets to Saving 20% to 50% on Baby Furniture, Equipment, Clothes, Toys, Maternity Wear and Much, Much More!* by Denise and Alan Fields, who wrote an equally valuable guide to saving money on wedding expenses (see the introduction to "Clothing"). In the format of their earlier opus, *Baby Bargains* describes the market for baby-related products, covers some of the issues like breastfeeding and paper vs. cloth diapers, and gives source after source for information and products. The Fields guarantee that you'll save $250 on the cost of your baby expenses, or they'll refund the cost of the book. Call 800-888-0385 to order, or see the introduction to "Clothing" for the mailing address.

The *Consumer Information Center* and *Superintendent of Documents* ("Books") offer publications devoted to baby-care advice and related information—usually free, or at a small cost. For other tips on buying baby goods, see the *Guide to Baby Products* and other books from Consumers Union in the current issue of *Consumer Reports*. See "Toys" for playthings and games, the "Computing" section of "Office" for entertainment software, and "Books" for literature for and about children.

FIND IT FAST

DIAPERS AND COVERS • **After the Stork, As A Little Child, Baby Bunz, Natural Baby, Snugglebundle**
NURSING CLOTHING • **After the Stork, Bosom Buddies, Natural Baby, Holly Nicolas, Snugglebundle**
CHILDREN'S CLOTHING • **After the Stork, As A Little Child, Baby Bunz, Baby Clothes Wholesale, Basic Brilliance, Natural Baby, Rubens & Marble, Snugglebundle**
TOYS • **After the Stork, Baby Bunz, Natural Baby**

AFTER THE STORK

1501 12TH ST. NW
P.O. BOX 26200
ALBUQUERQUE, NM
87104-6200
800-333-5437
505-243-9100
FAX: 505-243-6935

Catalog: free
Save: up to 40%
Pay: check, MO, MC, V, AE, Discover
Sells: children's clothing
Store: 4411 San Mateo, Albuquerque, NM; Monday to Saturday 10–8, Sunday 12–5

 (see text)

Real clothes for real kids from birth to 12 years old are sold at After the Stork, where cotton is king and prices are a friendly 25% to 40% below comparable retail. The 48-page color catalogs show playwear and sleepwear in snappy prints and kicky colors, so your kids can look hip without breaking your budget. The company has been price-shopped by pros who've found that you can assemble outfits that look like the upmarket Swedish brand, for less than half the cost. After the Stork has lots of T-shirts, sweats, long johns, pull-on pants, coveralls, dresses, rompers, and outerwear, as well as shoes, socks, sneakers, slippers, tights, underwear, and a choice bear or two. Check the size chart before you order—note that After the Stork sizes its clothing after shrinkage, so you don't have to order large—unless you're stockpiling against growth spurts.

Wholesale customers, request information on company letterhead; write to the attention of Kathy Thomas.

Special Factors: Satisfaction is guaranteed; returns are accepted.

AS A LITTLE CHILD

DEPT. W
10701 W. 80TH AVE.
ARVADA, CO 80005
303-456-1880

Brochure: free
Save: up to 30% (see text)
Pay: check or MO
Sells: diapers and diaper covers, etc.
Store: mail order only

As A Little Child celebrates children as one of life's great blessings, making baby's health and happiness its first order of business with a selection of environmentally positive diapering products that are kind to family budgets. The featured item is the Wabby, the only diaper cover made with Gore-Tex®, so it's both waterproof and "breathable." Since air can flow through the cover, baby's bottom stays cooler, which helps to prevent diaper rash. Wabbies are constructed to last, wash and dry quickly, and have newly designed closures that are strong and durable. The covers are offered in white, colors, and prints, sized from newborn to 34 pounds; they work well with Wabby diapers, which team all-cotton flannel with terrycloth for comfort and absorbency. Washcloths and mini-wipes are also available.

As A Little Child is offering readers a discount of 10% on their first order. Be sure to identify yourself as a WBMC reader when you order, and deduct the discount from the cost of the goods only. This WBMC reader discount expires February 1, 1997.

Special Factors: Quantity discounts are available.

BABY BUNZ & CO.

P.O. BOX 113-WB96
LYNDEN, WA 98264-0113

Catalog: $1
Save: up to 35%
Pay: check, MO, MC, V
Sells: diapering supplies and layette items
Store: mail and phone orders only

If you use cloth diapers instead of disposables, you may be overwhelmed by all the prefolded diapers and diaper "systems" on the market. One of the most popular diapering duos among the cloth set is a standard or fitted diaper with a natural-fiber cover. Baby Bunz & Co. has been selling the best-known covers, Nikkys, since 1982. Nikkys are made in soft lambswool, waterproof cotton, "breathable" poly, and vinyl-lined cotton, and are available in sizes from newborn to three years (up to 34 pounds). Training and all-night pants are also offered, and they're priced at up to 35% below retail.

The Baby Bunz 20-page color catalog also offers a variety of diaper styles—contour, prefolded, flat, and diaper doublers. The catalog includes guides to folding diapers and how to use Nikkys. Adorable Swedish layette wear, colorful cotton playsuits, baby buntings, cotton tights, lambskin and wool booties, pima cotton and Merino wool blankets, and a crib-sized lambskin are also featured. The natural theme is carried on with Aromatherapy for Kids, natural baby shampoo, Weleda baby-care products, bath sponges, and natural bristle baby brushes. You'll also find wooden rattles, natural-fiber soft toys, and an ideal lovey, "First Doll." Many other useful items are available, including a comfortable baby carrier, a "Boppy" baby pillow, and classic storybooks for children up to three years. These and other new additions to the latest Baby Bunz catalog include several guides on rearing healthy and happy children.

Canadian readers, please note: Only U.S. funds are accepted.

Special Factors: Satisfaction is guaranteed; unused returns are accepted within 30 days for replacement, refund, or credit.

BABY CLOTHES WHOLESALE

60 ETHEL RD. WEST
PISCATAWAY, NJ 08854
908-572-9520
908-842-2900

Catalog: $3
Save: up to 50%
Pay: check, MO, MC, V, AE, Discover
Sells: clothing for babies and children
Store: same address; also 70 Apple St., Tinton Falls, NJ

It's a shame to spend lots of money on children's clothing when they grow so quickly, especially when you don't have to: Baby Clothes Wholesale brings you everything from underwear to snowsuits for sizes newborn to seven, at savings of up to 50%. The company's 48-page color catalog features coveralls and rompers, sunsuits, terry sleepers and crawlers, creepers, bibs, receiving blankets, underwear, socks, overalls, party dresses, T-shirts, sweatsuits, turtlenecks, playsuits, cardigans, bonnets and caps, bathing suits, nightwear, vests, and bomber jackets. All of the clothing is first-quality, but some of the layette items (blankets, sheets, bibs, etc.) are irregular, and clearly indicated. Please note that orders under $50 are accepted, but a $5 handling fee is charged.

Canadian readers, please note: Only U.S. funds are accepted.

Special Factors: Satisfaction is guaranteed; quantity discounts are available; returns of unworn, unused, unwashed goods are accepted for exchange, refund, or credit; minimum order is $50.

BASIC BRILLIANCE

P.O. BOX 1719
PORT TOWNSEND, WA
98368
360-385-3835

Catalog: free
Save: up to 35%
Pay: check, MO, MC, V
Sells: clothing for children and mothers
Store: mail order only

Kids love brightly colored clothing they can really *play* in, and parents want it to last until they grow out of it—without costing a fortune. That's the concept behind Basic Brilliance, where "everything is cotton, garment-dyed, preshrunk, easy to wear and easy to care for." Most of the clothes are sized for 6 to 24 months and 2 to 8 (some to 10), and there are some great knockabout clothes for Mom—dresses, T-shirts, and leggings.

Kids have the run of the 12-page catalog, in cotton interlock snap rompers ($15), a hooded cardigan in French terry cotton ($18), ribbed pants ($10), loose empire-waisted jumper dresses ($16), leggings ($7.50), and lots of other great clothes at great prices. The colors in the current catalog are winners, too: royal, gold, berry, periwinkle, purple, butter, and the basics. You can't go wrong with the sizes, since there's a chart in the catalog for kids *and* their mothers, and everything is covered by an unconditional guarantee of satisfaction.

Please note: Only U.S. funds are accepted.

Special Factors: Satisfaction is guaranteed; returns are accepted.

THE NATURAL BABY CO., INC.

816 SILVIA ST., SUITE 800B-WBM6
TRENTON, NJ 08628-3299
800-388-BABY
609-771-9233
FAX: 609-771-9342

Catalog: free
Save: up to 30%
Pay: check, MO, MC, V, Discover
Sells: diapers, baby and children's clothing, nursing clothing, toys, remedies, etc.
Store: mail order only

Everything in The Natural Baby Co. catalog has been chosen with an eye to making children comfortable and keeping them healthy, without costing Mom and Dad a bundle. The Natural Baby Co. was established in 1983, and has a policy of supporting home-based businesses—so the quilt you buy here for your own baby may have been made by a mother of nine, and the wood cradles and toys crafted by carpenters "in between pouring out the Cheerios"!

The Natural Baby has built its business on cloth diapers and covers, beginning with the firm's own "Rainbow" diaper, a fitted cloth style (pinless, foldless) made of flannel-lined terrycloth ($29.95 per dozen). If you're on a tight budget, you can get the "Natural Baby Diapers" of bird's eye, from $15.75 a dozen. Diaper covers from Nikky's and The Natural Baby are available, as well as diaper pads and conventional cloth diapers. The catalog includes helpful sidebars on diapering with pinless covers, the cloth vs. disposables debate, and tips on preventing diaper rash.

There's much more for baby: a line of baby clothing from organically grown cotton, baby carriers, and sheepskin rugs and play balls, woolen crib blankets, flannel creepers, and Storkenworks shoes. The catalog offers some clothing for older kids, including long johns, Nikky's substantial underpants (in sizes to fit children up to 110 pounds), socks, sweaters, turtlenecks, and other goods. Mothers are treated to Leading Lady bras, and sportswear and nightwear designed to make nursing easier. Among the offerings are natural and homeopathic remedies for treating everything from cradle cap to poison ivy, as well as a splendid selection of wooden toys, dolls, rattles, balls, cradles, and other safe and nontoxic diversions.

Special Factors: C.O.D. orders are accepted.

HOLLY NICOLAS NURSING COLLECTION

DEPT. W
P.O. BOX 7121
ORANGE, CA 92613-7121
714-639-5933

Swatched Catalog: $1
Save: up to 50%
Pay: check, MO, AE
Sells: nursing clothing
Store: mail order only

This business was founded in 1983 by a former fashion model, who began by creating nursing dresses for the mothers of her grandchildren, Holly and Nicolas. The clothes she produces are well designed, incorporating concealed openings for nursing into the lines of the garments.

The catalog shows pretty, feminine blouses, dresses, and nightgowns designed for the nursing mother. The styles are classic: A stylish, sailor-collar dress in dark blue Oxford cloth, a square-neck blouse in blue shirting, and a basic blouse that comes in six colors are among the offerings. Prices are very reasonable: $20 for the nightgown with hidden openings for nursing, to $54 for a scallop-collar dress in black or blue, with a white collar. Samples of the actual fabrics are included in the brochure.

Holly Nicolas is offering readers of this book a 20% discount on the "Transition Dress," a flattering style that will see you through the nine months and nursing afterward, thanks to concealed openings. It's self-belted and comes in a wool or cotton/poly blend. Identify yourself as a reader when you order to take the discount. This WBMC reader discount expires February 1, 1997.

Special Factors: Returns are accepted within 30 days for exchange or refund.

RUBENS & MARBLE, INC.

P.O. BOX 14900-A
CHICAGO, IL 60614-0900

Brochure: free with self-addressed, stamped envelope
Save: up to 60%
Pay: check or MO
Sells: infants' clothing and bedding
Store: mail order only

Rubens & Marble has been supplying hospitals with baby clothes since 1890, and sells the same goods to consumers at up to 60% below regular retail prices. The babywear basics include undershirts in sizes from newborn to 36 months, with short, long, and mitten-cuff sleeves; they're offered in snap, tie, plain, and double-breasted slipover styles (many are seconds, with small knitting flaws). First-quality cotton/wool blend and preemie-sized cotton undershirts are available as well. Rubens & Marble also offers fitted bassinet and crib sheets, training and waterproof pants, kimonos, drawstring-bottom baby gowns, and terry bibs.

Special Factors: You *must* send a self-addressed, stamped envelope to receive the price list; seconds are clearly indicated; minimum order is one package (varying number depending on type of item).

SNUGGLEBUNDLE ENTERPRISES

DEPT. WBMC
6325-A FALLS OF NEUSE
** RD., #321**
RALEIGH, NC 27615
919-231-9615
FAX: 919-231-8137

Catalog: free
Save: up to 35%
Pay: check or MO
Sells: diapers, covers, children's clothing
Store: mail order only

The woman who runs this company offers literally dozens of diapering options, from EZ Bottoms® classic cotton flannel prefolded, to the popular Nikky lambswool covers. She's even assembled diaper samplers that allow you to test several methods at once, to see which one works best. Diaper liners and soakers, training pants, and cotton wipes are sold, as well as nursing pads, layette items, crib sheets and blankets, gowns, creepers, bibs, rompers, and more. Natural fibers prevail, chiefly cotton and wool, and Snugglebundle Enterprises features "green" (organic) cotton in a number of products.

In addition to diapers and layette items, the firm sells clothing for kids—brightly colored cotton in sturdy styles for boys and girls. The most recent sale supplement to the 16-page catalog offered 50% savings on irregular Ecosport parkas, and 35% off Sara's Prints. Earthlings, Family Clubhouse, Metrobaby, and Organic Baby brands are well represented.

Snugglebundle also carries a line of child/adult incontinence products; send a long, stamped, self-addressed envelope for more information.

Snugglebundle Enterprises is offering readers of this book a 5% discount on *nonsale merchandise* only, on orders totaling $25 or more in goods alone (not including shipping, handling, or any other charges). Identify yourself as a WBMC reader when you order. This WBMC Reader Discount expires February 1, 1997.

Special Factors: Satisfaction is guaranteed.

SEE ALSO

Alfax Wholesale Furniture • *institutional nursery and day-care center furniture* • **OFFICE**
Chock Catalog Corp. • *baby clothing and bedding* • **CLOTHING**
Clothcrafters, Inc. • *crib sheets* • **GENERAL MERCHANDISE**
Betty Crocker Catalog • *children's tableware, toys, games, and puzzles* • **GENERAL MERCHANDISE**
Michael C. Fina Co. • *sterling silver baby gifts* • **HOME: TABLE SETTINGS**
Gohn Bros. • *nursing bras, layette and baby goods* • **CLOTHING**
The Linen Source • *crib and juvenile bedding* • **HOME: LINEN**
L'eggs Hanes Bali Playtex Outlet Catalog • *maternity hosiery and underwear* • **CLOTHING**
Wicker Warehouse Inc. • *wicker nursery furniture, doll buggies* • **HOME: FURNISHINGS**

CRAFTS AND HOBBIES

Materials, supplies, tools, and equipment for crafts and hobbies

These firms can provide the materials for nearly any craft—miniatures, stenciling, basketry, clock making, wheat weaving, quilling, decoy painting, jewelry making, and much more. Some of these companies have been in business for generations and specialize in avocations that your local crafts shop may not even know exist. If you have a problem with a material or technique, most can provide assistance by phone. Ordering from a firm usually assures you a place on the mailing list, which means you'll probably receive the sales flyers, with savings of up to 70%. Save your catalogs, both for comparison shopping, and as sources of technical information.

The firms listed in the first part of this chapter are either general crafts suppliers with a very broad selection, or firms specializing in one item or type of goods—hobby models, feathers, parts for stuffed bears, stained glass supplies, bandboxes, etc. For help in locating a particular item, see "Find It Fast," below. If you're looking for a fiber, fabric, or related product, see "Textile Arts," right after this chapter. And if your interests run to carving, whittling, and bandsaw challenges, see "Woodcraft," following "Textile Arts."

If your craft or hobby involves the use of hazardous materials, find out about safety precautions; see the introduction to "Art Materials" for more information. For additional sources selling wooden toy parts, see the listings in "Tools." For lapidary equipment and findings, see the firms listed in "Jewelry."

FIND IT FAST

BASKETRY AND SEAT REWEAVING • **Caning Shop, Frank's Cane**

BOXES • **Boxes and Bows**

BRIDAL SUPPLIES • **Bailey's Wholesale**

DOLL- AND BEAR-MAKING • **Bolek's, CR's Bear and Doll**

FABRIC FLOWERS • **Bailey's Wholesale, Bolek's**

FEATHERS • **Gettinger**

GENERAL CRAFTS • **Artist's Club, Bailey's Wholesale, Bolek's, Circle Craft, Craft Resources, Think Ink, Vanguard**

GOURD CRAFT • **Caning Shop**

METAL DETECTING AND PROSPECTING • **Northwest Treasure Supply**

MODELS • **Model Expo**

POTPOURRI AND WREATHS • **Bolek's**

STAINED GLASS SUPPLIES • **Warner Crivellaro**

WOODWORKING PLANS AND SUPPLIES • **Artist's Club**

THE ARTIST'S CLUB

5750 N.E. HASSALO
PORTLAND, OR 97213
800-845-6507
FAX: 503-287-6916

Catalog: free
Save: up to 50%
Pay: check, MO, MC, V, AE, Discover
Sells: craft painting materials and supplies
Store: mail order only

The Artist's Club is devoted to artisans whose painting skills are applied to surfaces other than canvas, creating what might be called contemporary folk art. Half of the firm's 88-page color catalog is filled with books on painting flowers, decorating in the Victorian modes, Christmas and other holiday themes, creating clocks, decorating with gardening themes, painting jewelry, angel motifs, working with crackle medium, fabric painting, Americana, and more. Many of the complete project kits employ cute country designs done on wood forms, including eggs, clock blanks (which accept "fit up" clock works), and useful household items—napkin holders, keepsake boxes, step stools, tissue boxes, quilt racks, lap desks, menu boards, etc. Also available are paper maché forms and boxes, lovely hand-blown glass Christmas ornaments awaiting decoration, and lots of unpainted canvas items, including aprons, banners, fanny packs, Christmas tree skirts and stockings, photo albums, checkbook and notebook covers, and wastepaper baskets. The Club also offers a great selection of DecoArt, Delta, and Jo Sonja paints, and brushes by Bette Byrd, Loew Cornell, and Robert Simmons. Prices are discounted an average of 20% to 35%, and the regular sales catalogs yield greater savings.

There are plenty of project ideas and materials here for people working in other media, or noncrafters—anyone looking for beautiful, inexpensive Christmas ornaments (6 for $6.99), canvas tote bags, or wooden serving trays, for example.

Non-U.S. readers, please note: Only U.S. funds are accepted.

Special Factors: Satisfaction is guaranteed; returns are accepted within 30 days for exchange, refund, or credit.

BAILEY'S WHOLESALE FLORAL SUPPLY

**P.O. BOX 591W
ARCADIA, IN 46030
317-984-3663
FAX: 317-984-3663**

Catalog: $3, refundable
Save: up to 50%
Pay: check, MO, MC, V
Sells: silk flowers and bridal accessories
Store: mail order only

Bailey's Wholesale Floral Supply was founded in 1983 by Sharon Bailey, who was then running a part-time business designing silk floral arrangements. After finding that wholesale suppliers were reluctant to fill her small orders for silk flowers, she solved her problem by buying in volume—and sharing the considerable surplus and savings with other small businesses in the same position.

Her 18-page catalog shows a lovely selection of flowers—roses and buds, freesia, carnations, lilies of the valley, orchids, stephanotis, orchids, and more—and a variety of fabric foliage, including ferns, spider plants, Swedish ivy, and geranium leaves. Real dried foliage—baby's breath, eucalyptus, statice, etc.—is available, as well as supplies for wiring and arranging. If you're shopping for bridal accessories, check the savings on fans, lace parasols, ring pillows, tulle, lace, and other items. Most of the flowers are offered in any of dozens of colors, but Bailey's will also dye your flowers to order. A sampler of 32 flowers, one of each, costs $37, including shipping. And there's *no* minimum order!

Special Factors: Satisfaction is guaranteed; quantity discounts are available; returns are accepted for exchange, refund, or credit.

BOLEK'S CRAFT SUPPLIES, INC.

330 N. TUSCARAWAS AVE.
P.O. BOX 465
DOVER, OH 44622-0465
800-743-2723
216-364-8878
FAX: 216-343-9644

Catalog: $1.50
Save: up to 50%
Pay: check, MO, MC, V, Discover
Sells: general crafts supplies
Store: same address; Monday to Saturday 9–5

Bolek's is one of those amazing places that stocks 22 sizes of dolls' eyes, Aurora Borealis beads, carved wooden unicorns, and Bronze Schlappen chicken feathers. It's hard to imagine a craft *not* supplied here—jewelry making, beading, woodworking, ceramics, potpourri and fragrance blending, doll- and toy-making, Christmas ornaments, macramé, plastic canvas crafts, stenciling, styrofoam crafts, silk flowers, yarn crafts, and much more. Bolek's, in business since 1977, sells at prices up to 50% below those charged by local crafts supply stores for the same types of items. If you're looking for something you don't see in the 130-page catalog, write to Bolek's with a description or sample, and include a self-addressed, stamped envelope for a reply.

Canadian readers, please note: Only U.S. funds are accepted.

Special Factors: Authorized returns are accepted within 30 days for exchange, refund, or credit (refunds are subject to a 25% restocking fee); shipping is not charged on orders over $40 in the continental United States; C.O.D. orders are *not* accepted.

BOXES AND BOWS

P.O. BOX 773RW
CANBY, OR 97013
503-651-2500

Price List: free with SASE
Save: up to 50%
Pay: check or MO
Sells: hatboxes and bandboxes
Store: mail order only

Boxes and Bows sells handmade chipboard boxes, both oval and round bandboxes (from about 3" by 4" by 2-1/2" to about 6" by 8" by 4"), and oval and round hatboxes (from 12" to 18" in diameter). Both kinds of boxes are preassembled and ready to finish—with paint, fabric, paper, or another covering—and cost from $2.40 for the smallest bandbox to $8.75 for the largest hatbox. (Hatbox sets of similar sizes sell for over twice as much in other catalogs as they do here.) Whether you intend to decorate them for your own use, as gifts, for resale, or want to sell the unadorned boxes to other craftspeople, you'll get a great deal: Discounts of 20% are given on orders of $25 or more, and each shipment includes a free, illustrated guide to covering the boxes.

Special Factors: Minimum wholesale order is $25; C.O.D. orders are accepted.

THE CANING SHOP

926 GILMAN ST., DEPT.
  WBM
BERKELEY, CA 94710-1494
510-527-5010
FAX: 510-527-7718

Catalog: $1, refundable
Save: up to 30%
Pay: check, MO, MC, V, Discover
Sells: seat-reweaving, gourd-crafting, and basketry supplies
Store: same address; Tuesday to Friday 10–6, Saturday 10–2

 ¡Si!

The Caning Shop stocks the materials, tools, and instructions you'll need to restore your woven-seat chairs—or weave a basket from scratch. The firm was established by one of the authors of *The Caner's Handbook*. His more recent interest in gourds, an ancient craft, has culminated in *The Gourd Artist's Handbook* (coauthored with Ginger Summit). Other texts are available, as well as a line of gourd-related tools and supplies.

The 40-page catalog shows 15 kinds of prewoven cane webbing, which is used in modern and mass-produced seating. For older chairs, The Caning Shop offers hanks of cane in a full range of sizes, including binder cane, and also sells Danish seat cord, rawhide lacing, fiber rush, Hong Kong grass (sea grass), ash splint, Shaker tape, whole reed (for wicker), wicker braid, rattan, pressed fiber (imitation leather) seats, and tools. Basket makers should look here for kits, materials, hoops, and handles. And there are 20 pages of books and videos on both subjects. If you live in or near Berkeley, check the schedule of classes—"Pine Needle Basketry," "Gourd Masks," and "Miniature Rustic Furniture" were among those in a recent brochure.

Canadian readers, please note: Payment for the catalog and goods orders must be in U.S. funds.

Special Factors: Satisfaction is guaranteed; C.O.D. orders are accepted.

CIRCLE CRAFT SUPPLY

DEPT. WBMC
P.O. BOX 3000
DOVER, FL 33527-3000
813-659-0992
FAX: 813-659-0017

Catalog: $1
Save: up to 30%
Pay: check, MO, MC, V, Discover
Sells: general crafts supplies
Store: 13295 U.S. Hwy. 92, Dover, FL; Monday to Saturday 9–5

The 96-page catalog from Circle Craft Supply lists everything, from "abaca shapes" to zip-lock bags, that you'll need to indulge in any of scores of arts, crafts, and hobbies. Circle Craft was founded in 1982, and sells at discounts that average 20%, and reach 30% on some items. There are tools and materials here for a wide range of crafts and pastimes—beading, jewelry making, basketry, flower making, quick-count plastic canvas crafts, doll making, lamp making, clock making, Christmas ornaments, macrame, chenille crafts, and much more.

Special Factors: Authorized returns are accepted within 10 days; C.O.D. orders are accepted.

CRAFT RESOURCES, INC.

BOX 828
FAIRFIELD, CT 06430-0828
203-254-7702
FAX: 203-255-6456

Catalog: $1
Save: up to 50%
Pay: check, MO, MC, V
Sells: adult-oriented crafts kits
Store: mail order only

Craft Resources, founded in 1972, specializes in needlework projects in kit form and offers "the largest selection of adult-oriented crafts available." The 16-page color catalog shows kits for projects in latch hooking, needlepoint, long stitch, crewel, stamped and counted cross-stitch, string art, basketry, copper punching, wood crafts, and "stained glass" (sun catchers). The kits range from very basic designs for the beginner to more complex patterns, but a patient novice should be able to tackle any of these projects, with reasonable to impressive results. Most yield purely decorative items, such as the latch-hook blocks, but there are kits to help you create small rugs, afghans, picture frames, baby bibs, pillows, and baskets.

Craft Resources also sells yarn, embroidery floss, needlestitch canvas, knitting needles and crochet hooks, embroidery hoops, pillow forms, fiberfill batts, stencils, picture mats, and frames. The best prices are on the kits sold by the dozen—the per-kit price can drop from $3 to $1.25. Therapists and instructors will find these bargains invaluable, and they provide an ideal way for the rest of us to "try out" a craft without investing much money.

Special Factors: Satisfaction is guaranteed; unused returns are accepted within 60 days; minimum order is $10 with credit cards.

CR'S BEAR AND DOLL SUPPLY CATALOG

▬▬▬▬

BOX 8-WM61
LELAND, IA 50453
515-567-3652
FAX: 515-567-3071

Catalog: $2 (see text)
Save: up to 65%
Pay: check, MO, MC, V, Discover
Sells: doll- and bear-making supplies
Store: same address; Monday to Friday
8:30–3:30

Never considered trying your hand at making a doll or Teddy bear? Then you haven't seen the catalog from CR's Crafts. It's 120 pages of patterns, kits, parts, and the related miscellany that go into making some of the most adorable, collector-quality dolls and furry friends you'll find anywhere. If you don't fall in love with Sugar Britches, Barney Bear, or Bunnie, you're made of pretty stern stuff.

CR's Crafts sells everything you need to make any of hundreds of delightful creatures, including the fabric and fur, bodies and limbs, heads and faces, voice boxes and squeakers, armatures, wigs and hair, teeth, eyelashes, stuffing, music boxes, stands, books and manuals, and much more. Prices are competitive with other toy-making supply catalogs, and *very* low compared to finished products purchased elsewhere. CR's is also a good place to pick up parts and materials for repairing damaged dolls and stuffed toys, and a source for well-priced clothing, accessories, and furnishings for dolls and toys. CR's Crafts has been in business since 1981, and if you're in Leland, you're invited to drop in and see the stock of 4,000-plus items in person.

Special Factors: The catalog costs $2 if sent within the United States, $4 to Canada, and $7 to other countries (all in U.S. dollars).

FRANK'S CANE AND RUSH SUPPLY

P.O. BOX 3025
HUNTINGTON BEACH, CA
  92605-3025
714-847-0707
FAX: 714-843-5645

Catalog: free
Save: up to 40% (see text)
Pay: check, MO, MC, V, Discover
Sells: seat-reweaving supplies, furniture, kits, books, etc.
Store: 7252 Heil Ave., Huntington Beach, CA; Monday to Friday 8–5

Frank's has been in business since 1975, and the firm's comprehensive 40-page catalog of seat replacement materials includes over a dozen weaves of cane webbing as well as strand and binding cane, spline, fiber and wire-fiber rush, fiber wicker, Danish cord, oak and ash splints, round and flat reed, and fiber and real reed braid (often used as trim on wicker furniture). Frank's also sells rattan, basketry materials, raffia, sea grass, "tissue flex" (for rag coil baskets), wood hoops and handles, brass hardware, upholstery tools and supplies, dowels and wood crafts parts, and spindles and finials. Prices are competitive on these goods, and there are some bargains—Frank's sells the same decorative upholstery nails that cost $5.25 per hundred locally, for just $3. The catalog also has six pages of books on seat reweaving, woodworking, basketry, and upholstery.

The furniture kits include hardwood Shaker-style arm and side chairs, rocking chairs, and stools. Prices are reasonable: $12.50 for a stool kit, $30.50 for a child's ladder-back chair kit, and $64 for an adult's chair. (The furniture comes with enough fiber rush or flat fiber—your choice—to complete the seat.)

Special Factors: Minimum order is $10 with credit cards; C.O.D. orders are accepted.

GETTINGER FEATHER CORP.

_____

16 W. 36TH ST.
NEW YORK, NY 10018
212-695-9470
FAX: 212-695-9471

Price List and Samples: $2
Save: up to 50%
Pay: check or MO
Sells: feathers
Store: same address (8th floor); Monday to Thursday 8:30–5:30, Friday 8:30–3

Gettinger has been serving New York City's milliners and craftspeople since 1915 with a marvelous stock of exotic and common feathers. Even if you're not a creative type, you can add cachet to a tired hat with a few ostrich plumes, and Gettinger's feather boas are a dashing alternative to furs for gala occasions.

Pheasant, guinea hen, turkey, duck, goose, rooster, and peacock feathers are available here, loose or sewn (lined up in continuous rows of even length), by the ounce or the pound, beginning at $5 (loose) and $8 (sewn) per ounce. Pheasant tail feathers, 6" to 8" long, cost $13 per hundred; yard-long peacock feathers are priced at $25 per hundred; and pheasant hides cost $9 and up per skin. Feather boas are available, sold in two-yard pieces, as well as ostrich and marabou fans. And if you're reviving old feather pillows, you may be interested in the bedding feathers, which cost $10 to $45 per pound, depending on the quality (minimum five pounds).

Gettinger Feather is offering readers a discount of 5% on their first order. Be sure to identify yourself as a WBMC reader when you order, and deduct the discount from the cost of the goods only. This WBMC reader discount expires February 1, 1997.

Special Factors: Minimum order is $20.

MODEL EXPO, INC.

MOUNT POCONO
INDUSTRIAL PARK
P.O. BOX 1000
TOBYHANNA, PA
18366-1000
800-222-3876
717-839-2080
FAX: 717-839-2090

Catalog: $1
Save: up to 40%
Pay: check, MO, MC, V, AE
Sells: ship, plane, and car model kits and supplies
Store: mail order only

   ¡Sí!

If you've never considered building a model ship, you probably haven't seen Model Expo's catalog of models, parts, tools, and books. It's 92 pages of full-color photos of beautiful historical ship models, from transport vessels of ancient Egypt to Jacques Costeau's *Calypso*. In addition to the firm's own models (by its manufacturing arm, Model Shipways), the catalog shows lines from Amati, Billing, Constructo, Corel, Heller (plastic), Mamoli, and Mantua. Each of the featured models is described fully and rated according to difficulty (entry level, intermediate, or advanced). Well over half of the catalog is devoted to books (on model making, ship design and development, maritime history, naval aviation, and military topics), as well as historic and modern fittings, display cases and pedestals, shipwrights' tools, and hand and power tools. Both novice and experienced modelers will find much to interest them, and for those just taking up the hobby, Model Expo's guaranty will be reassuring: If you should break or lose a part during construction, Model Expo will replace it, free of charge!

Special Factors: Satisfaction is guaranteed; returns (except partially built kits) are accepted within 30 days for exchange, refund, or credit.

NORTHWEST TREASURE SUPPLY

Catalog: free
Save: 33% average
Pay: check, MO, MC, V, Discover
Sells: metal detectors and prospecting tools
Store: 3096 125th Ave. N.E., Bellevue, WA; by appointment only

DEPT. E52
P.O. BOX 52802
BELLEVUE, WA 98015-2802
206-881-7340
FAX: 206-885-7646

 ¡Si!

Whether you're a beachcomber who wants a little help, or a dedicated prospector setting up a dredging operation, Northwest Treasure Supply can equip your venture. "Detectorists" can start with an inexpensive model and add the "beginner's kit" of headphones, coil cover, trash-and-treasure bag, and a trowel, all for under $200. Recover enough coins to justify the cost, and you can upgrade. Prospectors can choose from scores of metal detectors by Fisher, Garrett, Keene, Minelab, Pro-Mack, Tesoro, and White's, and headphones by Cal-Rad, DepthMaster, and Koss. Once you've found the ore, you'll need recovery tools—knives, trowels, shovels, picks, scoops, etc.—and bags, sifters, and pans, as well as the tools and chemicals to test for the presence of gold and silver. Sluice boxes are sold, and Northwest Treasure Supply can work with you to determine the right dredging equipment for your needs. The firm offers over a dozen instructional videotapes on prospecting and metal detecting, and a long list of books on *where* to find old mines and stakes, hidden treasure, and even water. The people who run Northwest Treasure have been in the business since 1985, and can answer most questions on treasure hunting and panning.

Special Factors: Satisfaction is guaranteed; price quote by phone or letter; C.O.D. orders are accepted.

THINK INK

**A DIVISION OF CREATIVE
ENTERPRISES, INC.
7526 OLYMPIC VIEW DR.,
SUITE E
EDMONDS, WA
98026-5555
800-778-1935
206-778-1935**

Catalog: long self-addressed envelope with 55¢ postage
Save: up to 45% (see text)
Pay: check, MO, MC, V
Sells: thermography and embossing powders, Gocco printers, supplies, etc.
Store: same address

Think Ink features Print GOCCO's printing press silkscreen devices and embossing powders, which provide crafters with a great way to get custom prints inexpensively. Use clip-art designs, or if you can draw, GOCCOs will enable you to custom-color and print flyers, bulletins, cards, tote bags, T-shirts, and nearly anything else made of paper, fabric, wood, or leather. There are two Print GOCCO presses, the B6 model (with a 3-9/16" by 5-9/16" print area) for $99, and the B5 (with a 5-15/16" by 8-11/16" print area) for $360. Both models work by creating a master of your design that can be inked like a silkscreen and printed.

The Gocco Printer inks are offered in a wide range of colors and types, including 40cc tubes of textile ink (metallics, fluorescents, pastels, pearlescents, and basics are available), and enamel inks for nonporous surfaces. One application of the ink yields 80 to 100 prints. If you send a long, double-stamped (55¢), self-addressed envelope, Think Ink will send you Gocco-printed samples, a price list, and a brochure on the Print GOCCO printers. Rubber stamp artists should check the prices they're currently paying for embossing powders. Think Ink's powders do the same job, but are sold at bulk discount prices—as much as 60% to 70%, compared to the prices charged by rubber-stamp supply firms. The selection includes tinsels, glitter glosses, metallics, black, white, lavender pearl, Northern Lights, and many others.

Think Ink is offering readers of this book a one-time, 5% discount on first orders of the B5 or B6 GOCCO printer, or orders of embossing/thermography powders over $25. This WBMC reader discount expires February 1, 1997.

Special Factors: C.O.D. orders are accepted.

TOM THUMB WORKSHOPS

14100 LANKFORD
  HIGHWAY
P.O. BOX 357
MAPPSVILLE, VA 23407
804-824-3507
FAX: 804-824-4465

Price List: free with a long, stamped, self-addressed envelope
Save: up to 45% (see text)
Pay: check, MO, MC, V
Sells: potpourri, spices, herbs, oils, etc.
Store: same address (Rte. 13); Monday to Friday 9–5

Although they're both called potpourri, there's a world of difference between an artificially scented pile of dried things and dyed wood shavings, and a blend of flowers, herbs, spices, essential oils, and natural fixatives. Tom Thumb sells the ingredients and directions for making the real thing, from premixed blends like "Blackberry Royal" and "Woods and Roses," to a list of hundreds of herbs, spices, dried flowers, cones, and pods. The eight-page price list also shows a range of botanicals perfect for wreathes and arrangements—artemisia, eucalyptus, dried pomegranates, wheat, and lotus pods among them. Dozens of essential oils and blends are available in 1/8 ounce vials for $3.25, and the blended potpourri costs $6.50 for four ounces, or $19.50 per pound. These prices are 20% to 45% below those charged elsewhere for "house blends" of potpourri, and you can deduct 25% from the cost of the goods (with some exceptions) if your order is over $100. Tom Thumb also sells materials and equipment for drying and pressing flowers, spice jars and other containers, and the bookshelf includes a number of guides to aromatherapy, perfumery, and making wreathes, candles, and soap.

Wholesale buyers, please request the *bulk price list* and include a long, stamped, self-addressed envelope.

Special Factors: Satisfaction is guaranteed; returns are accepted within 30 days; minimum order is $15, $30 with credit cards.

VANGUARD CRAFTS, INC.

DEPT. WMC
P.O. BOX 340170
BROOKLYN, NY
11234-0003
718-377-5188
FAX: 718-692-0056

Catalog: $1, refundable
Save: up to 60%
Pay: check, MO, MC, V
Sells: crafts kits and materials
Store: 1081 E. 48th St., Brooklyn, NY; Monday to Friday 10–6, Saturday 10–5

Vanguard has been selling fun since 1959 through a 68-page color catalog of crafts kits and projects. Vanguard is geared to educators and others buying for classroom use, but it's a great source for rainy-day project materials at home.

You'll find kits and supplies for hundreds of crafts, including shrink art, foil pictures, grapevine wreaths, mosaic tiling, basic woodworking crafts, suncatchers, Styrofoam crafts, leatherworking, fabric flowers, decoupage, copper enameling, pom-pom crafts, stenciling, string art, crafts sticks projects, Indian crafts, clothespin dolls, calligraphy, and other diversions. Vanguard also features a line of kits inspired by the "spirit of the Southwest"—Santa Fe picture frames, "Pueblo" pottery, concho accessories, bead looms, kachina dolls, and more. Basic art supplies and tools—adhesives, scissors, paper, paint, pastels, hammers, craft knives, etc.—are also available. The prices are *very* reasonable, and the large selection makes it easy to meet the $25 minimum order.

Special Factors: Minimum order is $25.

WARNER-CRIVELLARO STAINED GLASS SUPPLIES, INC.

1855 WEAVERSVILLE RD.
ALLENTOWN, PA 18103
800-523-4242
610-264-1100
IN SPANISH: 800-523-4245
FAX: 610-264-1010

Catalog: $2 (see text)
Save: up to 50%
Pay: check, MO, MC, V, AE, Discover
Sells: stained-glass tools and supplies
Store: same address; Monday to Saturday
9–5 EST

Warner-Crivellaro serves the old art of stained glass with an 80-page catalog of glass sheets (Wissmach, Kokomo, Spectrum, Youghiogheny, and other types), bevels, glass cutting tools and machines, grinders, foil and foiling equipment, strips and spools of lead came, soldering tools and irons, patinas, flux, etching acid, finishing compound, cutting oil, and several pages of books and manuals. If you're new to the craft, see the starter kits, which begin at under $36 and include everything you need to begin a project. Once you've mastered a sun catcher or one of the beautiful bevel ornaments, you may be ready to tackle a lampshade.

Warner-Crivellaro publishes two other catalogs that you'll find helpful: a 55-page pattern catalog ($5 if ordered alone, $3 with an order, or free with a $50 order), and a 100-plus-page catalog (free with your first $50 order) of materials and supplies for more complex projects. But even the general catalog ($2) includes nearly four dozen lamp bases, most with a bronze-look or antique brass finish. The bases are fully wired and harped, and begin at under $16 for minis. Since reproduction lamps made in these styles usually fetch much more when they're sold in stores, consider saving by buying the base here and the shade elsewhere. The catalog shows other lamp and shade parts, including harps, vase caps, spiders, brass channel and bead edging, and two pages of solid bronze reproduction Tiffany lamp bases, which run from $140 to $775. Even the red oak frames sold here, which are designed to encase stained glass panels, can be employed by nonartisans to frame and finish other works of a similar thickness.

Please note: Orders sent to Alaska, Canada, and overseas must be paid in U.S. dollars or by credit card.

Special Factors: Authorized returns are accepted; minimum order is $25; C.O.D. orders are accepted.

SEE ALSO

The Astronomical Society of the Pacific • materials on astronomy topics •
BOOKS

Baron/Barclay Bridge Supplies • teaching and playing supplies for bridge •
TOYS

Dick Blick Co. • arts and crafts tools and supplies • **ART MATERIALS**

Caprilands Herb Farm • potpourri ingredients, pomanders, essential oils, etc. •
FARM

Ceramic Supply of New York & New Jersey, Inc. • ceramics and sculpting
materials, music box parts • **ART MATERIALS**

Crown Art Products Co., Inc. • supplies and equipment for silk screening,
stained glass, etc. • **ART MATERIALS**

Daleco Master Breeder Products • tropical and fresh-water fish supplies and
equipment • **ANIMAL**

Eloxite Corporation • jewelry findings, lapidary equipment, and clock-making
supplies • **JEWELRY**

Golfsmith International, Inc. • supplies for making golf clubs, including stains,
finishes, etc. • **SPORTS**

Hong Kong Lapidaries, Inc. • scarabs, inlaid intaglios, beads, and other crafts
materials • **JEWELRY**

House of Onyx, Inc. • semiprecious and precious gems, cabochons • **JEWELRY**

Leather Unlimited Corp. • leather, dyes, kits, etc. • **LEATHER**

Lixx Labelz • custom-designed labels • **GENERAL: CARDS**

M.C. Limited • steer hides • **HOME: DECOR**

Original Paper Collectibles • vintage fruit crate labels • **ART & ANTIQUES**

The Potters Shop Inc. • books on pottery and ceramics • **BOOKS**

San Francisco Herb Co. • dried flowers, potpourri ingredients, potpourri recipes,
etc. • **FOOD: BEVERAGES AND FLAVORINGS**

Storey's Books for Country Living • books and manuals on country crafts •
BOOKS

That Fish Place • aquarium supplies and equipment • **ANIMAL**

Triner Scale • pocket scale • **OFFICE**

University Products, Inc. • archival-quality collection storage, mounting, and display materials • **OFFICE: SMALL BUSINESS**

Weston Bowl Mill • unfinished wooden boxes, spool holders, etc. • **GENERAL
MERCHANDISE**

Textile Arts

Sewing and needlework of all kinds, and other crafts using textiles

Home sewing is enjoying a vogue these days, especially among women who need good business wardrobes but balk at the ludicrous prices of ready-to-wear. Sewing it yourself can not only save you money, but if you're skilled you'll get a custom tailor job, with the fabric and details *you* want. Every aspect of sewing—from the fabric and notions to the patterns to the machines themselves—has been improved over the past decade. The sources here can help you find the right tools and materials for your clothing project, but see the listings in "Home: Decor" for decorator fabrics.

If you do needlework and use DMC floss, you'll want the DMC Embroidery Floss Card in your files. This reference includes samples of each DMC floss color and a guide to which colors are available in pearl cotton in sizes 3, 5, and 8. (Most discount sources carry DMC floss, but few include color guides.) The American Needlewoman sells the DMC Floss Card; request the free catalog from The American Needlewoman, P.O. Box 6472-WBMC, Fort Worth, TX 76115.

For more firms selling fabric, notions, and sewing-crafts supplies, see the preceding listings in "Crafts and Hobbies."

FIND IT FAST

FUN FUR • **Monterey**
NOTIONS AND SEWING TOOLS • **Button Shop, Clotilde, A. Feibusch, Home-Sew, Newark Dressmaker, Park Slope, Rosemary's, Solo Slide, Taylor's, Thread Discount Sales**

TEXTILE ARTS, YARN, FABRIC • **Atlanta Thread, Connecting Threads, Dharma Trading, Fabric Editions, Fashion Fabrics Club, Fiber Studio, Fort Crailo, Global Village, Great Northern Weaving, J & J, Natural Fiber Fabrics, Oppenheim's, Rosemary's, Smiley's Yarn, Straw Into Gold, Thai Silks, Utex, Webs**

ATLANTA THREAD & SUPPLY

695 RED OAK RD.
  DEPT., WBMC 96
STOCKBRIDGE, GA 30281
800-847-1001
404-389-9115
FAX: 800-298-0403,
  404-389-9202

Catalog: $1
Save: up to 50%
Pay: check, MO, MC, V, AE, Discover
Sells: sewing tools, notions, and pressing equipment
Store: mail order only

Atlanta Thread, a division of a major distributor of sewing equipment, has been doing business since 1948, and boasts the lowest prices around on Gingher shears, Gosling drapery tapes, Kirsch drapery hardware, YKK zippers, and many other goods. This is a great source for quality supplies and equipment—coned thread, zippers and parts, custom tailoring linings and pads, buttons, Singer's sewing guides and professional tailoring manuals, cords, crinoline stiffening bands, fringe, hook-and-loop tape, professional pressing equipment—tables and boards, irons by Hi-Steam/Naomoto, Rheem, Rowenta,, and Sussman—and commercial-quality sewing machines, sergers, and parts. The 64-page catalog is illustrated, but if you need more information on a product, call and ask.

Special Factors: Satisfaction is guaranteed; returns are accepted within 30 days for exchange, refund, or credit; C.O.D. orders are accepted.

BUFFALO BATT & FELT CORP.

DEPT. WBMC
3307 WALDEN AVE.
DEPEW, NY 14043
716-683-4100, EXT. 130
FAX: 716-683-8928

Brochure and Samples: $1, refundable
Save: 40% plus
Pay: check, MO, MC, V
Sells: fiberfill, quilt batts, and pillow inserts
Store: mail order only

Buffalo Batt's "Super Fluff" polyester stuffing is so springy and resilient, the snowy-white samples nearly bounce out of the brochure. The firm has been in business since 1913, and sells this craft and upholstery stuffing by the case at savings of 40% or more on regular retail prices.

Super Fluff is manufactured in rolls 27" wide by 20 yards long and is the ideal filler for upholstery and crafts in which support and a down-like feel are desired. In addition to having high loft and nonallergenic properties, Super Fluff is machine washable and dryable, mildew resistant, and easy to sew. Buffalo Batt also sells Super Fluff in 12-ounce and two-pound bags, bulk rolls, pillow inserts (from 14" square to 24" square, and 12" by 16" and 14" by 18" rectangles), and both "traditional" and two-inch-thick "comforter-style" quilt batts. Ultra Fluff, a slick, premium fiberfill that gives a softer hand, was recently introduced; it's also available in ten-ounce bags and in bulk. Another new product, "thermobonded" quilt batt, is soft, dense, and flame retardant; it's available on 20-yard rolls. Buffalo Batt also sells "Soft Heart" Quallofil pillow inserts, in sizes from 14" to 26" square as well as the popular rectangles, and in bulk rolls.

The only negative is the minimum order of any two cases, which may be more than most single projects require. But it's a manageable amount for a home-based crafts business, quilting circle, cooperative, or for a major decorating project—or store the surplus for future use, or share with crafty friends!

Please note: Orders are shipped via UPS within the continental United States only.

Special Factors: Quantity discounts are available; minimum order is any two cases; C.O.D. orders are accepted.

THE BUTTON SHOP

P.O. BOX 1065-HM
OAK PARK, IL 60304
708-795-1234

Catalog: free
Save: up to 40%
Pay: check, MO, MC, V
Sells: buttons and sewing supplies
Store: 7023 Roosevelt Rd., Berwyn, IL; Monday to Friday 9–4, Saturday 10–2

The Button Shop, founded in 1900, stocks closures of all kinds, as well as trims, sewing machine parts, scissors, and other sewing tools and notions at savings of up to 50% on list prices or regular retail. Several pages of the 18-page catalog are devoted to buttons—anonymous white shirt buttons, clear waistband buttons, tiny buttons for doll clothes, classic four-hole coat and suit buttons, gilt heraldic buttons for blazers, designs for dressy clothing, Navy pea coat buttons, braided leather buttons for tweeds, and dozens of others, including baseball gloves and other novelty designs for children's clothing. If you want to custom-cover buttons with your own fabric, you'll find Maxant and Prym kits, as well as make-your-own fabric belt and buckle materials, gripper snaps and grommet sets, hooks and eyes of all types, zippers (including odd sizes to 108"), and Velcro by the inch and by the yard. The Button Shop sells all kinds of rickrack, bias tape, cording, white and black elastic (from 1/8" to 3"), replacement jacket cuffs, elbow patches, trouser pockets, shoulder pads, and other notions and supplies. Thread in cotton, cotton-covered polyester, and polyester is offered; the brands include Dritz, Fiskars, Gingher, Molnycke, Oncore, Prym, Singer, Talon, Wiss, and Wrights.

The Button Shop's comparatively deep inventory of sewing machine supplies and parts includes needles, presser feet, bobbins, bobbin cases, needle plates, buttonholers, motors, foot controls, light bulbs, and belts. The catalog descriptions are brief, and line drawings are the only illustrations. If you're not sure an item is the right one and need more information, call or write before ordering. You may also send a fabric swatch for the best color match if you're buying trim, thread, or buttons, and The Button Shop custom-makes zippers in lengths up to 120".

Special Factors: Returns are accepted within 30 days for exchange, refund, or credit; minimum order is $5, $10 with credit cards; C.O.D. orders are accepted.

CLOTILDE INC.

10086 SEW SMART WAY
B8031
STEVENS POINT, WI
54481-8031
800-772-2891
INTERNATIONAL:
715-341-2824
FAX: 715-341-3082

Catalog: free
Save: 20% average
Pay: check, MO, MC, V, Discover
Sells: sewing notions, tapes, etc.
Store: mail order only

Clotilde has been providing sewers with notions since 1971, and presents current offerings in a well-organized, 100-page color catalog. Clotilde's extensive collection of sewing tools and machine attachments (for both electronic and computerized models) makes it a great source for every home sewer.

Clotilde sells a broad range of sewing aids and equipment: ironing hams and boards, sewing and work tables, pattern design supplies, serging notions, scissors and cutters, quilting supplies, appliqué notions, and a large number of books, videos, and patterns. Everything is discounted 20% from regular retail, and throughout the catalog you'll find specials with further reductions. Clotilde has so many problem solvers and gadgets to make the hitherto difficult easy—like turning narrow fabric tubes, making even knife pleats, and cutting perfect circles— you'll want to have the catalog before you begin your next big project.

Wholesale customers must resell Clotilde's products to qualify for wholesale terms (40% to 50% off); minimum order is $100, no minimum quantities.

Special Factors: Satisfaction is guaranteed.

CONNECTING THREADS

5750 N.E. HASSALO
PORTLAND, OR 97213
800-574-6454
FAX: 503-287-6916

Catalog: free
Save: up to 40%
Pay: check, MO, MC, V, AE, Discover
Sells: quilting patterns, materials, and supplies
Store: mail order only

Connecting Threads answers the needs of "the busy quilter" with 48 pages of pattern and reference books, fabrics and batts, project plans, cutting and sewing tools, stencils, and equipment. If you haven't worked on a quilt in years, you may be surprised at the complexity and sophistication of the designs: Seminole patchwork, Amish miniatures, Sashiko (Japanese quilting), "photo" keepsake quilts, reverse appliqué, and Jewish quilting may be new to you. In addition to books, Connecting Threads offers EZ International's WaterFall and ColorBars ombréd cottons, stencils for both hand and machine quilting (top-stitching through the batt), and lots of other tools and sewing helpers. There are also books on related crafts—fabric painting, ribbon work, dolls, fabric ornaments, and "art" clothing. Savings average 25%, and both retail and discount prices are listed.

   Special Factors: Satisfaction is guaranteed; returns are accepted for exchange, refund, or credit.

DHARMA TRADING CO.

P.O. BOX 150916
SAN RAFAEL, CA
   94915-0916
415-456-7657
FAX: 415-456-8747

Catalog: free
Save: up to 50%
Pay: check, MO, MC, V, Discover
Sells: textile craft supplies and clothing "blanks"
Store: 1604 Fourth St., San Rafael, CA; Monday to Friday 8–5

The "whole earth" movement may have peaked in 1969, the year this firm was founded, but Dharma Trading has survived. The firm sells tools and materials for the textile arts—dyes, paints, resists, and fabrics—and declares, "We are the source for the tie-dye dyes used by most tie-dyers." The informative, 112-page catalog provides helpful tips on the features of the dyes and paints, application techniques and suggested fabrics, and even metric conversion charts and a shrinkage "estimator." Prices are good, running up to 50% off list or comparable retail.

Coloring agents by Deka, Dupont, Jacquard, Jones Tones, Pebeo (Orient Express), Peintex, Procion, Sennelier (Super-Tinfix), Setacolor, Versatex, and other firms are offered, as well as color remover, soda ash, urea, Synthrapol, gutta serti, and other resists. The tools include bottles and droppers for dye mixing and application, textile pens, tjantings, brushes (flat, foam, sumi), and steamers for setting dyes. Nearly half of Dharma Trading's catalog is devoted to silk and cotton clothing "blanks"—everything from cotton jester hats and silk earring blanks to cotton skirts, jackets, sweats, and more are shown in the current catalog. A list of cotton, rayon, and silk fabrics that have yielded good results with dyeing and painting is included in the catalog; samples (silk or cotton/rayon) are available for 25¢ each. Selected books dealing with fabric design, painting, screening, direct dyeing, batiking, tie-dyeing, and other techniques are also sold.

Special Factors: Quantity discounts are available; institutional accounts are available; C.O.D. orders are accepted.

FASHION FABRICS CLUB

Membership: $4.95 (see text)
Save: up to 50%
Pay: check, MO, MC, V
Sells: dress fabrics
Store: same address

10490 BAUR BLVD.
ST. LOUIS, MO 63132
314-993-3857
FAX: 314-993-5802

Fashion Fabrics Club speaks to the needs of home sewers who make their own clothing, but don't have the time to comb yard goods stores for the perfect fabric. Each month, Fashion Fabrics Club sends its members a brochure with over a dozen coordinated fabric swatches, discount coupons, and other offers. The fabrics are chosen to allow you to create coordinated outfits; a recent mailing featured selections from Koret, Tahari, and Eileen West, at $3.99 to $6.99 a yard. Care recommendations and "usual" selling prices are noted for each selection.

If you write to Fashion Fabrics Club, you'll receive the current packet of swatches and descriptions, with an order form; place an order, and you're automatically enrolled in the Club for a year. If nothing strikes your fancy but you'd like to receive the mailings, it will cost you $4.95 to join. All purchases are covered by the Club's pledge of satisfaction, and you'll receive discount coupons (including one for a $5 rebate on your first purchase) with each order you place, entitling you to savings on future orders.

Special Factors: Satisfaction is guaranteed; returns are accepted for exchange, refund, or credit; minimum order is $5.

A. FEIBUSCH COR- PORATION

30 ALLEN ST.
NEW YORK, NY 10002
212-226-3964
FAX: 212-219-1065

Information: price quote
Save: up to 50%
Pay: check or MO
Sells: zippers, thread, notions, and garment supplies
Store: same address; Monday to Friday 9:30–5, Sunday 10–5

Feibusch has been helping New Yorkers zip up since 1941, handling requests from the mundane to the exotic. Zippers of every conceivable size, color, and type are sold here—from minuscule dolls' zippers to heavy-duty closures for tents, luggage, and similar applications. If your requirements aren't met by the existing stock, Feibusch can have your zipper made to order. Talon and YKK zippers are available, and Feibusch also carries all-cotton and polyester thread in a full range of colors. There is no catalog, so *write* with your requirements: Describe what you're looking for or send a sample, specifying length desired, nylon or metal teeth, open or closed end, and other details. Enclose a scrap of fabric, if possible, to assure a good color match. Be sure to include a self-addressed, stamped envelope with your correspondence if you want to receive a reply. If you'd prefer to call with general information questions, note that Feibusch has salespeople who speak Chinese, French, and German, as well as Spanish!

Special Factors: Price quote by letter.

THE FIBER STUDIO

DEPT. WBMC
9 FOSTER HILL RD.
P.O. BOX 637
HENNIKER, NH 03242
603-428-7830

Book and Equipment Catalog: $1 (see text)
Save: up to 35%
Pay: check, MO, MC, V
Sells: knitting, spinning, and weaving equipment and supplies
Store: 9 Foster Hill Rd., Henniker, NH; Tuesday to Saturday 10–4, Sunday by chance

The Fiber Studio has been serving the needs of knitters, spinners, weavers, and doll makers since 1975 with a well-chosen line of tools and supplies, and great prices on yarn. The catalog lists looms, spinning equipment, and accessories by Ashford, Glimarkra, Harrisville Design, Leclerc, Louet, Norwood, and Schacht. The prices on these aren't discounted, but shipping is included on some models (see "Special Factors," below). Natural dyes, mordants, and a good selection of spinning fibers—from mohair tops to silk roving—are offered at competitive prices. (The sample card of current spinning fibers costs $4.) And scores of texts on knitting, spinning, and weaving are available.

The bargains here are on yarns, which are sold in two ways: through the stock shown in the yarn sample set ($5), and through the yarn closeouts. The stock yarns include rug wools, natural yarns, Superwash wool, Irish linen, cotton, silk, Shetland wool, mercerized cotton, and more, priced up to 35% less at The Fiber Studio than at other sources. Quantity discounts on these yarns run from 10% on orders over $100 to 20% on orders over $200. *After* you order the yarn card from The Fiber Studio, you can send $1 and four long, self-addressed envelopes with two stamps each, and ask to be put on the mailing list for the quarterly closeouts. If you can get to Henniker, you have a treat: the shop offers an extensive selection of beads from around the world, made of semi-precious stones, wood, bone, glass, horn, clay, and other materials, including trade beads. The Fiber Studio also sells Tibetan lambskins, of special interest to doll makers. These items aren't listed in the catalog, but you can make inquiries and order by phone.

Canadian readers, please note: Only U.S. funds are accepted.

Special Factors: Specify the *spinning fibers* ($4) or *yarns* ($5) sample set; shipping is not charged on most models of Harrisville Design, Leclerc, and Schacht looms; quantity discounts are available; minimum order is $15 with credit cards; C.O.D. orders are accepted.

FORT CRAILO YARNS COMPANY

P.O. BOX 10595
NEWBURGH, NY 12553
914-562-2698
FAX: 914-561-3623

Brochure and Samples: $2.80
Save: up to 35%
Pay: check, MO, MC, V, Discover
Sells: yarn for handweaving
Store: Broadway and Wisner Ave., Newburgh, NY; Monday to Friday 9:30–5

Fort Crailo Yarns, in business since 1963, sells four kinds of wool yarn and one of cotton, which are especially suited for hand weaving. Prices run up to 35% below those of comparable yarns sold elsewhere. The mothproofed, virgin wool yarn includes Crailo Rya (570 yd./lb., 33 colors), Crailo-Spun (700 yd./lb., 30 colors), Crailo Lite-Spun (1,700 yd./lb., 28 colors), and the very fine Crailo Worsted (4,900 yd./lb., 27 colors). Fort Crailo's cotton yarn is sold in 8-2, 3, 4, 5, and 6 ply, in 17 colors, and is suitable for warp or weft, and all the yarns are sold on half-pound cones. The colors are clear and true, and the range of weights makes Fort Crailo a good source for weavers of anything from fine fabrics to rugs.

Fort Crailo Yarns is offering readers a discount of 10% on their first order. Be sure to identify yourself as a WBMC reader when you order, and deduct the discount from the cost of the goods only. This WBMC reader discount expires February 1, 1997.

Special Factors: Quantity discounts are available.

GLOBAL VILLAGE IMPORTS

3439 N.E. SANDY BLVD.,
  #263-W
PORTLAND, OR
  97232-1959
503-236-9245
FAX: 503-233-0827

Brochure and Swatches: see text
Save: up to 50%
Pay: check or MO
Sells: Guatemalan ikat fabrics
Store: mail order only

Ikat is a type of weaving that uses tie-dyed warp threads to create striated designs that blend into overall patterns, which may be as subtle as

Zen or as colorfully riotous as a Mardi Gras parade. (Double ikats, in which both warp and weft threads are so dyed, represent a further refinement of the art.) Global Village has been selling handwoven Guatemalan ikats since 1988, and will send you an information packet and swatches of what's currently available for the sample fee—$5 (add $1 for international inquiries), refundable with purchase. Most of the fabrics are 36" wide, are woven by hand on large looms, and run from $9 to $15 per yard; the double ikats, hard to find at any price, are woven by the roll especially for Global Village. Upholstery-weight cottons, embroidered-look and brocade designs, and double ikats shot through with Lurex threads are also available. The firm's in-house designers have also created the "Western Star" collection—Navajo and cowboy saddle blanket motifs, redesigned and woven by hand in Guatemala. Quilters can take advantage of the "Quilter's Grabbag"—a generous pack of odds and ends, for $25 postpaid (note color preferences and minimum sizes needed, if applicable). The prices at Global Village are nearly 50% below the rates prevailing in New York City specialty shops. Fabric designers should take note of the company's custom weaving services, and wholesale inquiries are welcomed.

Special Factors: Minimum order is one yard; quantity discounts are available; C.O.D. orders are accepted.

GREAT NORTHERN WEAVING

Catalog and Samples: $1
Save: up to 50%
Pay: check, MO, MC, V
Sells: rug-weaving supplies and tools
Store: same address; Monday to Friday 9–4

1414 WEST F AVE. P.O.
BOX 462
KALAMAZOO, MI 49004
616-341-9752

The homey crafts of braiding and weaving rugs are served at Great Northern Weaving, which has been in business since 1985, and prices most items competitively—rags and filler cost up to 50% less here than elsewhere.

The 12-page catalog lists tools and materials for rug weaving and rug braiding. Braid-Aids, Braidkins, Braid-Klamps, Fraser rag cutters, reed and heddle hooks, shuttles, and warping boards are all available. The materials include coned cotton warp (8-4 ply) in over two dozen colors, all-cotton rug filler in 15 shades, 16-ply rug roping, new cotton "rags" on rolls, and loopers in bulk. Reference books are also available.

Canadian readers, please note: Payment must be made in U.S. funds.
Special Factors: C.O.D. orders are accepted.

HOME-SEW

DEPT. WM6
P.O. BOX 4099
BETHLEHEM, PA
  18018-0099
610-867-3833
FAX: 610-867-9717

Catalog: 50¢
Save: up to 70%
Pay: check, MO, MC, V
Sells: sewing and crafts supplies and notions
Store: mail order only

  ★ 🍁 (see text)

Home-Sew, which has been in business since 1960, offers savings of up to 70% on assorted laces and trims, as well as a wide range of sewing and crafts supplies. Home-Sew's 32-page catalog is well-organized and easy to use, with clear photographs of the trims and notions.

In addition to scores of laces (Cluny, Venice, nylon, poly, eyelet, etc.), Home-Sew offers elastic, satin and velvet ribbon, rickrack, tape, and appliqués. Specialty thread—for general sewing, overlock machines, carpets, and quilting—is available on cones and on spools. There are zippers, snaps, hooks and eyes, buttons, Velcro dots, belts and buckles, pins, needles, and scissors, as well as floss, adhesives, Styrofoam wreaths, spangles, beads, animal and doll parts, interfacings, and related items. If you're making your own curtains or slipcovers, check the prices on shirring and pleater tape, tasseled and moss fringe, cording, and related goods. Home-Sew makes it easy to see the trims before you buy—just join the Sample Club (50¢, order through the catalog), and you'll receive three mailings of lace, trim, ribbon, and elastics samples per year.

Wholesale customers, the minimum order is $100 for 25% off catalog prices; payment by check or money order only.

Canadian readers, please note: Send $1 (in Canadian funds) to Home-Sew Canada Inc., B.P./Box 87, 3285 1er Rue, Local 3, St. Hubert, Quebec J3Y 5S9, for the bilingual catalog.

Special Factors: Satisfaction is guaranteed; returns are accepted for exchange, refund, or credit; quantity discounts are available; shipping is not charged on orders over $45 that are paid by check or money order; minimum order is $5.

J & J PRODUCTS LTD.

117 W. 9TH ST., SUITE 111
LOS ANGELES, CA 90015
213-624-1840
FAX: 213-624-0134

Swatch Cards: $3 each, refundable (see text)
Save: up to 40%
Pay: check, MO, MC, V
Sells: woolen dress goods
Store: mail order only

Here are quality yard goods in beautiful colors, at competitive prices—gabardines, suitings, flannels, and other fine woolens. J & J showcases each type of fabric in a swatch booklet that costs $3, refundable with a purchase from that line.

In each booklet you'll receive a good-sized swatch, with smaller snippets to show the choice of colors. "Gabardine," $18 per yard, is offered in 45 colors; the mid-weight "Flannel" is shown in 17 shades; "Lightweight Wool Suiting" is a wool broadcloth offered in 32 colors, including turquoise and true red; and "Cashmere" features 20 fabrics, including a number of herringbones and tweeds, in beautiful shadings. You can order the swatch booklets by name for $3 each; the cost of each is refundable with a purchase from that particular booklet, and ordering information is included. The fabric is not inexpensive, but it has the luster and hand of fine-quality goods that wear well.

Special Factors: Satisfaction is guaranteed.

MONTEREY, INC.

P.O. BOX 271
JANESVILLE, WI 53547
800-432-9959

Price List: free with SASE (see text)
Save: up to 50%
Pay: check, MO, MC, V
Sells: fake-fur fabric
Store: 1815 E. Delavan Dr., Janesville, WI; Monday to Friday 8–4:30, Saturday 8–12 noon

Monterey, Inc. has been manufacturing deep-pile fur fabrics for a quarter of a century, and sells them at prices up to 50% below the usual retail. The brochure describes the fiber content of the different "fun" furs and lists the available colors, pile height, and ounces per yard. In addition to basic plush and shag, you'll find patterns and colors simulating the pelts of bear, seal, calf, tiger, and cheetah. Prices are given per cut yard, per yard on the roll (there are 15 to 20 yards per roll), and for quantity orders. Cut yards run from $8.50 to $15.50 per yard, and prices drop from there. You can buy the fabric in remnants (the Mill will choose the fur type) for $3.95 a pound, or $3.50 per pound by the carton (35 to 40 pounds). Stuffing for craft projects is available as well, at 69¢ a pound and up.

Please note: A set of samples is offered for $5, a worthwhile investment unless you're buying only remnants.

Special Factors: Minimum yardage order is one yard; minimum order is $25, $100 on orders shipped C.O.D.

NATURAL FIBER FABRICS DIRECT

10490 BAUR BLVD.
ST. LOUIS, MO 63132
314-993-3857
FAX: 314-993-5804

Membership: $4.95 (see text)
Save: up to 50%
Pay: check, MO, MC, V
Sells: natural-fiber fabrics
Store: same address

A year's membership in Natural Fiber Fabrics Direct costs $4.95, and brings you regular collections of about two dozen fabric swatches, with prices and fiber information. The cottons, silks, linens, woolens, and blends are dress and suit weight, and the prices are often 50% below those charged elsewhere for fabrics of similar quality. The mailings are sent about a season early, which gives you plenty of time to select a pattern and complete your clothing. The choices range from novelty knits and prints for playwear to dressy wovens for business clothing. You may recognize some of the fabrics, since they're also used in the workrooms of Campus Outfitters, Leslie Fay, Dan River, Schwartz Leibman, Spring Mills, and other makers. As an added service to members, Natural Fiber Fabrics matches most of the materials to Gutermann threads, which you can order with the fabric. And rebate coupons are issued for 5% of the value of fabric purchases (except clearance selections), further enhancing the values.

Please note: You must have your membership number to order; you'll find it above your name on the envelope in which the swatches are sent.

Non-U.S. readers, please note: Only U.S. funds are accepted.

Special Factors: Satisfaction is guaranteed; uncut returns are accepted for exchange, refund, or credit.

NEWARK DRESS-MAKER SUPPLY, INC.

6473 RUCH RD.
DEPT. WMI
P.O. BOX 20730
LEHIGH VALLEY, PA
  18002-0730
610-837-7500
FAX: 610-837-9115

Catalog: free
Save: up to 50%
Pay: check, MO, MC, V, Discover
Sells: sewing notions, crafts, and needlework supplies
Store: mail order only

Searching for specialty patterns, smocking guides, bear joints, alphabet beads, silk thread, or toy squeakers? Such requests are routine at Newark Dressmaker Supply, which offers trims, appliqués, scissors, piping, ribbon, lace, braid, twill, zippers, sewing gadgets, knitting supplies, name tapes and woven labels, interfacing, buttons, thread, floss, bias tape, rhinestones, wreath-decorating materials, supplies for making dolls and stuffed bears, fabric, upholstery materials, books and manuals, and much more. Among the brands of goods stocked here, you'll find Boye, Coats & Clark's, Dritz, Lily, Plaid, Sta-Flex, and Talon. "Sew Little" patterns for infants' and children's clothing are stocked, as well as "Great Fit" patterns for women's styles in sizes 38 to 60, and doll patterns from Putnam Pattern and other firms, and Folkwear patterns.

Newark Dressmaker has been in business since 1950 and is a great mail-order source for home sewers, since it offers a huge array of notions and other supplies, from glass-headed pins to yard goods, through the 60-page catalog. The prices are very competitive—up to 50% below regular retail on some items—and that doesn't count the 10% discount you get if your order totals $50 or more.

Wholesale customers, request the wholesale order form with the catalog; the minimum order is $125, and no specials, bonuses, or other offers apply to wholesale sales.

Canadian readers, please note: Only U.S. funds are accepted.

Special Factors: Satisfaction is guaranteed; minimum order is $20 with credit cards.

OPPENHEIM'S

**BOX 52
NORTH MANCHESTER,
 IN 46962-0052
219-982-6848
FAX: 219-982-6557**

Catalog: free
Save: up to 60%
Pay: check, MO, MC, V
Sells: yard goods, notions, crafts materials
Store: mail order only

The venerable Oppenheim's has been in business since 1875, and publishes a 64-page newsprint catalog of all kinds of crafts staples and specials. The firm's strength is fabrics, sold in cutaways, remnants, and by-the-yard cuts. The current catalog includes collection of calico, broadcloth, rib knits, Pendleton woolens, fun fur, denim, and other fabrics, in remnants and cutaways (sold by the lot or the pound). The yard goods will appeal to anyone looking for great prices on fabrics for crafts, plain clothing, and home decorating: Onasburg, shirting, sheeting, chambray, flannel, pillow ticking, cheesecloth, Pacific silver cloth, terry cloth, Rembrandt rug canvas and needlepoint canvas, bridal fabrics, velvet, rip-stop nylon, and stretch fabric for exercise wear are all offered in the lists of "staple" fabrics. Some of the fabrics are irregular; Oppenheim's will send you swatches (include a SASE with your request), and returns are accepted.

The catalog also includes an extensive roundup of notions—laces, ribbon, facings, cording, buckles, hook-and-loop tape, and more. Sewing tools, from seam rippers to sleeve boards, are featured, and there are lots of dolls and stuffed toy kits, appliqués, and preprinted quilt tops, pillows, and panels. If you're long on ideas and imagination but short on funds, Oppenheim's will be a welcome addition to your list of sources.

Special Factors: Satisfaction is guaranteed; returns (exceptions noted in catalog) are accepted within ten days for exchange, refund, or credit.

PARK SLOPE SEWING CENTER

297 SEVENTH AVE.
BROOKLYN, NY 11215
718-832-2556

Catalog: $3, refundable
Save: up to 40%
Pay: check, MO, MC, V
Sells: notions, sewing tools, fabric, etc.
Store: same address; Monday to Friday 10–7, Saturday 10–6, Sunday 12–5

Park Slope Sewing Center has been in business since 1991, serving the many quilters and home sewers in one of Brooklyn's enterprising neighborhoods. The woman who runs this shop is an accomplished seamstress, and something of a wizard at creating art from the computerized Elnas she sells. (The lower-priced line of Elnas is also available.) Visitors to the store will also find fabric, buttons, beads, trim, and patterns, and can take classes in quilting, machine techniques, and sewing basics. The 109-page catalog offers some of the products found in the store, as well as My Double dress forms, cabinets and carrying cases, sewing-room furniture, rubber stamps, supplies, books, videos, and more. The retail and discount prices are given for each item, and if you don't see what you're looking for, call—it may be available.

Special Factors: Satisfaction is guaranteed; price quote by phone or letter.

ROSEMARY'S SEWING SUPPLY

2299 T-DUNCAN RD.
MIDLAND, MI 48640
517-835-5388

Catalog with Swatches: $2
Save: 30% average
Pay: check or MO
Sells: cotton flannel, sewing notions, etc.
Store: mail order only

Six catalog pages, an order form, and a whole bunch of wonderful little swatches of flannel is what Rosemary sends for the $2 fee. Her specialty is all-cotton flannels, and adorable juvenile prints were among the stripes, florals, abstracts, and great range of solid colors in a recent mailing. The fabrics are described in the catalog; they're around $3 per 44"-wide yard. (Rosemary also sells flannel plaids, including yarn-dyed Lisbon flannels; include a long, double-stamped, self-addressed envelope with your request for samples of these.) Diaper flannel is offered in two widths, and if you make your own diapers, buy by the bolt for as little as $2.10 a yard. Scrap bundles and quilters' collections are also offered. You can stock up here on basics, like elastic, thread (spool and cone), needles and threaders, pins, buttons, quilt batts, scissors, seam rippers, muslin, and Pellon. If you're running a home-based business making layette items and flannel clothing, you'll appreciate the savings of up to 50% on fabric (compared to neighborhood sewing centers). Rosemary's has been in business since 1983, and offers extra discounts on quantity purchases.

Special Factors: Satisfaction is guaranteed.

SMILEY'S YARNS

DEPT. W
92-06 JAMAICA AVE.
WOODHAVEN, NY 11421
MAIL ORDER: 718-847-
   2185
STORE: 718-849-9873

Brochure: free with SASE
Save: up to 50% (see text)
Pay: check or MO
Sells: yarn for handknitting and crocheting
Store: same address; Monday to Saturday 10–5:30

Smiley's, where "Yarn Bargains Are Our Business," has been selling first-quality yarns at a discount since 1935. Each month, Smiley's offers a different "Yarn of the Month" selection at discounts from 30% to as much as 80% on list prices. Among the manufacturers represented are Aarlen, Alafoss of Iceland, Bernat, Bouquet, Grignasco, Hayfield, Ironstone, Jaeger, Lion Brand, Patons, Pingouin, Schachenmayr, Schaffhauser, Scheepjeswool, and Wendy. You can call or write for a price quote on goods by these firms, or inquire about knitting and crocheting yarns by other manufacturers—they may be available. Smiley's also offers a complete selection of Boye knitting and crocheting accessories at 50% off—knitting needles and crochet hooks, afghan hooks, stitch holders, etc. For samples of the current "Yarn of the Month" offering, send a long, stamped, self-addressed envelope once each month—or a dozen for the whole year. Requests without envelopes can't be honored.

Wholesale customers, inquire for terms.

Special Factors: Price quote by phone or letter with SASE; quantity discounts are available.

SOLO SLIDE FASTENERS, INC.

**P.O. BOX 378
8 SPRING BROOK RD.
FOXBOROUGH, MA 02035
800-343-9670
FAX: 800-547-4775**

Catalog: free
Save: up to 50%
Pay: check, MO, MC, V, AE
Sells: dressmaking and dry-cleaning equipment and sewing supplies
Store: mail order only

Solo Slide is a family-run business that's been supplying dressmakers, dry cleaners, tailors, and other clothing-care professionals with tools and equipment since 1954. Among the offerings in the firm's 58-page catalog are a number of items found in the "hard-to-find" sections of notions catalogs, at prices as much as 50% less.

Solo offers an extensive selection of zippers by Talon and YKK, zipper parts (slides and stops), straight pins in several sizes, snaps, hooks and eyes, machine and hand needles, buttons (dress, suit, metal, leather, etc.), thread on cones and spools, knit collars and cuffs for jackets, shoulder pads, elbow patches, belting, elastic, and other notions. Fine-quality linings, including Milium and Bemberg, are stocked, as well as pocket material. There are scissors in the most useful models from Gingher, Marks, and Wiss, pressing boards for sleeves and other specialty tasks, Qualitex pressing pads and other hams and rolls, and professional irons, pressers, and steamers by Cissell, Hi-Steam/Namoto, Rowenta, Panasonic, Spartan, and Sussman. The catalog also shows commercial/industrial sewing machines (blind stitch and lockstitch) and overlock machines by Babylock, Consew, Juki, Singer, and Tacsew. And don't miss the stain removers (including one for Magic Marker) that can save you trips to the dry cleaner.

Special Factors: Authorized, unused returns (except custom-ordered or cut goods) are accepted within 30 days for credit; minimum order is $30; C.O.D. orders are accepted.

TAYLOR'S CUTAWAYS AND STUFF

Brochure: $1
Save: up to 75%
Pay: check, MO, MC, V
Sells: cutaways and patterns
Store: mail order only

DEPT. WBMC-96
2802 E. WASHINGTON ST.
URBANA, IL 61801-4699

"Cutaways" are what's left when the pieces of a garment are cut from material. These scraps, sometimes running to a yard long, are perfect for doll clothing, piecework, quilting, and other crafts. Taylor's Cutaways, in business since 1977, offers bundles of polyesters, cottons, blends, calicos, and other assortments, as well as silk, satin, velvet, velour, felt, and fake fur cutaways. The brochure lists a wide variety of patterns and project designs for such items as draft stoppers, puppets, dolls, Teddy bears, pigs, ducks, and other animals. (Teddy bears seem to be a specialty; there are precut Teddies, mini sachet Teddies, velvet Teddies, Teddies made of cotton flannel, and Teddy bear adoption certificates sold in packs of 15.) Crocheting patterns for toys and novelties, iron-on transfer patterns, button and trim assortments, and toy eyes, joints, and squeakers are available.

The completely unskilled will appreciate Taylor's for the potpourri, already blended and scented, and the unscented dried flowers and plants, "Potpourri Magic" fixative, essential oils, and satin squares for making sachets. Prices of these and most of the other goods average 50% below comparable retail, and savings can reach as high as 75%. This seems an especially good source for anyone who makes sachets and potpourris, dolls, toys, pieced quilts, and bazaar items.

On the practical side, Taylor's sells "tea baglets," little fiber bags you fill with the tea of your choice and heat-seal with a household iron. (This is a great way to take a favorite loose tea with you when you travel.)

Wholesale customers, request the catalog on business letterhead or with your business card; minimum order is $20.

Special Factors: Quantity discounts are available.

THAI SILKS

252 STATE ST.
LOS ALTOS, CA 94022
800-722-SILK
IN CA: 800-221-SILK
415-948-8611
FAX: 415-948-3426

Brochure: free
Save: up to 50%
Pay: check, MO, MC, V, AE
Sells: silk fabric, scarves, lingerie, etc.
Store: same address; Monday to Saturday
9–5:30

¡Si! ★

Beautiful, comfortable silk is also affordable at Thai Silks, where the home sewer, decorator, and artist can save up to 50% on yardage and piece goods (compared to average retail prices). The large selection, which includes sueded silk, jacquard weaves, crepe de chine, bouclé, pongee, China silk, silk satin, raw silk, noil, silk rayon velvet, tapestry brocade, silk taffeta, prints, Dupioni silk, and upholstery weights. Hemmed white and colored silk scarves and neckties for painting and batiking, Chinese embroidered handkerchiefs, silk lingerie, kimonos, boxer shorts, pajamas, camisoles, and teddies are also available.

If you're a serious sewer or textile artist, consider joining Thai Silk's "Silk Fabric Club." For $20 a year, you'll receive four swatched mailings of new silks, and samples of closeouts. Thai Silks has been in business since 1964, and can answer your questions about fabric suitability for dyeing and specific uses.

Wholesale customers, the minimum order is 15 to 17 yards (if fabric); $100 in goods.

Special Factors: Satisfaction is guaranteed; samples are available (details are given in the brochure); authorized returns are accepted; C.O.D. orders are accepted; minimum order is 1/2 yard of fabric.

THREAD DISCOUNT SALES

10222 PARAMOUNT
 BLVD., DEPT. W
DOWNEY, CA 90241
310-928-4029
FAX: 310-928-1064

Price Sheets: free with long, stamped, self-addressed envelope
Save: up to 50%
Pay: check, MO, MC, V, AE, Discover
Sells: coned thread, sewing machines, and sergers
Store: same address; Monday to Saturday, 10–6

This firm sells machines and supplies for the serious sewer—sewing machines, sergers, overlock machines, and "coned" thread—at savings of up to 50% on list prices. Thread Discount Sales, in business since 1962, offers a batch of photocopied sheets as its catalog; they feature White and Singer sewing and overlock machines at an average 50% discount on list or original prices.

Among the coned thread available is all-purpose polyester thread, 6,000 yards of overlock at under $3 a cone in black and white ($3.49 in any of the 200 colors), and "super rayon" embroidery thread in 500-yard cones, in 500 colors, for $1.99. Most of the thread is offered in a full range of colors, which are listed by name and number (color charts are available for $1.50). In addition, Thread Discount Sales carries novelty metallics in a variety of colors, two sizes of nylon filament thread for "invisible" work, and "wooly" nylon in 200 colors at $2.99, regularly $5.99.

Please note: A shipping surcharge is imposed on orders sent to Alaska, Hawaii, Puerto Rico, and Canada.

Special Factors: Minimum order is six cones of thread (on thread orders; colors may be mixed).

UTEX TRADING ENTERPRISES

710 NINTH ST.
NIAGARA FALLS, NY 14301
716-282-4887
FAX: 716-282-8211

Price List: free with SASE
Save: up to 50%
Pay: check, MO, MC, V, AE
Sells: imported silk fabric
Store: same address; by appointment only

Utex was established in 1980 and offers textile artists, decorators, designers, and home sewers something special—over 200 weights, weaves, and widths of silk. The enormous inventory includes silk shantung, pongee, taffeta, tussah, crepe de chine, brocade, twill, habotai, peau de soie, lamé, and suiting. Most of the fabrics are 100% silk, and the price list includes a guide that recommends appropriate fabrics for specific purposes. Unprinted scarves and ties, silk thread, floss, yarns, and fine brushes and dyes for hand-painting are also stocked.

Canadian readers, please note: Utex's Canadian address is 111 Peter St., Suite 212, Toronto, Ontario, M5V 2H1; the phone number is 416-596-7565.

Utex Trading Enterprises is offering readers a discount of 10% on all orders. Be sure to identify yourself as a WBMC reader when you order, and deduct the discount from the cost of the goods only. This WBMC reader discount expires March 10, 1997.

Special Factors: Volume discounts are available; C.O.D. orders are accepted.

WEBS

DEPT. WBMC
P.O. BOX 147
NORTHAMPTON, MA
01061-0147
413-584-2225
FAX: 413-584-1603

Price Lists and Samples: $2 (see text)
Save: up to 60%
Pay: check, MO, MC, V, Discover
Sells: yarns and spinning and weaving equipment and books
Store: Service Center Rd. (half a mile off I-91), Northampton, MA; Monday to Saturday 9:30–5:30

Knitters and weavers of all types—production, hand, and machine—will find inspiration in the yarns from Webs, which has been selling natural-fiber yarn for up to 80% below the original prices since 1974. Webs' mailings offer conventional and novelty yarns of cotton, wool, linen, silk, rayon, and blends, sold in bags, coned, wound off, sometimes in balls, and in packs. (The packs come in assortments of 25, 50, and 100 pounds, at outstandingly low prices.)

Each set of samples is folded into a descriptive price sheet, which notes special considerations concerning supply, suitability for knitting or weaving, gauge, length per unit (e.g., yards per ball, cone, or pound), and prices and minimums. There are usually great buys, like mohair in choice colors, ribbon yarn in several hues, fine-quality cotton yarns in different weights and fashion colors, and all-wool rug yarn. The stock features Webs' own yarns, including mohair, rayon chenille, cottons, wools, and linens, in solid and variegated colors, as well as mill-ends, discontinued lines, and yarn overstock from such names as Berroco, Brunswick, Classic Elite, Knitting Fever, Phildar, Plymouth, and Reynolds. Savings can be boosted with an extra 20% discount if your yarn order totals $60 or more, or 25% on orders over $120. (Take note of the exceptions, marked "no further discount" or "NFD" in the price sheets.) Looms, spinning wheels, drum carders, and knitting machines are available at nondiscounted prices, although shipping is free on these items (which can be worth $25 to even $100, depending on where you live and the weight of the article).

Please note: State your craft—hand knitter, machine knitter, or weaver—when sending $2 for the price list and samples.

Special Factors: Shipping is not charged on looms, spinning wheels, drum carders, and knitting machines; quantity discounts are available; authorized returns are accepted within 30 days (a 15% restocking fee may be charged); minimum order is $20 with credit cards.

COMPANIES OUTSIDE THE UNITED STATES

The following firms are experienced in dealing with customers in the United States and Canada. They're included because they offer goods not widely available at a discount in the United States, because they have a better selection, or because they may offer the same goods at great savings.

Before ordering from any non-U.S. firm, please consult "The Complete Guide to Buying by Mail," page 583, for helpful tips. Pay for orders from foreign firms with a credit card whenever possible, so you'll have some recourse if you don't receive your order. For more information, see "The Fair Credit Billing Act," page 617.

MAURICE BRASSARD & FILS INC.

C.P. 4
PLESSISVILLE, QUEBEC
  G6L 2Y6
CANADA
819-362-2408
FAX: 819-362-2045

Catalog: $9.95 (see text)
Save: 35% average
Pay: check or IMO
Sells: weaving yarns, looms, etc.
Store: 1972 Simoneau, Plessisville, Quebec;
Monday to Friday 9–5

Maurice Brassard's catalog ($9.95) is a loose-leaf binder packed with two dozen pages of yarn samples, all neatly tied and labeled. Many of the descriptions are in French as well as English, and measurements are mixed—some are in grams, others ounces, some meters, others in feet. The prices translate into savings of 30% and more, on average.

The yarns include cotton warp in 2-8, 2-16, and 4-8, as well as bouclé, pearl cotton, polyester (2-8 and 2-16), Orlon, linen (natural, bleached, and dyed), cotton slub, Superwash wool, and a variety of novelty yarns. The color selection is superb, and the quality of the goods first-rate. Brassard also sells cloth strips for weaving, braiding, and other crafts, in cotton, nylon, acetate, and acrylic. In addition to yarn, Brassard stocks tools and equipment: cloth-cutting machines (to make strips), wool winders, and looms and accessories by Leclerc.

The catalog and ordering instructions have been written for Canadian orders, so if you're buying from the United States, call or write to get exact shipping costs *before* ordering. If you wish to review Brassard's prices before purchasing the catalog, request the price list, which is free.

Special Factors: Quantity discounts are available.

SEE ALSO

Campmor • tent zippers, Eureka yard goods, grommet kits, etc. • **SPORTS**
Derry's Sewing Center • sewing machines • **APPLIANCES**
Gohn Bros. • sewing and quilting notions and supplies • **CLOTHING**
Hancock's • quilters' fabrics, sampling club, notions, materials, etc. • **HOME: DECOR**
Homespun Fabrics & Draperies • ultra-wide cotton homespun, curtain sheers, and tow cloth • **HOME: DECOR**

Manny's Millinery Supply Co. • *millinery supplies, bridal supplies, etc.* • *CLOTHING*

Purchase for Less • *quilting and sewing books* • **BOOKS**

Sew Vac City • *sewing machines and sergers* • **APPLIANCES**

Sewin' in Vermont • *sewing machines and accessories* • **APPLIANCES**

Shama Imports, Inc. • *crewel-embroidered fabric* • **HOME: DECOR**

Suburban Sew 'N Sweep, Inc. • *sewing machines and sergers* • *APPLIANCES*

Woodcraft

Wood, tools, parts, plans, etc.

for woodworking

The ancient pleasures of working with wood—whittling, woodburning, marquetry, toy making, carving—all are honored by the firms listed here. If you enjoy making whirligigs or yard ornaments, duck decoys, wooden toy trains, or just refinishing furniture, you'll find the plans, patterns, reference works, toy parts, tools, hardware, stains, and finishes you need, at good to great prices. Related products, such as lamp parts, seat materials, clockworks, drawer organizers, and music boxes are sold by some of the firms. For listings of other companies that sell woodworking supplies and materials, see the listings in the main section of "Crafts" and "Tools."

CHERRY TREE TOYS, INC.

408 S. JEFFERSON ST.
P.O. BOX 369
BELMONT, OH 43718
614-484-4363
FAX: 614-484-4388

Catalog: $1
Save: up to 50%
Pay: check, MO, MC, V, Discover
Sells: woodworking and crafts supplies
Store: I-70, Exit 208, Belmont, OH; Monday to Saturday 9–5, Sunday 11–5

Cherry Tree Toys sells kits for delightful playthings, clocks, and door harps, as well as scores of wooden parts for your own designs. The company was founded in 1981 and prices its goods up to 50% below what toy and gift shops charge for similar items. The 68-page color catalog shows kits for dozens of whirligigs, musical banks, decorative clocks (depicting motifs ranging from trains to football helmets), door harps, wooden wagons and sleds, pull toys, miniatures, dollhouses, and "Wild West" wagons. Clock movements and markers, music boxes, and hundreds of wooden parts—wheels, spindles, smokestacks, beads, knobs, pulls, pegs, etc.—are offered as well. Cherry Tree sells plans, kits, and books on making toys, banks, dollhouses, whirligigs, clocks, and door harps, in addition to the supplies you'll need to finish the projects. See the collection of brass stencils in a range of holiday motifs, and the blank stencil sheets, Dover cut-and-use stencil sets, rubber stamps, paintbrushes and tole paint, and sets of gift tags, cards, and envelopes. If you're able, visit the factory outlet store in Belmont, where you'll find discontinued catalog items and seconds.

Special Factors: Satisfaction is guaranteed; returns are accepted within 30 days for exchange, refund, or credit; C.O.D. orders are accepted ($4.50 surcharge).

MEISEL HARDWARE SPECIALTIES

**P.O. BOX 70-MW
MOUND, MN 55364-0070
800-441-9870
FAX: 612-471-8579**

Catalog: $2
Save: up to 40%
Pay: check, MO, MC, V, Discover
Sells: hardware, wood crafts parts and plans
Store: 4310 Shoreline Dr., Spring Park, MN; Monday to Friday 9–6, Saturday 9–3

Woodworkers, toy makers, and creative souls should appreciate Meisel's 96-page color catalog of plans and project ingredients. Meisel has been in business since 1977, and prices routine items like lamp harps, wood screws, and foam brushes up to 40% below the going rate.

The catalog features woodworking plans for over 750 projects, including indoor and outdoor furniture, yard ornaments, silhouettes, toys, lamps, whirligigs, bird houses, useful things for the home, kitchen projects, and dollhouses. In addition to project plans for woodworking, there are parts and supplies for many projects, including 13 sizes of wooden wheels, Shaker pegs, dowels, plastic eyes, turned spindles, finials, wood furniture knobs, cork sheets, clock movements and parts, music boxes, and picture-hanging hardware. In addition to plans and parts, Meisel sells brass hardware, sandpaper, glues, stains, acrylic paints, and other finishing touches. The catalog is also a good source for fix-up materials—screw-hole buttons and furniture knobs, casters, magnetic cabinet catches, and furniture glides are all available.

Special Factors: Satisfaction is guaranteed; minimum order is $15 with credit cards; returns are accepted for exchange, refund, or credit.

TURNCRAFT CLOCKS, INC.

P.O. BOX 100MW
MOUND, MN 55364-0100
800-544-1711
FAX: 612-471-8579

Catalog: $2
Save: up to 30%
Pay: check, MO, MC, V, Discover
Sells: clock plans and movements
Store: 4310 Shoreline Dr., Spring Park, MN;
Monday to Friday 8–5

Clockmakers and woodworkers will enjoy Turncraft's full-color, 32-page catalog of clock plans, movements, and hardware components. Turncraft is celebrating nearly a quarter of a century of supplying home hobbyists with materials at savings of up to 30%.

You'll find over 130 clock projects in the catalog, as well as clock dials, time rings, bezels, mini-quartz movements, pendulum movements, chime and strike movements, clock hands, knobs and hinges, hangers, latches, brass decorations, weight shells, and quartz fit-ups. Paint and stains, glue, drill bits, plywood, walnut letters, numbers, and symbols are offered, making this a good source for both clockmakers and woodworkers.

Special Factors: Satisfaction is guaranteed; minimum order is $15 with credit cards.

VAN DYKE SUPPLY COMPANY

P.O. BOX 278
WOONSOCKET, SD 57385
605-796-4425

Catalog: $1
Save: up to 30%
Pay: check, MO, MC, V
Sells: restoration supplies and tools
Store: mail order only

The "Restorers" catalog from Van Dyke is 280 pages packed with the odd and innumerable things that a furniture doctor might need: moldings, veneering tools and adhesives, fiber and leather replacement seats, upholstery tools, a huge range of decorative wooden carvings and handles, and brass house and furniture hardware. Here are isinglass sheets (mica) for the wood-stove door window, bentwood chair components, an extensive selection of replacement chair and table legs, and carousel horse eyes. Van Dyke also sells Aladdin oil lamps and a wide selection of lamp parts, and shows two pages of suggested combinations of base, shade, and wiring options.

Van Dyke's offers discounts of 2% on prepaid orders of $25 or more, to 10% on orders over $1,000, and bulk pricing beyond that. But even without those discounts, the prices here are lower than those found in hardware stores and crafts shops for several of the same products, and the selection is unbeatable.

Special Factors: Satisfaction is guaranteed; returns of salable goods are accepted within 30 days; minimum order is $10.

WOODWORKER'S SUPPLY, INC.

5604 ALAMEDA PL. N.E.
ALBUQUERQUE, NM
87113
505-821-0500
FAX: 505-821-7331

Catalog: $2
Save: up to 30%
Pay: check, MO, MC, V, Discover
Sells: woodworking tools and equipment
Store: same address; Monday to Friday 8–5:30, Saturday 9–1; also 1125 Jay Ln., Graham, NC; and 1108 N. Glenn Rd., Casper, WY

Woodworker's Supply publishes a 56-page, color catalog of woodworking tools and hardware, priced up to 30% below comparable goods sold elsewhere. The company has been in business since 1972, selling basics—from abrasives to rolling table shapers—as well as a number of hard-to-find items. Typical offerings include drills (including cordless models), power screwdrivers, routers, saws (circular, jig, orbital, table, band, etc.), sanders (finish, belt, orbital, etc.), laminate trimmers, heat guns, biscuit joiners, power planes, grinders, jointers, drill presses, shapers, and other tools. The manufacturers represented include Bosch, Delta, Freud, Gerstner, Glit, Jorgensen, Porter-Cable, Ryobi, Sioux, Skil, and Woodtek, among others. Drawer slides by Alfit, Delta, and Knape & Vogt are carried, as well as Hettich hinges, coated-wire fixtures for custom kitchen cabinets, furniture and cabinet levelers, cassette storage tracks, halogen canister lights, wood project parts, veneers, butcher block, locks and latches, glue scrapers and injectors, steel wool-backed sheets for finish sanders, Preserve nontoxic wood finish, and Haas knock-down joint fasteners. A separate "Wood Finishing Supply Catalog" is packed with restoration products and finishes by Behlen, Franklin, Moser's, Old Village, Watco, and other firms. Like the best of such catalogs, Woodworker's Supply can give you as many ideas for new projects as it provides solutions to old woodworking problems.

Special Factors: Satisfaction is guaranteed; returns are accepted; minimum order is $5 ($25 to Canada).

SEE ALSO

The Bevers • wooden toy wheels, balls, etc. • **TOOLS**
BRE Lumber • cabinet-grade lumber • **HOME: IMPROVEMENT**
Metropolitan Music Co. • violin wood, stain, varnish, tools, etc. • **MUSIC**
World Abrasives Company, Inc. • abrasives of all types for wood, metal, ceramics, etc. • **TOOLS**

FARM AND GARDEN

Seeds, bulbs, live plants, supplies, tools, and equipment

The earliest mail-order catalog in this country is believed to have been a seed list, and if you're one of the nearly 70 million Americans who gardens, you probably use catalogs extensively to plan your garden. So you know that the mails (or UPS truck) can bring you a fantastic selection of bulbs, plants, flowers, herbs, and other growing things, as well as tools and equipment—often at considerable savings, compared to farm and garden centers. Choosing what to grow depends on what you want—an apple orchard, a little alyssum edging the walkways, a crop of asparagus, a windbreak at the property line—all require completely different kinds of resources. And they yield different benefits, from aesthetic (flowers) to nutritional (vegetables) to financial (market crops, property enhancement, etc.). Before you buy a single seed, make sure what you're planting is suitable for your climate or home environment. In addition to evaluating the light and drainage, test the soil. One of the best-known names in soil tests is LaMotte, which has been manufacturing soil test kits, reagents, and apparatus for analyzing water and air, as well as soil, for over 65 years. The best home gardener kit costs about $35, and a simplified version that tests just pH levels is available for about $10. The "LaMotte Soil Handbook" that comes with the kit includes a definition of soil nutrients and a "pH preference guide" for over 600 plants, shrubs, and trees. LaMotte's kits can be found in the spring and summer catalogs from Gardener's Supply, 128 Intervale Rd., Burlington, VT 05401. Gardener's Supply isn't a discounter, but offers a wealth of good and useful garden equipment and tools.

After you decide what you're going to do with your land or growing space, hit the books—horticultural literature is rich with masterworks on every aspect of the "whats" to grow and the "hows" of doing it. Hugh Johnson's *The Principles of Gardening* (Simon & Schuster, 1979), answers the "whys," giving you a grounding in the concepts and history that inform good garden planning. A bookshelf of the classics must also include Norman Taylor's *The Garden Dictionary* (updated as *The Encyclopedia of Gardening,* multi-volume) and *Taylor's Master Guide to Gardening* (Houghton Mifflin, 1994), all highly regarded references. *America's Garden Book* (New York Botanical Garden, Scribner's) and Rodale's *The Encyclopedia of Organic Gardening* are others prized for information and inspiration.

The business of preserving old plant varieties is the focus of *The Heirloom Gardener* (Sierra Club Books, 1984), by Carolyn Jabs. This wonderful guide to "living heirlooms"—endangered, rare, and nearly extinct fruit and vegetable varieties—includes a brief history of the business of seeds, information on "seed savers" and seed exchanges, finding lost varieties, capsule histories of some select heirloom varieties, seed research resources, tips on harvesting seeds, and other useful information. For information on this book and other titles, request the publications list from Sierra Club Mail-Order Service, 730 Polk St., San Francisco, CA 94109.

Kent Whealy's 422-page *Garden Seed Inventory* is something of a bible for vegetable seed savers. This book lists varieties alphabetically, describes each (height, appearance, variations, days to maturity), indicates which seed companies offer it, and also shows *how many* firms have offered that variety over the past few years—usually a declining number. The mandate is clear to seed savers: Buy, cultivate, and save those varieties! For price and ordering information on the current edition of the *Garden Seed Inventory,* send a request for the publication list with a long, self-addressed, stamped envelope to Seed Savers Exchange, RR 3, Box 239, Decorah, IA 52101.

If you're planning a "kitchen garden" that will yield enough to can, get the latest information and food-safety advice in *The Ball Blue Book,* the guide published by the folks who make canning jars and lids. In its 32nd edition, the book is so authoritative that it's recommended by the FDA. To receive a copy of the *Blue Book,* send $3.50 plus $1 for shipping and handling to Direct Marketing, P.O. Box 2005, Muncie, IN 47307. In addition to the books mentioned here, don't overlook the helpful consumer guides and how-to manuals published by HP Books, Ortho, and Sunset.

If you need farm machinery, see the listing of Central Michigan Tractor & Parts in "Auto." In addition to the Department of Agriculture publications, university cooperative extensions also disseminate technical information of use to farmers and production growers. Among those in the "Small Farms Series," published by the Northeast Regional Agricultural Engineering Service, the 34-page *Used Farm Equipment: Assessing Quality, Safety, and Economics* is a clear and well-illustrated overview of points to consider before making such a purchase. Write to Northeast Regional Agricultural Engineering Service, Cornell University, 152 Riley-Robb Hall, Ithaca, NY 14853 for a list of current publications and prices.

The U.S. government operates an information clearinghouse staffed by agricultural pros who can advise you on technical matters, including how to go organic ("sustainable agriculture" is part of the agency's mandate). Please try other sources, including your local extension agent, before calling; if you can't get help or adequate information, call ATTRA (Appropriate Technology Transfer for Rural Areas), at 800-346-9140, Monday to Friday, 8–5 CST.

If you're building your own greenhouse or cold frames, see Arctic Glass & Window Outlet ("Home: Improvement") for thermopane panels. Other garden-related products are sold by some of the companies listed in "Tools." And see the companies listed in the "Find It Fast" section of the "Home: Furnishings" chapter for lawn and patio furniture.

FIND IT FAST

BULBS, SEEDS, PLANTS • **Breck's, Butterbrooke, Caprilands, Carino, Dutch Gardens, Le Jardin, Mellinger's, J.E. Miller, Pinetree Garden, Scheepers, Sharp Bros., R.H. Shumway, Spring Hill, Van Bourgondien, Van Dyck's, Van Engelen**
DAYLILIES • **Daylily Discounters**
GREENHOUSES AND SUPPLIES • **Bob's Superstrong, Mellinger's, Turner**
PLANT MARKERS • **EON Industries**
ROSES • **Jackson & Perkins, Nor'East**
STRAWBERRIES • **Brittingham**

BOB'S SUPERSTRONG GREENHOUSE PLASTIC

BOX 42-WM
NECHE, ND 58265
204-327-5540

Brochure: $1 or two first-class stamps
Save: up to 40%
Pay: check or MO
Sells: greenhouse plastic and fastening systems
Store: same address; by appointment

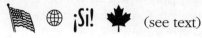 (see text)

Bob Davis and his wife, Margaret Smith-Davis, are resourceful gardeners who experimented with different materials while trying to create an inexpensive greenhouse and discovered that woven polyethylene makes an ideal greenhouse skin, even in harsh climes. Their experiences with the material were so successful that they decided to market it themselves. Their 14-year-old business, Bob's Superstrong Greenhouse Plastic (also known as Northern Greenhouse Sales), is a great source for other innovative gardeners who want to design their own greenhouses. They offer "superstrong" woven poly and two anchoring systems. One is "Cinchstrap," a bright-white, flat, flexible poly strapping material that can be used for permanent anchoring, abrasion reduction in installation, and as a replacement for wood lathing in greenhouse assembly. The other, "Poly-Fastener," is a channel-system anchor that uses a flat spline to secure the poly. Prices for the woven poly run from 16¢ to 25¢ per square foot, depending on the quantity ordered; the standard width is ten feet, but Bob can heat-seal additional widths together to create a wider swath. The Poly-Fastener runs between 53¢ and 58¢ a linear foot in 300' and 100' rolls (or $1 per foot for cut pieces), and the Cinchstrap costs 11¢ a linear foot on 100' rolls.

The 32-page catalog details several money-saving ideas to help further your savings, and stories from other customers show how they solved different design problems. The poly applications aren't limited to greenhouses: solar collectors, vapor barriers, storm windows, pool covers, and tent floors are other possibilities. Send $1 or two first-class stamps—or phone—for the informative catalog, which also offers water distillers for home use. Call if you have questions; please note the phone hours, below.

Canadian readers, please note: Write to Box 1450WM, Altona, Manitoba R0G 0B0, for literature.

Special Factors: Calls are taken daily between 6 A.M. and 8 P.M., CST; minimum order is $1; C.O.D. orders are accepted.

BRECK'S DUTCH BULBS

Catalog: free
Save: up to 50%
Pay: check, MO, MC, V, AE, Discover
Sells: Dutch flower bulbs
Store: mail order only

DEPT. CA9815A4
U.S. RESERVATION
  CENTER
6523 N. GALENA RD.
PEORIA, IL 61632
309-691-4616
FAX: 309-691-2632

Breck's has been "serving American gardeners since 1818" with a fine selection of flower bulbs, imported directly from Holland. The 52-page catalog is bursting with tulips, crocuses, daffodils, hyacinths, irises, jonquils, anemones, and wind flowers. Blooming period, height, color and markings, petal formation, and scent are all described in the text. Each order is shipped with the Breck's "Dutch Bulb Handbook," which covers naturalizing, planting, indoor growing, bulb care, and related topics. Discounts of up to 50% are offered on orders placed by July 31 for fall delivery and planting, and there are special savings on "samplers" and bulb collections.

Special Factors: Satisfaction is guaranteed; early-order discounts are available; returns are accepted for exchange, replacement, or refund.

BRITTINGHAM PLANT FARM, INC.

Catalog: free
Save: up to 75% (see text)
Pay: check, MO, MC, V
Sells: berry plants
Store: Rte. 346 and Phillip Morris Dr., Salisbury, MD; Monday to Friday 8–4:30, Saturday 8:30–12

DEPT. WBM5
P.O. BOX 2538
SALISBURY, MD 21802
410-749-5153
FAX: 410-749-5148

Brittingham, a family business established in 1945, specializes in berries. The firm's 32-page color catalog is packed with cultivation tips and handling guidelines, and details on Brittingham's participation in Maryland's strawberry certification program. (The strict standards assure you virus-free strawberry plants.) Strawberries dominate the offerings, with over two dozen varieties in the current catalog, for early through late yields. Prices begin at $9.25 for 25 plants, and top at $74.50 for 50,000 plants (you may mix up to five varieties; more expensive and patented varieties cost more). In addition to strawberries, Brittingham sells blackberries, raspberries, grapes, blueberries, asparagus, and rhubarb; quantity pricing also applies to these offerings.

Please note: Plants are not shipped to AK, CA, HI, NM, Canada, Mexico, or outside the continental United States.

Special Factors: Satisfaction is guaranteed; replacements, refunds, or credits are offered within a specified date (see catalog); minimum orders vary, depending on the item; C.O.D. orders are accepted.

BUTTERBROOKE FARM SEED CO-OP

78 BARRY RD.
OXFORD, CT 06478-1529
203-888-2000

Price List: free with long, self-addressed, stamped envelope
Save: up to 75%
Pay: check or MO
Sells: seeds
Store: mail order only

"Only pure, open-pollinated seeds will produce plants from which you can save seeds for planting another year." So says the straightforward price list from Butterbrooke Farm Seed Co-Op, where becoming "seed self-reliant" is one of several gardening objectives. Butterbrooke's members include organic farmers and seed savers, and the co-op has been in business since 1978. For just $12.50 per year, co-op members receive a 33% seed order discount, the quarterly Farm newsletter, "Germinations," advisory services, the opportunity to buy rare or heirloom seeds, and other benefits. This is no-frills gardening at its sensible best, from the selection of scores of seeds (a well-rounded kitchen-garden full) to the Farm's own "Home Garden Collection" for first-time planters—a group of vegetable favorites. The packets are measured to reduce waste: the standard size (65¢) will plant one to two 20-foot rows, and the large size ($1.50), three to four times that. All of the seeds are fresh, and they've been selected for short growing seasons. Butterbrooke also offers booklets on related topics—composting, making mulch, saving seeds—at nominal sums. You don't have to be a co-op member to buy from Butterbrooke, but the price of membership is low and the advice service alone should justify the expense.

Special Factors: C.O.D. orders are accepted.

CAPRILANDS HERB FARM

534 SILVER ST.
COVENTRY, CT 06238
203-742-7244

Brochure: free
Save: see text
Pay: check, MO, MC, V
Sells: live herbs and gifts
Store: same address; daily 9–5 except holidays

 (see text)

Caprilands offers live and dried culinary and medicinal herbs and a potpourri of herbaceous gifts, seasonings, and rite materials. The Farm is run by Mrs. Simmons, a herbalist of sixty years' standing, who provides a legendary luncheon program for visitors to her 18th-century farmhouse. (Reservations are essential; details on the program are given in the brochure.) In the years since its founding in 1929, Caprilands has become a respected source among collectors of hard-to-find herbs and those who dabble in "natural magic." Over 300 kinds of standard culinary herbs and less common plants are available, including Egyptian onions, rue, wormwood, mugwort, monardas, artemisia, santolinas, germander, lamb's ears, nepetas, ajuga, chamomile, woodruff, and many varieties of thyme ($2 to $3 per plant). Scented geraniums, roses, and flowers are also offered. (The plants are available at the Farm only, not by mail.) Packets of seeds for herbs and herbal flowers are available by mail for $1 each. Mrs. Simmons' own guides to the cultivation and use of herbs, including one of the bibles of herbal horticulture—*Herb Gardening in Five Seasons*—are sold through the brochure.

Caprilands offers a marvelous array of related goods: bronze sundials, wooden "good luck crows" for the garden, kitchen witches and costumed collectors' dolls, pomanders and sachet pillows, spice necklaces, wreaths, herbal hot pads, stoneware, note paper and calendars, and much more. Amid this olfactory plenty are two other great buys—rose petals and buds and lavender flowers for $12 per pound, compared to $15 and $22 in other catalogs; essential oils are also sold.

Wholesale customers, books *alone* are sold at wholesale, with a minimum order of 6 or 12 of the same title, discounted 10% to 40%.

Special Factors: Certain goods listed in the catalog are available only at the Farm.

CARINO NURSERIES

DEPT. WBMC
P.O. BOX 538
INDIANA, PA 15701
800-223-7075
FAX: 412-463-3050

Catalog: free
Save: up to 65%
Pay: check, MO, MC, V
Sells: evergreen seedlings and transplants
Store: mail order only

Carino Nurseries has been supplying Christmas tree farmers, nursery owners, and other planters with evergreen seedlings since 1947, and its prices and selection are excellent—savings of 60% are routine. The 36-page color catalog lists varieties of pine (Scotch, white, Mugho, Ponderosa, Japanese black, American red, and Austrian), fir (Douglas, Balsam, Canaan, Fraser, and Concolor), spruce (Colorado blue, white, Englemann, Black Hills, Norwegian, and Serbian), and white birch, dogwood, olive, black walnut, Chinese chestnut, Canadian hemlock, arborvitae, and other deciduous shrubs and trees.

Each 32-page color catalog entry includes a description of the variety, age, and approximate height of the plants, and the number of years spent in original and transplant beds. There are specials on ten-plant collections, but most of the seedlings are sold in lots of 100 at prices up to 65% below those of other nurseries. If you're buying 500 or more, Carino's prices drop 50%. Recommendations on selecting, planting, and shearing (for later harvest as Christmas trees) are given, and the shipping methods and schedule policies are detailed in the catalog as well.

Special Factors: Shipments are made by UPS; minimum order is 10 or 100 plants (see text).

DAYLILY DISCOUNTERS INTERNATIONAL

Catalog: $2
Save: up to 30% (see text)
Pay: check, MO, MC, V, AE, Discover
Sells: daylilies
Store: mail order only

RTE. 2, BOX 24
ALACHUA, FL 32615
904-462-1539
FAX: 904-462-5111

If you think that there are three kinds of daylilies—orange, yellow, and pink-and-white—Daylily Discounters will enlighten you. Between the voluminous text and the color photos, the firm's catalog covers 96 pages and includes details on the plant anatomy (including bracts and scopes), cultivation and disposal, and the hundreds of flowers themselves, from Agape Love to Yellow Lollipop. Companion perennials are available, as well as soil enrichers, plant tags, and reference books. If you're not familiar with daylilies, you'll find them quite varied in color, markings, and formation; many bear a resemblance to orchids, but they're much less tricky to cultivate. Daylilies are less expensive, and more modestly priced yet at Daylily Discounters. And once you're on the mailing list, watch for flyers on clearance sales, with further savings of up to 50%.

Non-U.S. readers, please note: Before ordering, obtain import permits (if required), as indicated in the catalog.

Special Factors: Quantity discounts are available; minimum order is $25.

DUTCH GARDENS, INC.

Catalog: free
Save: 30% average (see text)
Pay: check, MO, MC, V, AE
Sells: Dutch flower bulbs
Store: mail order only

DEPT. WMC6
P.O. BOX 200
ADELPHIA, NJ 07710
908-780-2713
FAX: 908-780-7720

Dutch Gardens publishes one of the most beautiful bulb catalogs around—over 175 color pages of breathtaking flower "head shots" that approximate perfection. Dutch Gardens has been in business since 1961, and its prices on flower bulbs are solidly below other mail-order firms and garden supply houses—30% less on average, and up to 50% on some bulbs and collections.

The fall planting catalog offers tulip, hyacinth, daffodil, narcissus, crocus, anemone, iris, snowdrop, allium, amaryllis, and other flower bulbs. The tulip selection alone includes single, double, fringed, parrot, lily, and peony types. The spring planting catalog showcases a dazzling array of lilies, begonias, dahlias, gladioli, peonies, tuberoses, anemones, freesia, hostas, and other flowers, and onions and shallots (for planting) are also available. Each Dutch Gardens catalog lists the size of the bulbs and the common and botanical names, height, planting zones, blooming period, and appropriate growing situations of each variety. A zone chart, guide to planting depth and bulb grouping, sun requirements, hints on naturalizing, rock gardening, terrace planting, indoor growing, and forcing are included.

Special Factors: Bulbs are guaranteed to bloom (conditions are stated in the catalog); bulb bonuses or discounts are available on quantity orders; shipping is not charged on orders over $40; minimum order is $20.

EON INDUSTRIES

107 W. MAPLE
P.O. BOX 11
LIBERTY CENTER, OH
  43532
419-533-4961

Brochure: free
Save: 35%-plus
Pay: check or MO
Sells: plant markers
Store: mail order only

EON Industries specializes in a useful garden item: metal plant markers. EON has been manufacturing markers since 1936, and currently offers four styles, at prices that begin at under $20 (plus shipping) for 100 10" Rose markers and run up to $29 per hundred (plus shipping) for the 20" Nursery style. (Volume pricing is available on large orders; inquire.) The markers create the impression of serious horticultural doings when staked among even common specimens, which is why upmarket garden catalogs carry them—at nearly twice the price!

Wholesale buyers, please send your inquiry on wholesale pricing on company letterhead, or fax to 419-533-6015.

Special Factors: Satisfaction is guaranteed.

FRED'S PLANT FARM

DEPT. WBMC
P.O. BOX 707
DRESDEN, TN 38225-0707
800-243-9377
901-364-5419
FAX: 901-364-3322

Catalog: free
Save: up to 50%
Pay: check, MO, MC, V, Discover
Sells: sweet potato plants and tobacco products
Shop (bonded warehouse): Hwy. 89 South, Rte. 1, Dresden, TN; Monday to Friday 8–5

Mr. Fred "Famous Since 1940" Stoker presides over "Fred's Plant Farm," which sells eight varieties of yams and sweet potato plants, with names like "Beauregard," "Oklahoma Reds," and "Jewell." The plant slips are well-priced—$50 per 1,000 plants in early spring, and from $15 per 50 plants to $400 for 10,000 later in the year. Mr. Stoker estimates typical local yields at an average of 300 bushels an acre, but much depends on the quality of the farming. The "Growers Guide" that accompanies your order gives detailed instructions on handling the slips, planting, cultivating the soil, harvesting, and storage of your crop, so it's well worth studying before you put spade to earth.

Mr. Stoker also sells an extensive line of tobacco—chewing, smoking, twists, and snuffing—at prices up to 50% below the branded versions. Be sure to specify whether you want the "sweet potato" or 40-page "tobacco" catalog when requesting information.

Special Factors: Inquire for information on quantity discounts; shipping is not charged; plants are shipped April 15 to July 1.

LE JARDIN DU GOURMET

P.O. BOX 75-WC
ST. JOHNSBURY CENTER,
  VT 05863
802-748-1446
FAX: 802-748-9592

Catalog: 50¢
Save: up to 50% (see text)
Pay: check, MO, MC, V
Sells: seeds, plants, and gourmet foods
Store: mail order only

   (see text)

If you like to cook, and if you have even a small patch of land on which you can grow things, you'll appreciate Le Jardin du Gourmet. Founded by a transplanted New York City chef who developed a business from growing his own shallots, Le Jardin is now run by his daughter and her husband. They share his appreciation of fine food—chestnut spread, chutney, fancy mustards, and Pompadour herbal teas are a few of the catalog offerings. The prices of some of these food items are very good, but the firm is listed here for one of the last great mail-order buys—the 25¢ seed packet.

Le Jardin du Gourmet sells seeds for hundreds of herbs, vegetables, peas, beans, and even some flowers: angelica, bok choi, pennyroyal, milk thistle, kohlrabi, dwarf corn, French endive, mache, salsify, German "beer garden" radishes, African pumpkins, Vidalia onions, fava beans, and forget-me-nots are all here. The 16-page catalog has a few line drawings and horticultural tips, as well as a recipe for scotched chestnut-bacon appetizers and a guide to making popcorn-on-the-cob in a microwave oven. If you're a novice gardener, invest a few quarters and test a number of "sample" packs of seeds, or play it safe with the live herbs and perennials also available from Le Jardin. The plants are sold in 2-1/4" pots, and suggestions for herb use and growth conditions are given in the catalog. Don't overlook the books on herbs and preserving food (canning, pickling, etc.), and good prices on plain and decorated balsam wreaths, roping, and small cut trees at Christmastime.

Canadian readers, please note: Only U.S. funds are accepted, and plants and bulbs are *not* shipped to Canada.

Special Factors: Minimum order is $15 with credit cards.

JACKSON & PERKINS

1 ROSE LANE, DEPT. 85B
MEDFORD, OR 97501
800-854-6200
FAX: 800-242-0329
TDD: 800-348-3222

Catalog: free
Save: up to 50%
Pay: check, MO, MC, V, AE, Discover
Sells: roses, bulbs, perennials, gifts, etc.
Store: mail order only

¡Si!

The subject is roses at Jackson & Perkins, which has been supplying gardeners nationwide since 1872. The horticultural classic absorbs three-fourths of the 60-page catalog—from miniatures and patio roses to classic hybrid teas, floribundas, and grandifloras. Jackson & Perkins is prominent in variety development, and has taken a number of "rose of the year" awards from All-American Rose Selections, an independent organization that ranks entries on how well they grow in diverse settings (they're tested in gardens all over the country).

Unlike many other catalogs, Jackson & Perkins notes the type of fragrance and the bud shapes of the roses, as well as plant height range, blossom size, number of petals, color, variety, patent notes, awards, and other data. In addition to a stunning collection of hybrid tea roses, Jackson & Perkins sells classic and striated floribundas, grandifloras, hedge roses, tree roses, patio roses (2" to 4" tall), and climbers. There are roses selected for their fragrance, exhibition roses, varieties from Germany and Denmark, David Austin's English roses, bush roses, and miniatures. And there are collections of favorites of each type, which are offered at extra savings.

Jackson & Perkins also sells daylilies and hybrid lilies, "garden classics"—hydrangeas, phlox, wisteria, lavender, astilbes, etc.—and begonias, ranunculus, and more. The catalog is peppered throughout with sundials, books, bronze garden plaques, trellises, and cast stone sculptures. And "The Basics," a guide to determining what you can plant in your area and how to space your roses, can be found with the order form. Follow the planting directions, and you should enjoy show-worthy roses—your gardening success is guaranteed!

Special Factors: Satisfaction is guaranteed; returns are accepted for exchange, refund, or credit.

MELLINGER'S INC.

DEPT. WBMC
WEST SOUTH RANGE RD.
NORTH LIMA, OH
  44452-9731
216-549-9861
FAX: 216-549-3716

Catalog: free
Save: up to 45%
Pay: check, MO, MC, V, Discover
Sells: seeds, bulbs, live plants, and home and garden supplies
Store: same address; Monday to Saturday 8:30–5 (June 16 to April); 8–6 (April to June 15)

Mellinger's publishes "the garden catalog for year-round country living," 112 pages of seeds, bulbs, live plants, reference books, greenhouses, garden supplies, and tools. Mellinger's, in business since 1927, has outstandingly low prices on some items, and nominal savings on others. The offerings include flower seeds and bulbs, potted trees and shrubs, shade tree and evergreen seedlings, herb plants, fruit trees, vegetable seeds and vines, tropical plants, and seeds for rare and unusual plants. Everything you'll need for successful cultivation is available, from seed flats to greenhouses. You'll find insect and animal repellents, plant fertilizers, soil additives, pruning and grafting tools, spades, cultivators, hoes, seeders, watering systems, cold frames, starter pots, planters and flower boxes, and related goods. In addition to chemical fungicides and insecticides, Mellinger's sells ladybugs, praying mantis egg cases, and other "natural" predators and beneficial parasites. Bird feeders and seed are also stocked.

Mellinger's stocks poly-skin greenhouses in small and commercial sizes, polyethylene (by the foot), and ventilation equipment, heaters, and thermostats. Books on topics from plant propagation and insect control to herbs and cooking are also available. The catalog includes a guide to hardiness zones, and a statement of the terms of the warranty covering plant orders.

Special Factors: Plants are warrantied for one year (see the catalog for terms); authorized returns are accepted (a 10% restocking fee may be charged); minimum order is $10 with credit cards.

J.E. MILLER NURSERIES, INC.

DEPT. WBM 5060 WEST LAKE RD.
CANANDAIGUA, NY 14424
800-836-9630
716-396-2647
FAX: 716-396-2154

Catalog: free
Save: up to 50%
Pay: check, MO, MC, V, AE, Discover
Sells: plants, shrubs, trees, and nursery stock
Store: same address; Monday to Friday 8–4:30 (daily during the spring)

Miller's spring and fall catalogs offer a full range of plants, seeds, bulbs, shrubs, and trees, at savings of up to 50%, compared to prices charged at garden centers. Miller Nurseries has been in business since 1936, and features a fall selection that includes russet apple, golden plum, grapes (including seedless varieties), red raspberry, blueberry, cherry, strawberry, and dozens of other fruit and nut trees, plants, and vines. Shade trees are offered, including poplar, locust, maple, and ash; and there are ornamental grasses and plants for the vegetable garden and some common flower bulbs as well. Garden supplies and equipment, including pruners, animal repellent, soil additives, wheelbarrows, mulch sheeting, etc., are also offered. The 64-page catalog includes horticultural tips, and each order is sent with Miller's 32-page planting guide. This firm has gotten rave reviews from several readers of this book, who've praised Miller's service and prices.

Please note: Orders are shipped to U.S. addresses only (not APO/FPO).

Special Factors: Trees and shrubs are sent as plants, guaranteed to grow; minimum order is $10 with credit cards.

NOR'EAST MINIATURE ROSES, INC.

P.O. BOX 307-WB
ROWLEY, MA 01969
508-948-7964
FAX: 508-948-5487

Catalog: free
Save: up to 30%
Pay: check, MO, MC, V
Sells: miniature roses
Store: 58 Hammond St., Rowley, MA; also
955 West Phillips St., Ontario, CA; Monday
to Friday 8–4, both locations

Nor'East publishes a 16-page catalog of its specialty, miniature roses, which are priced at $4.95 each, compared to over $7 for the same varieties sold elsewhere. (Nor'East doesn't tack on a per-plant handling fee, as does some of the competition.) Dozens of types of miniature bush roses are available, including micro-minis (4" to 8" tall at maturity), climbers, and tree roses (miniatures budded to understocks). The varieties are grouped by colors, which include reds, pinks, yellows, oranges, apricots, whites, mauves, and blends. Among the fancifully named specimens are old favorites and new entries: Good Morning America, Cupcake, Party Girl, Fireworks, and Ice Queen, to name a few. The catalog descriptions include height of the mature plant, blooming pattern and coloring, scent, suitable growth situations, and other information.

Nor'East offers quantity discounts and specially priced bonuses for large orders. "We pick 'em" collections are also offered—prices drop to $3.79 per plant if you let the firm make the selection. Nor'East offers other collections, including easy-to-cultivate choices, fragrant types, and a beginners' kit that includes pots and potting mix. Planting and care directions are sent with each order. And a selection of small vases and Sean McCann's book on miniature roses are available.

Special Factors: Returns of plants that fail to perform are accepted within 90 days for replacement; minimum order is $20 with credit cards.

PINETREE GARDEN SEEDS

Catalog: free
Save: up to 35%
Pay: check, MO, MC, V, AE, Discover
Sells: seeds, bulbs, plants, garden equipment, and books
Store: mail order only

P.O. BOX 300
NEW GLOUCESTER, ME
04260
207-926-3400
FAX: 207-926-3886

Pinetree Garden Seeds was established in 1979 to provide home gardeners with seeds in small packets, suitable for backyard gardens or horticultural experiments. The firm has far exceeded this mandate, with a 152-page catalog packed with well-chosen kitchen gadgets, gardening tools and supplies, books and other useful goods. But Pinetree's strength is the stock that built the business—over 700 varieties of vegetable and flower seeds, just a handful of which are treated. Of special interest are the "vegetable favorites from around the world," including radicchio, fava beans, snow peas, entsai, burdock, flageolet, cardoons, epazotes, and chiles. You'll also find plants and tubers for shallots, asparagus, berries, and potatoes. The flower section features seeds, tubers, and bulbs for annuals, perennials, everlastings, and wildflowers.

The tools and equipment run from kitchen and canning helps to hand tools. Fertilizers, Havahart traps, netting, and related goods are offered. Over 30 pages of the catalog are devoted to books, including a number of gardening literature classics, cookbooks, garden planners, and many other well-priced titles. Prices are quite competitive, and even the seed packets are backed by Pinetree's ironclad guarantee of satisfaction.

Canadian and non-U.S. readers, please note: The catalog costs U.S. $1.50 if sent to a non-U.S. address.

Special Factors: Satisfaction is guaranteed; returns are accepted for exchange, refund, or credit.

PRENTISS COURT GROUND COVERS

Brochure: $1
Save: up to 50%
Pay: check, MO, MC, V
Sells: live ground-cover plants
Store: mail order only

DEPT. WBM
P.O. BOX 8662
GREENVILLE, SC
29604-8662
803-277-4037

Prentiss Court, in business since 1978, offers a wide range of plants at up to 50% below nursery prices, and gives spacing and planting guides in the brochure. The current crop includes varieties of Cotoneaster, crown vetch, daylilies, Euonymus fortunei, fig vine, Hedera canariensis and helix, honeysuckle, hosta, jasmine, hypericum, Ophiopogon japonicus, Pachysandra terminalis, Parthenocissus, Trumpet creeper, and Vinca major and minor. In English, there are over 70 kinds of plants, including many types of ivy and flowering and berry-bearing ground cover. The plants are sold bare-root and/or potted, at prices that run from 41¢ for "Green Muscari," a liriope, to $5.70 for a large-blossomed hosta; most are under $1.

Ground cover provides an attractive, labor-efficient alternative to a conventional lawn—which may have to be "limed, aerated, re-seeded, fertilized, weed-treated, mowed, and raked," to quote the admittedly partisan but accurate president of Prentiss Court. Ground cover, on the other hand, should be mulched, not fertilized, and it seems to discourage weeds and pests all by itself. Follow the soil and light guidelines when selecting and planting, and you should be able to enjoy lush, low-maintenance grounds *without* chemical intervention.

Special Factors: Minimum order is 50 plants of the same variety.

JOHN SCHEEPERS, INC.

DEPT. WBM
P.O. BOX 700
BANTAM, CT 06750
203-567-0838
FAX: 203-567-5323

Catalog: free
Save: up to 30%
Pay: check, MO, MC, V, Discover
Sells: Dutch flower bulbs
Store: mail order only

John Scheepers has been in business since 1910, serving gardeners with premium, exhibition-quality Dutch bulbs of cultivated stock, at very good prices. Scheepers is affiliated with Van Engelen, which offers wholesale pricing on large orders (see that listing if you buy in 100-bulb lots). Scheepers' own prices are lower than market price, but the bulbs themselves—and the plants and blossoms—are significantly bigger.

The 48-page color catalog from Scheepers is heavy on tulips and narcissi: early-flowering Fosterianas, tulips from Asia Minor, trumpet narcissi, peony-like tulips, Giant Darwins, parrot tulips, and more. Like Van Engelen, Scheepers has a good selection of crocus, allium, fritillaria, iris, lilies, and other spring flower bulbs, as well as a number for shady, woodsy areas, and for holiday forcing. Bulb food, gifts, and books are available, and cultivating instructions are packed with each order. Most of the bulbs are sold in lots of ten, and the per-bulb price drops the more you order. The sales policy is similar to Van Engelen's, except the minimum order is just $25.

Wholesale customers, please call or write about placing large orders.

Special Factors: Quantity discounts are available; minimum order is $25.

SHARP BROS.
SEED CO.

396 SW DAVIS ST.-LADUE
CLINTON, MO 64735-9058
800-451-3779

Catalog: $1, refundable
Save: up to 30%
Pay: check, MO, MC, V
Sells: grasses, legumes, and wildflowers
Store: mail order only

Sharp Bros. sells the fruit of the plains—bluegrass and other grasses, prairie wildflowers, legumes, and other field crops. The "Catalog of Grasses, Legumes, Lawn Grasses, and Field Seeds" lists warm-season grasses by common name, with complete data on habit, color, preferred soil type, exposure, and other characteristics, and as many cold-season grasses. Some of the grasses are suited to forage, others erosion control, and general ground cover. Sharp Bros. also sells legumes, lawn grasses, certified field crops—soybeans, wheat, oats, barley, etc.—all under the Buffalo Brand label. You have to be familiar with the grasses to best use the catalog, but Sharp serves all kinds of buyers—"backyard gardeners," farmers, ranchers, conservation agencies, and prairie restoration groups, among others.

Special Factors: Quantity discounts are available; minimum order is one ounce of seed.

R.H. SHUMWAY
SEEDSMAN

P.O. BOX I-WH
GRANITEVILLE, SC 29829
803-663-9771
FAX: 803-663-9772

Catalog: free
Save: up to 50%
Pay: check, MO, MC, V, Discover
Sells: seeds, bulbs, and nursery stock
Store: Graniteville, SC; Monday to Friday 8:30–4 (open Saturday 8:30–1 in spring season only)

   (see text)

"Good Seeds Cheap" declares the cover of R.H. Shumway's catalog, which is full of old-fashioned *engravings* of flowers, fruits, and vegetables—there's not a photograph in sight. Shumway has been "The Pioneer American Seedsman" since 1870, and is notable for the number of old, open-pollinated seeds it carries, as well as new varieties.

The 64-page catalog features spring flower bulbs, many pages of berries, vines, beans, vegetable seeds, corn, onions, squash, tomatoes, and Shumway specialties—lawn grasses, grasses for pasturage and hay, millet and other "forage" seed, sorghums, Sudan grasses, clover, legumes, and alfalfa. Another specialty catalog, "Totally Tomatoes," offers over 300 varieties of tomato and pepper seeds, together with all of the supplies you'll need to grow America's favorite crop, at savings of 30% to 40%. Shumway offers over a dozen types of ornamental gourds—dishcloth gourds, small spoon, bird bone, dipper, bottle, and more. Herb seeds are available, for both culinary and ornamental plants—angelica, coriander, shiso, burnet, pyrethrum, upland cress, and cardoon, as well as the spice rack standards. Market gardeners and other small commercial growers should check Shumway's wholesale prices on bulk seed orders, or get together with gardener friends and combine orders to take advantage of the bulk pricing. Special offers and bonuses are sprinkled liberally throughout the catalog, which also offers a small selection of well-priced garden helpers.

Wholesale customers, the 124-page "HPS" catalog offers wholesale prices on flower and vegetable seeds to greenhouse growers and nursery operators. (Request this catalog by name on company letterhead.)

Special Factors: Satisfaction is guaranteed; quantity discounts are available; returns are accepted within 90 days for exchange or replacement; C.O.D. orders are accepted; minimum order is $15 with credit cards.

SPRING HILL NURSERIES

DEPT. NA9816A3
6523 N. GALENA RD.
PEORIA, IL 61632
309-691-4616
FAX: 309-691-2632

Catalog: free
Save: up to 50%
Pay: check, MO, MC, V, AE, Discover
Sells: flowers, bulbs, and shrubs
Store: mail order only

Spring Hill's parent company has been in business since 1849, supplying gardeners across the nation with plants and bulbs at discount prices. The 48-page color catalog is heavy on flower classics—irises, peonies, daffodils, carnations, hydrangeas, daylilies, phlox, and more—as well as ground cover, hostas, ferns, and other perennials. The descriptions include planting guidelines, mature size and characteristics, and site recommendations. Everything Spring Hill sells is backed by the firm's no-quibble guarantee of satisfaction, and the prices are good: specials on collections and quantity discounts bring the savings to as much as 50%, compared to typical nursery stock prices.

Special Factors: Satisfaction is guaranteed; quantity discounts are available.

TURNER GREEN-HOUSES

DEPT. 131

P.O. BOX 1260

GOLDSBORO, NC

27533-1260

800-672-4770, EXT. 131

FAX: 919-736-4550

Catalog: free
Save: up to 35%
Pay: check, MO, MC, V
Sells: greenhouses and accessories
Store: mail order only

Turner Equipment Company was founded in 1939, and has been producing greenhouses since 1957. Turner currently offers three basic series with a choice of options, or a total of 46 models. Prices average 25% less than the competition, and similar greenhouses in other catalogs sell for 35% more.

The three series include a 7'-wide lean-to, and two freestanding lines, 8' and 14' wide. Each greenhouse comes equipped with a ventilating system and aluminum storm door, and can be expanded lengthwise in four-foot increments. You can choose from a 6-mil polyethylene cover or fiberglass (warrantied for 20 years). Turner also sells electric and gas heaters, exhaust fans and air circulators, cooling units, greenhouse benches, thermometers, misters, and sprayers. In addition, the 20-page color catalog features well-chosen books on composting, organic gardening, greenhouse growing, herb cultivation, and related topics.

Special Factors: Satisfaction is guaranteed; authorized returns in original condition are accepted within 30 days for refund or credit (less freight); minimum order is $10.

VAN BOURGONDIEN BROS.

Catalog: free
Save: up to 40%
Pay: check, MO, MC, V, AE, Discover
Sells: flower bulbs and perennials
Store: mail order only

P.O. BOX 1000
BABYLON, NY 11702
800-622-9997
FAX: 516-669-1228

The 72-page spring and fall catalogs from Van Bourgondien offer a wealth of growing things for home, lawn, and garden at up to 40% less than other suppliers. Van Bourgondien was founded in 1919, and offers early-order discounts, bonuses, and specials on collections.

Both of the catalogs feature hosta and hybrid lilies, ground covers, and a wide range of flowers. Past fall issues have shown tulip, daffodil, hyacinth, iris, crocus, narcissus, anemone, allium, fritillaria, and other bulbs. Geraniums, delphiniums, shasta daisies, tiger lilies, lavender, flowering house plants, foxtails, black-eyed Susans, native ferns, and other greenery and flowers are usually offered. If you can't wait for the thaw, you can buy prepotted lilies of the valley, Aztec lily, paperwhites, amaryllis varieties, and crocus bulbs, all of which can be forced. The spring catalogs feature begonias, gladiolus, dahlias, caladiums, perennials, ferns, cannas, ground cover, and similar goods. Bulb planters and plant supplements are offered as well, and orders are shipped to the 48 contiguous United States.

Special Factors: Goods are guaranteed to be "as described" and to be delivered in perfect condition; quantity discounts are available.

VAN DYCK'S FLOWER FARMS, INC.

Catalog: free
Save: up to 50% (see text)
Pay: check, MO, MC, V, AE, Discover
Sells: Dutch flower bulbs
Store: mail order only

P.O. BOX 430
BRIGHTWATERS, NY
11718-0430
800-248-2852

Van Dyck's not only offers "wholesale Dutch bulbs," but also makes ordering a snap: Everything is sold in a "pack," whether it's one amaryllis or 35 mixed Iris Beauty bulbs. The catalog features these and other favorites—tulips, daffodils, crocuses, narcissi, hyacinths, alliums, fritillaria, ranunculus, and snowdrops. Anemones, crown imperials, daylilies, and other later-blooming flowers are offered. All of Van Dyck's bulbs are commercially cultivated, and the 100-page color catalog includes a hardiness guide and cultivation tips to help maximize the success of your plantings.

Special Factors: Satisfaction is guaranteed; quantity discounts are available; returns of bulbs are accepted for replacement; minimum order is 5 packs; delayed billing is available, subject to credit approval.

VAN ENGELEN INC.

■

STILLBROOK FARM
DEPT. WBM
313 MAPLE ST.
LITCHFIELD, CT 06759
203-567-8734
FAX: 203-567-5323

Catalog: free
Save: up to 50%
Pay: check, MO, MC, V, Discover
Sells: flower bulbs
Store: mail order only

Van Engelen, in business since 1971, is the wholesale affiliate of John Scheepers, another vendor of Dutch flower bulbs. Scheepers serves the needs of gardeners buying fewer than 50 of the same bulb at the same time, but Van Engelen sells most bulbs in lots of 50 or 100, and requires a $50 minimum order. If you can meet the minimum, you'll have the choice of over 500 different varieties of tulip, narcissus, crocus, daffodil, anemone, allium, freesia, iris, fritillaria, hyacinth, amaryllis, and lilies, all of which are shown in the 28-page catalog. These are Dutch-cultivated bulbs, and while Van Engelen's prices are on a par with those of two other bulb discounters, Van Engelen's plants are taller and have bigger flowers. In addition to buying bulbs à la carte, you can choose from several collections that are priced below listed wholesale. Each has from 215 to 525 bulbs, and if you like the selection of varieties and colors, they're a real buy. Please note that Van Engelen states that, "Complaints may be entertained if made within *10 days* after receipt of goods," which is something of an industry standard.

Special Factors: Quantity discounts are available; minimum order is $50.

SEE ALSO

Arctic Glass & Window Outlet • glass panels for cold frames, greenhouses • *HOME: IMPROVEMENT*

Central Michigan Tractor & Parts • used and rebuilt parts for tractors and combines • *AUTO*

Clothcrafters, Inc. • knee pads, gardening aprons, porous plastic sheeting • *GENERAL MERCHANDISE*

Dairy Association Co., Inc. • livestock liniment • *ANIMAL*

Daleco Master Breeder Products • kits for yard ponds • *ANIMAL*

Manufacturer's Supply • replacement parts for lawnmowers, rototillers, trimmers, tractors, etc. • *TOOLS*

Northern Hydraulics, Inc. • trimmers, tractors, lawnmower parts, garden carts, log stackers, lawn sweepers, etc. • *TOOLS*

Red Hill Mushrooms • mushroom-growing kits • *FOOD*

Storey's Books for Country Living • books and manuals on farm and garden topics, homesteading, etc. • *BOOKS*

That Fish Place • live aquarium plants • *ANIMAL*

Zip Power Parts, Inc. • lawnmower parts • *TOOLS*

FOOD AND DRINK

Foods, beverages, and condiments

Sales of food by mail are projected to grow to over $2 billion in 1996, reflecting an increase in food savvy and the demand for authentic ingredients. The dominant mail-order foodstuffs are cheese, fruit, and nuts, as well as preserves and condiments, coffee, tea, and seasonings. The listings here are representative: You'll find caviar and Italian truffles, Mexican and Lebanese foods, giant pistachio nuts, Vermont maple syrup, and more from the firms listed here—at savings that run to 80%. Consider them when making out gift lists—a few packets of rare herbs, a tin of trail mix, sunny grapefruit in the dead of winter—even modest gifts can be delightful. If you want to maximize your savings, choose a popular food like pecans or dried fruit, buy it in bulk, and package it yourself. Or try your hand at making herb-infused vinegars and oils. The firms listed here sell the ingredients for all of these and more; please note that the specialists in coffee, tea, herbs, and spices are listed in the next section, "Beverages and Flavorings."

If you'd like to improve your diet and cut food costs, a food co-op may be the answer. If you don't have one nearby, send a long, stamped, self-addressed envelope to Co-Op Directory Services, 919 21st Ave. South, Minneapolis, MN 55404. You'll receive a list of food co-ops across the country, and the contact information for local wholesalers who can advise you on setting up your own co-op. (The *National Green Pages* from Co-Op America has some of this information; see the description in the introduction of "General.")

Even if you can't manage a natural, whole-foods diet, you can save money just by eating better: One researcher who studied the effects of a diet with no more than 30% of the calories derived from fat (the government-approved level) found that it was *cheaper* to eat leaner, by an average of about $275 per year, per person. Great to know, but how to you get there? In the early 1990s, the FDA recast its dietary guidelines, throwing out the famous "four food groups" for the better-balanced "pyramid." The U.S. Department of Agriculture (USDA) has prepared a helpful, 30-page brochure, "The Food Guide Pyramid" (HG-252); request it by name and number form the U.S. Department of Agriculture, Human Nutrition Information Service, 6505 Belcrest Rd., Hyattsville, MD 20782 (include a long, stamped, self-addressed envelope). As simple as the pyramid seems, changes in the government's food labeling regulations are not. Some of the best ongoing sources of information that sort food facts from fallacies are newsletters: *Nutrition Action Healthletter,* published by the Center for Science in the Public Interest (CSPI), broke the stories about the high-fat content of Chinese and Mexican restaurant food. It's a fearless champion of truth in advertising, which is what you'd expect of a Ralph Nader publication. Subscriptions are currently $24 per ten-issue year; write to CSPI-Circulation, 1875 Connecticut Ave. NW, Suite 300, Washington, DC 20009 for updated information. Another helpful newsletter, *Environmental Nutrition,* summarizes abstracts and current food-health controversies and findings, with good, balanced reporting. A 12-issue year is currently $24 from *Environmental Nutrition,* P.O. Box 420057, Palm Coast, FL 32142-9585.

Once you've figured out what to eat, you can learn how to cook it with less fat, salt, and sugar with Jane Brody's *Good Food Guide* and *Good Food Gourmet,* which are full of recipes for old favorites reformulated to reduce calories and sodium. Retraining your palate is one thing, but before you trade their Fruit Loops for steamed millet, see *What Are We Feeding Our Kids?* by Michael Jacobsen, CSPI's executive director. It examines the politics and marketing techniques used to sell food to children, and proposes methods of reducing the influence of the industry. For more information, write to CSPI at the address above.

In addition to nutrition, food safety is a big concern among consumers. Warm weather gives rise to "picnic anxiety," and the fall brings "stuffing fears," common concerns about handling troublesome foods properly. Help is just a call or letter away:

- **The American Dietetic Association** answers questions on all aspects of food safety; 800-366-1655, Monday to Friday 10 A.M. to 5 P.M., ET, for a registered dietitian; recordings are on 24 hours a day.

- **USDA Mcat and Poultry Hotline** answers your questions on safe handling of meat and poultry; 800-535-4555, in DC 202-720-3333 (both TDD); Monday to Friday 10 A.M. to 4 P.M., November 1–30 and the weekend before Thanksgiving, 9 A.M. to 5 P.M., Thanksgiving Day 8 A.M. to 2 P.M., all ET.

- **Butterball**, the turkey company, lays on four dozen food-service professionals to answer your questions on how to handle, cook, carve, and store the big bird. United States and Canada: 800-323-4848; TDD: 800-833-3848; both English and Spanish are spoken. November 1 to the day before Thanksgiving, 9 A.M. to 9 P.M., the weekend before, 9 A.M. to 7 P.M., Thanksgiving Day, 7 A.M. to 7 P.M.; weekdays after Thanksgiving to Christmas, 9 A.M. to 7 P.M.

- *A Quick Guide to Safe Food Handling,* a USDA publication, gives guidelines on food handling and charts of cooking requirements for different meats and egg dishes—plus one that gives the projected shelf life of refrigerated and frozen foods. Send a long, stamped, self-addressed envelope to the USDA at the address given above, with your request for HG-248.

- *Get Hooked on Seafood Safety*, published by the FDA, covers risks and safety precautions for buying, handling, storing, and preparing fish. A copy can be ordered from the Consumer Information Center, listed in "Books."

- **The FDA's Seafood Hotline** dispenses answers to your specific questions on fish-related safety issues; call 800-FDA-4010 Monday to Friday 12 P.M. to 4 P.M. ET.

- When you're ordering food by mail, keep food safety in mind. Don't purchase highly perishable or temperature-sensitive items like chocolate, soft cheese, fruits, vegetables, and uncured meats during the summer, unless you have them shipped by an express service and plan to eat them immediately.

FIND IT FAST

CHEESE • **Gibbsville**
COFFEE AND TEA • **Festive Foods, The Maples**
GOURMET FOODS • **Aux Delices, Caviarteria, Festive Foods**
HERBS, SPICES, FLAVORINGS • **Festive Foods, Karen's Kitchen**
MAPLE SYRUP • **Palmer's, Elbridge C. Thomas**
MUSHROOMS • **Aux Delices, Festive Foods, Jaffe Bros., Northwestern, Red Hill**
NUTS, DRIED FRUITS • **Bates Bros., Durey-Libby, The Maples**
ORGANIC AND NATURAL FOODS • **Deer Valley, Jaffe Bros., Walnut Acres**

AUX DELICES DES BOIS INC.

14 LEONARD ST.
NEW YORK, NY 10013
800-666-1232212-334-1230
FAX: 212-334-1231

Catalog: free
Save: up to 50%
Pay: check, MO, MC, V
Sells: mushrooms, truffles, greens, etc.
Store: same address; Monday to Thursday
9–7, Friday 9–6, Saturday 10–2 (Nov. 1 to
May 15)

 (see text)

Aux Delices des Bois sells a wonderful selection of in-season gourmet ingredients from its Lower Manhattan quarters, at prices up to 30% below the competition. The specialty here is mushrooms, both dried and fresh (see the "Fungus by Fax" section of the order form for details on getting prices and ordering). Mousseron, morel, porcini, chanterelle, and black trumpet mushrooms are available dried; powdered porcini, morels, and chanterelles are also sold. The fresh mushrooms include most of the dried varieties, as well as cauliflower mushrooms, charbonnier, hedgehog, matsutake, yellowfoot, oyster, crimini, portobello, enoki, "hen of the woods," white trumpet, shiitake mushrooms, and many others. Also available on a seasonal basis are Black Perigord and Alba White truffles, but you can buy truffle-infused oil year 'round. Wild rice, white asparagus from France, Cavaillon melons, and greens (herbs and mesclun, pea shoots, sunflower sprouts, etc.) are also on the menu. All of the produce is shipped by overnight delivery, and Aux Delices also offers gift baskets and three months of mushrooms, which you can give to yourself or a truly deserving friend. The firm has been in business since 1987 and is serious about mushrooms: Aux Delices is a member of the New York Mycological Society and the North American Truffling Society.

Please note: Only nonperishable goods are sent out of the United States.

Special Factors: See order form for details on pricing mushrooms.

BATES BROS. NUT FARM, INC.

15954 WOODS VALLEY RD.
VALLEY CENTER, CA 92082
619-749-3333
FAX: 619-749-9499

Price List: free with self-addressed, stamped envelope
Save: up to 50%
Pay: check, MO, MC, V
Sells: nuts, dried fruits, and candy
Store: same address; daily 8–5; also Terra Nova Plaza, 358 E. H St., #604, Chula Vista, CA; every day, 10–7:30

Nuts are the featured item at Bates, which was founded in 1971 and grows some of what it sells. Price checks have shown savings of almost 50% on selected items, compared to the competition.

Bates' four-page brochure lists the standard almonds, walnuts, peanuts, cashews, pecans, and mixes, as well as macadamia nuts, filberts, pignolias, sunflower seeds, and pistachios. You can buy them raw, roasted and salted, smoked, and saltless. The dried fruits include apricots, raisins, dates, papaya, figs, banana chips, pineapple, and coconut, as well as other sweets. These are the ingredients for trail mix, which Bates also sells ready-made, as well as granola, wheat germ snacks, popcorn, and old-fashioned candy—malted milk balls, English toffee, nut brittle, taffy, candy corn, and licorice ropes, among others. And look here for good prices on glacé fruit: fruitcake mix, cherries, colored pineapple wedges, orange and lemon peel, and citron. Gift packs are available year-round.

Special Factors: C.O.D. orders are accepted.

CAVIARTERIA INC.

502 PARK AVE.
NEW YORK, NY 10022
800-4-CAVIAR
IN NY 212-759-7410
IN CA 800-287-9773
FAX: 718-482-8985

Catalog: free
Save: up to 30%
Pay: MO, MC, V, AE
Sells: caviar and gourmet foods
Store: same address (store and tasting bar);
also 247 N. Beverly Dr., Beverly Hills, CA;
Monday to Saturday 9–6, both locations

Caviarteria, established in 1950, brings its line of caviar to the world through a 12-page catalog. This family-run business stocks every grade of Caspian Beluga, Oscetra, and Sevruga caviar (fresh and vacuum-packed), plus American sturgeon, whitefish, trout, and salmon caviar. Prices begin at about $16 per ounce for Kamchatka bottom-of-the-barrel vacuum-packed and run up to $275 for 3-1/2 ounces of "Ultra" Beluga. Price comparisons of Caviarteria's Beluga Malassol to those of another caviar-by-mail firm show you can save as much as 40% here, and even the caviar servers are already priced lower than usual retail.

The catalog lists other gourmet treats: whole sides and "center cut" packages of smoked Scottish salmon, Icelandic gravlax, fresh pâté, foie gras from France, game meats (buffalo, venison, wild boar, and pheasant), and other delicacies. Caviarteria recently moved the New York City store to the larger shop on Park Avenue, and opened a tasting bar. How about Champagne by the glass (flutes of Taittinger for $6!), or a caviar sampler with toast points, or smoked salmon sandwiches are among the temptations. The Beverly Hills branch also features Champagne and wine, and Caviarteria will ship Champagne anywhere in California overnight, and send caviar, foie gras, and other delights for next-day deliery *anywhere*.

Special Factors: Satisfaction is guaranteed; minimum order is $25 with credit cards.

DEER VALLEY FARM

R.D. 1, BOX 173
GUILFORD, NY 13780
607-764-8556

Catalog: $1
Save: up to 40% (see text)
Pay: check, MO, MC, V
Sells: organic and natural foods
Store: Rte. 37, Guilford, NY; Monday to Friday 8–5; 19B Ford Ave., Oneonta, NY; Monday to Saturday 9:30–5:30, Thursday 9:30–8:30; and 64 Main St., Cortland, NY; Monday to Saturday 9:30–5:30, Thursday 9:30–8:30

Deer Valley Farm, which has been in operation since 1947 and is certified organic by New York State Natural Food Associates, sells a full line of foods—from baked bread and cookies to wheat middlings. Whole grains, flours, cereals, nut butters, crackers, fruits, pasta, herbs and spices, tea, soy milk, preserves, and yeast and other baking ingredients are usually available. You can buy "organically grown" meats here at substantial savings: hamburger, typically priced at $4.50 to $6 per pound in health food stores, costs $3.49 per pound, and the trimmed sirloin is $6.29 a pound; veal, pork, lamb, and even fish are also available. Deer Valley sells raw milk cheese, and the cheddar is only $3.29 to $4.89 per pound, less than some of the supermarket varieties. The only drawback here is the minimum order, $150, necessary to reap savings of 25% to 40% on the prices you'd pay if buying the same goods from your local health food store. But if you get your friends together, you can meet that amount easily with a combined order—just be prepared for an impromptu feast when the cartons arrive!

Special Factors: Deliveries are made by Deer Valley truck in the New York City area (elsewhere by UPS); minimum order is $15, $150 for wholesale prices.

DUREY-LIBBY EDIBLE NUTS, INC.

100 INDUSTRIAL RD.
P.O. BOX 345
CARLSTADT, NJ 07072
201-939-2775
FAX: 201-939-0386

Flyer: free
Save: up to 50%
Pay: check or MO
Sells: nuts
Store: mail order only

Durey-Libby, established in 1950, picks and processes "delicious fresh nuts you don't have to shell out a fortune for." You can't eat fancy tins, stoneware crocks, and rattan baskets, so if you're buying nuts, why not *pay* for nuts—and nothing but. Durey-Libby's no-frills price list features walnuts, pecans, cashews, almonds, macadamia nuts, pistachios, and cocktail mixes, packed in bags and vacuum tins. The prices are up to 50% less than those charged by gourmet shops and many food catalogs. The smallest units are three-pound cans, which will give you enough for cooking and snacking.

If you identify yourself as a reader of this book when you order, you may deduct 10% from your order total (computed on the cost of the goods only). This WBMC reader discount expires February 1, 1997.

Special Factors: Satisfaction is guaranteed; shipping is not charged on orders within the contiguous United States.

FESTIVE FOODS OF THE ROCKIES

DEPT. WBMC-96
P.O. BOX 49172
COLORADO SPRINGS, CO
80949-9172
719-594-6768
FAX: 719-522-1672

Catalog: free
Save: up to 75% (see text)
Pay: check, MO, MC, V, AE
Sells: baking ingredients, fancy foods, herbs and spices, etc.
Store: mail order only

  ¡Sí!

Festive Foods of the Rockies has been supplying serious home cooks and bakers with fine ingredients since 1984, and offers a number of items not often seen in other fancy foods catalogs. There are 20 pages of temptations, from pure Belgian chocolate to St. Dalfour sugarless fruit conserves. Festive Food's per-ounce prices of the bulk-packed herbs are much lower than those charged at the supermarket: eight ounces of pure vanilla extract cost $7.50 here, while just *two ounces* of extract cost $5.39 locally. The 16-ounce pack of Old Bay seasoning is $4.25 here, compared to $3.13 for six ounces, and mild curry powder costs $3.70 for eight ounces here, while one ounce of McCormick's runs $1.85—a difference of 75%. Savings on the other goods vary, depending on the item and amount ordered.

Festive Foods offers a wide range of products, including pastry and baking ingredients, chocolate and cocoa, extracts, essential oils of plants and spices, a wide variety of herbs and spices in spice-jar "refill" packs as well as the more economical bulk sizes, seasoning blends, tea (black, green, herbal, and flavored), dried mushrooms, maple syrup, sun-dried tomatoes, flavored champagne vinegars, and dried fruits. Among notable products are French coffee extract, Tahitian vanilla beans, pine nuts, asafetida powder, horseradish powder, fine sea salt, Chaat Masala, chutneys, and mushroom powder. If you enjoy cooking and eating, stock up—Festive Foods will pay shipping if your order totals $100 or more.

Special Factors: Satisfaction is guaranteed; shipping is not charged on orders over $100; returns are accepted for exchange, refund, or credit.

GIBBSVILLE CHEESE SALES

W-2663 CTH-00
SHEBOYGAN FALLS, WI
53085-2971
414-564-3242
FAX: 414-564-6129

Price List: free
Save: up to 30%
Pay: check or MO
Sells: Wisconsin cheese and summer sausage
Store: same address (6 miles south of Sheboygan Falls on Hwy. 32); Monday to Saturday 7:30–5

Gibbsville Cheese Sales is a standout even in Wisconsin, the Dairy State, where *everyone* produces cheese. The company's prices are appetizingly low—as little as $2.45 a pound for mild cheddar in five-pound bulk packaging. Several types of Old Wisconsin summer sausage and beef sticks are also offered, in addition to well-priced gift packages for a variety of budgets and tastes.

Gibbsville has been in business since 1933, and produces the most popular kinds of cheese, including Cheddar (mild, medium, aged, super-sharp white, garlic, and caraway), Monterey Jack (including Jacks flavored with salami, hot pepper, dill, and vegetables), and Colby (including salt-free). You can buy Cheddar and Colby in "Economy" boxes of ten pounds, or in bulk with as little as a pound. Five pounds of rindless Colby cost $2.45 a pound, and prices of other cheeses are just as reasonable. If you can get to the store in Gibbsville, you can even watch the production process through a viewing window. In addition to the cheeses of its own manufacture, Gibbsville Cheese sells Swiss (baby, medium, aged, and lace), Provolone, Muenster, Parmesan, Romano, Mozzarella, Gouda, Pine River Cold-Pack Cheese Spreads (including Sharp Cheddar, Swiss Almond, Port Wine, Smoked, etc.), and Blue, Limburger, and Lone Elm String Cheeses. The price list indicates which cheeses are "lower in fat," and includes several "lite" versions of favorites.

Please note: Shipments are not made during summer months (approximately June to September).

Special Factors: Price quote by letter with SASE.

JAFFE BROS., INC.

P.O. BOX 636-W
VALLEY CENTER, CA
92082-0636
619-749-1133
FAX: 619-749-1282

Catalog: free
Save: up to 50%
Pay: check, MO, MC, V, Discover
Sells: organically grown food
Store: (warehouse) 28560 Lilac Rd., Valley Center, CA; Sunday to Thursday 8–5, Friday 8–3

Jaffe Bros., established in 1948, sells organically and naturally grown dried fruit, nuts, seeds, beans, grains, nut butters, honey, and many other organically grown items, through the 20-page catalog. Prices average 30% below comparable retail, but there are greater savings on certain items, and quantity discounts are offered on many goods. Jaffe's products are marketed under the Jaybee label, and virtually all of them are grown "organically" (without fumigants or poisonous sprays and with "nonchemical" fertilizers) or "naturally" (similarly treated but not fertilized).

You'll save on wholesome foods here—dried peaches, Black Mission figs, Monukka raisins, papaya, dates of several types, almonds, pine nuts, macadamias, nut butters, brown rice, flours and grains, seeds for eating and sprouting, 15 kinds of peas and beans, unheated honey, coconut, jams, juices, carob powder, salad oil, olives, herb teas, and much more. (Most of the produce is packed in two- and five-pound units and larger.) The catalog also lists dehydrated mushrooms, sun-dried tomatoes, canned olives, organic spaghetti sauce, low-salt dill pickles and sauerkraut, organic whole wheat pasta, kosher maple syrup, organic applesauce, and even a biodegradable peppermint-and-castile soap/shampoo. If you'd like to bestow goodness upon a friend, be sure to see the group of gift assortments—nicely packaged selections of favorites, at reasonable prices.

Wholesale customers, please request the "wholesale" catalog on your company letterhead; minimums (pounds or number of items) apply.

Special Factors: Quantity discounts are available; problems should be reported to Jaffe within ten days of receipt of goods; store is closed Saturdays; C.O.D. orders are accepted.

KAREN'S KITCHEN

43 RANDOLPH RD., SUITE 757
SILVER SPRING, MD 20904
301-236-5992
FAX: 301-236-5993

Catalog: $1, deductible
Save: up to 70%
Pay: check or MO
Sells: food and seasonings
Store: mail order only

Karen's Kitchen is the brainchild of a resourceful working mother turned entrepreneur, who developed low-cost alternatives to commercial mixes like Hamburger Helper. Karen's Kitchen publishes a newsletter, which includes recipes for different mixes with cost breakdowns of the from-scratch product and the branded equivalent. It's possible to save up to 75% on some mixes—if you do the processing yourself. The quarterly newsletter is well worth the yearly $14 fee ($17 in Canada, $22 other non-U.S. countries). But the catalog alone ($1) will be appreciated by anyone who enjoys cooking.

There are 24 pages of organic peas and beans, grains and grain products, whole wheat and corn-flour pasta, dried fruits, dehydrated vegetables, herbs, spices, seasoning blends, flavors, extracts, and an impressive list of teas. Among the current offerings are anasazi beans, quinoa, whole-wheat artichoke pasta, dried cherries and dried sliced dehydrated Formosan mushrooms, whole white peppercorns, Beau Monde and Souvlaki seasoning blends, Chinese Monastery tea, sherry-flavored black tea, and Benchley tea bags. In the back of the catalog are lists of ingredients of every seasoning blend and herbal tea, so you can customize them to your own taste. Karen also sells customized product labels for resellers, ginseng products, essential oils, natural herbs, and herbal extracts. The best prices are on the one- and five-pound sizes, although the two-ounce size of Karen's spices beats the supermarket spice prices by up to 70%!

Canadian readers, please note: Only U.S. funds are accepted.

Wholesale customers should contact Karen's Kitchen for prices on specific items bought in bulk.

Karen's Kitchen is offering readers a 10% discount on first orders from the retail catalog only. Be sure to identify yourself as a WBMC reader when you order. This WBMC reader discount expires June 1, 1997.

Special Factors: Satisfaction is guaranteed; quantity discounts are available; minimum order is $10, $100 for bulk.

THE MAPLES FRUIT FARM, INC.

P.O. BOX 167
CHEWSVILLE, MD 21721
301-733-0777

Catalog: $1, refundable
Save: up to 50%
Pay: check, MO, MC, V, Discover
Sells: dried fruit, nuts, coffee, gift baskets, etc.
Store: 13144 Pennsylvania Ave., Hagerstown, MD; Monday to Thursday 9–6, Friday 9–7, Saturday 8–5

The 16-page catalog of dried fruits, nuts, coffee, tea, and sweets from Maples Fruit Farm pictures an early view of the Farm, which has been operated by the same family for 200 years. The prices here are mouth-watering—savings of 25% to 50% were found on selected items. The dried fruits include apricots, dates, pears, peaches, and pineapple. (Fruits prepared with sulphur dioxide are clearly indicated in the catalog.) Raw and roasted (salted and unsalted) nuts are offered, including cashews, almonds, peanuts, pecans, macadamia nuts, filberts, black walnuts, and a number of others, including trail mix. Two pounds of raw pecans from Maples are half as expensive than those from a specialty pecan source, and the roasted macadamia nuts, honey-roasted peanuts, and cashews are all better buys here. Among sweets, Maryland grade-A amber maple syrup costs less than the syrup offered by competitors (who sell Canadian and New York state products). Maples Fruit Farm also sells 38 kinds of gourmet coffee, roasted fresh at the firm's gourmet shop daily, and tea from Benchley, Celestial Seasonings, and Twinings.

Reasonably priced gift baskets are available, and if you can stock up or share orders, check the *wholesale* prices on cases. Don't miss the store if you're in the Hagerstown area—drop in to smell the coffee roasting, and sample some of the 5,000 gourmet treats on the shelves.

Please note: The Maples accepts faxes over the regular phone line—but call before transmitting.

Special Factors: Satisfaction is guaranteed; minimum order is $25 (excluding shipping).

PALMER'S MAPLE SYRUP

BOX 246
PALMER LANE
WAITSFIELD, VT
 05673-9711
802-496-3696

Brochure and Price List: free
Save: 33% plus (see text)
Pay: check or MO
Sells: maple syrup, cream, and candy
Store: Mehuron's Market and Bisbee's Hardware, Waitsfield, VT

Everett Palmer has been sugaring since he was ten years old, and in early spring he heads for the woods to draw the sap that will be transformed into a season's worth of maple syrup. He's still using the sugar house that his grandfather built 160 years ago! The Palmers' brochure describes the entire process, including grading and canning, and gives the recipe for the raised doughnuts that Mrs. Palmer serves to visitors who drop by during the sugaring season.

And the Palmers are nice when it comes to the price, which at this writing is $11.40 a quart, compared to $16.95 for the same grade of Vermont syrup sold through another gourmet foods catalog. Even the Palmers' highest per-ounce price, for half pints, is lower by a third than what other mail-order firms are charging. The Palmers sell three grades of syrup—light amber (Fancy), medium amber (A), and dark amber (B)—at the same price. If you like a very delicate flavor, try the Fancy grade; grade B has a strong "mapley" flavor that suits some palates and purposes (cooking and baking) more than the other two grades. Maple cream and candies may also be available; see the price list for information.

Please note: The pint-size "log cabin" tins hold 16.9 ounces, the half-pint tins, 4.5 ounces.

Special Factors: Orders are shipped worldwide.

RED HILL MUSHROOMS

P.O. BOX 4234
GETTYSBURG, PA 17325
800-822-4003
717-337-3038
FAX: 717-337-3936

Price List: free
Save: up to 30%
Pay: check, MO, MC, V
Sells: fresh mushrooms and growing kits
Store: 1540 Biglerville Rd., Gettysburg, PA

¡Si!

Shiitake and oyster mushrooms enjoyed a great vogue in fashionable food several years ago, and have subsequently found a permanent home in the dishes of many good cooks. Red Hill Mushrooms sells oyster mushrooms, which have a fine, delicate flavor, and the slightly nutty Shiitake, which is crunchy when raw. The price at this writing is competitive—$10 a pound for Shiitake, $8 for oyster mushrooms—and they're offered in three- and five-pound boxes. Red Hill is also home to the "Shiitake Log Kit" ($25), a compressed sawdust log enriched with wheat germ and millet and infused with Shiitake spawn. Follow the care directions given in the literature, and you should be rewarded with as many as four crops of Shiitake. When the log ceases to produce, you can crumble it up and use it as mulch in your garden!

Special Factors: Minimum order is $25.

SULTAN'S DELIGHT, INC.

P.O. BOX 140253
STATEN ISLAND, NY
10314-0014
718-720-1557

Catalog: free with a stamped, self-addressed envelope
Save: up to 50%
Pay: check, MO, MC, V, Discover
Sells: Middle Eastern foods and gifts
Store: mail order only

Sultan's Delight specializes in authentic Middle Eastern food specialties, sold at excellent prices—up to 50% below comparable goods in gourmet shops. The firm was established in 1980, and offers both raw ingredients and prepared specialties, including the Near East and Sahadi lines of foods. See the catalog if you're looking for canned tahini, couscous, tabouleh, fig and apricot jams, stuffed grapevine leaves, bulghur, green wheat, orzo, fava beans, ground sumac, Turkish figs, or pickled okra. You'll also find olives, herbs and spices, jumbo pistachios and other nuts, roasted chick peas, halvah, Turkish delight, marzipan paste, olive oil, Turkish coffee, fruit leather, filo, feta cheese, and other specialties. Cookbooks for Greek, Lebanese, and Middle Eastern cuisine are available, as well as Turkish coffee pots, waterpipes, inlaid backgammon sets, and other intriguing items.

Sultan's Delight is offering readers of this book a 10% discount on their first order (computed on the goods total only). Identify yourself as a reader when you order. This WBMC reader discount expires March 31, 1997.

Special Factors: Minimum order is $15.

ELBRIDGE C. THOMAS & SONS

RTE. 4, BOX 336
CHESTER, VT 05143
802-263-5680

Brochure: $1
Save: up to 50% (see text)
Pay: check or MO
Sells: Vermont grade-A maple syrup
Store: by appointment

Mr. Thomas makes and sells the nectar of New England—pure, grade-A Vermont maple syrup. He's been in business since 1938, and his prices on large sizes are as much as 50% lower than those of his competitors—

and even better than those charged for lesser grades. The stock is pure and simple: Vermont maple syrup, grade A, available in half-pint, pint, quart, half-gallon, and gallon tins. (Plastic containers are available upon request.) Maple sugar cakes, which make irresistible gifts, are also offered (by special order only). The brochure includes a number of suggestions for using maple syrup in your favorite foods—maple milk shakes, maple ham, frosting, and baked beans are just a few examples.

Special Factors: Quantity discounts are available; prices are subject to change without notice.

WALNUT ACRES ORGANIC FARMS

DEPT. 9621
WALNUT ACRES RD.
PENNS CREEK, PA 17862
800-433-3998
FAX: 717-837-1146

Catalog: free
Save: up to 40%
Pay: check, MO, MC, V, Discover
Sells: organically grown foods, natural toiletries, cookware, etc.
Store: Penns Creek, PA; Monday to Saturday 9–5, Sunday 12–5

Walnut Acres Organic Farms, in business since 1946, sells organically grown foods, nutritional supplements, cookbooks, and related items. Most of the goods are produced at Walnut Acres, grown on "500 acres of chemical-free soil." The 56-page color catalog presents the bounty in full, appetizing color: grains, cereals, granola, bread and pancake mixes, flours, seeds and nuts, nut butters, soups, salad dressings, sauces, pasta, dried fruits, juices, honeys, and other goods. Herbs and spices, relishes, dehydrated vegetables, canned fruits, vegetables, and beans, powdered milk, crackers, jams and preserves, cheeses, and baked goods are also offered. Walnut Acres sells nutritional supplements and some natural toiletries and unguents as well, and a variety of products "friendly to the environment."

Walnut Acres is known for its quality and selection, but savings of 30% to 40% are possible on the dried fruits and nuts, compared to other mail-order sources. Walnut Acres sells its nuts, seeds, grains, cereals, and dried fruits in bulk packages (three and five pounds) at additional savings.

Wholesale customers must be doing business as stores, or selling for resale; request the wholesale catalog on company letterhead.

Special Factors: Products are guaranteed to be as represented.

WOOD'S CIDER MILL

RD #2, BOX 477
SPRINGFIELD, VT 05156
802-263-5547

Brochure: free with SASE
Save: up to 50% (see text)
Pay: check, MO, MC, V
Sells: cider jelly and syrups
Store (farm): call for appointment

The Wood family has maintained a farm in Vermont since 1798 and today produces wonderful, cider-based treats for mail-order customers. The prices here are better than reasonable—in fact, Wood's cider jelly can be found selling in other catalogs at prices nearly twice as high as those charged by the Woods themselves! And another firm's cider jelly costs over twice as much for the same amount.

The Cider Mill is best known for its jelly, which is made of evaporated apple cider. From 30 to 50 apples are needed to make the cider that's concentrated in just one pound of jelly, but you'll understand why when you taste it on toast or muffins, or try it with pork and other meats as a condiment. Boiled cider is also available; it's a less-concentrated essence that is recommended as a base for a hot drink, as a ham glaze, and as a topping for ice cream and pancakes. For pancakes, however, try the cider syrup, a blend of boiled cider and maple syrup. (It's also outstanding as a basting sauce for Thanksgiving turkeys, and even roast chicken.) Straight maple syrup is also produced on the farm.

Special Factors: Satisfaction is guaranteed; returns are accepted for exchange or refund; quantity discounts are available; minimum order is four jars.

Beverages and Flavorings

Coffee, tea, infusions and tisanes, herbs, spices, seasonings, and condiments

Herbs, spices, coffee, and tea are mail-order naturals, and all of them are available from the firms listed here. You can save up to 90% on the cost of herbs and spices by buying them from discounters, but that won't help you if you don't know how to use them. Even the smaller savings on coffee and tea won't mean as much if you're not using the best brewing techniques. The following resources are accessible, colorful, and they all include recipes:

The Complete Book of Herbs, by Lesley Bremness, and *The Complete Book of Spices,* by Jill Norman, are guides to identifying, storing, and using herbs and spices. Coffee lovers will appreciate *The Perfect Cup,* by Timothy James Castle, which covers selecting, serving, and tasting the magic bean. *The Afternoon Tea Cookbook,* by tea authority Michael Smith, includes history and great recipes for the proper English interlude. At this writing, all of these books are available from Jessica's Biscuit (see the listing in "Books"). Don't overlook the books and tips mentioned in the catalogs of these vendors, and see the listings in the foregoing chapter, "Food and Drink," for other firms selling coffee, tea, and seasonings.

FIND IT FAST

COFFEE AND TEA • *CMC, Cordon Brew, Grandma's Spice Shop, Northwestern Coffee Mills, Old Town Gourmet, Rafal Spice, Simpson & Vail*
HERBS, SPICES, FLAVORINGS • *Bickford, Brew City, CMC, Grandma's Spice Shop, E.C. Kraus, Mr. Spiceman, Northwestern Coffee Mills, Old Town Gourmet, Penzeys', Rafal Spice, San Francisco Herb, The Spice House, Spices Etc.*
WINE- AND BEER-MAKING • *Brew City, E.C. Kraus*

BICKFORD FLAVORS

19007 ST. CLAIR AVE.
CLEVELAND, OH
44117-1001
216-531-6006
FAX: 216-531-2006

Price List: free
Save: up to 40% (see text)
Pay: check, MO, MC, V
Sells: flavorings
Store: same address; Monday to Friday 9–5

Bickford, established in 1914, makes and sells its own concentrated flavorings, from naturally derived oils, leaving out the usual alcohol and sugar that you'll find in other "pure" essences. Over 100 flavorings are offered, from almond to wintergreen. Vanilla is sold here in white, dark, and regular versions. (The white vanilla won't tint your angel food cake or meringues.) All of Bickford's flavorings are sold in one-ounce bottles for $2.29, which is competitive pricing, but the good buys are pints ($19.95) and larger sizes. (Vanilla is also sold in bottles of two, four, and eight ounces.) In addition to an unparalleled selection of flavorings, Bickford also sells about 100 exotically flavored oils (ginger, peach, caramel, and sherry oil are all available), food colorings, chlorophyll, and carob syrup.

Special Factor: Orders are shipped worldwide.

BREW CITY SUPPLIES, INC.

P.O. BOX 27729
MILWAUKEE, WI 53227
414-425-8595
FAX: 414-425-8595

Catalog: free
Save: up to 50%
Pay: check, MO, MC, V
Sells: home-brewing equipment
Store: mail order only

You can start a *real* microbrewery right in your own kitchen, with the help and guidance of the folks at Brew City. This four-year-old firm is dedicated to the proposition that anyone can brew a batch of beer, and leads you through the process of turning malt, water, yeast, and hops into pilsner in "Nine Easy Steps" and dozens of books and videos.

Brew City offers beginner kits with everything you need to set up operation for under $40, and all of the supplies you'll need: yeast by

YeastLab, malt extracts from all over the globe, including Australia (Coopers), Belgium (Brewferm), Britain (John Bull, and Munton Fison), Germany (Ireks-Arkady), Holland (Laaglander), Ireland (Mountmellich), Scotland (Glenbrew), and the United States (Premier). Sugars, yeasts, additives, and pellet hops are sold, as well as soda pop extracts (cola, cream, birch beer, orange, etc.). The 32-page catalog also shows an extensive selection of equipment and tools—grain mills, boilers, fermenters, paddles, bottles, cappers, keg taps, labels, and even steins are available. The prices are "guaranteed lowest," and the informative catalog teaches you the role of "wort chillers," "sparging bags," and other strangely named devices.

Brew City Supplies is offering readers a discount of 10% on their first order. Be sure to identify yourself as a WBMC reader when you order, and deduct the discount from the cost of the goods only. This WBMC reader discount expires February 1, 1997.

Special Factors: Satisfaction is guaranteed.

THE CMC COMPANY

P.O. BOX 322
AVALON, NJ 08202
800-CMC-2780
FAX: 609-861-0043

Catalog: free
Save: up to 50%
Pay: check or MO
Sells: gourmet seasonings
Store: mail order only

If you're one of the legion of home cooks who'd love to replicate the great flavors of Mexican and Eastern restaurant cuisine, you've just found the source for the flavorings that make the dishes authentic. CMC has been in business since 1990 with a seasonings line that features Mexican chiles (dried, powdered, canned, etc.), and hot sauces, moles (rojo, verde, poblano, pepian), as well as such specialties as Mexican dried shrimp, chorizos, masa harina, and cooking utensils for Mexican dishes. CMC's Thai food selection includes sambals (which are like relishes), tamarind paste, trassi (dried shrimp paste), half a dozen curry pastes, Kaffir lime leaves, jasmine rice, and all of the sauces—fish, oyster, satay, sriracha, etc.—that make Thai food transcendental. Your efforts at inspired Indian food will be improved by tandoori paste and Patak chutneys, black cumin seed, chapati flour, a great selection of individual curry spices, ghee (clarified butter), and the other ingredients sold here. And there are Szechuan spices, and Busha Browne's Jamaican Specialties (pukka hot sauce, hot pepper sherry, jerk sauce and seasoning, etc.). Many of CMC's spices and flavorings are hard to find elsewhere, and therefore hard to comparison-price, but several products—garam masala, basmati rice, and lemon grass powder, for example—were found to be 10% to 50% less expensive here than at other gourmet sources.

Wholesale customers, please note that discounts are given to resellers and food-service professionals.

The CMC Company is offering readers a discount of 10% on their orders. Be sure to identify yourself as a WBMC reader when you order, and deduct the discount from the cost of the goods only. This WBMC reader discount expires February 1, 1997.

Special Factor: Keep the catalog since it's updated with inserts until the next printing.

CORDON BREW

309 N.BALSAM ST.
RIDGECREST CA 93555
619-229-9060

Price List: free
Save: up to 30%
Pay: check, MO, MC, V
Sells: coffee and brewing accessories
Store: mail order only

 (see text)

Cordon Brew, established in 1991 to cater to the whims of budget-minded coffee connoisseurs, delivers high-altitude Arabica beans in scores of straight and blended coffees, decaffeinated and flavored brews, and organically grown coffee. The straight coffees run from Brazil Santos to Tanzanian Peaberry and include Kenya AA, Mocha, Java Estate, and Kona Fancy. Cordon Brew offers blends in roasts from French to Espresso, a good selection of decaffeinated beans, and the choice of flavored beans is really inspired—or have Hawaiian Hazelnut, Cookies 'n Cream, and Pecan coffees become commonplace?

In addition to beans, Cordon Brew sells bean grinders and coffee-makers, the Bodum "Bistro" plunger-style coffee press, canvas tote bags, and mugs. All of the equipment is sold at good discounts, and the prices of the coffee beans average $1 to $3 per pound less than those charged by the typical gourmet coffee shop.

Cordon Brew is offering readers a free pound of Colombia Supremo beans if their first order totals $40 or more, before adding shipping. Be sure to identify yourself as a WBMC reader when you order. This WBMC reader discount expires February 1, 1997.

Special Factor: Minimum order is 3 lb. coffee or $15 in equipment.

GRANDMA'S SPICE SHOP

DEPT. B
P.O. BOX 472
ODENTON, MD 21113
410-672-0933
FAX: 410-674-4640

Catalog: $1, refundable
Save: up to 60%
Pay: check, MO, MC, V
Sells: herbs, spices, coffee, tea, etc.
Store: mail order only

Once upon a time, a real Grandma—rocking chair and all—ran this gourmet emporium. Since its sale several years ago, the firm has expanded the range and depth of the stock to include coffee from Havana, Nougatine coffee (flavored with hazelnut oil), Jasmine tea from Fukien province, beet powder, raspberry leaves, and herbal Worcestershire sauce among other items. The 26-page inventory includes coffees (regular, flavored, and decaffeinated), loose teas (green, black, flavored, decaffeinated) and rare estate teas, Benchley teabags, a large herb and spice selection, cocoa, herbal vinegars and honeys, hot sauces, McCutcheon preserves, and fruit-sweetened preserves. Spice racks, mortar and pestle sets, gift baskets, and Melitta travel sets are all available. The herbs and spices afford the best savings, up to 60% if bought in bulk (half or full pounds). Coffee and tea connoisseurs should see the catalog for the unusual and rare varieties (which are not sold at a discount).

Three full catalog pages are devoted to potpourri, sachets, and related ingredients—simmering spice blends, cedar moth mixes, bath herbs, pomander rolling mixes, pinecones, dried flowers, potpourri oils, and bath oils (stock scents and custom blends are available). Prices of the smaller sizes are competitive with bath and gift shops; as with the herbs, you'll save the most on the potpourri and ingredients when you buy by the pound.

Grandma's Spice Shop is offering readers of this book a 10% discount on first orders. Identify yourself when your order. This WBMC reader discount expires June 1, 1997.

Special Factor: Minimum order is $15.

E.C. KRAUS WINE & BEERMAKING SUPPLIES

P.O. BOX 7850-WC
INDEPENDENCE, MO
64054
816-254-7448

Catalog: free
Save: up to 40%
Pay: check, MO, MC, V
Sells: wine- and beer-making supplies
Store: 733 S. Northern, Independence, MO; Monday to Friday 8–5:30, Saturday 9–1

E.C. Kraus, founded in 1967, can help you save up to half of the cost of wine, beer, and liqueurs by producing them yourself. The firm's 16-page illustrated catalog features supplies and equipment for the home vintner and brewer, beginner or an experienced: malt and hops, fruit and grape concentrates, yeasts, additives, clarifiers, purifiers and preservatives, fruit acids, acidity indicators, hydrometers, bottle caps, rubber stoppers, corks and corkscrews, barrel spigots and liners, tubing and siphons, steam juicers, fermenters, fruit presses, dried botanicals, and much more. The T. Noirot extracts can be used to create low-priced liqueurs, and there are books and manuals to provide help if you want to learn more. If you're just getting started, you may find the Kraus "Necessities Box"—equipment and supplies for making five gallons of wine or four gallons of beer—just what you need.

Special Factor: Local ordinances may regulate production of alcoholic beverages.

MR. SPICEMAN, INC.

210-11 48TH AVE.
BAYSIDE, NY 11364
718-428-7202

Catalog: $1, deductible
Save: up to 94%
Pay: check, MO, MC, V
Sells: herbs, spices, seasonings, and candy
Warehouse: same address; Friday 8–12 noon

Mr. Spiceman publishes a catalog that runs from soup to nuts, but is best known for great buys on herbs, spices, and other seasonings. Founded in 1965, this firm supplies restaurants, delis, and fine food outlets, as well as consumers, at savings that average from 40% to 60%. The catalog lists over 130 herbs and spices, available in small and bulk packaging, including ground allspice, cayenne pepper, ground cumin, curry powder, paprika, and other basics. Mr. Spiceman sells unusual seasonings, such as achiote, juniper berries, cilantro leaves, and freeze-dried chives, as well as marinade mixes, pasta sauces, barbecue sauces, crystallized ginger, Knorr soup and sauce mixes, marinating sauce, Gravy Master flavoring, 4C products, and Virginia Dare extracts and flavorings. A number of kitchen gadgets are available, including a nutmeg grater and several peppermills.

The prices are good, and Mr. Spiceman is bettering them for new customers. As a reader of this book, you may deduct 10% from your first order (computed on the goods total only). This WBMC reader discount expires February 1, 1997.

Special Factors: Call before visiting the warehouse location; minimum order is $10, $25 with credit cards.

NORTHWESTERN COFFEE MILLS

MIDDLE RD.
BOX 370
LA POINTE, WI 54850
800-243-5283
715-747-5825
FAX: 715-747-5405

Catalog: free
Save: 30% average
Pay: check, MO, MC, V, AE
Sells: coffee, tea, herbs, spices, coffee filters, and coffee flavors
Store: 217 North Broadway, 2nd Floor, Milwaukee, WI; Monday to Friday 10–5:30, Saturday 10–4

If coffee is America's drink, Wisconsin may be harboring a national treasure. It's the home of Northwestern Coffee Mills, which set up shop in 1875 in a town better known for a different sort of brew. Northwestern begins with top-quality Arabica, and roasts each type of bean separately to develop its optimum flavor.

The 12-page catalog describes each of the blends, straights, dark roasts, and decaffeinated coffees, noting relative strength, body, aroma, and flavor. Among the blends are American Breakfast, North Coast Blend (a strong, after-dinner coffee), Mocha Java, a New Orleans chicory blend, and Island Blend, a favorite of local restaurateurs that "stands up well when heated for hours on end." There are fancy straights, including Brazil Santos, Costa Rica Tarrazu, Kenya AA, Colombia Excelso, and Sumatra Lintong. Puerto Rico Yauco Selecto is available, as well as estate-grown Java and Hawaiian Kona, Yemen Mocha Mattari (the *real* mocha from Yemen), and other rare straight coffees. Decaf drinkers can choose from water-processed blends and straights. Coffee filters for all types of drip and percolator systems are sold, including Chemex, Melitta, and the Wisconsin-made "Natural Brew" unbleached filters. Northwestern also maintains a premium tea department. The catalog describes how tea is grown and processed, tea grading, and the types of teas Northwestern sells: flavored, black, green, oolong, and decaffeinated. The varieties include Ceylon, Indian Assam, Indian Darjeeling, Irish Breakfast, Russian Caravan, Japan Sencha, "China Dragon Well Panfired Leaf," and Orange Spiced tea, among others. Northwestern's prices on single pounds of coffee or four-ounce packages of tea are market-rate, but the firm will sell both to consumers at bulk rates. There are price breaks at 5, 10, and 25 pounds, and since coffee in whole-bean form will keep well for several months in the freezer, it makes sense to order as much as you can store.

Last but not least, Northwestern sells herbs, spices, and other flavorings in supermarket sizes and in bulk. Several capsicums (peppers) are offered, and dried vegetables (garlic granules, horseradish powder, mushrooms, etc.), blended salt-free and salted seasonings, and natural extracts (vanilla, almond, cocoa, cinnamon, orange, etc.) are also listed. You can use these extracts, says Northwestern, to create flavored coffees (which it does not sell).

Special Factors: Satisfaction is guaranteed; quantity discounts are available; returns are accepted within one year for exchange, refund, or credit.

THE OLD TOWN GOURMET

#9, PATIO MARKET N.W.
ALBUQUERQUE, NM
  87104
800-484-9631, EXT. BEAN
  (2326)
505-842-5643

Price List: free with long, stamped, self-addressed envelope
Save: up to 30%
Pay: MO, MC, V
Sells: coffee, tea, chiles, gourmet food, etc.
Store: same address (in Old Town, Albuquerque); daily 10:30–5 (except Monday, January–March)

The Old Town Gourmet has been selling New Mexican gourmet specialties at the same location in Albuquerque since 1952. The firm roasts, blends, and flavors its own Arabica coffee beans, and incorporates native nuts in several, including "Southwest Piñon," a three-bean blend with piñon nuts that is the store's most popular blend. The store also stocks a vast assortment of dried New Mexican chiles, which are offered whole or ground, as well as chile-flavored products—jams, jellies, salsas, vinegars, bread and cake mixes, and even chile peanut butter (touted as an excellent marinade for chicken or fish). The Old Town Gourmet also carries flavored teas, and will custom gift baskets for an additional fee. For chile connoisseurs and specimen collectors, this firm's specialty in New Mexican varieties offers a special attraction. If you have the opportunity to visit the store, you'll find it in Albuquerque's "old" section, in one of the town's original adobe buildings.

The Old Town Gourmet is offering readers a discount of 10% on their first order. Be sure to identify yourself as a WBMC reader when you order, and deduct the discount from the cost of the goods only. This WBMC reader discount expires February 1, 1997.

Special Factors: Satisfaction is guaranteed; shipping is included (ground UPS) on orders sent within the 48 contiguous states.

PENDERY'S INC.

1221 MANUFACTURING
DALLAS, TX 75207
800-533-1870
214-741-1870
FAX: 214-761-1966

Catalog: $2
Save: up to 50%
Pay: check, MO, MC, V, AE, Discover
Sells: herbs, spices, and Mexican seasonings; teas and botanicals
Store: 304 E. Belknap St., Fort Worth; also Galleria Mall and Inwood Village, 5450 W. Lovers Lane, Dallas, TX

 ¡Si!

Pendery's has been spicing up drab dishes since 1870 and can add the authentic touch of real, full-strength chiles to your Tex-Mex cuisine for a fraction of the prices charged by gourmet shops. The firm's 72-page catalog describes the origins of the company and its contributions to the development of Tex-Mex chile seasonings. It's not a coincidence that "those captivating capsicums" occupy five catalog pages and include pods, ground peppers, and blends. Scores of general and specialty seasonings and flavorings are offered, including fajita seasoning, jalapeño peppers, and spice-rack standards from allspice to white pepper. Among the unusual or hard-to-find ingredients available here are masa harina, Mexican chocolate, annatto, horseradish powder, Worcestershire powder, dehydrated cilantro, corn shucks for tamales and cornhusk dolls, and dried diced tomatoes. The catalog also offers handsome, handblown Mexican glassware, dried flowers and other potpourri ingredients, and related gifts. Prices of the spices are far lower than those charged by gourmet stores and supermarkets—up to 50% less on some of the specialty seasonings.

Special Factor: Orders are shipped worldwide.

PENZEYS' SPICE HOUSE

Catalog: free
Save: 35% average (see text)
Pay: check, MO, MC, V
Sells: spices, herbs, and seasonings
Store: same address; Monday to Friday 9–5, Saturday 9–3

1921 S. WEST AVE.
WAUKESHA, WI 53186
414-574-0277
FAX: 414-574-0278

Penzeys' Spice House is a family-run firm that "grinds and blends our spices weekly to ensure freshness," something no one else in the business seems to be doing. The selection is extraordinary—there are 11 forms and types of cinnamon, for example. Penzeys', established in 1957, prices even one-ounce sizes of seasonings at below-supermarket rates and offers savings of up to 40% on full pounds.

The informative, 36-page catalog begins with adobo seasoning and ends with vanilla beans. In between, you'll find Brady Street Cheese Sprinkle, Bicentennial "Rub" Seasoning (an early American blend), cassia buds from China, cardamom, chili peppers (rated for heat in Skoval units), tandoori chicken seasoning, fenugreek seeds, mulled wine spices, "Old World Seasoning," pot herbs for soups and stews, Spanish saffron, seasonings for salad dressings and homemade sausages, star anise, taco seasoning, French tarragon, and many other straight seasonings and blends. (Nearly three dozen are offered in salt-free versions, and Penzeys' Spice House also offers a line of soup bases.) The descriptions include provenance, ingredients in the blends, and suggested uses. Recent editions of the catalog have included a number of recipes, including a retinue for Thanksgiving dinner, spicy cheese bread, pan-seared tuna steaks, and sauerbraten.

The Penzeys offer several appealing gift packages, including "Spicy Wedding," "Great Baker's Assortment," "Indian Curries," and a "Spice Replacement" set (when "the love of your life has left you taking all of your spices, maybe your house burned down or was just swept away by a tornado/hurricane"). Zassenhaus pepper mills and inexpensive jars for herb and spice storage are also available.

Special Factors: Satisfaction is guaranteed; price quote by phone or fax; returns are accepted for exchange, refund, or credit.

RAFAL SPICE COMPANY

**2521 RUSSELL
DETROIT, MI
313-259-6373
FAX: 313-259-6220**

Catalog: free
Save: up to 57%
Pay: check, MO, MC, V, Discover
Sells: coffee, tea, flavorings, cookbooks, etc.
Store: same address; Monday to Saturday 7–4

If you have a weakness for Cajun and Creole dishes, you'll love Rafal Spice, which charges up to 57% less than a New Orleans mail-order firm selling the identical foods. Rafal Spice also sells coffee and tea in a range of blends and flavors, and well-priced herbs and spices, from alfalfa leaves to za'atar powder. Rafal offers a number of very uncommon ingredients, like bladderwrack, devil's claw tuber powder, hawthorn berries, sanicle, skunk cabbage root, and powdered soy sauce.

Among the food and flavorings brands you'll find in the 72-page catalog are Angostura, Bell's, Buckeye, Clancy's, Crystal, Gayelord Hauser, Jamaican Hell, Konriko, Lawry's, Mrs. Dash, Mrs. Wages, Old Bay, Trappey, Wright's, and Zatarain's. Liquid Spice by Dilijan, Lorann flavorings and extracts, food coloring, kitchen tools, spice grinders, labels, storage jars, Melior and Melitta coffee makers, filters, tea infusers, and six pages of cookbooks wrap up the catalog. The shipping is computed fairly (on weight and distance), and the catalog even includes a few recipes.

Please note that botanicals not intended for consumption are indicated in the catalog with an asterisk.

Special Factors: Satisfaction is guaranteed; allow 3 weeks for delivery of order; minimum order is $10.

SAN FRANCISCO HERB CO.

**250 14TH ST., DEPT. W
SAN FRANCISCO, CA
94103
800-227-4530
415-861-7174
FAX: 415-861-4440**

Catalog with Potpourri Recipes: free
Save: 50% plus
Pay: check, MO, MC, V
Sells: culinary herbs, teas, spices, and potpourri ingredients
Store (wholesale outlet): same address; Monday to Friday 10–4

Reader-recommended San Francisco Herb is known for excellent prices and a great selection of herbs, spices, potpourri ingredients, fragrance oils, botanicals, and teas. San Francisco Herb was founded in 1973 and is primarily a wholesaler, but anyone who meets the $30 minimum order can buy here, too.

The culinary herbs and spices range from the routine—allspice, cinnamon, marjoram, tarragon—to such uncommon seasonings as spice blends for Greek foods and cilantro leaf. Among the botanicals are alfalfa leaf, balsam fir needles, chamomile, kelp powder, lavender, orris root, pine cones, rosebuds, pennyroyal, spearmint leaf, and yerba maté. (Some of these can be consumed, and others can't; check with a reliable information source before assuming botanicals are safe for food use.) Recipes for mulling spice blend, no-salt flavor enhancers, bouquet garni, and garam masala (a spice blend used in Indian cuisine) are all available on request.

The catalog also features dozens of recipes for sachets and simmering and jar potpourris. The "Hollyberry Christmas Jar Potpourri" has a delectable scent and lovely combination of colors, and "Plantation Peach" is delightfully fruity. If you're not experienced in making potpourri, try some of the recipes to become more familiar with blending colors and fragrances.

The spices and botanicals are sold by the pound (selected items are available in four-ounce units), with quantity discounts of 10% on purchases of five pounds or more of the same item. San Francisco Herb also sells glass vials and spice jars, flavored teas in bulk, dehydrated vegetables, shelled nuts, sprouting seeds, and such miscellaneous food goods as lemon powder, arrowroot powder, bacon bits, pine nuts, and roasted chicory root.

Special Factors: Satisfaction is guaranteed; volume discounts are available; authorized returns are accepted within 15 days (a 15% restocking fee may be charged); minimum order is $30; C.O.D. orders are accepted.

SIMPSON & VAIL, INC.

P.O. BOX 309
38 CLINTON ST.
PLEASANTVILLE, NY
10570-0309
800-282-TEAS
914-747-1336
FAX: 914-741-6942

Catalog: free
Save: up to 30%
Pay: check, MO, MC, V
Sells: coffees, teas, brewing accessories, and gourmet foods
Store: same address; Monday to Friday 9–5:30, Saturday 9–4:30

Simpson & Vail, established in 1929, sells gourmet coffees at prices lower than those charged by many New York City bean boutiques. Over 50 coffees are offered, including American (brown), French, Viennese, and Italian roasts, Kenya AA, Tanzanian Peaberry, Hawaiian Kona, Sumatra Mandehling Kasho, wood-roasted Brazil Santos, and other straight coffees and blends. The water-process decaffeinated line includes American-style roast, espresso, Mocha Java, Tip of the Andes, and others. Coffee-making gear and supplies by Krups and Melitta are available.

The tea department features over 80 varieties, among them the classics of England and the East, blends, naturally flavored connoisseur teas (raspberry, vanilla, watermelon, coconut, etc.), and selected decaffeinated teas. You'll also find tea accessories—infusers and balls, strainers, and filters—as well as bone china mugs, tea cozies, and warmers. And Simpson & Vail also stocks butter cakes from Vermont, Scottish shortbread, fudge sauces, soups by Abbott's, preserves, jams, marmalades, Patak Indian foods, and the delectable lines of Italian foodstuffs and condiments from Balducci's and Dean & Deluca.

Readers of this book may deduct 10% of the goods total from their first order only. Remember to identify yourself as a WBMC reader when you order. This WBMC reader discount expires February 1, 1997.

Special Factors: All beans are ground to order; gift packages are available.

SPICES, ETC.

P.O. BOX 5266
CHARLOTTESVILLE, VA
  22906
800-827-6373
804-293-9410
FAX: 800-827-0145

Catalog: free
Save: up to 75% (see text)
Pay: check, MO, MC, V, Discover
Sells: herbs, spices, tea, etc.
Store: mail order only

Spices, Etc., in business since 1991, offers a wealth of seasonings through a 64-page catalog, from straight bulk-packaged herbs and spices at savings of up to 65%, a great collection of sauces—diablo, curry, bay, barbecue, jerk, Thai, key lime, peanut, and more. The spice blends cover a wide culinary range, from celery salt and apple pie seasonings to garam masala, pesto, and exotic speciality blends. Chilies, popcorn seasonings, fruit essences, "Liquid Spices" (concentrate in soybean oil), dehydrated vegetables, bulk-packaged teas, hot pepper sauces, mustards, and other edibles are available. There are pages of grinders, mortar-and-pestle sets, spice racks, and empty jars in several sizes. Gift assortments and seasoning collections are also offered.

Special Factors: Quantity discounts are available.

SEE ALSO

Cabela's Inc. • *freeze-dried foods, trail packs* • **SPORTS**
Campmor • *dehydrated camping food, beef jerky, etc.* • **SPORTS**
Caprilands Herb Farm • *live and dried herbs, herbal vinegars, and teas* • **FARM**
Don Gleason's Campers Supply, Inc. • *freeze-dried food for camping and survival* • **SPORTS**
Le Jardin du Gourmet • *gourmet foods, live herb plants, etc.* • **FARM**
New England Cheesemaking Supply Company, Inc. • *cheese-making supplies and equipment* • **HOME: KITCHEN**
The Paper Wholesaler • *catering supplies, restaurant paper goods, disposable tableware* • **GENERAL MERCHANDISE**
Plastic BagMart • *plastic food storage bags* • **OFFICE: SMALL BUSINESS**
Storey's Books for Country Living • *cookbooks and manuals on food preservation* • **BOOKS**

Survival Supply Co. • *dehydrated and "survival" food* • **SPORTS**

Taylor's Cutaways and Stuff • *tea "baglets" for making your own teabags* • **CRAFTS: TEXTILE ARTS**

Triner Scale • *pocket scale* • **OFFICE**

U.S. Toy Company, Inc. • *penny candies* • **TOYS**

Weston Bowl Mill • *sugar buckets and butter churns* • **GENERAL MER-CHANDISE**

Zabar's & Co., Inc. • *gourmet foods and condiments* • **HOME: KITCHEN**

GENERAL MERCHANDISE, BUYING CLUBS, AND GOOD VALUES

Firms and buying clubs offering a wide range of goods and services

Most of the firms listed in this chapter offer such a diverse selection that it might be confusing to put them elsewhere: everything from mosquito netting to potpourri turns up. Go through the listings carefully, since there are some real finds here, and countless answers to the question of what to give for Christmas, birthdays, and other occasions. (See the section following this chapter, "Cards, Stationery, Labels, and Check-Printing Services," for firms specializing in those goods.)

Shopping has become much easier thanks to 800 lines. Those toll-free numbers also yield travel and lodging reservations, banking and investment assistance, product information and advice, and a wide range of services. Several guides are available to help you find the number you need—and to save you the 75¢ fee you're charged in some parts of the country every time you dial 800-555-1212. These guides include:

- The *AT&T Toll-Free 800 Consumer Directory* is a big help in finding 800 numbers quickly; it has over 60,000 listings, from "accountants" to "yarn." The current consumer edition costs $14.99 at this writing (plus shipping, handling, and applicable sales tax), and can be ordered by calling 800-426-8686 between 8 A.M. and 6 P.M., ET. (A listing of 120,000 business-to-business numbers is also available from AT&T; inquire for the current price.)
- Another directory that's packed with listings of manufacturers, catalogers, and sources of consumer information is *Catalyst*, billed as "The National Consumer Guide." It offers over 200 pages of infor-

mation for thousands of companies, special discounts and free catalogs, and a product index to help you locate specific items. The official cost of a two-issue, year's subscription is about $20, but call 800-234-6348 for current rates.

- The *National Green Pages™*, from Co-Op America, lists "green" companies—firms that meet the organization's standards for social and environmental responsibility. This 136-page guide runs from "advertising services" to "wood," and includes a list of steps you can take in your own life to help build a sustainable society. The current edition costs $6.95 from Co-Op America, 1612 K St. NW, Suite 600, Washington, DC 20006; 202-872-5307. (The *National Green Pages™* is free to Co-Op America members; individuals pay $20, businesses, $60; request membership information from the address above.)

Finding ways to save on all the things you buy—food, clothing, housing, transportation, education, insurance, vacations, and even luxury goods—is covered in *Cut Your Spending in Half: How to Pay the Lowest Price for Everything,* by the editors of Rodale Press (Rodale Books, 1994). It's a mine of information and ideas that can help you buy smarter and cheaper. Unfortunately, you can surrender all of your gains if you don't know how to handle a problem—whether it's fighting a bad utility bill, returning a defective product, or negotiating a 30-year mortgage. *Getting Unscrewed and Staying That Way* (Klein, Klein and Walsh, 1993) covers the range of remedies you have in curing problems that can crop up in the course of any transaction. Both books make valuable additions to the consumer reference bookshelf.

FIND IT FAST

BASKETS • **New England Basket**
CANVAS AND FLANNEL PRODUCTS • **Clothcrafters**
COUPON PREMIUMS • **Betty Crocker Catalog**
COUNTRY ACCENTS • **Gooseberry Patch, Tender Heart**
GIFTS • **Anticipations, Bennett Bros., Gooseberry Patch, Grand Finale, Tender Heart**
PARTY GOODS • **Paper Wholesaler**
WOODENWARE • **Weston Bowl Mill**

AARP

601 E. ST. N.W.
WASHINGTON, DC 20049
202-434-2277

Information: inquire
Save: up to 40% (see text)
Pay: check, MO, MC, V
Sells: membership (see text)
Store: mail order only

The AARP, or American Association of Retired Persons, is a not-for-profit organization dedicated to improving the lives of older Americans, especially in the areas of finance and health. Membership is open to anyone aged 50 or older, retired or not, at a cost of just $8 a year. Among the benefits are subscriptions to the bimonthly *Modern Maturity* and the monthly *AARP Bulletin,* the opportunity to buy low-cost supplemental health insurance, auto and homeowner insurance, obtain the AARP VISA card (15.6% APR, $10 annual fee), the AARP Motoring Plan (affiliated with Amoco Motor Club), group travel programs coordinated with American Express, publications on health topics, discounts on hotels and car rentals, and access to a pharmacy-by-mail. (See the listing for Retired Persons Services in "Medicine" for more details.)

When you write to the AARP for membership information, you can request the group's publication, "Prescription for Action," a 68-page guide to approaching health-care issues on a collective, community level. It gives guidelines and ideas for conducting price-comparison surveys of prescription drugs, compiling directories of physicians in your area who accept Medicare/Medicaid, cataloging services for seniors, having a voice in government, and promoting proven alternative-care options and long-term home care. The book is a compendium of ideas, resources, and references—a great source for health-care activists.

Special Factors: Inquire for information.

AMERICAN SCIENCE & SURPLUS

3605 HOWARD ST., DEPT.
WBM-96
SKOKIE, IL 60076
708-982-0870
FAX: 800-934-0732

Catalog: free
Save: up to 95%
Pay: check, MO, MC, V
Sells: industrial and scientific surplus goods
Store: 5696 Northwest Hwy., Chicago, IL;
also Rte. 38, East of Kirk Rd., Geneva, IL;
6901 W. Oklahoma Ave., Milwaukee, WI;
Monday to Friday 10–6, Thursday 10–9, Saturday 9–5, Sunday 11–5

American Science & Surplus offers a wide variety of surplus wares through witty catalogs that are published about seven times yearly. The firm has been selling surplus since 1937, and offers that blend of the strange and useful that is catnip to fans of surplus goods: everything from "humongo scissors and son" (a big and a small pair of scissors), to a baggie sized to fit a motorcycle.

Past catalogs have shown small DC motors, staplers, grow-your-own butterfly kits, microscopes, lasers, magnets, pharmaceutical bottles, collections of drive belts, feather hatbands, dozens of kinds of tape, whetstones, irregular body parts, DPDT switches, telescoping antennas, pumps, casters, glow-in-the-dark bats, piano hinges, Chinese riffler tools, aircraft drill bits, and magnifying lenses. (Please *don't* expect to find these particular items in the catalogs you receive—these are surplus goods, and stock is limited.) The descriptions, which are droll and explicit, note the original and possible uses for the products, as well as technical data, when available. Savings on original and if-new prices can reach 95%.

Special Factors: Satisfaction is guaranteed; returns are accepted within 15 days; minimum order is $10 in goods.

ANTICIPATIONS

9 ROSS SIMONS DR.,
   DEPT. WBMC
CRANSTON, RI 02920-4476
800-556-7376
FAX: 800-896-8181

Catalog: free
Save: up to 50%
Pay: check, MO, MC, V, AE, DC, Discover
Sells: gifts, home accents, etc.
Store: mail order only

Anticipations is 48 pages of treasures to delight your friends and grace your own home, at savings that average 25% on comparable retail. Produced by Ross-Simons (see the listing in "Jewelry"), Anticipations features fine and faux jewelry, carpets, home furnishings, holiday decorations, china, mirrors, framed art prints, children's gift items, Limoges boxes, and much more. Not everything is priced at a discount, but savings on selected furnishings, home accents, and table settings run as high as 45%. Anticipations maintains the same service standards as its parent company, featuring "white glove treatment" (in-home delivery of large pieces of furniture), and a swatching service for upholstered goods.

Special Factors: Satisfaction is guaranteed; returns are accepted within 30 days.

BENNETT BROTHERS, INC.

30 E. ADAMS ST.
CHICAGO, IL 60603
ORDERS: 800-621-2626
312-263-4800
FAX: 312-621-1669

Catalog: free
Save: up to 40%
Pay: check, MO, MC, V, Discover
Sells: jewelry, appliances, electronics, luggage, furnishings, etc.
Store: same address: Monday to Friday 8:15–5 (see the catalog for holiday shopping hours); also 211 Island Rd., Mahwah, NJ: Monday to Saturday 9–5:30

At the turn of the century, much of Bennett Brothers' business was in jewelry, gems, and watches. They're still a big part of the company's trade, but Bennett's current offerings, shown in the annual *Blue Book*, also include furnishings, leather goods, electronics, cameras, sporting goods, and toys.

The *Blue Book* is 100 color pages of name-brand goods, of which jewelry comprises over a third of the offerings—wedding and engagement bands, pearls, pins and bracelets, necklaces, and other pieces featuring all kinds of precious and semiprecious gems, as well as charms, lockets, medallions, anniversary jewelry, Masonic rings, and crosses and religious jewelry. The watch department offers models from Armitron, Benrus, Casio, Citizen, Gitano, Jules Jurgensen, Pulsar, Seiko, and Timex.

Bennett Brothers offers a fine selection of clocks, timepieces, and weather instruments. Silverware and chests, silver giftware, tea sets, pewterware, and fine china are also sold. The catalog shows kitchen cutlery sets, cookware sets, small kitchen appliances, microwave ovens, barbecue grills, vacuum cleaners, air machines, exercise equipment, sewing machines, personal-care appliances, bed linens, towels, tablecloths, and luggage. The leather goods department includes briefcases and attaché cases and luggage from Amity, Atlas, Gralnick & Son, Monarch, Samsonite, Winn, and York.

The *Blue Book* also features a large group of personal electronics and office supplies—clock radios, portable cassette players, stereo systems and components, TVs and video equipment, phones and answering machines, cameras, projectors, telescopes, binoculars, pens, globes, cash registers, calculators, typewriters, safes, files, and office furnishings. Home furnishings are also available, including patio furniture. The catalog includes Bachmann and LGB collectors' trains, Cox radio-controlled cars and planes, playing cards, and board games. There are also exercise machines, golf clubs, basketballs, fishing rods, and croquet sets. Metal detectors, flashlights, weathervanes, lawnmowers, chain saws, and other tools round out the offerings.

Bennett's prices are listed next to "suggested retail" prices throughout the book. Price comparisons of several goods substantiated Bennett's guideline prices (suggested retail), and the savings of 30% to 40%. Corporate buyers should contact Bennett Brothers for details on the firm's corporate gift programs, which can provide incentives at price levels from $16 to $1,000.

Special Factors: Authorized returns are accepted within ten days for exchange or credit.

CLOTHCRAFTERS, INC.

**DEPT. WM96, O. BOX 176
ELKHART LAKE, WI 53020
414-876-2112
FAX: 414-876-2112**

Catalog: free
Save: up to 40%
Pay: check, MO, MC, V
Sells: home textiles
Store: mail order only

  ⊕

This firm, established in 1936, sells "plain vanilla" textile goods of every sort, from cheesecloth by the yard to flannel patches for cleaning guns. The 20-page catalog is packed with inexpensive, useful things: pot holders, chefs' hats, bouquet garni bags (12 for $4), salad greens bags, fabric coffee filters, striped denim place mats, cotton napkins ($12 a dozen), hot pads, aprons, and supermarket produce bags ($9 for 6). Clothcrafters has a great selection of well-priced kitchen tools, including parchment paper, rubber spatulas, spatter lids, radiant heat plates, and other handy utensils.

You'll also find laundry bags, tote bags, flannel shoe bags, woodpile covers and firewood carriers, garment bags, cider-press liners, computer covers, flannel polishing squares, and mosquito netting. The bed and bath department offers cotton duck shower curtains, lightweight cotton terry towels and bath wraps, terry tunics, barbers' capes, flannel sleeping bag liners, and flannel crib sheets. Textile artists should check this source, since many of these items can be painted, embroidered, dyed, and otherwise embellished.

Gardeners will find the "PlyBan" porous plastic sheeting ideal for protecting newly planted rows from frost and insects ($9 for 4' by 50'). Clothcrafters also sells mosquito-netting helmets, multi-pocketed aprons, and denim knee pads—add an old shirt and dungarees, and you'll be ready to tackle the back forty.

Canadian readers, please note: Only U.S. funds are accepted.

Special Factors: Satisfaction is guaranteed; returns are accepted for exchange, refund, or credit.

BETTY CROCKER CATALOG

Catalog: 50¢
Save: up to 70% (see text)
Pay: check, MO, MC, V, Discover
Sells: table settings, kitchenware, house-wares, toys, etc.
Store: mail order only

P.O. BOX 5371
MINNEAPOLIS, MN 55460
612-540-2212
FAX: 612-540-7432

Betty Crocker, one of the most successful marketing creations in the history of prepared foods, has an image built on helping homemakers make the most of their time and money. All of her mixes and snacks—from Hamburger Helper to Nature Valley Granola Bars—as well as General Mills products bear coupons good for "Betty Crocker Catalog Points," which can be collected and applied toward the purchase of items from the Betty Crocker catalog. And if you've never sent the 50¢ requested for the catalog, do it now—the coupons you've been collecting (or tossing out with the empty packages) are worth big savings on a wide range of goods.

The catalog features tableware, including Oneida Community flatware and china from Franciscan, Johnson Brothers, Pfaltzgraff, and Royal Doulton. Flatware chests are available, as well as Armetale serving pieces, all sorts of bakeware, Betty Crocker, Regal, and T-Fal cookware, cutlery, kitchen gadgets, a line of scissors, and the Betty Crocker cookbook collection. And there are pages of educational toys, games, and puzzles, several patterns of children's tableware, and home entertaining helps like bridge tables and chairs, popcorn bowls, and beechwood accessories and snack tables.

Each item has two prices: the "no points" price (like regular retail), and the "Thrift" price, which you pay if you ante up a lot more points. For example, a five-piece place setting of Oneida highest-quality 18-8 stainless steel flatware, with a suggested sale price of $32.95, costs just $9.99—plus 65 Betty Crocker points. The LUX loud-ring kitchen timer costs $8.95 with 20 points, $11.95 without. And the points are easy to acquire—they're on all of the over 200 General Mills food products, and the catalog itself comes with 100 free points, plus over $8 in food coupons!

Special Factors: Satisfaction is guaranteed; returns are accepted for exchange, refund, or credit.

GOOSEBERRY PATCH

4 NORTH SANDUSKY ST.
P.O. BOX 190
DELAWARE, OH 43015
614-369-1554
FAX: 614-363-7225

Catalog: $3
Save: up to 30%
Pay: check, MO, MC, V
Sells: "country" gifts and crafts
Store: mail order only

The gift world is divided into two spheres—big and little. It's the "medium" gift, with more impact than a stocking stuffer but not enough to dent your budget, that always eludes. That's what makes Gooseberry Patch such a welcome find, especially if you and your intended recipient like things with a country accent. The firm's 64-page catalog is printed on paper the color of sugar cookies, and its contents are as sweet and wholesome: heart wreaths of canella berries, big bags of potpourri tied with ribbon, gift baskets tailored to specials tastes—filled with herbs, vanilla beans, flower seeds, tea, or bath infusions; wooden watermelon wedges, collectors' dolls, foam eggs and balls wrapped in country fabrics, cookie cutters in the shapes of everything from sunflowers and carrots to angels and crows, and tin cat silhouettes to perch on shelf or windowsill are just a few of the gifts currently available. A number of items cost under $10—festive "scent" baskets, antiqued tin hearts, a cat rubber stamp, and homespun heart coasters, for example—and there are dozens of great choices for under $20. If you're ordering by phone, be sure to ask about specials and new items that may not be pictured.

Special Factors: Satisfaction is guaranteed; price quote by phone or letter; returns are accepted for exchange, refund, or credit; minimum order is $15 with credit cards.

GRAND FINALE

SUBSCRIPTIONS DEPT.
P.O. BOX 620049
DALLAS, TX 75262-0049
800-955-9595

Catalog: $3, year's subscription, refundable on first purchase
Save: 25% to 70%
Pay: MC, V, AE, Discover
Sells: upmarket and name-brand goods
Store: mail order only

Your catalog fee brings you a year of "luxury for less," 48-page catalogs of special values, clearance items, and closeouts from well-known mail-order houses. It's possible to save up to 70% on the original selling or list prices through Grand Finale, which has been in business since 1980.

Past catalogs have featured designer clothing, shoes, handbags, hand-embroidered table linens, hand-hooked rugs, Lane occasional furniture, cashmere sweaters, needlepoint pillows, quilts, and Christmas decorations. Almost every catalog offers Limoges bibelots, coasters, designer bed linens, rugs, cookware, flatware, fine china and crystal, and women's clothing. There's usually a sale section in the catalog featuring exceptional bargains; quantities of these items are limited, so order promptly. The quality is consistently high, and Grand Finale provides a gift boxing service ($3) and can forward presents to recipients directly.

Special Factors: Satisfaction is guaranteed; quantities are limited, so order promptly; returns are accepted for exchange, refund, or credit.

NEW ENGLAND BASKET CO.

P.O. BOX 1335
N. FALMOUTH, MA 02556
508-759-2000
FAX: 508-295-8299

Catalog: $3
Save: up to 50%
Pay: check, MO, MC, V
Sells: baskets, bows, and ribbons
Store: #19, Patterson Brook Rd., West Wareham, MA

New England Basket Co. offers a great line of country basket models, as well as traditional woven willow baskets. The 20-page color catalog showcases a diverse array of styles, colors, and finishes. Dimensions of each basket are given, and there are two prices—for one set or piece, or for one case. In addition to their obvious uses as decorative accents and a place for chips or rolls, consider baskets as great gift containers, closet organizers, flowerpot holders, toy catchalls—the list is endless.

New England Basket Co. also offers a great line of ribbon and bows—both satin and curling ribbon, and pom-pom and star bows, in a wide range of colors. These and the gift tags are so well priced that it pays to stock up for the holidays. And if you're considering starting a gift-basket business, see the heat sealing machines, cellophane sheets and excelsior, and other supplies—all you add is fruit and cheese!

Special Factors: Satisfaction is guaranteed; quantity discounts are available; authorized returns are accepted (a 15% restocking fee is charged) for exchange, refund, or credit.

THE PAPER WHOLE-SALER

17800 N.E. FIFTH AVE.

NORTH MIAMI, FL 33162

305-651-6900

FAX: 305-651-6300

Catalog: $3
Save: up to 40%
Pay: check, MO, MC, V, Discover
Sells: party supplies, restaurant disposables
Store: (warehouses) same address; also 2638 S.W. 28th Lane, Coconut Grove; 410 W. 49th St., Hialeah; and 8259 W. Flagler, Miami, FL

The Paper Wholesaler, in business since 1983, sells restaurant and party and entertaining supplies and related goods in case lots and "retail packs," at discounts of up to 40% on the regular prices. The 32-page color catalog is full of table goods, decorations, and the little things that add fun to festive occasions: paper plates and napkins in vibrant colors and snappy designs, including ensembles for children's birthdays, wedding parties, and showers; plastic cutlery and cups, tablecloths, doilies, balloons, crepe paper, party hats, streamers and pennants, favors, and other novelties. Guest towels and toilet paper are sold here, as well as a good selection of candles, hors d'oeuvre picks and drink stirrers, cocktail napkins with amusing slogans, wrapping paper, gift bags, bows and ribbon, and invitations in upbeat designs and colors.

The Paper Wholesaler has a "serious" section for restaurateurs and caterers, which includes a selection of cake-decorating supplies, cake pans, deli and bakery containers, commercial-sized rolls of foil and poly film, ice scoops and bar tools, carafes, syrup pitchers, ash trays, and even the brooms, mops, and buckets you'll need when the guests are gone. And there's food—restaurant-sized containers of Pepperidge Farm Goldfish, Hellmann's mayonnaise, Orville Redenbacher popcorn, Planter's peanuts, and other condiments and snacks. The catalog includes tips on party planning, and the order form even features shopping lists so you don't overlook anything.

Special Factors: Satisfaction is guaranteed; returns of unopened, unused goods are accepted within 30 days for exchange, refund, or credit.

TENDER HEART TREASURES, LTD.

10525 "J" ST.
OMAHA, NE 68127-1090
800-443-1367
402-593-1313
FAX: 402-593-1316

Catalog: free
Save: 30% to 50%
Pay: check, MO, MC, V, AE, Discover
Sells: handcrafts and gifts
Store: mail order only

Tender Heart Treasures has a staggering collection of crafts, seasonal display and decorations, and home accents, at prices that are a solid 30% to 50% below retail. (In fact, if you're a craftsperson you'll find the low prices a little depressing, since they're *retail*—the wholesale prices are 40% to 60% lower.) The 74-page color catalog features hundreds of gifts, display pieces, and seasonal decorations: bears of all types in costume and the buff, "welcome" signs and hospitality plaques, hatboxes, dolls and figurines, angels, electrified kerosene lamps, bent-wire decorations, baskets, floppy-eared bunnies in cute outfits, picture frames, bird houses, twig doll furniture, planters, wooden apples and other fruit, wreaths, miniatures, and lots more. In addition to terrific prices, Tender Heart Treasures makes ordering a breeze—there's no minimum, and shipping charges are easy to compute to any destination.

Wholesale inquiries should be made to 800-443-1367; a copy of your resale tax certificate will be required with your first order.

Special Factors: Satisfaction is guaranteed; quantity discounts are available; authorized returns are accepted within 30 days for exchange, refund, or credit; C.O.D. orders are accepted.

TERRY'S VILLAGE

**DEPT. 452 P.O. BOX 2309
OMAHA, NE 68103-2309
800-200-4400
402-331-5511
FAX: 800-723-9000
TDD (RELAY): 800-833-
7352**

Catalog: free
Save: up to 54%
Pay: check, MO, MC, V, AE, Discover
Sells: gifts, home accessories, and crafts
Store: mail order only

What wonderful catalogs arrive from Terry's Village, full of decorative treats to make your home special for the holidays, and mark the seasons throughout the year. The spring edition is full of bunnies celebrating Easter, shown on tin boxes that can be filled with candy, outside their own miniature village, and on banners, wreathes, and soap dishes. Cherub wall and shelf statues, terra-cotta birdbaths, handpainted mushroom finches, muslin dolls, candles, and vegetable-shaped soup crocks describe the range of gifts and accents. The Christmas edition shows angels of every type, Nativity scenes, beautiful collector dolls, resin Santas and grand Santas in gold with fur trim, winter villages (including a porcelain gingerbread version), ornaments, water globes, and even wrapping paper and ribbon assortments. The prices are so low that it sometimes costs more to make a craft item yourself than it does to buy it as a finished product here. For holiday gifts, favors, hostess presents, home decor and even resale (depending on the prices prevailing in your area), don't buy elsewhere until you've check the Terry's Village catalog.

Special Factors: Satisfaction is guaranteed; returns are accepted within 30 days for exchange, credit, or refund.

WESTON BOWL MILL

P.O. BOX 218-WBMC
WESTON, VT 05161-0218
802-824-6219
FAX: 802-824-4216

Catalog: $1, refundable
Save: up to 30%
Pay: check, MO, MC, V
Sells: woodenware and wooden household items
Store: Main St. (Rte. 100), Weston, VT; daily 9–5

Weston Bowl Mill has been known since 1960 for its wooden salad bowls, but the Mill produces hundreds of other wooden items for use throughout the home. Prices of many of the goods run about 30% below comparable retail, and savings are even better on selected goods. Almost everything is available with and without finish (oil or lacquer): The popular salad bowls, thick curves milled from a solid piece of maple or birch, are offered in sizes from 6" to 20" across. You can save by buying the seconds (when available), but note that sales are final—no returns are accepted on seconds.

Weston sells much more for dining table and kitchen, including birch plates and trays, maple lazy Susans, salt-and-pepper shakers, cheese plates, knife racks, tongs, a great selection of carving and cutting boards, and carbon steel knives. The 26-page catalog offers a wide variety of other home items, including shelves with brackets, towel and tissue holders, spoon racks, pegged coat racks, a large selection of wooden boxes, quilt racks, benches, stools, wooden fruits and vegetables, sugar buckets and churns, and baskets. Weston's bird feeders and whirligigs are well priced; likewise the delightful group of wooden toys—vehicles, tops, puzzles, game boards, cradles, and other classics—that are oil-finished. And the "country store" department includes "magic" massagers, lap boards, door stops and window props, outlet plates, spool holders, bells, yardsticks, and many other useful items.

Special Factors: Minimum order is $5, $20 with credit cards.

SEE ALSO

Acme Premium Supply Corp. • *premium merchandise* • **TOYS**
Baron/Barclay Bridge Supplies • *bridge-playing gifts* • **TOYS**
Bruce Medical Supply • *dining, dressing, bathing, and other aids for the disabled and motor-impaired* • **MEDICINE: SPECIAL NEEDS**
Business Technologies, Inc. • *cash registers* • **OFFICE**

Caprilands Herb Farm • herb charts, note cards, potpourri, pomanders, etc. • **FARM**

Michael C. Fina Co. • silver and crystal giftware • **HOME: TABLE SETTINGS**

Gohn Bros. • Amish "general store" goods • **CLOTHING**

Kaye's Holiday • holiday ornaments • **TOYS**

Oriental Trading Company, Inc. • gifts, novelties, etc. • **TOYS**

Paradise Products, Inc. • wide variety of party goods • **TOYS**

Pendery's Inc. • potpourri ingredients and gifts • **FOOD: BEVERAGES AND FLAVORINGS**

La Piñata • piñatas • **TOYS**

Plexi-Craft Quality Products Corp. • acrylic furniture, accessories, and gifts • **HOME: FURNISHINGS**

Rafal Spice Company • potpourri ingredients, oils, etc. • **FOOD: BEVERAGES AND FLAVORINGS**

Nat Schwartz & Co., Inc. • bridal registry for gifts • **HOME: TABLE SETTINGS**

Albert S. Smyth Co., Inc. • giftware, bridal and gift registry • **HOME: TABLE SETTINGS**

Surplus Center • tools, electrical components, security equipment • **TOOLS**

Survival Supply Co. • "survivalist" gear, books, and food • **SPORTS**

Think Ink • inexpensive thermographic color hand printers • **CRAFTS**

Thurber's • gifts, collectibles, and Christmas ornaments • **HOME: TABLE SETTINGS**

U.S. Box Corp. • ribbons, bows, gift wrap, etc. • **OFFICE: SMALL BUSINESS**

U.S. Toy Company, Inc. • toys, games, and novelties • **TOYS**

Wag-Aero Group of Aircraft Services • aviation-related gifts • **AUTO**

Cards, Stationery, Labels, and Check-Printing Services

Greeting and correspondence cards,
personal and business stationery, mailing
and novelty labels, related services, and
check-printing services

Once upon a time, cards were something you bought for special occasions and the big three—Mother's Day, Father's Day, and Christmas. You chose between Hallmark and American Greetings and bought them at the local drugstore. All that changed in the 70s when small, independent card companies introduced "real" sentiments and "soft touch" cards. We now have a $4 billion industry that celebrates every remotely memorable life event and holiday, at prices that have risen from 35¢ and 50¢ to $2 to $3 *each*. If you send cards regularly, you can save considerably by buying from the firms listed here—50% and more on the cost of the same type of cards if bought individually. (And when you buy by the box, you have cards whenever you need them.) Companies that manufacture cards usually offer personal stationery, labels, and related goods—luggage tags, printed napkins and party goods, desk organizers, calendars, etc.—as well. In addition to the firms listed here, you can get good buys on cards from museum shops. Many of them run mail-order specials after Christmas, with special assortments and bonuses that bring per-card prices to well under $1 each.

Another great way to save money effortlessly is by having your next order of checks printed by one of the companies listed here. You can choose from some great designs and pay well under $15 for the same number of checks that would run $45 or more when ordered through the bank. The editor of this book has used two of the services listed here without a hitch; Current even updated the account data format in her checks to conform to her bank's newest protocols, despite the fact that she sent them an old sample check. Send for information from these firms when you're a couple of months from needing new checks. When you receive them, file the brochures with the bank's reorder reminder, or tape a note to yourself (about the new check sources) on top of the "time to reorder" notice in your last book of existing checks. Then pull the file, place your order with one of the check-printing services, and save an easy 50%.

FIND IT FAST

CARDS AND STATIONERY • **American Stationery, Current**
LABELS • **Current, Lixx Labelz**
CHECK-PRINTING SERVICES • **Check Store, Checks in the Mail, Image Checks, Current**
WEDDING STATIONERY • **American Stationery**

THE AMERICAN STATIONERY CO., INC.

DEPT. W
P.O. BOX 207
PERU, IN 46970
800-822-2577
FAX: 317-472-5901

Catalog: free
Save: up to 45%
Pay: check, MO, MC, V, AE, Discover
Sells: personalized stationery
Store: mail order only

The American Stationery Co. offers an excellent selection of personalized stationery, at prices up to 45% below those charged by other firms for comparable goods and printing. The company has been in business since 1919, and also produces "The American Wedding Album," a 52-page color catalog with a wide range of wedding invitations and accessories.

The correspondence selections include embossed sheets and notes in four colors, deckle-edged and plain sheets and envelopes in white and pastels, and heavyweight Monarch sheets, business envelopes, and "executive" stationery of heavyweight, chain-laid paper. The styles range from traditional to casual-but-tasteful, for both business and personal correspondence. There are great buys here, including the "Typewriter Box" of 100 printed sheets and the same number of printed envelopes for $20, as well as informals and notes in contemporary and calligraphic typefaces, notepads in spiffy designs, and a choice of ink colors—navy, teal, and gray, as well as the standard range. Stationery for children, personalized memo pads, bill-paying envelopes, bordered postcards, gummed and self-sticking return-address labels, and related goods are shown in the 48-page color catalog.

Special Factors: Satisfaction is guaranteed; returns are accepted for replacement or refund.

THE CHECK STORE

790 QUAIL ST.
P.O. BOX 5145
DENVER, CO 80217-5145
800-424-3257

Brochure: free
Save: up to 50%
Pay: check or MO
Sells: check-printing services
Store: mail order only

The Check Store offers over 20 personal check designs, chiefly classic marble-grain and safety backgrounds and soft-focus illustrations—clowns, wildlife, mountain views, puppies, flowers, nature scenes, and Western motifs among them. The standard introductory offer—200 wallet-style checks with single-copy deposit tickets for $4.95—is being offered at this writing, and self-duplicating checks and printer-friendly (continuous-form and laser) designs are available at a higher price. The brochure of business check styles shows general and multipurpose, payroll, itemized invoice, and checks with voucher stubs, in three-to-a-page, continuous-form, and laser printer formats, beginning at $19.95 for 300 nonduplicating checks. Confidentiality of all of your bank data is guaranteed.

Special Factors: Satisfaction is guaranteed.

CHECKS IN THE MAIL

Brochure: free
Save: up to 50%
Pay: check or MO
Sells: check-printing services
Store: mail order only

5314 NORTH IRWINDALE
AVE.
IRWINDALE, CA 91706
800-733-4443

  ¡Si!

The designs offered by Checks in the Mail are the liveliest available from the big check-printing firms. The "Stars and Stripes" check, for example, doesn't confine its flag to the upper-left corner—this banner spans the whole check face. Ageless party girl Betty Boop does a cameo on one, richly colored fish swim across "Ocean Wonder," and a personal favorite, "Ransom," adds a playful touch to every bill payment. There are over two dozen designs for personal checks, offered in wallet and carbonless duplicate styles, and in three-to-a-page desk sets. Business checks are available in a choice of formats, as well as continuous-feed and laser printer checks; request the "business" or "computer" brochures separately.

Prices begin at $4.95 for 200 wallet-style personal checks (the introductory offer), and run up to $29.95 for a desk set of 300 duplicate checks. Script lettering and rush delivery are extra. The checks are guaranteed to be printed to your bank's standard, and confidentiality of your bank data is assured.

Special Factors: Satisfaction is guaranteed.

CURRENT, INC.

Catalog: free
Save: up to 57%
Pay: check, MO, MC, V, AE, Discover
Sells: stationery, gifts, wrapping paper, cards, check-printing services
Store: outlets in CA, CO, and OR

1005 E. WOODMAN RD.
COLORADO SPRINGS, CO
80941
800-525-7170
719-593-5900

Current, in business since 1950, publishes a monthly, 68-page color catalog of stationery, gifts, and household items in appealing designs, many exclusive to Current, ranging from animal and nature scenes to quilt motifs and other Americana. All-occasion and holiday cards are available, as well as notepads, personal cards and stationery, gift wrapping, ribbon, stickers, recipe cards and files, toys, games, organizers, kitchen helps, calendars, memo boards, mugs, and other gifts. Current's "Expressions of Faith" catalog features Christian-oriented cards, gifts, and products for children. Prices are very reasonable, and discounts are given based on the number of items ordered.

Current's Check Product Division also offers check-printing services: 21 designs, which are priced up to 50% below what your bank probably charges you. Business checks are offered in four colors, two type styles, with dozens of stock graphic designs, in binder or checkbook style. And since Current is one of the printers that *banks* use, your checks are guaranteed to be accepted at any U.S. bank. For information and current special offers, see the check-printing brochure that's sent with the catalog, or call or write for information.

Special Factors: Satisfaction is guaranteed; sliding discounts of 20% and more are offered on orders of 12 or more items; returns are accepted.

IMAGE CHECKS, INC.

P.O. BOX 548
LITTLE ROCK, AR
  72203-0548
800-562-8768

Brochure: free
Save: up to 50%
Pay: check or MO
Sells: check-printing services
Store: mail order only

Image Checks has over 40 years of experience in printing checks for businesses, and offers a great choice of options in check and record formats. In addition to general disbursement checks, Image Checks sells payroll and voucher versions, in standard (desk) and computer (continuous-form and laser printer) styles. Savings vary, depending on the format, options (custom logo or ink color), and amount you're buying, from about 30% to 50%, compared to bank prices.

Special Factors: Phone lines are staffed Monday to Friday 8 A.M. to 4:30 P.M., CT.

LIXX LABELZ

BOX 74679K
2803 W. 4TH AVE.
VANCOUVER, BC V6K 1R0
CANADA
800-595-5499

Catalog: $4CAD, $3US (see text)
Save: up to 30%
Pay: check or MO
Sells: customized labels, bookplates, stationery, rubber stamps
Store: mail order only

Put an end to blah correspondence with Lixx Labelz, custom-printed labels for your letters, books, wine bottles, and what-have-you. Other firms put your name on a gummed or self-adhesive label, and some throw in an initial or cute motif, but Lixx Labelz offers you over 280 graphics showcased in the catalog (a free brochure of the firm's most popular designs is also available). The design focus is a meeting of *Wild Kingdom* and modern calligraphy—great hand-lettered type styles and a choice of scores of animals, from giant pandas and other endangered species to geckos, house cats, and otters. Hearts, hydrangeas, maple leaves, hot-air balloons, stars, Teddy bears, and food and wine designs are also available. The labels are large, running from about 1" by 3" to about 3" by 4", and they're printed on recycled, self-adhesive paper. Considering the size and the custom options, the Lixx Labelz prices— $12-CAD for 200 of the smallest size to $25-CAD for 200 of the largest bookplate size—are very reasonable. Lixx Labelz has developed an order form that makes it easy to specify exactly what you want, but if you don't find something to your liking among the stock designs, no problem—the firm will use your own copyright-free art to create the label you had in mind. Notepads and stationery are also available, and the most popular Lixx designs are now offered in rubber stamps.

For those whose needs are declarative, there's the line of "Just Cause Labelz" (separate catalog, $1). The categories include Junk Mail Cures, Mother Earth, Animal Rights, Recycling, Vegetarianism, and Pollution; memorable mottos abound.

U.S. readers, please note: Payment is accepted in U.S. funds, at a discount on the Canadian dollar rate (25% at this writing).

Special Factors: Label orders are not accepted via phone; orders take up to 6 weeks to arrive.

SEE ALSO

Dover Publications, Inc. • *cards, labels, graphics, posters, etc.* • ***BOOKS***

Online Services

Computer-based shopping, communication, and information services

You can attend an auction, buy stock shares, do thesis research, communicate with friends in New Zealand, learn a new language, enjoy a movie, play bridge, and do tens of thousands of other things just sitting at your computer, thanks to the miracle of online services and networks. Before describing the former, you may find it helpful to learn a little bit about the latter.

A BRIEF HISTORY OF THE NET

Online services wouldn't exist without computer networking, and it's hard to think of networking without a nod to the great one: The Internet. The story of the Net begins in the 60s, as the Department of Defense proposed an alliance with an assortment of university brainpower, to create a network that would permit researchers to share research data across computers "live." The prototype, ARPANET, was unveiled in 1969, and its first connection succeeded at linking computers at four California universities. The Net grew exponentially, joining research labs, universities, and government agencies in a network that crossed the country and spanned the globe. It's noteworthy that even in its germinal stages, computer games and nonacademic "chat" were as popular with the scientists as the opportunity to collaborate with contemporaries on far-flung continents. As the medium evolved, crude bulletin boards (the electronic equivalent of cork) gave way to USENET newsgroups (opinion forums) and conferences (live online discussions), which are two of the services most popular with users today.

THE WORLD WIDE WEB

The Net had plenty of engineers when it was built, but no MBAs. The highly technical, noncommercial milieu in which the enterprise was conceived and flourished still influences the way the Net works, and may be the key to the biggest problem facing the neophyte who wants to explore its resources. It has been said that if something can be imagined, it can be found on the Net. Figuring out *how* to locate what you need is the Net's Achilles heel. The Net has the quality of something organic, constantly mutating, that defies conventional organization. But the World Wide Web (aka the Web, WWW, and W3) is changing that. The Web is a system that ties together the zillions of huge and tiny network servers (the command centers of the network) that make up the Net, using graphics and video and hypertext "links." These connections take you from one file or "place" to another that has related information, where you may find other links, and so on—and each document or newsgroup or other site can be on a different computer, anywhere in the world.

BROWSERS

The Web is a *system,* and what makes it work are *browsers,* software navigators that deliver the Web as organized multimedia—sound, graphics, and full-format text. The best-known browser at this writing is Mosaic, which is sold in Internet-in-a-Box kits and a la carte; the other leader is Netscape Navigator, which is usually used by businesses. The promise that the Web and Mosaic and other browsers represent—access to information for all—is part of what's made politicians wax mystical about the creation of the Information Superhighway. The trouble is that even with a browser, experienced computer programmers report problems with finding what they're looking for.

At this point, the best strategy for getting acquainted with the Net is to make your first stop one of the big online services (see below). But if you want to tackle the Net, bravo! Following are several books on how to do it. If one doesn't help, try another, and remember: The rewards for making it easy for millions of people to navigate the Net successfully are so great, that *someone* will come up with the "dream browser." Until then:

GUIDES TO THE INTERNET AND RELATED REFERENCES

- *The Internet Companion: A Beginner's Guide to Global Networking,* by Tracy Laquey (Addison-Wesley), is introduced by Al Gore and takes you through the process of making connections and performing searches. The text edition is also sold with a networking disk.

- *The Online User's Encyclopedia: Bulletin Boards and Beyond,* by Bernard Aboba (Addison-Wesley), manages to be big and deep and lots of fun, covering both Mac and Windows Net surfing with lots of graphics and command examples. Extensive bibliographies, reviews of software and books, a guide to cable configuration, and lists of BBSes, conferences, online resources, UNIX tips, and a glossary are great extras. Register for the book online and you can download the updates.
- *Internet Starter Kit for Macintosh,* by Adam C. Engst (Hayden Books), has strong recommendations from Mac Net pros, who praise the scope of the text and the fact that it comes with MacTCP, a program for creating a personal account on the Net, which will cost you twice the price of the book if you buy it in a software store as a program!
- *The Whole Internet User's Guide and Catalog,* by Ed Krol (O'Reilly & Associates, Inc., 1995), is an excellent, accessible guide that defines the Internet and covers access, file transfers, e-mail, newsgroups, navigating, performing searches, the Web, and troubleshooting problems. The "catalog" of the book lists hundreds of intriguing Net sites, from "aeronautics" (NASA's Langley Research Center) to "zymurgy" (sources for home-brewed beer). A detachable card of basic UNIX commands ends this useful volume.
- The *Dummies* books, as in "DOS for," "Windows for," and "Modems for," also carries titles on modems, the Internet, and CompuServe. If you like the format, check out the most recent titles.

ONLINE SERVICES

What they are: The online services discussed here are provided by giants like America Online and CompuServe. They're freestanding networks with gateways to the Net and their own browsers for the Web, but they aim to provide such a wide array of consumer services, information, and entertainment that you won't feel the need to stray.

How to use them: At this writing, if you have a 386 computer (or higher) running Windows 3.1 (or higher), at least 4Mb space on your hard drive, 4Mb RAM, a Hayes-compatible modem (9600 baud or higher), a standard (non-PBX) phone line, a VGA monitor that supports 256 colors, a mouse, and a credit card, you can open an account on America Online (AOL) or CompuServe (CS) (Macintosh requirements differ). You'll also need the service's software; see the descriptions of the services, below, for details. Once you're online, you can scroll and click your way through the service, reading news headlines, booking airline tickets, completing a homework assignment with some help from *Compton's Encyclopedia,* buying mutual shares, downloading this week's *Time,* posting a review of a current restaurant to a bulletin board—you can do these and thousands of other things, all within the domain of just one online service.

Shopping: The first thing you buy online is time—a certain number of hours for a set fee, and an hourly rate for time beyond that allotment. Surcharges apply for premium services, much like cable TV. Study the service's pricing policy carefully, and keep track of the time you spend online. Read the manual for timesaving shortcuts. Online, time really *is* money.

Both America Online and CompuServe have shopping services, which offer a range of computer and consumer products at a discount. Whether the general user will come to prefer buying by computer more than by catalog remains to be seen, but a lot of firepower is betting on the possibility. MCI has announced that it's breaking ground on an electronic mall, and will provide high-speed data links to businesses. The Home Shopping Network has bought the Internet Shopping Network, and QVC Network Inc. will be retailing on the Net as well. The Microsoft Network will mirror the look and feel of Windows 95, the latest evolution in its operating system. Creating a seamless transition from one environment to another is just one of several singular features that may make Microsoft Network a serious contender for the time and money now spent on other services. Regardless of the names of the contenders, the explosive growth of networking assures a proliferation of "electronic malls" and other spending opportunities. As screen graphics and picture resolution improve, the experience of looking through an online catalog will come closer to the "manual" version. The potential environmental benefits of doing business without paper, ink, and gasoline are so significant that every "green" cataloger should invest in making it work.

E-mail: In addition to shopping, the online services offer e-mail, which is reportedly the most-used application on the Net. E-mail uses the memorandum as its format—you have a blank for the name and address, a "re" blank, a section in which you can keystroke your thoughts (or paste them from another document), and options, like carbon copies, receipt notification, file attachments, etc. Type your message, address it, and click the "send" button—that's e-mail at its most basic. E-mail is powerful, but plain: You can send it to thousands of people at the same time, but you can't underline a single word in the letter. E-mail has addressing protocols that differ, depending on where you're sending mail from and to. And e-mail and all text communications have their own code of behavior governing addressing, punctuating, emphasizing, and even mailing your letters. The cheapest and easiest way to learn about the rules of your online services is to is read the manual (RTM) and download the file of frequently asked questions (FAQ). If you chat online with other, more experienced users and wonder aloud about basics, you'll probably get the same advice—with the same acronyms. E-mail protocol, commonly used contractions, and the language of "emoticons," punctuation symbols arranged to represent facial expressions, are the subject of *Smiley's,* by David W. Sanderson, and *!%@:: A Directory of Electronic Mail Addressing & Networks,* by Donnalyn Frey and Rick Adams (both titles from O'Reilly & Associates, 1993).

Security: At this writing, there is no assurance that any data on the Net is safe from hackers and "phone phreaks." When you go online, you usually have to set up an account that bills one of your credit cards; to reduce temptation to someone bold enough to steal data, use a card with a low ($1,000 or lower) line of credit, and *never* use a debit card. To protect all of the users and avoid legal hassles when using e-mail, you should know that the content of your letters may be read by others. Most of the online services have guides to what's okay and what's out of bounds, and if you have questions, the sysop (who plays the role of hall monitor, den mother, and traffic supervisor) should be able to help.

Basics: All of the online services offer email, news, popular publications, shopping, weather, financial services, chats and forums, and connections to the World Wide Web and the Internet. The pricing structures vary from one to another, which makes comparisons tricky unless you cost out based on "real life" use patterns. The following firms emerged as clear winners on that basis, with savings of 62% to a whopping 94%, compared to other online services that are competing for the same market. Because the services are constantly adding and expanding features and content and restructuring pricing and rates, these listings will become outdated quickly. Check the most current review of the major services by reading computer magazines like *PC World* and *PC Magazine* for an update on what's on offer.

AMERICA ONLINE INC.

**8619 WESTWOOD
CENTER DR.
VIENNA, VA 22182-2285
800-827-6364
703-448-8700**

Registration Software: free
Save: up to 94% (see text)
Pay: MC, V, AE
Sells: online services
Store: mail order only
E-mail: postmaster@aol.com

When America Online Inc. was founded in 1985 by Steve Case, it took him the next five years to make the 100,000-member mark. These days, AOL adds that many new accounts in less than a month, and could easily exceed 2.5 million by early 1996.

America Online has long been appreciated for its snazzy interfaces, which make it more "friendly" to users accustomed to good graphics and production. America Online allows you to use up to five screen names per account, making it a great fit for families and individuals running small businesses. It's also very focused on the idea that AOL is a community, and its wildly popular chat rooms and forums are neighborhoods within that larger realm. The pricing structure is friendly, too: $9.95 per month with five hours free access, and $2.95 per hour after that. These fees are for activity in the "Member Services" area; e-mail (with address-book function) is free, but surcharges apply if you're having it converted to a fax or to paper mail. AOL's connections to the Net include USENET newsgroups, Telnet, FTP, Gopher, the Web, and WAIS data bases.

AOL's "People Connection" supports a wide range of interests and opinions, and there's no reason to guess at facts with a reference section that includes the Library of Congress, the Bible, *Compton's,* the *Smithsonian,* and *National Geographic.* The news and publications include *U.S. News & World Report, New York Times, Chicago Tribune, Atlantic Monthly, Woman's Day,* and CNN, UPI, Reuters, and other wire sources. The Entertainment section brings you TV, radio, movies, music, games, columns, and more, and there's a separate section, "Kids Only," especially for children. You can look up product ratings in *Consumer Reports* and make a purchase through Shopper's Advantage, or recalculate your mortgage, check a stock quote, or buy a block of Morningstar mutual funds through "Marketplace" and "Personal Finance." Sports, education, travel, weather, and computing interests are all served with forums, product offerings, data bases, and much more. One of AOL's strongest draws is the "Clubs and Interests" department, which has established online "communities" of people with needs and interests ranging from coping with multiple sclerosis to launching a one-person business. Advice and support are given freely, and it's easy to see why this form of communication is so valuable to people who have mobility problems or who are physically isolated.

The support materials that you receive with your America Online membership are skeletal, and purchasing *The Official America Online Tour Guide,* by Tom Lichty (Ventana Press), is recommended; you'll have the chance when you register your account, or you can locate it elsewhere at a discount.

Special Factors: Ask for the risk-free trial offer; per-minute surcharges apply to users outside the contiguous United States.

COMPUSERVE INFORMATION SERVICE

5000 ARLINGTON
  CENTRE BLVD.
COLUMBUS, OH 43220
800-848-8199
614-457-8600

Registration Software: free
Save: up to 94% (see text)
Pay: direct debit, MC, V, AE, Discover
Sells: online services
Store: mail order only
E-mail: 70006,101@compuserve.com

CompuServe, founded in 1979, is the old guard of the online services—what it lacks in luscious interfaces, it makes up for in solid document libraries, well-established forums, CD-ROM capabilities, and business-related services. CompuServe has over 2.5 million subscribers in 138 countries, and is the service of choice for most businesses. The rates at this writing are $8.95 per month for unlimited time on basic services, and $4.80 per hour *and up* for extended services. (You'll receive some good support materials free, as well as the CompuServe Magazine.) CompuServe's celebrated e-mail allows you to send files, connect to over a dozen kinds of mail systems on the Net, and offers a "return receipt" option. At this writing, CompuServe gives you a $9 monthly credit toward e-mail, which costs 15¢ for the first 7,500 words (prices and pricing structure may change).

CompuServe's basic services include membership support (account information, help lines, etc.), e-mail and CS classifieds, the Electronic Mall, games and trivia, investment information, news from the Associated Press, U.S. National Weather Service reports, sports, HealthNet online medical information resource, *Consumer Reports,* Peterson's College Database, Grollier's encyclopedia, EAAsy Sabre® (for travel reservations), Zagat restaurant reviews, and more. CompuServe's forums are strong on the professional side—doctors, lawyers, educators, entrepreneurs, publicity directors, court reporters, engineers, broadcast professionals, computer enthusiasts, etc. all have their own spots—but human sexuality, disabilities, trademark and copyright research, dissertation abstracts, and military and veteran forums and data bases are a few of the other offerings. The shopping opportunities include catalog companies, whose catalogs can be downloaded onto CD-ROM, and "Shopper's Advantage," which has some of the best prices around on computer products, electronics, and appliances (there is a yearly charge for membership).

If you're looking for information data bases and serious discussion, CompuServe is still out front with its forums and document libraries, whether they're about SSI or SDI. At this writing, CompuServe is the best choice for business and home-based-business use. The coming support of Internet use that will allow you to upload and download files from the Net (FTP), and actually log onto other computers on the Net (Telnet), will strengthen this focus.

Special Factors: Please note that you have limited use of the system until you receive your permanent ID number.

HEALTH AND BEAUTY

Cosmetics, perfumes, and toiletries; vitamins and dietary supplements

You can save a solid 30% on your cosmetic and beauty needs and still get the same name brands featured in beauty emporiums and department stores when you buy by mail. Products may be in perfectly good but discontinued colors, promotional sizes or packaging, or have some other attribute that distinguishes them from the full-size, full-price product. Another source for savings is Sally Beauty Supply, a network of beauty-supply stores across the country that sell to both consumers and cosmetologists. Find the store nearest you by calling 800-284-SALLY; once you're familiar with the products, you may be able place phone orders instead of shopping in the store. Good discounts on perfumes are somewhat elusive; the savings tend to be closer to 20% off list, and if the discounts are deeper, the scent may be specially packaged, a gray-market product, or counterfeit. (Examine the packaging carefully.) You may find a bargain in "copycat" scents, which are produced by Essential Products. If you like their version, you'll save up to 90% on the cost of the real thing.

The storm of controversy surrounding what used be known as "vitamins and minerals" is never-ending, and since they're not regulated as drugs by the FDA, supplements are listed here. You can stay informed about the vitamin debate, as well as research findings in nutrition and general medical issues through the health sections of papers and newsweeklies, but you'll find more focused coverage in such specialty newsletters as the monthly *University of California at Berkeley Wellness Letter* ($24 per year in the United States; to subscribe, write to P.O. Box 420148, Palm Coast, FL 32142, or call 904-445-6414). If you're going to take nutritional supplements or anything else to augment your diet and improve your sense of well-being, be sure to consult your primary-care physician, especially if you're already taking medication or have a health problem.

For more information on nutritional health resources, see the introduction to "Food and Drink"; for firms selling related products, see the listings in "Medicine."

FIND IT FAST

EXERCISE EQUIPMENT • **Creative Health**
PERFUME AND BEAUTY PRODUCTS • **Beautiful Visions, Essential Products, Fragrance International, Holbrook Wholesalers, Kettle Care, Scente Perfumerie**
SUNGLASSES • **Sunglasses U.S.A.**
VITAMINS • **Freeda, Hillestad, PIA**

BEAUTIFUL VISIONS

**105 ORVILLE DR.
BOHEMIA, NY 11716
800-645-1030
FAX: 516-567-9072**

Catalog: free
Save: up to 90%
Pay: check, MO, MC, V, Discover
Sells: cosmetics and preparations
Store: same address; Monday to Friday 9–5, Saturday 9–4

 ¡Si!

Beautiful Visions, which has been in business since 1977, sells beauty essentials from top manufacturers at up to 90% off list prices. Each issue of the 80-page catalog brings you cosmetics, skin-care products, and perfumes from Almay, Aziza, Chanel, Charles of the Ritz, Coty, Jōvan, L'Oreal, Max Factor, Maybelline, Prince Matchabelli, Revlon, Vidal Sassoon, and other manufacturers. Current fashion shades are stocked, as well as the basics. The catalog also features vitamins and minerals, grooming tools, fashion jewelry, and gifts, all at very reasonable prices.

Special Factors: Satisfaction is guaranteed; returns are accepted.

CREATIVE HEALTH PRODUCTS

DEPT. WBMC
5148 SADDLE RIDGE RD.
PLYMOUTH, MI 48170
800-742-4478
313-996-5900
FAX: 313-996-4650

Catalog: free
Save: 30% average
Pay: check, MO, MC, V, AE, Discover
Sells: fitness equipment, related medical devices
Store: mail order only (see text)

Creative Health Products has been selling health, fitness, and exercise equipment since 1976, and carries some of the best product lines available. Savings vary from item to item, but average 30% on list or regular retail prices. The 14-page catalog lists current models of stationary bicycles, ergometers, rowers, stair climbers, and accessories by Altero, American Diagnostic, Baseline, Cateye, Dicor, Lafayette, Lange, Monark, Novel, Oglend-Bodyguard, Omron/Marshall, Quinton, Spirit, and Tunturi. There are pulse/heart rate monitors from Biosig Instruments, Cardio Sport, CIC, Nissei, and Polar, Skyndex body-fat calipers, Jamar strength and flexibility testers, and professional scales by A&D, Detecto, Health-O-Meter, Metro, and Seca. Stethoscopes, Tadeka blood pressure testers (sphygmomanometers), otoscopes, ophthalmoscopes, and books on health and fitness are also sold, and the catalog includes guides on buying different types of devices. Please note that this is professional equipment and, even with discounts, the prices are not low. Creative Health welcomes questions about any of the products, and can help you find the best equipment for your needs. Although primarily a mail-order firm, Creative Health welcomes visitors (weekdays, 9–5), so drop by if you're in the area (call first for directions).

Special Factors: Quantity discounts are available; institutional accounts are available; C.O.D. orders are accepted.

ESSENTIAL PRODUCTS CO., INC.

90 WATER ST.,
DEPT. WBM
NEW YORK, NY
10005-3587
212-344-4288

Price List and Sample Cards: free with SASE (see text)
Save: up to 90% (see text)
Pay: check or MO
Sells: "copycat" fragrances
Store: same address; Monday to Friday 9–6

"We offer our versions of the world's most treasured and expensive ladies' perfumes and men's colognes, selling them at a small fraction of the original prices." Essential was founded in 1895 and markets its interpretations of famous perfumes under the brand name of "Naudet."

Essential Products stocks 50 different copies of such costly perfumes as Beautiful, Coco, Eternity, Giorgio, Joy, L'Air du Temps, Obsession, Opium, Passion, Poison, White Diamonds, and Ysatis, as well as 23 "copycat" colognes for men, from Antaeus to Zizanie. A one-ounce bottle of perfume is $20 (1/2 ounce, $11.50), and four ounces of any men's cologne cost $11. When you write to Essential Products, please identify yourself as a WBMC reader, which entitles you to five free "scent cards" of Essential's best-selling fragrances. The sample cards give an idea of how closely the Naudet version replicates the original, but you should try the product to evaluate it properly. You must also enclose a long, stamped, self-addressed envelope for the set of samples.

Special Factors: Satisfaction is guaranteed; returns are accepted within 30 days for refund; minimum order is $20.

FRAGRANCE INTERNATIONAL, INC.

**398 E. RAYEN AVE.
YOUNGSTOWN, OH 44505
800-877-3341
800-543-3341
216-747-3341
FAX: 216-747-7200**

Catalog: free
Save: up to 30% average (see text)
Pay: check, MO, MC, V, Discover
Sells: men's and women's scent
Store: mail order only

Living well may be the best revenge, but doing it at a discount goes one better. Fragrance International can help you carve an average of 28% to 33% off your next purchase of men's or women's scent, whether you're buying full-strength perfume, eau de parfum, eau de toilette, cologne, after shave, body cream, lotion, dusting powder, or deodorant. Not every scent is offered in every form, but the current list includes hundreds—from Adolfo to Yves Saint Laurent's "Y" for women, and Aramis to Zizanie for men. In addition, a selection of bath salts and shower gels, cosmetic bags, manicure accessories, cosmetic trays, makeup mirrors, and other beauty and bath accessories is available. Be sure to check the flyers of specials for closeouts and other special buys, at savings of 50% and more. And please note the minimum order requirement: $50 if you pay by credit card.

Special Factors: Minimum order is $50 with credit cards.

FREEDA VITAMINS, INC.

36 E. 41ST ST.
NEW YORK, NY
10017-6203
800-777-3737
212-685-4980
FAX: 212-685-7297
TDD: 800-777-3737

Catalog: free
Save: up to 40%
Pay: check, MO, MC, V, AE, Discover
Sells: dietary supplements and prescriptions
Store: Freeda Pharmacy, same address; Monday to Thursday 8:30–6, Friday 8:30–4

 ¡Si! © ★ ✓

Freeda, a family-run operation, has been manufacturing vitamins and minerals in its own plant since 1928. Freeda is dedicated to providing the purest possible product, and its formulations are free of coal tar dyes, sulfates, gluten, starch, animal stearates, pesticides, sugar, and artificial flavorings, and are suitable for even the strictest vegetarian or Kosher diet. The Zimmermans, who run the firm, put an extra tablet in every bottle just to be nice. There are savings of up to 40% on some of Freeda's supplements—and the WBMC reader discount makes this the best vitamin buy around.

The 36-page catalog lists vitamins, minerals, multivitamins, and nutritional products, which are available in a dizzying choice of combinations and strengths. The vitamin "families" include A and D, B, C, and E; among the minerals are calcium, iron, magnesium, potassium, selenium, and zinc; amino acids, proteins, and other dietary extras are offered. Freeda is listed here not for its megadose formulations, but because of its emphasis on quality production and additive-free goods. It's great to find a source for children's (and adults') vitamins made without sugar, coal tar dyes, sulfiting agents, animal stearates, sulfates, or artificial flavorings. (Freeda's chewable vitamins are naturally flavored, and there is an unflavored version for children on restricted diets. All of the Freeda vitamins are approved by the Feingold Association.) Needless to say, the Freeda catalog is free of the preposterous claims and misleading information often given by supplement sellers. And wonderful as all of this is, it's still important to check with your health-care professional before taking supplements and to avoid megadoses unless they're specifically recommended.

Freeda is offering readers of this book a special discount of 20% on all orders. You must mention WBMC to take the discount, which should be computed on the cost of the goods only, and can't be combined with other discounts and specials. This WBMC reader discount expires December 31, 1997.

Special Factors: Courtesy discounts are given to health-care professionals; most major health plans are honored; C.O.D. orders are accepted.

HILLESTAD INTER-NATIONAL, INC.

P.O. BOX 1770

AV 178 U.S. HWY. 51 NORTH

WOODRUFF, WI 54568

715-358-2113

FAX: 715-358-7812

Catalog: $1
Save: up to 40%
Pay: check, MO, MC, V, Discover
Sells: nutritional supplements, toiletries, and cleaning products
Store: same address; Monday to Friday 8–5

You can get "factory-direct" prices on the "Harvest of Values," "Nutri-Game," and Hillestad lines of vitamins, minerals, and other supplements by ordering from the manufacturer, who's been in business since 1959. Prices here are up to 40% lower than those charged elsewhere for comparable goods.

Hillestad offers good selection of vitamins and minerals through a comparatively hype-free catalog. There are multivitamin and mineral formulations for adults, chewable versions for children, vitamins A, B-complex, C, and E; a "stress" formula; and chelated iron, bone meal, lecithin, alfalfa, amino acids, protein, and antioxidants. Hillestad also sells a host of herbs, pet vitamins, garlic concentrate in capsules, vitamin E cream and aloe body lotion, shampoo, cream rinse, and liquid "soapless" soap, a biodegradable, phosphate-free cleanser for dishes, hand-washables, and general cleaning. Complete label data on most products are given in the catalog.

Special Factors: Satisfaction is guaranteed; all goods are guaranteed against defects in manufacturing; returns are accepted within 30 days.

KETTLE CARE

DEPT. WBMC
710 TRAP RD.
COLUMBIA FALLS, MT
59912
406-892-3294

Catalog: $1, refundable
Save: up to 30% average (see text)
Pay: check, MO, MC, V
Sells: natural skin-care and bath products
Store: mail order only

Every skin-care empire ever built began with someone at the stove, turning improbable ingredients into the stuff of dreams. That's the business of Kettle Care, where natural products and botanicals are combined to create moisturizers, facial creams, facial scrubs, lotions, balms, and other things to soothe your skin and spirit. The eight-page catalog features lavender liquid castile-based facial soap, five botanically scented massage oils, hand-saving Worker's Creme, natural facial scrubs, lotion for normal-to-oily complexions, Aromatherapy Facial Creme, and pure essential oils. Herbal sleep and dream pillows, bath herbs, and woodsy herbal sachets are part of the "Herbal Pleasures" section. The prices are very reasonable: Kettle Care's Herbal Aid Creme with cocoa butter and almond oil costs $8 for two ounces, while Caswell-Massey's Almond Night Cream costs nearly $15 for the same amount. Among the other good buys are quarter ounces of essential and fragrance oils for $5 and jars of naturally flavored lip balm for $2. You can buy everything individually, or take advantage of the sample sets and discounted "packs" of four or six of the same kind of item. (See Special Factors, below, for details on Kettle Care's recycling program; many products are available packaged in glass.) The catalog lists the ingredients of most of the products, and includes directions for use. And there's a guide to which skin-care products suit which complexion types, so you can develop your own treatment line and regimen.

Wholesale customers: The minimum order is $35, and the discounts average 45% to 50% off catalog prices.

Special Factors: Satisfaction is guaranteed; returns are accepted for exchange, refund, or credit; C.O.D. orders are accepted; 25¢ credit given for every container returned.

PIA DISCOUNT VITAMINS

Catalog: free
Save: 20% minimum
Pay: check, MO, MC, V, AE
Sells: supplements, homeopathic remedies, vitamins, etc.
Store: mail order only

708 SAWMILL RIVER RD.
ARDSLEY, NY 10502
800-662-8144
914-693-3632
FAX: 914-693-3557

There are plenty of companies selling generic lines of vitamins, but the 24-page newsprint catalog from PIA offers name-brand vitamins, minerals, and remedies, at a minimum savings of 20% on list. The formulations are not given, but they're easy to locate when you visit your health-food store or pharmacy to price shop.

The catalog begins with Alacer ascorbates and ends with zinc lozenges, and offers savings on Bach Flower remedies (hard to find at a discount), Boiron, FutureBiotics, Good 'N Natural, Kwai, Kyolic, Medicine from Nature, Nature's Way, Gary Null's products, Schiff, Solgar, and Twinlab. The name of the product, form (caplet, tablet, etc.), potency, and amount are given, with the retail and discounted prices. If you don't see what you're looking for, call PIA to see whether it can be ordered.

PIA Discount Vitamins is offering readers a discount of 10% on their first order. Be sure to identify yourself as a WBMC reader when you order, and deduct the discount from the cost of the goods only. This WBMC reader discount expires February 1, 1997.

Special Factors: Satisfaction is guaranteed; price quote by phone or letter; online with CompuServe and Prodigy.

SCENTE PERFUMERIE INC.

255 FIFTH AVE., 3RD FL.
NEW YORK, NY
  10016-6516
212-889-8681
FAX: 212-725-2562

Catalog: $2, refundable
Save: up to 35%
Pay: check, MO, MC, V, AE
Sells: perfumes and Lancôme products
Store: mail order only

You don't buy fragrances to put a sales commission in a stranger's pocket, you buy them because you like the way they make you—or someone else—smell. So if you don't need the "help" you'll get at the department store counter, skip it: Buy from Scente Perfumerie, and save up to 33% on the prices you usually pay.

This firm's 48-page catalog ($2, refundable with purchase) doesn't have glossy photos or provocative descriptions; it's just a no-frills list of men's and women's scents, their forms (perfume, cologne, after shave, etc.), and the retail and discount prices. The latest edition offered popular and hard-to-find fragrances among the hundreds, including Boucheron, Decadence, Dunhill, Sublime, Tea Rose, and Zibeline. If you'd love to have a large "wardrobe" of scents but can't afford it even at a discount, see the listing of about 70 perfumes and colognes that are available in miniature bottles or sample sizes, from under $3. (They're also great for travel, stocking stuffers, and for the person who uses scent too rarely to justify a bigger bottle.)

Please note: All orders are shipped via UPS, and returns are accepted *only* as stated in "Special Factors," below.

Special Factors: Satisfaction is guaranteed; authorized returns of product that has not been used, in manufacturer's original box and packaging, are accepted within 30 days for refund or credit; minimum order is $20; French-speaking sales reps are on staff.

SUNGLASSES U.S.A., INC.

469 SUNRISE HWY.
LYNBROOK, NY 11563
800-USA-RAYS
FAX: 516-599-4825

Catalog: free
Save: up to 33%
Pay: check, MO, MC, V, Discover
Sells: Ray-Ban sunglasses
Store: same address; Monday to Friday
10–5:30

Sunglasses U.S.A. sells Ray-Ban sunglasses at 33% to 50% off suggested retail. The catalog includes information on the lens material, color, and protection factors against glare and ultraviolet light. The Ray-Ban lines currently available include Classic Metals, Killer Loop (shields), Traditionals and Premier Traditionals, Wayfarers, Leathers, Tortuga, Cats, Marine Line, and Retrospecs. The price list includes sizing and style numbers, making it easy to be sure you're buying the right model.

Sunglasses U.S.A. is offering readers a discount of 10% on all orders. Be sure to identify yourself as a WBMC reader when you order, and deduct the discount from the cost of the goods only. This WBMC reader discount expires December 31, 1997.

Special Factors: Shipping and handling cost a flat $2 per order.

SEE ALSO

Adventures In Cassettes • *motivational audio cassettes* • **BOOKS: RECORDINGS**

Baby Bunz & Co. • *natural bathing toiletries for babies* • **CLOTHING: MOTHER AND CHILD**

Better Health Fitness • *exercise equipment* • **SPORTS**

Caprilands Herb Farm • *potpourri ingredients, essential oils, etc.* • **FARM**

Dairy Association Co., Inc. • *Bag Balm liniment* • **ANIMAL**

Deer Valley Farm • *nutritional supplements and natural toiletries* • **FOOD**

Jaffe Bros., Inc. • *Jaybee brand soap/shampoo* • **FOOD**

The Natural Baby Co., Inc. • *homeopathic and natural remedies* • **CLOTHING: MOTHER AND CHILD**

Penzeys' Spice House • *salt-free seasonings* • **FOOD: BEVERAGES AND FLAVORINGS**

Retired Persons Services, Inc. • *vitamins, beauty products, shampoo, etc.* • **MEDICINE**

Walnut Acres Organic Farms • *natural toiletries, nutritional supplements* • **FOOD**

— HOME —

Decor

Floor coverings, wall and window treatments, lighting, upholstery materials, tools, and services

his section of the "home" decor chapter—immediately following this introduction—covers treatments for windows, walls, and furnishings. Look here for firms selling fabric, stock and custom blinds and shades, wallpaper and borders, and drapery hardware and painting accessories. Some of the firms sell a wide range of products (see "Find It Fast," below), but if you're looking for lamp and shade specialists, you'll find them in "Lighting," immediately after this section; for floor coverings, see "Rugs, Carpeting, and Flooring," following that.

Doing your own decorating instead of hiring someone is a time-honored tradition, and there are scores of books on interior design written specifically for consumers, such as *Interior Design on Your Own,* from Consumer Reports Books. *Interior Design,* by John F. Pile (Harry N. Abrams, Inc., 1988), is a sumptuous, oversized guide to classics old and new, that includes design fundamentals. Shelter magazines (*House Beautiful, Metropolitan Home, World of Interiors,* etc.) can be great sources for ideas, but beware the chic totem: Tizio lamps, the Atelier "red and blue" chair, banana plants, overdone windows, and Pirelli floors have all enjoyed endorsement as "timeless" by the design establishment, but have become clichés nonetheless. Focus on styles that *you* find refreshing and beautiful—products with good materials and workmanship—and you'll make better buying decisions.

If you haven't already done so, set up files for each room you're decorating. Keep your budget, floor plan, measurements, paint chips, swatches, sources, and other reference materials there. One designer strongly recommends taking a series of "before" pictures. When shot from different perspectives, they can help you see the room's strengths, as well as its failings. If nothing else, it will be gratifying to see the contrast when all of your work is done!

Until recently, access to the best fabrics, furnishings, and accessories has been limited to design professionals ("to the trade"). Over the last few years, products that were once available to licensed designers exclusively are now offered by discounters and retail decorators. They sell to consumers who've shopped the showrooms and read the shelter magazines, want the best, and are willing to pay for it. Some decorators now offer their buying services (with or without design consultations), enabling consumers to purchase once-unavailable fabrics, accessories, and furnishings, sometimes at a discount.

All of this sounds good—consumers become educated, discounters respond with access to more products, manufacturers sell more goods, small design firms increase their business. A retailing success? Not according to the manufacturers, some of which threaten to pull their product lines from discounters and nontraditional sellers if their brand or trade names appear in ads, or even in editorial mentions, like the listings in this book. Because of this problem (which affects a number of other industries, not just the home furnishings trade), some brand names may not appear in a merchant's listing, even when that brand is available. To determine whether a firm offers a line not noted in the listing, call or write the company.

In addition to the firms listed in this section, you'll find firms that sell clocks, mirrors, mattresses, lamps, and related goods in the "Furnishings" chapter—see the "Find it Fast" section in the introduction for a thumbnail guide.

FIND IT FAST

DECORATOR FABRIC • **Dorothy's, Fabric Center, Fabrics by Phone, Hancock Fabrics, Home Fabric Mills, Homespun Fabrics, Marlene's, Shama, Silk Surplus**
DECORATOR TRIM • **Fabric Center, Hancock Fabrics**
WINDOW AND WALL TREATMENTS • **American Discount, Benington's, Custom Window, Dorothy's, Hang-It-Now, Harmony, Homespun Fabrics, Interiors Guild, Robinson's, Shibui, Silver, Wells Interiors**

AMERICAN DISCOUNT WALL AND WINDOW COVERINGS

1411 FIFTH AVE.,
  DEPT. WBM
PITTSBURGH, PA 15219
800-777-2737, EXT. 103
FAX: 412-471-3347

Information: price quote
Save: up to 73% (see text)
Pay: check, MO, MC, V, AE, Discover
Sells: wall coverings, fabrics, and window treatments
Store: same address; Monday to Friday 8:30–5, Saturday 8:30–1

American Discount Wall and Window Coverings, whose parent firm was founded in 1916, offers savings of up to 73% on the best in decorator wall and window treatments. Most of the wall coverings are discounted 35% to 50%; upholstery and decorator fabrics are priced 10% to 35% below regular retail here. Custom window treatments by Bali, Del Mar, Flexalum, Graber, HunterDouglas, Joanna, Kirsch, Levolor, Louver-Drape, Nanik, and Verosol are discounted 25% to 73%.

Among the wall covering firms and designers represented are Boussac of France, Carefree, Eisenhart, Essex, Fashon, Greeff, Imperial, Judscott, Katzenbach and Warren, Kingfisher, Kravet, Ralph Lauren, Carey Lind, Mayfair, Mirage, Sandpiper, Sanitas, Seabrook, Sunworthy, United, Van Luit, Walltex, Westgate, Winfield, and York—and there are scores more.

Special Factors: All goods are first quality; returns (except cut rolls, borders, custom wall coverings, and custom window treatments) are accepted within 20 days (a 25% restocking fee is charged).

BENINGTON'S

DEPT. WBMC
1271 MANHEIM PIKE
LANCASTER, PA 17601
800-252-5060
717-299-2381
FAX: 717-299-4889

Information: price quote
Save: up to 83%
Pay: check, MO, MC, V, AE, Discover
Sells: wall coverings and carpeting
Store: same address; 5 other outlets in PA and VA

Benington's observes that "decorating is exciting when you can get what you want at a price you can afford," and aims to deliver with discounts of up to 83%. The firm incorporates wall coverings, decorator fabrics, and carpeting under one roof, representing the major names in all three industries. Call with the name of the manufacturer, the pattern book name or number, style, color, and amount you'll require, to receive a price quote. Extra-wide commercial wall coverings are also available. Prices average 50% below list, and if you're ordering large quantities, you may receive deeper discounts.

Benington's is offering readers a discount of 5% on *all* orders. Be sure to identify yourself as a WBMC reader when you order, and deduct the discount from the cost of the goods only. This WBMC reader discount expires February 1, 1997.

Special Factors: Price quote by phone, fax, or letter; wall coverings (except commercial or institutional orders) are shipped free within the continental United States.

CUSTOM WINDOWS & WALLS

DEPT. WBMC
32525 STEPHENSON HWY.
MADISON HEIGHTS, MI
  48071
800-772-1947
FAX: 810-583-9897

Brochure: free
Save: up to 75%
Pay: check, MO, MC, V, Discover
Sells: wall coverings, window treatments, decorator fabrics
Store: mail order only

After deliberating over window treatments and wallpaper patterns, go the final step and get the best price. Custom Windows & Walls, which is the mail-order division of a firm in business since 1908, should definitely be on your list of sources. Upon request, Custom will send you manufacturers' brochures describing the available lines, along with a measuring guide, samples, and a list of discount prices. The firm offers window treatments by Comfortex, Del Mar, Graber, HunterDouglas (Duette), Kirsch, Levolor, and LouverDrape, as well as its own "Window Express" 1" mini and 1/2" micro blinds and vertical blinds in a choice of scores of colors and materials, at 50% to 75% below list price. If you're shopping for verticals, don't miss "It's in the Mail," a new line offered in PVC and fabric at very low prices. Wall coverings from Birge, Carefree, Imperial, Seabrook, Sunwall, Van Luit, Warner, York, and other manufacturers are available, as well as coordinating fabrics and the full line of Croscill wall coverings and accessories. Prices are discounted to 50% plus below list, and a price-quote form is included in the information packet. Please note that all of the window treatments are made to order and are not returnable. Measure and *remeasure* carefully before ordering.

Custom Windows & Walls is offering readers a discount of 10% on orders of Window Express brand mini blinds and verticals. Be sure to identify yourself as a WBMC reader when you order, and deduct the discount from the cost of the goods only. This WBMC reader discount expires February 1, 1997.

Special Factors: Quantity discounts are available.

DOROTHY'S RUFFLED ORIGINALS, INC.

8112 MARKET ST.
WILMINGTON, NC 28405
910-686-8000
FAX: 910-686-8029

Catalog: $4
Save: up to 80% (see text)
Pay: check, MO, MC, V, AE, Discover
Sells: decorator fabrics and custom services
Store: same address; also Roswell, GA; Charlotte, and Goldsboro, NC; Cincinnati, OH; Myrtle Beach, SC; and Newport News and Richmond, VA

Dorothy's Ruffled Originals celebrates the swags, poufs, jabots, flounces, and flourishes of the fully dressed window with a large collection of custom- and ready-made draperies, bed linens, table toppers, pillows, nursery linens, shower curtains, canopies, and all the hardware and rods you need to put things in place.

Dorothy's "Designs for the Home" catalog ($4) features full-color showcases of Dorothy's designs, coordinated in room settings. These creations have a Southern glamour and add a distinctly feminine touch to a room. Dorothy uses a generous six-to-one ratio of yardage to finished ruffle in many of her creations in this collection, which produces dense, luxurious gathers—most draperies are only half as voluminous. The catalog includes a guide to the fabrics Dorothy offers, and detailed price and measurement guides.

The prices of the custom work aren't *cheap,* but they're reasonable, compared to local decorating shops.) The "Economy Line" features single ruffled curtains and valances in a "lighter fullness" at a lower cost. And a wide selection of pleated shades, blinds, and verticals is available for 80% off list. If you can sew, see the good buys on Dorothy's fabric—

200 different chintzes, eyelets, moirés, laces, etc.—as well as romantic florals, damask-print solids, stripes and paisleys, "wallpaper" prints on fabric, and more, from about $3 to $11 a yard. Don't miss the hardware section in the back of both catalogs, which has an excellent selection of rods, brackets, finials, supports, sashes, shelves, and other drapery fittings.

Wholesale customers, a tax I.D. number is required, and discounts run up to 20%.

Special Factors: Satisfaction is guaranteed; returns of defective goods are accepted for exchange, refund, or credit; minimum order is 1 yard fabric; C.O.D. orders are accepted.

THE FABRIC CENTER, INC.

DEPT. WBMC
485 ELECTRIC AVE.
FITCHBURG, MA 01420
508-343-4402
FAX: 508-343-8139

Catalog: $2
Save: up to 50%
Pay: check, MO, MC, V
Sells: interior decorator fabrics
Store: (showroom) same address; Monday to Saturday 9–5:30

The Fabric Center has been in business since 1932, selling fine fabrics for home decorating at savings of up to 50% on suggested list prices. Fabrics for upholstery and window treatments are available, including lines from Robert Allen, American Textile, Paul Barrow, Covington, George Harrington, Kravet, Peachtree, Waverly, and many others. The firm's splendid 164-page color catalog ($2) features hundreds of fabrics from a wide range of manufacturers, shown in room settings and grouped with complementary patterns and colorways. The catalog descriptions include fiber content, width, vertical repeat, and a usage code to help you determine if the material is appropriate for draperies, home accessories, or upholstery. And The Fabric Center's "Sampling Service" allows you to try the fabric in your home before you order. The 3" by 4" samples cost 15¢, the 8" by 10" pieces are 50¢, and 24" by 27" samples cost $3.95 each. (The price of each $3.95 sample can be credited to each $50 in goods ordered.) Don't miss the scores of trim—tassels, bullion fringe, cording, brush fringe, tiebacks, and more—in colors chosen to complement the widest decorative range.

In addition to the latest designs in home fashion, The Fabric Center stocks cotton moiré in 26 colors ($6.98 per yard at this writing), 60 shades of cotton/poly chintz, dozens of tapestries, over 20 lace fabrics (suitable for curtaining), cotton/linen-blend solids and prints, and drapery sheers and linings. Prices are very reasonable—solid color chintz costs $4.98 a yard at this writing.

Special Factors: Minimum order is one yard.

FABRICS BY PHONE

P.O. BOX 309, DEPT. 200
WALNUT BOTTOM, PA
17266
800-233-7012, EXT. 25

Brochure and Samples: $3
Save: up to 50%
Pay: check, MO, MC, V
Sells: decorator fabrics and custom window treatments
Store: Fabric Shop, 120 N. Seneca St., Shippensburg, PA

Fabrics by Phone has been doing business since 1937, as the mail-order arm of a decorating store, and suggests that you call with manufacturer's name and fabric colorway for price and availability information. Fabrics by Phone also makes custom draperies and accessories, including bedspreads, coverlets, dust ruffles, pillows, tablecloths, and more. For more on these services, send $3 for the literature, price list, and swatches.

Special Factors: Price quote by phone or letter with SASE; minimum order is three yards (on goods not in stock).

HANCOCK'S

DEPT. WBMC
3841 HINKLEVILLE RD.
PADUCAH, KY 42001
800-845-8723
FAX: 502-442-3152

Catalog: $1, refundable
Save: up to 60%
Pay: check, MO, MC, V, Discover
Sells: decorator fabrics, pillow forms, quilting supplies, etc.
Store: same address; Monday to Friday 9:30–8, Saturday 10–6, Sunday 1–5

You might not expect "America's Largest Fabric Store" to be found in Paducah, Kentucky, but the folks at Hancock's will enlighten you.

They've pulled together a 72-page color catalog of the best sellers on the retail floor there, hundreds of fabrics that represent the most popular looks in decorating today, from traditional to eclectic design. And they sell them at prices 50% to 70% below suggested retail.

The catalog includes a color shot of the fabric, the name of the design (but not the maker), and the price per yard; width, fiber content, and repeat information are not given consistently. But if you've been going through the shelter magazines and going through swatch books, you'll recognize much of what you see—except the prices. Hancock's sampling service charges 50¢ for drapery-weight goods and 75¢ for upholstery fabric (in 9" squares), and provides cuttings of solid colors upon request. If you're looking for a good selection of solid colors, see the choice of chintzes, warped sateen, jacquards, and other offerings. In addition, Hancock's sells trim (brush and loop fringe, bullion, cording, tassels, etc.), drapery lining (under $3 a yard at this writing), pillow forms (up to 30" square in polyfil, and 20" square in duck and goose down feather, for under $13), fusible backing for roller shades, heavy felt, and will do custom lamination for under $5 a yard.

Hancock's separate catalog for quilters is 32 pages of notions, tools and equipment, materials, batts, thread, and more. You'll find quilters' collections of fabric by Bernartex, Concord, Alexander Henry, Hoffman, John Kalder, P&B, South Seas, VIP, and West Point; a broad selection of interfacing, basic fabrics (from bridal satin to heavy canvas), and sewing and quilting products by Coats & Clark, Dritz, Gingher, Hobbs, Mundial, Olfa, Schmetz, and June Taylor. Savings on list average 60% plus, and you can join Hancock's swatch club for monthly snippets of Hancock's newest fabrics (see the catalog for details).

Special Factors: All goods are first quality; special orders are accepted.

HANG-IT-NOW WALLPAPER STORES

10,517F N. MAIN ST.
ARCHDALE, NC 27263
800-325-9494
910-431-6341
FAX: 910-431-0449

Information: price quote
Save: 40% average
Pay: check, MO, MC, V, AE, Discover
Sells: wall coverings and decorator fabrics
Store: same address; also 4620 W. Market St., Greensboro, NC; Monday to Friday 9–6, Saturday 9–3, both locations

Hang-It-Now Wallpaper, established in 1981, sells wall coverings at savings of 30% to 65% on list prices. A limited selection of decorator fabrics is also available, at discounts of up to 40%. All major brands of wall coverings (plus strings, grass cloth, and borders) are offered here, including Color House, Crutchfield, Eisenhart, Faslon, Imperial, Katzenbach & Warren, Carey Lind, Sanitas, Seabrook, Sunworthy, United, Van Luit, Warner, and York, among others. Hang-It-Now specializes in providing wall coverings to retail establishments, and has done numerous installations for furniture retailers and decorators.

Special Factors: Only first-quality goods are sold; shipping is not charged on orders sent within the continental United States.

HARMONY SUPPLY INC.

P.O. BOX 313
MEDFORD, MA 02155
617-395-2600
FAX: 617-396-8218

Information: price quote
Save: up to 60%
Pay: check, MO, MC, V
Sells: wall coverings, window treatments, decorator fabrics
Store: 18 High St., Medford, MA; Monday to Saturday 8–5:30, Thursday 8 A.M.–9 P.M.

Harmony Supply, in business since 1949, can give your home a face-lift at a discount with savings of up to 60% on wallpaper, coordinating fabrics, and window treatments. Harmony carries over 2,500 designs and patterns of wallpaper, grass cloth, and string cloth, including Laura Ashley, Imperial, Ralph Lauren, Van Luit, and many others. Harmony Supply also sells made-to-measure mini, micro, vertical, and pleated shades and blinds by Flexalum, Graber, HunterDouglas, Kirsch, Levolor, Louverdrape, and Verosol. You'll save the most on goods that are currently in stock, but even special orders are discounted up to 60%, and everything Harmony sells is first quality. Call or write for a price quote, since there's no catalog or price list.

Special Factors: Satisfaction is guaranteed; returns (except custom blinds) are accepted within 30 days (a 25% restocking fee is charged on special-order goods).

HOME FABRIC MILLS, INC.

━━━━━━━

882 S. MAIN ST.
P.O. BOX 888
CHESHIRE, CT 06410
203-272-3529
FAX: 203-272-6686

Information: price quote free
Save: up to 40%
Pay: check, MO, MC, V (see text)
Sells: decorator fabrics and custom services
Store: same address; also Rte. 202, Belchertown, MA; and 443 Saratoga Rd., Rte. 50, Scotia, NY; Monday to Wednesday 10–9, Thursday to Saturday 10–5

Home Fabric Mills has been in business since 1968 and is a good source for the home decorator who's unsure of what type of fabric is best for a particular project, or the person who's trying to match a color.

The three Home Fabric Mills stores are stocked with thousands of bolts of upholstery and drapery materials, lining, trims, and workroom supplies from Bloomcraft, Conso, Covington, Graber, Kaufmann, Kirsch, Lanscot-Arlen, Waverly, Wolf, and other manufacturers. Only first-quality goods are sold, and Home Fabric Mills will sell in half-yard increments—great to know if you're still deciding on your fabrics. Swatches are also available on request.

Please note: Credit card payments are accepted on out-of-state mail orders only.

Home Fabric Mills is offering readers a discount of 20% on first orders. Be sure to identify yourself as a WBMC reader when you order, and deduct the discount from the cost of the goods only. This WBMC reader discount expires February 1, 1997.

Special Factors: Price quote by phone or letter; minimum order is 1/2 yard.

HOMESPUN FABRICS
& DRAPERIES

P.O. BOX 3223-WBM
VENTURA, CA 93006
805-642-8111
FAX: 805-642-0759

Price List and Samples: $2
Save: up to 50%
Pay: check, MO, MC, V
Sells: 10'-wide fabric, draperies, accessories, and services
Store: mail order only

 (see text)

Homespun Fabrics & Draperies has a solution to some of the biggest drapery headaches—bulkiness, sun rot, the expense of dry cleaning, and the hassle of pleater hooks among them. Homespun Fabrics sells all-cotton material that's ten feet wide, or about 105" to 109" after shrinkage. The fabric includes homespun, hobnail, barley, and monk's cloth weaves, in white and natural. The width makes the fabric perfect for "seamless draperies," and even eliminates some of the finishing work. Homespun Fabrics manufactures all styles of draperies (suitable to the fabric), and can also custom-make "fanpleat" draperies. These operate on a track system that's hung from the ceiling or mounted on the wall, with a buckram header tape with nylon tabs that engage the track. The drapery folds are 4 or 5" deep, so the stackback (the area covered by the curtain when it's drawn back) that would be 37" deep with conventional pinch-pleat draperies is only 11" deep with the fan-pleat system. Made in Homespun Fabrics' heavyweight cottons, this system produces handsome, neutral window coverings that give you maximum glass exposure. They have a crisp, tailored appearance that's ideal for modern decor and office settings, and are machine washable and dryable, and guaranteed against sun rot for seven years.

In addition to the heavy cottons, Homespun Fabrics offers open-weave casement fabric (tow cloth), wide muslin, and both regular-width and ultrawide semisheers—batiste, voile, and bouclé slub, in lots of colors. Homespun can create the draperies, or you can do it yourself—and you'll find helpful books on home decorating and guides to making fan-pleat draperies, slipcovers, bedspreads, table linens, and accessories.

Special Factors: Returns are accepted within ten days for exchange, refund, or credit.

INTERIORS GUILD, INC.

P.O. BOX 99352
CLEVELAND, OH 44199
800-496-2634

Information: price quote
Save: up to 75%
Pay: MC, V, AE, Discover
Sells: wall coverings, window treatments, fabric, etc.
Store: mail order only

Interiors Guild brings you the best names in wall and window treatments—and their complementing fabrics, borders, and accessories—at savings of 40% to 75%. The parent company of this newly minted firm began business in 1890, and is teaching its corporate progeny the secret to a long and prosperous life: Offer qualified and personalized design assistance, a broad selection of merchandise, free shipping, and competitive prices. Your job? Have the manufacturer's book name and pattern number at hand when you call, and an estimate of how many square feet you need if you're buying wall coverings; have the window measurements written down if you're ordering blinds or shades. Interiors Guild sells popular wall covering lines by Colorall, Eisenhart, Imperial, Sanitas, Warner, and other makers, and window treatments by Del Mar, Hunter-Douglas, and Levolor. Call for price quotes or to place an order from Monday to Friday 9 A.M. to 12 midnight, Saturday and Sunday 9 A.M. to 9 P.M., ET.

Please note: Free delivery is offered within the contiguous United States only.

Special Factors: Satisfaction is guaranteed; price quote by phone, fax, or letter; shipping is not charged (see text).

MARLENE'S DECORATOR FABRICS

301 BEECH ST., DEPT. 2J
HACKENSACK, NJ 07601
800-992-7325
201-843-0844
FAX: 201-843-5688

Flyer: free with stamped, self-addressed envelope
Save: up to 60%
Pay: check, MO, MC, V
Sells: decorator fabrics
Store: mail order only

Marlene's Decorator Fabrics has been selling upholstery, slipcover, and drapery goods since 1946, and can save you up to 60% on the list prices of fabrics by Robert Allen, Artmark, Paul Barrow, Berger, Boussac of France, Manuel Canovas, China Seas, Clarence House, Colefax & Fowler, Greeff, Kasmir, Kravet, Ralph Lauren, Lee Jofa, Sanderson, Schumacher, Stout, Stroheim & Roman, Waverly, Wesco, and many others. Write or call for a price quote, or send a self-addressed, stamped envelope with a sample if you're not sure of the manufacturer or pattern, or to request a brochure. Specify the yardage needed and whether you're interested in upholstery, drapery, or other decorator fabric.

Special Factors: Minimum order is 4 yards retail, 25 yards wholesale.

M.C. LIMITED FINE LEATHERS

DEPT. WBM
P.O. BOX 17696
WHITEFISH BAY, WI 53217
414-263-5222
FAX: 414-263-5508

Brochure and Price List: free
Save: up to 40%
Pay: check, MO, MC, V
Sells: steer hides and hide pillows
Store: mail order only

  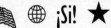

Whether your home style is New Western, chromed modern, 90s eclectic, or Neolithic, there's nothing like steer hide to add decorative depth. M.C. Limited offers processed skins in full hides (36 square feet on average, 5' to 6' wide by 7' to 8' long) in eight natural colors for $235. This is nearly 40% below prices by two New York City leather suppliers for comparable skins. M.C. Limited also makes steer hide pillows backed with pigskin suede, which are offered plain or with fringe, tassels, medallions, or other embellishments. Sizes range from 6" by 13" to 24" square, priced from $35 to $175. Custom options—down filling, steer-hide backs, special shapes and sizes—are also available. M.C. Limited notes that all of its hides are byproducts of the beef industry, and are not claimed from animals raised primarily for their skins. A special new tanning process is reputed to render the hides "soft and beautiful" as they age, so they won't stiffen, dry out, and lose hair.

Special Factors: Satisfaction is guaranteed; authorized returns (except pillows) are accepted (a percent restocking fee is charged) within 30 days.

ROBINSON'S WALLCOVERINGS

DEPT. 6LY
225 W. SPRING ST.
P.O. BOX 427
TITUSVILLE, PA 16354-0427
800-458-2426
814-827-1893
FAX: 814-827-1693

Catalog: $2
Save: up to 50%
Pay: check, MO, MC, V, AE, Discover
Sells: wallpaper, borders, decorator fabrics, and accessories
Store: 339 W. Spring St., Titusville; also 3506 Liberty Plaza, Erie; 1720 Wilmington Rd., Rte. 18, New Castle, PA

Robinson's has been in business since 1919, and sells both vinyl-coated and solid vinyl wallpaper, coordinating borders, and fabrics that are suitable for use throughout the home. The catalog also offers tools and supplies for installation, as well as decorating accents to complement your scheme. Robinson's provides color photographs that show how different designs look when they're installed—a very helpful feature. Free samples of any wall coverings shown in the catalog are available. Prices are competitive—an average of $7.49 for a single roll of wallpaper, and $6.99 for five yards of border trim.

Patterns not shown in the catalog are available through Robinson's Custom Order Department at savings of 30% off book price. See the catalog for details, or call with manufacturer's name, book name, pattern number, price code, and suggested retail price, to receive a quote.

Special Factors: Satisfaction is guaranteed; returns are accepted within 30 days for exchange or refund; minimum order is $15 with credit cards.

SHAMA IMPORTS, INC.

Brochure: free
Save: up to 50%
Pay: check, MO, MC, V
Sells: crewel fabrics and home accessories
Store: mail order only

DEPT. WBM-96
P.O. BOX 2900
FARMINGTON HILLS, MI
    48333-2900
810-478-7740

Shama Imports, which began business in 1982, offers good prices on Indian crewel fabrics and home accessories. Crewel is hand-embroidered on hand-loomed cotton, offered here in traditional serpentine flower-and-vine motifs and other distinctive designs, in a range of colors. The eight-page color brochure that shows the patterns also includes decorating suggestions. Background (unembroidered) fabric is also available by the yard, and Shama stocks crewel chair and cushion covers, tote bags, bedspreads, and tablecloths as well. All of the fabric is 52" wide and can be washed by hand or dry-cleaned. Samples are available for $1 each; those showing one-fourth of the complete pattern cost $5 (refundable). The brochure lists the pattern repeats for all of the designs.

Special Factors: Satisfaction is guaranteed; uncut, undamaged returns are accepted within 30 days for refund or credit; C.O.D. orders are accepted.

SHIBUI WALLCOVERINGS

Brochure and Samples: $4
Save: up to 40%
Pay: check, MO, MC, V
Sells: imported grass cloth and "natural" wall coverings
Store: mail order only

DEPT. WBM-96
P.O. BOX 1268
SANTA ROSA, CA 95402
800-824-3030
707-526-6170
FAX: 707-544-0719

Shibui, which has been doing business since 1966, sells fine wall coverings made of natural materials—jute, grasses, corks, strings, and textiles.

Shibui stocks imported jute-fiber grass cloth, rush cloth, textile papers, textured weaves, and string wall coverings. The $4 brochure fee includes samples, and larger pieces are available upon request. The string wall coverings include several that look like silk at a fraction of the price, and there are lots of wonderful wall coverings of woven grasses backed by paper of contrasting colors. Paper-hanging tool kits, adhesives, and lining paper are also stocked, and a protective coating is available.

Special Factors: Satisfaction is guaranteed; shipping is not charged on orders over $100; single and double rolls can be cut from regular bolts (not returnable); returns are accepted within 30 days; C.O.D. orders are accepted.

SILK SURPLUS

DEPT. 55
37-24 24TH ST.
LONG ISLAND CITY, NY
  11101
718-361-8500, EXT. 55
FAX: 718-361-8311

Information: price quote
Save: up to 75% (see text)
Pay: check, MO, MC, V, AE
Sells: discontinued decorator fabric and trim (see text)
Store: same address; Monday to Saturday 10–5:30, Sunday 12–5; also 223 and 235 E. 58th St., New York; 1215 Northern Blvd., Manhasset; 449 Old Country Rd., Westbury; 281 Mamaroneck Ave., White Plains; and Elm Ave. N., Rte. 22, Millerton, NY

Silk Surplus is well-known to budget-minded New Yorkers who covet luxurious upholstery and drapery fabrics because it's where they can save up to 75% (and sometimes even more) on sumptuous Scalamandré and Boris Kroll closeouts and fabrics from other mills. Silks, cottons, velvets, woolens, chintzes, brocades, damasks, and other weaves and finishes are usually available from Silk Surplus, which opened its doors in 1962. Walk-in customers can select from among the bolts in any of the six Silk Surplus shops. But if you're buying by mail, you must know exactly which Scalamandré or Boris Kroll fabric you want, and in which color. If it's there, you're in luck. You may also send the store a fabric sample with a query. This is a great shopping stop on a trip to New York City, but only serious searchers for Scalamandré or Boris Kroll closeout fabrics should contact the store intending to buy by mail. If you're a design professional, you may ask for an additional trade discount.

Special Factors: Price quote by phone or letter with SASE; sample cuttings are free; all sales are final; minimum order is 3 yards.

WELLS INTERIORS INC.

7171 AMADOR PLAZA DR.
DUBLIN, CA 94568
800-547-8982
FAX: 510-829-1374

Catalog: free
Save: up to 85%
Pay: check, MO, MC, V
Sells: window treatments and accessories
Store: same address; Monday to Friday 10–6, Saturday 10–5, Sunday 12–4; 19 other stores in CA and OR (see the catalog for locations)

Wells Interiors has been in business since 1980, guarantees "the lowest prices" on its goods, and will beat any other dealer's price down to cost on a wide range of top brands. Discounts can run up to 85% on retail prices on Levolor's mini blinds, verticals, wood blinds, and similar styles by other manufacturers, such as Bali, Del Mar, Graber, HunterDouglas, Joanna, LouverDrape, Jenny Lynn, M&B, amd Windsor. Kirsch woven woods, pleated shades, decorator roller shades, verticals, and miniblinds are also available.

The catalog includes a guide to the lines currently available, and includes instructions on measuring your windows and installing the blinds. Details of the firm's warranty are given in the catalog as well.

Special Factors: Written confirmation is required on phone orders.

Lighting

Residential indoor and outdoor lighting fixtures, lamp shades, and related goods

The artful use of lighting ranks with color in the success of a room, but it's one of the biggest design challenges. None of the firms listed here can tell you how to light your home, but you'll find the basics in interior design textbooks and decorating manuals, and the books mentioned in the introduction to "Home: Decor," preceding this section. *Lighting Style,* by Kevin McCloud (Ebury Press, 1995), showcases a wide range of possibilities. You'll find another authority in your own observations of lighting that pleases you—whether it's good general illumination, glare-free task lighting for reading or needlework, a combination of the two in a kitchen, subdued but reader-friendly lamps in a bedroom or library, or outdoor lighting that improves security while highlighting the architecture. Note how effects are created, and work with the fixtures you have to try out new ideas—raise or lower the wattage, alter the shading, change the location of the lamp, use tinted bulbs, etc. Study the optimal *placement* and *height* of light fixtures, which have distilled to rules of measurement in interior design textbooks. You can do so much with lamps (floor, table, swag, desk, etc.) and conventional ceiling fixtures (canopy and chandelier), that you might not think of retrofitting high-hats, eyeballs, or other recessed fixtures when you review your home lighting. Consider them when you want to update a track system, increase hallway lighting discreetly, or create a special effect with a spotlight or wall-washer.

The firms listed here sell lighting for the home—lamps, ceiling fixtures, bathroom and kitchen lighting, patio and walkway lighting, building lanterns, etc.—and related electrical accessories, shades, and replacement parts. Some also sell ceiling fans and attachments. Discounts average about 30% to 40% on name-brand goods, and the firms that manufacture their own fixtures sell at competitive prices.

FIND IT FAST

CEILING FANS • **American Light Source, Main Lamp**
CRYSTAL CHANDELIERS • **King's Chandelier, Luigi Crystal**
REPLACEMENT PRISMS, HURRICANES, BOBECHES • **King's Chandelier, Luigi Crystal**

AMERICAN LIGHT SOURCE

5211D WEST MARKET ST.,
   SUITE 803
GREENSBORO, NC 27409
800-741-0571

Catalog: $5, refundable (see text)
Save: up to 40%
Pay: check, MO, MC, V, AE
Sells: light fixtures and ceiling fans
Store: mail order only

American Light Source has been in business for several years, selling lighting fixtures for every room of the house (and porch and patio, too), at savings of up to 40%. Over 100 major manufacturers are represented, and the $5 catalog fee brings you a thick showcase of lighting fixtures, ceiling fans, and accessories. If you know what you want, just call or write with the manufacturer's name and model number of the piece to receive a price quote. Please note the $150 minimum order requirement.

Special Factors: Satisfaction is guaranteed; price quote by phone or letter; minimum order is $150.

BRASS LIGHT GALLERY, INC.

DEPT. WBMC
131 S. 1ST ST.
MILWAUKEE, WI 53204
800-243-9595
FAX: 414-271-7755

Catalog: $6, refundable (see text)
Save: 20% average (see text)
Pay: check, MO, MC, V
Sells: lighting fixtures
Store: same address; Monday to Friday 9–5, Saturday 10–3

After you've seen the fixtures from Brass Light Gallery, you'll know why you've held off buying from other sources. Not only are the materials and workmanship here of superior quality, but the designs have that satisfyingly "right" quality that's so often lacking in lighting fixtures. For example, the Mission-style hanging, wall, and table lamps are executed with that odd combination of nearly Japanese proportion and angles and Western rigidity that makes sense of the whole style. (If you're accustomed to "chunky" Stickley-style fixtures, you'll see the difference immediately.) Brass Light Gallery's "Goldenrod" and "Continental" collections include Mission/Prairie styles, chandeliers in polished brass with cased glass shades, double wall sconces, and much more. The alabaster chandeliers, sconces, and table lamps are actually less expensive than comparable fixtures from the 20s and 30s—when you can find them, intact and unchipped, in antiques stores. Also, the firm's "Prismatics" collection for kitchens and lofts features vintage heavy, ribbed glass shades, retrofitted with different styles of brass or metal poles, or other fixtures for low and angled ceiling mounts. The glass and finish options for many of the pieces make it possible to create truly individual fixtures, or faithful interpretations of the originals. The Brass Light Gallery's catalog—over 100 pages of lighting, plus technical specifications—has been designed for use by homeowners, interior designers, and architects. (The catalog costs $6, refundable with purchase, but a 12-page color brochure is free on request.) Prices here average 20% below retail, but the fixtures are much better quality than those being sold by Brass Light Gallery's competitors—so the values are much better as well.

Special Factors: Satisfaction is guaranteed.

GOLDEN VALLEY LIGHTING

274 EASTCHESTER DR.,
  #117A
HIGH POINT, NC 27262
800-735-3377
910-882-7330
FAX: 800-760-6678

Catalog: $5, refundable (see text)
Save: up to 50%
Pay: check, MO, MC, V
Sells: lighting fixtures, floor and table lamps
Store: mail order only

   ¡Si!

Golden Valley, a company founded in 1989 and run by veterans of the lighting industry, offers savings of up to 50% on lighting fixtures and ceiling fans. You can call to order, or send $5 (refundable with purchase) for Golden Valley's 170-page color catalog featuring chandeliers, ceiling fixtures, sconces, fluorescents, bathroom and vanity strip lighting, and more. Or you can request a price quote: Call when you've decided what you want (have the manufacturer's name, model number, color, finish, and any other details at hand). When you're ready to order, you can make a deposit of 50% of the cost of the fixture, and pay the balance before shipment, or prepay the entire amount and expedite the order.

Special Factors: Price quote by phone or letter with SASE.

KING'S CHANDELIER CO.

DEPT. WBM96
P.O. BOX 667
EDEN, NC 27288-0667
910-623-6188
FAX: 910-627-9935

Catalog: $3.75
Save: up to 50%
Pay: check, MO, MC, V
Sells: Czech, Venetian, and Strass crystal chandeliers
Store: Hwy. 14 (Van Buren Rd.), Eden, NC; Monday to Saturday 10–4:30

The Kings have been designing and producing chandeliers since 1935 and offer their designs through the 90-page catalog. There are light fixtures to suit every taste, at prices for all budgets.

The catalog shows page after page of chandeliers, candelabras, and wall sconces in a range of styles: Victorian, "colonial," contemporary, and many variations on the classic lighting fixture dripping with prisms, pendalogues, faceted balls, and ropes of crystal buttons. Austere styles with brass arms and plain glass shades are also available, as well as the Kings' own magnificent designs made of Strass crystal. Prices begin at about $125 for a brass single sconce and go up to $14,500 for the palatial Strass Royal Belvedere. Options include different finishes on the metal parts, hurricane shades or candelabra tapers, and candelabra bulb sockets. Replacement parts for these lighting fixtures are stocked as well.

Since a catalog can't show the chandeliers to their best advantage, King's will create a videotape of the lighting fixtures that interest you— preferably not more than six models. The VHS tapes are available for a $25 deposit, refundable on return.

Special Factors: Satisfaction is guaranteed; returns are accepted within five days for refund or credit.

LUIGI CRYSTAL

7332 FRANKFORD AVE.
PHILADELPHIA, PA 19136
215-338-2978

Catalog: $1.50, refundable
Save: up to 50%
Pay: check, MO, MC, V, AE, Discover
Sells: crystal lighting fixtures
Store: same address; Monday to Friday
9–5:30, Saturday 10–4

Luigi Crystal may be located in the land of Main Liners, but its heart belongs to Tara. Luigi has been creating crystal lighting fixtures since 1935, and the prices are surprisingly low—under $200 for a full-sized chandelier, for example. The 44-page catalog shows each candelabra, chandelier, sconce, and hurricane lamp in black-and-white photographs. Many of the styles are formal and ornate, heavily hung with prisms and pendalogues and set in marble or faceted crystal bases. Several lamps feature globe shades, gold cupid bases, "Aurora" crystal prism shades, and even stained glass. At the other end of the spectrum are simple "Williamsburg chimney lamps" for under $50 a pair, and several graceful five-arm chandeliers.

If you're searching for replacement parts for your own fixtures, see the catalog for glass chimneys, bobeches, strung button prisms, drop prisms in several styles (3" to 8" long), and pendalogues. In addition to those models, Luigi's workshops can produce designs to your specifications; call or write to discuss details and prices.

Please note: The minimum order on goods sent outside the United States and Canada is $1,000.

Special Factors: Orders are shipped worldwide ($1,000 minimum order).

MAIN LAMP/LAMP WAREHOUSE

1073 39TH ST.
BROOKLYN, NY 11219
718-436-8500
FAX: 718-438-6836

Information: price quote
Save: up to 50%
Pay: check, MO, MC, V, AE, Discover
Sells: lighting fixtures and ceiling fans
Store: same address; Monday, Tuesday, and Friday 9–5:30, Thursday 9–8, Saturday and Sunday 10–5

Main Lamp/Lamp Warehouse, established in 1954, is noted for its comprehensive inventory of lamps, lighting fixtures, and ceiling fans, all of which are sold at everyday discounts of up to 50%. Call or write for prices on lighting fixtures, lamps, and track lighting by Fredrick Cooper, Crystal Clear, Halo, Kichler, George Kovacs, Lenox Lamps, Rembrandt, Stiffel, and other major names. Ceiling fans by Casablanca, Emerson, and other firms are also stocked.

Special Factors: Price quote by phone or letter with SASE; store is closed Wednesdays; minimum order is $50.

Rugs, Carpeting, and Flooring

All kinds of floor coverings, padding and underlays, tiles, flooring, etc.

Large rugs and wall-to-wall carpeting can represent the biggest single expense in redecorating a room. Saving up to 50% on the cost of the rug and padding is easy through the firms listed here. They're based in North Carolina and Dalton, Georgia, close to the carpet mills that turn out millions of miles of broadloom every year.

Before you order wall-to-wall carpeting, make sure you have someone local who can install it. (It's almost impossible for a novice to do a good job, and a poor one leads to shifting, rippling, and uneven wear.) Choice of carpet weave, fiber, and color depend on where it's going, the purpose of the room or area and the anticipated foot traffic, and overall decor. Interior design textbooks (see the introduction of "Home: Decor" for references) usually discuss the difference in fiber and construction, as well as appropriate sites for different types of carpeting. For information on installation, maintenance, and a stain-removal guide, send a long, stamped, self-addressed envelope to The Carpet and Rug Institute, Box 2048, Dalton, GA 30722.

For more firms selling rugs and carpeting, see the "See Alsos" at the end of the chapter, and those mentioned under *Rugs and Carpeting* in "Find it Fast" in the introduction of "Home: Furnishings."

BEARDEN BROS. CARPET & TEXTILES CORP.

DEPT. WBMC
4109 SOUTH DIXIE HWY.
DALTON, GA 30721
800-433-0074
FAX: 706-277-1754

Catalog: $2 (see text)
Save: up to 50%
Pay: check, MO, MC, V, AE, Discover, Bearden Brothers charge card
Sells: carpeting, rugs, padding, and vinyl flooring
Store: same address; Monday to Friday 8:30–6

Bearden Bros. Carpet & Textiles set up shop in 1989 in Dalton, "Carpet Capital of the World," joining hundreds of other companies devoted to manufacturing carpet. Bearden sells carpeting and flooring lines from scores of mills, including Aladdin, Armstrong, Beaulieu, Bigelow, Cabin Craft, Citation, Cumberland, Evans and Black, Galaxy, Horizon, Interloom, J.P. Stevens, L.D. Brinkman, Lees, Mohawk, Philadelphia, Salem, Shaw, and World—and that's just a few of the many brands available.

You can call with the manufacturer's name, style name, and color codes, and number of square yards you plan to buy and ask for a price quote, or send a carpet sample if you don't have that information. Bearden Bros. also sells its own line of flooring and carpet products, as well as reproduction Oriental, Victorian, and contemporary designs, braided rugs, border designs, and even brass stair rods. A 32-page catalog of rugs—braided, flat weave, designer, Oriental, etc.—is available for $2 (regularly $4); mention WBMC when you send for it. Bearden ships carpeting to all 50 states and countries around the world, and offers special discounts to religious institutions and carpet dealers.

Special Factors: Written confirmation of phone orders is required; quantity discounts are available.

CHARLES W. JACOBSEN, INC.

LEARBURY CENTER
401 N. SALINA ST.
SYRACUSE, NY 13203
315-422-7832
FAX: 315-422-6909

Catalog: free
Save: see text
Pay: check, MO, MC, V
Sells: new and antique Oriental rugs
Store: same address; Monday to Saturday 10–5, Monday and Thursday 10–8

Charles W. Jacobsen, Inc. has over 70 years of experience in the sale of fine Oriental rugs, and publishes a color portfolio of a sampling of rugs selected from the 8,000 the firm has in inventory. Rug collectors know Jacobsen for the company's stock and good prices, but both are worth considering if you're buying a rug for your home and want something more than run-of-the-mill.

Jacobsen's stock-in-trade is handwoven carpets, of recent vintage, from India, Pakistan, Romania, Turkey, Iran, Afghanistan, China, and other countries (subject to trade restrictions and availability). The sizes vary with the type of rug, but most are available from 2' by 3' to 9' by 12', with some available in sizes to 12' by 20'; many of the designs are also made as runners. If you've been shopping for good, machine-made reproductions of Oriental rugs, you'll be familiar with some of the names: Kashan, Herez, Tabriz, Sarouk, Abadeh, Sarabend, Bijar, Ferraghan, Shirvan, and Bokhara are some of the most commonly known. Even if you think your budget relegates you to no more than a good copy of a handmade rug, check here before you buy. In some cases, Jacobsen's prices on the new rugs—made completely by hand, with wool or silk pile, often with some vegetable dyes (which lend a mellow quality to the rug over time)—are not much higher, and are lower than those charged for comparable examples by other rug merchants.

Buying a one-of-a-kind *anything* by mail can be tricky, but Jacobsen will work with you to get it right: The questionnaire provided with the catalog captures information about your preferences, room requirements, and budget; based on this information, you'll be sent slides of rugs that best suit your needs. When you've settled on a selection, you can have the rug sent on approval to try in the intended setting—the only way to be sure it's the right choice.

Special Factors: Satisfaction is guaranteed.

JOHNSON'S CARPETS

3239 S. DIXIE HWY.
DALTON, GA 30720
800-235-1079, EXT. 601
706-277-2775
FAX: 706-277-9835

Brochure: free
Save: up to 80%
Pay: check, MO, MC, V, AE, Discover
Sells: vinyl and wood flooring, carpeting, area rugs, and padding
Store: same address; Monday to Friday 8–5, Saturday 9–1

Johnson's has arrangements with over 40 carpet mills and flooring makers that allow it to offer carpet and vinyl and wood flooring lines from a wide range of manufacturers, at prices up to 80% below those charged by department stores and other retail outlets. If you've decided on your floor covering, call or write with the name of the manufacturer, the style name or number, and the square yardage required. Johnson's also creates its own "custom designer" rugs, and can produce patterns to match wallpaper or furnishings—samples are shown in the catalog (available upon request). Padding, adhesives, and tack strips for installation are also available.

A deposit is required when you place your order, and final payment must be made before shipment (common carrier is used). Both residential and commercial carpeting needs are served here—details on the products and sales policy are given in the brochure.

Special Factors: Orders are shipped worldwide.

PARADISE MILLS, INC.

P.O. BOX 2488
DALTON, GA 30722
800-338-7811, EXT. 618
706-226-9266
FAX: 706-226-9061

Catalog: free (see text)
Save: up to 60%
Pay: check, MO, MC, V, Discover
Sells: carpeting and vinyl and wood flooring
Store: mail order only

The eight-page brochure from Paradise Mills is packed with tips on buying carpeting (effects of color contrasts in your decor, a comparison of tufting types and their relative merits, how to find the style information on a carpet sample, etc.), and it includes complete details on the company's sales policy. Paradise is sited in Dalton, the carpet capital of the United States, and the company's relationships with major mills mean discounts of up to 60% on carpeting and flooring by Aladdin, Armstrong, Cumberland, Diamond, Galaxy, Horizon, Lees, Philadelphia, Queen, Salem, Shaheen, World, Wunda Weave, and many others. In addition, Paradise sells its own line of carpet, and offers customized rugs—either any of the preset designs in your choice of colors or completely original patterns. (You can have your carpeting matched to your wallpaper, or replicate nearly any other image in the firm's warrantied nylon plush.) Please note that orders must be paid before delivery, and carpet samples are available for $5 each.

Special Factors: Quantity discounts are available; authorized returns are accepted within 30 days for exchange, refund, or credit; minimum order is $10.

VILLAGE CARPET & FLOOR COVERING

3203 HWY. 70 S.E.
NEWTON, NC 28658
704-465-6818

Brochure: free
Save: up to 50%
Pay: check or MO
Sells: carpeting and padding
Store: same address, off I-40 near Hickory

Village Carpet & Floor Covering offers well-known names in carpeting—Aladdin, Bigelow, Cabin Crafts, Cumberland, Galaxy, Horizon, Mohawk, Philadelphia, Salem, Sutton, Wunda Weave, and others, at discounts of up to 50%. Padding and underlays are also available. All of the carpeting is first quality, and shipping is made by common carrier. If you have difficulty getting style information or calculating the amount you need, just ask—the salespeople deal with these problems regularly.

Special Factors: Satisfaction is guaranteed; quantity discounts are available.

WALL'S KARASTAN CARPET CENTER

**4309 WILEY DAVIS RD.
GREENSBORO, NC 27407
800-877-1955
FAX: 910-292-3601**

Information: price quote
Save: up to 40%
Pay: check, MO, MC, V
Sells: Karastan rugs
Store: same address (Exit 120, I-85)

Karastan has built its name on fine, Axminster-loomed Oriental rugs that are reproductions of the originals, but less expensive and of consistent quality. The Original Karastan Collection of classic designs has been in existence since 1928, and each rug in the group is guaranteed against manufacturing defects for 20 years from date of purchase. Wall's Karastan Carpet Center sells both first-quality Karastans, and "mill trials," which are the first rugs of a particular run. Mill trials are not seconds, but may have some flaw that's "imperceptible in 99% of the rugs"—one or two colors may be off shades, for example. Wall's has been in business since 1933 and provides dealer warranties on all the rugs it sells, including mill trials. Prices on the first-quality rugs are up to 40% below regular retail or list, and the mill trials are discounted further (but are not always available in every design and size). Shipments are made by UPS, and to save you even more money, Wall's is paying the freight on all first-quality Karastan rugs, and is including the Durahold pad at no charge. Call or write to Wall's if you need advice, or when you're ready to order.

Special Factors: Returns are accepted.

WAREHOUSE CARPETS, INC.

P.O. BOX 3233
DALTON, GA 30719
800-526-2229
706-226-2229
FAX: 706-278-1008

Brochure: free
Save: up to 50%
Pay: check or MO
Sells: carpeting, vinyl flooring, and padding
Store: Walnut Ave. (Exit 136 off I-75), Dalton, GA; Monday to Friday 8–5

Warehouse Carpets began in 1977 as a carpeting wholesaler, and has since moved into retail mail order, offering customers savings of as much as 50% on carpeting and floor coverings. Call for a quote if you're shopping for carpeting from Aladdin, Cabin Crafts, Columbus, Coronet, Downs, Evans & Black, Galaxy, Horizon, Interloom, Mannington, Philadelphia, Queen, Salem, Sutton, or World; or vinyl flooring from Armstrong, Congoleum, Mannington, or Tarkett. And if you'd like to save an average of 50% on rug padding, Warehouse Carpets can provide several types.

Can call or write with the names of the manufacturer and style of the carpeting you want, and follow with a 50% deposit (check or money order). The balance is due when the goods are ready for shipment, which is made by common carrier, and the brochure and information sheet include details of the terms.

Special Factors: All goods are first quality; price quote by phone or letter; orders are shipped worldwide (except Canada).

SEE ALSO

American Frame Corporation • *sectional frames and mats* • **ART MATERIALS**

Anticipations • *home accents, furniture, etc.* • **GENERAL MERCHANDISE**

Arctic Sheepskin Outlet • *sheepskin rugs* • **CLOTHING**

Bedroom Secrets • *window treatments, home accessories* • **HOME: LINEN**

BRE Lumber, Inc./Rare Earth Hardwoods • *flooring, cabinet-grade lumber, decking, and paneling* • **HOME: IMPROVEMENT**

Buffalo Batt & Felt Corp. • *throw pillow inserts and upholstery stuffing* • **CRAFTS: TEXTILE ARTS**

The Caning Shop • *seat-weaving materials, replacement seats, upholstery supplies* • **CRAFTS**

The Deerskin Place • *sheepskin rugs* • **CLOTHING**

Defender Industries, Inc. • *teak kitchen and bath accessories* • **AUTO**

Domestications • *home accents, window treatments, etc.* • **HOME: LINEN**

Eldridge Textile Co. • *window treatments, slipcovers, etc.* • **HOME: LINEN**

Excalibur Bronze Sculpture Foundry • *reproduction art lamps, vases, etc.* • **ART & ANTIQUES**

Frank's Cane and Rush Supply • *seat-reweaving materials, upholstery supplies, etc.* • **CRAFTS**

The Furniture Showplace • *lamps, decorator accessories, etc.* • **HOME: FURNISHINGS**

Global Village Imports • *upholstery-weight ikat fabrics* • **CRAFTS: TEXTILE ARTS**

Goldberg's Marine Distributors • *teak kitchen and bath accessories* • **AUTO**

Gooseberry Patch • *country crafts and home accents* • **GENERAL MERCHANDISE**

Home-Sew • *upholstery supplies* • **CRAFTS: TEXTILE ARTS**

Leather Unlimited Corp. • *sheepskin rugs* • **LEATHER**

The Linen Source • *window treatments, home accents* • **HOME: LINEN**

Loftin-Black Furniture Company • *mirrors* • **HOME: FURNISHINGS**

M&E Marine Supply Company, Inc. • *teak boat accessories for kitchen and bath* • **AUTO**

Monarch • *radiator enclosures* • **HOME: IMPROVEMENT**

Murrow Furniture Galleries, Inc. • *lamps* • **HOME: FURNISHINGS**

Newark Dressmaker Supply, Inc. • *upholstery supplies* • **CRAFTS: TEXTILE ARTS**

Quality Furniture Market of Lenoir, Inc. • *lamps, decorator fabrics, etc.* • **HOME: FURNISHINGS**

Shuttercraft • *interior and exterior wooden window shutters* • **HOME: IMPROVEMENT**

Stuckey Brothers Furniture Co., Inc. • *clocks, mirrors, etc.* • **HOME: FURNISHINGS**

Thai Silks • *upholstery-weight silk fabrics* • **CRAFTS: TEXTILE ARTS**

Utex Trading Enterprises • *upholstery-weight silk fabric* • **CRAFTS: TEXTILE ARTS**

Warner-Crivellaro Stained Glass Supplies, Inc. • *lamp bases and parts* • **CRAFTS**

Furnishings

Household furnishings of all types, including outdoor furniture, office furnishings, and services

You can save as much as 50% on suggested retail by ordering your furniture from North Carolina, the manufacturing center of the industry. The discounters don't take the staggering markups that make furnishings and home accessories prohibitively expensive in department and furniture stores. This doesn't endear them to the furniture manufacturers; in fact, it's becoming common for manufacturers to do everything they can to make it difficult for discounters to sell by mail, by forbidding them to trade outside designated "selling areas" and sometimes prohibiting the firms from having 800 phone lines. (Manufacturers elicit compliance by threatening to refuse to fill the discounters' orders.) This practice has the effect of limiting trade, and raising the prices we all have to pay. To avoid creating problems for the discounters, while giving access to the best buys possible, all brand names have been *omitted* from these listings. But most of the firms listed here can take orders for furniture and accessories from hundreds of manufacturers, can supply catalogs, brochures, and swatches, and give decorating advice over the phone.

It's smart to use the "in-home delivery service" when a firm offers it, since your furniture will be uncrated exactly where you want it, and if there are damages, you'll see them right away and can contact the company while the shipper is there to find out what to do.

For other firms that sell furnishings and decorative pieces for the home, see the "Home: Decor" and "General Merchandise." Some of the companies listed here also sell lines of office furniture, but see "Office and Business" for a more comprehensive selection.

FIND IT FAST

ACRYLIC FURNITURE • **Plexi-Craft**
BEDDING AND MATTRESSES • **Carolina Interiors, Murrow, Parkway, Priba, Quality Furniture Market, Stuckey Brothers, Triad Furniture**
BRASS BEDS • **Barnes & Barnes, Parkway, Priba**
CLOCKS • **Barnes & Barnes, Parkway, Stuckey Brothers**
COUNTRY FURNISHINGS • **Pine Factory, Marion Travis**
DECORATOR FABRIC • **Barnes & Barnes, Furniture Patch, Priba**
LAMPS AND LIGHTING • **Barnes & Barnes, Furniture Patch, Parkway, Priba, Stuckey Brothers, Triad Furniture, Wicker Warehouse**
LAWN AND PATIO FURNISHINGS • **Barnes & Barnes, Loftin-Black, Parkway, Priba, Quality Furniture Market, Stuckey Brothers, Triad Furniture, Wicker Warehouse**
LEATHER FURNITURE • **Priba, Wellington's**
MIRRORS • **Barnes & Barnes, Furniture Patch, Hunt Galleries, Parkway, Stuckey Brothers, Triad Furniture, Wicker Warehouse**
MODERN FURNISHINGS • **Genada Imports**
OFFICE FURNISHINGS • **Barnes & Barnes, Furniture Patch, Harvest House, Don Lamor, Ephraim Marsh, Parkway, Priba, Shaw Furniture, Sobol House**
RUGS AND CARPETING • **Carolina Interiors, Furniture Patch, Priba**
TABLE PADS • **Factory Direct Table Pad, Parkway**
UNFINISHED FURNITURE • **Marks Sales, Marion Travis**
VICTORIAN REPRODUCTIONS • **Heirloom Reproductions**
WALL TREATMENTS • **Carolina Interiors**
WICKER FURNITURE • **Ellenburg's Furniture, Fran's Wicker, Wicker Warehouse**

BARNES & BARNES FINE FURNITURE

190 COMMERCE AVE.
SOUTHERN PINES, NC
28387
800-334-8174
910-692-3381
FAX: 910-692-0998

Brochure: free
Save: up to 55%
Pay: check, MO, MC, V, Discover
Sells: home furnishings
Store: same address; Monday to Friday 9–5, Saturday by appointment

Barnes & Barnes has been selling home furnishings and accessories since 1980 and can save you up to 55% on the suggested retail prices on pieces from a long list of manufacturers. In addition to hundreds of furniture lines that include patio furniture, brass beds, and office furniture, Barnes & Barnes sells lamps, mirrors, clocks, and decorator fabric from a number of prominent firms. A deposit of 50% is required to place an order, and the rest is due upon delivery. Shipping charges are collected on delivery. For a roster of the available manufacturers and details on the firm's sales policy, request the free brochure.

Special Factors: Price quote by phone or letter.

CAROLINA INTERIORS

115 OAK AVE.
KANNAPOLIS, NC 28081
704-933-1888
FAX: 704-938-2990

Brochure: free
Save: up to 60%
Pay: check or MO
Sells: home furnishings and accessories
Store: same address (I-85, Exit 63); Monday to Saturday 9–6; three other locations in NC

Carolina Interiors is run by several veterans of the furnishings trade, whose relationships with over 350 manufacturers help assure discounts of 30% to 60%. If you're traveling through North Carolina near Canyon Village, locate the Fieldcrest Cannons factory outlet store, and you'll find Carolina Interiors next door with over 250,000 square feet of furnishings, wall and floor treatments, rugs, and bedding. You can call or write for a price quote if you know what you want, and to request the brochure that lists a number of the available brands and details the sales policy. Carolina Interiors requires a 30% deposit (protected by surety bond) when you place the order, and features in-home delivery in most areas.

Special Factors: Price quote by phone, fax, or letter.

ELLENBURG'S FURNITURE

Catalog: $6
Save: up to 60%
Pay: check, MO, MC, V
Sells: home furnishings
Store: same address

1-40 STAMEY FARM RD.
P.O. BOX 5638
STATESVILLE, NC 28687
704-873-2900

Ellenburg's Furniture specializes in wicker from the top names in home furnishings, but the firm also sells some of the country's most popular lines of American-style furniture, from scores of manufacturers. The $6 catalog fee brings you a sheaf of brochures from different makers, a price list, details on Ellenburg's sales policy, and current specials. A 25% deposit is required when you place your order, and delivery is available from Ellenburg's own van service, a furniture carrier, or common carrier. Savings run from 40% to 50% on retail, and up to 75% on sale items and closeouts.

Special Factors: Returns of damaged and defective goods only are accepted.

FACTORY DIRECT TABLE PAD CO.

Prices and Samples: $1
Save: up to 50%
Pay: check, MO, MC, V, Discover
Sells: custom-made table pads
Store: mail order only

1501 W. MARKET ST.
INDIANAPOLIS, IN 46222
800-737-4194
FAX: 317-631-2584

Factory Direct's spiffy little color brochure states that about half of the cost of a custom-made table pad is the fee paid to the person who measures the table. For $1, Factory Direct Table Pad will send you a guide to doing this yourself, as well as several sample swatches of the table pad top, which can be made in pebble-grain or smooth finish, in plain colors or in wood grain, in different thicknesses. Factory Direct has been in business since 1982, and warrants its table pads for 7, 15, or 20 years. Complete details of the terms of sale are given in the literature.

Special Factors: Authorized returns are accepted within 15 days.

FRAN'S WICKER & RATTAN FURNITURE, INC.

**295 RTE. 10E
SUCCASUNNA, NJ 07876
201-584-2230
FAX: 201-584-7446**

Catalog: $2
Save: up to 30%
Pay: check, MO, MC, V, AE, Discover
Sells: wicker and rattan furniture and accessories
Store: same address; Monday to Friday 9–5:30, Wednesday and Thursday till 8:30, Saturday 9–6, Sunday 12–5

Fran's Wicker is in its third generation of family management, having grown from a basket importer to one of the best local sources for wicker and rattan furniture. The 58-page color catalog is packed cover to cover with furniture and decorative accessories in natural and painted wicker, and a more limited selection of rattan. If you're looking for a seating and table set for porch or patio, or your living or dining room, you'll find dozens here. The styling runs from Victorian curves to modern shapes. Breakfast sets, bedroom furniture, étagères, rockers, TV carts and entertainment centers, office furniture, trunks, plant stands, bookcases, magazine racks, hampers, mirrors, lamps, and baskets are offered. There are a number of pieces for children, including a bassinet, changing table, chairs and tables, rockers, and toy chests. The catalog details your options in cushion coverings and delivery, and the "lowest price" guarantee.

Special Factors: Satisfaction is guaranteed.

THE FURNITURE PATCH OF CALABASH, INC.

DEPT. WBMC
10283 BEACH DR. SW
P.O. BOX 4970
CALABASH, NC 28467
910-579-2001
FAX: 910-579-2017

Brochure: free
Save: up to 40%
Pay: check, MO, MC, V
Sells: furniture, lighting, carpeting, accessories
Store: same address; Monday to Saturday 9–5:30

The Furniture Patch of Calabash invites you to spend some time at their showroom when you're in the area visiting Myrtle Beach, but if you can't make the trip, help is available by mail. The Furniture Patch represents several hundred manufacturers of home (indoor and outdoor) and office furnishings, decorator fabric, lighting, mirrors, rugs and carpets, and decorative accessories. The brochure includes a partial listing of some of the best names in home and industrial design, and savings run up to 40%. Details on the sales policy and ordering guidelines are included, and the sales assistants can answer any other questions you may have, and give you quotes on specific items you're pricing. The Furniture Patch has been in business since 1990, and provides in-house (van) delivery to all states in the continental United States.

Special Factors: Returns of transit-damaged goods are accepted for repair or replacement.

THE FURNITURE SHOWPLACE

356 DANIEL RD.
SPINDALE, NC 28160
704-287-7106
FAX: 704-287-8785

Brochure: free with SASE
Save: up to 55%
Pay: check, MO, MC, V
Sells: home furnishings and accessories
Store: same address (60 miles west of Charlotte, NC); Monday to Saturday 9–5

The Furniture Showplace (formerly Furniture Barn) is a family-owned firm that sells fine furnishings and decorative accessories at great prices, and prides itself on prompt handling of orders and excellent delivery service. The Furniture Showplace, established in 1970, represents hundreds of manufacturers that are listed in the brochure, which also includes details on the terms of sale. Spindale is 60 miles west of Charlotte, so if you're in the area, drop by—there's a "mini-barn" for children and a 20,000-square-foot showroom.

Special Factors: Price quote by phone or letter with SASE; shipment is made by "a professional delivery specialist"; a 33% deposit is required on all orders.

GENADA IMPORTS

DEPT. W-96
P.O. BOX 204
TEANECK, NJ 07666
201-790-7522
FAX: 201-790-7522

Catalog: $1
Save: up to 40%
Pay: check, MO, MC, V
Sells: Danish, modern, and traditional furniture
Store: mail order only

Genada has been in business since 1968, selling Danish modern furniture in its most American incarnation: low-slung, teak-finished chairs and couches, with loose-cushion backs and seats of tweed-covered foam. The style has weathered fad and fatigue quite well, and the furniture's basic appeal is only enhanced by its low prices. Armchairs begin at under $100, and couches start at under $170 (armless divans from $120).

Genada isn't limited to Scandinavian design; the catalog shows reproductions of the Eames chair and other modern classics, folding chairs with woven rope seats and backs, knock-down bookcases and cabinets, butcher block tabletops and bases, convertible foam-block chairs and sofas, gateleg tables with chairs that store in the base, and bentwood chairs. The catalog also features modern chairs by Paoli Chair Co., suitable for home or office, as well as several handsome styles in molded teak, walnut, and rosewood finishes, from about $300 and up. Imported armoires, patio furniture, "country" kitchen furniture, freestanding wall units, computer workstations, desks, VCR carts, and bar stools are all available. If you're shopping for a bridge table with folding hardwood chairs, you'll find several reasonably priced styles here.

Special Factors: Price quote by phone or letter; specify upholstery and finish materials when ordering.

HEIRLOOM REPRODUCTIONS

1834 W. FIFTH ST.,
   DEPT. WMC
MONTGOMERY, AL
   36106-1516
800-288-1513
FAX: 205-263-3313

Catalog: $2, refundable
Save: up to 55%
Pay: check, MO, MC, V
Sells: Victorian and French reproduction furniture, clocks, etc.
Store: same address; Monday to Saturday 10–5

If a button-tufted, damask-covered, center-medallion camelback sofa speaks to you, you have a weakness for Victorian decor. But as anyone who's tried to find *good* examples of the style knows, they're hard to come by at a reasonable price. Enter Heirloom Reproductions, where gooseneck rockers, fainting sofas, and bustle chairs are stock in trade. The 64-page catalog and other literature feature clear, black-and-white photos of classic parlor sets—sofas and marble-topped occasional tables—and curio cabinets, entertainment centers, hall trees, armoires, dining room sets, bedroom furniture, folding screens, and other pieces. The copy includes dimensions, some notes on construction features, and prices, which are discounted 40% to 50% from list. Prices include your choice of finish, which you may select from several options, and fabric, available in damasks, brocades, prints, tapestries, and velvets. Heirloom Reproductions also sells classic Victorian table lamps with crystal bases and fringed shades, and Howard Miller clocks and collectors' cabinets. If you need help in choosing the best pieces for your decorating scheme, consult the staff designer, who can also give you complete details on fabrics, construction, and the firm's sales policy.

Special Factors: Swatches are available on request; orders are shipped from the factory by insured truck.

HUNT GALLERIES, INC.

Catalog: $8, refundable (see text)
Save: up to 30%
Pay: check, MO, MC, V
Sells: upholstered furniture
Store: same address

2920 HWY. 127 N.
P.O. BOX 2324 WBMC
HICKORY, NC 28603
800-248-3876
704-324-9934

Hunt Galleries, a family business that was founded half a century ago, has become a full-fledged manufacturer of a complete line of upholstered furniture. Hunt's catalog and price list are models of clarity—every piece is shown in color, fully described with complete measurements. (The catalog fee of $8 is refundable with a purchase, but you may request the free brochure for basic sales information.) Most of the line is seating—sofas, love seats, chaises, chairs, armchairs, sectionals, dining room chairs, tuffets, ottomans, benches, vanity stools, etc., most of traditional design—but Hunt Galleries also offers upholstered headboards, mirrors, and even sofa tables.

The price list specifies charges for upholstery in your fabric (COM) versus different grades of Hunt's material, as well as options, including fabric lining, casters, swivel rocker mechanisms, seat filling choices (poly foam, down and feather blends, blends with innersprings, and foam with springs), and quilting. And the catalog shows the quality points of the furniture itself—doweled and glued hardwood frames, hand-tied coil springs, deep padding, etc. The terms of sale are detailed in the price list, including the shipping alternatives: truck, inside delivery, and UPS (when possible). If you still have questions, just give the Hunts a call!

Special Factors: Satisfaction is guaranteed.

DON LAMOR INC.

2220 HWY. 70 EAST
BH9 HICKORY FURNI-
    TURE MART
HICKORY, NC 28602
704-324-1776

Information: price quote
Save: up to 40%
Pay: check, MO, MC, V
Sells: home and office furnishings
Store: same address; Monday to Friday 9–6,
Saturday 9–5

Don Lamor lays claim to "North Carolina's largest display of fine home furnishings," and is an authorized dealer for a number of prominent manufacturers. The sales consultants can assist you in selecting the right furnishings for your needs, and require a 50% deposit on your order (the balance is due before the order can be shipped). Both home and office furnishings, rugs, and accessories and occasional pieces are available.

Special Factors: Price quote by phone or letter.

LOFTIN-BLACK FURNITURE COMPANY

111 SEDGEHILL DR.
THOMASVILLE, NC 27360
800-334-7398
910-472-6117
FAX: 910-472-2052

Brochure: free
Save: up to 50%
Pay: check, MO, MC, V
Sells: furnishings, bedding, and accessories
Store: same address; Monday to Saturday
8:30–5:30; also 214 N. Main St., High Point,
NC

Loftin-Black, founded in 1948, delivers selection, service, and savings. The firm offers fine home, office, and patio furniture and accessories from hundreds of companies, including the top names in furnishings. Check here before ordering mirrors, table pads, and bedding—they're also available, at sizable savings. The brochure includes a brands listing and general sales information (a 50% deposit is required when ordering, and the balance is due upon delivery). Loftin-Black will provide in-home delivery and setup, although you can engage a common carrier if you prefer. If you're in the Thomasville area, drop in and see Loftin-Black's 14,000 square feet of furniture on display.

Special Factors: Price quote by phone or letter; delivery (in-home) is made by Loftin-Black's van service.

MARKS SALES CO., INC.

DEPT. AB
609 E. 81ST ST.
BROOKLYN, NY 11236
718-763-2591

Catalog: $2 (see text)
Save: up to 50%
Pay: check or MO
Sells: unfinished, assembled furniture
Store: mail order only

Two dollars brings you the Marks Sales catalog, 62 pages of clear, sepia-toned photographs of over 100 pieces of reproduction antiques that await your finishing hand. The flavor is Continental—side chairs and armchairs and matching counter and bar stools with graceful legs, rush seats, and cane backs, imposing cane-back "tub" chairs with lion's head-arms, settles with serpentine ladderbacks and carved aprons, Chinese Chippendale styles, bombé chests, and even tables, desks, and semanieres are among the offerings. Every piece is made in Spain or Italy from beechwood and arrives completely assembled and sanded (these are not kits), ready for paint or stain and finish. Seats are made by hand of rush, cane, or muslin-covered foam. Prices are wholesale; if you finish your selection yourself, you can create a custom look for a modest investment, compared to buying the same pieces in local decorator shops.

Please note: Catalogs are sent via bulk mail and take up to three weeks to arrive; if you want yours sooner, add $1.25 for first-class postage.

Canadian readers, please note: Only U.S. funds are accepted.

Special Factors: Satisfaction is guaranteed; authorized returns are accepted within 20 days for full refund, less cost of freight.

EPHRAIM MARSH CO.

DEPT. 362
P.O. BOX 266
CONCORD, NC
28026-0266
800-992-8322
704-782-0814
FAX: 704-782-0436

Catalog: $5, refundable
Save: up to 40%
Pay: check, MO, MC, V
Sells: fine home and office furnishings
Store: mail order only

Between decorating indecision and budget restraints, furnishing a home can be a daunting affair. What you need is a friend with good taste and a decorator's discount—or Ephraim Marsh.

After surveying the offerings of hundreds of furniture manufacturers nationwide, Ephraim Marsh selects a number of pieces for its own production. Since the furniture is made to order, you can select the finish (depending on the options available), and most of the upholstered furniture can be made with your material (COM), or a choice from Ephraim Marsh's swatches. The 130-page catalog includes straightforward descriptions of the quality points of each group of furniture—whether solid wood or veneers are used, the type of joinery, finish, upholstery details, etc. What distinguishes Ephraim Marsh from other furnishings purveyors is the respect for good design and creature comfort that's shaped the collection. Each piece has been chosen for some combination of utility, charm, and beauty. Unless you're a diehard modernist, you'll find something to enhance your own rooms here: State-occasion mahogany ball-and-claw dining tables, a plain maple "Grandma's Kitchen" breakfront, a lovely yew "drum" table, Chinese Chippendale sofas and wing chairs, and even leather-upholstered furniture for bar and boardroom are just a few of the hundreds of offerings.

The prices are not *cheap*—this is "Furniture for the Long-Term Investor." But pieces of comparable quality sell elsewhere for 25% to 50% more, and it's wonderful to have the option of custom upholstery. Ephraim Marsh has been in business since 1956, and is enjoying a steady trade despite lean times in the home furnishings market—which is the best endorsement possible.

Special Factors: Authorized returns in original condition (except COM upholstery jobs) are accepted.

MURROW FURNITURE GALLERIES, INC.

DEPT. WBMC
P.O. BOX 4337
WILMINGTON, NC 28406
910-799-4010
FAX: 910-791-2791

Brochure: free
Save: up to 60%
Pay: check, MO, MC, V
Sells: home furnishings, bedding, and accessories
Store: 3514 S. College Rd., Wilmington, NC; Monday to Friday 8:30–5:30, Saturday 9–5:30; also The Furniture Patch of Calabash, 10283 Beach Dr. SW, Calabash, NC; Monday to Saturday 9–5:30

Murrow Furniture Galleries, founded in 1979, sells furnishings, bedding, and accessories from over 500 manufacturers (listed in the brochure; a color catalog showcasing a broad range of styles is also offered). The extensive selection of brands and consistently good savings make this one of the best furniture discounters around. If you're able to visit the store in Wilmington, you'll find five gallery showrooms of 45,000 square feet, with fine furnishings and accessories on display. Delivery options and terms of sale are detailed in the brochure.

Special Factors: Price quote by phone or letter; deposit is required.

PARKWAY FURNITURE GALLERIES

P.O. BOX 2450
BOONE, NC 28607
704-264-3993
FAX: 704-262-3530

Catalog: free
Save: up to 50%
Pay: check or MO
Sells: home and office furnishings, decorative accessories
Store: Hwy. 105 South, Boone, NC; Monday to Saturday 8–5

Parkway Furniture Galleries has published a lovely 18-page color catalog showcasing a sample of the home furnishings, patio furniture, lamps, clocks, mirrors, table pads, bedding, and decorative accents that are available. Parkway has been in business since 1979 and represents over 200 manufacturers, at savings of 40% to 50%. The sales policy is detailed in the brochure, which also lists the manufacturers that are represented. Van line service is available, with in-home setup.

Special Factors: Satisfaction is guaranteed; price quote by phone or letter.

PINE FACTORY

————————

P.O. DRAWER 672
ASHLAND, VA 23005
804-798-9156

Brochure: free
Save: up to 30%
Pay: check, MO, MC, V, Discover
Sells: pine furniture
Store: 60 stores nationwide in AL, CT, DE, FL, GA, LA, MD, MI, NJ, NY, OH, PA, SC, TN, and VA; locations listed in the literature

If you like the warm look of pine and plain, clean lines, you'll like the furniture from Pine Factory. This national chain is based in the east, but will ship anywhere in the country. Pine Factory can furnish the whole house: couches and coffee tables, entertainment units, TV carts, easy chairs, dining sets, hutches and corner cupboards, beds and bureaus, wardrobes and nightstands, bunkbeds and trundles, desks and computer stands, and office furnishings are among the scores of items available. The price list that's sent with the color brochure illustrates each piece with a line drawing, and includes dimensions. Since the oil finish can be renewed by simply applying another coat and scratches can be covered with a bit of stain, this is the perfect furniture for a young, active family—and the price is right, compared to similar offerings from other firms. If you live near one of the Pine Factory stores, your order will be delivered by van and assembled (if necessary) in your home; outside the Pine Factory delivery area, common carrier is used.

Special Factors: All furniture is covered by a limited warranty.

PLEXI-CRAFT QUALITY PRODUCTS CORP.

514 W. 24TH ST.
NEW YORK, NY
  10011-1179
212-924-3244
FAX: 212-924-3508

Catalog: $2
Save: up to 50%
Pay: check, MO, MC, V
Sells: acrylic furnishings and accessories
Store: same address; Monday to Friday 9:30–5

Plexi-Craft manufactures its own line of premium acrylic goods, and prices them at up to 50% less than what department and specialty stores charge for comparable items. The 16-page catalog shows acrylic furnishings and accessories of all kinds. There are a number of tables—dining, cocktail, Parsons, TV, snack, and side—and the models with separate bases may be ordered with glass instead of acrylic tops. Several rolling bars are available, as well as chairs, pedestals, computer stands, vanities and stools, luggage racks, magazine units, and telephone tables. Desk sets, kitchen organizers and paper towel holders, and bathroom fixtures round out the selection, and there's an antistatic cleaner and a polish formulated for acrylic to keep everything gleaming. Plexi-Craft, founded in 1972, also accepts orders for custom work.

   Special Factors: Price quote by phone, fax, or letter on custom work.

PRIBA FURNITURE SALES AND INTERIORS

P.O. BOX 13295
GREENSBORO, NC 27415
910-855-9034
FAX: 910-855-1370

Brochure: free
Save: up to 50%
Pay: check, MO, MC, V, Discover
Sells: furniture, accessories, bedding, carpeting, etc.
Showroom: 210 Stage Coach Trail, Greensboro, NC; Monday to Friday 9–5:30, Saturday 9–5

Priba's 40,000-square-foot showroom is a must-see if you're in the High Point/Greensboro area, but if you're not planning to travel, Priba will bring the furnishings to you. The firm has been in business since 1972, and represents over 300 manufacturers of home furnishings, including bedroom and dining room suites, leather, patio furniture, lamps and accessories, carpeting, decorator fabrics, wall coverings, and mattresses. The choice of manufacturers tends to the upmarket end of the scale, and a number are usually listed as "to the trade only" in decorator magazines. Send for the brochure for details on Priba's sales policy, and call for price quotes or for assistance in making your selection. Savings run up to nearly 50% on list or regular retail, and Priba uses van-line service, so your furniture will be uncrated and set up within your home.

Special Factors: Credit cards are accepted for deposits only; shipping charge is calculated on a minimum weight of 150 pounds.

QUALITY FURNITURE MARKET OF LENOIR, INC.

■■■■■■■

2034 HICKORY BLVD. S.W.
LENOIR, NC 28645
704-728-2946
FAX: 704-726-0226

Information: price quote
Save: up to 47%
Pay: check, MO, MC, V
Sells: furnishings, bedding, and accessories
Store: same address; Monday to Saturday 8:30–5

Quality Furniture Market, in business since 1955, takes its name seriously: You're invited to check the firm's ratings with Dun and Bradstreet, the Lyons listing, and the Lenoir Chamber of Commerce (800-737-0782) before you buy. The firm's magnificent selection is offered at prices that are 20% over cost, compared to the usual 110% to 125% markups.

Quality Furniture sells indoor and outdoor furniture, bedding, and home accessories by literally hundreds of firms. The list of brands is given in the brochure, as well as terms of sale and other conditions. Readers have written to say they were very pleased with Quality's prices and the firm's in-home delivery service. If you're traveling near Lenoir, drop by and get lost in the three floors of furniture galleries and display rooms.

Special Factors: Price quote by phone or letter with SASE; all orders must be prepaid before shipment; shipment is made by common carrier or in-home delivery service.

SHAW FURNITURE GALLERIES, INC.

131 W. ACADEMY ST.
RANDLEMAN, NC 27317
910-498-2628
FAX: 910-498-7889

Brochure: free
Save: up to 50%
Pay: check, MO, MC, V
Sells: home and office furnishings
Store: same address; Monday to Friday 9–5:30, Saturday 9–5

The Shaw family has been selling furniture at a discount since 1940 and represents over 300 manufacturers; the large inventory can be seen in Shaw's showroom in Randleman. (If you're able to visit, let the company know you're coming—they'll pick up the cost of your lodging, based on a minimum purchase.) Shaw's brochure includes a partial listing of the available brands, but inquire if you're pricing a piece of furniture or an item by a manufacturer not mentioned, since it may be carried. Shaw's references and the terms of sale are detailed in the brochure, and please note that while down payments of up to 30% may be charged to your credit card, final payments must be made by certified check or money order. Shipment is made by Superior Delivery Service, which is co-owned by Shaw.

Special Factors: Price quote by phone or letter with SASE; shipments are made by Superior Delivery Service (owned by Shaw's management); minimum order is $100.

SOBOL HOUSE OF FURNISHINGS

RICHARDSON BLVD.
P.O. BOX 219
BLACK MOUNTAIN, NC 28711
704-669-8031
FAX: 704-669-7969

Brochure: free
Save: up to 50% plus
Pay: check or MO
Sells: home and office furnishings
Store: same address

Sobol House has been saving informed consumers on their furniture purchases since 1971, and the firm's low prices have helped build a clientele worldwide over the years. Although Sobol carries contemporary furnishings, the firm's specialty is traditional, 18th century, and country styles, from the most prominent names in the business. Sobol can help you make your selection—with advice and manufacturers' catalogs—and gives price quotes on specific items. Both sidewalk and in-house delivery are available, and details of the sales policy are given in the brochure and order form.

Special Factors: Price quote by phone or letter.

STUCKEY BROTHERS FURNITURE CO., INC.

RTE. I, BOX 527
STUCKEY, SC 29554
803-558-2591
FAX: 803-558-9229

Information: price quote
Save: up to 50%
Pay: check or MO
Sells: indoor and outdoor furnishings and accessories
Store: same address; Monday to Friday 9–6, Saturday 9–5

Stuckey is South Carolina's answer to High Point—it sells a full line of furniture and accessories at North Carolina prices and has been doing business by mail since 1946. Furnishings and accessories, including patio and office furnishings, are available from over 300 manufacturers. Lines of clocks, lamps, mirrors, and bedding are offered as well. Request the brochure that details the sales terms and shipping options (van line or common carrier).

Special Factors: Price quote by phone or letter with SASE.

MARION TRAVIS

P.O. BOX 292
STATESVILLE, NC 28687
704-528-4424
FAX: 704-528-3526

Catalog: $1
Save: up to 50%
Pay: check, MO, MC, V
Sells: country chairs, benches, and tables
Store: 354 S. Eastway Dr., Troutman, NC; Monday to Thursday 8–3:30, Friday 8–12 noon

You can pay hundreds of dollars for an oak pedestal table at your local antique shop, and search every tag sale in the state for a matched set of ladder-back chairs. Or you can send $1 to Marion Travis for the catalog that shows these and other furnishings. The ten pages of black-and-white photographs show country furniture, including a large selection of ladder-back chairs with woven cord seats. There are armchair and rocker styles and children's models, beginning at under $25. Plain, slat-seat kitchen chairs and a classic oak kitchen table with utility drawer are shown, as well as a porch swing and Kennedy-style rockers with cane backs and seats. The prices cited are for unfinished furniture, but Marion Travis will stain and finish your selection in natural, oak, or walnut for a surcharge. If you're in the vicinity of Troutman, you can receive a 25% discount on most items by going to the store, making a purchase, and taking it with you, unboxed.

Special Factors: Authorized returns of defective goods are accepted within 30 days.

TRIAD FURNITURE DISCOUNTERS

3930 HIGHWAY 501
MYRTLE BEACH, SC 29577
800-323-8469
803-236-3660
FAX: 803-236-1534

Information: price quote
Save: up to 50%
Pay: check, MO, MC, V, Discover
Sells: home and office furnishings
Store: same address; Monday to Friday 10–6, Saturday 10–5

 ¡Si!

Triad's brochure lists nearly 100 major manufacturers of home, office, and outdoor furniture, lamps, mirrors, and bedding, which Triad offers at savings of up to 50% on the suggested list prices. (When you've decided on the style and price range of what you're shopping, Triad will send manufacturers' brochures at no cost.) Triad's sales policy—50% down on placing the order, the balance before shipment—is standard among Carolina's furniture discounters. Triad gives you a firm delivery charge (not an estimate), and all shipments are delivered in-house with setup. You can write for the brochure, which includes the partial list of manufacturers, or call for a price quote on specific items.

Special Factors: Price quote by phone or letter.

WELLINGTON'S FURNITURE, INC.

P.O. BOX 2178
BOONE, NC 28607
800-262-1049
704-264-1049
FAX: 704-265-1049

Catalog: free
Save: up to 50%
Pay: check, MO, MC, V, Discover
Sells: leather furniture
Store: 2301 Blowing Rock Rd., Boone, NC; Monday to Saturday 10–5:30

Wellington's 72-page catalog showcases leather chairs, ottomans, sofas, sleepers, sectionals, and recliners from nearly a dozen manufacturers. Styles range from traditional English Chesterfields and wing chairs to sleek contemporary pieces, and Wellington's offers a variety of options in cushion construction, arm tailoring, and even leg and foot styles. The catalog describes the quality points of the furniture, defines leather terms, and details the sales policy. A "Swatch Request" form is included in the catalog, so you can sample the leather.) Wellington's offers a more generous guarantee of satisfaction than many furniture marketers, discounts everything up to 50% below manufacturers' list prices, and runs frequent promotions. Designers are welcome to inquire for special pricing (tax numbers are required).

Please note: A 50% deposit is required when placing the order, and only half of the purchase price total may be charged to a credit card. Deliveries are insured and include in-home setup.

Special Factors: Returns are accepted for credit (freight and restocking fees apply).

WICKER WAREHOUSE INC.

195 S. RIVER ST.
HACKENSACK, NJ 07601
201-342-6709
FAX: 201-342-1495

Catalog: $5, refundable
Save: up to 50%
Pay: check, MO, MC, V, Discover
Sells: wicker furniture and accessories
Store: same address; Monday to Saturday 10–6, Wednesday till 7, Thursday till 9

Why comb antique stores and flea markets for vintage wicker furniture when you can find freshly minted versions of the same styles, in pristine condition, at comparable prices? Wicker Warehouse, established in 1978, sells current styles by the top names in the business, including lines treated to withstand the elements—so you don't have to drag everything inside the garage when it starts raining. The 64-page color catalog shows great groupings for sun porch and summer home, and wicker-embellished bedroom furnishings, mirrors, lamps, dining chairs, stools, nursery accoutrements, bathroom accessories, trunks, and even doll buggies. Fabric and finish options are shown as well. The prices are 30% to 50% below list, and orders are shipped anywhere within the continental United States.

Special Factors: Satisfaction is guaranteed; price quote by phone or letter.

SEE ALSO

Alfax Wholesale Furniture • *office and institutional furnishings* • **OFFICE**
American Discount Wall and Window Coverings • *upholstery and decorator fabrics* • **HOME: DECOR**
Anticipations • *home furnishings and accents* • **GENERAL MERCHANDISE**
Bedroom Secrets • *home furnishings* • **HOME: LINEN**
Bennett Brothers, Inc. • *small selection of home furnishings* • **GENERAL MERCHANDISE**
Business & Institutional Furniture Company, Inc. • *office and institutional furniture* • **OFFICE**
Cole's Appliance & Furniture Co. • *home furnishings* • **APPLIANCES**
Coppa Woodworking Inc. • *Adirondack chairs, screen doors* • **HOME: IMPROVEMENT**
Custom Windows & Walls • *decorator fabrics* • **HOME: DECOR**
Eldridge Textile Co. • *custom-upholstered headboards, ottomans, footstools, etc.* • **HOME: LINEN**
Excalibur Bronze Sculpture Foundry • *"art" furniture* • **ART & ANTIQUES**
The Fabric Center, Inc. • *upholstery and decorator fabrics* • **HOME: DECOR**
Fabrics by Phone • *upholstery and decorator fabrics* • **HOME: DECOR**
Frank Eastern Co. • *office furniture* • **OFFICE**
Frank's Cane and Rush Supply • *small selection of unfinished furniture kits* • **CRAFTS**
Harmony Supply Inc. • *decorator fabrics* • **HOME: DECOR**
Home Fabric Mills, Inc. • *upholstery and drapery fabrics* • **HOME: DECOR**
Marlene's Decorator Fabrics • *upholstery and drapery fabric* • **HOME: DECOR**
Shama Imports, Inc. • *crewel upholstery fabric and cushion covers* • **HOME: DECOR**

Silk Surplus • upholstery and drapery fabric • **HOME: DECOR**
Improvement and Maintenance
___

Hardware, tools, equipment, supplies,

and materials

Buying a home is probably the largest single investment that you'll make during your lifetime, so the rewards for doing your homework before you sign the contract can be significant. Even if you've bought real estate before, go over the basics before you buy again: contract obligations with agents and buyers, mortgage types and bridge loans, assessments and inspections, caveats, zoning and environmental restrictions, deeds and titles, etc.

If you're looking for the ideal community, check the guides: *The Hundred Best Small Towns in the U.S.* and *Places Rated Almanac* look at statistical indices: The cost of living, housing availability, climate, medical facilities, arts and recreational opportunities, and other criteria are tallied as part of the final recommendations. Once you've chosen the spot, do the research: subscribe to the local newspaper, drop in on public hearings on land and water use, attend a couple of community events, and study maps and surveys of the area. Learn as much as possible about the local history (including fires, floods, manufacturing and farming sites, water and sewerage systems, etc.), as well as plans for future development, tax hikes, and changes in the local economy. *Country Bound,* by Marilyn and Tom Ross (Communication Creativity, 1992) gives lots of useful advice on this whole process of evaluation. When you're ready to look for property, you'll find *How to Buy a House, Condo, or Co-op,* from Consumer Reports Books, a great primer; *Finding & Buying Your Place in the Country,* by Les and Carol Scher, is one of several popular guides to realizing that dream (available from Storey Communications; see the listing in "Books"). *The Home Buyer's*

Kit and *The Home Seller's Kit,* by Edith Lank, walk you through both sides of the transactions, with lots of checklists and charts to keep you organized. And *Your New House: The Alert Consumer's Guide to Buying and Building a Quality Home,* by Alan and Denise Fields, focuses on building—258 pages on what puts the "con" in "construction," and how to avoid and solve every problem that can arise. See the mention of *Bridal Bargains* in the introduction to "Clothing" for ordering information.

After buying, furnishing, and decorating your house, you have to keep it. Keeping house means maintaining it against those ills that befall even the finest homes: roof leaks, clogged gutters, damp basements, peeling paint, and a hundred other problems. Keeping it clean and in good repair can be a never-ending task, so doing it faster, better, and cheaper is a common goal. Consumers Union publishes several books that can help, including *Year-Round House Care, The Complete Guide to Home Repair and Maintenance, Home Security* (on locks, alarms, etc.), and *How to Clean Practically Everything.* (See the current issue of *Consumer Reports* to order, or check your local bookstore.) Reader's Digest Books offers *The Family Handyman® Helpful Hints: Quick and Easy Solutions, Timesaving Tips, Tricks of the Trade* (1995), nearly 400 well-organized pages of great ideas for doing everything from setting up a workshop to repairing masonry. Time Life's *How Things Work in Your Home (And What to Do When They Don't)* is over 20 years old, but still a great help in do-it-yourself repairs. Because design advances and computerization are not discussed, this book will be of most help if you have older appliances. Time-Life's current series, "New Home Repair and Improvement," updates the first edition of the series, which was released in the 70s. You can order a "customized" library of any of the 20 titles—from *Adding On* to *Walls and Ceilings*—that meet your needs from Time-Life, 800-621-7026 (Monday to Friday 9 A.M.–9 P.M., ET), or look for volumes at your library or book sales.

For sources selling related goods, see the listings in "Home: Decor" and "Tools."

FIND IT FAST

ARCHITECTURAL DETAILS • **Oregon Wooden Screen Door, Shuttercraft**
INSULATED GLASS PANELS • **Arctic Glass**
LUMBER AND FLOORING • **BRE Lumber**
PLUMBING FIXTURES • **Baths from the Past, CISCO, Faucet Outlet, LIBW**
RADIATOR ENCLOSURES • **ARSCO, Monarch**
SCREEN DOORS AND WINDOWS • **Coppa Woodworking**

ARCTIC GLASS & WINDOW OUTLET

DEPT. WB
565 CO. RD. T
HAMMOND, WI 54015
800-428-9276
715-796-2292
FAX: 715-796-2295

Catalog: $4, refundable
Save: up to 50%
Pay: check, MO, MC, V, Discover
Sells: exterior doors, windows, skylights, glass panels
Store: I-94 at Hammond Exit, 35 miles east of St. Paul, MN; also Hamilton Ave., Eau Claire, WI; Monday to Thursday 8–8, Friday 8–5, Saturday 9–5

Joseph Bacon began his business after discovering that surplus patio door panes doubled perfectly as passive solar panels in the greenhouse he was building—and cost up to 50% less. Since founding Arctic Glass in 1979, he's watched it outgrow several facilities and increase revenues 2,000%. In fact, Mr. Bacon has shipped to 49 of the 50 states—he's just waiting for that order from Hawaii!

Arctic Glass sells surplus patio door panels from two of the best-known manufacturers in the business. Different types of double panes are available (some with low E coating), most of the glass is 3/16" thick, and all of the panes are double-sealed. The many suitable applications and uses for those panels are listed in the literature. Arctic also stocks Velux skylights and the complete line of Kolbe & Kolbe doors and windows—wood-framed casements, tilts, slider, direct-set, eyebrow, and fanlight windows and a variety of doors. Weather Shield wood and vinyl windows and doors, Therma-Tru doors, and Velux skylights are also available.

Prices average 10% to 50% below list, and all of the panels are guaranteed against leakage or failure for ten years. The warranty terms and installation instructions, including retrofitting, are detailed in the literature. If you have any questions, you can talk them over with Mr. Bacon himself.

Special Factors: Shipments are made to 49 of the 50 states; quantity discounts are available; minimum crating charge is $50 for mail orders; returns are accepted within 30 days for exchange, refund, or credit; minimum order is $50.

ARSCO MANUFAC-TURING COMPANY, INC.

Catalog: free
Save: up to 35%
Pay: check, MO, MC, V, Discover
Sells: radiator enclosures
Store: same address; Monday to Friday 8–4

3564 BLUE ROCK RD.
CINCINNATI, OH 45247
800-543-7040
513-385-0555

"Once you own ACE Radiator Enclosures, you won't ever catch yourself staring at those naked radiators...." So reads the brochure from ARSCO Manufacturing, which makes enclosures for conventional steam radiators, fan coil units, and fin tube (baseboard) heaters. If you live within 600 miles of Cincinnati, ARSCO will send someone to measure your radiator; farther afield, you can use the guide ARSCO provides and do it yourself.

Standard sizes run up to 42" high and 96" long (larger sizes can be made), and there are 14 stock colors of paint enamel, although custom color matches can be provided for a fee. Other options include special notches, doors, or cutouts for valve access, a built-in humidifier pan, insulated tops, and adjustable legs for uneven floors.

Prices are a solid 35% below those charged by local sources for the same kinds of enclosures, and if your unit is measured by ARSCO's personnel, the fit is guaranteed. If you're measuring it yourself, do it twice and then again, since the enclosures are all made to order, and are *not* returnable.

Special Factors: Enclosures are not returnable.

BATHS FROM THE PAST, INC.

83 EAST WATER ST.
ROCKLAND, MA 02370
800-697-3871
617-335-2445
FAX: 617-871-8533

Catalog: free (see text)
Save: up to 30%
Pay: check, MO, MC, V
Sells: bathroom and kitchen hardware
Store: mail order only

Nothing completes a period bathroom like authentic hardware—brass spigots and porcelain shower roses, telephone-style tub fillers and tall overflow drains—but nothing breaks a budget faster. Baths from the Past makes it more affordable to buy these, as well as kitchen faucets, shower curtain rods, Victorian porcelain bathroom sinks, and bathroom accessories, at prices up to 30% below other sources (for comparable quality and finish—chrome, polished brass, and polished lacquered brass). The finishes are guaranteed for ten years, and the fixtures themselves are covered by a lifetime guarantee against failure or defective workmanship.

Special Factors: Satisfaction is guaranteed.

BRE LUMBER, INC./ RARE EARTH HARDWOODS

6778 EAST TRAVERSE
  HWY.
TRAVERSE CITY, MI 49684
800-968-0074
616-946-0043
FAX: 616-946-6221

Information: price quote
Save: up to 30%
Pay: check, MO, MC, V, Discover
Sells: lumber, hardwood flooring, inlays, etc.
Store: same address; Monday to Friday 8–5, Saturday 8–12 noon

Home remodeling involves endless dilemmas, like realizing that prefinished parquet floor tiles have their merits, but you want a *real* floor. If that's out of line with the budget, BRE Lumber may be able to help.

BRE sells the genuine article, at a price better than those of other specialty dealers (though you won't beat the floor-in-a-box prices). BRE's stock includes cabinet-grade lumber flooring, wide-plank flooring, paneling, molding, stairs, parts, and "dimensional lumber." Dozens of species of flooring woods are available, include maple, Padauk, Cocobolo, Bubinga, Jatoba (Brazilian cherry), Wenge, and teak, among others, and the stock is "long and clear." Tatajuba decking (Brazilian teak), which is said to be five times harder than redwood, is also available, as are inlay borders and feature strips. BRE has been in business since 1987 and can save you up to 30% on the delivered cost of the flooring, and sometimes more, depending on prices prevailing in your area. If you're planning to build or remodel, get BRE's current price list and samples ($15 plus shipping) and consider all the options before buying veneer-faced particle board. If you can't get what you need from stock, take advantage of BRE's custom mill-work services.

Special Factors: Price quote by phone, fax, or letter with SASE.

CISCO

CHANUTE IRON &
SUPPLY CO.
1502 W. CHERRY ST.
CHANUTE, KS 66720-1005
316-431-9289
FAX: 316-431-7354

Information: price quote
Save: up to 40%
Pay: check, MO, MC, V
Sells: plumbing supplies and fixtures
Store: same address; Monday to Friday 8–5, Saturday 8–12 noon

CISCO stocks a full range of fixtures and equipment for plumbing, heating, and air conditioning. CISCO has been selling plumbing supplies, fixtures, and tools since 1941 and offers a portion of the inventory by mail at savings of 25% to 40%. Delta and Moen faucets, Insinkerator garbage disposers, Burnham boilers, Miami Carey medicine chests and accessories, and whirlpools and fixtures by Aqua Glass, Aquatic, and Jason are available. There are Elkay, Moen, and Swanstone sinks, Crane fixtures, Cal-Spas and saunas, spa and swimming pool accessories and parts (no chemicals), tools by Rigid, and the professional line of tools by Makita. Replacement parts for all types of faucets are also stocked.

Please note: No catalog is available.

Special Factors: Price quote by phone, fax, or letter with SASE; minimum order is $25; CISCO pays freight on UPS-shippable items over $100.

COPPA WOOD-WORKING INC.

1231 PARAISO AVE.
SAN PEDRO, CA 90731
310-548-4142
FAX: 310-548-5332

Catalog: $1
Save: up to 40%
Pay: check, MO, MC, V
Sells: Adirondack furniture, screen doors, windows, etc.
Store: mail order only

Coppa Woodworking is a small firm that manufactures Adirondack-style furniture, screen doors, and window screens in a variety of finishes, woods, and other options, at prices up to 40% below those charged elsewhere for comparable products. (You know you're dealing directly with the craftsmen when the catalog itself smells of fresh lumber!) Classic low-slung, slat-back Adirondack chair styles are featured, from the children's model for about $30 to the "fanback" for under $70 to a 51-inch-wide love seat for about $100. All of the seating and complementing footrests and side tables are made of unfinished pine that can be stained (white, blue, or green) for a small fee. Old-fashioned butcher block tables with 2-1/2" red-oak tops begin at $126, and other woods and custom-painted bases are available.

The other side of Coppa's business is screen doors, window screens, and sidelights (panels); the doors can be produced in over 100 styles to suit every decor. A number of options are available, including wood choice (Douglas fir, sugar pine, red oak, mahogany), stain and varnish, single or double-door fixtures, custom sizes, built-in pet doors, and a choice of fiberglass screening materials (including heavy-duty cat-proof mesh). Prices begin at a mere $34 for the plainest style in pine, and custom charges are quite reasonable. And if you'd like a feature or detail not mentioned, be sure to ask, since Coppa may be able to provide.

Special Factors: Satisfaction is guaranteed; returns are accepted.

THE FAUCET OUTLET

P.O. BOX 547
MIDDLETOWN, NY 10940
800-444-5783
FAX: 914-343-1617

Catalog: $1
Save: up to 33%
Pay: check, MO, MC, V
Sells: bathroom and kitchen faucets
Store: mail order only; phone hours Monday to Friday 8–8, Saturday 9–2, Sunday 10–3, ET
E-mail: faucet@faucet.com

We don't spend much time thinking about those things that deliver water from the pipes into the shower, tub, or sink, so when they need replacing it's a shock to discover how many there are, and how much they cost. Thank goodness for The Faucet Outlet.

This mail-order concern specializes in spigots, spouts, knobs, connections, hot water dispensers, and related items by Alsons, American Standard, Chicago Faucets, Delta, Elkay, Grohe, Jado, Kohler, Moen, Price Pfister, St. Thomas Creations, Speakman (shower heads), Swanstone, and other firms. A selection of bathroom accessories for the disabled— elevated toilet seats, grab bars and rails, benches, and flush levers—are also available. The 64-page catalog features a sampling of products from a number of manufacturers, as well as valuable service information and The Faucet Outlet's sales policy. (A separate catalog of NuTone chimes, fans, intercoms, security videos, and medicine cabinets is also available.) You can send $1 for the catalogs, or if you know exactly what you want or don't see the model you're looking for, call with the stock or item number for a price quote. (Check before ordering to make sure your fixtures comply with local codes and are compatible with existing plumbing.) Discounts on faucets are 33% on manufacturers' list prices at this writing, but are subject to change and may vary from line to line.

Please note: The catalog fee, usually $2, is $1 to readers of this book, so be sure to mention WBMC when you send for it.

Special Factors: Authorized returns are accepted.

LIBW

717 E. JERICHO TPKE.,
  SUITE 294
HUNTINGTON STATION,
  NY 11746
800-553-0663
FAX: 516-694-3494

Literature: $5, credited to order(see text)
Save: up to 33%
Pay: check, MO, MC, V
Sells: bathroom fixtures and accessories
Store: mail order only

Renovating that old bathroom can run into large sums fast, so it's nice to be able to economize on more than just the towels. LIBW helps you save on the fixtures themselves, with discounts averaging 25% to 33% on faucets, sinks and pedestals, toilets and bidets, medicine cabinets, mirrors, whirlpools, and even door and cabinet hardware. LIBW has been in business since 1989, and represents Altmans, American Standard, Artistic Brass, Baldwin, Century, Domus, Dornbracht, Eljer, Eurotec, Franke, Grohe, Hansgrohe, Jacuzzi, Jado, Kohler, Miami Carey, Nutone, Omnia, Pearl, Price Pfister, St. Thomas, Sunrise Specialty, and scores of other manufacturers. You can send for the literature ($5, credited to your order), or write or call for quotes and shipping charges on specific items. Please note that price quotes are for payments by check or money order and represent a 5% discount.

Special Factors: Price quote by phone or letter; a 5% discount is given on orders paid by check or money order.

MONARCH

DEPT. WBMC
2744 ARKANSAS DR.
BROOKLYN, NY 11234
201-796-4117
FAX: 201-796-7717

Brochure: $1, refundable with order
Save: up to 35%
Pay: check, MO, MC, V
Sells: all-steel radiator enclosures
Store: mail order only

If you're tired of looking at the exposed ribs of the radiators in your home, consider enclosures. They not only render the unsightly heating fixtures more decorative, but also help to direct the heat into the room.

Monarch sells enclosures in two dozen styles, from a basic grillwork design to an elaborate enclosure that includes shelves. Monarch's enclosures are constructed of heavy steel, and price comparisons show savings of up to 35%. There is a choice of colors in baked enamel, including wood-grain finishes. Monarch's literature includes a guide to measuring your radiator prior to ordering. (Please note that, like window treatments and other goods ordered to measure, the enclosures are not returnable.)

Special Factors: Most enclosures can be shipped by UPS; larger enclosures are shipped via common carrier.

OREGON WOODEN
SCREEN DOOR

2767 HARRIS ST.
EUGENE, OR 97405
503-485-0279
FAX: 503-484-0353

Brochure and Price List: $3
Save: up to 30%
Pay: check, MO, MC, V
Sells: wooden screen and storm doors
Store: same address

The satisfying "thock" of a wooden screen door closing is one of the many small sounds of a great summer day. Revive this lovely component of a well-tailored home with the help of Oregon Wooden Screen Doors, which sells 30 door styles, but allows you to amend the designs with your choice of spandrels, brackets, and other embellishments. The categories break down into "Ornamental," "Classic," "Muscular," and the "Designers Collection." They range in complexity from "Settler," a straightforward, two-panel door, to "Wright's Delight," a tribute to the master architect. Each door is constructed of 1-1/4" thick, vertical-grain fir, with mortise-and-tenon and dowel joinery, for strength and warp resistance. Wood-framed screen and storm inserts are available, and all of the wood is primed with wood preservative—you provide the final finish. Solid brass hardware can be ordered with your door, or you can obtain it locally.

Prices begin at under $200 for the kit versions of the simplest styles, to several hundred for the most elaborate. Since the doors are made to measure, this approximates a custom job—at a prefab price! If you have questions about any aspect of design or construction, or want a fully customized design, the staff will be pleased to help.

Special Factors: Authorized returns are accepted.

SHUTTERCRAFT

DEPT. WBM
282 STEPSTONE HILL RD.
GUILFORD, CT 06437
203-453-1973
FAX: 203-245-5969

Brochures: free with SASE
Save: up to 30%
Pay: check, MO, MC, V
Sells: interior and exterior house shutters and hardware
Store: same address; Monday to Friday 9–5

Authentic, "historic" exterior wood shutters with movable louvers are sold here at prices well below those charged for custom-milled shutters. An added advantage: They look more substantial than the vinyl versions, and the firm's literature points out that "real wood shutters are naturally ventilating and do not cause the wood siding behind them to rot." Shuttercraft's white pine and cedar shutters can be bought in widths up to 36", in lengths to 144", and in shapes that include half-circle tops, Gothic arches, and cutouts in the raised panels. (A pine tree is shown, but Shuttercraft will execute your pattern for $10 per pair of shutters.) Also available are fixed-louver shutters, exterior raised-panel shutters in Western cedar, interior plantation styles, S-shaped holdbacks, and shutter hinges (both fixed and lift-off styles). Shuttercraft will prime, paint, trim, and rabbet your shutters for a fee; details are given in the brochures.

Special Factors: Shipping is not charged on orders totaling $400 or more.

SEE ALSO

AAA-Vacuum Cleaner Service Center • *floor-care machines and supplies* • **APPLIANCES**
ABC Vacuum Cleaner Warehouse • *floor-care machines and supplies* • **APPLIANCES**
Clegg's Handyman Supply • *home fix-up items, plumbing and electrical supplies, etc.* • **TOOLS**
Clothcrafters, Inc. • *mosquito netting and flannel polishing cloths* • **GENERAL MERCHANDISE**
King's Chandelier Co. • *replacement parts for chandeliers* • **HOME: DECOR: LIGHTING**
Manufacturer's Supply • *woodburning furnaces and heaters* • **TOOLS**
Midamerica Vacuum Cleaner Supply Co. • *floor-care machines, supplies, and parts* • **APPLIANCES**

Percy's Inc. • garbage disposals • **APPLIANCES**

Safe Specialties, Inc. • safes for home, office, and business • **OFFICE**

Sewin' in Vermont • floor-care machines • **APPLIANCES**

Staples, Inc. • cleaning products, janitorial supplies, paper towels, brooms, trash bags, etc. • **OFFICE**

Value-tique, Inc. • safes for home, office, and business • **OFFICE**

Water Warehouse • swimming pool maintenance equipment and supplies • **SPORTS**

Kitchen

Cookware, bakeware, restaurant equipment, and food storage

This chapter includes companies selling everything from measuring spoons to commercial ranges, frequently at discounts of 30% to 50% on the regular retail prices. For other kitchen electronics, see "Appliances"; for kitchen tools and linens, see the next chapter, "Linen"; and look in "Books" for cookbooks. In addition, a number of firms that sell specialty ingredients and cookware are listed in the "Food and Drink" chapter—including several that offer stupendous buys on herbs, spices, and other flavorings.

FIND IT FAST

CHEESE-MAKING EQUIPMENT • **New England Cheesemaking Supply**
COMMERCIAL FIXTURES • **Fivenson, Kaplan Bros., Peerless**
GOURMET COOKWARE • **Broadway Panhandler, Open House, Professional Cutlery, Zabar's**

BROADWAY PANHANDLER

477 BROOME ST.
NEW YORK, NY 10013
212-966-3434

Information: price quote (see text)
Save: up to 40%
Pay: check, MO, MC, V, AE
Sells: cookware, cutlery, kitchenware, bakeware
Store: same address; Monday to Friday 10:30–6, Saturday 11–7, Sunday 12–6

The Broadway Panhandler is located just blocks from the Bowery, New York City's commercial kitchenware district, but it draws a steady stream of trade in those who like Broadway Panhandler's mix of high-end home cookware with well-chosen professional equipment. Although there is no catalog, you can call or write for prices on appliances and equipment by All-Clad, Bodum, Bourgeat, Braun, Calphalon, Chicago Metallic, Le Creuset, Cuisinart (machines), Kaiser, KitchenAid, Krups, Omega, Pavoni, Pelouze, and Vollrath. Broadway Panhandler's knife department includes lines by Global, Lamson & Goodnow, Sabatier, and Wüstof-Trident (price lists and manufacturers' brochures may be available for the cutlery). If you're able to visit the store, you'll also find cookbooks, serving pieces, kitchen linens, candy molds, baking supplies, and lots of baskets and gadgets. Savings vary by brand and season, but open-stock cutlery is about 30% off at this writing, and selected cookware lines are discounted up to 35% off list.

Special Factors: Price quote by phone or letter.

COLONIAL GARDEN KITCHENS

DEPT. CGZ4182
HANOVER, PA 17333-0066
800-323-6000

Catalog: $2
Save: up to 40%
Pay: check, MO, MC, V, AE, Discover
Sells: kitchen equipment and household helps
Store: mail order only

Colonial Garden Kitchens is one of the Hanover Direct, Inc. companies offering moderately priced gadgets, as well as name-brand appliances, at a discount. A third or more of the goods in the color catalog are usually on "sale" at 20% to 40% below their regular prices. And every catalog features the latest in kitchen appliances, specialty cookware and utensils, work units and food storage containers, serving and entertaining equipment, hard-to-find cleaners, bed and bath organizers, and lots of other things that are handy to have around the house. The West Bend Bread and Dough Maker and Pasta Express machines, the DeLonghi toaster oven, commercial oven mitts, microwave bacon crispers, and cast-iron muffin tins are among the popular products that have appeared in past catalogs. Everything is backed by the CGK's guarantee of satisfaction.

Special Factors: Returns are accepted for exchange, refund, or credit.

FIVENSON FOOD EQUIPMENT, INC.

324 S. UNION ST.
TRAVERSE CITY, MI
  49684-2586
800-632-7342
616-946-7760
FAX: 616-946-7126

Catalog: $3, refundable
Save: up to 60%
Pay: check, MO, MC, V, AE, Discover
Sells: food and beverage equipment and furnishings for restaurant, bar, camp, club, church, concession, office, etc.
Store: same address; Monday to Friday 9–5, Saturday 10–12

Fivenson has been selling restaurant, concession, pizza, ice cream, bakery, institutional, bar, grocery, and ventilation equipment and furniture to the food-service industry since 1937 and offers consumers the same products at prices up to 60% below list. Fivenson's catalog features ranges, ovens, steamers, fryers, and toasters by Dean, Frymaster, Garland, Savory, Toastmaster, U.S. Range, Vollrath, and Amana microwave ovens. There are Regal coffee urns, commercial blenders from Hamilton Beach, as well as dishwashers, cooling units of every description from Delfield, Traulson, True, Ultra, and Victory; Pelouze scales; and sinks, lunchroom furniture, bakery racks, equipment for popcorn, hot dog, and concession stands. Fivenson also sells office coffee service sets, smoke-reduction equipment, air doors, ice makers, cleaning tools, chafing dishes, restaurant china, and other supplies. (The china and glassware are sold by the case only.) Since the $3 catalog is a brief 16 pages, you'll save money if you can decide what you want and then call, fax, or write Fivenson for a price quote.

Special Factors: Price quote by phone or letter with SASE; kitchen layout and design services are available; minimum order is $25.

KAPLAN BROS. BLUE FLAME CORP.

523 W. 125TH ST.
NEW YORK, NY
10027-3498
212-662-6990
FAX: 212-663-2026

Brochure: free with SASE
Save: up to 50%
Pay: check or MO
Sells: commercial restaurant equipment
Store: same address; Monday to Friday 8–5

Kaplan Bros. Blue Flame Corp., established in 1953, sells commercial restaurant equipment at discounts of up to 50% on list prices and will send you manufacturers' brochures on request for a self-addressed, stamped envelope. Blue Flame is best known as a source for Garland commercial stoves, including the popular six-burner model that costs over $2,705 at list, but $1,252 here. (Garland's Residential Range model is available.) Garland fryers, ovens, griddles, and salamanders are stocked, as well as Frymaster and Pitco fryers, and equipment by Blickman, Blodgett, Dynamic Cooking System, MagiKitchin, Prince Castle, and Vulcan.

Please note: Goods are shipped to "mainland U.S.A." only—no orders can be shipped to Alaska, Hawaii, Canada, or APO/FPO addresses.

Special Factors: Request brochures by name of manufacturer; if purchasing a stove for residential installation, have kitchen flooring, wall insulation, and exhaust system evaluated before ordering and upgrade if necessary.

KITCHEN ETC.

DEPT. WBM96
P.O. BOX 1560
NORTH HAMPTON, NH
03862-1560
603-964-5174
FAX: 603-964-5123

Catalog: free
Save: 30% average
Pay: check, MO, MC, V, Discover
Sells: tableware and kitchenware
Store: West Hartford, CT; Burlington, Dedham, Natick, and Peabody, MA; Nashua and North Hampton, NH; and South Burlington, VT (see the catalog for locations)

Kitchen Etc. has put together a great, 104-page catalog of fine and everyday china, cutlery, and serving pieces that brings you helpful buying information, as well as prices that usually run from 20% to 40% below regular retail. The firm has been doing business since 1983, and has eight stores throughout New England.

The catalog features fine and casual dinnerware patterns from Blue Danube, Dansk, Franciscan, Hutschenreuther, International, Johnson Brothers, Lenox, Mikasa, Nikko, Noritake, Pfaltzgraff, Roma, Royal Doulton, Royal Worcester, Studio Nova, and Wedgwood. The available patterns are listed, as well as a guide to the shape of each piece, present and future availability (if known), and suggested retail and discount prices. Stemware from Atlantis Block, Gorham, Lenox, Mikasa, Miller Rogaska, Noritake, and Royal Doulton is sold. Stainless steel and silverplate flatware is available from Gorham, Mikasa, Oneida, Pfaltzgraff, Reed & Barton, Wallace, and Yamazaki.

The catalog offers cookware and serving pieces from All-Clad, Calphalon, Circulon, Farberware, Le Creuset, Revere, and T-Fal. If you're looking for cutlery, check the prices on knives from Chicago Cutlery, Farberware, J.A. Henckels, and Wüstof-Trident. Selected kitchen appliances are also available, including pasta bowl sets, woks, pizza stones, glassware, Tex-Mex items, and hard-to-find tools. Special orders are accepted on some goods, so if you don't see what you're looking for in the catalog, call to see whether the firm can get it. Kitchen Etc. also maintains a bridal registry service.

Special Factors: Satisfaction is guaranteed; price quote by phone or letter.

NEW ENGLAND CHEESEMAKING SUPPLY COMPANY, INC.

Catalog: $1
Save: up to 80% (see text)
Pay: check, MO, MC, V
Sells: cheese-making supplies and equipment
Store: same address; Monday to Friday 8–4 (call first)

DEPT. WBM
P.O. BOX 85
ASHFIELD, MA 01330-0085
413-628-3808
FAX: 413-628-4061

Making cheese at home is one of the few do-it-yourself endeavors with a nominal price tag that doesn't require a significant time or skills investment. New England Cheesemaking Supply, in business since 1978, can provide you with all the tools and materials you'll need to produce hard, soft, and semi-soft cheeses, at savings of up to 80% on the prices charged by supermarkets and specialty stores for the same kinds of cheeses.

Soft cheese is the easiest to make, and may be the cheapest, since you can get as much as two pounds of cheese from a gallon of milk. Milk sells for $1.30 a half gallon in some parts of the country, and flavored soft cheeses often cost $4.50 to $7.00 per pound, or as much as $2.80 for packaged, four-ounce varieties. So, by using the "Gourmet Soft Cheese Kit," you can recoup the $15.95 cost, plus the price of the milk, after making as little as two pounds of soft cheese. This kit is designed for the beginner and comes with cheese starter, cheesecloth, a dairy thermometer, and recipes. It can be used to make *crème fraiche* as well as *fromage blanc*—generic soft cheese—in as little as ten minutes. (If you use skim milk, you can produce low-calorie, low-cholesterol cheese, and omit the salt for sodium-restricted diets.)

New England Cheesemaking Supply also sells a "basic" cheese kit (for ricotta, Gouda, Monterey Jack, cheddar, etc.), and others for making mozzarella and goat cheese. Rennet (animal and vegetable), a large selection of starter and direct-set cultures, lipase powders, mold powder, cheese wax, cheesecloth, thermometers, molds for shaping hard and soft cheese, and several books on cheese production are offered. Experienced cheese producers should see the 16-page catalog for the machinery as well: a home milk pasteurizer and Wheeler's hard cheese press are available. The woman who runs this firm is an experienced cheese producer and can answer your questions by phone or letter.

Special Factors: Price quote by phone or letter with SASE; minimum order is $20 with credit cards; C.O.D. orders are accepted; online with Prodigy.

OPEN HOUSE
━━━━━━━━━━━━━

200 BALA AVE.
BALA-CYNWYD, PA 19004
610-664-1488

Information: price quote
Save: up to 40%
Pay: check, MO, MC, V
Sells: flatware, stemware, cookware, etc.
Store: same address; Monday to Saturday 10–5

Open House has been doing business since 1960, and prices its collection of tableware, cookware, cutlery, and linens at up to 40% below list or usual retail prices. There is no catalog, but you can call for a price quote on goods from All-Clad, Arabia, Calphalon, Chantal, J.G. Durand, Fitz & Floyd, Guzzini, Libbey, Mikasa, Nikko, Schott-Zwiesel, Tri-Chef, and other makers. If you're trying to find the best price on name-brand cookware or table settings, give this firm a call—it may be available.

Special Factors: Minimum order is $25.

PEERLESS RESTAURANT SUPPLIES

DEPT. WBMC
1124 S. GRAND BLVD.
ST. LOUIS, MO 63104
800-255-3663
314-664-0400
FAX: 314-664-8102

Catalog: $8.25
Save: 40% average
Pay: check, MO, MC, V
Sells: commercial cookware and restaurant equipment
Store: same address; Monday to Friday 8–5, Saturday 9–12 noon

The hefty Peerless catalog—yours for $8.25—has everything you need to set up a professional kitchen or restaurant dining room, except the food. Since so many of the appliances and utensils can do double duty in home kitchens, the catalog makes a good investment if you're planning any significant kitchenware purchases.

Peerless represents over 2,000 manufacturers of everything from diner sugar shakers to walk-in refrigerators: tableware, trays and carts, bar accessories, restaurant seating, table linens and kitchen textiles, cookware, ranges and ovens, refrigerators, sinks, worktables, cleaning supplies and equipment, ice machines, dishwashers, and much more. Sample offerings include Libbey glassware, Hall and Buffalo china, cutlery by Dexter Russell, WearEver pots and pans, Vollrath stainless steel stock pots and chafing dishes, Rubbermaid's professional line of janitorial storage and food-service containers, Pelouze food scales, Hamilton Beach and Waring professional bar appliances, Peerless' own commercial cleaners and polishes, Metro wire shelves, Market Forge steamers, and Robot Coupe food processors. Peerless also sells cooking equipment by Castle, Dean, Frymaster, Hobart, Montague, Southbend, and Vulcan; commercial microwave ovens from MenuMaster and Panasonic; refrigeration from Delfield, Ice-O-Matic, Kelvinator, Raetone, Scotsman, Traulsen, and True; Eagle sinks, In-Sink-Erator commercial disposers, ventilation equipment, and much more. Peerless offers UL-approved zero-clearance ranges for home kitchens, from Garland, Imperial, Viking, and Wolf.

If you know what you want by manufacturer and model number, you can call or write for a price quote—but the catalog is worth the $8.25 fee if you're buying more than a couple of items. Food-service professionals should note the services Peerless can provide, including facility design, installation, construction supervision, concept development, and equipment leasing. Used kitchenware is available at big savings, and if you get to St. Louis, stop in and check out the "Bargain Room," which features closeouts.

Special Factors: Quantity discounts are available; authorized returns are accepted within 30 days for exchange, refund, or credit (a 10% restocking fee may be charged, or 20% on special orders); minimum order is $50.

PROFESSIONAL CUTLERY DIRECT

DEPT. WBM6
170 BOSTON POST RD.,
   SUITE 135
MADISON, CT 06443
800-859-6994
203-458-5015
FAX: 203-458-5019

Catalog: $2, refundable
Save: up to 42%
Pay: check, MO, MC, V
Sells: kitchen cutlery, cookware, cookbooks, etc.
Store: mail order only
E-mail: pcd@connix.com

Serious cooks require commercial-quality equipment, which is what you'll find in the 40-page catalog from Professional Cutlery Direct. It's geared to cooks who know the merits of high-carbon stainless steel (it resists corrosion and can be sharpened), or why wood cutting boards are better than plastic (the latter actually promote the breeding of bacteria!). No matter what your experience level, you'll warm to everyday discounts of 20% to 30%, with specials reaching as much as 42% off list.

PCD's stock includes several lines by Cuisine de France Sabatier, F.Dick, Forschner/Victorinox, Lamson & Goodnow, Gerber Balance Plus, and Wüstof-Trident: boxed sets, sharpeners and steels, blocks with and without knife sets, wall-mounted knife holders and magnetic strips, professional roll-packs (used by teachers and caterers), and Forschner/

Victorinox attaché cases with 14 or 24 pieces, including a kullenschliff slicer. Hardwood cutting boards are available in several sizes and styles, as well as Eagleware commercial aluminum cookware, Chaudier commercial stainless cookware, Bourgeat professional copper cookware, Enclume pot racks, and professional cookbooks.

The PCD catalog includes product information to help you choose the cutlery that's best for your needs, as well as details on the volume discount plan offered on Forschner/Victorinox knives—5% on orders over $200 to 20% for orders over $600. And there's a cap on shipping—$12.75 at this writing, no matter how much you buy!

Special Factors: Price quote by phone or letter; quantity discounts are available on selected items; returns of most items are accepted within 30 days for exchange, refund, or credit; minimum order is $10.

ZABAR'S & CO., INC.

**2245 BROADWAY
NEW YORK, NY 10024
212-496-1234
FAX: 212-580-4477**

Catalog: free
Save: up to 50%
Pay: check, MO, MC, V, AE
Sells: gourmet food, cookware, and housewares
Store: same address; Monday to Friday 8–7:30, Saturday 8 A.M.–8 P.M., Sunday 9–6; housewares mezzanine daily 9–6

¡Si!

Zabar's, thought of by many as New York City's ultimate deli, offers the better part of North America a sampling from its famed counters and housewares mezzanine via a 62-page catalog. Zabar's has been around since 1934, and offers savings of up to 50% on name-brand kitchenware, and competitive prices on foodstuffs.

Past catalogs have offered smoked Scottish, Norwegian, and Irish salmon, plum pudding, peppercorns, Bahlsen cookies and confections, pâtés, mustards, crackers, escargot, Lindt and Droste chocolate, Tiptree preserves, Dresden stollen, olive oil, prosciutto and other deli meats, and similar gourmet fare. The cookware selections include Mauviel hotel-weight copper pots and pans (send a postcard for a price list); Calphalon, Cuisinart Commercial, Le Creuset, Magnalite, and Spring of Switzerland equipment; Krups and Simac machines, DeLonghi, Krups and Melitta coffee makers, KitchenAid food processors, Mouli kitchen tools, and products by Henckels, T-Fal, Wagner, Wüstof-Trident, and other firms. Zabar's distinguishes itself among kitchenware vendors for the enormous selection of goods and the substantial discounts. The catalog features a representative selection from the store, and price quotes are given over the phone—if you don't see it in the catalog, just call.

Special Factors: Minimum order is $15.

SEE ALSO

Bernie's Discount Center, Inc. • microwave ovens and kitchen appliances • **APPLIANCES**

Bruce Medical Supply • food preparation equipment for those with limited strength and mobility • **MEDICINE: SPECIAL NEEDS**

Cabela's Inc. • camping cookware, stoves, implements • **SPORTS**

CISCO • garbage disposals, sinks, etc. • **HOME: IMPROVEMENT**

Clothcrafters, Inc. • kitchen textiles and kitchen utensils • **GENERAL MERCHANDISE**

Coppa Woodworking Inc. • butcher block tables • **HOME: IMPROVEMENT**

The CMC Company • cookware for Mexican and Asian specialties • **FOOD: BEVERAGES AND FLAVORINGS**

Cordon Brew • coffee makers and brewing equipment • **FOOD: BEVERAGES AND FLAVORINGS**

Betty Crocker Catalog • cutlery, cookware, and kitchen gadgets • **GENERAL MERCHANDISE**

Current, Inc. • canning labels, recipe boxes, etc. • **GENERAL: CARDS**

Grandma's Spice Shop • spice racks, wine racks, mortar and pestle sets, teapots, etc. • **FOOD: BEVERAGES AND FLAVORINGS**

Jessica's Biscuit • cookbooks • **BOOKS**

E.C. Kraus Wine & Beermaking Supplies • bottle washers, cherry pitters, funnels, corkscrews • **FOOD: BEVERAGES AND FLAVORINGS**

Lixx Labelz • custom-designed kitchen labels • **GENERAL: CARDS**

LVT Price Quote Hotline, Inc. • microwave ovens, major appliances, etc. • **APPLIANCES**

Mr. Spiceman • kitchen gadgets • **FOOD: BEVERAGES AND FLAVORINGS**

The Paper Wholesaler • disposable bakeware and cake-decorating supplies • **GENERAL MERCHANDISE**

Penzeys' Spice House • pepper mills and spice jars • **FOOD: BEVERAGES AND FLAVORINGS**

Percy's Inc. • major appliances • **APPLIANCES**

Plastic BagMart • garbage can liners • **OFFICE: SMALL BUSINESS**

Rafal Spice Company • kitchen gadgets, cookbooks • **FOOD: BEVERAGES AND FLAVORINGS**

S & S Sound City • microwave ovens • **APPLIANCES**

Simpson & Vail, Inc. • *teapots, coffee makers, grinders, filters, etc.* • *FOOD:*
BEVERAGES AND FLAVORINGS
Sultan's Delight, Inc. • *Turkish coffee pots and cups, mamoul and falafel molds,*
mortars and pestles • *FOOD*
Walnut Acres Organic Farms • *cookware, bakeware, serving pieces, etc.* •
FOOD
West Marine • *galley gear* • *AUTO*
Weston Bowl Mill • *woodenware, knives, and kitchen helpers* • *GENERAL*
MERCHANDISE

Linen

Bed, bath, and table textiles, accessories, and services

Retailing tradition honors January as white-sale month, but there's no reason to wait: You can buy your sheets, towels, pillows, and table linens from discounters who sell at savings of up to 60% every day, year-round. Some of the companies listed here offer both first-quality and irregular goods, and some sell only first-quality—ask before placing your order to be sure you're getting what you want. In addition to goods from the major mills, several of the firms can provide sheets to fit water beds, sofa beds, and oddly shaped mattresses, will rejuvenate down pillows and comforters, and make shower curtains, pillows, bed skirts, and coordinating lamp shades to match your sheets or bedroom fabric.

You can coax extra years of wear from bed, bath, and table textiles by treating them right, so follow the manufacturers' care instructions and avoid chlorine bleach and overdrying. Protect your down-filled bedding with duvets or pillow slips, and when you have to wash down, use mild detergent, warm water, and the machine's gentle settings. Use fabric bags for storage instead of plastic, which will hold humidity, and don't store down-filled goods in cedar or camphor since the down will pick up those odors permanently.

BEDROOM SECRETS

DEPT. 96WBMC
310 E. MILITARY
P.O. BOX 529
FREMONT, NE 68025
800-955-2559
402-727-4004
FAX: 402-727-1817

Catalog: $2
Save: up to 40%
Pay: check, MO, MC, V, AE, Discover
Sells: linens for bed and bath
Closeout Store: 605 Broad St., Fremont, NE

Bedroom Secrets specializes in ensemble dressing for bedroom and bath, for a polished, pulled-together look. The 60-page catalog is a rich mix of floral motifs, tailored patterns, Southwestern designs, and much more—furniture, pictures, and other goods are also offered. Most of the linen designs are offered in sheet sets, comforters, accent pillows, window treatments, and many are presented with coordinating bath accoutrements—shower curtains, towels, rugs, hampers, and even matching mirrors and toothbrush holders. Bedroom Secrets represents some of the best-known names, including Laura Ashley, Bill Blass, Collier Campbell, Croscill, Di Lewis, Revman, and Sanderson. Discounts on many items average 30%, but some lines are priced nearly 40% below regular retail. And there's another advantage to buying here: The custom department can round out your decorating scheme with made-to-order window treatments, dust ruffles, chairs and benches, and whatever else you need to complete your rooms. Coordinating fabrics and wall coverings are available, as well as window treatments and home furnishings. Fabrics and wall coverings from Waverly are featured in the latest catalog from Bedroom Secrets ($2).

Special Factors: Satisfaction is guaranteed; resalable returns are accepted within 30 days; minimum order is 3 yards (if fabric).

DOMESTICATIONS

DEPT. DOM8779
P.O. BOX 41
HANOVER, PA 17333-0041
800-962-2211, EXT.
  DOM8779

Catalog: free
Save: up to 75%
Pay: check, MO, MC, V, AE, Discover
Sells: bed, bath, and table linens, dinnerware, gifts, etc.
Store: mail order only

Domestications, Hanover Direct's home style catalog, offers a colorful selection of goods for bed, bath, and table, plus well-priced home decorating accents. The full-color catalog emphasizes sheets and bedding, with traditional florals, a spectrum of solids, classic contemporary designs, and an assortment of the latest juvenile patterns. In addition to an ever-expanding line of Domestications' private-label designs, there are selections from the best names in the business, including Bill Blass, Cannon, Fieldcrest, Martex, Louis Nichole, Dan River, Springmaid, J.P. Stevens, and Wamsutta. Choose from a full selection of all-cotton and cotton-blend sheets, blankets, bedspreads, and comforters, as well as down comforters, pillows, mattress pads, and hard-to-find items like sofa-bed sheets. The rest of the catalog features a variety of fashion-forward home accessories—tablecloths, window treatments, lamps, carpets, tableware, and even occasional furniture. Prices run from market rate to bargain basement.

    Special Factors: Satisfaction is guaranteed; returns are accepted; minimum order is $20 with credit cards.

ELDRIDGE TEXTILE CO.

277 GRAND ST., DEPT. L
NEW YORK, NY 10002
212-925-1523
FAX: 212-219-9542

Catalog: $3 refundable
Save: up to 40%
Pay: check, MO, MC, V, Discover
Sells: bed, bath, and table linens
Store: same address; Sunday to Friday
9–5:30

 ¡Sí!

Eldridge has been selling soft goods and housewares since 1940, and offers mail-order customers savings of up to 40% on bed, bath, and table linens. Fully coordinated ensembles are available from Laura Ashley, Bill Blass, Cameo, Collier Campbell, Croscill, Crown Crafts, DiLewis, Faribo, Fieldcrest, Home Innovations, Martex, Newmark (bath rugs), Pacific Designs, Phoenix (down products), Revman, André Richard, Richloom, Saturday Knight, Springmaid, Thomasville, Utica, Wamsutta, Eileen West, and other firms. Some of the best-selling sheet and towel lines are featured in the 32-page color catalog, as well as upholstered headboards, ottomans, footstools, and Surefit couch and chair slipcovers.

Special Factors: Price quote by phone or letter with SASE; returns of unused goods are accepted for refund or credit; minimum order is $25.

HARRIS LEVY, INC.

278 GRAND ST., DEPT. WBM
NEW YORK, NY 10002
800-221-7750
212-226-3102
FAX: 212-334-9360

Catalog: free
Save: up to 60%
Pay: check, MO, MC, V, AE
Sells: bed, bath, and table linens; kitchen and closet accessories
Store: same address; Monday to Thursday 9–5, Friday 9–4, Sunday 9–4:30

 ¡Si! ★

Harris Levy, established in 1894, is one of the plums of New York City's Lower East Side—a firm that sells the crème de la crème of bed, bath, and table linens at savings of up to 60%. One-of-a-kind and imported items are available in the store, and *none* of the stock is seconds or discontinued merchandise. What makes Levy special are things like heavy Matelasse blanket covers at about half the price charged by luxury linens catalogs, a sleep connoisseur's choice of pillows, and even mundane items like bath mats in fresh designs.

Harris Levy's imports include Egyptian cotton percale and linen sheets, English kitchen towels, Irish damask tablecloths, and bedding from Switzerland, England, France, and Italy—all worth a trip to the store. Mail-order shoppers can call or write for the free catalog or price quotes on bed and bath linens from the major names: Cannon, Croscill, Crown Crafts, Fieldcrest, Martex, Palais Royal, Revman, Springmaid, J.P. Stevens, and Wamsutta. The catalog also gives a sampling of Harris Levy's large selection of bath accessories, shower curtains, rugs, towels, closet organizers, storage products, hangers, and travel accessories. Levy specializes in custom services and can provide monogramming and sheets in special sizes and shapes, tablecloths, dust ruffles, curtains, pillowcases, and other products from stock sheets or your own fabric.

Please note: Phone orders are accepted Monday to Friday 10–4.

Special Factors: Price quote by phone, fax, or letter with SASE; store is closed Saturdays.

THE LINEN SOURCE

5401 HANGAR CT.
P.O. BOX 31151
TAMPA, FL 33634
800-431-2620
CUSTOMER SERVICE:
  813-243-6170
FAX: 813-882-4605

Catalog: free
Save: up to 35%
Pay: check, MO, MC, V, AE, Discover
Sells: bed linens, home accessories
Store: mail order only

 ¡Sí!

Why wait for a white sale when you can restyle your bedroom at a discount any day of the year? The 72-page catalog from The Linen Source features the latest fashions in bed dressing, with an emphasis on bold colors and strong graphics, and rich, romantic ensembles. You'll find current designs in sheets, comforters, and accessories by Laura Ashley, Burlington House, Crown Crafts, Dakotah, Fieldcrest/Cannon (Court of Versailles, Adrienne Vittadini). Gear, Martex, Dan River (Alexander Julian), Springmaid, Utica, Wamsutta, and other names. Patchwork quilts and window treatments are shown, as well as vases, statuary, framed prints, rugs, lamps, tableware, and even night wear. The best savings are on sheet sets, but most of the other products are competitively priced—20% to 35% off regular retail.

Special Factors: Satisfaction is guaranteed; returns are accepted.

J. SCHACHTER CORP.

5 COOK ST.
BROOKLYN, NY
11206-4003
800-INTO-BED
718-384-2732, 2754
FAX: 718-384-7634

Catalog: $1, refundable
Save: up to 40%
Pay: check, MO, MC, V, Discover
Sells: down-filled bedding, linens, and custom services
Store: same address; Monday to Thursday 9–5, Friday 9–1:30

Schachter has been making comforters and pillows for the bedding industry and recovering old comforters for private customers since 1919. Custom work is featured in the firm's 12-page catalog, but stock goods are also available. Schachter specializes in custom jobs: Comforters, coverlets, bed ruffles, pillow shams, duvets, and shower curtains are popular requests, and Schachter will take your sheets and create quilted blanket covers, or lightweight summer quilts, with them. Filling choices for the comforters include lamb's wool, polyester, white goose down, and a nonallergenic synthetic down alternative. Schachter carries bed and bath linens by the major mills—Cannon, Croscill, Fieldcrest, Martex, Springs Industries, J.P. Stevens, and Wamsutta—and labels from France, Germany, England, Switzerland, Italy, and Belgium—Bruna, Palais Royal, Peter Reed, Sferra, and Sufolla. Carter cotton bath rugs, and blankets by Atkinson, Chatham, Early's of Whitney, Faribo, and Hudson Bay are offered. Schachter's own stock comforters and accessories are all available, and the firm can recover and sterilize old down pillows and comforters.

Special Factors: Store is closed Saturdays.

SEE ALSO

Baby Bunz & Co. • crib bedding • **CLOTHING: MOTHER AND CHILD**
Campmor • sleeping bags, sleeping bag liners • **SPORTS**
Chock Catalog Corp. • crib and bassinet bedding • **CLOTHING**
Clothcrafters, Inc. • plain cotton sheets, towels, table linens, etc. • **GENERAL MERCHANDISE**
Gettinger Feather Corp. • pillow feathers • **CRAFTS**
Gohn Bros. • sheets and blankets • **CLOTHING**
Kitchen Etc. • table linens • **HOME: KITCHEN**

Plexi-Craft Quality Products Corp. • *acrylic bathroom accessories* • **HOME: FURNISHINGS**

Retired Persons Services, Inc. • *waffle-type foam bed pads* • **MEDICINE**

Rubens & Marble, Inc. • *bassinet and crib sheets* • **CLOTHING: MOTHER AND CHILD**

Shama Imports, Inc. • *crewel-embroidered bedspreads* • **HOME: DECOR**

Table Settings

China, crystal, glass, flatware, woodenware, and related goods

Buying active patterns of tableware is as easy as picking up the phone and calling one of the firms listed here. But if your pattern—in china, crystal, or silver—is discontinued, you'll have to turn to a specialist. Two of these firms—Beverly Bremer and Buschemeyer—sell discontinued silver flatware (also called "estate" silver). If you're missing pieces of a china or crystal pattern, write to Replacements, Ltd., 302 Gallimore Dairy Rd., Greensboro, NC 27400-9723, or call 910-275-7224. Replacements has over 250,000 pieces in stock, and can help you identify your pattern if you're not sure of the name. The China Connection is another such source for discontinued china patterns, by such manufacturers as Castleton, Haviland, Lenox, and Noritake. Send details on the maker, pattern, and piece you're trying to match to The China Connection, 329 Main St., P.O. Box 972, Pineville, NC 28134.

BARRONS

P.O. BOX 994
NOVI, MI 48376-0994
810-348-7050
FAX: 810-344-4342

Catalog: free
Save: up to 65%
Pay: check, MO, MC, V, Discover
Sells: tableware and giftware
Store: mail order only

Barrons has been selling fine tableware since 1975 and offers savings of up to 65% on the list prices of china, crystal, flatware, and gifts and stocks over 1,500 patterns. Past catalogs have showcased popular lines of china from Block, Fitz & Floyd, Franciscan, Gorham, Hutschenreuther, Johnson Brothers, Lenox, Mikasa, Minton, Nikko, Noritake, Royal Albert, Royal Doulton, Royal Worcester, Spode, Waterford, and Wedgwood. Crystal from Atlantis, Gorham, Lenox, and Mikasa is offered, and you can save on stainless steel, silver plate, and sterling flatware from Dansk, Gorham, International, Kirk-Stieff, Lunt, Mikasa, Oneida, Reed & Barton, Towle, Wallace, and Yamazaki. Royal Doulton figurines, Gorham crystal gifts, Towle silver serving pieces, and other collectibles and accessories are also sold at a discount.

Special Factors: Satisfaction is guaranteed; returns are accepted within 30 days for exchange, refund, or credit.

BEVERLY BREMER SILVER SHOP

DEPT. WBMC
3164 PEACHTREE RD., N.E.
ATLANTA, GA 30305
404-261-4009

Information: inquire (see text)
Save: up to 75%
Pay: check, MO, MC, V, AE, Discover
Sells: new and estate silver flatware, holloware, gifts, etc.
Store: same address; Monday to Saturday 10–5

  ¡Si!

Beverly Bremer herself presides over this shop, which has an astounding inventory of American and Continental sterling, from new flatware to old loving cups. "The store with the silver lining," which opened in 1975, is worth a detour if you're traveling anywhere around Atlanta. But if you can't get there, call or write with your needs—Beverly Bremer does nearly half her business by mail, and is now completely computerized. Just request a current inventory list of your flatware pattern.

The briskest trade is done in supplying missing pieces of sterling silverware in new, discontinued, and hard-to-find patterns. The brands represented include Buccellati, Gorham, International, Jensen, Kirk-Stieff, Lunt, Odiot, Old Newbury Crafters, Oneida, Reed & Barton, Schofield, Frank Smith, State House, Tiffany, Towle, Tuttle, Wallace, Westmoreland, and other firms. If you know the pattern name, call to see whether the piece you want is in stock; you can also send a photocopy of both sides of a sample piece if you're unsure of the pattern. Beverly Bremer will send you a printout of the available pieces in your pattern, and a brochure profiling the company.

Although the shop's specialty is flatware, the shelves and cases sparkle with vases, epergnes, picture frames, candlesticks, jewelry, christening cups, thimbles, and other treasures. Silver collectors should note that over 1,000 patterns are carried in stock here, "beautiful as new," and Ms. Bremer says that, unless noted, there are no monograms on the old silver. (She doesn't sell silver on which monograms have been *removed,* either.) She recommends against resilvering old silver plate as "not a wise use of your money," and notes that sterling holds its value over time. How many other investments can do that—and enhance your dinner table as well!

Special Factors: Sterling silver pieces are bought; appraisals are performed.

BUSCHEMEYER SILVER EXCHANGE

515 S. FOURTH AVE.
LOUISVILLE, KY 40202
800-626-4555
FAX: 502-589-9628

Information: price quote (see text)
Save: up to 50%
Pay: check, MO, MC, V, AE, DC, Discover
Sells: new and discontinued flatware and holloware
Store: same address; Monday to Friday 10–5, Saturday 10–4

Buschemeyer, in business since 1865, can help you save on purchases of new flatware—sterling, silverplate, and holloware. But if you're looking for a discontinued pattern, Buschemeyer also may have what you need. The firm stocks "all active and inactive sterling and silver plate flatware," including current American-made sterling patterns, and will hold your want list if what you're looking for isn't currently available. You can call, write, or fax for a price quote on active silver lines, and call (if you know the pattern) about discontinued pieces, or send a photocopy of the front of a teaspoon or fork if you're not sure of the name. Please remember to include your name, address, phone number, and any other information you have about the piece with your query.

Special Factors: Orders are shipped worldwide.

CHINA CABINET, INC.

DEPT. WBMC
24 WASHINGTON ST.
TENAFLY, NJ 07670
800-545-5353
201-567-2711

Catalog: $2, refundable
Save: up to 50%
Pay: check, MO, MC, V, Discover
Sells: tableware
Store: same address; Monday to Saturday
10–6

China Cabinet, in business since 1988, represents scores of manufacturers of fine china, crystal, and flatware. In addition to such widely available brands as Dansk, Gorham, Orrefors, Royal Doulton, and Wedgwood, China Cabinet offers goods from Baccarat, Ceralene Limoges, Arthur Court, Gien, Godinger, Haviland Limoges, Jacques Jugeat, Silvestri, and Wilton, among others. Savings run up to 50%, and giftware from selected manufacturers is offered as well as place settings and serving pieces. China Cabinet is publishing a catalog ($2, refundable), which was not available for review, but the firm also gives price quotes by phone and letter.

China Cabinet, Inc. is offering readers a discount of 5% on their first order of anything *except silver flatware*. Be sure to identify yourself as a WBMC reader when you order, and deduct the discount from the cost of the goods only. This WBMC reader discount expires February 1, 1997.

Special Factors: Minimum order is $25 with credit cards.

CHINA-SILVER-CRYSTAL

5700 MAYFIELD RD.
CLEVELAND, OH 44124
800-653-5668
FAX: 216-473-2040

Brochure: free
Save: up to 60%
Pay: check, MO, MC, V, Discover
Sells: tableware, collectibles, gifts, etc.
Store: mail order only

China-Silver-Crystal represents the best names in tableware, at prices it guarantees are the lowest, offers a bridal registry service, and a great incentive to buy *all* of your china and crystal here: the "Lifetime Half-Price Replacement Offer." Purchase 12 place settings of dinnerware, or

24 pieces of crystal stemware all at once, and should a piece break while the pattern is active, China-Silver-Crystal will replace it at 50% off the manufacturer's prevailing suggested selling price (51% of the shards must be returned to CSC to validate the claim). The terms of the warranty are given in the several pages of literature you'll receive from CSC, as well as the brands list, which runs from Astral crystal to Yamazaki silverware, and includes David Winter cottages, Hummel and Lladró figurines, Mont Blanc pens, Seiko timepieces, and Belleek giftware. There are also four pages of excellent tips on caring for your crystal, silver, and china—nice lagniappe. The firm has been in business since 1977, and goes one better than the usual "we'll beat any advertised price" claim: China-Silver-Crystal will beat *price quotes* from other companies.

Special Factors: Lowest prices guaranteed; price quote by phone or letter; all goods are first quality.

THE CHINA WAREHOUSE

P.O. BOX 21807
CLEVELAND, OH 44121
800-321-3212
216-831-2557

Catalog: free
Save: up to 50%
Pay: check, MO, MC, V
Sells: tableware and gifts
Store: mail order only

The China Warehouse has been in business since 1983 and offers "all major china and crystal lines," as well as flatware, decorative accessories, giftware, and collectible figurines. The brands include Armetale, Block, Gorham, Lenox, Noritake, Orrefors, Reed & Barton, Riedel, Royal Doulton, Sasaki, Spode, Towle, Wallace, Waterford, Wedgwood, and dozens of others, in china, crystal, and stainless and sterling flatware. A catalog is available, but you can also call or write for a price quote.

Special Factors: Orders are shipped worldwide.

COINWAYS/ANTIQUES LTD.

**475 CENTRAL AVE.
CEDARHURST, NY 11516
800-645-2102
516-374-1970
FAX: 516-374-3218**

Information: price quote
Save: up to 75%
Pay: check, MO, MC, V, AE, DC, Discover
Sells: new and used sterling flatware
Store: same address; Monday to Friday
10–5:30, Wednesday 10–7:30, Saturday 10–4

Coinways/Antiques Ltd. should be on your list of firms to call when the garbage disposer claims one of your good teaspoons—especially if it's from an old or discontinued pattern. Coinways, which has been in business since 1979, sells both new and used ("estate") sterling flatware, by the piece or in full sets.

You'll save up to 75% on the suggested retail or market prices of silver manufactured by Alvin, Amston, Dominick & Haff, Durgin, Easterling, Gorham, International, Kirk-Stieff, Lunt, Manchester, National, Oneida, Reed & Barton, Royal Crest, State House, Tiffany, Towle, Tuttle, Wallace, Westmoreland, F.M. Whiting, and other firms. If you're replacing a piece in an old pattern that's still active, try to find a piece of the same vintage. (Over the years, some manufacturers have reduced the amount of silver they use in each piece, so that a fork made today will be lighter and feel less substantial than the same piece, circa 1930.) If you write to Coinways for a quote, note the name of the piece, its length and shape, and include a photocopy of the design if you don't know the pattern name.

Coinways/Antiques Ltd. is offering readers a discount of 5% on all orders of estate sterling flatware. Be sure to identify yourself as a WBMC reader when you order, and deduct the discount from the cost of the goods only. This WBMC reader discount expires February 1, 1997.

Special Factors: Orders are shipped worldwide.

MICHAEL C. FINA CO.

580 FIFTH AVE.
NEW YORK, NY 10036
800-BUY-FINA
718-937-8484
FAX: 718-937-7193

Catalog: free
Save: up to 60%
Pay: check, MO, MC, V, AE, Discover
Sells: jewelry, tableware, and giftware
Store: 3 W. 47th St., New York, NY; Monday to Friday 9:30–6, Thursday 9:30–7, Saturday 10:30–6

Nearly half of Michael C. Fina's 40-page holiday catalog is devoted to jewelry—rings embedded with diamonds and emeralds, strands of pearls and gold link necklaces, wedding bands, and modern silver jewelry and accessories are representative of the selection. Fina, which has been in business since 1935, is well known to New Yorkers for its great prices on jewelry.

Fina also offers an impressive line of tableware, including china by Aynsley, Bernardaud Limoges, Ceralene Raynaud Limoges, Dansk, Fitz and Floyd, Franciscan, Ginori, Gorham, Haviland Limoges, Johnson Brothers, Lenox, Mikasa, Minton, Noritake, Portmeirion, Rosenthal, Royal Crown Derby, Royal Doulton, Royal Worcester, Spode, Thomas, Villeroy & Boch, and Wedgwood. Crystal stemware from Atlantis, Baccarat, Gorham, Lenox, Miller Rogaska, Noritake, Orrefors, Royal Doulton, Sasaki, Stuart, and Waterford is available. Fina also sells flatware from Dansk, Gorham, International, Kirk-Stieff, Lunt, Mikasa, Oneida, Reed & Barton, Retroneu, Towle, Wallace, and Yamazaki. Sterling silver baby gifts, picture frames, carriage clocks, and silver dressing table accessories are usually available, and Fina maintains a bridal registry.

Special Factors: Satisfaction is guaranteed; returns (except engraved or personalized items) are accepted within three weeks for exchange, refund, or credit.

FORTUNOFF FINE JEWELRY & SILVER-WARE, INC.

P.O. BOX 1550
WESTBURY, NY 11590
516-294-3300
FAX: 516-873-6984

Catalog: $2
Save: up to 50%
Pay: check, MO, MC, V, AE, DC
Sells: jewelry, tableware, and giftware
Store: 681 Fifth Ave., New York, and 1300 Old Country Rd., Westbury, NY; also Paramus Park Mall, Paramus, West Belt Mall, Wayne, and 441 Woodbridge Center Dr., Woodbridge, NJ

In addition to spectacular buys on fine jewelry and watches, Fortunoff is a top source for place settings in stainless, silver plate, and sterling silver. Attractive groups of silver giftware—chafing dishes, tea and coffee services, candlesticks, ice buckets, picture frames, and antique vanity accessories—appear frequently in the catalogs. Flatware from Empire Silver, International, Kirk-Stieff, Lauffer, Mikasa, Oneida, Reed & Barton, Retroneu, Roberts & Belk, Supreme, Towle, C.J. Vander, and Yamazaki is available—call for prices on specific patterns. Some of the Fortunoff stores carry a broader variety of products, including outdoor furniture, leather goods, decorative accents for the home, linens for bed and bath, organizers, and similar items.

Special Factors: Price quote on flatware by letter with self-addressed, stamped envelope; minimum order is $25; orders are not shipped outside the United States.

JAMAR

1714 SHEEPSHEAD BAY
RD.
BROOKLYN, NY 11235
718-615-2222

Information: price quote
Save: up to 40%
Pay: check, MO, MC, V
Sells: tableware
Store: same address; Monday to Saturday 11–5:30

Jamar offers the best names in china, crystal, and silver, as well as gifts and collectibles. If you know the patterns and pieces you're looking for, you can call for a quote; Jamar doesn't have a catalog, but will beat any other advertised price.

Special Factors: Store is closed Mondays during the summer.

THE JOMPOLE COMPANY, INC.

330 SEVENTH AVE.
NEW YORK, NY 10001
212-594-0440
FAX: 212-594-4444

Information: price quote
Save: up to 40%
Pay: check or MO
Sells: tableware, figurines, watches, and pens
Store: same address; Monday to Friday 9–5

Jompole has been in business since 1913 and offers a fine selection of table settings, giftware, and writing instruments, at savings of up to 50%. The china lines include Bernardaud Limoges, Coalport, Denby, Franciscan, Hutschenreuther, Lenox, Mikasa, Minton, Pickard, Royal Copenhagen, Spode, and Wedgwood, among others. Crystal stemware is available from Baccarat, Fostoria, Gorham, Kosta Boda, Orrefors, Rosenthal, Val St. Lambert, and Waterford, and there's flatware from Alvin, Community, Fraser, International, Georg Jensen, Kirk-Stieff, Lauffer, Lunt, Oneida, Reed & Barton, Supreme Cutlery, Towle, Tuttle, Wallace, and other firms. Jompole may have figurines and collectibles by some of the same firms, as well as Hummel, Lladró, Norman Rockwell, and Swarovski. Call or write for prices on these, as well as on pens and pencils from Cross, Mont Blanc, Parker, and Waterman, and watches by Borel, Cartier, Heuer, Patek-Philippe, Rolex, and Seiko. Jompole also carries premium items for businesses—"from balloons and lollipops to diamonds and furs"—and invites inquiries from interested firms.

Special Factors: Price quote by phone or letter with SASE; institutional accounts are available.

KAISER CROW INC.

3545 G. SO. PLATTE RIVER
   DR.
ENGLEWOOD, CO 80110
303-781-6888
FAX: 303-781-5982

Catalog: free
Save: up to 57%
Pay: check, MO, MC, V, AE, Discover
Sells: flatware
Store: mail order only

  ¡Si!

Kaiser Crow has been in business since 1985 and sells at discounts of up to 57%. The 48-page color catalog shows specials on Oneida's Community, Heirloom, and gold-accented stainless flatware lines, at savings of more than 50% on list prices. A great selection of gifts—Limoges boxes, collectible figurines, vases, garden accessories, silver chests, baby gifts, serving pieces, woven throws, carpets, placemats, etc.—is also offered. Call or write for a price quote if you don't see what you're looking for.

Special Factors: Satisfaction is guaranteed.

MEIEROTTO'S MIDWESTERLING

4311 N.E. VIVION RD.
KANSAS CITY, MO
   64119-2890
816-454-1990 (SEE TEXT)
FAX: 816-454-1605

Information: inquire
Save: up to 50%
Pay: check or MO
Sells: replacement sterling flatware
Store: same address; Monday to Saturday
10–6 (closed Wednesday and Sunday)
E-mail: CS: 72712,3527@compuserve.com

Meierotto's MidweSterling is home to over half a million pieces of sterling flatware, in both discontinued and current patterns. (New silverplate and stainless flatware, china, crystal, and giftware are also sold.) Meierotto's offers a lowest-price guarantee on the flatware, maintains a bridal registry, and accepts layaways (20% down). Send a long, stamped, self-addressed envelope for a price-quote form, which includes a guide to standard flatware shapes and sizes. If what you want isn't in stock, Meierotto's will search for it. The firm also buys used silver (inquire for information), and performs silverware repairs and knife reblading.

Please note: Meierotto's is closed on Wednesdays and Sundays.
Special Factors: Satisfaction is guaranteed; price quote by phone, fax, or letter; layaway orders are accepted (20% deposit).

MESSINA GLASS & CHINA CO. INC.

P.O. BOX 307
ELWOOD, NJ 08217
800-515-7176
609-561-1474

Catalog: $2, refundable (see text)
Save: up to 50%
Pay: check, MO, MC, V, AE
Sells: tableware and collectibles
Store: Rte. 30 (White Horse Pike), Elwood, NJ; Monday to Friday (except Thursday) 10–3, Saturday 10–4 (closed Thursday and Sunday)

Fine china and stoneware, stainless and sterling flatware, crystal stemware, and collectibles are among the offerings at Messina Glass & China, which has been in business since 1959. Please request specific manufacturers' catalogs, or a price quote if you know the pattern/piece you want. Messina carries tableware and gifts by Atlantis, Block, Dansk, Fitz & Floyd, Franciscan, Galway, Gorham, Johnson Brothers, Lenox (including lamps), Miller Rogaska, Minton, Noritake, Oneida, Pfaltzgraff (stoneware, china, and stainless flatware), Pickard, Reed & Barton, Retroneu, Royal Albert, Royal Crown Derby, Royal Doulton, Royal Worcester, Spode, Wedgwood, and Yamazaki, among others. If you're looking for a piece in a recently discontinued pattern, try here—it may be available. Messina also sells monogrammed barware, stemware, and crystal serving trays.

Please note: The $2 catalog fee (refundable with a purchase) brings you *manufacturers'* literature—you must specify the brand and line you're interested in. If you know what you want, you can simply call or write for a price quote.

Messina is offering readers free shipping on orders of $150 or more sent within the 48 contiguous states. Be sure to identify yourself as a WBMC reader when you order to claim the exemption. This WBMC reader offer expires February 1, 1997.

Special Factors: Specify which manufacturers' catalogs you want.

MIKASA OUTLET STORE

25 ENTERPRISE AVE.
SECAUCUS, NJ 07096
201-867-2354

Information: inquire (see text)
Save: up to 50%
Pay: check, MO, MC, V, AE, Discover
Sells: Mikasa tableware and gifts
Store: same address; Monday to Saturday
10–6, Thursday 10–9, Sunday 10–6

¡Si!

Mikasa manages to strike the balance between fashion-forward style and affordability in china, crystal, flatware, and gifts. Although some of Mikasa's most popular china patterns feature flowers and abstract geometrics rimming the plates and banding the cups ("High Spirits," "Tapestry Garden"), the full range includes much more sedate, traditional designs ("Gold Tiara," "Merrick," "Yardley"). The flatware and crystal patterns complement the selection, and are also mid-priced for upper-end table settings.

The Mikasa store sells both first-quality Mikasa tableware at a discount, and has a clearance room with seconds and discontinued patterns. If you can't visit, call with the pattern name, name of the piece (e.g., white wine goblet, dinner knife, dessert plate, etc.), and the quantity you'd like to buy. If it's in stock or can be obtained, you'll receive a price quote and shipping estimate. Don't delay in ordering, especially if the pattern or piece has been discontinued, because stock moves quickly here.

Special Factors: Authorized returns are accepted for exchange, refund, or credit.

ROGERS & ROSENTHAL, INC.

━━━━━━━

2337 LEMOINE AVE.,
  SUITE 101
FORT LEE, NJ 07024-0212
201-346-1862
FAX: 201-947-5812

Information: price quote
Save: up to 50%
Pay: check or MO
Sells: tableware
Store: mail order only

  (see text)

Rogers and Rosenthal, two old names in the silver and china trade, represent the business of this firm: the best in table settings at up to 60% below list prices. Rogers & Rosenthal has been in business since 1930, selling flatware (stainless, plate, and sterling) by top manufacturers. The brands include Fraser, Gerber, Gorham, International, Jensen, Kirk-Stieff, Lauffer, Lunt, Oneida, Reed & Barton, Sasaki, Frank Smith, Supreme, Towle, Tuttle, Wallace, and Yamazaki. There are china and crystal lines by Aynsley, Bernardaud Limoges, Block, Coalport, Franciscan, Gorham, Hutschenreuther, Lauffer, Lenox, Mikasa, Noritake, Pickard, Portmeirion, Rosenthal, Royal Copenhagen, Royal Doulton, Royal Worcester, Spode, and Wedgwood. Silver baby gifts, Lladró and other figurines, and pewter holloware are also stocked. Please write or call for a price quote—*there is no catalog.*

Canadian readers, please note: Only special orders are shipped to Canada.

Special Factors: Price quote by phone or letter with SASE; returns are accepted for exchange.

RUDI'S POTTERY, SILVER & CHINA

180 RTE. 17 NORTH
PARAMUS, NJ 07652
201-265-6096
FAX: 201-265-2086

Information: price quote
Save: up to 50%
Pay: check, MO, MC, V, Discover
Sells: tableware
Store: same address; Monday and Saturday 10–5:30, Tuesday to Friday 10–9

Rudi's has been in business since 1968, and in the intervening years has expanded the firm's stock to include some of the finest goods available at savings of up to 60% on list. China, crystal, and flatware are stocked here; the silverware brands include Gorham, International, Kirk-Stieff, Lunt, Reed & Barton, Towle, Tuttle, and Wallace. Rudi's china dinnerware and crystal stemware lines include Arzberg, Baccarat, Belleek, Bernardaud Limoges, Coalport, Fitz and Floyd, Galway, Gorham, Kosta Boda, Lalique, Lenox, Mikasa, Minton, Noritake, Orrefors, Rosenthal, Royal Copenhagen, Royal Doulton, Royal Worcester, Sasaki, Spode, Stuart, Wedgwood, and Yamazaki. Call or write for a price quote on your pattern or suite.

Special Factor: Price quote by phone or letter with SASE.

NAT SCHWARTZ & CO., INC.

DEPT. WB16
549 BROADWAY
BAYONNE, NJ 07002
800-526-1440
FAX: 201-437-4903

Catalog: free
Save: up to 50%
Pay: check, MO, MC, V, Discover
Sells: tableware, giftware, and housewares
Store: same address; Monday to Friday 9:30–6, Thursday 9:30–8, Saturday 10–5

Nat Schwartz & Co., established in 1967, publishes a 32-page catalog filled with fine china, crystal, flatware, housewares, and gifts that represent just a fraction of the firm's inventory. Schwartz's china and giftware department offers Arzberg, Aynsley, Belleek, Bernardaud, Bing & Grøndahl, Block, Edward Marshall Boehm, A. Raynaud (Ceralene) Limoges, Dansk, Denby, Christian Dior, Fabergé, Fitz and Floyd, Franciscan, Gien

Limoges, Ginori, Haviland Limoges, Hermes, Hummel, Hutschenreuther, Johnson Brothers, Ralph Lauren, Lenox, Lladró, Mikasa, Minton, Mottahedah, Muirfield, Nao by Lladró, Nikko, Noritake, Pickard, Poole Pottery, Portmeirion, Swid Powell, Rosenthal, Royal Copenhagen, Royal Crown Derby, Royal Doulton, Royal Worcester, Sasaki, Spode, Thomas, Villeroy & Boch, Vista Allegre, Wedgwood, Wilson Armetale, and other firms. Crystal suites and gifts by Atlantis, Baccarat, Ceska, Daum, Christian Dior, Fabergé, Galway, Gorham, Lenox, Miller/Rogaska, Noritake, Swid Powell, Rosenthal, Royal Doulton, St. Louis, Sasaki, Stuart, Tipperary and Waterford are available, among others. Also featured are flatware and holloware by Buccellati, Jean Couzon, Cuisinart, Dansk, Empire, Farberware, W.M.F. Fraser, Gorham, International, Kirk-Stieff, Ralph Lauren, Lunt, Oneida, Swid Powell, Reed & Barton, Retroneu, Ricci, Sambonet, Sheffield, Towle, Tuttle, Wallace, and Yamazaki. Among the housewares lines are Braun, Le Creuset, Cuisinart, Farberware, KitchenAid, Krups, and Wüstof-Trident. Schwartz provides a number of valuable services, including coordination of silver, crystal, and china patterns, gift and bridal registry, and a corporate gift program. Gift wrapping is offered at no extra charge, and hand engraving is now available. You can send for the catalog, or call for a price quote.

Special Factors: Satisfaction is guaranteed; price quote by phone, fax, or letter; special orders are accepted with a nonrefundable 20% deposit (unless the order is canceled while still on back order); undamaged returns are accepted within 30 days (a restocking fee may be charged).

ALBERT S. SMYTH CO., INC.

DEPT. WM96
29 GREENMEADOW DR.
TIMONIUM, MD 21093
800-638-3333
410-252-6666
FAX: 410-252-2355

Catalog: free
Save: up to 50%
Pay: check, MO, MC, V, AE, Discover
Sells: tableware, giftware, and jewelry
Store: same address; Monday to Saturday 9–5, Thursday 9–9

All that gleams and glitters can be found at Smyth, at savings of up to 50% on comparable retail and list prices. Smyth has been doing business since 1914, and has a well-regarded customer service department. The 24-page color catalog features a wide range of jewelry, including diamonds, strands of semiprecious beads, colored stone jewelry, and pearls. Watches by Krieger, Movado, Omega, Rado, Seiko, Tag Heuer, and Vuarnet have been offered, as well as Mont Blanc pens, mahogany jewelry chests, Waterford giftware, Virginia Metalcrafters gifts, and Kirk-Stieff pewter and silver gifts.

Tableware and home decorative accents are sold here at impressive savings, including such items as British carriage clocks, Baldwin brassware, and fine picture frames. You'll find pewter candlesticks, coffee sets, punch bowls, and place settings by Aynsley, Gorham, Kirk-Stieff, Lenox, Noritake, Reed & Barton, Royal Doulton, Spode, Towle, Villeroy & Boch, Wallace, Waterford, and Wedgwood among the offerings.

Smyth maintains a bridal registry and provides gift consultations and a gift-forwarding service. The catalog shows a fraction of the inventory, so write or call for a price quote if you don't see what you're looking for.

Special Factors: Satisfaction is guaranteed; returns (except personalized and custom-ordered goods) are accepted within 30 days.

THURBER'S

2256-C DABNEY RD.
RICHMOND, VA 23230
800-848-7237
FAX: 804-278-9480

Catalog: $1
Save: up to 60%
Pay: check, MO, MC, V, AE, Discover
Sells: tableware, giftware, and Christmas ornaments
Store: same address

The 24-page color catalog from Thurber's showcases both fine tableware and gifts, but you can call or write year-round for quotes on specific items. Thurber's has been in business since 1985, selling gifts and the accoutrements of gracious living at up to 60% off list prices. Place settings and other tableware by Dansk, Fraser, Gorham, International, Kirk-Stieff, Lenox, Lunt, Miller Rogaska, Minton, Noritake, Oneida, Portmeirion, Reed & Barton, Royal Doulton, Royal Worcester, Spode, Tirschenreuth, Towle, Villeroy & Boch, Wallace, Wedgwood, and Yamazaki are available as well, at savings of up to 60%. And the holiday catalog features a lovely selection of limited-edition Christmas ornaments, and plates.

Special Factors: Satisfaction is guaranteed; returns are accepted within 30 days for exchange, refund, or credit.

WINDSOR GIFT SHOP

233-237 MAIN ST.
MADISON, NJ 07949
800-631-9393
201-377-7273
FAX: 201-377-0103

Catalog: $1
Save: up to 30%
Pay: check, MO, MC, V, AE, Discover
Sells: table settings, gifts, collectibles, etc.
Store: same address; Monday to Saturday 9:30–5:45, Thursday 9:30–8:45

Windsor Gift Shop's color catalog begins with Baccarat crystal and ends with collectors' Christmas ornaments. Between the covers are 28 pages of stemware and gifts by Atlantis, Astral, Cristal de Sevres, Kosta Boda, Orrefors, Rosenthal, Royal Doulton, Saint Louis, Villeroy & Boch, and Waterford, and dinnerware and gifts by Arzberg, Bernardaud and Ceralene Limoges, Richard Ginori, Haviland Limoges, Hutschenreuther, Lenox, Mottahedeh, Noritake, Pickard, Rosenthal, Royal Copenhagen, Royal Doulton, Royal Worcesterchire, Spode, Thomas, Villeroy & Boch, and Wedgwood. Silverware and holloware by W.M. Fraser, Gorham, International, Kirk-Stieff, Lunt, Oneida, Reed & Barton, Wallace, and Yamazaki are also available. Silver chests, trivets, paperweights, clocks, vases, decanters, perfume bottles, vanity accessories, cachepots, baby gifts, and a small selection of jewelry appear in the catalog as well. (Windsor shows just a sampling of the available tableware; call for information on pieces not illustrated.) Not every line or item is discounted, but savings can reach over 40% on selected lines and pieces. Windsor also maintains a bridal registry, and a corporate gift department.

Special Factors: Satisfaction is guaranteed; authorized returns are accepted.

SEE ALSO

Bruce Medical Supply • *dining aids and cutlery for those with limited strength or muscle control* • **MEDICINE: SPECIAL NEEDS**
Betty Crocker Catalog • *china, stemware, and flatware* • **GENERAL MERCHANDISE**
Fivenson Food Equipment, Inc. • *restaurant appliances, tableware, and serving pieces* • **HOME: KITCHEN**
Kitchen Etc. • *tableware* • **HOME: KITCHEN**
Harris Levy, Inc. • *table linens* • **HOME: LINEN**

Paradise Products, Inc. • *party supplies, doilies, disposables, etc.* • **TOYS**

Pendery's Inc. • *Mexican glassware* • **FOOD: BEVERAGES AND FLAVOR-INGS**

Ross-Simons Jewelers • *china, crystal, and silver tableware* • **JEWELRY**

Weston Bowl Mill • *wooden plates, trays, and tableware* • **GENERAL MER-CHANDISE**

INSURANCE AND CREDIT

Consumer insurance and
credit information sources

"**I**nsurance" is the price of protecting yourself or others from absorbing the entire cost of misfortune and disaster. As no one's favorite topic, it's rivaled by "credit," the business of borrowing money. They're two of life's necessary expenses, but they're amazingly variable in cost. Since it's possible to save a considerable sum on car, health, home, and life insurance and consumer credit, it repays investing a few evenings studying some consumer literature on the subject (see the sources listed below). If you don't turn up new savings, it means you've already made the best choices possible!

Whether you're buying insurance or borrowing credit, the same money-saving strategies apply, overall: Determine the type of product that best fits your needs and situation, then shop price and terms among reliable providers.

Before consulting books that deal exclusively with insurance or credit, get a grounding in finance basics. You can begin with the government publication offered from the Consumer Information Center and the Superintendent of Documents (see the listings in "Books.") The following books are excellent primers on consumer finance, including insurance and credit. If you don't really understand how bonds work, or how to calculate your net worth and set a retirement savings plan, these books will help show you.

- *Making the Most of Your Money,* by the eminently reliable Jane Bryant Quinn (Simon & Schuster, 1991), takes you from assessing your financial situation to choosing a bank, writing a will, creating a budget, buying insurance, owning a home, paying for education, investing, and retirement planning. Because the topics naturally flow into one another, you can use it as a workbook, as well as a general reference.

- *Personal Finance for Dummies™,* by Eric Tyson (IDG Books, 1994), is another in the "Dummies" series of books that use a forgiving approach with pop overtones and lots of cartoons and graphics to teach—in this volume—about savings and interest, consumer credit and debt issues, financial planning and budgets, mortgages, insurance, investments, retirement planning, and related money issues that stymie many of us. There are cute icons in the margins that highlight "technical stuff," tips, warnings, points to keep in mind, special caveats, and related products and services that are "Dummies Approved." Despite the friendly face, this book packs lots of information wallop and may appeal to those looking for a hip, humorous approach to finance. Investment novices should check the "Dummies" volume on mutual funds for the same kind of guidance.

- *The Wall Street Journal Guide to Understanding Personal Finance,* by Kenneth M. Morris and Alan M. Siegel (Lightbulb Press, Inc., 1992) takes the graphical approach further with full-color photographs of *everything,* from the front and back of a canceled check to the anatomy of a mutual-funds index. This approach is very helpful to those who are phobic about forms and charts; it breaks things down into their comprehensible elements and explains how they work. Banking, credit and interest, financing a home, insurance, financial planning, investing, and taxes are covered.

In addition to these sources, see *Cut Your Spending in Half,* which is described in the introduction to "General Merchandise."

INSURANCE

Where once we depended on an insurance agent for our education, we now have Ralph Nader, *Consumer Reports,* and personal-finance writers to explain the mechanics of insurance and how to make good choices. Use their resources, and you may profit: The editor of this book was able to save over $800 on her home insurance (with no loss in necessary coverage) with the help of a few good tips and reference works.

- The books on general consumer-finance topics, above, all cover insurance basics and are a good way to get acquainted.
- *Winning the Insurance Game: The Complete Consumer's Guide to Saving Money* (Knightsbridge Publishing Co., 1990) teams con-

sumer advocates Ralph Nader and Wesley J. Smith in 538 pages on the general mechanics of insurance, and in-depth sections on auto, health, home, and life insurance, summaries of government benefits, and notes on how to document and file claims and resolve disputes. Appendixes of bad bets, government insurance agencies, information organizations, and sample policy terms cover all the bases.

- *The Guide to Buying Insurance: How to Secure the Coverage You Need at an Affordable Price,* by David L. Scott (Globe Pequot Press) covers life, health, car, home, and liability insurance, with lots of commonsense advice.
- *The National Insurance Consumer Helpline* can answer questions on all aspects of insurance, from car to COBRA. Call 800-942-4242 or 703-549-8050, Monday to Friday 8 A.M. to 8 P.M., ET.
- Get a package deal: Ask the insurer about discounts for handling more than one policy—homeowner and auto, for example—and you may save up to 15%.
- Raise the deductibles: Home and auto policies make you pay more if the insurer has to cover the first $500 to $1000 of loss or damage. If you can afford to cover a high deductible yourself, you'll save significantly on your premiums.
- Lengthen the waiting/coverage period: Disability coverage is cheaper if you're willing to defer the date when coverage begins, or limit the duration of payout.

When it comes to understanding *health and life insurance,* you *must* do your homework. Where there were once "whole" and "term" life insurance policies are now a variety of complex investment and estate-planning tools. The resources listed above evaluate the forms of life insurance; for more information, see the resources below:

- The *Life Insurance Handbook,* by Jerry Gilbert (Consumer Reports Books), explains the differences among insurance products and teaches you how to find the one that's right for your needs.
- Price shop: When you've decided on the *kind* of life or health insurance you need, you can hire *Quotesmith Corp.* to feed your request to its computers for a printout of 25 to 50 policies meeting your requirements. You can also get all of the ratings on a single insurance carrier ($15 extra). Quotesmith has over 300 insurance companies on file, and covers medigap and long-term care policies, as well as life and standard health insurance. You can still work with a broker after running a quote, but the printout should help you to negotiate the best price.

- Check the ratings: In addition to Quotesmith's ratings check, *Insurance Forum,* an industry newsletter, compiles a yearly master listing of the ratings of about 1,700 insurance providers (life and health). The issue is updated in the spring; send a $10 check or money order to Insurance Forum, Inc., P.O. Box 245, Ellettsville, IN 47429, and request the "annual ratings issue."
- Skip the broker: Save on fees and sales commissions by buying life insurance directly from the insurer. Term and cash-value insurance policies are sold directly to consumers by USAA Life Insurance Co. (800-531-8000), or Ameritas Life Insurance Corp. (800-552-3553).

The time to think about saving on your *auto insurance* is before you buy your next vehicle. If you're in the market for a new car, be sure that you account for typical insurance costs for any vehicle you consider. Even an old clunker can have high rates if it's prone to needing repairs or is on the list of cars thieves target for parts. The books on general insurance topics (listed previously) all cover cars, and the following information can help as well:

- The Chartered Property Casualty Underwriters Society publishes "Understand Your Auto Insurance Policy and Get the Most for Your Money" and "Team Up with Your Insurance Adjuster When You File a Claim" (home or auto). They're free on request; send a long, stamped, self-addressed envelope for each pamphlet to Chartered Property Casualty Underwriters Society, Box 3009, Malvern, PA 19355.
- The Comprehensive Loss Underwriting Exchange (CLUE) will send you a copy of the last five years of your reported auto insurance claims for $8. Get your history before you apply for insurance, both to avoid omitting an incident you've forgotten, and to make sure the record is accurate. Call 800-456-6004 for more information or to order a report.

Home, or property insurance, may cover aspects of auto-related problems—the theft of personal property from your car, for example—so make sure you understand the provisions of both. In addition to consulting the general references on insurance listed earlier in this section, study the actual policy you receive. Make a list of questions as they occur to you, then work through them with your broker. Make sure you understand the limitations of your coverage, and adjust or change it to cover your needs.

Buying the right amount of insurance coverage requires knowing how much it would cost to rebuild your home and replace the contents.

Local contractors can help you determine the cost of rebuilding, or your insurance broker may have a formula that does the math.

"Taking Inventory" is the name of a very helpful form from the Insurance Information Institute. It's an inventory work sheet, broken down room by room, with lists of typical items and furnishings, and a blank for their purchase date and cost. This is for a *general* inventory and wouldn't cover fine-arts or antiques scheduling, but will give you the foundation for finding replacement values. Request the brochure by name from Insurance Information Institute, 110 William St., New York, NY 10038; include a long, stamped, self-addressed envelope.

See the mention of the Chartered Property Casualty Underwriters Society, and National Insurance Consumer Helpline for more assistance in filing claims and understanding your policy.

CREDIT

"Credit" is the right to borrow on the strength of your promise to pay, and "interest" is the cost of exercising that right. The most commonly used forms of credit is the revolving charge account, followed by car loans. Together, they accounted for $838 *billion* in American consumer debt in 1994. The average outstanding balance is $1,700, and at an average card rate still around 18%, that's a hefty contribution to the issuer's profit margin.

The following resources offer credit-shopping tips, comparison results, and techniques to help you maximize card value, not cost:

- *The Ultimate Credit Handbook: How to Double Your Credit, Cut Your Debt, and Have a Lifetime of Great Credit,* by Gerri Dettweiler (Plume/Penguin Books, 1993) has garnered endorsements by Congressional representatives and the president of the National Consumer League. Ms. Dettweiler was long the Executive Director of Bankcard Holders of America, and covers everything from "the secrets of a great credit rating" to "a lifetime strategy for great credit." No matter how badly you've managed credit in the past, this book will help you figure out where you stand and what you need to do to improve your situation. The explanation of how the credit industry works equations for computing your "safe" debt load can help you spot your best credit buy and shoulder debt responsibly.
- Bankcard Holders of America (BHA), a membership organization, performs quarterly reviews of credit-card offerings to find those offering the lowest rates and best terms. The most recent list costs $4; it's a big help in figuring out whether to jump, consolidate, or "churn" (transfer balances to new cards offered at low introductory

rates, from cards that are raising their rates). BHA also offers a computer-based "Debt Zapper" service: Complete the form BHA sends you, providing current credit-card debt information and the $15 fee, and you'll receive a printout detailing how much to pay on each debt to minimize interest. The Zapper showed BHA members who participated in the trial of the service how to save an average of 25% on their credit costs. Send a long, stamped, self-addressed envelope for membership information and a list of current publications and services, to BHA, Customer Service, 524 Branch Dr., Salem, VA 24153.

- RAM Research compiles monthly lists of the best credit-card offers; copies are available for $5 each. Request RAM's *CardTrack* from RAM Research, Box 1700, Frederick, MD 21702.
- Consumer Credit Counseling Services (CCCS) has over 1,000 offices nationwide to help the troubled credit consumer. If you're having problems, get in touch; this private foundation will work with you to craft the best plan of action credit-wise, for a nominal fee, or free. For the location of the CCCS office nearest you, call 800-388-2227.

Car loans, mortgages, and other consumer-credit issues will be covered in the next edition of *WBMC*.

JEWELRY, GEMS, AND WATCHES

Fine, fashion, and costume jewelry; loose stones, watches, and services

You'll find everything from inexpensive neck chains to investment-grade gems here, at savings of 20% to 75%. You'll also find companies that sell to amateur and professional jewelry makers, and sometimes supply pieces in finished form.

Before making a financial commitment of any magnitude, make sure you know what you're buying. *All About Jewelry: The One Indispensable Guide for Buyers, Wearers, Lovers, Investors,* by Rose Leiman Goldenberg (Arbor House Publishing Co., 1983), covers precious and semi-precious stones, pearls, metals, and other materials used in jewelry. For an inside look at the business, try *Modern Jeweler's Consumer Guide to Colored Gemstones,* by David Federman (Modern Jeweler Magazine, 1990), with dazzling color photographs by Tino Hammid. A gemlike production in its own right, it reveals the intrigue and chicanery that shape each stone's market, and discusses irradiation and heat treatment of gems. Write to Modern Jeweler, Vance Publishing Corporation, P.O. Box 1416, Lincolnshire, IL 60069-9958 for the current price and ordering information if you can't find it locally.

The FTC has established guidelines for the jewelry trade and publishes pamphlets for consumers that discuss the meanings of terms, stamps and quality marks, and related matters. Request "Gold Jewelry," "Bargain Jewelry," and "Guidelines for the Jewelry Industry" from the Federal Trade Commission, Public Reference Office, Washington, DC 20580.

If you need help in finding an appraiser, contact the American Society of Appraisers at 212-687-6305. The Society will locate an appraiser in your area and have that person contact you, at no charge. (The Society's senior members have at least five years of experience and are required to pass an exam; they handle all "appraisables," not just jewelry.)

The Gemological Institute of America (GIA) can tell you what should appear on a GIA report and confirm whether an appraiser has been trained by the organization. For more information, write to the Gemological Institute of America, Inc., 1180 Avenue of the Americas, New York, NY 10036. There is also a GIA office in California, at P.O. Box 2110, 1660 Stewart St., Santa Monica, CA 90406.

The Jewelers' Vigilance Committee can tell you whether your dealer is among the good, the bad, or the ugly. This trade association monitors the industry and promotes ethical business practices. For more information write to the Jewelers' Vigilance Committee, 1180 Avenue of the Americas, 8th Fl., New York, NY 10036.

DIAMONDS BY RENNIE ELLEN

15 W. 47TH ST., RM. 401
NEW YORK, NY 10036
212-869-5525

Catalog: $2
Save: up to 75%
Pay: check, MO, teller's check, bank draft
Sells: stock and custom-made jewelry
Factory: visits by appointment only

It's hard to believe that you can buy diamond engagement rings wholesale, but that's Rennie Ellen's business. You can save up to 75% on the price of similar jewelry sold elsewhere by buying here. Rennie Ellen is honest, reputable, and personable, and she's been cutting gems since 1966.

Rennie Ellen sells diamonds of all shapes, sizes, and qualities, set to order in platinum or gold. The color catalog shows samples of Ms. Ellen's design work, including rings, pendants, and earrings set with diamonds. Engagement and wedding rings are a specialty, and the cards and notes from grateful young marrieds that line her office walls testify to her success. The factory is open to customers by appointment only.

Special Factors: Price quote by phone or letter; a detailed bill of sale is included with each purchase; returns are accepted within five working days; minimum shipping, handling, and insurance charge is $15 (sent by registered mail).

ELOXITE CORPORATION

DEPT. 4
P.O. BOX 729
WHEATLAND, WY 82201
307-322-3050
FAX: 307-322-3055

Catalog: $1
Save: up to 75%
Pay: check, MO, MC, V
Sells: jewelry findings
Store: 806 Tenth St., Wheatland, WY; Monday to Friday 8:30–4, Saturday 8:30–3

Eloxite has been selling jewelry findings, cabochons, beads, and other lapidary supplies since 1955. Prices here are up to 75% below those charged by other crafts sources for findings and jewelry components. Jewelry findings with a Western flair are featured: bola ties and slide medallions, belt buckles and inserts, and coin jewelry are prominent offerings. Also shown are pendants, rings, earrings, lockets, tie tacks, and pins made to be set with cabochons or cut stones, as well as jump rings, chains, pillboxes, screw eyes, and ear wires. The stones themselves are sold—cut cubic zirconia and synthetic gemstones and oval cabochons of abalone, agate, black onyx, garnet, opal, obsidian, jasper, and malachite. A recent catalog included loosely strung gemstone bead necklaces and jewelers' tools and supplies.

Sandwiched between the pages of jewelry components are quartz clock movements and blanks for clock faces, clock hands, and ballpoint pens and letter openers for desk sets. Discounts are available on most items, and specials are usually offered with orders of specified amounts.

Special Factors: Quantity discounts are available; undamaged returns are accepted within 15 days for exchange or refund (a $2 restocking fee may be charged); minimum order is $15; C.O.D. orders are accepted.

HONG KONG LAPIDARIES, INC.

Catalog: $3, refundable
Save: up to 50%
Pay: check, MO, MC, V
Sells: jewelry supplies and loose stones
Store: mail order only

2801 UNIVERSITY DR.
CORAL SPRINGS, FL 33065
305-755-8777
FAX: 305-755-8780

  ¡Si!

Hong Kong Lapidaries, established in 1979, sells a wide range of precious and semiprecious stones in a variety of forms. The 52-page catalog lists items of interest to hobbyists as well, and the prices run as much as 70% below comparable retail.

Thousands of cabochons, beads, loose faceted and cut stones, and strung chips of pearl, garnet, amethyst, onyx, abalone, and other kinds of semiprecious stones are offered through the catalog, which comes with a separate 12-page color brochure that shows representative pieces. Egyptian clay scarabs, coral, cameos, cubic zirconia, yellow jade, cloisonné jewelry and objets d'art, 14K gold-filled and sterling silver beads, and ball earrings are available. Hobbyists should note the necklace thread—100% silk or nylon—in a score of colors and 16 *sizes*—plus stringing needles.

Special Factors: Satisfaction is guaranteed; price quote by fax; quantity discounts are available; returns are accepted within 12 days; minimum order is $50; C.O.D. orders are accepted.

HOUSE OF ONYX, INC.

Catalog: free
Save: up to 60%
Pay: check, MO, MC, V, Discover
Sells: investment-grade stones, jewelry, and gifts
Store: 120 Main St., Greenville, KY; Monday to Friday 9–4

THE AARON BUILDING
GREENVILLE, KY
42345-0261
800-844-3100
502-338-2363
FAX: 502-338-9605

The House of Onyx publishes a large tabloid catalog filled with reports on the gem industry and listings of diamonds and other precious stones, as well as specials on gifts and jewelry. Imported gifts and jewelry from Mexico, China, and India have been offered in the past, including Aztec onyx chess sets, ashtrays, bookends, vases, statuettes, and candlesticks. Cloisonné and vermeil beads, jewelry, and artware, and carvings of soapstone, rose quartz, tiger's eye, Burmese jadeite, lapis lazuli, carnelian, turquoise, and agate are usually available. The jewelry includes semiprecious bead necklaces, freshwater and cultured pearls, and diamond and gemstone rings, earrings, and pendants, from department-store grade to fine one-of-a-kind pieces. Collectors of crystals and mineral specimens should check here for amethyst, fluorite, quartz, pyrite, and other geodes and samples.

House of Onyx has been in business since 1967, and offers a wide range of investment-quality stones, with discounts of 50% and 60% offered on parcels of $2,000 to $12,500. The investment stones account for much of the business here, and the catalog is packed with useful information and commentary on gems and investing.

Special Factors: Satisfaction is guaranteed; investment gemstones are sold with an unlimited time return guarantee and a "100% purchase price refund" pledge; other returns are accepted within 30 days; minimum order is $25.

NATURE'S JEWELRY

27 INDUSTRIAL AVE.,
DEPT. NJ-106E
CHELMSFORD, MA
01824-3692
800-333-3235
FAX: 800-866-3235

Catalog: free
Save: up to 40% (see text)
Pay: check, MO, MC, V, AE, Discover
Sells: fashion and novelty jewelry
Store: mail order only

No matter what your personal style, taste, or budget, you'll find a bauble to suit your fancy in the Nature's Jewelry catalog. Each issue has nearly 100 pages of classic, theme, and holiday jewelry and accessories, including strands of semiprecious stones, preserved wildflower jewelry, pins and watches with environmental themes, jewelry for the season—from "star" bow earrings in red and green for Christmas to a cuff of enamelled hearts for Valentine's Day—and much more, at very affordable prices. Many of the designs are exclusives, so they're hard to compare to other jewelry, but prices on items at Nature's Jewelry are up to

50% lower than those charged elsewhere for similar pieces. Many of the pierced earrings are priced under $10, and a large proportion of other pieces cost under $20.

If you'd like to be able to wear fresh flowers every day, you'll love the collection of handmade, handpainted stone-and-resin buds and blossoms. Past catalogs have shown lilacs, roses, irises, pansies, poppies, and other flowers, and there's even a line of *preserved* blossoms in earrings, pins, and pendants. Love pigs? They're here, to adorn your ears or dress, as well as cows, sheep, lots of cats, horses, dinosaurs, dolphins, whales, pandas, fish, birds, dragonflies, coyotes, frogs, and many other animals. Nature's Jewelry sells dozens of pierced ear "illusions," figures and animals that appear to go *through* the earlobe. There are $10 tennis bracelets, golf-motif jewelry, pieces of nature (real parsley, four-leaf clovers, maple leaves, etc.) dipped in 24K gold, and chunks of "beach glass" made into beautiful, jewel-like necklaces and earrings. Every catalog has much more, with lots of new additions in each issue, and sale pages with dozens of pieces at 50% off.

Special Factors: Satisfaction is guaranteed; returns are accepted for exchange, refund, or credit.

ROSS-SIMONS JEWELERS

DEPT. WBMC
9 ROSS-SIMONS DR.
CRANSTON, RI 02920-4476
800-556-7376
FAX: 800-896-8181

Catalog: free
Save: up to 40%
Pay: check, MO, MC, V, AE, DC, Discover
Sells: jewelry, tableware, and giftware
Store: Kittery, ME; Atlanta, GA; Las Vegas, NV; and Barrington, Providence, and Warwick, RI

Ross-Simons has 40 years of experience in the jewelry business, and the firm's color catalog showcases a wide selection of jewelry items. Half of each issue is also devoted to fine china, flatware, and crystal. Prices are discounted up to 40% below suggested list and regular retail, and you can call directly for a quote if you're shopping for a specific item.

Stylish jewelry is the strong suit here: Precious and semiprecious stones in myriad settings, cubic zirconia pieces, sterling silver, cultured pearls, and 18K gold plate. Ross-Simons also sells watches by the top names in timepieces; call for a price quote on any well-known line.

Fine china, crystal, silver, and gifts complete the catalog, which features patterns from Bernardaud Limoges, Ceralene Limoges, Fitz & Floyd, Gorham, Haviland, Lenox, Mikasa, Noritake, Royal Doulton, Wedgwood and many more. Crystal is available from some of the same manufacturers, as well as Atlantis, Baccarat, Miller Rogaska, Orrefors, and St. Louis. Ross-Simons also sells flatware—stainless, silver plate, and new sterling—by Gorham, International, Kirk-Stieff, Lunt, Oneida, Reed & Barton, Towle and Wallace. Commemoratives from Bing & Grøndahl, Hummel, and other makers are available, as well as other gifts. Bridal registry services are available.

Special Factors: Satisfaction is guaranteed; returns (except personalized items) are accepted within 30 days for exchange, refund, or credit.

SIMPLY DIAMONDS

DEPT. A
P.O. BOX 682
ARDSLEY, NY 10502-0682
800-552-2728
914-693-2370
FAX: 914-693-2446

Catalog: free
Save: up to 50%
Pay: check, MO, MC, V, AE
Sells: diamond jewelry
Store: mail order only
E-mail: CS: 75224,1032@compuserve.com

The Simply Diamonds catalog is just eight pages long, but it features such a universally attractive line of gold and diamond jewelry that you're almost certain to find pieces you'd like to give, or to receive. Diamond-studded heart pendants and rings, bow earrings, circle pins, initial pendants, diamond link bracelets, religious jewelry, and kids charms are among the choices. (The unique gold and diamond children's name bracelets would be a perfect gift for mother or grandmother.) Prices are as low as $65 for a lovely Baroque pendant drop with a tiny diamond, and all of the gold is solid 14K. In addition to what's shown in the catalog, Simply Diamonds can fulfill other diamond needs—including engagement rings—at a discount, thanks to the parent company's involvement in the diamond district of New York City. GIA, EGL, and IGI certificates are available.

Special Factors: Satisfaction is guaranteed; returns are accepted within 30 days for exchange, refund, or credit; C.O.D. orders are *not* accepted.

SEE ALSO

Antique Imports Unlimited • vintage jewelry and watches • **ART & ANTIQUES**

Bennett Brothers, Inc. • costume and fine jewelry and watches • **GENERAL MERCHANDISE**

Berry Scuba Co. • underwater timepieces • **SPORTS**

Central Skindivers • underwater timepieces • **SPORTS**

Ceramic Supply of New York & New Jersey, Inc. • jewelry findings • **ART MATERIALS**

Michael C. Fina Co. • fine jewelry and watches • **HOME: TABLE SETTINGS**

Fortunoff Fine Jewelry & Silverware, Inc. • fine jewelry and watches • **HOME: TABLE SETTINGS**

Paul Fredrick • men's jewelry • **CLOTHING**

The Jompole Company, Inc. • fine watches • **HOME: TABLE SETTINGS**

Manny's Millinery Supply Co. • hat pins • **CLOTHING**

Professional Cutlery Direct • Swiss Army watches • **HOME: KITCHEN**

Nat Schwartz & Co., Inc. • fine jewelry • **HOME: TABLE SETTINGS**

Albert S. Smyth Co., Inc. • fine jewelry and watches • **HOME: TABLE SETTINGS**

LEATHER GOODS

Small leather goods, handbags, briefcases, attaché cases, luggage, trunks, and services

The firms listed here stock everything you should need to tote your effects around town, to the office, and farther afield. In addition to handbags, briefcases, suitcases, trunks, and small leather goods, some of the firms also sell cases for musical instruments and portfolios for models and artists.

If you're buying luggage, consider the pros and cons of different luggage materials: waterproof, puncture-proof materials and lockable closures are good considerations. Wheeled suitcases help bridge the distances in mammoth hub airports, and built-in, partly recessed wheels that are designed to avoid jamming in conveyor belts are the best bets. The Rollaboard, by Travelpro Luggage, is engineered to allow pieces to be attached together and rolled around as a unit, and sized to fit under airline seats and in overhead bins. (Ace Luggage and Gifts sells the Rollaboard Travelsystem at a discount.) Whatever style suitcase you use, make it as thief-proof as possible: Use small combination locks, since pros who work airports have masters to popular keyed models; bind your luggage with webbed belting, which will keep clamshell suitcases from springing open if their locks fail, and prevents easy access by anyone rifling the luggage while it's in transit. Keep a list of the contents of the suitcase with you in case your luggage is lost, since the list will help to identify the suitcase, and can be used for insurance valuation.

Companies that sell small leather goods and handbags are also listed in "Clothing," portfolios and display cases and binders are available from some of the companies listed in "Art Materials," and companies selling travel accessories are listed in "Travel."

431

ACE LUGGAGE AND GIFTS

2122 AVE. U
BROOKLYN, NY 11229
800-DIAL ACE
718-891-9713
FAX: 718-891-3878

Catalog: $2, refundable (see text)
Save: up to 40%
Pay: check, MO, MC, V, AE
Sells: luggage and leather goods
Store: 2122 Ave. U, Brooklyn, NY; Monday to Saturday 10–6, Thursday 10–8 (extended hours in December)

  (see text)

Ace, which was established in 1961, sells luggage by American Tourister, Andiamo, Boyt, Delsey, French, Hartmann, Lark, Lucas, Samsonite, LeSport Sac, Travelpro (Rollaboard), Tumi, and Wings at discounts of up to 40%. Briefcases and attaché cases by Boyt, Eagle Creek, Hartmann, Jansport, Lodis, Schlesinger, Scully, and Tumi, are available, as well as handbags and small leather goods by Etienne Aigner, Bosca, and Garys. You'll find travel alarms, Swiss Army knives, lighters, pens, and other small luxuries by Colibri, Cross, Mont Blanc, Seiko, Victorinox (Swiss Army) and Waterman in the store. The 36-page catalog that's published during the holiday season features gift merchandise, but catalogs and price quotes on the luggage and leather goods are available throughout the year. And special discounts *may* be possible for corporate and quantity orders.

Readers in Canada and abroad, please note: Orders are shipped via UPS.

Special Factors: Price quote by phone.

AL'S LUGGAGE

2134 LARIMER ST.
DENVER, CO 80205
303-295-9009
303-294-9045
FAX: 303-296-8769

Catalog: $2, refundable
Save: up to 50%
Pay: check, MO, MC, V, AE, Discover
Sells: leather goods and luggage
Store: same address; Monday to Friday 8:30–5:30; Saturday 8:30–5

The $2 catalog fee (refundable with purchase) brings you a sheaf of photocopied materials from Samsonite, including price lists, ordering instructions, and shipping rate charts. Al's Luggage has been selling leather goods and luggage since 1948, and carries Diane Von Fursten-berg, Jordache, Lion Leather, London Fog Luggage, Members Only, Platt, Stebco, Winn, and WK. In addition to current lines of suitcases, overnight bags, cosmetics cases, totes, wardrobes, duffels, and garment bags, Al's offers business cases, portfolios, and even camcorder carrying cases. The catalog shows only Samsonite models, which are sold here for 30% to 50% below list prices. If you're shopping for an item by another manufacturer, call or write for a price quote.

Special Factors: Price quote by phone or letter with SASE; C.O.D. orders are accepted.

JOBSON'S LUGGAGE WAREHOUSE

666 LEXINGTON AVE.
NEW YORK, NY 10022
800-832-7706
212-355-6846
FAX: 212-753-3295

Catalog: free
Save: up to 75%
Pay: check, MO, MC, V, AE, Discover
Sells: luggage, leather goods, and accessories
Store: same address; Monday to Saturday 9–6

Jobson's Luggage Warehouse has served New York City since 1949, and makes its "warehouse-priced" inventory available to customers world-wide through a very clear, 32-page catalog. Jobson's sells luggage, attaché cases, backpacks, laptop cases, and accessories by Air Express, American Tourister, Atlas, Boyt, Delsey, Eastpack, Eiffel, Perry Ellis, Hartmann, Jansport, Lark, Lion, Lucas, Paolo Marino, Samsonite, Schlesinger, Skyway, Travelpro, Tumi, Zero Halliburton, and other man-ufacturers. Jobson's has a great selection of business cases, choice small leather goods, desk and travel accessories, manicure sets, pens by Cross and Mont Blanc, and gifts. You can send for the catalog, or if you have the model and color information for a piece by any of the firms men-tioned here, call or write for a price quote.

Jobson's Luggage Warehouse is offering readers a discount of 10% on their first order. Be sure to identify yourself as a WBMC reader when you order, and deduct the discount from the cost of the goods only. This WBMC reader discount expires December 31, 1997.

Special Factors: Satisfaction is guaranteed; price quote by phone or letter; unused returns are accepted within 30 days for exchange, refund, or credit.

LEATHER UNLIMITED CORP.

DEPT. WBMC96

7155 CTY. HWY. B

BELGIUM, WI 53004-9990

414-994-9464

FAX: 414-994-4099

Catalog: $2, refundable

Save: up to 50%

Pay: check, MO, MC, V, Discover

Sells: leathercraft supplies and equipment and finished products

Store: same address; Monday to Friday 7–3:30

Here's a catalog for the beginner, the seasoned leather worker, and the rest of us. It offers all sorts of leather-crafting supplies, from kits to raw materials, as well as leather cleaners and conditioners, a line of bags, business cases, small leather goods, and even black-powder (shooting) supplies. Leather Unlimited has been in business since 1970, and offers substantial savings on crafts supplies, beginning with leather—sold by the hide, or in pieces. The weights run from fine lining grade to heavy belting leather, in a variety of finishes and colors. There are laces, belt blanks, key tabs, and dozens of undyed embossed belt strips; these are matched by hundreds of belt buckles, which run from embossed leather buckles to a line with organization logos and sporting themes. The 80-page catalog features dozens of kits for making all sorts of finished goods, plus stamping tools, punches, carvers, rivets, screws, snaps, zippers, lacing needles, sundry findings, leather-care products and dyes by Fiebing's, and Missouri River patterns for making authentic Native American and frontier-style clothing.

Among the finished products available here are sheepskin rugs, slippers, mittens, hats, and purses made of sheepskin and deerskin, duffels and sports bags, leather totes, and wineskins. Leather Unlimited is an authorized dealer for Harley-Davidson buckles, and also sells top-grain belt leather business cases, portfolios, wallets, and other small leather goods. And the firm recently added a line of books on Indian lore, crafts, and related topics. The prices are outstandingly low—up to 50% below comparable retail on some items—and extra discounts are given on quantity or volume purchases.

Leather Unlimited Corp. is offering readers a discount of 10% on their first order. Be sure to identify yourself as a WBMC reader when you order, and deduct the discount from the cost of the goods only. This WBMC reader discount expires February 1, 1997.

Special Factors: Satisfaction is guaranteed; authorized returns are accepted within ten days; minimum order is $40.

THE LUGGAGE CENTER

960 REMILLARD CT.
SAN JOSE, CA 95122
800-450-2400

Information: price quote
Save: see text
Pay: MO, MC, V, AE
Sells: luggage, business cases, and travel accessories
Store: locations in Bakersfield, Berkeley, Burlingame, Citrus Heights, Dublin, Emeryville, Fresno, Los Gatos, Mountain View, Pleasant Hill, Redwood City, Sacramento, San Francisco, San Jose (four), San Rafael, Vacaville, Visalia, and Walnut Creek, CA

  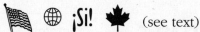 (see text)

The Luggage Center can save you up to 50% off the manufacturers' suggested list prices on the top names in luggage, and even more when the firm is running a sale. The latest lines from well-known makers are available, including Andiamo, Atlantic, Atlas, Briggs & Riley, Delsey, Eagle Creek, Lark, Lifestyles International, London Fog, Ricardo, Samsonite, Skyway and Tumi. Business cases, garment bags, and travel accessories are carried as well; call or write for a price quote.

Canadian readers, please note: Orders to Canada are shipped via UPS.

Special Factors: Returns are accepted within 30 days.

NEW ENGLAND LEATHER ACCESSORIES, INC.

187 GONIC RD.
ROCHESTER, NH 03866
603-332-0707
FAX: 603-332-4526

Catalog and Samples: $5, refundable
Save: up to 30%
Pay: check, MO, MC, V, Discover
Sells: leather handbags and accessories
Store: same address; Monday to Saturday 9–5

The 12-page catalog from New England Leather is illustrated with line drawings and photographs of its handsome leather bags and accessories, which are priced up to 30% below comparable leather goods. The $5 catalog fee also brings you a handful of butter-soft leather samples that show you the color range—tobacco, mallard green, brown, wine, and black.

Dozens of handbags and small leather items are available, mainly classic envelopes, hobo bags, knapsacks, and variations on simple pouch designs. The bags are lined, constructed with brass hardware, and treated to repel rain. Prices run from under $30 for a clutch purse to $198 for an enormous "mailbag." New England Leather has been in business since 1976, continuing on in the tradition of the region, which was once the leather-working capital of the country. Everything produced by the firm is 100% American made.

Special Factors: Returns are accepted.

J. TIRAS CLASSIC HANDBAGS, INC.

4252 RICHMOND AVE.
HOUSTON, TX 77027
800-460-1999
713-840-1999
FAX: 713-840-1988

Catalog: $2, refundable
Save: up to 80% (see text)
Pay: check, MO, MC, V, AE
Sells: designer handbag look-alikes
Store: same address; Monday to Saturday 10–5

Great design, fine workmanship, and top-notch materials are what justify paying hundreds of dollars for bags by Bottega Venetta, Louis Vuitton, Salvatore Ferragamo, Bally, Donna Karan, Judith Leiber, and other designers. But if you had the chance to buy a look-alike for up to 80% less, would *you* insist on the real thing?

Jerome and Jeannie Tiras have been building their business since 1989 on the obvious answer, with a great lineup of copies of handbags by well-known designers, *sans* trademarks, logos, etc. If you know the originals, you'll recognize the copies—but not the prices, which average $80 to $160 for the leather copies, and begin at $75 for a gold evening bag and run to $750 for a leopard-patterned miniaudiere done completely in rhinestones and crystals. (The inspirations for many of the evening bags are Judith Leiber's creations, which routinely fetch $950 to thousands of dollars for jewel-encrusted specimens. The "everyday" bags are copies of designer originals selling for $300 to $2,000.) Tiras' 28-page color catalog shows nearly 200 handbags, totes, change purses, wallets, belts and buckles, key chains, evening compacts, purse mirrors and combs, and other little luxuries, as well as a small group of beautiful fashion jewelry. Look for these in the current catalog, as well as details on bonus referral or purchase programs that Tiras may be running.

Special Factors: Unused returns (except sale items) are accepted within 10 days for exchange, refund, or credit; minimum order is $50.

SEE ALSO

Bennett Brothers, Inc. • small leather goods, luggage, and luggage carts • **GENERAL MERCHANDISE**
Dairy Association Co., Inc. • Tackmaster leather balm • **ANIMAL**
The Deerskin Place • deerskin leather goods • **CLOTHING**
A. Feibusch Corporation • replacement luggage-weight zippers • **CRAFTS: TEXTILE ARTS**
Gander Mountain, Inc. • backpacks and lightweight luggage • **SPORTS**
Holabird Sports • racquet-sports bags • **SPORTS**
IMPCO, Inc. • leather conditioner • **AUTO**
Justin Discount Boots & Cowboy Outfitters • leather-care preparations • **CLOTHING: FOOTWEAR**
M.C. Limited • steer hides and hide pillows • **HOME: DECOR**
United Pharmacal Company, Inc. • leather-care products • **ANIMAL**

MEDICINE

Prescription and over-the-counter
drugs, hearing aids, contact lenses and
eyeglasses, etc.

Buying medication by mail is convenient, and it can be less expensive than having prescriptions filled at the local drugstore. Even generic drugs may be cheaper by mail, affording you savings of up to 60% on some commonly prescribed remedies. But because not all medications are discounted, price out each prescription you have filled. One book that *every* person who takes medication should have is *Worst Pills Best Pills II,* by Dr. Sidney Wolfe, 690 pages on drugs commonly prescribed to older Americans and a list of 119 others to avoid. In the same activist spirit, *Getting the Best from Your Doctor,* by Wesley J. Smith, helps you choose a practitioner, understand your rights and the role of medical insurance, and use the medical system to your benefit. *Worst Pills Best Pills II* ($15) and *Getting the Most from Your Doctor* ($10) can be ordered from Public Citizen Publications, 2000 P. St. NW, Suite 600, Washington, DC 20036. You can also check a doctor's credentials through the American Board of Medical Specialties; call 800-776-2378 Monday to Friday 9–6, ET, to find out whether the doctor in question is board certified, and when he received certification and in what field of practice. And if you or someone you care for is going to be hospitalized, Karen Keating McCann's *Taking Charge of Your Hospital Stay* (Plenum Publishers, $24.95, 800-221-9369) can guide you through the process, with checklists, resources, definitions, and advice on avoiding billing problems.

Hearing aids, contact lenses, and other commonly used aids are featured in this chapter as well. Please let your doctor know if you're using mail-order suppliers for hearing aids or lenses, so he or she can make sure the lenses fit properly or that the hearing aid makes the right kind of correction.

For savings on breast forms, and products for persons with limited mobility, chronic conditions, and convalescent and post-op patients, see "Special Needs," immediately following this chapter.

For nutritional supplements, toiletries, and over-the-counter preparations, see the listings in "Health and Beauty."

FIND IT FAST

CONTACT LENSES AND SUPPLIES • **Contact Lens Replacement Center, General Lens, National Contact Lens Center**
EYEGLASSES AND FRAMES • **Hidalgo, Precision Optical, Prism Optical**
HEARING AIDS • **Ric Clark**
PRESCRIPTION DRUGS • **Medi-Mail, Retired Persons Services**

RIC CLARK COMPANY

36658 APACHE PLUME DR.
PALMDALE, CA 93550
805-947-8598
FAX: 805-947-4854

Catalog: free
Save: 50% plus
Pay: check or MO
Sells: hearing aids
Store: mail order only

Ric Clark Company's catalog features six hearing aid models, designed for varying degrees of hearing loss. Ric Clark's aids are suitable for losses from mild to severe and include in-the-ear models, "compression" aids designed to "cushion" sudden loud noises, and standard models. Prices are about half those charged by hearing-aid dealers, and a $10 deposit entitles you to a month's free trial, after which you may return the aid for a complete refund or keep it and pay the balance. Batteries and repairs are also available. Ric Clark Company recommends that you see a physician before buying an aid; you must sign a waiver if you don't provide a physician's note stating that you need an aid.

Special Factors: Satisfaction is guaranteed; all aids are warrantied; a budget payment plan is available.

CONTACT LENS REPLACEMENT CENTER, INC.

P.O. BOX 1489, DEPT. 96
MELVILLE, NY 11747
800-779-2654
516-491-7763
FAX: 516-643-4009

Price List: free with SASE
Save: up to 50%
Pay: check, MO, MC, V, Discover
Sells: contact lenses and sunglasses
Store: mail order only

Contact Lens Replacement Center, in business since 1986, sells contact lenses of every type at savings of up to 50%. The replacement lenses include hard, soft, planned-replacement, disposable, and gas-permeable types. Toric, bifocal, and aphakic lenses are also available. The brands include Barnes Hind/Hydrocurve, Bausch & Lomb, Boston, Ciba, Coopervision, CSI, Fluorex, Fluoroperm, Hydron/Ocular Sciences, Johnson & Johnson, Paraperm, Sunsoft, and Wesley-Jessen. All soft, planned-replacement, and disposable lenses are shipped in factory-sealed containers. Hard and gas-permeable lenses are made to order. Please note: This is a *replacement* service—not for first-time lens wearers—and you must supply a current prescription for the lenses you are now wearing. The prices are so low that it may make sense to discontinue lens insurance and rely on this service if you lose or damage your contacts—the Center's staff can help you determine the least expensive way to replace your prescribed lenses. And there are *no* membership fees of any kind. Sunglasses by Randolph Engineering, Ray-Ban, Revo, Serengeti, Sun Cloud, and Vuarnet are also available, at discount prices. Call with the specific model name and number for a price quote.

Special Factors: Price quote by phone or letter with SASE.

GENERAL LENS CORPORATION

Catalog: free (see text)
Save: up to 75%
Pay: check, MO, MC, V, AE, Discover
Sells: replacement contact lenses
Store: mail order only

DEPT. WBM
14350 N.E. 6TH AVE.
NORTH MIAMI BEACH, FL
33161-2907
800-333-5367
305-653-9229
FAX: 305-653-7986

General Lens Corporation makes it easy to save up to 75% on replacement contact lenses from Allergan Hydron, Bausch & Lomb, Ciba Vision, CooperVision, Johnson & Johnson, Ocular Science, Sola/Barnes Hind, Wesley-Jessen, including lines of disposables and planned-replacement lenses. (GLC can also supply gas-permeable, hard, bifocal, and special-order lenses by Boston, Kontour, Metro Optics, Sunsoft, Unilens, and other manufacturers.)

To order, you simply provide GLC with the name and phone number of your eye doctor; GLC's doctor will get your current prescription and send you fresh lenses. The catalog prices are up to 75% less than what you may have been paying, and you can save even more by becoming a GLC member ($25 for two years). Members receive special offers and up to 30% in extra discounts, and only members can participate in GLC's referral program, through which you can earn free lenses by referring friends who then become members, too. And the usual $5 fee for the Automatic Replacement Program, especially helpful for people who wear disposables, is waived for members. If you have questions about any of GLC's programs or services, call toll-free for information.

Special Factors: Unopened, factory-sealed returns are accepted within 30 days for exchange, refund, or credit.

HIDALGO, INC.

DEPT. WB
45 LA BUENA VISTA
WIMBERLEY, TX 78676
512-847-5571
FAX: 512-847-2393

Catalog: free
Save: up to 60%
Pay: check, MO, MC, V, AE, Discover
Sells: prescription eyeglasses, sunglasses, binoculars, watches, knives, etc.
Store: Wimberley North Too Shopping Center, Wimberley, TX; Monday to Friday 9–5, closed Saturday

Hidalgo's 64-page catalog makes ordering your eyeglasses by mail seem so easy, you'll wonder why you haven't tried it before. Hidalgo has been in business since 1967 and understands the concerns of the person who's buying glasses by mail. The catalog includes detailed descriptions of the frames, lenses, and special coatings, and includes a "Consumers' Guide to Sunglasses" that answers just about every question you can think of. There are instructions on taking your "pupil distance" measurements, and a chart that shows the light transmission data on the lenses sold by Hidalgo. The "try-on program" allows you to order up to three frames and try them out *before* ordering your glasses—a great feature for people who have a hard time finding frames that fit or flatter.

Hidalgo's own frames dominate the selection, and there are sunglasses by Bausch & Lomb, Nikon, Ray-Ban, Revo, and Serengeti, as well as replacement parts for Ray-Ban. The lens options include a choice of materials (glass, plastic, etc.), colors, coatings, and UV protection. Terms of Hidalgo's warranty are stated clearly in the catalog, as well as details of the "try-on" program. The prices are as much as 40% less than regular retail on the nonprescription eyewear, and 50% or more below customary charges for prescription glasses.

Special Factors: Returns in new, unused condition are accepted within 30 days for exchange, refund, or credit.

MEDI-MAIL, INC.

P.O. BOX 98520
LAS VEGAS, NV 89193-8520
800-793-4726

Brochure: free
Save: see text
Pay: check, MO, MC, V
Sells: prescription drugs and health-care products
Store: mail order only

Medi-Mail is a national membership pharmacy-by-mail/phone that offers name-brand prescription drugs and over-the-counter health products at competitive prices. The firm's 48-page catalog answers general questions on buying prescription drugs by mail, and lists scores of generic over-the-counter remedies, nutritional supplements, and beauty preparations. Among other services, Medi-Mail provides a refill slip (when appropriate) and an itemized receipt with each prescription, and will send you a printout of your past orders on request.

Special Factors: Price quote by phone.

NATIONAL CONTACT LENS CENTER

4930 PINECROFT WAY
SANTA ROSA, CA
95404-1311
800-326-6352
707-538-4444
FAX: 707-538-7766

Brochure: free
Save: up to 75%
Pay: check, MO, MC, V, Discover
Sells: soft and gas-permeable contact lenses
Store: same address; Monday to Friday 9–5

National Contact Lens Center, established in 1974, can save you up to 75% on your next pair of contact lenses. You must be an experienced lens wearer to buy here, since the firm can't provide, through the mail, the fitting and monitoring services needed by first-time wearers. No membership fees are ever charged.

National Contact Lens Center sells all the major soft contact lens brands, including lines by American Hydron, Bausch & Lomb, Boston, Ciba, Coopervision, Johnson & Johnson (Acuvue), Ocular Science, Pilkington/Barnes Hind, and Wesley-Jessen. Colored, standard, extended-wear, disposable, planned-replacement, and opaque lenses are offered, as well as toric (for astigmatism) lenses. Hard and gas-permeable lenses are also available. Savings can reach 75%, depending on the lens and manufacturer, and every lens is backed by National Contact Lens Center's 30-day replacement guarantee honored even if the vials are opened.

Special Factors: Satisfaction is guaranteed; price quote by phone; returns are accepted within 30 days for replacement, exchange, refund, or credit.

PRECISION OPTICAL

DEPT. WBMC96
507 2ND AVE.
ROCHELLE, IL 61068
815-562-2174

Catalog: free
Save: up to 30%
Pay: check, MO, MC, V, AE
Sells: nonprescription reading glasses
Store: mail order only

If you're having trouble seeing the fine—or not so fine—print, see your eye doctor. *Then* get the 12-page catalog from Precision Optical. In it, you'll find about 20 eyeglass styles for men and women, all with nonprescription magnifying lenses (what are usually known as "reading glasses"). The catalog includes a guide to finding the strength you need; Precision Optical offers eight levels, or diopters, from 1.25 to 3.25. The glasses are covered by the firm's guarantee, so if they're not right, check the catalog (it has a guide to diagnosing strength problems), and exchange them until you get a pair that works for you. The frames are contemporary and attractive, and both full- and half-lens styles are available. Precision Optical has been in business since 1946 and sells eyeglass cases, magnifying lenses, loupes, and eyeglass repair kits.

Special Factors: Satisfaction is guaranteed; returns are accepted within 30 days for exchange, refund, or credit.

PRISM OPTICAL, INC.

10992 N.W. 7TH AVE.,
 DEPT. WC96
NORTH MIAMI, FL 33168
305-754-5894
FAX: 305-754-7352

Catalog: $2, refundable
Save: up to 70% (see text)
Pay: check, MO, MC, V, AE, Discover
Sells: prescription eyeglasses, contact lenses, and sunglasses
Store: same address; Monday to Friday 8:30–5

 ¡Si!

Prism Optical has been selling prescription eyeglasses by mail since 1959, and publishes a 20-page color catalog that shows over 100 eyeglass frames for men, women, and children, discounted an average of 30% to 50%. Frames (and designer sunglasses) from Armani, Bollé, Carrera, Cazal, Christian Dior, Gucci, Anne Klein, Neostyle, Polo, Ray-Ban, Revo, and Serengeti are available. One of the benefits of ordering from Prism is being able to choose from a number of lens options, including photochromic lenses, polycarbonate (ultra-thin) lenses, permanently tinted lenses, lenses with gray mirror-finish, and UV-filtering coating and scratch-resistant coating. The lens styles include single-vision and bifocal lenses, trifocals, and "invisible" bifocals, among others. Prism guarantees that the glasses will fit correctly, and the catalog provides guides to gauging the correct size of the temple and bridge pieces.

Prism Optical also sells prescription contact lenses at prices up to 70% below those charged elsewhere. The firm sells "all brands," factory-sealed and guaranteed against defects. Call Prism with your prescription informationn for availability and price informationn.

Special Factors: Satisfaction is guaranteed; returns are accepted within 30 days for refund or credit; C.O.D. orders are accepted.

RETIRED PERSONS SERVICES, INC.

DEPT. 493000

500 MONTGOMERY ST.

ALEXANDRIA, VA

  22314-1563

ORDERS AND INFO:

  800-456-2277

FAX: 800-456-7631

TDD: 800-933-4327

Catalog: free
Save: see text
Pay: check, MO, MC, V, Discover
Sells: prescription drugs and OTC products
Store: mail order only

Retired Persons Services, Inc., is the mail-order pharmacy of the American Association of Retired Persons (AARP). Ordering from the AARP Pharmacy is a benefit of membership in the AARP, which may be the smartest $8 you ever spend (see the listing for the AARP in "General Merchandise"). The catalog offers nutritional supplements, over-the-counter remedies, analgesics, supplies for diabetics, nail clippers and scissors, support hosiery and foot-care products, dental-care items, hearing aid batteries, and much more. Prices of generic and branded prescription drugs are given by phone (800-456-2226) Monday through Friday, 7 A.M. to 7 P.M. and Saturday, 9 A.M. to 1 P.M. You may also speak directly with a pharmacist (800-456-2277) if you have questions. If you're an ostomy patient, call 800-284-4788 for the separate Ostomy Care Catalog. Medical information leaflets for seniors are provided with most prescriptions, and computerized prescription histories are available for tax and insurance purposes. RPS will call your doctor for you on prescription drug refills, and the AARP Pharmacy also participates in major prescription drug insurance plans. Orders are filled on an invoice basis—you'll be billed, instead of paying when you place the order.

Special Factors: Satisfaction is guaranteed; returns (except prescription drugs) are accepted for exchange, refund, or credit.

Special Needs

*Products and services for persons with
limited mobility, chronic medical conditions,
and convalescent and post-op patients*

When the *Americans with Disabilities Act* was passed in 1990, it was lauded as long-overdue legislation that would eliminate discrimination and barriers for persons with disabilities. What's emerging as the law is invoked and enforced is the story of how the law is applied, and a shaping of the very understanding of what constitutes a disability. To begin learning about the terms and titles, read the act itself. It's available from the Department of Justice's ADA helpline, 800-514-0301, TDD 800-514-0388. John Wiley & Sons has published the *Pocket Guide to the ADA* ($19.95), and AARP will send "Accessibility: It's Yours for the Asking" if you send a postcard requesting Publication D15520 from AARP Fulfillment, P.O. Box 22796, Long Beach, CA 90801-5796.

For purposes of this book only, and not constituting any definition, general vision correction (prescription and nonprescription eyeglasses, contact lenses, etc.) and hearing aids are found in the main section, "Medicine," just preceding this. This section features companies that serve more specialized needs—for diabetics, ostomates, persons with incontinence problems, post-surgery supplies and prostheses, etc.

When meeting the challenge of a long-term illness or a change in motor or sensor ability, you often need information—on coping, on care, on different therapies—as much as specialized products. The not-for-profit groups founded around fund-raising and education functions for individual diseases and conditions—arthritis, cancer, diabetes mellitus, multiple sclerosis, cystic fibrosis, spina bifida, and AIDS are a few of the best-known—can often help to refer you to local support groups and networks, specialists, related groups, and other information sources. (Your medical specialist should be able to give you the name of the biggest groups or foundations.) You can also search "Books in Print" for titles on the subject, read related medical journals, and find facts and friends on some of the online services. America Online's "Disabilities Forum" unites users with diverse disabilities, to talk about practical and philosophical issues. They hold dozens of "chats" each week, on everything from attention deficit disorder and autism to fibromyalgia and muscular dystrophy. Even the individual who can join an in-person support group will find benefit from these discussions, in which every aspect of the illnesses or condition may be discussed, support and suggestions freely exchanged. CompuServe also hosts a Disabilities Forum, for both the disabled and for their friends and family members, and there are separate forums for AIDS, cancer, and diabetes. But for hard information, nothing beats the Internet itself, with data bases on disability aid (through the University of Michigan), recordings for the blind and deaf education (through the University of Wisconsin), issues affecting the disabled, and directories of bulletin-board services and published materials. For a listing of these resources, see *The Internet Yellow Pages,* by Harley Hahn and Rick Stout (Osborne McGraw-Hill, 1995), or a similar directory of Internet resources; get the most current edition.

FIND IT FAST

BREAST FORMS • **Bosom Buddy**
GADGETS • **Comfort House**
INCONTINENCE PRODUCTS • **Medical Supply**
NURSING HOME CLOTHING • **Senior's Needs**
OSTOMY AND TRACHEOSTOMY SUPPLIES • **Bruce Medical**
SUPPORT HOSIERY AND GARMENTS • **Bruce Medical, Support Plus**

BOSOM BUDDY BREAST FORMS

B & B COMPANY, INC.
DEPT. WC01
2417 BANK DR.
P.O. BOX 5731
BOISE, ID 83705-0731
800-262-2789
208-343-9696
FAX: 208-343-9266

Brochure: free
Save: up to 50% (see text)
Pay: check, MO, MC, V, Discover
Sells: breast prostheses
Store: mail order only

B & B has been producing the "Bosom Buddy Breast Form," a comfortable, reasonably priced external breast form, since 1976. The form is weighted and shaped to ideal dimensions with cushioned pillows, each of which contains 1-1/2 ounces of tiny glass beads. (The weight may be adjusted by adding or removing pillows.) The form itself is all-fabric (no silicone or plastic is used), made of nylon softened with fiberfill, with an all-cotton backing that rests next to your skin. Bosom Buddy is interchangeable (fits both left and right sides), available in sizes from 32AAA to 46DDD, and it costs $65 ($70 for sizes DD and DDD). These prices are about 50% below silicone models. The brochure gives complete details, and B & B's staff can answer any questions you may have by phone.

Wholesale customers, the minimum order is three breast forms, or $100.

Special Factors: Satisfaction is guaranteed; returns are accepted.

BRUCE MEDICAL SUPPLY

Catalog: free
Save: up to 60%
Pay: check, MO, MC, V
Sells: ostomy, tracheostomy, diabetic, and general medical products
Store: mail order only

DEPT. 10736
411 WAVERLY OAKS RD.
WALTHAM, MA 02154
800-225-8446
FAX: 617-894-9519

The Bruce Medical Supply catalog is a valuable aid to persons who are in need of home health products, including those needing goods for laryngectomies, colostomies, ileostomies, urostomies, or mastectomies, as well as diabetes, arthritis, incontinence, or special dietary restrictions. Bruce Medical Supply, which has been in business since 1978, also stocks products designed to make all sorts of routine tasks easier.

The 64-page catalog offers a comprehensive range of ostomy supplies, diabetes monitoring supplies and equipment, bathtub safety benches, tub grips, wheelchairs, walkers, canes, crutches, magnifying glasses, reading glasses, blood pressure kits, stethoscopes, compresses, and similar products. Most of the goods are from well-known firms, including Ames, Amoena, Convatec, Hollister, Johnson & Johnson, Kimberly Clark, Mentor, Procter & Gamble, and 3M.

Books on related topics, and general nursing and caretaker supplies are available. The catalog also features a good selection of dining, food preparation, dressing, grooming, and bathing aids for persons whose range of movement or strength is limited.

Special Factors: Satisfaction is guaranteed; price quote by phone or letter; goods are shipped in unmarked boxes; C.O.D. orders are accepted.

COMFORT HOUSE®

189 FRELINGHUYSEN AVE.
NEWARK, NJ 07114-1595
201-242-8080
FAX: 201-242-0131

Catalog: free
Save: up to 30% (see text)
Pay: check, MO, MC, V, Discover
Sells: all-around helpful tools and gadgets
Store: mail order only

Here are 40 pages of products designed to make the little things easier for everyone, beginning with the catalog itself, which is printed in a big, clear typeface. Comfort House® sells things like cleaning tools with extension poles, that anyone might find useful, as well as electric vegetable peelers and power-seat lifters, designed specifically for those with limited strength and mobility. There are doorknob turners, dressing aids, various gripping devices, exercisers, sleeping and bathing aids, travel accessories, gardening tools, and much more. Comfort House® is not a *discount* catalog, although a couple of price-checks showed savings of up to 32% on some of the body-care products; this is simply a great collection of products that can help people perform everyday tasks more easily and more safely, as well as coping with changed conditions.

Special Factors: Satisfaction is guaranteed; returns in unused condition are accepted within 60 days.

MEDICAL SUPPLY CO., INC.

P.O. BOX 250
HAMBURG, NJ 07419-0250
800-323-9664
201-209-8448
FAX: 201-209-4799

Price List: free with SASE
Save: 30% average
Pay: check or MO
Sells: diapers, underpads, disposable briefs
Store: mail order only

Coping with incontinence is easier now that Attends, Depends, and similar products have come onto the market. But these products aren't cheap, so it's great to find a source for incontinence products at a discount. Medical Supply Co. has been in business since 1977, selling Depends briefs and Chux underpads at savings of up to 50%. For example, Depends selling for 90¢ each in a local drugstore are sold here as

"Incontinence Pants" at 50¢ each (in cases of 50). The Chux underpads run from 13¢ to 41¢ each (sold in cases), depending on the size. Medical Supply accepts Medicaid (in Delaware and New Jersey only) and does not charge shipping on orders delivered in Connecticut, New Jersey, New York, and Pennsylvania. (Customers in other states pay UPS charges collect.)

Medical Supply Co. is offering readers of this book a 10% discount on first orders. Be sure to identify yourself when you order, and take the discount on the goods total. This WBMC reader discount expires February 1, 1997.

Special Factors: Shipping is not charged on deliveries to CT, NJ, NY, and PA; inquire about Medicaid acceptance (if applicable); minimum order is one case.

SENIOR'S NEEDS, INC.

THE BASIC APPAREL CO.
68 STILES RD.
SALEM, NH 03079
800-777-2006 (WEEKDAYS)
FAX: 800-875-1405

Catalog: free
Save: up to 40%
Pay: check, MO, MC, V, AE
Sells: adaptive apparel
Store: mail order only

Senior's Needs was founded to create a source for attractive, well-priced clothing for nursing home residents. The 32-page catalog shows a broad selection of "adaptive apparel" for men and women, in easy-fitting styles and easy-care fabrics. There are quite a few dusters and housedresses, most in back-snap style, and shirts and pants for men. Jackets, nightwear, jogging suits, sweaters, footwear, hosiery, and accessories are offered in both men's and women's styles. Some of the conventionally styled underwear is offered in large sizes—half slips to size 3X, bras to 52DD, and panties to 15 for women, and men's undershirts and shorts to size 4X.

The catalog is geared to people who take care of the clothing needs of nursing home residents and the prices are great—under $28 for dresses, back-snap slips for less than $8, and men's cutaway slacks for $23 are a few examples. Extra-low prices are offered on the Senior's Needs "budget" specials, but there's no choice of color or style.

Special Factors: Satisfaction is guaranteed; authorized returns are accepted; shipping is not charged on orders sent to nursing facilities.

SUPPORT PLUS

99 WEST ST., DEPT.
  WBM96
P.O. BOX 500
MEDFIELD, MA 02052
800-229-2910
508-359-2910
FAX: 508-359-0139

Catalog: free
Save: up to 30%
Pay: check, MO, MC, V, AE, Discover
Sells: support hosiery, therapeutic apparel, foot products, comfort footwear
Store: same address; Tuesday, Thursday, Saturday 10–1

Support Plus has been in business since 1972, and offers an extensive selection of supportive hosiery and undergarments for men and women, as well as comfortable leather footwear. Discounts average about 15%, but some items are priced 30% less than regular retail.

If your physician recommends or prescribes support (elastic) hosiery, you'll find this catalog a helpful guide to what's available. Support Plus offers panty hose, stockings, knee-highs, and men's dress socks in different support strengths. (The compression rating for each style is given in the catalog descriptions.) Among the brands sold here are Bauer & Black, Berkshire, Futuro, Hanes, T.E.D., and Support Plus' own line. Maternity, cotton-soled, control-top, open-toe, and irregular styles are available.

Support Plus also sells posture pads for chairs and beds, joint "wraps" for applications of heat and cold, Dale abdominal and lumbrosacral supports, Futuro braces and joint supports, and personal-care products and bathing aids—eating and dressing implements, bedding, underpads and disposable pants, bath seats and rails, and toilet guard rails. The catalog also features a collection of comfort-styled shoes and slippers for women by Barefoot Freedom, Clinic Shoe, Foot Saver, Daniel Green, Munro, and Soft Spots, in standard and hard-to-fit sizes.

Support Plus is currently offering a bonus-with-purchase on Bauer & Black hosiery, and runs other specials regularly; although the B & B offer may be discontinued, check the catalog for other deals.

Special Factors: Price quote by phone; unworn returns are accepted.

SEE ALSO

Bailey's, Inc. • first-aid kits • **TOOLS**
Campmor • snake bite kits, variety of first-aid kits • **SPORTS**

Chock Catalog Corp. • *snap-back women's clothing* • **CLOTHING**

Creative Health Products • *fitness equipment, blood pressure kits, skinfold calipers, etc.* • **HEALTH**

Defender Industries, Inc. • *first-aid kits, marine safety gear* • **AUTO**

The Faucet Outlet • *bathroom fixture aids for disabled persons* • **HOME: IMPROVEMENT**

Freeda Vitamins, Inc. • *dietary supplements* • **HEALTH**

Goldberg's Marine Distributors • *first-aid kits, marine safety gear* • **AUTO**

Hillestad International, Inc. • *dietary supplements* • **HEALTH**

No Nonsense Direct • *nurses' hosiery* • **CLOTHING**

Okun Bros. Shoes • *nurses' shoes* • **CLOTHING: FOOTWEAR**

Omaha Vaccine Company, Inc. • *biologicals and pharmaceuticals for livestock* • **ANIMAL**

Orion Telescope Center • *telescopes* • **CAMERAS**

Plastic BagMart • *zip-top plastic bags* • **OFFICE: SMALL BUSINESS**

S & S Sound City • *closed-caption decoders* • **APPLIANCES**

Scope City Inc. • *telescopes* • **CAMERAS**

Snugglebundle Enterprises • *child/adult incontinence products* • **CLOTHING: MOTHER AND CHILD**

United Pharmacal Company, Inc. • *animal biologicals and vet instruments* • **ANIMAL**

World Wide Aquatics • *post-mastectomy swimsuits* • **SPORTS**

MUSIC

Instruments, supplies, and services

Professional musicians rarely pay full price for their instruments, and if you buy from the same sources they use, neither will you. The firms listed here sell top-quality instruments, electronics, and supplies, and while they usually serve the knowledgeable, they can assist you even if you're a musical neophyte. If you catch the clerks during a lull in store trade, you can usually get the same kind of help over the phone—but please understand that they're usually very busy. Some of the stores take trade-ins, some rent instruments, and most sell used equipment.

By purchasing from these sources, you can save hundreds of dollars on top-rate equipment, and if you're equipping a band, you might save enough money to buy the van and pay the roadies. Get the best equipment you can—instruments can last a lifetime, and the resale market for quality pieces is good. Buy wisely today and you may be selling your "vintage" ax to Elderly Instruments or Mandolin Brothers 20 years down the road for several times what you paid!

FIND IT FAST

ACCORDIONS • **Accordion-O-Rama**
DRUMS • **American Musical, Sam Ash, Lone Star, Thoroughbred Music**
FRETTED INSTRUMENTS • **American Musical, Metropolitan Music, Shar, Thoroughbred Music, Weinkrantz**
GENERAL, SCHOOL, AND MARCHING BAND INSTRUMENTS • **Giardinelli, Interstate Music, Kennelly Keys, National Educational Music, West Manor**

GUITARS AND ELECTRONICS • *American Musical, Sam Ash, Carvin, Discount Music, Kennelly Keys, Manny's, Thoroughbred Music*
PIANOS AND ORGANS • *Altenburg*
REEDS • *Discount Reed*
SHEET MUSIC • *Patti Music*
STRINGS • *Thoroughbred Music*
VINTAGE INSTRUMENTS • *Elderly Instruments, Mandolin Brothers*

ACCORDION-O-RAMA, INC.

DEPT. WBMC
307 SEVENTH AVE.
NEW YORK, NY 10001
212-675-9089
212-206-8344

Catalog: $1, refundable (see text)
Save: up to 40%
Pay: check, MO, MC, V
Sells: accordions, accessories, and services
Store: same address (20th Floor); Tuesday to Friday 10–5, Saturday 11–3

Accordion-O-Rama, in business since 1950, has an extensive inventory of new and rebuilt accordions and concertinas that are all sold at a discount. Accordion-O-Rama is an authorized dealer and factory-service center for several leading brands, and can customize your instrument to meet your requirements—including MIDI. Concertinas and accordions—electronic, chromatic, diatonic, and piano—are offered here at considerable savings. Accordion-O-Rama carries its own line, as well as instruments by Arpeggio, Avanti, Cordovox, Crumar, Dallape, Elka, Excelsior, Farfisa, Ferrari, Gabbanelli, Galanti, Guerrini, Hohner, Polytone, Sano, Scandalli, Solton, Sonola, Paolo Soprani, Vox, and other firms. The catalog features color photos of individual models with specifications. New and reconditioned models are stocked, and accordion synthesizers, amps, speakers, generators, organ-accordions, and accordion stands are available.

When you write for information, be sure to describe the type of accordion that interests you. In addition to the color catalog ($1), you can request the black-and-white catalog, which is free, or order a video: The "Demonstration" video provides a tour of Accordion-O-Rama and the "Basics of MIDI" tape gives an introduction to MIDI. Either tape can be purchased for $25 or both for $45 (postpaid in the United States).

Accordion-O-Rama is offering readers of this book an extra 2% discount on purchases of new, full-size models. Identify yourself as a reader when you order. This WBMC reader discount expires February 1, 1997.

Special Factors: Trade-ins are welcomed; wholesale prices are based on volume.

ALTENBURG PIANO HOUSE, INC.

━━━━━━

1150 EAST JERSEY ST.

ELIZABETH, NJ 07201

800-526-6979

FAX: 908-527-9210

Brochure: free

Save: 35% minimum

Pay: check, MO, MC, V, AE

Sells: pianos and organs

Store: same address; Monday to Friday 9–9, Saturday 9–6, Sunday 12–5; also Asbury Park, Montclair, Toms River, and Trenton

The Altenburg Piano House has been doing business since 1847, and it's run today by a descendant of the founder. Altenburg sells pianos and organs by "almost all" manufacturers, including its own models and lines by Baldwin, Hammond, Kawai, Kimball, and Mason. Prices are at least 35% below list or suggested retail, and if you write to Altenburg for literature, you'll receive information on its own line of pianos— upright, grand, and console models. Complete specifications are listed for each piano, including details on the encasing, keys, pin block, bridges, soundboard, action, strings, hammer felt, and warranty. If you're in the area of Elizabeth, New Jersey, drop by the Art Deco showroom and hear an Altenburg—they've been recommended by no less than Franz Liszt! And if you're pricing a name-brand model, call or write with the name of the piano or organ for price and shipping details.

Special Factors: Orders are shipped worldwide.

AMERICAN MUSICAL SUPPLY

P.O. BOX 152
SPICER, MN 56288
800-458-4076

Catalog: free
Save: up to 70%
Pay: check, MO, MC, V, Discover
Sells: musical instruments and recording equipment
Store: Victor's House of Music: 235 Franklin Ave., Ridgewood, NJ 07540-3295

  ¡Si!

Forget the brass and woodwinds—American Musical Supply is rock and roll all the way. The 96-page catalog opens with Shure and Audio-Technica mics, and ends with Roland mixers. Recorders, speakers, amps, headsets, signal processors, monitors, DAT and CD players and recorders, equalizers, mastering decks, pedals and effects boxes, cables, pickups, tuners, and other accessories are offered. Guitars are featured as well—the latest acoustic and electric models from Charvel, Fender, Gibson, Ibanez, Martin, and Washburn. The percussion section includes drums by Pearl and Tama, as well as cymbals, chimes, cowbells, and other esoteric instruments. American Musical Supply sells electronic keyboards and accessories, books, manuals, and videos on technique, making music with MIDI, Recorded Versions Guitar transcriptions, and much more. Prices run up to 70% below list, although discounts vary from item to item. AMS is the mail-order division of Victor's House of Music, a third-generation family business. If you need advice on the best equipment for your music, they should be able to help.

Special Factors: Minimum order is $10; C.O.D. orders are accepted.

SAM ASH MUSIC CORP.

DEPT. WBMC
P.O. BOX 9047
HICKSVILLE, NY 11802
800-4-SAM ASH
IN CANADA 800-726-2740
516-333-8700

Information: inquire
Save: up to 40%
Pay: check, MO, MC, V, AE, Discover
Sells: instruments and electronics
Store: 401 Old Country Rd., Carle Place, NY; Monday and Friday 10–9, Tuesday to Thursday, and Saturday 10–6; also New Haven CT; Forest Hills, Huntington Station, White Plains, Brooklyn, and New York, NY; and Cherry Hill, Edison, and Paramus, NJ

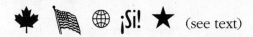 ¡Si! ★ (see text)

In 1924, violinist and bandleader Sam Ash opened a musical-instrument shop in Brooklyn. The company is still family-run, but now boasts ten stores and patronage by superstars, schools and institutions, and recording studios, as well as the music-making general public. Regular half-off specials are a feature here, so don't buy anywhere else until you've given Sam Ash a call.

Musical instruments, musical electronics, karaoke, music software, sound systems, electronic keyboards, recording equipment, disk jockey equipment, digital home pianos, specialized lighting, and accessories are available from hundreds of manufacturers, including Akai, AKG, Armstrong, Audio-Technica, Bach, Benge, Bose, Buffet, Bundy, Casio, Cerwin-Vega, Charvel, Conn, dbx, DigiTech, DOD, Electro-Voice, E-Mu, Ensoniq, Fender, Gemeinhardt, Gibson, Guild, Ibanez, Jackson, JBL, JVC, Karaoke (sing-along machines), Kawai, King, Klipsch, Kurzweil, Leblanc, Ludwig, Marshall, Martin, Mesa-Boogie, Noble & Cooley, Ovation, Paiste, Pearl, Rickenbacker, Roland, Sabian, Selmer, Sennheiser, Shure, Paul Reed Smith, Sony, Suzuki, SWR, Tama, Takamine, Tascam, Technics, Toa, Yamaha, and Zildjian. Sheet music is stocked, repairs and service are performed, and trade-ins are accepted at the stores.

Please note: For a Spanish-speaking sales representative, call 212-719-2299.

Special Factors: Minimum order is $25.

CARVIN CORP.

12340 WORLD TRADE DR.
SAN DIEGO, CA 92128
800-854-2235
FAX: 619-747-0743

Catalog: free
Save: up to 50%
Pay: check, MO, MC, V, AE, Discover
Sells: Carvin instruments and accessories
Store: same address; Monday to Friday
8:30–5; also 7414 Sunset Blvd., Hollywood,
and 1907 N. Main St., Santa Ana, CA; Monday to Friday 10–7, Saturday 10–6, both locations

 ¡Si! ★

Carvin manufactures its own line of instruments and equipment, made to exacting standards. You'll find the specifications, features, and individual guarantees of each instrument noted in the 56-page color catalog; prices are up to 40% less than those of comparable models. You'll also find luminaries of the pop and jazz music world shown throughout the catalog, alongside Carvin equipment—Chet Atkins, David Roe, Bunny Brunel, Greg Allman, and Stanley Clarke are a few.

Mixers, amps, mikes, monitor systems, and electric guitars are offered here, as well as professional-quality guitars designed for the requirements of professional musicians. All of Carvin's instruments and equipment are sold under a ten-day free trial arrangement. Servicing and performance testing is done free of charge during the warranty period, and warranties range from one to five years, depending on the item.

Special Factors: Satisfaction is guaranteed; returns are accepted for refund; minimum order is $25 with credit cards.

DISCOUNT MUSIC SUPPLY

DEPT. WB
41 VREELAND AVE.
TOTOWA, NJ 07512-1120
201-942-9411
FAX: 201-890-7922

Catalog: free
Save: 35% average
Pay: check, MO, MC, V
Sells: musical accessories
Store: mail order only

Rock guitarists should see the 40-page catalog from Discount Music Supply, which sells guitars, strings, and related accessories. DMS sells guitars by Goya/Martin and Hondo, speakers by Celestion, amps by Gorilla and Hondo; the Pignose amp, DiMarzio and Seymour Duncan, Fender, and Select pickups, Audio-Technica and Shure mikes, Sabine's Chromatic Autotuner, Conquest and SpectraFlex cables, Nady devices, Hamilton stands, guitar cleaning products, and effects boxes by Boss and DOD. Studio systems and components by Boss and DigiTech are offered, as well as Hohner and Huang harmonicas and Fender picks. If you use strings by Augustine, Ernie Ball, La Bella, D'Addario, D'Angelico, Darco, Fender, GHS, Guild, Dean Markley, Martin, Maxima, S.I.T., or Vinci, see the catalog for enormous savings.

Discount Music Supply, in business since 1986, can save you an average of 35% on list prices, and much more on selected items and lines. Quantity discounts on strings, for example, can reduce list prices by nearly 70%. Discount Music Supply doesn't list the entire inventory, so if you don't see what you're looking for, call, write, or fax your inquiry.

Special Factors: Quantity discounts are available; authorized returns are accepted within 14 days for exchange, refund, or credit; minimum order is $20.

DISCOUNT REED COMPANY

24307 MAGIC MOUNTAIN PKWY., # 181

VALENCIA, CA 91355

800-428-5993

805-294-9437

FAX: 805-294-9762

Price List: free

Save: up to 45%

Pay: check, MO, MC, V

Sells: reeds for musical instruments

Store: mail order only

Discount Reed sells just that—"mail order reeds at fantastic savings"—through the four-page price list. The firm, which began business in 1980, sells woodwind reeds by the box, priced up to 45% less than the list prices—which represents really big savings if you're used to buying reeds one at a time. Reeds for all types of clarinets and saxophones are stocked, as well as reeds for oboes and bassoons, in strengths from 1 to 5-1/2 (soft to hard). The names include Grand Concert, Dave Guardala, Fred Hemke, Java, Jones (double reeds), Marca, Mitchell Lurie, La Mode, Olivieri, Prestini, Rico, V-12, V-16, Vandoren, and La Voz. (If you're looking for a reed not listed in the flyer, call or write, since it may be available.) In addition, Discount Reed sells Harrison and Vandoren reed cases, reed trimmers, La Voz reed guards, Blue Note sax straps, swabs, and other accessories.

Special Factors: Satisfaction is guaranteed; minumum order is $20 with credit cards.

ELDERLY INSTRUMENTS

P.O. BOX 14210-WM96
LANSING, MI 48901
517-372-7890, EXT. 123
FAX: 517-372-5155

Catalog: free (see text)
Save: 33% average
Pay: check, MO, MC, V, Discover
Sells: new and vintage musical instruments, books, videotapes, and recordings
Store: 1100 North Washington, Lansing, MI; Monday to Wednesday 11–7, Thursday 11–9, Friday and Saturday 10–6

  ¡Si!

Elderly Instruments has an extraordinary selection of in-print, hard-to-find recordings of all types of music, from folk and bluegrass to jazz and classical, listed in the closely printed 106-page "Recordings" catalog. (For a sample of Elderly's picks, call "Dial-a-Ditty-a-Day," several minutes of an Elderly selection: 517-372-1212, touch-tone required.) Elderly Instruments also sells books on dance, repair and construction of instruments, music history, folklore, and even songbooks and videotapes (request the "Books, Videos, and Instructional Tapes" catalog).

Despite the impressive publication department, this firm has built 23 years of business on vintage instruments. Epiphones, Fenders, Martins, Dobros, Gibsons, Rickenbackers, and other electric and acoustic guitars have been offered in the past, as well as banjos, violins, mandolins, and other fretted instruments. (There are two additional catalogs—"Electric" and "Acoustic," for new guitars and effects of each type. Request the catalog that better answers your needs.) Elderly Instruments also sells new instruments, lays claim to the title of world's largest dealer of new Martin guitars, and is among the top 20 Gibson dealers. You'll find a good selection of equipment here by Alvarez-Yairi, Boss, Collings, Crate, DiMarzio, Dobro, DOD, E.S.P., Fender, Gibson, Guild, Martin, Sigma, Steinberger, Stelling, Taylor, and Yamaha, among other names. The monthly "vintage used instruments list" is sent free with catalog orders, or you may subscribe for $12 ($25 outside the United States and Canada). Prices are as low as 50% off list, and everything is covered by the Elderly Instruments guarantee of satisfaction (see the catalog for details).

Please note: Mail-order hours are Monday to Saturday, 9–5.

Special Factors: Satisfaction is guaranteed; unused, authorized returns are accepted within five days for exchange, refund, or credit; minimum order is $10.

GIARDINELLI BAND INSTRUMENT CO., INC.

7845 MALTLAGE DR.
LIVERPOOL, NY 13090
800-288-2334
315-652-4792
FAX: 315-652-4534

Catalog: free
Save: up to 50%
Pay: check, MO, MC, V, AE, Discover
Sells: brasses, woodwinds, and accessories
Store: same address; Monday to Friday 9–7

Giardinelli has been selling fine brasses and woodwinds since 1948, and publishes a 134-page catalog with an exhaustive listing of brass instruments, woodwinds, and accessories for both. Trumpets, flugelhorns, trombones, French horns, euphoniums, tubas, clarinets, flutes, piccolos, saxophones, oboes, and bassoons are all available. The brands include Bach, Besson, Buffet, Bundy, Courtois, DEG, Emerson, Farkas, Gemeinhardt, Getzen, Holton, Humes & Berg, Leblanc, Schilke, Selmer, Signet, Denis Wick, Yamaha, Yanigasawa, and others. Mouthpieces, mutes, reeds, metronomes, tuners, cases, stands, cleaning supplies, and books round out the catalog, and Giardinelli features its own line of fine stock and custom mouthpieces for brasses. Savings run up to 50%, and the customer service department can assist you if you have questions or need advice.

Special Factors: Satisfaction is guaranteed; returns are accepted for exchange, refund, or credit; institutional accounts are available.

INTERSTATE MUSIC SUPPLY

P.O. BOX 51315
NEW BERLIN, WI 53151
800-982-BAND
FAX: 414-786-6840

Catalog: free (see text)
Save: up to 60%
Pay: check, MO, MC, V, Discover
Sells: instruments, electronics, and accessories
Store: Cascio Music Co., 13819 W. National Ave., New Berlin, WI; Monday to Thursday 10–8, Friday 10–5:30, Saturday 10–4:30

Interstate Music Supply is a division of Cascio Music Company, which has been in business since 1949. IMS serves everyone's musical needs, beginning with schools and music teachers. The 200-page *School Discount Catalog* lists a wide range of equipment, at savings of up to 60%. Everything from woodwind reeds and corks to full lines of brass, woodwind, percussion, and stringed instruments is available, including repair kits and parts, cleaning supplies, neckstraps, cases, storage units, music stands, stage lighting, sound systems, piano labs, and even riser setups for bands and orchestras. There are great buys on goods from Anvil, Bach, Blessing, Buffet, Bundy, Dynamic, Emerson, Engelhardt, Fender, Fostex, Franz, Gemeinhardt, Gibson, Holton, Korg, Kramer, Leblanc, Ludwig, Mesa-Boogie, Orff, Ovation, Pearl, Peavey, Roland, Sansui, Schilke, Seiko, Selmer, Trace-Elliot, Vandoren, Vito, Yamaha, and Zildjian. Interstate Music also produces three other catalogs: *Guitars* and *Drums*, 64 pages each of guitar/bass and percussion instruments and accesories, and *Interfaith Musical Supplies* Church and Temple Catalog, which features electronics, instruments, and enough noisemakers (bongos, tone chimes, autoharps, tambourines, cymbals, etc.) to raise the roof. But if you don't see what you want, call or write—it may be available.

Special Factors: Satisfaction is guaranteed; price quote by phone or letter with SASE; returns are accepted within ten days for exchange, refund, or credit; institutional accounts are available; minimum order is $25.

KENNELLY KEYS MUSIC, INC.

20505 HWY. 99
LYNNWOOD, WA 98036
800-426-6409
206-771-7020
FAX: 206-670-6713

Information: price quote
Save: up to 40%
Pay: check, MO, MC, V, AE, Discover
Sells: musical instruments and accessories
Store: same address

Kenelly Keys Music, in business since 1960, offers discounts of up to 40% on the retail prices of instruments and accessories. The brass and woodwind names represented here include Altus, Blessing, Buffet, Burbank, Canadian Brass, Getzen, Holton, Keilworth, LeBlanc, Powell, Schilke, and Yanagisawa. The guitar, keyboard, percussion, and combo departments carry EV, Gibson, Godin, Hamer, Heritage, LP, Mackie, Marshall, Martin, Ovation, Pearl, Seagull, Sonor, Soundtech, and Takamine. Kennelly Keys Music offers a full line-service department for repairs, tune-ups, and questions, and provides "dealer prep" on all instruments it sells. There is no catalog, so call or fax with inquiries and for price quotes; product literature is available.

Special Factors: Institutional accounts are available; authorized returns are accepted; minimum order is $25.

LONE STAR PERCUSSION

10611 CONTROL PLACE
  DR.
DALLAS, TX 75238
214-340-0835
FAX: 214-340-0861

Catalog: free with a long, self-addressed, stamped envelope
Save: 40% average
Pay: check, MO, MC, V, Discover
Sells: percussion instruments
Store: same address; Tuesday to Friday 9:30–5:30, Saturday 9:30–2

Concert, marching, jazz, and rock percussion—Lone Star stocks it all. This firm has been doing business with individuals and institutions worldwide since 1978, and publishes a 48-page catalog that lists drums and heads, cases, drumsticks, keyboard mallets, cymbals, castanets, gongs, tambourines, triangles, wood blocks, bells, percussion for Latin music, and much more. The brands include American Drum, Balter, Deschler, Vic Firth, Gambal, Tom Gauger, Goodman, Grover, Hinger, R. Holmes, Holt, Latin Percussion, Linwood, Ludwig, Malletech, Musser (Ludwig), Payson, Pearl, Premier, Pro-Mark, Regal Tip, Remo, Ross, Sabian, Silverfox, Spectrasound, Tama, Yamaha, Zildjian, etc. In the unlikely event you don't see what you're looking for among the thousands of items listed, call or write—it's probably available.

Special Factors: Satisfaction is guaranteed; authorized returns are accepted within two weeks (a restocking fee of up to 20% may be charged); institutional accounts are available.

MANDOLIN BROTHERS, LTD.

629 FOREST AVE.
STATEN ISLAND, NY
  10310-2576
718-981-3226, 981-8585
FAX: 718-816-4416

Catalog: free
Save: up to 35%
Pay: check, MO, MC, V, AE, Discover
Sells: new and vintage fretted instruments and accessories
Store: same address; Monday to Saturday 10–6
E-mail: Mandolin@ix.netcom.com
CS: 74352,2715@compuserve.com

Mandolin Brothers has been selling vintage fretted instruments at good prices since 1971, and offers select new instruments at a standard discount of 35% from list prices. The 84-page catalog is packed with listings of vintage guitars, mandolins, mandolas, banjos, electric basses, and other stringed instruments. Part of the catalog is devoted to new equipment—guitars, mandolins, banjos, electronics, and accessories. The instruments carried include Benedetto, Breedlove, Collings, D'Angelico, D'Aquisto, Deering, Dobro, Flatiron, Franklin, Gibson, James Goodall, Guild, Heritage, Hofner Basses, Kentucky, Larrivee, Lowden, Martin, National Reso-Phonic, OME, Ovation, M.V. Pedulla, Jose Ramirez, Bart Reiter, Rich & Taylor (banjos), Rickenbacker, Santa Cruz, Steinberger, Stelling, Taylor, Trace (acoustic amps), Wildwood, and Yamaha. There are pickups by DiMarzio, EMG, and Seymour Duncan, travel guitars, cables, strings, straps, frets, mutes, capos, books, videos, and more. Written instrument appraisals and repairs are available, and Mandolin Brothers ships in-stock instruments on a three-day approval basis—and that includes vintage equipment. If you're in the Staten Island area, be sure to visit the well-stocked showroom, an official site on the "New York Music Trail," and try out the instruments.

Special Factors: Satisfaction is guaranteed; returns are accepted within three days.

MANNY'S MUSIC MAILBOX

ATTN: MAILBOX MUSIC
156 W. 48TH ST.
NEW YORK, NY 10036
212-869-5172
FAX: 212-391-9250

Catalog: free
Save: up to 50%
Pay: check, MO, MC, V, AE, DC, Discover
Sells: instruments, electronics, and accessories
Store: same address; Monday to Saturday 10–6; also Audio Technique, 1600 Broadway, New York, NY

  ¡Si!

Manny's has been selling musical instruments since 1935, and it's rare that this store on New York City's "Music Row" doesn't have a rock luminary or two checking out the equipment. The 104-page Manny's Music Mailbox catalog (call for a copy) testifies to the firm's illustrious history as a purveyor to the stars, and showcases a fraction of the stock. Manny's runs sales regularly, bringing the standard 30% discounts up to 50%. You can see the catalog, or call for a price quote on instruments, electronics, and accessories, from amps and mixers to fine woodwinds and brass instruments, by Art, Bach, Buffet, Casio, DOD/Digitech, EMG, Fender, King, Gibson, Hohner, Ibanez, JBL, Korg, Leblanc, Ludwig, Marshall, Martin, Music Writer (NoteStation), Ovation, Pearl, Peavey, Roland, Shilke, Steinberger, Tascam, Washburn, and Yamaha. Manny's also has a complete computer department. You'll find just about anything you need here (except grand pianos and accordions), and if an item isn't stocked, Manny's can probably get it for you.

Special Factors: Price quote by phone, fax, or letter with SASE.

METROPOLITAN MUSIC CO.

P.O. BOX 1415
STOWE, VT 05672
802-253-4814
FAX: 802-253-9834

Catalog: $1.25
Save: up to 50%
Pay: check or MO
Sells: stringed instruments and accessories
Store: mail order only

Metropolitan Music Co., in business since 1928, sells stringed instruments and accessories through the 40-page catalog and maintains a workshop for repairs and adjustments. There are some "student" quality instruments here, but most of the models are chosen for professional musicians. Metropolitan carries John Juzek violins, violas, cellos, and basses, and bows by F.N. Voirin, Glasser, and Emile Dupree. Bridges, pegs by Taperfit and other firms, bow hair and parts, fingerboards, necks, chin rests, Resonans shoulder rests, Ibex tools, strings, cases, and bags are all stocked. This is an excellent source for the experienced musician who is familiar with the instruments and accessories. Books on instrument repair and construction are available, as well as a fine selection of wood, parts, and tools. The prices listed in the catalog are subject to discounts of 30% to 50%.

Special Factors: Price quote by phone or letter with SASE; minimum order is $15.

NATIONAL EDUCATIONAL MUSIC CO.

DEPT. WBMC
1181 RTE. 22
MOUNTAINSIDE, NJ 07092
908-232-6700
FAX: 908-789-3025

Catalog: free
Save: up to 60%
Pay: check, MO, MC, V, AE
Sells: instruments and accessories
Store: mail order only

NEMC has been supplying schools with new band and orchestra instruments since 1957, at savings of up to 60% on list prices. NEMC sells brass, woodwind, stringed, and percussion instruments by Alpine,

Amati, Bach, Blessing, Buffet, Bundy, Decatur, DEG, F.E. Olds, Fox, Gemeinhardt, Getzen, Holton, International Strings, John Juzek, Korg, Larilee, Leblanc, Lewis, Ludwig, Meisel, Mirafone, Pearl, F.A. Reynolds, Ross, Schreiber, Selmer, Signet, Vito, and other makers. The 60-page catalog also offers imported master violins and violas, as well as cases, stands, strings, bows, and other accessories. NEMC provides "the longest warranty in the industry" on woodwinds, drums, and brass and stringed (except fretted) instruments.

Canadian readers, please note: Only U.S. funds are accepted.

Special Factors: Returns (of instruments) are accepted within seven days (a restocking fee may be charged); minimum order is $50.

PATTI MUSIC COMPANY

414 STATE ST., DEPT. WC
MADISON, WI 53703
608-257-5877
FAX: 608-257-5847

Catalog: $3 (see text)
Save: 20% average
Pay: check, MO, MC, V, Discover
Sells: sheet music, music books, teaching methods and aids, metronomes, etc.
Store: same address; Monday to Saturday 9:30–5:30

One of the hardest items to find at a discount is sheet music, but that's the raison d'être of Patti Music Company's mail-order department. Patti Music has been in business since 1936, and publishes a 124-page catalog of sheet music and books and methods for piano and organ, and a selection of metronomes and tuners. Savings on the sheet music run around 15%, and the metronomes are discounted up to 33%.

Piano methods, ensembles, and solos are among the 11,000 titles featured, from scores of music publishers from Alfred to Yorktown Music Press. The catalog lists organ music for religious holidays, Christmas music and Broadway shoes, and flashcards, manuscript paper, theory books, and other teaching aids. The proficiency levels of the music and instructional material run from beginner to advanced. In addition to sheet music, there are key-wound, quartz, and electronic metronomes from Franz, Matrix, Seiko, and Wittner, and chromatic tuners by Seiko.

Please note: The $3 catalog fee is waived for music professionals requesting a copy on letterhead or enclosing a business card.

Special Factors: Discounts are available through the catalog only, not in the store.

SHAR PRODUCTS COMPANY

P.O. BOX 1411
ANN ARBOR, MI 48106
800-248-7427
800-793-4334 (CUSTOMER
    SERVICE)
800-438-4538 (FINE
    INSTRUMENTS)
FAX: 313-665-0829

Catalog: free
Save: up to 50%
Pay: check, MO, MC, V, Discover
Sells: sheet music, stringed instruments, videos, accessories
Store: 2465 S. Industrial Hwy., Ann Arbor, MI; Tuesday to Friday 9–6, Saturday 9–5

 (see text)

"Shar is managed by knowledgeable string players and teachers, who are sympathetic to the needs of the string community" states the firm, which has been in business since 1962, and prices its goods up to 50% below list or full retail prices. The 64-page general catalog gives equal time to stringed instruments and to the firm's extensive collection of classical music videos and accessories. If you play violin, viola, cello, or bass, see the catalog for the cases, bows, chin and shoulder rests, strings, bridges, tailpieces, pegs, music stands, humidifying tubes, endpins, and other supplies and equipment. Student violins by Fischer, Hoffman, Schneider, and Suzuki are available, as well as a large collection of new, old, and rare violins by master violin makers.

The accessories catalog features hundreds of books of sheet music, manuals, videotapes, and audiocassettes. (The separate sheet music catalog, with thousands of titles, is available for $2.) Shar sells the Suzuki books and records line, videotapes of master artists (Casals, Segovia, Pavarotti, Heifetz, and others) in performance, classical recordings on CD, and sheet music for a wide range of instruments. Not all goods are discounted, but savings overall average 30%, and selected lines are offered at further savings periodically.

Canadian readers, please note: Personal checks are not accepted.

Special Factors: Satisfaction is guaranteed; C.O.D. orders are accepted.

THOROUGHBRED MUSIC

Catalog: free
Save: up to 40%
Pay: check, MO, MC, V, AE, Discover
Sells: music electronics and accessories
Store: three stores in Clearwater, Sarasota, and Tampa, FL

5511 PIONEER PARK BLVD.
TAMPA, FL 33634
800-800-4654
813-889-3871
FAX: 813-881-1896

Serious rock musicians and studio engineers should see the 114-page catalog from Thoroughbred Music, which showcases amps, CD and DAT players and recorders, drum machines and effects boxes, MIDI equipment, special-effect lighting, matador timbales, and hundreds of other electronics and instruments (guitars and bass, banjos, mandolins, drums, etc.). The manufacturers represented include Akai, Audio Technica, dbx, Fostex, Gibson, Guild, Hartke, Ibanez, Jackson, Klipsch, Lexicon, Mackie, Marshall, Ovation, Pearl, Rickenbacker, Roland, Shure, Takamine, Tama, Tascam, Yamaha, and Zildjian. The catalog ends with eight pages of instructional books, tapes, and videos.

If you're in the Clearwater area, stop in to see who's playing at Thoroughbred's Kapok Pavilion. Catalog customers enjoy the same "guaranteed low prices" enjoyed in the store, and if you don't see what you're looking for, call—it may be available.

Special Factors: Satisfaction is guaranteed; price quote by phone or letter.

WEINKRANTZ MUSICAL SUPPLY CO., INC.

870 MARKET ST.,
SUITE 1265
SAN FRANCISCO, CA
94102-2907
415-399-1201
FAX: 415-399-1705

Catalog: free
Save: up to 50%
Pay: check, MO, MC, V
Sells: stringed instruments and accessories
Store: same address; Monday to Friday 9–5, PST

Stringed instruments are the whole of Weinkrantz's business—violins, violas, cellos, and basses. Weinkrantz, founded in 1975, prices the instruments and accessories 30% to 50% below suggested retail. The 40-page catalog lists the available instruments and outfits, cases, music stands, metronomes, bows, strings, and other supplies. There are several pages of strings alone, including Jargar, Kaplan, Pirastro, Prim, and Thomastik. Weinkrantz carries violins and violas by T.G. Pfretzschner, Roma, Ernst Heinrich Roth, and Roman Teller. Cellos by these firms and Karl Hauser, Wenzel Kohler, Lothar Semmlinger, and Anton Stohr are cataloged, as well as basses from Enesco, Roth, and Emanuel Wilfer. Instruments from well-known smaller workshops are also in stock, but not cataloged because of limited production. Call or write with specific requests.

If you don't want to buy an outfit, you can order the bow, case or bag, rosin, string adjusters, and other equipment à la carte. Strings, bow hair, chin rests, bridges, metronomes, and tuners are all sold at a discount. Instrument bags and cases by Gewa, Gordge, Jaeger, Reunion Blues, and Winter are also available.

Canadian readers, please note: Only U.S. funds are accepted.

Special Factors: Satisfaction guaranteed (see the catalog for the policy on strings); minimum order is $10 with credit cards; orders are shipped worldwide (to select destinations).

WEST MANOR MUSIC

831 EAST GUN HILL RD.
BRONX, NY 10467-6109
718-655-5400

Price List: free
Save: 45% average
Pay: check, MO, MC, V
Sells: musical instruments
Store: same address; Monday to Friday 9–4, Saturday 10–3 (in June and Sept.)

  ¡Si!

West Manor Music has been supplying schools and institutions with musical instruments since 1952, and offers a wide range of equipment at average discounts of 45%. The 16-page catalog lists clarinets, flutes, piccolos, saxophones, oboes, trumpets, trombones, French horns, cornets, flugelhorns, euphoniums, Sousaphones, violas, violins, cellos, guitars, pianos, drums, cymbals, xylophones, glockenspiels, and other instruments. Drum stands and heads, strings, reeds, cases, music stands, metronomes, mouthpieces, and other accessories are sold. The brands represented include Alpine, Amati, Armstrong, Artley, Benge, Besson, Blessing, Buffet, Bundy, Conn, DEG, Fender, Fox, Gemeinhardt, Holton, King, Leblanc, Ludwig, Meisel, Noblet, Olds, Premier, Sabian, Selmer, Signet, Vito, and Zildjian, among others. All of the instruments sold are new, guaranteed for one year. West Manor also offers an "overhaul" service for popular woodwinds and brasses, and can perform repairs as well.

Special Factors: Quantity discounts are available; minimum order is $25, $100 with credit cards.

SEE ALSO

Adventures in Cassettes • *greatest hits compilations* • **BOOKS: RECORDINGS**
Audio House • *used CDs* • **BOOKS: RECORDINGS**
Berkshire Record Outlet, Inc. • *classical recordings* • **BOOKS: RECORDINGS**
Cherry Tree Toys, Inc. • *music box parts* • **CRAFTS: WOODCRAFT**
Dover Publications, Inc. • *classical music scores* • **BOOKS**
Wholesale Tape and Supply Company • *tape duplicating machines and equipment* • **APPLIANCES**

OFFICE AND BUSINESS

Office machines, furniture, and supplies; printing and related services

If you're using a single source for your office needs, you're probably paying more than you should on supplies, printing, furnishings, and the countless things you need to keep your business going. You can begin a cost-control program by having your buyer send for the catalogs listed here, to build a file of discount sources for most of your needs.

If you're the head of a small business, you might consider buying printed envelopes from the U.S. Postal Service. The USPS and the Stamped Envelope Agency, a private concern, offer envelopes with embossed stamps (postage) in windowed or plain styles, size 6-3/4 or 10, with up to seven lines of printing (maximum of 47 characters per line), at about the cost of the postage and a box of envelopes—which is like getting the printing free. Ask for PS Form 3203 from your local post office. You can also order stamps by mail or phone, from sheets of 25 to coils of 500. Ask for PS Form 3227 at your local post office, or call 800-STAMP-24 to order by phone (Discover, MasterCard, and VISA are accepted).

Several of the firms listed here sell computers and supplies, but hardware and software specialists are listed in the next section, "Computing." Look there for vendors of computers, peripherals, software, computing furniture, paper goods, supplies, and services.

For bulk pricing on garbage bags, mailroom supplies, and other packaging materials, see the listings in "Office: Small Business," following "Computing."

For office furnishings, see the "Find it Fast" listing in the introduction to "Home: Furnishings."

FIND IT FAST

BUSINESS CARDS, STATIONERY, FORMS • **Brown Print, Paper Access, Pennywise**
CASH REGISTERS • **Business Technologies, Quill**
GENERAL OFFICE SUPPLIES • **Mail Center USA, OfficeMax, Pennywise, Quill, Viking**
OFFICE FURNITURE • **Alfax, Business & Institutional Furniture, Factory Direct Furniture, Frank Eastern, National Business Furniture, Office Furniture Center, OfficeMax, Pennywise, Quill, Staples, Viking**
OFFICE MACHINES • **OfficeMax, Quill, Staples**
POSTAL SCALES • **Triner Scale**
RECYCLED GOODS AND RECYCLING CONTAINERS • **Business & Institutional Furniture, Factory Direct Furniture, Quill, Viking**
SAFES • **Safe Specialties, Value-tique**

ALFAX WHOLESALE FURNITURE

370 SEVENTH AVE.,
   SUITE 1101
NEW YORK, NY
   10001-3981
800-221-5710
212-947-9560
FAX: 212-947-4734

Catalog: free
Save: up to 51%
Pay: check, MO, MC, V, AE
Sells: office and institutional furniture
Store: mail order only

¡Si!

Alfax has been selling office furnishings since 1946 and does a brisk business with institutional and commercial buyers, especially schools and churches. The best discounts are given on quantity purchases, but even individual items are reasonably priced.

The 108-page color catalog shows furnishings for offices, cafeterias, libraries, conference rooms, and even religious institutions. Tables and chairs are offered in several styles, as well as a range of files and literature storage systems. There are several pages of institutional nursery and child-care furnishings, play centers, cots, and accessories. Pulpits and lecterns, stackable padded pews, P.A. systems, trophy cases, carpet mats, lockers, hat racks, park benches, heavy steel shelving, prefabricated office and computer stations and workstations are just a few of the institutional furnishings and fixtures available. Representative brands include Abco, Bevis, Bretford, D.M.I., Globe, Harvard, High Point, Krueger, Lyon Metal, Samsonite, and Sauder. Many products have home applications, and all of the equipment is designed for years of heavy use.

Special Factors: Satisfaction is guaranteed; institutional accounts are available.

BROWN PRINT & CO.

P.O. BOX 935
TEMPLE CITY, CA 91780
818-286-2106

Price List and Samples: $2
Save: up to 40%
Pay: check or MO
Sells: custom-designed business cards
Store: mail order only

Brown Print & Co. has been designing and printing business cards and stationery since 1966 and offers the person looking for something different just that. Mr. Brown, the proprietor, will send you a generous assortment of actual samples, ranging from black glossy stock and gold foil with iridescent metallic colors to standard black and white cards with raised inks and artwork. Fold-overs and other unusual formats are also available. Mr. Brown's talents would be wasted on someone who wanted a conventional card; his specialty is unusual design, and he enjoys working with his customers to create "the amusing, the novel, and other effective visual concepts."

Special Factors: Quantity discounts are available; minimum order is 500 cards; online with Prodigy.

BUSINESS & INSTITUTIONAL FURNITURE COMPANY, INC.

■

BOX 92069
MILWAUKEE, WI
  53202-0069
414-272-6080
FAX: 414-272-0248

Catalog: free
Save: up to 50%
Pay: check, MO, MC, V, AE, Discover
Sells: office and institutional furnishings
Store: 605 N. Broadway Ave., Milwaukee, WI; Monday to Friday 9–5

Although the best prices at B & I are found on quantity purchases, even individual pieces of furniture and office equipment are competitively priced. The 84-page catalog is geared for those who are furnishing offices, but many items are appropriate for home use as well. B & I has been in business since 1960, and offers a lowest-price guarantee (see the catalog for terms). Office furniture is featured, including desks, files, bookcases, credenzas, and panels and panel systems (for office partitioning). The seating runs from stacking lunchroom chairs to leather-upholstered ergonomic executive thrones—reception, clerical, specialty, folding—they're all here. There are data and literature storage units, computer workstations, waste cans, mats, announcement boards, outdoor furniture, energy-saving devices, and much more. Over 250 brands are represented, and B & I can provide space planning and design services, free of charge.

Special Factors: "15-year, no-risk guarantee"; quantity discounts are available.

BUSINESS TECHNOLOGIES, INC.

426 W. FIFTH ST.
DUBUQUE, IA 52001
319-556-7994
FAX: 319-556-2512

Catalog: free
Save: 33% average
Pay: company check, MO, MC, V, AE
Sells: cash registers and related supplies
Store: same address; Monday to Friday
8:30–5

Business Technologies makes ringing up sales its business, selling Sharp cash registers, and supplies for virtually all makes of cash register. The firm was established in 1985, and will send you manufacturers' brochures, a guide to selecting the right register for your needs, and a roster of optional accessories that will help you customize the register to the needs of your business. Even the "simple" machines have programmable tax and percentage capabilities, and the top-of-the-line models are built-in bookkeepers and gofers: one system can enable a restaurant to keep track of employees' tips, track its guests' balances, and even transmit an order to a kitchen printer. Management reports, credit authorization, currency conversion, scanner functions, and other features are available, depending on the model. Prices at Business Technologies are an average of 33% below list, and the firm provides technical support, a one-year warranty, and free programming.

Special Factors: Price quote by phone, fax, or letter; minimum order is $10.

FACTORY DIRECT FURNITURE

P.O. BOX 92967
MILWAUKEE, WI 53202
800-972-6570
414-289-9770
FAX: 414-289-9946

Catalog: free
Save: up to 70%
Pay: check, MO, MC, V, AE
Sells: office furniture and institutional equipment
Store: mail order only

The 64-page catalog from Factory Direct Furniture features some of the best buys around on office furniture, filing cabinets, bookcases, seating, workstations, storage units, office panel systems, and institutional furnishings. Factory Direct Furniture has been in business since 1974, and carries ergonomic seating for the executive as well as support staff, a full range of files, panel systems, computer workstations and work centers, bulletin and announcement boards, reception furniture, lockers, stacking chairs, and conference furniture. The manufacturers represented include Allied, Balt, Bevis, BPI (office panels), Diversified, DMI, Edsal, Excel, FireKing, Ghent, Global Furniture, Globe, Hale, Harvard, High Point, Integra, Jefsteel, Krueger, La-Z-Boy, Lee, MLP, National, Planto, SafCo, Samsonite, Sauder, Sentry (safes), Signore, Sirco, Stylex, and Virco, among others. Savings of 40% are routine, and a number of items are tagged 70% below manufacturers' list prices.

Please note: Factory Direct Furniture offers a seven-year guarantee on everything it sells, normal wear and tear excepted. See the catalog for details on the warranty and the firm's "meet or beat" pricing policy.

Special Factors: Satisfaction is guaranteed; quantity discounts are available; institutional accounts are available.

FRANK EASTERN CO.

599 BROADWAY
NEW YORK, NY
10012-3258
212-219-0007
FAX: 212-219-0722

Catalog: $1
Save: up to 60%
Pay: check, MO, MC, V
Sells: office, institutional, and computer furniture
Showroom: same address; Monday to Friday 9–5

 ¡Si!

Frank Eastern, in business since 1946, offers furnishings and equipment for business and home offices at discounts of up to 60% on list and comparable retail. Specials are run in every 72-page catalog. Frank Eastern's offerings include desks, chairs, filing cabinets, bookcases, storage units, computer workstations, and wall systems and panels. Seating is especially well represented: ergonomic, executive, clerical, drafting, waiting room, conference, folding, and stacking models in wood, leather, chrome, and plastic were all shown in the most recent catalog. Ergonomic seating is a Frank Eastern specialty, and the prices here are a good 25% less than those listed in two comparable office-supply catalogs. Manufacturers represented include Allied, BPI, Global Furniture, Globe Business, Jefsteel, Sauder, and Sirco. Don't overlook good buys on solid oak bookcases, wall organizers, lateral filing cabinets, and mobile computer workstations.

Special Factors: Satisfaction is guaranteed; quantity discounts are available; minimum order is $75 with credit cards.

MAIL CENTER USA

MED TECH PLAZA
8666 HUEBNER RD.,
SUITE 100-WBM
SAN ANTONIO, TX 78240
210-641-9844
FAX: 210-641-9795

Catalog: $5 (see text)
Save: up to 70%
Pay: check, MO, MC, V, AE, Discover
Sells: office supplies and equipment, mail-room supplies, etc.
Store: 32 locations in Austin and San Antonio, TX

Mail Center USA runs a fleet of mailing centers in San Antonio and Austin, but is listed here for its mail-order office-supply business. You'll save 30% to 40% on *everything* in the big catalog ($5), and up to 70% on products featured in the quarterly sales catalogs, which are free to customers who order at least once a year.

The big, full-color catalog runs to 328 pages and offers everything in office needs, from accordion files to ZIP-code directories. The manufacturers represented include AccuFax, Bates, Canon, Curtis, Day Runner, Fellowes, G.E., Hewlett Packard, ITT, Ledu, Maxell, Mont Blanc, Panasonic, Pollenex, Qume, Rolodex, Stabilo, 3M, Trend Enterprises, and Verbatim, among others. Mail Center USA offers great discounts, which cover printing services as well (greeting cards, order forms, checks, labels, business stationery, etc.).

Special Factors: Satisfaction is guaranteed; authorized returns are accepted for exchange, refund, or credit; institutional accounts are available; minimum order is $15; the company is online with Prodigy.

NATIONAL BUSINESS FURNITURE, INC.

735 N. WATER ST.

P.O. BOX 92952

MILWAUKEE, WI 53202

414-276-8511

FAX: 414-276-8371

Catalog: free

Save: 31% to 64%

Pay: check, MO, MC, V, AE

Sells: office and computer furnishings

Store: mail order only

You can furnish your office for less through the 132-page catalog from National Business Furniture, which offers everything from announcement boards to portable offices at savings of up to 64%. NBF has been in business since 1975 and sells office systems, desks and tables for every purpose, credenzas, bookcases, shelving, computer workstations, desk organizers, literature racks, service carts, lockers, floor mats, reception furniture, and much more. The selection is super: There's a range of filing cabinets, and an extensive line of seating, including executive, clerical, luxury, ergonomic, conference, folding, stacking, and reception chairs. The manufacturers include DMI, Fire King, Global, Globe, Harvard, High Point Furniture, KI, La-Z-Boy Chair, National Office Furniture, Riverside, Safco, Samsonite, Sauder, Signore, and Stylex, among others.

Special Factors: Price quote by phone or letter with SASE; quantity discounts are available.

OFFICE FURNITURE CENTERS, INC.

135 BEAVER ST.

WALTHAM, MA 02154

800-343-4222

617-893-7300

FAX: 617-893-1505

Catalog: free

Save: up to 50%

Pay: check, MO, MC, V, AE

Sells: office furnishings

Store ("mini-showroom"): 370 Seventh Ave., Suite 1101, New York, NY

The 48-page catalog from Office Furniture Center offers attractive chairs, desks, workstations, filing cabinets, bookcases, partition systems, and other business furniture. Office Furniture has been in business since 1985, and sells at discounts that average about 35%, and reach 50% on some goods. The brands include Belcino, Bevis, Bush, DMI, Globe, Haskell, High Point, Lee, Meilink, Signore, Stacor, and Stylex, among others. Office Furniture Center's arrangements with over 250 manufacturers help ensure prompt shipment of your order.

Special Factors: Quantity discounts are available.

OFFICEMAX, INC.

3605 WARRENSVILLE CENTER RD.
SHAKER HEIGHTS, OH 44122-5203
800-788-8080

Catalog: free
Save: up to 70%
Pay: check, MO, MC, V, AE, Discover, OfficeMax account
Sells: office supplies and equipment
Store: stores nationwide (call for nearest location); Monday to Friday 8 A.M.–9 P.M., Saturday 9–9, Sunday 11–6 (Sunday hours vary by location)

OfficeMax, with over 350 locations, is one of the country's largest office products superstore chains. The stores themselves offer discounts of up to 70% on thousands of office and computer products, while the 220-page color catalog showcases the best-selling items—from paper clips to computers—and includes list prices, the OfficeMax discount prices, and your savings. You'll recognize the brands: Acco, Avery, Bush, Compaq, Cross, Dennison, Digital, Eldon, Epson, Global, Hewlett Packard, IBM, Lotus, Macintosh, Mont Blanc, O'Sullivan, Rolodex, Sentry, Smead, Texas Instruments, and Xerox are a few. If you don't see what you want in the catalog, it can probably be special-ordered from the master catalog at all OfficeMax stores. Shipping is free on orders of $100 or more if you're within the trading area of an OfficeMax store. Call for locations, and the current catalog.

Special Factors: Satisfaction is guaranteed; returns are accepted in the original packaging, with receipt, within 30 days of purchase; shipping is free on orders of $100 or more within designated store areas; C.O.D. orders are accepted.

PAPER ACCESS INC.

———

23 W. 18TH ST.
NEW YORK, NY 10011
800-PAPER-01
212-463-7035
FAX: 212-463-7022

Catalog: free
Save: up to 50%
Pay: check, MO, MC, V, AE
Sells: specialty papers for desktop publishing, labels, etc.
Store: same address

Paper Access, a new entry in the burgeoning laser printing supplies market, offers a winning pairing of good prices with great selection. The 64-page color catalog runs from recycled papers to presentation envelopes, and includes granite, laid, marbled, embossed, watermarked, neon, vellum, deckle-edge, parchment, Oriental, acid-free, foil, and graduated color papers, card stock, brochure forms, labels, folders, mailers, and more. The prices better those of other laser paper specialists by 10% to 50%. Paper Access' color/pattern choice is also superior to what the firm's most prominent competitor offers. These are top-of-the-line papers from well-known names—Beckett, Crane, Cross Pointe, Fabriano, Gilbert, Hammermill, Letraset, Neenah, James River/Curtis, Riverside, Simpson, Strathmore, Wausau, and Zanders. And to make sure you know exactly what you're ordering, there's the "Paper Access Kit" ($25), with over 500 different full-size paper samples, and some envelopes. On top of everything, shipping is free on most orders!

Special Factors: Satisfaction is guaranteed; shipping is not charged on orders within the continental United States; returns are accepted for exchange, refund, or credit.

PENNYWISE OFFICE PRODUCTS

———

4350 KENILWORTH AVE.
EDMONSTON, MD 20781
301-699-1000
FAX: 301-277-6700

Catalog: free
Save: up to 65%
Pay: check, MO, MC, V, AE
Sells: office supplies and equipment
Store: mail order only

Pennywise is a new entry in the discount office supply arena, but it honors the formula that works: Low prices on everyday office needs, and free shipping on qualifying orders. Place an order from the 64-page catalog of specials, and you'll receive the "big book" that showcases over 18,000 products. Both list and the Pennywise discount prices are listed, and a number of items that are usually sold by the box are available here by the piece—helpful if your pens keep drying up before you can use them. In addition to supplies, Pennywise sells office furniture, electronics, some peripherals, and business services—rubber stamps, business cards and stationery, printed envelopes and binders, embossing stamps, imprinted pens and gifts, and more. Orders of $25 or more (with some exceptions) are delivered free within the United States, and open accounts are available.

Wholesale buyers, please note: Pennywise *does not* sell goods for resale.

Special Factors: Satisfaction is guaranteed; shipping is not charged.

QUILL CORPORATION

P.O. BOX 94080
PALATINE, IL 60094-4080
708-634-4800
FAX: 708-634-5708

Catalog: free (see text)
Save: up to 80%
Pay: check, MO, MC, V (see text)
Sells: office supplies and equipment
Store: mail order only

Quill, founded in 1956, offers businesses, institutions, and professionals savings of up to 80% on a wide range of office supplies and equipment. There are real buys on Quill's house brand of office and computer supplies, which are comparable in performance and quality to name brands costing much more. The monthly 56-page catalogs feature general office supplies and equipment, including files, envelopes, mailers, and ribbons and elements for typewriters, word processors, and computer printers. In addition to everyday needs—labels, scissors, paper trimmers, pens and pencils, etc.—Quill sells copiers and supplies, word processors, telephones, fax machines, binders and machines, dictating machines, accounting supplies, chairs, and much more. The computer lines include computers and peripherals, disk drives, network products, software, surge suppressors, disks, and storage units. The brands available through Quill include Ashton-Tate, Citizen, Diablo, Epson, Everex, Hammermill, Hewlett Packard, Honeywell, IBM, Logitech, Lotus, Olivetti, Panasonic, Sanyo, Star, Texas Instruments, Ventura, and Word-Perfect, among others. Quill also runs a stationery department with great prices on custom-imprinted business stationery, labels, and forms.

Please note: Quill does business with companies and professionals. Terms (30 days net) are available to qualified businesses.

Special Factors: Satisfaction is guaranteed; institutional accounts are available; returns are accepted.

SAFE SPECIALTIES, INC.

10932 MURDOCK RD.,

SUITE 104-05A

KNOXVILLE, TN 37922

800-695-2815

615-675-2815

FAX: 615-675-2850

Catalog: $2
Save: 30% average
Pay: check, MO, MC, V, AE, Discover
Sells: home and office safes
Store: same address; Monday to Friday 9–6

Safe Specialties, Inc., has been selling home and office safes since 1989, and offers popular home and office models at an average of 30% off list prices. If you're shopping for a depository safe, pistol box, gun safe, secured box for your RV or truck, a data or diskette safe, in-wall or in-floor safe, fire-resistant file cabinet, or other model, try Safe Specialties: Models from Amsec, Cannon, Crystal Vault, DeCoy, FireKing, Ft. Knox, Hayman, Homak, Liberty, Meilink, Star, and other firms are available, at competitive prices. Money-handling equipment—cash drawers, coin counters, money bags, and related products—are also offered.

Safe Specialties is offering readers a discount of 2% on their first order paid by check or money order, not credit card. Be sure to identify yourself as a WBMC reader when you order, and deduct the discount from the cost of the goods only. This WBMC reader discount expires February 1, 1997.

Special Factors: Inquire for information on shipping rates and methods.

STAPLES, INC.

**ATTN: MARKETING
   SERVICES
100 PENNSYLVANIA AVE.
P.O. BOX 9328
FRAMINGHAM, MA
   01701-9328
800-333-3330
FAX: 508-370-8750**

Catalog: free
Save: 50% average
Pay: check, MO, MC, V, AE, Discover, Staples Charge
Sells: office supplies, furniture, and business machines
Store: 130 stores in CA, CT, DC, DE, MA, MD, NH, NJ, NY, OH, PA, RI, and VA (locations are listed in the catalog)

Staples delivers "The Price Revolution in Office Products," an office superstore with deep discounts on every item. Staples was founded in 1986 and has earned a loyal following among buyers for small and home offices, as well as larger firms. Staples publishes a 200-page catalog of products with the "catalog list" prices and the Staples price. These are not closeouts, seconds, or unbranded goods, but first-quality products from Acco, Adams (forms), Alvin, Apple Computer, AT&T, Bates, Brother, Canon, Casio, Cross, Curtis, Dell, Dennison Carter's, Eldon, Esselte, Faber Castell, GBC, Globe-Weis, Hammermill, Hewlett Packard, IBM, Maxell, Mont Blanc, Murata, Olympus (recorders), Panasonic, Parker, Phone-Mate, Ricoh, Rolodex, Rubbermaid, SCM, Sentry (safes), Sharp, Sony, Southworth (paper), Texas Instruments, 3M, Vanguard, Velobind, Verbatim, Waterman (pens), and Wilson Jones, among others. You can order office furniture, computers and supplies, paper and forms, filing supplies, business cases, calendars, pens and pencils, adhesives, mailing room supplies, janitorial products, fax machines, copiers, phones and phone machines, and much more through the catalog or by phone. If there's a trade-off for the savings and product choice, it's in *options,* like color or odd sizes.

Staples offers a free, no-obligation membership card that entitles you to extra savings on selected items. A separate Staples charge card is also available, and you can apply for either through the catalog.

Special Factors: Returns in original packaging are accepted within 30 days for exchange, refund, or credit; minimum order is $15 with credit cards.

TRINER SCALE

2842 SANDERWOOD
MEMPHIS, TN 38118
901-363-7040
FAX: 901-363-3114

Flyer: free
Save: 30% (see text)
Pay: check, MO, MC, V, Discover
Sells: manual and electronic scales
Store: same address; Monday to Friday
8–4:30

Triner Scale, which was founded in 1897, sells a full line of mechanical and electronic scales. Triner also sells a pocket scale, a precision instrument that weighs things (up to four ounces). A finger ring permits the scale to hang while measurements are taken; the thing to be weighed is secured with an alligator clip. Suggested uses include postage determination (a rate chart is included), food measurement, lab use, craft and hobby use, and weighing herbs. It's a useful item to have on hand, and it can give you accurate readings of postage costs. The pocket scale costs under $10, and the electronic mini-scales, $125; inquire for information.

Wholesale buyers: Quantity pricing begins at $6.50 for 1 to 249 units.
Special Factors: Shipping is not charged.

TURNBAUGH PRINTERS SUPPLY CO.

104 S. SPORTING HILL RD.
MECHANICSBURG, PA
17055-3057
717-737-5637

Catalog: $1
Save: see text
Pay: check or MO
Sells: printing supplies and new and used equipment
Store: same address; Monday to Friday 8–4

Turnbaugh offers the printer working in the manner of Gutenberg new and used presses, type, and related equipment and supplies. Savings on used equipment are as much as 70%, compared to the prices of new goods. Turnbaugh's stock is listed in *Printer's Bargain News,* a broadside that is published every two years.

Turnbaugh has been in business since 1931, and sells printing presses of every vintage, including hand, antique, treadle, and power (but not computerized) presses; offset machines, paper trimmers, stapling machines, folders, booklet stitchers, punching machines, numbering machines, and related equipment. Goods by Baltimore, Chandler & Price, Gordon, and Kelsey show up frequently. The catalog descriptions include the general condition and bed dimensions of the presses. Type, leads, rules, leaders, quoins, keys, spacers, gauge pins, printers' saws, composing sticks, cold padding cement, ink, type cleaner, rollers, type cabinets and cases, engraving tools, bone paper folders, embossing powder, paper stock, shipping tags, and other goods are offered as well.

Special Factors: Price quote by letter with SASE; *no printing services are available;* minimum order is $10.

20TH CENTURY PLASTICS, INC.

3628 CRENSHAW BLVD.
LOS ANGELES, CA 90016
213-731-0900
FAX: 213-735-9901

Catalog: free
Save: up to 35%
Pay: check, MO, MC, V, AE, Discover
Sells: photo albums and accessories, binders, organizers, etc.
Store: mail order only

  ¡Si!

20th Century Plastics helps you save your memories with a wide selection of archival photo and slide storage sheets and albums, as well as safekeepers for your collections of stamps, baseball cards, recipes, and periodicals. The 48-page, color catalog also features a variety of binders and report covers, as well as photo albums, video- and audiocassette portfolios, static-proof floppy disk storage, and business-card files. The prices of the archival quality photo storage products are excellent, and there are especially good prices on the albums. Whether you're organizing snapshots at home or creating a storage and filing system for a large office, you'll find solutions at 20th Century Plastics.

Special Factors: Satisfaction is guaranteed; returns are accepted within 30 days for exchange, refund, or credit.

VALUE-TIQUE, INC.

P.O. BOX 67, DEPT. WBM
LEONIA, NJ 07605
201-461-6500

Catalog: $1 (see text)
Save: 25% plus
Pay: check, MO, MC, V, AE, DC, Discover
Sells: Sentry safes, fireproof files, media safes and storage chests
Store: Discount Safe Outlet, 117 Grand Ave., Palisades Park, NJ; Monday to Friday 9–5, Saturday 9–1

Value-tique has been selling home and office safes since 1968, and offers a range of well-known brands at discounts of 25% and more. Your savings are actually greater because Value-tique also pays for shipping. And the $1 catalog fee (cash is requested) buys a $5 credit certificate, good on any purchase. Value-tique sells Sentry Safes, the EDP Media-Safe and media chests for computer disk storage, a standard home and office safe, and different wall safes. Elsafe, Fichet-Bauche, Gardall, Knight, and Star safes are also available, as well as Pro-Steel gun safes. Models include wall and in-floor safes, cash-drop safes, and many others for home and business use. If you're not sure of the best type for your security purposes, call Value-tique to discuss your needs. Before ordering, *measure* to be sure the safe will fit the intended location.

Special Factors: Shipping is free in the contiguous United States.

VIKING OFFICE PRODUCTS

13809 SO. FIGUEROA ST.
LOS ANGELES, CA 90061
213-321-4493
FAX: 310-327-2376

Catalog: free (see text)
Save: up to 60%
Pay: check, MO, MC, V, AE
Sells: office supplies, furniture, computer supplies, stationery
Store: mail order only

¡Si!

Viking Office Products began business in 1960, and sells office supplies, furnishings, and computer supplies at discounts of up to 60%. The semi-annual, 450-page general catalog features daily office needs, from pens and markers to ergonomic seating and filing cabinets, all of which are sold at a discount. The brands represented include Avery, BIC, Boston, Canon, Eaton, Faber Castell, IBM, La-Z-Boy, Pendaflex, Pentel, Rubbermaid, Smead, Sony, 3M, Toshiba, and Wilson Jones, as well as Viking's own label. Once you place an order, you'll receive the monthly sale catalogs, with extra-deep discounts on everyday office needs.

Special Factors: Satisfaction is guaranteed; institutional accounts are available; shipping is free on orders over $25 (to the contiguous 48 United States).

VULCAN BINDER & COVER

KEY WBM
BOX 29
VINCENT, AL 35178
800-633-4526
205-672-2241
FAX: 205-672-7159

Catalog: free
Save: up to 40%
Pay: check, MO, MC, V, AE
Sells: binders and supplies
Store: mail order only

Three-ring binders can be quite pricey at stationery stores, which is why it makes sense to buy from the manufacturer. Vulcan can save you up to 40% on all of your binder needs, from light-duty models with flexible covers to heavy-duty binders with 3" D-rings. Vulcan's 48-page catalog also shows magazine files, zippered binders, catalog binders, 19-ring styles, pocket sizes, tabbed inserts, notepad holders, report covers, page protectors, cassette cases, and business cases and leather luggage. Custom imprinting is available on the binders and tabbed dividers.

Special Factors: Satisfaction is guaranteed; quantity discounts are available; returns are accepted within 15 days for exchange, refund, or credit; minimum order is $25.

SEE ALSO

Ace Luggage and Gifts • attaché cases and briefcases • **LEATHER**
The American Stationery Co., Inc. • custom-printed stationery, notepads, and envelopes • **GENERAL: CARDS**
Bernie's Discount Center, Inc. • phones, phone machines, fax machines, copiers, calculators, etc. • **APPLIANCES**
Dick Blick Co. • flat files and display equipment • **ART MATERIALS**

Current, Inc. • check-printing services • **GENERAL: CARDS**

Delta Publishing Group, Ltd. • wholesale magazine subscriptions • **BOOKS**

Jerry's Artarama, Inc. • ergonomic chairs and flat files • **ART MATERIALS**

The Jompole Company, Inc. • pen and pencil sets, premiums, etc. • **HOME: TABLE SETTINGS**

Don Lamor Inc. • office furnishings • **HOME: FURNISHINGS**

Leather Unlimited Corp. • leather attaché cases, card cases, portfolios, etc. • **LEATHER**

Loftin-Black Furniture Company • office furnishings • **HOME: FURNISH-INGS**

The Luggage Center • business cases • **LEATHER**

LVT Price Quote Hotline, Inc. • calculators, typewriters, phones, fax machines, pens, etc. • **APPLIANCES**

Ephraim Marsh Co. • fine executive furnishings • **HOME: FURNISHINGS**

Plastic BagMart • trash can liners • **OFFICE: SMALL BUSINESS**

Plexi-Craft Quality Products Corp. • acrylic racks, desk accessories, etc. • **HOME: FURNISHINGS**

S & S Sound City • phones and phone machines • **APPLIANCES**

Sobol House of Furnishings • contract furnishings • **HOME: FURNISHINGS**

Stuckey Brothers Furniture Co., Inc. • office furnishings • **HOME: FUR-NISHINGS**

Think Ink • inexpensive thermographic color hand printers • **CRAFTS**

Triad Furniture Discounters • office furnishings • **HOME: FURNISHINGS**

Turnkey Material Handling, Inc. • parts bins, office and institutional furnishings, and fixtures • **TOOLS**

U.S. Box Corp. • product packaging for resale • **OFFICE: SMALL BUSINESS**

University Products, Inc. • archival-quality storage supplies for microfiche and microfilm; library supplies and equipment • **OFFICE: SMALL BUSINESS**

Wholesale Tape and Supply Company • mailing supplies for tapes • **APPLIANCES**

Computing

Computers, peripherals, software, supplies, furniture, and accessories

If you're a first-time computer buyer or want to upgrade your current system, learn as much as you can from as many sources as possible. Attend demonstrations of new products, watch colleagues at work with different systems and programs, and ask questions. Don't assume that any software will perform as promised, no matter who's vouching for it. Evaluate your current and anticipated requirements as carefully as possible, since buying the right equipment and software the first time is the best money spent. Determine what you'll be doing with the computer and what you'd like to be able to do in six months. How much RAM will the software and operating system require? Would an entertainment-oriented system be the best choice (supporting CD ROM, sound, and enhanced video)? Are you buying for individuals who travel, deskbound workers, or both? Is a combination of separate notebooks and desktop systems practical, or would docking stations work best? Consult the repair shop of a large computer outlet to get an idea of how much repairs run on different types of equipment, and evaluate manufacturers' warranties and service contracts offered by the resellers *before* committing yourself to added expense. Whatever you decide, use a good-quality surge suppressor or UPS, and back up your disks!

COMPUTER DISCOUNT WAREHOUSE

CDW COMPUTER
CENTERS, INC.
2840 MARIA AVE.
NORTHBROOK, IL
60062-2026
800-800-4CDW
708-465-6000
FAX: 708-291-1737

Catalog: free
Save: up to 50%
Pay: check, MO, MC, V, Discover
Sells: computers, peripherals, software, etc.
Store: same address; also 315 W. Grand
Ave., Chicago, IL

  (see text)

CDW is one of the country's top resellers of AST computers, but also sells products by everyone else, from Aldus to Wyse: Acer, Borland, Canon, Epson, Hayes, Hewlett-Packard, IBM, Intel, Logitech, Maxtor, Motorola, NEC, Pacific Data, Toshiba, UDS, and WordPerfect, among others. CDW has been in business since 1982 and publishes a 40-page catalog, but you can call for price quotes on desktops, towers, notebooks, hard drives, Kingston memory upgrades, coprocessors, monitors, printers, scanners, UPS systems, and popular software—utilities, spreadsheets, graphics, data management, communications, and networking programs. The catalog details the sales policy (including returns), so it's a good idea to request it before placing an order.

Please note: A $25 handling fee is charged on orders shipped outside the United States.

Special Factors: Price quote by phone or letter; C.O.D. orders are accepted.

DARTEK COMPUTER SUPPLY CORP.

DEPT. WBMC
949 LARCH AVE.
ELMHURST, IL 60126
800-832-7835
708-832-2100
FAX: 708-941-1106
TDD: 708-941-8601

Catalog: free
Save: up to 60%
Pay: check, MO, MC, V, AE, Discover
Sells: PC and Macintosh supplies and equipment
Store: mail order only
E-mail: AOL: dartek1@aol.com

Dartek can save you on the equipment you need to make the most of your PC or Mac, at up to 60% on the regular or list prices on many products. Dartek has been serving the industry since 1980 and offers everything from software to workstations. The 132-page PC catalog and the 100-page Mac catalog show both handheld and desktop scanners and accessories, magnetic media, fax modems, hard and CD ROM drives, wire shelving, keyboards, printers and accessories, Mac cases, monitor arms, mice, joysticks, and much more, by Adobe, Brother, Hayes, Hewlett Packard, IOMEGA, Magnavox, Maxell, Microsoft, Novell, O'Sullivan, Seagate, Syquest, and 3M, among others. Dartek sells a wide range of software, including desktop publishing (type, layout, clip art, photography, graphics, etc.), word processing, time management, accounting, spreadsheet, legal, mailing list and database, virus detection, utilities, disk management, communications, information/reference, languages, and Mac tutorials. And there are all the supplies you'll need to stay productive—cables, power conditioners, disks and disk storage, data cartridges, toner cartridges for laser printers (regular, refillable, and remanufactured), ribbons, banner paper, labels, binding equipment, computer care and maintenance equipment, security devices, and device connections (fax switches, music on hold, phone interruption blockers, etc.), also at savings.

Dartek Computer Supply is offering readers a 10% discount on their first order. Be sure to identify yourself as a WBMC reader when you order. This WBMC reader discount expires February 28, 1997.

Special Factors: Satisfaction is guaranteed; quantity discounts are available; authorized returns are accepted (a restocking fee may be charged) within 45 days for exchange, refund, or credit; institutional accounts are available; minimum order is $25; C.O.D. orders are accepted.

DAYTON COMPUTER SUPPLY

6501 STATE RTE. 123 N.
FRANKLIN, OH 45005
800-735-3272
513-743-4060
FAX: 513-743-4056

Catalog: free
Save: up to 50%
Pay: MC, V, Discover
Sells: toner cartridges, diskettes, cables, printer ribbons, etc.
Store: same address; Monday to Friday 8–5

Dayton Computer Supply, also known as DCS, can save you and your company up to 50% on your computer supply needs. In business since 1979, DCS offers a comprehensive selection of supplies for computers, printers, copiers, and other office machines. DCS is also among the top 50 toner cartridge remanufacturers in the nation, producing cartridges for hundreds of laser printers and copiers, from Apple to Xerox. DCS also offers new cartridges from the original manufacturers, such as Apple, Canon, Epson, Hewlett-Packard, IBM, Okidata, Panasonic, Toshiba, and Xerox.

If you're looking for buys on magnetic media, see DCS. The firm's bulk computer disks meet or exceed ANSI standards, and are backed by the DCS guarantee. DCS also sells diskettes, data cartridges, from BASF, Dysan, KAO, Maxell, Sony, 3M, and Verbatim. DCS carries a full line of cabling supplies and accessories, such as printer cables, internal and external drive cables, switch boxes, gender changers and adapters, surge protection devices, mice and mouse supplies, printer stands, disk storage boxes, etc. And DCS remains one of the largest ribbon distributors in the nation, stocking ribbons for over 10,000 printers, and specializing in hard-to-find ribbons. "If we can't find it...it probably cannot be found," say DCS management.

Please note: Orders are shipped to Canada via UPS only, and shipped to APO/FPO addresses by U.S. mail.

Dayton Computer Supply is offering readers a 5% discount on all orders. Be sure to identify yourself as a WBMC reader when you order. This WBMC reader discount expires February 1, 1997.

Special Factors: Satisfaction is guaranteed; price quote by phone; quantity discounts are available; C.O.D. orders are accepted; institutional accounts are available.

EDUCALC CORPORATION

27953 CABOT RD.
LAGUNA NIGUEL, CA
   92677
800-677-7001
714-582-2637
FAX: 714-582-1445

Catalog: free
Save: up to 40%
Pay: check, MO, MC, V, Discover
Sells: calculators, palmtops, PDAs, note-
books, peripherals, books, software, etc.
Store: same address; Monday to Friday 8–5

  ¡Si!

EduCALC, in business since 1976, specializes in calculators and peripherals that maximize the functions of the Hewlett Packard 48G calculator
series and HP95/100/200LX palmtop computers, and the HP Omni-
Book. Canon, Sharp, and Texas Instruments calculators are also carried,
and used calculators are available. The savings average 25%, but some
items are discounted up to 40%; trade-ins are available for some calcula-
tor/palmtops—inquire for information.

When hooked up to the appropriate peripherals, the HP calculators
can be linked to PCs, receive messages by satellite, edit programs, save
data on RAM cards, develop programs, perform language translations,
and analyze mathematical, scientific, engineering, and business data
with the aid of software cards. The equipment currently available
includes printer/plotters, modules, interface units, RAM/ROM cards, disk
drives, adapters, and personal (portable) diaries. Stands, covers, keyboard overlay systems, ribbons, printing paper, disks, plotter pens, and
other supplies are offered as well. The 68-page catalog should be noted
for its comprehensive bookshelf—both general and calculator-related
reference texts on astronomy, navigation, engineering, higher mathematics and statistics, programming, and computer systems and languages are listed. The catalog descriptions are comprehensive, easy to
understand, and include product specifications. For more information,
an automated calculator/palmtop news line is available 24 hours a day;
call 714-582-3976.

Special Factors: Satisfaction is guaranteed; returns are accepted
within 30 days.

EDUCORP COMPUTER SERVICES

7434 TRADE ST.
SAN DIEGO, CA
  92121-2410
800-843-9497
619-536-9999
FAX: 619-536-2345

Catalog: free
Save: up to 75%
Pay: check, MO, MC, V, AE, Discover
Sells: CD-ROM software and Macintosh shareware
Store: mail order and by chance

If you've been looking for a reason to take the plunge into CD-ROM technology, you've got it in the compact, 144-page catalog from EDUCORP. There are over 700 titles, including *Lunicus* and *Myst*, reference material (*Grollier's Encyclopedia* and *The View from Earth*), and educational titles. EDUCORP also carries a wide variety of desktop publishing and graphic design tools, such as stock-photo CDs, background textures, and clip-art CDs.

But CD-ROM represents only half of the business at EDUCORP, which has been serving the Macintosh world since 1984. The rest of the stock here is an enormous collection of shareware, priced from $3.99 to $6.99 per disk, depending on the quantity ordered. The shareware library includes DAs, games, HyperCard stacks, and more, from an init file that says "bye bye" when you shut down your Mac, to MacPorkBarrel, a game that involves catching bills dropped from the Capitol building while dodging (and bribing) IRS auditors. The shareware is available on floppy, or the complete collection on two CDs.

If you're intrigued by the possibilities, see for yourself with EDUCORP's "samplers": The EDUCORP CD Sampler includes demos of over 100 of the most popular titles the company carries; the Photo CD Sampler has a thumbnail index of every photo CD EDUCORP sells; and the Clip Art CD Sampler does the same with clip art titles. At under $10 each, they're a great way to make sure you know what you're buying! And EDUCORP will "meet or beat" any advertised price on the CD-ROMs themselves.

Special Factors: Quantity discounts are available *for dealers*; authorized returns are accepted within 30 days (a 25% restocking fee may be charged); institutional accounts are available; minimum order is $20 with credit cards.

EGGHEAD DISCOUNT SOFTWARE

P.O. BOX 185
ISSAQUAH, WA 98027-7007
800-EGGHEAD
TDD: 800-949-3447

Catalog: free
Save: up to 65%
Pay: check, MO, MC, V, AE, Discover
Sells: software and computer accessories
Store: 78 stores in CT, DC, FL, GA, MA, MD, NC, NJ, NY, PA, RI, and VA; locations are listed in the catalog

If you live in the Northeast, you probably know Egghead Discount from its stores, which offer a broad selection of software for IBM-compatible and Macintosh systems, at savings of up to 60%. Egghead's frequent two-week sale catalogs feature nearly 50 pages of extra discounts on popular programs and things like joysticks, mice, toner cartridges, and other necessities. But you don't have to go to the store for the savings, or limit yourself to the 1,400 or so programs on the shelves there: Egghead will give you the same good deals on mail and phone orders, as well as access to over 20,000 additional programs and 40,000 other items. For an extra 5% discount on everything you buy, become a "CUE" member—it's free, and you'll receive a membership card entitling you to the 5% discount, plus a quarterly newsletter filled with tips and savings. In addition to the exhaustive selection and good prices, Egghead usually has the latest releases as soon as they're available. Call for a price and shipping quote if you know exactly what you want, or request a catalog for the current specials.

Special Factors: Satisfaction is guaranteed; returns are accepted within 30 days for exchange, refund, or credit; institutional accounts are available.

800-SOFTWARE, INC.

1003 CANAL BLVD.
RICHMOND, CA 94804
510-412-9020
FAX: 510-412-1550

Catalog: free
Save: up to 50%
Pay: check, MO, MC, V, AE
Sells: software, hardware, and network products
Store: same address; Monday to Friday 9–5, Saturday 10–2

800-Software has won recommendations from computer users who appreciate 800's prices, selection, and technical support. The company's well-designed, 154-page catalog lists programs for PCs, Macintosh computers, and some UNIX products, including data bases, graphics, utilities, operating systems, personal finance programs, spreadsheets, desktop publishing programs, and word processing software. There are lines and products by Alpha, Amdek, Apple, AST Research, Borland, Central Point Software, Computer Associates, Digital, Fox & Geller, Funk Software, Hayes, IMSI, Intel, Lotus, Micropro, MicroSoft, Novell, Oasis Systems, Paperback Software, Quadram, Revelation Technology, Software Solutions, Toshiba, Word Perfect, XyQuest, and many others. You'll also find boards, buffers, graphics cards, keyboards, mice, monitors, printers, surge suppressors, modems, and other peripherals and accessories for PCs. Specials are run on a frequent basis, and the catalog is a great source for information on what's new in word processing, spreadsheet, data management, educational, and other types of programs.

Corporate and government buyers, please note: Free post-sale technical support is provided.

Special Factors: Authorized returns are accepted within 30 days (a 10% restocking fee may be charged); institutional accounts are available; quantity discounts are available.

LYBEN COMPUTER SYSTEMS, INC.

**5545 BRIDGEWOOD
STERLING HEIGHTS,
 MI 48310
800-493-5777
810-268-8100
FAX: 810-268-8899**

Catalog: free
Save: up to 70%
Pay: check, MO, MC, V
Sells: computer supplies
Store: mail order only

Lyben Computer Systems, Inc. has been in business since 1982 and offers a full range of computer accessories, supplies, and peripherals. Lyben can save you up to 70% on the suggested retail price on goods from such companies as Boca, Panasonic, Sony, 3M, and Tripplite, to name a few. Lyben's 268-page color catalog runs from batteries to work stations and wrist pads, with all of your computer needs in between— magnetic media, storage units, cleaning tools and products, shredders, binding systems, memory upgrades, cables, switches, game cards, modems, buffers, network products, software and CD ROM, printers, and much more. The seasonal, 48-page catalogs just a sample of the thousands of items Lyben sells—if you don't see what you're looking for, call or write—it may be available.

Special Factors: Minimum order is $15; C.O.D. orders are accepted.

MACWAREHOUSE

DEPT. WBM96
P.O. BOX 3013
1720 OAK ST.
LAKEWOOD, NJ
  08701-3013
800-255-6227
FAX: 908-905-9279

Catalog: free
Save: up to 50%
Pay: check, MO, MC, V, AE, Discover
Sells: Macintosh software and peripherals
Store: mail order only

Whether you're a dedicated Macintosh user or are toying with making a cross-platform leap, you'll want to see the 190-page catalog from MacWarehouse. More than a roundup of current releases and enhancements, MacWarehouse offers an upgrade service (competitive and live) for a wide range of programs, an extensive line of enhancements and memory upgrades, network media, monitors, video cards, online service packages, and a broad range of accessories, tools, cables, hardware, and little things to make your Mac sing—including MIDI connections, video imaging kits, and sound-recording systems! And MacWarehouse has an equally impressive selection of software and programs: word processing, data base systems, utilities, accounting, graphics, project managers, spreadsheets, fonts, multimedia packages, security systems, and much more. The products run from Access PC to Zephyr Palettes, and the discounts are a satisfying 25% to 50%—and even more on specials and bundled software.

Special Factors: Price quote by phone or letter; authorized returns are accepted; institutional accounts are available; C.O.D. orders are accepted; online with CompuServe.

MARYMAC INDUSTRIES, INC.

22511 KATY FRWY.
KATY, TX 77450-1598
713-392-0747
800-231-3680
FAX: 713-574-4567

Information: see text
Save: 15% plus
Pay: check, MO, MC, V, AE, DC, Discover, Radio Shack card
Sells: Radio Shack and Tandy products
Store: same address; Monday to Friday 8–6

Marymac lays claim to title of "world's largest independent authorized computer dealer," and is able to offer discounts of 15% and more on *anything* in the Radio Shack/Tandy catalog. (Get a copy from your local dealer, or request one from Tandy Catalog, 300 One Tandy Center, Fort Worth, TX 76102—Marymac doesn't mail the catalog.) Price quotes are given on computers, peripherals, fax machines, cellular phones, phone machines, TVs, audio components, scanners, and other goods under the Radio Shack and Tandy labels. Marymac was founded in 1976 and has a "meet or beat" pricing policy. Shipping and insurance are not charged on most items delivered within the continental United States.

Special Factors: Shipping and insurance are included on most items sent within the contiguous United States; C.O.D. orders are accepted; minimum order is $25; online with GEnie.

MEI/MICRO CENTER

1100 STEELWOOD RD.
COLUMBUS, OH
43212-9972
800-634-3478
614-481-4417
FAX: 614-486-6417

Catalog: free
Save: up to 75%
Pay: check, MO, MC, V, Discover
Sells: data storage, ribbons, paper, etc.
Store: mail order only

MEI/Micro Center founded its business in 1986 on great buys on magnetic media, which are still here, in the 52-page catalog—diskettes, data cartridges, flopticals and optical disks, Bernoulli and Syquest cartridges, and accessories. The brands include Dysan, Iomega, Precision, 3M, Verbatim, and MEI's own label—all offered at excellent discounts. You'll also find media storage units, backup units, sound cards, surge suppressors, printer supplies (ribbons, toner cartridges, inkjet modules, etc.), CD-ROM drives and some hardware—fax/modems, mice, and even a laptop. Check the pricing on the paper: laser stock, certificates and brochure papers, business cards, parchment, labels, and transparencies are all offered.

Please note: MEI/Micro Center doesn't ship goods outside the United States and Canada, and does not ship boxes of paper by the U.S. Postal Service.

Special Factors: Satisfaction is guaranteed; returns are accepted for exchange, refund, or credit; C.O.D. orders are accepted.

MICRO WAREHOUSE, INC.

DEPT. WBM96
P.O. BOX 3014
1690 OAK ST.
LAKEWOOD, NJ
 08701-3014
800-367-7080
FAX: 908-905-5245

Catalog: free
Save: up to 59%
Pay: check, MO MC, V, Discover
Sells: computers, software, and peripherals
Store: mail order only

There's one way to keep up with the new releases, upgrades, innovations in peripherals, and other developments in computing—find a source to do it for you. MicroWarehouse not only leads with the latest releases, it also gives you great prices on everything it sells. The 136-page catalog is packed with software for DOS, Windows, OS/2, and other environments, as well as modems, fax machines, scanners, disk drives, expansion devices, printers, monitors, memory upgrades, and much more. The software runs the gamut from word processing and integrated communications to data bases, utilities, graphics, and more—you'll find everything from Act! contact management software to Zoom fax modems. The Upgrade Warehouse division can handle both live and competitive upgrades, making it easy to keep on top of changes as they're released. And if you want more information on a given product, the Fax Facts service will send it directly to your fax. All of this, and savings of up to 50%, have helped establish MicroWarehouse as a leading supplier—along with its MacWarehouse division, which handles the needs of Apple owners, and Data Comm Warehouse, for networking solutions specialties. Request the catalog that best serves your needs: Micro, Mac, or Data Comm.

Special Factors: Authorized returns of defective items are accepted within 120 days for exchange, refund, or credit; institutional accounts are available; C.O.D. orders are accepted; online with CompuServe.

MISCO

ONE MISCO PLAZA
HOLMDEL, NJ 07733
800-333-5640
908-264-1000
FAX: 908-888-9449

Catalog: $4
Save: up to 40%
Pay: check, MO, MC, V, AE
Sells: computer software, peripherals, and accessories
Store: mail order only

MISCO's "In-Stock Guarantee" helps assure you that the warehouse will have what you want, when you need it. The 164-page catalog is strong on computer accessories—keyboard drawers, wrist rests, laptop bags, etc.—and ergonomically designed chairs and workstations. MISCO also offers a good selection of media and storage, toner cartridges and paper, software, peripherals for stand-alone and networked PCs, input devices, modems, monitors, memory boards, SCSIs and hard drives, scanners, printers, fax machines, telephones, line drives, cables and connectors, and much more. This is a great source for anyone running a home office, and bigger businesses can contact MISCO's Bid Department for volume discounts.

Special Factors: Quantity discounts are available; returns are accepted; minimum order is $30; C.O.D. orders are accepted.

NEW MMI CORP.

DEPT. WBMC01
2400 REACH RD.
WILLIAMSPORT, PA 17701
800-233-8950
FAX: 717-327-1217

Catalog: free
Save: up to 40%
Pay: check, MO, MC, V, Discover
Sells: computers, peripherals, and software
Store: New MMI Corp., 2400 Reach Rd.,
Williamsport, PA; Monday to Friday 9–6, Saturday 10–3

New MMI Corp. has been in business since 1987, selling computer systems, disk drives, boards, monitors, printers, modems, software, and accessories by a number of manufacturers, at savings of up to 40%. New MMI provides technical assistance before and after the sale, is an authorized dealer for everything it sells, and an authorized repair center for Apple, AST, Compaq, Epson, Hewlett-Packard, Okidata, and Panasonic. The 64-page color catalog shows a wide selection of current releases and includes specifications; if you don't see what you're looking for in the catalog, call, fax, or write for a price quote—it may be available. The firm's bulletin board service can be accessed by dialing 717-327-9952 (2400 baud and up), or 717-327-9953 (1200 to 2400 baud).

Special Factors: Authorization is required for returns (a restocking fee may be charged); C.O.D. orders are accepted.

THE PC ZONE

17411 N.E. UNION
HILL RD.
REDMOND, WA
98052-6716
800-258-2088
206-883-3088
FAX: 206-881-3421

Catalog: free
Save: up to 50%
Pay: check, MO, MC, V, AE, Discover
Sells: DOS and Windows software and hardware
Store: mail order only

The PC Zone combines two lines in one 48-page catalog: DOS Zone and the Windows Zone (a separate Mac Zone catalog is also available). Software stars here—the latest releases for personal productivity, communications, networking, data bases, desktop publishing, utilities, spreadsheets, word processing, graphics, fonts, multimedia, and more—over 2,000 products at last count. PC Zone includes a number of entertainment and games packages, and a minutely printed list of software that's available but not featured. In addition, PC Zone sells memory upgrades of different types, CD-ROM drives, OCR devices and scanners, monitors, mice, modems, backup devices, printers, other peripherals and accessories, and much more. Request the PC or Mac catalog, and if you don't see what you're looking for, call—it may be available but not listed.

Special Factors: Authorized returns are accepted; institutional accounts are available; C.O.D. orders are accepted.

ROCKY MOUNTAIN COMPUTER OUTFITTERS

**100 FINANCIAL DR.
KALISPELL, MT 59901
800-367-4222
406-758-8000
FAX: 800-881-3090**

Catalog: free
Save: up to 50%
Pay: check, MO, MC, V, AE, Discover
Sells: IBM and Macintosh software, peripherals, etc.
Store: mail order only
E-mail: CS: 76635,660@compuserve.com

NEC monitors, productivity tools, DAT drives, and the latest presentation programs—they're all here at Rocky Mountain Computer Outfitters, where the employees are also users. (They swear that the whole catalog is put together with Mac technology: "No paste-up. No stripping. No kidding.") Given the Mac's repute as a graphics and publishing tool, this isn't earth shattering, but it *is* nice to know that the staff actually uses what they sell, and can help you to find the best product for your needs. The catalogs are big on current Mac and Windows software—workgroup, word processing, spreadsheet, design, publishing and layout, data base, time management, entertainment, education, and more. CD-ROM drives, memory chips, and high-speed modems are strong, as well as Radius monitors, DayStar digital accelerators, and scanners. Prices are discounted, and the Rocky Mountain staff is proud of being able to answer "your cross-platform questions," as well.

Special Factors: Authorized returns (except special orders and clearance items) are accepted for exchange, refund, or credit; online with America OnLine and CompuServe.

BEN TORRES RIBBON COMPANY

590 E. INDUSTRIAL RD.,
UNIT 15
SAN BERNARDINO, CA
92408-3946
909-796-5559

Price List: free
Save: up to 40%
Pay: check or MO
Sells: refilled and new printer ribbons and toner cartridges
Store: same address; Monday to Friday 9:30–4:30

Ben Torres can sell you the company's own printer ribbons at prices about 40% below the going rate, or refill your used ribbon cartridges at savings of over 50%. Torres' ribbon price list runs from Anadex to Toshiba, and includes scores of printer models. New ribbons are available for most models, and all of the Torres ribbon cases are refillable (please note that some cartridges can't be opened without breaking them). Laser cartridges for Apple, Canon, Hewlett Packard, and other printers are refilled as well. (Check the terms of your printer's warranty or service contract before sending in your empties, to make sure using reconditioned cartridges doesn't invalidate it.) The firm uses only the original cartridge you send (no substitutes), refills with extra toner, includes a test-pattern printout using the refilled cartridge, and guarantees your satisfaction. The price list includes specifics on what to send and what to exepct. Torres has been in business since 1979, and guarantees your "satisfaction with impressions" of the ribbons—whether new or refilled.

Wholesale customers, there is no separate price list, so call or write for quotes on large orders.

Canadian readers, please note: Only U.S. funds are accepted.

Special Factors: Satisfaction is guaranteed; returns are accepted within 30 days for exchange, refund, or credit.

SEE ALSO

The Astronomical Society of the Pacific • *astronomy-related computer programs* • **BOOKS**
Business & Institutional Furniture Company, Inc. • *computer workstations* • **OFFICE**
Clothcrafters, Inc. • *cotton computer covers* • **GENERAL MERCHANDISE**
Frank Eastern Co. • *computer workstations* • **OFFICE**

Genada Imports • *computer workstations* • **HOME: FURNISHINGS**

Jerry's Artarama, Inc. • *computer workstations* • **ART MATERIALS**

Jobson's Luggage Warehouse • *laptop cases* • **LEATHER**

Mail Center USA • *computer peripherals, disks, and accessories* • **OFFICE**

National Business Furniture, Inc. • *computer workstations* • **OFFICE**

Plexi-Craft Quality Products Corp. • *acrylic computer stands* • **HOME: FURNISHINGS**

Quill Corporation • *computers, peripherals, software, etc.* • **OFFICE**

Safe Sepcialties, Inc. • *data and diskette safes, lockboxes, etc.* • **OFFICE**

Staples, Inc. • *computer disks, data binders, workstations, software, etc.* • **OFFICE**

20th Century Plastics, Inc. • *static-proof disk storage* • **OFFICE**

Viking Office Products • *computer supplies, peripherals, and furniture* • **OFFICE**

Small Business

Products and services for businesses

Whether you're running a small office or just drafting the plans for your first venture, maximize every dollar you spend by buying from firms that will sell to you at "bulk" discounts, or wholesale. The companies listed here can help you hold down costs even if you can't compete with the buying power of the Fortune 500. None of the firms requires a resale certificate—at most, they ask you to send your catalog request on letterhead, or enclose your business card. But many impose minimum orders and have less generous return policies than those offered by consumer-oriented mail-order firms, so order accordingly.

Over the past few years, there's been enormous growth in "alternative" purchasing—buying clubs, members-only warehouses, barter organizations, and co-ops. Explore the options available to you and find the right combination of vendors and services for your needs; there's usually no single "right" source, and it's up to you to determine the balance between paying list price and pushing for the deepest discounts on *everything*.

ASSOCIATED BAG COMPANY

400 W. BODEN ST.
MILWAUKEE, WI
53207-7120
800-926-6100
FAX: 800-926-4610

Catalog: free
Save: up to 40%
Pay: check, MO, MC, V
Sells: packaging supplies
Store: mail order only

Bags, boxes, bubble pack—that's just the beginning of what's available from Associated Bag Company. The well-designed, 48-page catalog features packaging materials for a range of purposes: rolls and envelopes of bubble pack, foam sheeting, corrugated boxes and rolls, cloth drawstring bags, a wide range of zip-lock bags, mailing tubes and envelope, sealing tape, stretch wrap, shrink wrap, packing peanuts, antistatic bags, and much more. Both recycled and recyclable "green" products are noted throughout the book. Dispensers for tape and paper, shrink guns, and other equipment are also available. Prices average 20% less than those charged by other packaging suppliers, and savings are greater on quantity buys.

In addition to the customary commercial uses, these products are suited to a number of household tasks, including one very costly undertaking—moving. Get the boxes locally but handle the packing yourself with wrapping materials from Associated Bag, and you can save several hundreds of dollars in materials and labor. Just make sure your homeowner policy, or the moving company, will still provide coverage if there's breakage.

Special Factors: Satisfaction is guaranteed; quantity discounts are available; returns are accepted; minimum order is $25.

PLASTIC BAGMART

904 OLD COUNTRY RD.
WESTBURY, NY 11590
516-997-3355
FAX: 516-997-1836

Catalog: free with SASE
Save: up to 60%
Pay: check, MO, MC, V
Sells: plastic bags
Store: same address; Monday to Friday 9–5, Saturday 9–3

Plastic BagMart, established in 1980, offers plastic bags in sizes most frequently used in homes, offices, and industry. Prices are up to 60% lower than those charged by supermarkets and variety stores for smaller lots. The BagMart stocks plastic bags in sizes from 2" square to 50" by 48", one to four mils thick. Garbage and trash cleanup bags, kitchen and office waste-can bags, food-storage bags, recycling bags, large industrial-type bags, zip-top styles, plastic shopping bags, compactor, garment, and other types are available. The bags are sold in case lots only (100 to 1,000 bags per case, depending on the size). The 12-page catalog features the most popular lines, but if you don't see what you need, write with particulars.

Plastic BagMart is offering readers of this book a 5% discount on their *first* order (computed on the goods total only). This WBMC reader discount expires February 1, 1997.

Canadian readers, please note: Orders are shipped by UPS only.

Special Factors: Satisfaction is guaranteed; price quote by letter with SASE; returns are accepted within ten days; minimum order is one case.

UNIVERSITY PRODUCTS, INC.

DEPT. F132
P.O. BOX 101
HOLYOKE, MA 01041-0101
800-628-1912
FAX: 800-532-9281

Catalog: free (see text)
Save: up to 30%
Pay: check, MO, MC, V, AE. DC, Discover
Sells: archival-quality materials
Store: mail order only

You may not know it, but anarchy reigns on your bookshelves, in the pages of your photo albums, and among the works of art on your walls.

It's sad, but true: most of us store and display our precious belongings in materials and under conditions that damage them, sometimes irreparably.

Help is available from University Products, which publishes the comprehensive *Archival Quality Materials Catalog*. University Products has been selling conservation and library supplies to institutions since 1968 and does business with preservation-minded individuals and institutions who want to protect their collectibles and other treasures. Both the materials used in display and storage, and the conditions under which we keep them affect the long-term "health" of many collectibles. Problems with spotting, discoloration, and damage may be seen in stamps, antique textiles, comic books, baseball trading cards, postcards, scrapbooks, photographs, sheet music, and even currency. To meet the need for safe storage of these goods, University Products sells acid-free manuscript boxes and interleaving pages, files, photo albums and Mylar page protectors, archival storage tubes, slide and microfiche storage materials, mounting materials and adhesives, an extensive selection of acid-free papers of all types, storage cases and cabinets, dry mount and framing equipment, and related tools and supplies. The catalog includes valuable information on conservation basics for a range of materials and collectibles. Since a "basic retouching" of an old photograph can cost over $100, each dollar spent in preservation can save a hundred in restoration—*if* restoration is possible.

Special Factors: Satisfaction is guaranteed; quantity discounts are available; institutional accounts are available.

U.S. BOX CORP.

1296 MCCARTER HWY.
NEWARK, NJ 07104
201-481-2000
FAX: 201-481-2002

Catalog: free
Save: up to 60%
Pay: check, MO, MC, V
Sells: resale packaging
Store: mail order only

 ¡Si!

U.S. Box Corp. has been selling packaging—boxes, bags, canisters, and displays—since 1948. This is primarily a business-to-business firm, but it offers products that consumers use routinely: wrapping paper, tape, gift boxes, ribbon, and mailing bags, for example. Prices are as much as 60% lower here than those charged for comparable items in variety and stationery stores. Volume discounts run from 5% on orders over $500 up to 15% on totals of $2,500 plus. Samples of the goods may be purchased at unit cost plus $2 shipping; this is recommended, since returns are not accepted.

U.S. Box Corp.'s 76-page color catalog shows plain and decorated corrugated cardboard mailers, boxes, shopping bags, gift and presentation boxes, poly bags, rigid plastic boxes, plastic display cases, showcase and window displays, and a full line of velvet boxes, inserts, and stands for jewelry sale and display. Both consumers and businesses should see the selection—and prices—of U.S. Box Corp.'s colorful excelsior, cellophane, gift wrap and gift tins, bows and package decorations, ribbons, and tissue paper. Consolidate your packaging needs and you'll easily meet the $150 minimum order—the current catalog includes computer disk mailers, all-purpose gift stickers (just 5¢ each), gold and silver cord-handled bags, gold folding gift candy boxes, hatbox sets, hinged partitioned plastic boxes (perfect for notions, hardware, and small parts), and jewelry display pieces, many of which could double as jewelry collection organizers.

Special Factors: Returns are not accepted; minimum order is $150.

SEE ALSO

Business Technologies, Inc. • *cash registers* • **OFFICE**
Current, Inc. • *gift wrapping paper and ribbon* • **GENERAL: CARDS**
Hunt Galleries, Inc. • *custom-upholstered furnishings for institutions, designers, etc.* • **HOME: FURNISHINGS**
The Jompole Company, Inc. • *pen and pencil sets, premiums, etc.* • **HOME: TABLE SETTINGS**
New England Basket Co. • *ribbon, bows, gift tags, baskets, etc.* • **GENERAL MERCHANDISE**
Oriental Trading Company, Inc. • *fund-raising and promotional items* • **TOYS**
Turnkey Material Handling, Inc. • *parts bins, office and institutional furnishings, and fixtures* • **TOOLS**
U.S. Toy Company, Inc. • *gifts, premiums, fund-raising items* • **TOYS**
Yazoo Mills, Inc. • *shipping tubes* • **ART MATERIALS**

SPORTS AND RECREATION

Equipment, clothing, supplies, and services
for recreational activities

If the high price of recreation equipment seems unsporting to you, you've turned to the right place. Discounts of 30% are standard among many of the suppliers listed here, who sell clothing and equipment for cycling, running, golfing, skiing, aerobics, racquet sports, skin and scuba diving, camping, hunting, hiking, basketball, triathaloning, soccer, and other endeavors. Racquet stringing, club repairs, and other services are usually priced competitively as well. Buying your gear by mail may be the only sport that repays a nominal expenditure of energy with such an enhanced sense of well-being.

If you've been sedentary for some time, have a complete physical before beginning any workout program or sport. Stop and cool down if you're in pain, but don't give up. You can make running, aerobics, and racquet sports easier on your joints by wearing properly fitted shoes, learning correct foot placement, and working out on a resilient surface. Low-impact aerobics, fast-paced walking, and swimming are less stressful than running, calisthenics, and traditional sports. Getting fit should be a pleasure, and if you take the time to find an enjoyable, challenging sport or workout routine, cardiovascular health and vigor will be more easily won.

FIND IT FAST

CAMPING • **Campmor, Gander Mountain, Survival Supply**
CYCLING • **Bike Nashbar, Performance Bicycle Shop**
EXERCISE EQUIPMENT • **Better Health**
GOLF • **Austad's, Custom Golf Clubs, Golf Haus, Telepro**

HUNTING • **Bowhunters Warehouse, Cabela's, Cheap Shot, Deer Shack, Gander Mountain, Sport Shop, Wiley's**
INLINE SKATES • **Sailboard Warehouse**
RACQUET SPORTS • **Holabird**
SNOWBOARDING • **Sailboard Warehouse**
SOCCER • **Soccer International**
SWIMWEAR AND POOL SUPPLIES • **Water Warehouse, World Wide Aquatics**
VOLLEYBALL • **Spike Nashbar**
WALKING • **Walk USA**
WATER SPORTS • **Bart's, Berry Scuba, Central Skindivers, Overton's, Performance Diver, Sailboard Warehouse**

AUSTAD'S GOLF

DEPT. 50114
P.O. BOX 1428
SIOUX FALLS, SD
  57196-1428
800-759-4653, EXT. 50114

Catalog: free
Save: up to 30%
Pay: check, MO, MC, V, AE, DC, Discover
Sells: golf equipment and apparel
Store: 1600 Rte. 83, Oak Brook, IL; 7485 France Ave. South, Edina, and 648 NE Hwy. 10, Blaine, MN; also Tenth and Cleveland, Sioux Falls, SD

Austad's Golf, established in 1963, features clubs and other equipment designed to meet the golfing needs and fit the budgets of all kinds of golfers. Training aids, accessories, carts—everything to help you enjoy your game can be found in Austad's catalog. And Austad's own clothing line, Linksport, will keep you fashion-forward on the course, without costing you a fortune.

  Special Factors: Satisfaction is guaranteed; online with CompuServe and Prodigy.

BART'S WATERSPORTS

P.O. BOX 294-WBM
NORTH WEBSTER, IN
  46555
800-348-5016
FAX: 219-834-4246

Catalog: free
Save: up to 40%
Pay: check, MO, MC, V, AE, Discover
Sells: water-sports and marine/boating
equipment and accessories
Store: Hwy. 13, North Webster, IN; Monday
to Saturday 9–6

The thrills of water sports are cheaper at Bart's, where wet suits, skis, and marine products cost up to 40% below list, and clearance items are offered at even greater savings. Bart's has been in business since 1971, and backs every sale with a guarantee of satisfaction. The 64-page color catalog features name-brand water skis, personal watercraft accessories, and marine equipment for boats. Wakeboarders can choose from pages of boards and accessories, and there's a large selection of floats, tubes, and other inflatables. Ski vests and wet suits for men, women, and children are offered, in addition to wet suit accessories, swimwear for men and women, T-shirts, sunglasses, gloves, boat lifts, and boat/PWC covers. Brands include Body Glove, Body Guard, Connelly, Eagle, Intensity, O'Brien, Skiwarm, Slippery When Wet, and others.

Special Factors: Satisfaction is guaranteed; quantity discounts are available; returns are accepted within 60 days.

BERRY SCUBA CO.

DEPT. W-96
6674 N. NORTHWEST
  HWY.
CHICAGO, IL 60631
800-621-6019
312-763-1626
FAX: 312-775-1815

Catalog: free
Save: up to 40%
Pay: check, MO, MC, V, AE, Discover
Sells: scuba-diving gear
Store: same address; also North Pier Mall,
Chicago; Lombard and Palatine, IL; and
Atlanta, GA

Berry, "the oldest, largest, and best-known direct-mail scuba firm in the country," carries a wide range of equipment and accessories for diving and related activities. Shop here for regulators, masks, wet suits, fins, tanks, diving lights, strobes, underwater cameras and housing, Citizen diving watches, pole spears, and other gear and accessories for underwater use. The brands include Bay Side, Chronosport, Citizen, Cyalume, Dacor, Deep Sea, Desco, Global, Henderson, Ikelite, Mako, Mares, Nikon, Parkway, Poseidon, Princeton, Scuba Systems, Sea & Sea, Seatec, Sherwood, T.U.S.A., Timex, Trident, Undersea Guns, Underwater Kinetics, U.S. Divers, U.S. Tech, and Viking, among others. Berry does business on a price-quote basis, but will send you the free catalog, on request.

Special Factors: Orders are shipped worldwide.

BETTER HEALTH FITNESS

5302 NEW UTRECHT AVE.
BROOKLYN, NY 11219
718-436-4693
FAX: 718-854-3381

Information: inquire
Save: up to 20%
Pay: check, MO, MC, V, AE
Sells: exercise equipment
Store: same address; Monday to Wednesday 10–6, Thursday 10–8, Sunday 12–5 (closed Friday and Saturday)

Whether you're buying a stationary bicycle for rainy-day workouts or outfitting an entire gym, you'll get it for less at Better Health. The firm has been selling top-of-the-line models since 1977, including Alva (ballet barres), Barracuda, Bodyguard, Cal-Gym, Century, Cybex, Detecto, Everlast, Fitness Master, Healthometer, H.W.E. Massage, Landice, Life Fitness, Monark (cycles), Multi Sport (gyms), Pacemaster (treadmills), Parabody, Penco (lockers), Pro-Form, Quinton, Titan, Trek Fitness, Trotter (treadmills), Tunturi, and Vectra. You can save up to 20% on the regular prices of equipment by these and other manufacturers. Call or write for quotes on treadmills, ski machines, multi-station units, free-weights, benches, aerobic and tumbling mats, dance studio equipment, saunas, locker room equipment, boxing equipment, massage recliners, and related goods. Gym layout and design services are available to local customers.

Special Factors: Satisfaction is guaranteed; price quote by phone or letter with SASE; authorized returns are accepted within 15 days for exchange, refund, or credit; minimum order is $50.

BIKE NASHBAR

4111 SIMON RD.,
  DEPT. WBM6
YOUNGSTOWN, OH
  44512-1343
800-NASHBAR
FAX: 800-456-1223

Catalog: free
Save: up to 30%
Pay: check, MO, MC, V, Discover
Sells: bicycles, accessories, apparel, and equipment
Store: same address

Bike Nashbar, one of the country's top sources for casual and serious cyclists, publishes a 70-plus-page catalog that runs from rain parkas to panniers, sold at "guaranteed lowest prices." Bike Nashbar has been in business since 1973 and sells its own line of road, touring, and ATB bikes, which have features usually found on more expensive models. There are full lines of parts and accessories, including saddles from Avocet, San Marco, and Vetta, gears, brakes, chain wheels, hubs, pedals, derailleurs, handlebars, and other parts by Campagnolo, Control Tech, Dura-Ace, Shimano, SR, and other firms. Panniers and bags, racks, helmets, protective eyewear, gloves, tires and tubes, wheels, toe clips, locks (Nashbar and Kryptonite), handlebar tape, grips, tire pumps, lights, and other accessories are offered. Bike Nashbar also features a large selection of cycling clothing, both its own label, and Cannondale, Hind, Insport and Tinley, as well as shoes by Avocet, Diadora, Look, Saucony, Scott, Sidi, Specialized, Time, and Vittoria. The catalog includes a good bit of technical information, and if you need more assistance, just call.

Special Factors: Satisfaction is guaranteed; technical advice is available; online with America Online.

BOWHUNTERS WAREHOUSE, INC.

1045 ZIEGLER RD.
P.O. BOX 158
WELLSVILLE, PA 17365
800-735-2697
717-432-8611
FAX: 717-432-2683

Catalog: free
Save: up to 40%
Pay: check, MO, MC, V, Discover
Sells: equipment for bow hunting, hunting, and archery
Store: same address; Monday to Friday 9–5, Wednesday 9–9, Saturday 9–1

You can save up to 40% on a complete range of supplies for bow hunting, bow fishing, archery, and hunting through the 144-page catalog from Bowhunters Warehouse, which has been in business since 1974. The catalog features a large selection of bows and arrows, as well as points, feathers, bow sights, rests, quivers, targets, bow-hunting books and videotapes, game calls, camouflage clothing and supplies, shooting equipment, and other gear for outdoor sports. Accra, Bear, Beman, Browning, Darton, Delta, Easton, Golden Eagle, Hoyt, Martin, PSE, Saunders, and other manufacturers are represented. Bowhunters Discount Warehouse also builds arrows to order, and the catalog includes a complete description of the features and available options for custom arrows. Specifications are included with the information on the hunting equipment, making this a good reference as well as a source for real savings.

Special Factors: Authorized returns are accepted; minimum order is $15; C.O.D. orders are accepted.

CABELA'S INC.

812 13TH AVE.
SIDNEY, NE 69160
308-254-5505
FAX: 308-254-6102
TDD: 800-695-5000

Catalog: free
Save: up to 40% on list prices
Pay: check, MO, MC, V, AE, Discover
Sells: hunting, fishing, and camping gear
Store: I-80, Exit #59, Sidney, NE; also E. Hwy. 30, Kearney, NE; Monday to Saturday 8–8, Sunday 12 noon–5:30, both locations

Cabela's, the "world's foremost outfitter" of fishing, hunting, and outdoor enthusiasts, has been praised by several readers. Cabela's catalog pricing represents savings of up to 40% on regular retail on some goods, but *do not ask for discounts.*

Cabela's sells rods, reels, and tackle from well-known manufacturers, including Berkley, Blue Fox, Daiwa, Fenwick, Abu Garcia, G. Loomis, Mitchell, Shakespeare, and Shimano. There's an extensive selection of lures, line, tackle boxes, hooks, nets, and other fishing gear, and pages of Minn Kota electric boat motors, electronics by Eagle, Humminbird, Interphase, and Seacom, boat covers, boat seats, Sea Eagle dinghies, Starcraft fishing boats, down riggers, winches, batteries, and trailer parts. Fishing is the strong suit in the spring and summer catalogs, but a comparable range of hunting equipment is offered in other issues.

General outdoor needs are served by the camping department: Eureka tents, sleeping bags and mats, gear bags, backpacks, cookware and kitchen equipment, heavy-duty flashlights, Pentax and Tasco binoculars, Hobie and Ray-Ban sunglasses, hunting knives, and related products are offered. And there's a good selection of outdoor clothing, including waders, camouflage wear, fishing vests and hunting jackets, snakeproof boots, moccasins, bush jackets, parkas, jeans, and more. The 258-page color catalog includes complete product descriptions and specifications, but if you need help with your selection or are buying for someone else, the customer service department can assist you.

Special Factors: Satisfaction is guaranteed; price quote by phone; returns are accepted for exchange, refund, or credit.

CAMPMOR

P.O. BOX 997
PARAMUS, NJ 07653-0997
201-445-5000

Catalog: free
Save: up to 50%
Pay: check, MO, MC, V, AE, Discover
Sells: camping gear and supplies
Store: 810 Rte. 17 N., Paramus, NJ; Monday to Friday 9:30–9:30, Saturday 9:30–6

Campmor's 144-page catalog is full of great buys on camping goods, bike touring accessories, and clothing. You'll save up to 50% on clothing by Borglite Pile, Columbia Interchange System, Sierra Designs, Thinsulate, and Woolrich, as well as duofold and Polypro underwear, Sorel and Timberland boots, and other outerwear. Swiss Victorinox knives are offered at 30% off list, and Buck knives, Coleman cooking equipment, Sherpa snowshoes, Silva compasses, Edelrid climbing ropes, and books and manuals on camping and survival are available. You'll also find tents and sleeping bags by Coleman, Eureka, Moonstone, The North Face, Sierra Designs, Slumberjack, Wenzel, and Campmor's own lines, as well as backpacks by JanSport, Kelly Camp Trails, and Peak. Campmor has been in business since 1946, and it is worth a trip if you're in the Paramus area.

Special Factors: Returns are accepted for exchange, refund, or credit; minimum order is $20 on phone orders.

CENTRAL SKINDIVERS

160-09 JAMAICA AVE.
JAMAICA, NY 11432-6111
718-739-5772
FAX: 718-739-3679

Information: price quote
Save: up to 40%
Pay: check, MO, MC, V, AE, Discover
Sells: SCUBA-diving equipment
Store: same address; Monday to Saturday 10–6:30

 ¡Si!

Central Skindivers, in business since 1952, sells diving gear at savings of up to 40%, including tanks from Dacor, Sherwood, and U.S. Divers, and a full range of regulators, masks, fins, gauges, computers, suits, and other gear. There are buoyancy jackets from Beuchat, Dacor, Seaquest, Seatec, Sherwood, Tabata, and U.S. Divers, and watches and timers from Chronosport, Citizen, Heuer, and Seiko. Central Skindivers has no catalog, so call for a price quote.

Special Factors: Shipping is not charged; minimum order is $50.

CHEAP SHOT, INC.

1797 RTE. 920
CANONSBURG, PA 15317
412-745-2658
FAX: 412-745-4265

Catalog: free
Save: 33% plus
Pay: check or MO
Sells: ammunition
Store: Gun Runner, 950 S. Central Ave., Canonsburg, PA; Monday to Friday 8–8, Saturday 8–5, Sunday 10–4

Cheap Shot, "shooters serving shooters since 1978," offers savings of 33% and more on the usual prices of ammo and reloading components from CCI, Federal, Hornady, Remington, and Winchester. The 16-page catalog also offers a "reloading library," with several manuals on the subject. Because Cheap Shot specializes in ammo and buys in volume, the discounts are better than those offered by many hunting catalogs.

Please note: Federal regulations on age and identification requirements are stated in the catalog, and you must provide signature and drivers' license number in order to purchase ammunition.

Special Factors: Authorized returns are accepted (a 20% restocking fee may be charged); C.O.D. orders are accepted (a 25% deposit is required).

DEER SHACK

7155 CTY. HWY. B
DEPT. WBMC96
P.O. BOX E
BELGIUM, WI 53004-0905
800-443-3337
414-994-9818
FAX: 414-994-4099

Catalog: $2
Save: up to 30%
Pay: check, MO, MC, V, Discover
Sells: deer-related and hunting products
Store: mail order only

   ✓

This catalog is devoted to the culture of the deer hunter, where a camo gun sock is listed under "Great Stocking Stuffers," and the audiotapes include *Vocabulary of Deer*. Much of the 64-page color catalog shows handsome gifts—limited edition prints of hunting scenes, handpainted bronzes, mirrors and home accents adorned with shed antlers, and signs, mats, plaques, desk accessories, belt buckles, mugs, and humorous literature. The hunting gear includes bow and gun accessories, decoy and scent supplies, game transport and processing supplies, Hatchbag vehicle liners, camo wear and blinds, tree stands, maps, and books and tapes covering everything from locating game to tanning the hides.

Deer Shack is offering readers a discount of 10% on anything they buy, on any order until this offer expires. Be sure to identify yourself as a WBMC reader when you order, and deduct the discount from the cost of the goods only. This WBMC reader discount expires February 1, 1997.

Special Factors: Satisfaction is guaranteed; returns (except personalized goods) are accepted for exchange, refund, or credit.

GANDER MOUNTAIN, INC.

DEPT. WBMC
P.O. BOX 6
WILMOT, WI 53192
800-558-9410
FAX: 800-533-2828
TDD: 800-558-3554

Catalog: free
Save: up to 35%
Pay: check, MO, MC, V, AE, Discover
Sells: hunting, fishing, camping, reloading, archery, and boating gear
Store: Merrillville, IN; Flint and Utica, MI; Duluth and St. Cloud, MN; Appleton, Brookfield, Eau Claire, Madison, Wausau, and Wilmot, WI

Gander Mountain is reader-recommended as a great source for outdoor sports gear and clothing, getting high marks for selection and service. Prices are also reliably good—savings of up to 35% can be found on different items, although not everything is discounted. Fishing and hunting are Gander Mountain's focus, served through the 200-plus-page color catalog of equipment and clothing. The rod and reel department offers gear by Berkley, Big Jon, Browning, Cannon, Daiwa, Eagle, Fenwick, Abu Garcia, Johnson, Mitchell, Penn, Quantum, Shakespeare, Shimano, Zebco, and under Gander Mountain's own name. There are lures by Bagley's, Mepps, Normark, and many other firms, and fishing line, nets, tackle boxes, rod cases, and other gear. Boat seats, covers, winches, bilge pumps, Minn Kota and other motors, Cannon downriggers, depth finders, recorders, radios, sonar devices, and Humminbird electronics are all offered as well.

Hunters will find a similar range of products for their sport: CVA black-powder rifles, Lyman and MEC reloaders, Ram-line magazines, Hastings, Mossberg, and Remington replacement barrels for shotguns, Gun Guard gun cases, Treadlok gun safes, Michaels holsters, practice equipment, shell boxes, and related goods. Spotting scopes, hunting binoculars, mounts, and tripods by Bausch & Lomb, Bushnell, Leupold, and Tasco are also available.

Gander's video department offers Warburton and other tapes on big game hunting, shooting and handling guns, game calls and hunting techniques, training hunting dogs, hunting wild birds, and fishing for bass, walleye, and trout. Specialty clothing for both hunting and fishing—waders, hunting and shooting jackets, camouflage wear—is carried, as well as rugged clothing. Chamois cloth shirts, rain suits, leather jackets, and footwear for men and women from Acme, Browning, Danner, Dexter, Heartland, Hi-Tec, Hodgman, Long Haul, Maine Classic, Merrell, Minnetonka, Nike, Ridge, Rockport, Rocky, Sorel, and other firms is available, plus Bushnell sunglasses, backpacks and luggage, camp cookware, sleeping bags, tents, Buck knives, pet beds, and other outdoor gear.

Special Factors: Satisfaction is guaranteed; C.O.D. orders are accepted.

DON GLEASON'S CAMPERS SUPPLY, INC.

9 PEARL ST.
P.O. BOX 87
NORTHAMPTON, MA
01061-0087
413-584-4895
FAX: 413-586-8770

Catalog: free
Save: up to 30%
Pay: check, MO, MC, V
Sells: camping supplies and equipment
Store: same address; Monday to Friday 9–5:30, Thursday til 8:30, Saturday 9–5

Don Gleason has been helping America hit the trail since 1957, with everything from tents to trowels. The firm's 80-page catalog is packed with good buys on equipment—tents and screen houses by Comet, Eureka, The North Face, Sierra Designs, and Walrus, sleeping bags by The North Face, Slumberjack, and White Stag, Winnebago air mattresses, tarps, blankets, primus stoves and cookware, Coleman and Gott coolers, first aid kits, Buck knives, duffles, and backpacks and rucksacks by Camp Trails, Caribou, Eagle Creek, JanSport, and The North Face. Don Gleason has an excellent selection of tent stakes and grommet kits, seals and other tent-mending supplies, hook-and-loop fastening, bungee cords and bungee-by-the-yard, camp toilets, cots, compasses, flashlights, insect repellents, axes, picks, and even gold-panning equipment. Savings run up to 50%, and there are volume discounts of 10% and 15% on the freeze-dried food from Alpine Aire, Backpacker's Pantry, Dri-Lite Foods, and Mountain House. See the catalog for details of the no-hassle warranty.

Special Factors: Satisfaction is guaranteed; quantity discounts are available; returns are accepted for exchange, refund, or credit; minimum order is $10 with credit cards.

GOLF HAUS

700 N. PENNSYLVANIA
LANSING, MI 48906
517-482-8842

Price List: free
Save: up to 60%
Pay: check, MO, MC, V,
Sells: golf clubs, apparel, and accessories
Store: same address; Monday to Saturday
9–5:30

    (see text)

Golf Haus has "the absolute lowest prices on pro golf clubs" anywhere —up to 60% below list—and stocks goods by every major manufacturer. All of the models sold here are available nationwide, which means that, unlike the "exclusive models" offered by a number of discounters, the goods at Golf Haus can be price-shopped fairly. There are clubs, bags, putters, balls, and other golf equipment and supplies by Cobra (including the "King Cobra" line), Dunlop, Hogan, Lynx, MacGregor, Ping, PowerBilt, Ram, Spalding, Tiger Shark, Titleist, Wilson, and other firms. There are Bag Boy carts, Etonic shoes, gloves, umbrellas, spikes, scorekeepers, visors, rain suits, tote bags, socks, and much more.

Golf Haus is offering readers of this book a gift of knit club head covers (for woods), with each purchase of a complete set of clubs (woods and irons). Identify yourself as a reader when you order. This WBMC reader discount expires February 1, 1997.

Special Factors: Shipping and insurance are included on orders shipped within the continental United States; minimum order is $50.

GOLFSMITH INTERNATIONAL, INC.

11000 N. IH35
AUSTIN, TX 78753
800-456-3344
512-837-4810
FAX: 512-837-1245

Catalog: free
Save: up to 50%
Pay: check, MO, MC, V, Discover
Sells: customized golf clubs, components, accessories, and repair equipment
Store: same address; Monday to Friday 7–7, Saturday 8–7, Sunday 9–7

   ¡Si!

Golfsmith International's accessories catalog, *The Golf Store*, features the firm's own line of Golfsmith clubs. Golfsmith can make woods and irons in any flex, length, weight, or grip size. The Golf Store catalog brings you 60 pages of putters, specialty clubs, bags, balls, clothing, footwear, gloves, pull carts, and other accessories, including instructional videos and books. Golfsmith, which opened its doors in 1967, offers savings of up to 50% on the cost of comparable name-brand products.

The 228-page *Clubhead and Components* catalog offers a complete selection of golf club heads for woods, irons, and putters, as well as grips, shafts, refinishing supplies, and tools, as well as instruction manuals. Golfsmith conducts the Harvey Penick Golf Academy, and also offers four different training programs in making, repairing, and fitting clubs, for every level of experience. All of the courses are conducted at Golfsmith's complex in Austin, Texas.

Non-U.S. readers, please note: Orders must be paid in U.S. funds.

Special Factors: Request each catalog desired by name; C.O.D. orders are accepted.

HOLABIRD SPORTS

9220 PULASKI HWY.
BALTIMORE, MD 21220
410-687-6400
FAX: 410-687-7311

Brochure: free
Save: up to 40%
Pay: check, MO, MC, V, AE, Discover
Sells: racquet sports equipment and athletic footwear
Store: same address; Monday to Friday, 9–5, Saturday 9–3

Buy here and get the "Holabird Advantage": equipment for racquet sports at up to 40% below list prices, service on manufacturers' warranties, and free stringing with tournament nylon on all racquets. If you're in the Baltimore area, drop by and try out a racquet on Holabird's indoor court.

Holabird has been in business since 1981, and carries tennis racquets by scores of firms, including Donnay, Dunlop, Estusa, Fischer, Fox, Head, Mizuno, Prince, Pro-Kennex, Rossignol, Slazenger, Spalding, Wilson, Wimbledon, Yamaha, and Yonex. There are tennis balls by Dunlop, Penn, and Wilson, ball machines by Lobster, Prince, and Tennis Master, and footwear by Adidas, Asics, Avia, Converse, Diadora, Fila, Head, K-Swiss, New Balance, Nike, Prince, Reebok, Wilson, and others.

Racquetball players should check the prices on racquets by E-Force, Ektelon, Head, Pro-Kennex, Spalding, and Wilson. The squash department features racquets by Black Knight, Dunlop, Ektelon, Fox, Head,

Pro-Kennex, Prince, Slazenger, Spalding, and Wilson, and eye guards by Black Knight, Ektelon, Leader, and Pro-Kennex. Pros can save their clubs sizable sums on court equipment and maintenance supplies, such as court dryers, tennis nets, ball hoppers, and stringing machines.

Holabird also stocks a full line of basketball, cross-training, aerobic, running, walking, and hiking shoes, as well as sandals, T-shirts, socks, caps, sunglasses from Ray-Ban, and Timex sport watches. See the monthly eight-page catalog for specials, or call or write for a price quote.

Special Factors: Authorized returns (except used items) are accepted within seven days; online with Prodigy.

OVERTON'S SPORTS CENTER, INC.

DEPT. 57612
P.O. BOX 8228
GREENVILLE, NC 27835
800-334-6541
919-355-7600
FAX: 919-355-2923

Catalog: free
Save: up to 40%
Pay: check, MO, MC, V, AE, Discover
Sells: boating accessories and water sports goods
Store: 5343 South Boulevard, Charlotte; 111 Red Banks Rd., Greenville; and 1331 Buck Jones Rd., Raleigh, NC

Overton's lays claim to title of "World's Largest Water Sports Dealer," selling a wide range of equipment for boating, water skiing, snorkeling, and other avocations at up to 40% off list. Overton's was established in 1975, and publishes three catalogs: The 132-page, color *Water Sports* catalog features skis and accessories ranging from junior trainers to experts' tricks, jumpers and slaloms by Connelly, EP, Jobe, Kidder, O'Brien, and other firms. Wetsuits, apparel, knee boards, water toys, inflatables, snorkeling accessories, boating accessories, books, videotapes, and personal watercraft accessories are also offered. The 48-page swimwear and apparel catalog, "Kristi's," features such names as De La Mer, Bendigo, Venus, Solar Tan Thru, Point Conception, OP, O'Neill, Take Cover, Club Sportwear, and many more. The look is California young, with eye-popping prints dominating the collection.

The 200-page Discount Boating Accessories answers your boating needs with a wide range of products: boat seats and covers, safety equipment, instruments, electronics, hardware, cleaners, fishing equipment, clothing, fuel tanks, and performance accessories. The brands include Apelco, Aqua Meter, Brinkman, Eagle, Humminbird, Interphase, Ray Jefferson, Maxxima, Newmar, PowerWinch, Shakespeare, and Si-Tex, among others. The equipment catalogs give both the list or comparable retail, and Overton's discount prices.

Canadian readers, please note: Only U.S. funds are accepted.

Special Factors: Satisfaction is guaranteed; quantity discounts are available; unused returns are accepted within 30 days for exchange, refund, or credit; C.O.D. orders are accepted.

PERFORMANCE BICYCLE SHOP

P.O. BOX 2741
CHAPEL HILL, NC
27515-2741
800-727-2453
FAX: 800-727-3291

Catalog: free
Save: up to 40%
Pay: check, MO, MC, V, Discover
Sells: bicycle parts and cycling apparel
Store: 31 stores in CA, CO, IL, MD, NC, OR, PA, VA, and WA

Serious cyclists are familiar with Performance Bicycle Shop for the company's line of bicycling parts, accessories, and clothing. The firm's parts department is well stocked with components by Campagnolo, Look, Mavic, Shimano, Time, and other firms. Performance has been in business since 1981 and offers a large selection of cycling clothing, as well as helmets, cycling shoes, gloves, panniers, and hundreds of products to enhance performance. The brands represented in the 80-page color catalog include Avocet, Bell, Dia Compe, Giro, Nike, Profile, Scott USA, Shimano, Specialized, Thule, and Vetta, among others. In-line skates (Rollerblades) and camping gear are also available.

Special Factors: Satisfaction is guaranteed.

PERFORMANCE DIVER®

DEPT. WBMC
P.O. BOX 2741
CHAPEL HILL, NC
27514-2714
800-933-2299
FAX: 800-727-3291

Catalog: free
Save: up to 50%
Pay: check, MO, MC, V, Discover
Sells: scuba equipment and apparel
Store: mail order only

Performance Diver®, established in 1990, publishes the largest catalog of quality scuba gear in the United States, with a full line of scuba equipment, accessories, and apparel. You'll find regulators, gauges, BDCs, wetsuits, and a wide variety of accessories in the 44 pages. Although many of the items are manufactured by the same companies that sell under well-known labels in dive shops, they're available here under the Performance name at savings of up to 50% on comparable retail. The catalog emphasizes technologically advanced design, with the latest fibers and construction methods used to maximize performance, comfort, and safety. You don't have to dive to appreciate the good selection of Citizen and Seiko watches, Guy Harvey T-shirts, Supplex trunks and Lycra tanks, or duffel bags—but any recreational activity that features "treasure recovery bags" in multiple sizes is definitely worth a look.

Special Factors: Satisfaction is guaranteed; returns are accepted for exchange, refund, or credit.

SAILBOARD WARE-HOUSE, INC.

300 S. OWASSO BLVD.,
   DEPT. WBMC
ST. PAUL, MN 55117
612-482-9995
FAX: 612-482-1353

Catalog: free
Save: 35% average
Pay: check, MO, MC, V, AE, Discover
Sells: windsurfing, snow-boarding, inline skating, and kayaking equipment
Store: same address; Monday to Friday 10–8, Saturday 9–2; also Hood River, Oregon; Monday to Saturday 9–9, Sunday 9–6 (April 1–October 1); and Boston, MA; Monday to Saturday 11–7

Put wind and water together, and you have the prime ingredients for the thrilling sport of windsurfing, also known as sailboarding. The right equipment helps, which is what you'll find at Sailboard Warehouse—at discounts that average 35%, but run much deeper on sale items and special purchases. Sailboard Warehouse, better known as "The House" to devotees, has been in business since 1982, selling light to heavy wind sailboards, sails, masts, harnesses, fins, and a broad selection of windsurfing apparel. The 40-plus-page catalogs feature equipment by Bailey, BIC, DaKine, Fanatic, Freedom Maui, Maui Magic, Mistral, NeilPryde, O'Brien, SeaTrend, Simmer, Tiga, Topsails, Weichart, Windcatcher, Windsurfing Hawaii, and other manufacturers. The boards run from entry-level to custom models for pros, and the catalog includes numerous informative sidebars on choosing equipment and evaluating construction and materials. Automaxi car racks, windsurfing books and videos, and wet suits, drysuits, harnesses and other accessories by Bare, Body Glove, O'Neill, and Ronny are also available.

The House also answers your winter sports needs with a full line of snowboards from Aggression, Apocalypse, Heavy Tools, Joyride, Kemper, Limited, Mistral, One, Pyramid, Rad Air, and Staple; boots by Agis, Alpina, Airwalk, and Grunge, and related equipment. And if the day brings neither wind nor snow, strap on a pair of Kinetics or Rollerblade inline skates (sold here at a discount), and take on the pavement instead!

Please note: Phone hours are Monday to Friday 8–6, Saturday 9–1, CST.

Sailboard Warehouse is offering readers a discount of 5% on first orders. Identify yourself as a WBMC reader when you order, and deduct the discount from the cost of the goods only. This WBMC reader discount expires May 1, 1997.

Special Factors: Satisfaction is guaranteed; shipping is not charged on orders of two or more boards; authorized returns are accepted within 20 days for exchange, refund, or credit.

SIERRA TRADING POST

DEPT. WBMC-96
5025 CAMPSTOOL RD.
CHEYENNE, WY
82007-1802
307-775-8000
FAX: 307-775-8088

Catalog: free
Save: up to 70%
Pay: check, MO, MC, V, Discover
Sells: outdoor clothing and equipment
Store: same address; Monday to Saturday 9–6, Sunday 12–6; also 2000 Harvard Way, Reno, NV; Monday to Saturday 10–7, Sunday 11–5

  ⊕ (see text)

Sierra Trading Post, established in 1986, offers casual and outdoor clothing and camping gear in a charming, 32-page catalog. Sierra is essentially a mail-order outlet store that sells closeouts, overruns, and special purchases at savings of up to 70%. Rugged clothing and outerwear, shoes for hiking and running, great pants and shorts, socks, sweaters, underwear, and even comfortable dresses are among the offerings. Name brands pepper the catalog—Asolo, Columbia, Duofold, Hanes, Hind, Kelty, Lowe, Marmot, New Balance, The North Face, Sportif USA, and Vasque are among the manufacturers represented in past mailings. Sleeping bags, backpacks, and tents are also available.

Non-U.S. readers, please note: Orders are shipped outside the United States (via USPS) to APO/FPO destinations, Canada, and Japan only.

Special Factors: Satisfaction is guaranteed; returns are accepted for exchange, refund, or credit.

SOCCER INTER-
NATIONAL, INC.

P.O. BOX 7222,
  DEPT. WBM-96
ARLINGTON, VA
  22207-0222
703-524-4333

Catalog: $2, refundable (see text)
Save: up to 30%
Pay: check or MO
Sells: soccer gear, accessories, and gifts
Store: mail order only

  (see text)

Soccer International, founded in 1976 by a rabid soccer buff, publishes an 18-page color catalog of game-related items ranging from professional equipment to novelties. The savings run up to 30% on some goods, compared to the prices charged by other firms, but generally average about 20% less. The catalog is a must-see for any soccer enthusiast or friend of one, since it's a great resource for gifts as well as gear. (Consider the $2 an investment, since there's a $5 gift certificate included with the catalog, which will be recouped on your first order.)

You'll find a number of balls here from Adidas, Brine, Mikasa, and Umbro, plus a variety of jerseys and T-shirts. PVC leg shields and ankle guards, a ball inflator, nets and goals, practice aids, and a great selection of books and videotapes on coaching, game strategy, and soccer rules are available. If you're stuck on the sidelines, you'll want Lava Buns, the stadium cushion: Pop it in the microwave for a few minutes, and it will keep your bottom warm for hours. Soccer International also sells soccer-design pillows, soccer-theme games, radios, door mats, mugs, ties, cloissoné pins, bumper stickers, doorknobs, and a lamp. This is where you'll find the World Cup 1994 video highlights (of most of the games), poster, tie, and playing cards, as well as replica team jerseys of four of the top soccer-playing countries. Soccer-loving puzzle buffs will enjoy the challenge of Mordillo jigsaw puzzles from Germany, which run from 500 to 2,000 pieces. (Mordillo's book of soccer cartoons, also available, is a classic.) And you can add a touch of the jungle to your game with "wild balls," patterned with leopard, cheetah, tiger, zebra, or panther designs, in sizes 3, 4, or 5.

Canadian readers, please note: Orders must be paid in U.S. funds, drawn on the Canadian postal service, or on a U.S. bank.

APO/FPO readers, please note: Orders are not shipped to APO/FPO addresses during November or December.

Institutional buyers, please note: Catalog prices are mainly for single items, but Soccer International's specialty is sales to teams, leagues, clubs, and schools. If you're buying in multiples for a group, let the company know when you request the catalog.

Special Factors: Minimum order is $15; shipping is not charged on orders over $35 sent within the contiguous United States.

SPIKE NASHBAR

4111 SIMON RD., DEPT. WBM6
YOUNGSTOWN, OH 44512
800-774-5348
FAX: 800-456-1223

Catalog: free
Save: up to 40%
Pay: check, MO, MC, V, Discover
Sells: volleyball gear and apparel
Store: mail order only

Spike Nashbar, established in 1990, offers savings of up to 40% on competition volleyball gear, clothing, and accessories. The 40-page color catalog offers over two dozen balls for indoor and outdoor play, from Brine, Mikasa, Molten, Sideout, Spalding, Tachikara, and Wilson (Redsand). Over two dozen lines of clothing are offered, and several nets and net systems are available, including one from Park and Sun for under $96 and "the best portable net system available," the Spectrum series, which costs about $236. There are volleyball shoes for men and women by Asics, Kaepa, Mizuno, Power, and Reebok beginning at under $40. Sport bras, socks, T-shirts, shorts, duffels, sport watches, and sunglasses from Bausch & Lomb and Bollé are also sold, as well as vital knee protection from Asics and Body Glove. If you've ever watched or played serious volleyball, you'll know why they're part of the standard uniform of the game. Spike Nashbar has a "best price" policy; see the catalog for details.

Canadian readers, please note: Only U.S. funds are accepted.

Special Factors: Satisfaction is guaranteed; returns are accepted for exchange, refund, or credit.

SPORT SHOP

DEPT. WBMC
P.O. BOX 340
GRIFTON, NC 28530
919-746-8288
FAX: 919-746-8296

Catalog: $1
Save: up to 50%
Pay: check, MO, MC, V, Discover
Sells: hunting gear and accessories
Store: Hwy. 11 N., Grifton, NC; Monday to
Saturday 8–5

Hunting is the sport served here, with bow-hunting and bow-fishing equipment and accessories, black-powder rifles and supplies, and much more offered through a 64-page catalog. Sport Shop has been in business since 1955, and sells at discounts of up to 50% off suggested list or regular retail.

Bow-hunters enjoy a wide selection of bows for all ages and abilities, including models by Bear, Darton, Pearson, and PSE. Arrows and shafts from Berman and Easton are available, as well as arrow cases, quivers, arrow-making supplies, archery tools, Cobra bow sights, scopes, releases, arrow rests and plungers, arm guards, gloves, and other equipment for the serious hunter. Sport Shop sells both bull's eye and animal (picture) targets, and arrow broad heads and points by Muzzy, Wasp, and Zwickey. Tree stands, camouflage paint, scent killer and dispensers, turkey and deer calls, and camouflage headgear, Rocky boots, and Walls camo pants and jackets are available, and Sport Shop also sells bow-fishing supplies, Daisy air guns, Thompson Center blackpowder rifles, and accessories. Nearly two dozen videos on hunting technique are offered.

If you foresee buying more than $400 in hunting gear over the next two years, consider joining Sport Shop's Frequent Buyer club. The $20 fee entitles you to a 5% merchandise discount on all orders you place for two years.

Special Factors: Returns are accepted for exchange, refund, or credit; minimum order is $15 with credit cards.

SURVIVAL SUPPLY CO.

▬▬▬▬▬

P.O. BOX 1745-WM
SHINGLE SPRINGS, CA
95682

Catalog: $2
Save: up to 30% (see text)
Pay: check, MO, MC, V
Sells: camping and outdoor gear, survival supplies, etc.
Store: mail order only

Survival Supply serves two distinct but overlapping markets: outdoors enthusiasts and survivalists. The firm's 44-page catalog is heavy on emergency food and gear, and there are books on everything from combat ammunition to Caribbean tax havens. Everything is offered at prices that average 25% below regular retail, and quantity discounts are available on food items.

Survival Supply began business in 1988 and offers an extensive selection of dehydrated foods, including goods from Backpackers Pantry, Ready Reserves, and Stone Mill Farms. Survival Supply's survival kits can keep one or two persons going for 3 to 30 days, or a party of four sustained for up to a year. A seven-day food kit for four costs about $250 at this writing, and includes water purification tablets, stoves and fuel, a cooking kit, 30 candles and waterproof matches, and much more, besides the food. In addition, Survival Supply offers a small selection of camp stoves and lanterns, mess kits, flashlights, camp saws and shovels, gas masks, knives, first-aid kits, duffels, camouflage BDUs, and survival guides—from genuine military manuals to handbooks on poaching.

If you do the purchasing for an institution, corporation, city, or county with an emergency preparedness program, you can call, fax, or write for the corporate price list. It features a number of kits for large-scale emergencies—the "five member search and rescue" and "25 person disaster and trauma first aid" kits are examples. Water pouches and drums and nitrogen-packed dehydrated foods are available, as well as MRE rations, or Meals Ready to Eat. Please note that you must be from a *qualifying group* to receive the price list.

Survival Supply is offering readers a discount of 2% on first orders. Identify yourself as a WBMC reader when you order, and deduct the discount from the cost of the goods only. This WBMC reader discount expires February 1, 1997.

Special Factors: Quantity discounts are available.

TELEPRO GOLF SHOP

17622 ARMSTRONG AVE.
IRVINE, CA 92714-5791
800-333-9903
FAX: 714-261-5473

Brochure: free
Save: up to 40%
Pay: check, MO, MC, V, Discover
Sells: golf clubs
Store: Shamrock Golf Shops in Lakewood, Los Angeles, Palos Verdes, Pasadena, and Santa Ana, CA; addresses are listed in the brochure

Telepro, a division of Shamrock Golf Shops and an affiliate of Teletire (see "Auto"), sells first-quality golf clubs and accessories at savings of up to 40%. Telepro has been in business since 1976, and sells clubs by Callaway, Cobra, Hogan, Lynx, Mizuno, Ping, Shamrock, Taylormade, Titleist, Wilson, Yonex, and other manufacturers. Bags and other accessories are sold at varing discounts. The brochure includes a questionnaire on your golfing style, which helps Telepro determine the best clubs for your game.

Special Factors: Satisfaction is guaranteed; returns (except special orders) are accepted within 30 days (a 10% restocking fee may be charged).

WALK USA

6150 NANCY RIDGE. RD.
SAN DIEGO, CA
  92121-3209
800-255-6422

Catalog: free
Save: up to 50%
Pay: check, MO, MC, V, AE
Sells: walking clothing, shoes, and accessories
Store: mail order only

If you've had it with shin splints and runner's knee, it's time to slow it down. Mother was right—walking *is* good exercise—and because it's much easier on your joints, it's become very popular over the last few years. Walk USA serves both dedicated strollers and race-walkers with easy-fitting sport suits, lightweight fleece separates, Supplex shorts, Supplex stirrup and Lycra ankle-length tights, Jogbra sports bras, athletic socks, and accessories. Walking shoe models from Avia, Brooks, K-Swiss, New Balance, Rockport, Ryka, and Saucony are sold at an average discount of 30% off list, and the 16-page color catalog also shows hats and gloves for winter workouts, mesh safety vests with reflective stripes, sunshields and watches with lap monitors, and the ice/heat packs, joint supports, and Sorbothane insoles you may need if you get carried away. And you may do just that after mastering world-class race-walking techniques with the help of one of Walk USA's videos. If you need background music but find your running tapes are too fast, you can take your pick tapes mixed for different walking speeds and styles. Not everything is discounted, but the prices are competitive with those charged for comparable private-label workout wear elsewhere.

Special Factors: Satisfaction is guaranteed; returns are accepted for exchange, refund, or credit; C.O.D. orders are accepted.

WATER WAREHOUSE

801 LUNT AVE.
ELK GROVE VILLAGE, IL
  60007
800-574-7665
FAX: 708-952-8754

Catalog: $2
Save: up to 50%
Pay: check, MO, MC, V, Discover
Sells: swimming pool supplies and equipment
Store: mail order only

Swimming pools have two lives—summer and winter—and Water Warehouse sells supplies and equipment for both seasons, at savings of up to 50% on list or comparable retail. Here are all the chemicals you need to keep the water safe, and cut down on maintenance: Monarc chlorinating tabs, oxidizers (shocks), rust and scale preventers, algaecides, pH balancers, and other agents. You'll also find water-testing kits, pool skimmers, vacuums, thermometers, filters, and brushes, and the tools for enjoying the fruits of your labor—inflatable loungers, sport tubes, kiddie "riders," flippers, water balls, and diving games. When the weather turns cool, Water Warehouse helps out with high-speed pool pumps (for quick draining), repair kits for vinyl liners, winterizing plugs (to save the skimmer), covers for all pool shapes and sizes, and water sleeves to hold the covers down. The 52-page color catalog features these products and more, from names like Arneson, Polaris, Teledyne, and Weber, and there are seasonal sales that lower the discount prices even further.

Special Factors: Satisfaction is guaranteed; returns are accepted within 30 days for exchange, refund, or credit.

WILEY OUTDOOR SPORTS, INC.

DEPT. WBMC 1996
1808 SPORTSMAN LN.
HUNTSVILLE, AL 35816
205-837-3931
FAX: 205-837-4017

Catalog: free (see text)
Save: 30% average
Pay: check, MO, MC, V, Discover
Sells: hunting, camping, and outdoor gear and equipment
Store: 1808 Sportsman Lane, Huntsville, AL; Monday to Friday 9–6, Saturday 9–4:30

This family-run business has been outfitting hunters with a full range of equipment and gear since 1953, and offers savings that average 30%, but can run as high as 50% on certain items and lines. Wiley specializes in hunting, reloading, camping, and optical equipment, and serves the dedicated outdoors enthusiast. The catalog includes a good selection of tents, backpacks, knives, binoculars, and clothing, as well as the hunting equipment. The firm prides itself on its commitment to good service and lifelong customer relationships, and invites serious inquiries only about its goods.

Special Factors: Satisfaction is guaranteed; unused returns are accepted within 10 days for exchange, refund, or credit; minimum order is $25; C.O.D. orders (via UPS only) are accepted.

WORLD WIDE AQUATICS

DEPT. WBMC
10500 UNIVERSITY CEN-
    TER DR., SUITE 250
TAMPA, FL 33612-6415
800-726-1530
813-972-0818
FAX: 813-972-0905

Catalog: free
Save: up to 50%
Pay: check, MO, MC, V, AE, Discover
Sells: swimwear and accessories
Store: mail order only

Buying a swimsuit is one of the top ten Most Dreaded Shopping Activities, in part because of the convergence of large expanses of skin, fluorescent lights, and endless mirrors. Swimsuit styles are also problematical—they're often cut to reveal more than comfort and reputation allow. World Wide Aquatics solves all of these problems, and offers savings of up to 50% on selected suits as well.

The firm's 48-page color catalogs show swimsuits, trunks, shorts, and coverups for men, women, and children from Arena, Hind, Hydro-Fit, Ocean, Quintana Roo, Speedo, and Tyr. The styles run from racing-sleek to skirted, full-coverage models, including a line designed for post-mastectomy wear. The sizes run from children's 4 to women's size 24, men's to a 40-inch waist. "Aqueous" shoes for use in the pool and water-exercise equipment are also available. World Wide Aquatics sells workout wear by Dolphin and Speedo (including triathalon clothing that goes from bike to beach), wet suits, swimming goggles, bathing caps, and competition equipment and books.

World Wide Aquatics has been in business since 1972, and offers deep discounts on multiples of 12 of selected suits—ideal for schools and swim clubs. See the catalog for details, or if you know the style you want from one of the manufacturers listed here, call for availability and a quote.

Special Factors: Satisfaction is guaranteed; new, unused returns (except books and videos) with hangtags and labels are accepted in the original packaging for exchange, refund, or credit.

SEE ALSO

Astronomics/Christophers, Ltd. • spotting scopes for bird watching • **CAMERAS**
Bruce Medical Supply • small selection of fitness equipment • **MEDICINE: SPECIAL NEEDS**
The Button Shop • zippers for tents and sleeping bags • **CRAFTS: TEXTILE ARTS**
Car Racks Direct • car racks for sports equipment, boats, etc. • **AUTO**
CISCO • swimming pool accessories and parts • **HOME: IMPROVEMENT**
Clothcrafters, Inc. • flannel gun-cleaning patches, mosquito netting, sleeping bag liners • **GENERAL MERCHANDISE**
Creative Health Products • exercise equipment • **HEALTH**
Dance Distributors • dancewear, gymnastics shoes, etc. • **CLOTHING**
Defender Industries, Inc. • water sports accessories • **AUTO**
E & B Marine Supply, Inc. • water skis • **AUTO**
Ewald-Clark • binoculars • **CAMERAS**
A. Feibusch Corporation • replacement tent zippers • **CRAFTS: TEXTILE ARTS**

Leather Unlimited Corp. • *black-powder supplies, suede duffel bags* • **LEATHER**

Mardiron Optics • *binoculars and spotting scopes* • **CAMERAS**

Mass. Army & Navy Store • *government surplus camping and survival gear* • **CLOTHING**

Newark Dressmaker Supply, Inc. • *replacement zippers for sleeping bags and tents* • **CRAFTS: TEXTILE ARTS**

Okun Bros. Shoes • *sports shoes* • **CLOTHING: FOOTWEAR**

Orion Telescope Center • *binoculars* • **CAMERAS**

Racer Wholesale • *auto racing safety equipment and accessories* • **AUTO**

Ruvel & Company, Inc. • *government surplus camping supplies and survival goods* • **TOOLS**

Safe Specialties, Inc. • *gun safes and pistol boxes* • **OFFICE**

Scope City Inc. • *field binoculars, spotting scopes* • **CAMERAS**

Sportswear Clearinghouse • *athletic apparel* • **CLOTHING**

State Line Tack, Inc. • *saddle and tack, riding clothing, etc.* • **CLOTHING**

TOOLS, HARDWARE, ELECTRONICS, ENERGY, SAFETY, SECURITY, SURPLUS, AND INDUSTRIAL GOODS

Materials, supplies, equipment, and services

This chapter offers the do-it-yourselfer, woodworker, hobbyist, woodcutter, and small-time mechanic a wealth of tools and hardware, some of it at rock-bottom prices. Replacement parts for lawnmowers, trimmers, garden tractors, snowmobiles, snow throwers, blowers, go-carts, minibikes, and even plumbing and electrical systems are available from these companies. The tools run from hex wrenches and fine wood chisels to complete work benches and professional machinery, and the hardware includes hard-to-find specialty items as well as nuts and bolts.

When you're working, observe safety precautions and use goggles, dust masks, respirators, earplugs, gloves, and other protective gear as appropriate. (A number of these firms sells safety equipment.) Keep your blades sharpened and make sure your tools, hardware, and chemicals are kept out of the reach of children and pets. If you're using a chain saw, make sure it's fitted with an approved antikickback device (contact the manufacturer for recommendations).

For more tools and related products, see "Crafts and Hobbies," "General Merchandise," and the "Improvement" section of "Home."

FIND IT FAST

ABRASIVES • *Red Hill, World Abrasives*
LOGGING EQUIPMENT • *Bailey's, H & H, Zip Power Parts*

SAFETY GEAR • *Bailey's*
SURPLUS GOODS • *H & R, Ruvel, Surplus Center*
TOOLS AND HARDWARE • *The Bevers, Camelot, Chown, H & R, Harbor Freight, Northern Hydraulics, Tool Crib, Tools on Sale, Wholesale Tool*

ALL ELECTRONICS CORP.

DEPT. WBMC
P.O. BOX 567
VAN NUYS, CA 91408-0567
800-826-5432
818-904-0524
FAX: 818-781-2653

Catalog: free
Save: up to 60%
Pay: check, MO, MC, V, Discover
Sells: surplus electronics and tools
Store: 905 S. Vermont Ave., Los Angeles, CA; Monday to Friday 9–5, Saturday 9–4; also 14928 Oxnard St., Van Nuys, CA; Monday to Friday 9–6:30, Saturday 9–5

Electronics hobbyists will appreciate the 64-page catalog from All Electronics, which has been in business since 1967. Every issue features a huge number of surplus parts, hardware items, and tools: semiconductors, transducers, heat sinks, sockets, cables and adapters, fans, plugs, switches, solenoids, relays, capacitors, piezoelectric elements, fuses, resistors, transformers, potentiometers, keyboards, computer fans, PC boards, and hard-to-find and one-of-a-kind items are typical offerings. While much of the stock is for electronics hobbyists, the catalogs usually offer such items as telephone cords and jacks, TV and video accessories, screwdrivers, soldering irons, hemostats, and rechargable batteries.

Special Factors: All parts are guaranteed to be in working order; returns are accepted within 30 days; minimum order is $10.

BAILEY'S

44650 HWY. 101
P.O. BOX 550
LAYTONVILLE, CA 95454
800-3-BAILEY
FAX: 707-984-8115

Catalog: $2 (5 issues)
Save: up to 70%
Pay: check, MO, MC, V, AE, Discover
Sells: woodcutting and reforestation supplies; outdoor and work clothing
Store: same address; Monday to Friday 6–7, Saturday 9–5; also 1520 S. Highland Ave., Jackson, TN; Monday to Friday 6–7, Saturday 9–5 (TN)

 ¡Sí! (see text)

Bailey's, one of the country's best sources for "mail-order woodsman supplies, at discount prices," stocks a large number of goods everyone will find useful—specialty boots, leather conditioners, outdoor clothing, and safety gear. Campers and even urbanites will appreciate the well-priced outerwear (Filson jackets and pants, flannel shirts, rain slickers, etc.), and the first-aid kits and portable fire extinguishers. In addition, there are boot dryers, E.A.R. plugs and headset noise mufflers, and work gloves.

The 84-page color catalog (free on request, $2 for a five-issue year's subscription) features woodcutting equipment (including chain saws), and lists Oregon and Bailey brand chain reels and bars for saws by Homelite, Husqvarna, McCulloch, Pioneer, and Stihl. Silvey chain grinders, spark plugs, automatic measuring tapes, guide bars, bar and chain oil, bar wrenches and files, and other tools are available. Bailey's stocks a full line of heavy-duty calked leather, rubber, and PAK-insulated boots, as well as Vibram and Air Bob boots, all available with and without steel toes. There is climbing gear, log splitters, Alaskan saw mills and Woodbug portable small-log sawmills, chainsaw-powered winches, firefighting equipment, and reforestation supplies (including seedlings). Bailey's is the place to call if you have questions about your chain saw. Savings run as high as 60% on goods in the general catalog, and even more on items offered in the sales flyers.

Canadian readers, please note: Bailey's NRI number is 23079956.

Special Factors: Call the California office for Spanish-speaking sales reps.

THE BEVERS

P.O. BOX 12
WILLS POINT, TX
75169-0012
214-272-8370

Catalog: $2, refundable
Save: up to 50%
Pay: check or MO
Sells: hardware and woodworking parts
Store: mail order only

The Bevers have been selling hardware and parts for household use and crafts projects since 1977, offering a useful mix of items for the hobbyist and do-it-yourselfer. The catalog offers goods for woodworking, construction, and household repairs: steel and brass wood screws with round and flat heads, lock and flat washers, a full range of eye bolts and squared screw hooks, Tap-Lok threads, machine screws with a choice of head styles, hex heads and carriage bolts, cotter pins, brass-plated hinges, picture hangers, lag screws, countersinks, doweling drill bits, clamps, and rotary and sandpaper drums for drills. There's a good selection of wooden parts for making toys and repairing furniture, including wood balls, toy wheels, Shaker pegs, pegboards, game pieces, golf tees, screw-hole buttons, knobs and pulls, and turned finials and spindles. Unfinished candle cups, napkin rings, honey dippers, egg cups, round boxes, blocks, and balls await the finishing touch of the craftsperson. The Bevers carry a number of hard-to-find items, so consult the catalog if you're having trouble locating a special screw or toy part.

Special Factors: Price quote by letter with SASE on quantity orders.

CAMELOT ENTERPRISES

P.O. BOX 65, DEPT. W
BRISTOL, WI 53104-0065
414-857-2695

Catalog: $2, refundable
Save: up to 60%
Pay: check, MO, MC, V
Sells: fasteners, tools, and hardware
Store: 8234 199 Ave. (facing Hwy. AH), Bristol, WI; Tuesday to Friday 8–6, Saturday 8–12; other hours by appointment only

Camelot, founded in 1983, sells "quality fasteners, hardware, and tools direct to the craftsman" at savings of up to 60%, through a 29-page catalog that's jam-packed with garage and workshop necessities. Camelot carries a full range of nuts (hex, K-lock, wing, stop, etc.), bolts (hex-head, machine, carriage), screws (wood, lag, drywall, machine), washers, grease fittings, cotter pins, anchors, and other hardware. And you don't have to buy by the pound to get wholesale prices—Camelot packages the hardware in counts of 10, 25, 50, 100, etc. Camelot's tools include screwdrivers, punches, air tools, pliers, snips, rasps, and other hand and power tools for hobbyist and machinist by Astro, Best Tool, Cal-Van, Camelot, Chicago Pneumatic, Excalibur, General, Ingersoll Rand, Lisle, Milton, Milwaukee, and Truecraft, among others. Shop equipment, Excalibur fastener sets, Marson pop rivets, and Camelot's own twist drills and fasteners are also sold at competitive prices.

Camelot is offering readers of this book a 5% discount on orders of $50 or more (excluding shipping and sales tax) *except* closeouts and items in the "Customer Only" sales flyers. Please identify yourself as a reader when you order. This WBMC reader discount expires February 1, 1997.

Special Factors: Satisfaction is guaranteed; price quote by letter only; returns are accepted within ten days for replacement, refund, or credit; no collect calls are accepted.

CHOWN HARDWARE

333 N.W. 16TH AVE.
P.O. BOX 2888
PORTLAND, OR 97208
800-547-1930
FAX: 800-758-7654

Catalog: free
Save: up to 45%
Pay: check, MO, MC, V, AE, Discover
Sells: tools and hardware
Store: same address; Monday to Friday 7–5, PT

Chown, a family operation founded in 1879, offers businesses and consumers wholesale pricing on tools, hardware, and home-improvement products from over 200 vendors. The 326-page catalog is chock-full of the kinds of things the corner hardware store either doesn't carry, or promises to get: specialty screwdriver bits and saws for weekend projects, wrenches and vise-grips for every job, Ames shovels, scoops, and rakes, door locks and latch sets by Baldwin, Corbin, Jado, and Schlage, and much more. Chown stocks all the basics, as well: builders' hardware, bathroom fixtures, hand and power tools and accessories from Black & Decker, Bosch, Delta, Franklin Brass, Knape & Vogt, Norton, Porter-Cable, Shop-Vac, Stanley, Toolmark, and scores of other firms are represented. The catalog is indexed, but not priced; you can call for quotes on the items you need, or request the separate "supplemental budget price list." Chown keeps all of the catalog items in stock and ready to ship, and will take special orders on products that are not part of regular inventory.

Special Factors: Quantity discounts are available; authorized returns (except special orders) are accepted within 45 days for exchange, refund, or credit; minimum order is $10 if on account.

CLEGG'S HANDYMAN SUPPLY

■

DEPT. W96
P.O. BOX 732
OREM, UT 84059-0732
801-221-1772

Catalog: $3, refundable
Save: 30% average
Pay: check or MO
Sells: hardware, home fixtures, etc.
Store: mail order only

Clegg's is a family-run firm, dedicated to the "frugal home handyperson," offering a wide variety of hardware, plumbing and electrical products, and sundry home fix-up items. These are the kinds of things that drive you to the hardware store in the middle of Saturday afternoons—cord switches, wood toilet seats, faucet parts, door stops, deadbolt locks, flashlights, molly bolts, switch boxes, augers, phone jacks, and much more—over 900 items at this writing. The prices average 30%-plus below suggested or regular retail, and if your order totals $50 or more, shipping is free. Clegg's has been in business since 1992, and prides itself on responding to the needs of its customers. The firm's 40-plus-page catalog should prove a great help to any do-it-yourselfer with limited access to a good hardware store. You can call for a price quote on items not found in the catalog, and Clegg's can often help you to locate those hard-to-find parts.

Special Factors: Satisfaction is guaranteed; quantity discounts are available; shipping is not charged on orders over $50; returns are accepted within 90 days; phone orders are not accepted.

ENCO MANUFACTUR-
ING COMPANY

DEPT. WBMC
5000 W. BLOOMINGDALE
   AVE.
CHICAGO, IL 60639
800-860-3400
312-745-1500
FAX: 800-860-3500

Catalog: free
Save: up to 50%
Pay: check, MO, MC, V, Discover
Sells: machining tools and hardware
Store: same address; also AZ, CA, FL, GA,
IL, MN, NH, OH, TX, and WA (see catalog
for locations)

If the notion of saving big on lathes and mills has you riveted, read on. Enco, one of the country's biggest suppliers of machine shop equipment, gives you access to lathes, mills, grinders, cutting tools, woodworking equipment, fabricating equipment, hand tools, air compressors, measuring tools, books, and more. Enco has 54 years of experience in distributing shop equipment, and the 400-page catalog is a valuable reference—and prices are routinely 30% to 50% below list or comparable retail here.

Special Factors: Quantity discounts are available; institutional accounts are available; minimum order is $25; C.O.D. orders are accepted.

H & H MANUFAC-
TURING & SUPPLY CO.

P.O. BOX 692
SELMA, AL 36701-0692
334-872-6067
FAX: 334-872-0813

Catalog: free
Save: up to 60%
Pay: check or MO
Sells: chain-saw parts and logging equipment
Store: 111 Hwy. 80 E., Selma, AL; Monday to
Friday 7–5, Wednesday 8–12 noon

H & H Manufacturing runs a mail-order firm known as "Saw Chain" that's been offering savings of up to 60% on saw chain and other logging needs since 1964. You can buy the chain, guide bars, and sprockets here for chain saws by Craftsman, John Deere, Echo, Homelite, Husqvarna, Jonsered, Lombard, McCulloch, Olympic, Pioneer, Poulan, Remington, Stihl, and other firms. The chain is sold in a range of pitches and gauges, and both gear-drive and direct-drive sprockets to fit all models are stocked. Swedish double-cut files, Esco rigging products, Windsor and Tilton saw chain and bars, wire rope, logging chokers, slings, and other logging equipment is also available. Remember to include all requested information when ordering chain and sprockets—make and model, chain pitch, gauge, number of drive links, type of bar, and length.

Special Factors: Chains, bars, files, and sprockets are guaranteed to last as long as or longer than any other make; returns are accepted for replacement; C.O.D. orders are accepted.

H & R COMPANY

18 CANAL ST.
P.O. BOX 122
BRISTOL, PA 19007-0122
215-788-5583
FAX: 215-788-9577

Catalog: $5, year's subscription, refundable
Save: up to 50%
Pay: check, MO, MC, V, Discover
Sells: new and surplus electromechanical, robotic, and optical components
Store: mail order only

H & R Company, formerly known as Herbach & Rademan, was established in 1934 and offers surplus bargains—chiefly electronics, robotics, optics, and intriguing mechanical devices. The 52-page catalogs have offered capacitors, lasers, motors, power supplies, compressors, fans, test equipment, relays, resistors, air and hydraulic cylinders, solenoids, transformers, and similar equipment. Computer components, including monitors, keyboards, cables, and power line filters, are usually available. H & R also sells goods that nearly anyone, electromechanically inclined or not, can use: educational kits, phone accessories, digital scales, heavy-duty outlet strips and surge suppressors, model trains and cars, closed-circuit TV components, goggles, robotics components, compasses, cabinet slides, tool cases and cabinets, magnets, weather balloons, and reference books on technical topics. Product specifications are given in the catalog.

Please note: The minimum is $500 on orders shipped outside the United States and Canada.

Special Factors: Satisfaction is guaranteed; price quote by phone, fax, or letter; returns with original packing materials are accepted within 30 days; minimum order is $25, $500 on orders outside the United States and Canada.

HARBOR FREIGHT TOOLS

3491 MISSION OAKS BLVD.
P.O. BOX 6010
CAMARILLO, CA 93011
800-423-2567
FAX: 805-388-0760

Catalog: free
Save: up to 80%
Pay: check, MO, MC, V, AE, Discover
Sells: tools, hardware, industrial equipment, machinery
Store: same address; also Bakersfield, El Cajon, Carmichael, Chula Vista, Escondido, Fresno, Hemet, Hesperia, Lancaster, Modesto, Redding, Reseda, Riverside, Sacramento, Salinas, Santa Maria, Santa Rosa, Sparks, Stockton, Vallejo, and Visalia, CA; Lexington, KY; and Las Vegas, NV

Great prices on everything from air compressors to woodworking equipment is what you'll find in the 116-page catalog from Harbor Freight Tools, which offers workshop necessities at savings of up to 80% on list and comparable retail. Specials are run frequently, making this a valuable source for the hobbyist, do-it-yourselfer, and professional shop.

The latest catalog offered air tools, compressors, hand tools for all kinds of work, automotive repair and maintenance equipment, shop equipment, power tools and supplies, metalworking, welding and plasma cutting tools, woodworking machines and tools, generators, engines, pumps, and even a roundup of useful things for home and garden—post hole diggers, stud sensors, push brooms, ladders, paint sprayers, and more. AEG, Black & Decker, Bosch, Campbell Hausfeld, Central Forge, Central Pneumatic, Chicago Electric, Chicago Pneumatic, Cummins, Delta, Dewalt, Homelite, Honda, Makita, Milwaukee, Pittsburgh, Porter-Cable, Quincy, Ryobi, Sentry, Skil, Stack-On, Stanley, Wayne, and WEN are among the brands represented.

Special Factors: Shipping is free on orders over $50 delivered within the continental United States.

MANUFACTURER'S SUPPLY

Catalog: free
Save: up to 50%
Pay: check, MO, MC, V, Discover
Sells: replacement parts for lawnmowers,
snowmobiles, chain saws, etc.
Store: mail order only

DEPT. WBMC-96
P.O. BOX 167
DORCHESTER, WI
54425-0167
800-826-8563
FAX: 800-294-4144

Manufacturer's Supply is the source for the parts you'll need to get all kinds of things functioning again, at prices up to 50% below list or comparable retail. Consult the 200-page catalog for original replacement parts for equipment by Arctic Cat, Briggs & Stratton, Comet, Dayco, Hahn, Hoffco, Husqvarna, Oregon, Tecumseh, and other makers, for chain saws, lawn mowers, motorcycles, snowmobiles, ATVs, snow throwers, trimmers, trailers, and rototillers. Logging safety equipment (hard hats, chaps, and boots), as well as sprockets and nose assemblies, chains, grinders, files, air filters, T-wrenches, starter springs, carburetor parts, and guide bars (for dozens of saw brands) are available.

In addition, Manufacturer's sells parts for standard and riding lawn mowers, as well as semipneumatic tires for mowers and shopping carts, wheelbarrows, and hand trucks. The firm stocks wheels, hubs, bearing kits, roller chains, sprockets, clutches, belts, and other goods for trailers, minibikes, go-carts, riding mowers, snow throwers, rototillers, garden tractors, and ATVs. The snowmobile parts include everything from lubricants to windshields—carburetors, fuel filters, cleats, tracks, studs, pistons, gaskets, drive belts, wear rods, slides, suspension springs, and engines, among other items. Also available are wood-chopping tools, Woodchuck wood-burning furnaces, and Magic Heat air circulators and chimney-cleaning brushes. Manufacturer's Supply has been in business since 1960, and welcomes inquiries on products not shown in the catalog.

Special Factors: Authorized, unused returns are accepted within 30 days (a 20% restocking fee may be charged); minimum order is $10; C.O.D. orders are accepted.

NORTHERN HYDRAULICS, INC.

P.O. BOX 1499,
DEPT. 17806
BURNSVILLE, MN 55337
800-533-5545
FAX: 612-894-0083

Catalog: free
Save: up to 50%
Pay: check, MO, MC, V, Discover
Sells: do-it-yourself items, power tools, etc.
Store: Cutler Ridge, Ft. Myers, Miami North, and West Dade, FL; Jonesboro, Marietta, and Norcross, GA; Des Moines, IA; Burnsville, Brooklyn Center, Maplewood, Minnetonka, Rochester, Rogers, Spring Lake Park, and West St. Paul, MN; Charlotte, Colfax, Matthew, and Raleigh, NC; Greenville, SC; Knoxville, TN; Garland, Richardson and San Antonio, TX; Newport News, Richmond and Virginia Beach, VA; and Menomonee Falls, WI

Northern Hydraulics makes it easy to save up to 50% on gas engines, pressure washers, generators, trailer parts, painting and welding equipment, tarps, air tools and compressors, winches, power tools, farm and garden and RV equipment, and much more. The 64-page catalog offers a good selection of tools and equipment for home and commercial workshop, for farm, garage, rental store, construction firms, warehouses, and light industrial operations. You'll find tow hoes, shop hoists and presses, parts washers, log splitters, Homelite and McCulloch chain saws, hydraulic pumps and parts by J.S. Barnes and Parker. Vertical- and horizontal-shaft replacement gas engines from Briggs & Stratton, Honda, Kohler, and Tecumseh are offered, for tillers, mowers, and lawn tractors. Air compressors by American IMC and Campbell-Hausfeld are offered, as well as air tools from Chicago Pneumatic, Ingersoll-Rand, and Northern Hydraulics' own line.

Northern also sells go-carts and parts, tires, casters and wheels, RV equipment, tractor lamps and seats, sandblasting and painting equipment, trailer parts, hand and power tools by Black & Decker, Bosch, Makita, Skil, and others. The lawn and garden equipment includes gas trimmers, cultivators, garden carts, agpumps, mower tires, blowers, sprayers, tillers, and much more. Georgia Boots, gloves, and other protective items are also available. And you'll find boating accessories, personal security devices such as lights and alarms, cordless phones, solar fences, and electronic fences, all at discount prices.

Northern invites your inquiries about two specialty catalogs it publishes: *Herter* for waterfowl hunting supplies, and *RV Direct* for RV accessories.

Special Factors: Authorized returns are accepted for exchange, refund, or credit.

RED HILL CORPORATION

P.O. BOX 4234
GETTYSBURG, PA 17325
800-822-4003
717-337-3038
FAX: 717-337-3936

Catalog: free
Save: up to 50%
Pay: check, MO, MC, V
Sells: abrasives and hot-melt adhesives
Store: Supergrit® Abrasives, 1540 Biglerville Rd., Gettysburg, PA

 ¡Si!

Red Hill's business is the rough stuff that gets things smooth—abrasives. The company was founded in 1978 and offers a wide range of abrasives and refinishing products at prices up to 50% below regular retail. The 28-page catalog includes belts (aluminum oxide, silicone carbide, and zirconia on cloth backing) in 19 sizes, plain-back, hook-and-loop, and pressure-sensitive sanding disks, paper disks for orbital sanders, sheets, sleeve and drums, sanding screens, rolls, and foam-core sanding blocks. Red Hill's "Perma Sand," tungsten carbide grit bonded to a metal substrate, promises to last up to 100 times longer than conventional papers. In addition, the catalog offers abrasives for vibrating hand sanders, RAKSO's paper-backed steel wool sheets (to mount on sanders, for finishing work), felt-backed sanding disks that work with a hook-and-loop fastening system, abrasive cords and tapes (for getting into crevices). Triangles for Bosch and Ryobi triangular sanders are sold in bags of 25 for 20¢ to 35¢ each, respectively, about half the price of regular retail. The catalog also lists auto-body refinishing products, masking tape, tack cloths, and a stick for cleaning sanding belts when the grit gets clogged—a money saver in itself. Red Hill has introduced NicSand Sanding Gel in grits 3000, 5000, and 10,000, which is sold in a kit with a pad that attaches to electric drills (under $10). The gel is great for polishing marble or glass tabletops or your car, or for deglossing surfaces between finishes. And you'll find glue guns and glue sticks here—and at $5 a pound for five pounds of sticks (white clear, amber clear, and super amber), they cost just a third of the going rate at the typical hardware store, and the savings increase on larger quantities.

Please note: Spanish, Italian, French, and German are spoken here.

Special Factors: Price quote by phone or letter on special order sizes; quantity discounts are available; minimum order is $25; C.O.D. orders are accepted.

RUVEL & COMPANY, INC.

4128-30 W. BELMONT
 AVE., DEPT. WBMC
CHICAGO, IL 60641
312-286-9494
FAX: 312-286-9323

Catalog: $2
Save: up to 70%
Pay: check, MO, MC, V
Sells: government surplus
Store: same address; Monday to Friday 10–4:30, Saturday 10–2

Ruvel, established in 1965, is the source to check for good buys on government-surplus camping and field goods. U.S. Army and Navy surplus goods are featured in the 64-page catalog, including G.I. duffel bags, high-powered binoculars, leather flying jackets, mosquito netting, M65 field jackets, U.S. Marine Corps shooting jackets, dummy grenades, U.S. Army technical manuals, and similar items. Past catalogs have offered Israeli and M9 gas masks, Kevlar helmets, hammocks, snowshoes, strobe lights, mess kits, dinghies, nightsticks, snowshoes, U.S. Army blankets, parade gloves, first-aid kits, packboards, and duffel bags. Ruvel is noteworthy for its low prices and extensive stock of real surplus—there are hundreds of "genuine" government-issue items available here, and many intriguing, useful surplus things that are increasingly hard to find these days.

Special Factors: Order promptly, since stock moves quickly.

SURPLUS CENTER

P.O. BOX 9\82209
LINCOLN, NE 68501-2209
800-488-3407
FAX: 402-474-5198

Catalog: free
Save: up to 85%
Pay: check, MO, MC, V, AE, Discover
Sells: new and surplus industrial goods, hardware, etc.
Store: 1015 W. "O" St., Lincoln, NE; Monday to Friday 8–5, Saturday 8–12

Surplus Center, established in 1933, publishes a 180-page catalog that's a treasury of parts for the "build-it-yourselfer." One third of the catalog features hydraulic equipment of all types, including cylinders, valves, pumps, and motors, as well as hoses, filters, and tanks. Also featured are pressure washers, blowers, winches, electrical motors of all kinds, electrical generators, air compressors, surveying equipment, spray pumps, vacuum pumps, gearboxes, gas engines, and more. Heavy-duty 400-amp DC welders are available, as well as sandblasters, inverters, multimeters, battery chargers, and a full line of residential and commercial burglar alarms. Some of the goods are real government surplus, but most are brand new bargains. If you have any questions about an item, you can call Surplus Center's staff technicians for information.

Special Factors: Authorized returns are accepted (a restocking fee may be charged); C.O.D. orders are accepted.

TOOL CRIB OF THE NORTH

P.O. BOX 1716
GRAND FORKS, ND
58208-3720
800-358-3096
FAX: 701-746-2857

Catalog: $3
Save: up to 50%
Pay: check, MO, MC, V, Discover
Sells: tools and hardware
Store: Bismarck, Fargo, Grand Forks, and Minot, ND; locations are given in the catalog

Do-it-yourselfers, hobbyists, contractors, and industrial buyers are among the numerous customers of Tool Crib, which has been in business since 1948. The firm offers a broad range of tools, industrial and shop equipment, and supplies—ladders, pumps, generators, motors, woodworking equipment, saws, compressors, abrasives, concrete-handling equipment, trailers, and much more. You can send $3 for the 208-page catalog, or call or write for price quotes on items by Black & Decker, Bosch, Delta, Emglo, Freud, Hitachi, Kawasaki, Makita, Milwaukee, Porter-Cable, Powermatic, Ryobi, Senco, Skil, Stanley, Target, David White, and any other major manufacturer. Whether you're shopping for a circular saw or an adjustable scaffold system, you'll find it at Tool Crib—at up to 50% off list price. The catalog includes line drawings, products specifications, and both list and discount prices for most items, which makes it a good reference as well as a buying tool.

Canadian readers, please note: Only U.S. funds are accepted.

Special Factors: Satisfaction is guaranteed; shipping is not charged (with some exceptions) on orders over $75.

TOOL HAUZ INC.

122 E. GROVE ST.
P.O. BOX 1288
MIDDLEBORO, MA
  02346-1288
800-533-6135
508-946-4800
FAX: 508-947-7050

Brochure: free
Save: up to 50%
Pay: check, MO, MC, V
Sells: tools and hardware
Store: same address and 57 Crawford St., Needham, MA

The six-page "bargain list" from Tool Hauz Inc. features the best names in woodworking and power tools, at discounts that sometimes beat even those of the "wholesale" sources. You'll find everything from Estwing hammers and Stabila levels to Greenbull ladders and Rosseau saw stands—routers, drills, screw guns, disc sanders, and power saws; all types, by Delta, Hitachi, Jepson, Makita, Metabo, Milwaukee, Panasonic, Porter-Cable, Ryobi, and Skil. Supplies and hardware, including abrasives, saw blades, hole saws, screws, drill bits, tarps, tool aprons, and related goods are stocked as well. Call for the price list, or a price quote if you know the model you're looking for.

Special Factors: C.O.D. orders are accepted.

TOOLS ON SALE™

SEVEN CORNERS HARDWARE, INC.
216 W. SEVENTH ST.
ST. PAUL, MN 55102
800-328-0457
FAX: 612-224-8263

Catalog: free
Save: up to 50%
Pay: check, MO, MC, V, Discover
Sells: tools for contractors, masons, and woodworkers
Store: same address; Monday to Friday 7–5:30, Saturday 7–1, CT

If you can't get to St. Paul to visit Seven Corners Hardware, where there are "over 35,000 items on the floor," you can do business with the firm's mail-order division, Tools on Sale™. The parent company was founded in 1933, and specializes in tools for contractors and woodworkers.

The Tools on Sale™ catalog is one of the last great freebies in America—456 pages of name-brand tools, at discounts of up to 50%. You'll find everything from air compressors to workbenches here, from manufacturers that include Black & Decker, Bosch, Delta, Dewalt, Dremel, Elu, Freud, Hitachi, Jorgensen, Makita, Milwaukee, Porter-Cable, Rigid, Ryobi, Senco, Skil, 3M, and David White, among others. If you're looking for stair templets, Werner ladders and scaffolding, demolition hammers, moisture meters, water stones, mechanics' cabinets, or just want to *see* 18 pages of construction aprons and nail bags, look no farther. And there are 13 pages of books, videos, and manuals on everything from making a hobbyhorse to building a home. Free freight on orders shipped to the United States (except Alaska and Hawaii) is an added bonus.

Special Factors: Shipping is not charged on orders shipped within the contiguous United States; authorized returns are accepted for exchange, refund, or credit.

TREND-LINES, INC.

135 AMERICAN LEGION HWY.

P.O. BOX 9117

REVERE, MA 02151-9117

617-853-0225

FAX: 617-853-0226

Catalog: $1
Save: up to 30%
Pay: check, MO, MC, V, Discover
Sells: woodworking tools and hardware
Store: 63 stores in CT, MA, ME, NH, NY, RI, and VT; locations are listed in the catalog

Trend-Lines has been in business since 1981, selling complete lines of tools and hardware to professional woodworkers, at savings of up to 30%. The 68-page color catalog shows a wide range of woodworking tools and parts, including saws (jig, miter, band, reciprocating, scroll, radial-arm, and chain); drills, routers, trimmers, planers, jointers, sanders, nibblers, polishers, grinders, bits, blades, and other accessories. Bosch, Delta, DeWalt, Forstner, Freud, Hitachi, Makita, Milwaukee, Porter-Cable, Reliant, Ryobi, Shopcraft, Skil, Wagner, and other popular names are represented. The catalog also shows full lines of supplies such as abrasives (sheets, belts, and disks), lubricants, adhesives, paste stains and varnishes, wood plugs and buttons, toy wheels, dollhouse kits, and hand tools and cabinet hardware. Woodworking manuals and plans are also sold.

Special Factors: Satisfaction is guaranteed; returns of unused goods in the original packaging are accepted within 30 days for exchange, refund, or credit; C.O.D. orders are accepted.

TURNKEY MATERIAL HANDLING CO.

500 FILLMORE AVE.
P.O. BOX 1050
TONAWANDA, NY
  14151-1050
800-828-7540
FAX: 800-222-1934

Catalog: free
Save: up to 50%
Pay: check, MO, MC, V, AE, Discover
Sells: commercial and industrial furnishings, storage units, etc.
Store: mail order only

 ⊕ ¡Si!

Turnkey's line is geared for industrial and commercial applications, but the sturdy storage units and other equipment sold here have home applications as well. Turnkey has been doing business since 1946, and publishes a 96-page catalog that features shelving and storage bins in a huge selection of sizes and styles. You'll find everything from small parts bins, ideal for hardware storage, to 108-drawer steel wall cabinets, plus plastic bin-and-frame arrangements. The catalog also shows mats and runners, workbenches, stainless-steel rolling carts, suspension files, lockers, flat and roll files, moving pads, canvas tarps, security gates, hand trucks, rolling ladders, trash cans, stretch wrap, zip-lock bags, power-failure lights, recycling centers, and many other products. Turnkey has expanded its line of shipping products, which include a wide range of padded mailers, bubble-pack, kraft paper, packing labels and envelopes, strapping tape, and other needs.

Special Factors: Satisfaction is guaranteed; authorized returns (except custom-made items) are accepted (a 20% restocking fee may be charged); minimum order is $25.

WHOLESALE TOOL CO., INC.

P.O. BOX 68
12155 STEPHENS DR.
WARREN, MI 48089-3962
810-754-9270

Catalog: free
Save: 30% average
Pay: check, MO, MC, V, Discover
Sells: tools, hardware, and machinery
Store: same address; also Tampa, FL; Indi-anapolis, IN; Stoughton, MA; Charlotte, NC; Tulsa, OK; and Houston, TX (see catalog for locations)

Wholesale Tool has been bringing good prices and a great tool selection to hobbyists and industry since 1960, through the 752-page "Full-Line Catalog." This hefty tome runs from Toyota forklifts to Crescent wrenches, and is a treasury for do-it-yourselfers as well as woodworkers, machinists, contractors, and surveyors. Wholesale Tool is geared to the professional, as you can see from the collection of reference works—no Sunset guides to building decks, but *Die Design Fundamentals,* the 24th edition of *The Machinery Handbook,* a guide to world screw threads, and *Creep Feed Grinding* are here, among others. Wholesale Tool represents both popular commercial brands and industrial suppliers: Black & Decker, Brown & Sharpe, Brubaker Tool, Chicago Pneumatic, Desmond, Dorian Tool, Dremel, Florida Pneumatic, Fowler, General, G.E., Hanson, Heinrich, Jorgensen, Lufkin, Master, Merit, Milwaukee, Minute Man, Mitutoyo, Norton, Porter-Cable, Rigid, Ryobi, Shop-Vac, Starrett, 3M, Vise-Grip, Wesco, and Yuasa, among others. The comprehensive product descriptions include model number, technical specifications, Wholesale Tool's price, and sometimes the list price. Savings average 30%, and the catalog features several pages of clearance and odd-lot items, which are sold below cost.

Special Factors: Authorized returns are accepted within 30 days (a 10% restocking fee may be charged); minimum order is $25.

WORLD ABRASIVES COMPANY, INC.

P.O. BOX 5266
OLD BRIDGE, NJ
08857-5266
908-583-9700

Catalog: $1.25, refundable
Save: up to 60%
Pay: check or MO
Sells: abrasives and sanding materials
Store: mail order only

World Abrasives sells all kinds of sanding products and related goods, including hard-to-find sizes and types of abrasives. The firm has been in business since 1972 and can answer just about any question you may have on abrasives. World Abrasives stocks sanding belts for wood, metal, and plastic, as well as waterproof belts for wet grinding glass and ceramics, in grits from 16 to 1000, in a wide range of sizes. There are sanding disks, sheets, rolls of sanding materials, grinding wheels and points, wire wheels, and buffing wheels. The belts are sold in lots of ten, disks in lots of 25, and sheets in packages of 25, but there are small assortments for single jobs as well. Carborundum, Midwest, 3M, and World's own line are represented, and polishing compounds, oil and honing stones, 3M dust masks, goggles, disk adhesives, and belt cleaners are stocked. World Abrasives also sells tubing cutters, hack saws, utility knives, punches, chisels, files, X-Acto knives, drill bits and burs, gloves, and other handy tools. Prices are low, even in small quantities, and custom abrasives can be produced for special applications.

Special Factors: Satisfaction is guaranteed; minimum order is $20.

ZIP POWER PARTS, INC.

DEPT. WBM
P.O. BOX 10308
ERIE, PA 16514-0308
800-824-8521
FAX: 800-983-PART

Catalog: free
Save: up to 45%
Pay: check, MO, MC, V, Discover
Sells: parts for chain saws, lawn mowers, snowmobiles, etc.
Store: 2008 E. 33rd St., Erie, PA; Monday to Friday 8–5, Saturday 9–1

If you own a chain saw, Zip Power Parts may be an old friend. In business since 1962, Zip Power Parts is one of the country's best sources for chain-saw parts, with a 28-page catalog of saw chain, bars, bar guards, and sprockets to fit all makes and models of chain saws. Saw chain grinders, chain saw repair parts, and small engine parts are all available, and there are shop tools for filing and grinding, wedges, lubricants, "mini-mills," hand tools, manuals, safety clothing and equipment, and woodcutting accessories. Additional parts for lawnmowers—mufflers, air filters, blades, starter rope and handles, fuel lines and filters, points, condensers, electronic ignitions, etc.—are listed in the catalog.

Special Factors: All products are guaranteed against defects in materials and workmanship; returns are accepted; minimum order is $25; C.O.D. orders are accepted.

SEE ALSO

Alfax Wholesale Furniture • institutional furnishings and fixtures • **OFFICE**
American Science & Surplus • surplus tools, electronics, etc. • **GENERAL MERCHANDISE**
Arctic Glass & Window Outlet • replacement patio door panes and passive solar panels • **HOME: IMPROVEMENT**
Cahall's Brown Duck Catalog • work clothing and rugged footwear • **CLOTHING**
Cherry Tree Toys, Inc. • wooden toy parts, hardware, etc. • **CRAFTS: WOODCRAFT**
CISCO • professional power tools • **HOME: IMPROVEMENT**
Clothcrafters, Inc. • shop aprons, woodpile covers, tool holders • **GENERAL MERCHANDISE**
Crutchfield Corporation • security systems for car and home • **APPLIANCES**

Defender Industries, Inc. • wood treatment products, marine hardware • **AUTO**

Frank Eastern Co. • industrial and institutional supplies and furnishings • **OFFICE**

Goldberg's Marine Distributors • wood treatment products, marine hardware • **AUTO**

Knapp Shoes Inc. • work shoes and boots • **CLOTHING: FOOTWEAR**

LIBW • bathroom fixtures, cabinet and door hardware • **HOME: IMPROVE-MENT**

Meisel Hardware Specialties • wooden craft parts and brass hardware, woodworking plans • **CRAFTS: WOODCRAFT**

Metropolitan Music Co. • tools and supplies for making musical instruments • **MUSIC**

Northwest Treasure Supply • metal detectors and prospecting equipment • **CRAFTS**

Okun Bros. Shoes • work and safety footwear • **CLOTHING: FOOTWEAR**

S & S Sound City • surveillance equipment • **APPLIANCES**

Shuttercraft • shutter-hanging hardware • **HOME: IMPROVEMENT**

Staples, Inc. • fire extinguishers • **OFFICE**

Todd Uniform, Inc. • work clothing and footwear • **CLOTHING**

Woodworker's Supply, Inc. • wooden craft parts and brass hardware, woodworking plans and tools • **CRAFTS: WOODCRAFT**

TOYS AND GAMES

Juvenile and adult diversions

One of the greatest challenges for many budget-conscious parents is spending a "reasonable" amount of money on toys. The Power Rangers generation is articulate and well-informed on the features of the latest diversions. Gaining the upper hand takes work: Consider limiting the number of ads your children see by reducing their exposure to commercial television. Foster interests in activities that are built around imagination instead of gimmicks and props. To add toys to your child's life without expense, join or start a toy library. The USA Toy Library Association, established nearly a decade ago, helps individuals and communities start and support their own collections. Toy libraries often benefit children with special needs or disabilities, and may be brought to children by van—but they also can be established in the corner of the local public library. For more information about support materials and joining the USA-TLA, send a long, stamped, self-addressed envelope to USA Toy Library Association, 2530 Crawford St., Suite 111, Evanston, IL 60201.

One of your best defenses against crass materialism is to replace watching TV with reading. You can expand on your efforts by making *Zillions,* published by Consumers Union, part of their literary diet. This "Consumer Reports for Kids" is an ad-free guide to products, money management, and smart buying for shoppers from 8 to 13 years old. Help educate the next generation—buy a young friend a subscription. Write to Zillions, Subscription Dept., Box 51777, Boulder, CO 80322-0777, for rate information, or see the current issue of *Consumer Reports*. And Constructive Playthings currently offers *365 TV-Free Activities You Can Do with Your Child,* by Steve and Ruth Bennett, another resource in the battle of the box.

BRIDGE SUPPLIES • **Baron/Barclay**
CHILDREN'S TOYS • **Acme Premium, Constructive Playthings, Oriental Trading, Stickers 'n' Stuff, U.S. Toy**
ORNAMENTS • **Kaye's Holiday**
PARTY GOODS • **Acme Premium, Oriental Trading, Paradise Products, La Piñata, Stickers 'n' Stuff, U.S. Toy**
STICKERS • **Stickers 'n' Stuff**

ACME PREMIUM SUPPLY CORP.

DEPT. WBM
4100 FOREST PARK BLVD.
ST. LOUIS, MO 63108-2899
800-325-7888
314-531-8880
FAX: 800-999-5799

Catalog: free
Save: up to 50%
Pay: check, MO, MC, V, Discover
Sells: toys, novelties, and premium goods
Store (showroom): same address

Acme Premium is listed here because so much of what it offers is toys, games, and novelties. The 176-page color catalog is bursting with stuffed animals, balloons, games, and other diversions, but please note that Acme's targeted customers are businesses, clubs, churches, and carnivals. Acme also states that its merchandise "is not intended for use by children under five years of age," a caveat well worth noting.

But Acme offers a number of items everyone can use, at very good prices—flashlights, and pens and pencils, for example. Acme merged with Ace Novelty last year, and their combined catalog features licensed sports novelties—caps, T-shirts, basketballs, key chains, and more—as well as the great stuffed toys Acme's always sold: naturalistic animals, Troll-kins®, wizards, and dogs with sunglasses, to name just a few. Complete details of the sales policy are given in the catalog.

Special Factors: Authorized returns are accepted (a restocking fee may be charged).

BARON/BARCLAY BRIDGE SUPPLIES

**3600 CHAMBERLAIN
  LANE, SUITE 230
LOUISVILLE, KY
  40241-1989
800-274-2221
502-426-0410
FAX: 502-426-2044**

Catalog: free
Save: up to 50% (see text)
Pay: check, MO, MC, V
Sells: bridge playing and teaching materials
Store: mail order only

Baron/Barclay Bridge Supplies carries materials and equipment for every kind of bridge player, from novice to old hand. Baron/Barclay was established in 1946, and stocks hundreds of books on bridge, and sells them at quantity discounts of up to 50%. Over half of the 64-page color catalog is devoted to teaching manuals and texts, books on strategy and bidding, bridge history and reference texts, and complete courses in bridge. Videotapes and instructional software are also available, as well as a great choice of playing cards, scoring cards and club forms, recap sheets, and a variety of gifts and equipment—bridge-motif china, scarves, jackets, magnetic card sets, games, jewelry, watches, pens and pencils, and even electronic bridge games.

Special Factors: Satisfaction is guaranteed; quantity discounts are available; returns are accepted within 30 days for exchange, refund, or credit (videotapes and software for exchange only).

CONSTRUCTIVE PLAYTHINGS

U.S. TOY COMPANY, INC.
1227 E. 119TH ST.
GRANDVIEW, MO
64030-1117
816-761-5900
FAX: 816-761-9295

Catalog: free (see text)
Save: up to 30% (see text)
Pay: check, MO, MC, V
Sells: toys and educational products
Store: Garden Grove, CA; Denver and Englewood, CO; Apopka, FL; Skokie, IL; Leawood, KS; North Wales, PA; and Carrollton, TX

Constructive Playthings sells wholesome, growth-oriented diversions for children, and makes a "lowest price guarantee" on everything it carries (see the catalog for details). Constructive Playthings has been in business since 1953, and features brightly colored, washable, durable toys, from activity centers and baby's first music box to teepees for backyard fun and a scaled-down kitchen, complete with sink. The toys are made to withstand lots of play; in fact, Constructive Playthings also sells directly to schools and child-care institutions (the school edition of the catalog costs $3). Before giving in to this year's TV spinoff character, see if you can't get your children interested in these games and diversions instead—they'll outlast seasonal fads and are easier on your budget.

Special Factors: Satisfaction is guaranteed; returns are accepted for exchange, refund, or credit; institutional accounts are available.

KAYE'S HOLIDAY

DEPT. WBMC96
6N021 MEREDITH RD.
MAPLE PARK, IL 60151
708-365-2224
FAX: 708-365-2223

Catalog: $1 for 2 issues (see text)
Save: up to 75% plus
Pay: check, MO, MC, V
Sells: holiday ornaments
Store: mail order only

Tired of missing those post-Christmas clearances with the half-price buys on ornaments? Here's a sale that never stops: Kaye's Holiday, where decorations for Christmas, Easter, Halloween, and other holidays are priced from 20% to 75% below regular retail (and sometimes well below *wholesale*) every day. Kaye has been in business since 1982, and sends out a workmanlike set of photocopies showing handmade ornaments of blown glass, fabric, straw, and wood, tagged at $1 to $5 each. These are the same ornaments that can be found in import shops and gift catalogs selling for three times as much. (Kaye's even sells famous-name European blown-glass ornaments, at great savings.) Ornaments make wonderful gifts and keepsakes, and they're great to give when you're dropping in on people during the holidays.

Kaye's Holiday is offering readers one paper holiday garland (various types, Kaye's choice; minimum value, $2) and the next catalog for $1, shipping included. Spefify "WBMC Special" when you order; limit one per household. This WBMC reader offer expires December 31, 1997.

Special Factors: Order as early as possible for the best choice.

ORIENTAL TRADING COMPANY, INC.

DEPT. 539
P.O. BOX 3407
OMAHA, NE 68103
800-228-0475
402-331-6800
FAX: 800-327-8904

Catalog: free
Save: up to 75%
Pay: check, MO, MC, V, AE, Discover
Sells: party goods, novelties, etc.
Store: mail order only

¡Si! ★

Before you throw another party or plan a single fund-raising event, see the catalog from Oriental Trading. It's a novelty shop in 98 pages, crammed with everything from balloons and stickers to spun glass bridal favors, resin animals and figurines, party favors, tickets, bingo supplies, penny candies, ribbon, inflatables, stuffed toys, masks, glow-in-the-dark jewelry, tropical drink stirrers, stars and stripes yoyos, costumes, card assortments, and lots more. Most of the products are sold by the dozen, gross, pound, or other multiple, at prices that are easily 50% below what individual items cost in party goods stores—and often even cheaper. Seasonal catalogs with special holiday selections are released regularly. Oriental Trading has been in business since 1932, and has a separate department devoted to fund-raising activities that can help you make the most of your event.

Special Factors: Quantity discounts are available; authorized returns (except food, candy, and costumes) are accepted within five days for exchange, refund, or credit.

PARADISE PRODUCTS, INC.

DEPT. WBMC
P.O. BOX 568
EL CERRITO, CA
94530-0568
510-524-8300
FAX: 510-524-8165

Catalog: $2
Save: up to 50%
Pay: check, MO, MC, V
Sells: party paraphernalia
Store: mail order only

Paradise Products has been sponsoring bashes, wingdings, and festive events since 1962, when it began selling party products by mail. The 104-page catalog is a must-see for anyone throwing a theme event. The firm sells materials and supplies for over 100 different kinds of events, including celebrations of Oktoberfest, the 50s, the Gold Rush, Presidents' Day, St. Patrick's Day, fiestas, "Las Vegas Night," Hawaiian luaus, pirate parties, Super Bowl celebrations, wedding, graduations, and July Fourth parties. Balloons, streamers, tissue balls and bells, party hats, banquet table coverings, crepe paper by the roll, pennants, garlands, and novelties are among the items available. Paradise's prices are as much as 50% below those charged by other party-supply stores, depending on the item and the quantity ordered.

Special Factors: Goods are guaranteed to be as represented in the catalog; shipments are guaranteed to arrive in time for the party date specified (terms are stated in catalog); minimum order is $30.

LA PIÑATA

NO. 2 PATIO MARKET,
OLD TOWN
ALBUQUERQUE, NM
87104
505-242-2400

Brochure: $1
Save: up to 30%
Pay: check, MO, MC, V, Discover
Sells: piñatas and paper flowers
Store: same address; Monday to Saturday 10–6, Sunday 11–5 (winter); Monday to Saturday 10–9, Sunday 11–5 (summer)

   ¡Sí! ✓

La Piñata is a marvelous source for piñatas, the hollow papier-mâché animals and characters that are traditionally filled with candy and broken by a blindfolded party guest. Prices here are low, running from $3.50 to $60 each. The stock includes superheroes like Batman and Superman, Sesame Street characters, Spiderman, pumpkins, Santa, snowmen, witches, stars, reindeer, and other seasonal characters. And there are all sorts of animals, including bears, burros, bulls, elephants, unicorns, tigers, pigs, kangaroos, and cows. La Piñata, which has been in business since 1955, also carries inexpensive, colorful paper flowers in several sizes.

La Piñata is offering readers a discount of 10% on all orders. Be sure to identify yourself as a WBMC reader when you order, and deduct the discount from the cost of the goods only. This WBMC reader discount expires February 1, 1997.

Special Factors: Price quote by phone or letter; C.O.D. orders are accepted.

STICKERS 'N' STUFF INC.

Catalog and Samples: $2
Save: up to 80%
Pay: check, MO, MC, V
Sells: novelty stickers
Store: mail order only

DEPT. WBM
P.O. BOX 430
LOUISVILLE, CO
80027-0430
303-604-0422
FAX: 303-666-5553

Stickers 'n' Stuff, founded in 1980, sells a wide variety of adorable stickers: prism (rainbow effect), chrome (foil background), hologram (like the emblem on your credit card), fuzzies, and neon stickers. The designs include lots of bears, cats, balloons, rainbows, wild animals, sports figures, troll dolls, holiday themes (Christmas, Thanksgiving, Valentine's Day, etc.), and the American flag. In addition, Stickers 'n' Stuff sells metallic-striped band-aids in heart shapes, sticker collecting books, sticker "earrings," endangered species stickers, and even scratch 'n' sniff stickers. Parents, teachers, and day-care workers may derive the most benefit from a stash of assorted stickers, skillfully deployed on a rainy day. Thanks to this firm, stickers that cost 25¢ in the toy store cost as little as 4¢ here, or an average of 8¢ for the Sampler Assortment of 366 stickers. You can save even more on half or full cases, which are usually bought for resale. And you can try them out before you order:

$2 brings you the catalog and a generous batch of stickers, enough to last a couple of Saturday afternoons!

Special Factors: Satisfaction is guaranteed; quantity discounts are available; returns are accepted for exchange, refund, or credit.

U.S. TOY CO., INC.

1227 E. 119TH ST.
GRANDVIEW, MO 64030
816-761-5900
FAX: 816-761-9295

Catalog: $3
Save: up to 70%
Pay: check, MO, MC, V
Sells: novelties and fund-raising items
Store: Garden Grove, CA; Denver and Englewood, CO; Apoka, FL; Skokie, IL; Leawood, KS; North Wales, PA; and Carrollton, TX (see catalog for locations)

It's always party time at the U.S. Toy Company, where masks, costumes, favors, festive tableware, streamers and decorations, games, grab bag prizes, little toys and novelties, penny candy, jewelry, stuffed animals, inflatables, balloons, hats, crowns, and other fun things are available at discounts of up to 70% on regular retail. In addition to party goods grouped by theme—Halloween, St. Patrick's Day, Easter, Mardi Gras, etc.—the 128-page U.S. Toy catalog has everything you need for your own carnival (except the rides), bingo hall, casino (play money included), or other fund-raising event. Some products are sold in cases or large lots, but much is available in small quantities—making this a great source for parents, teachers, camp directors, and anyone else looking for inexpensive party materials.

Special Factors: Institutional accounts are available; minimum order is $25.

SEE ALSO

American Science & Surplus • educational materials for elementary-grade sciences • **GENERAL MERCHANDISE**

The Bevers • wooden wheels, balls, and other components for toy making • **TOOLS**

Cherry Tree Toys, Inc. • wooden toy kits, parts, and plans • **CRAFTS: WOODCRAFT**

Betty Crocker Catalog • *educational toys, games, and puzzles* • **GENERAL MERCHANDISE**

CR's Crafts • *doll- and toy-making supplies and parts* • **CRAFTS**

Dover Publications, Inc. • *cut-and-assemble projects, stickers, dioramas, etc.* • **BOOKS**

A. Feibusch Corporation • *zippers for doll clothing* • **CRAFTS: TEXTILE ARTS**

The Fiber Studio • *doll-making fibers* • **CRAFTS: TEXTILE ARTS**

Gohn Bros. • *dominos, "Dutch blitz," and other games* • **CLOTHING**

Gooseberry Patch • *collectors' country dolls* • **GENERAL MERCHANDISE**

Home-Sew • *doll and stuffed animal parts* • **CRAFTS: TEXTILE ARTS**

Meisel Hardware Specialties • *wooden wheels and other toy parts, toy plans* • **CRAFTS: WOODCRAFT**

Monterey, Inc. • *fun fur yardage and remnants for toys* • **CRAFTS: TEXTILE ARTS**

The Natural Baby Co., Inc. • *wooden toys* • **CLOTHING: MOTHER AND CHILD**

Newark Dressmaker Supply, Inc. • *supplies for making dolls and toys* • **CRAFTS: TEXTILE ARTS**

The Paper Wholesaler • *party supplies* • **GENERAL MERCHANDISE**

R.C. Steele Co. • *dog trivia, dog-breed playing cards, etc.* • **ANIMAL**

Taylor's Cutaways and Stuff • *kits and patterns for making dolls and toys* • **CRAFTS: TEXTILE ARTS**

Wasserman Uniform Company, Inc. • *USPS-related banks and collectibles* • **CLOTHING: FOOTWEAR**

Wicker Warehouse Inc. • *wicker doll buggies, reproduction miniatures* • **HOME: FURNISHINGS**

Woodworker's Supply • *wooden toy parts, plans, and dollhouse plans* • **CRAFTS: WOODCRAFT**

TRAVEL

There are all kinds of ways to save on travel, depending upon the nature of the traveler and the trip. This chapter includes listings of information sources, discount travel brokers, money-saving accommodations, and travel-related services. In addition, membership in professional organizations, unions, buying clubs, and other groups may entitle you to travel discounts and services—check your benefits package to find out.

CONSOLIDATORS/BUCKET SHOPS

Consolidators, also known as bucket shops, are travel wholesalers who buy cruise slots, blocks of rooms, and plane seats from airlines, hotels, and charter agents, and resell them for less than the hotels, airlines, or often the charter operators themselves are willing to accept for individual tickets or rooms. Travel agents are big customers of consolidators, but individuals may buy from them too, which will often save them 20% to 30% on APEX fares and much more on full economy tickets.

Unitravel Corporation, one of the oldest consolidators in the business, books flights in the United States and Europe and sells directly to individuals. Contact Unitravel about a month before you anticipate traveling, and allow for some uncertainty since tickets might not be available until shortly before the day of departure. Call 800-325-2222 or 314-727-8888 for more information.

Council Charter, another consolidator, has been in business for over 40 years and is affiliated with the Council on International Educational Exchange, a not-for-profit travel concern. For information on Council Charter's current offerings, call 800-223-7402 or 212-661-0311.

Nouvelle Frontiers is an off-price travel broker that sells to consumers as well as to travel agencies. For information, call 212-779-0600, or 800-366-6387. You can also try *Travac Tours and Charters,* at 212-563-3303, or 800-872-8800, and *European-American Travel,* at 800-848-6789, or 202-789-2255.

DISCOUNT TRAVEL AGENTS

Simple common sense tells you that commissions pegged to the selling price of a ticket may be something of a disincentive to getting travel agents to find you the lowest fare. On top of this problem is the real difficulty in getting "hard" information in a market that literally changes overnight, every night. Inexperienced and undermotivated travel agents can be impaired on both counts, for which you pay the price.

You can improve the odds of getting the lowest rate by pricing your trip with at least three travel agents and asking for the cheapest fare. Make sure you know just what you're buying *before* you buy it. Ask for a statement of the agency's cancellation policy, and get it in writing if the travel agent is booking your trip through a tour operator.

The problems with agents make *Travel World* (also known as *Farefinders*) worth checking before your next trip. This travel agency is run by Annette Forest, who's been in the business for over a decade and uses a wide range of information sources to find the lowest fares. Travel World will search for the best rates on travel by air, train, or ship, as well as cruises and tours to any destination worldwide. You can buy your tickets and book reservations through Travel World, but it's optional—there's no obligation for the fare-finding services. Ms. Forest also teaches hands-on college classes for aspiring travel agents at Travel Smart, and invites inquiries on her course. Write to Travel World, 11899 West Pico Blvd., West Los Angeles, CA 90064, or call 213-479-6313 for information.

Eleventh-hour travels can be the most costly, so try *800-FLY-ASAP* before booking at full fare with a local agent. This firm works to deliver a seat at the lowest possible price, on short notice. Call the company's name—800-359-2727.

If you're just interested in a good price on a cruise, give *Cruises Worldwide* a call. This travel agency will send you a printout of last-minute opportunities (from three-day getaways to 14 days on the high seas), as well as cruises scheduled up to a year from now. Discounts run from 5% to 50% on the published rates, and major lines are well represented. For information or the current printout, call 800-6-CRUISE, fax 714-975-1849, or write to Cruises Worldwide, 16585 Von Karman, Irvine, CA 92714 (there is a $1 fee for the information).

Other cruise discounters include *Cruise Time,* which has two offices: 1 Hallidie Plaza, Suite 406, San Francisco, CA 94102; 800-338-0818, fax 415-391-1856, and 301 Maple Ave. W., Suite H, Poplar Bldg., Vienna, VA 22180; 800-627-6131, fax 703-255-9652. And *World Wide Cruises* also books at a discount; 8059 W. McNab Rd., Ft. Lauderdale, FL 33321; 800-882-9000, or 305-720-9000, fax 305-720-9112.

STANDBY TRAVEL

If you can be flexible in your plans, consider the world of standby travel. It really is a last-minute affair, but it can be one of the cheapest ways to fly.

Airhitch is an old friend among travelers who favor 11th-hour departures. The firm has offices in several large cities, but does most of its business by mail. You first phone for information, have a registration form sent to you, apply for the desired dates or range (which must be at least five days long), and call for availability on the Wednesday before your desired departure dates. The procedure is involved, but it works. Airhitch also runs Calhitch and Sunhitch, companion services providing discount runs to East/West coast and Caribbean/Mexican location, respectively. The friendly phone system at Airhitch has been programmed to dispense all the details of the standby program. Make sure you have pen and paper at hand before calling 800-372-1234, or 212-864-2000.

Access International also books standby flights from New York to points in Europe. It works on a registration/fee basis, and publishes a brochure that describes the services. Call 212-333-7280 for information.

LODGING AND DINING DISCOUNTS

Entertainment Publications runs very successful programs featuring accommodations and meals at discounts, in the United States and abroad. To join, you purchase the directory suited to your travel and entertainment needs; the directory comes with a membership card, which is presented to validate the offer. At this writing, *Travel America at Half Price* costs $32.95; the *National Hotel and Dining* edition, covering over 2,800 hotels in the United States and Canada, costs $38; and there are 119 other guides for individual cities and different regions of the country and Canada. The potential savings are enough to justify getting a directory if you travel at all, since the big guides cover over 4,000 lodging sources in the United States, Canada, Mexico, and the Caribbean and entitle you to 25% price breaks on meals in over 1,000 restaurants around the country. And *Entertainment Europe,* features coupon offers on dining and hotels in nearly 150 cities. For more information and prices, write to Entertainment Publications, Inc., 2125 Butterfield Rd., Troy, MI 48084, or call 800-477-3234 or 800-285-5525 (313-637-8400 in MI).

Taste Publications International runs another popular program that nets savings on dining, entertainment, and accommodations. *America at 50% Discount,* $49.95 yearly, offers savings of up to 25% on rack rates at participating hotels, discounted meals at selected locations, plus reduced-price movie passes (offered by mail for United Artists, Loews, and other major chains). For more information, call 800-248-2783 or

410-825-3463, or write to Taste Publications International, 1031 Cromwell Bridge Rd., Baltimore, MD 21202.

Great American Traveler offers discounts at about 1,500 hotels nationwide; membership is $29.95, but you can upgrade to the "Golf Access" membership for $20 more, netting you 50% discounts on courses in North America, among other benefits. Call 800-548-2812, fax 205-979-1038, or write to Colonial Vacations, 1945 Hoover Ct., Birmingham, AL 35226.

Membership in the *International Travel Card,* also known as ITC, costs $36 a year and features savings of up to 50% on over 1,500 hotels nationwide. For more information, call 800-342-0558, or write to ITC, 6001 N. Clark St., Chicago, IL 60660.

And as a general tip on saving money when booking hotel accommodations, always ask whether a special rate is available. You can often take advantage of promotions as nebulous as a "shopper's special" that one Chicago hotel holds regularly; anyone who claims to be in Chicago to shop is entitled to 50% off—but you have to know about the program to claim the discount!

CONNECTIONS

Most travelers insist on the lowest possible prices for airline tickets, but squander comparatively large sums on the last leg of the journey—the trip from the airport to the hotel. Avoid this pitfall with the help of *Crampton's International Airport Transit Guide,* which lists schedules and rates of taxis, car services, trains, buses, car-rental agencies, and other connections from airports worldwide to nearby cities. The pocket-sized guide costs under $5, is updated yearly, and is sold by The Complete Traveller Bookstore (see "Other Resources," following). You may also contact the publisher, Salk International Travel Premiums, Inc., at P.O. Box 1388, Sunset Beach, CA 90742, or 213-592-3315, for more information.

EDUCATIONAL TRAVEL

Combining education with travel isn't a new concept, but *Elderhostel* brings it to a specific group—those 60 and over—and does it so successfully that it's created a loyal group of followers who plan their travel around Elderhostel programs. The organization was founded in 1981 and currently offers programs in hundreds of colleges in the United States, Canada, and overseas—from Australia to Germany. There are study cruises, "RV" programs for hostelers who are bringing their own accommodations (tent or RV), and "Intensive Studies" programs that offer more in-depth courses, as well as the popular courses held on campuses around the country. Previous catalogs have offered programs as diverse as "Christmas Around the World" at Lakeland Community

College, "The Role of the U.S. Intelligence in a Democracy" at Southern Utah University, "The Magic of Opera" at Eckerd College in St. Petersburg, Forida, and "Cults in America" at the Cape May Institute in New Jersey. The price is right: Programs in the United States currently run about $250 to $295 each, and include everything except transportation—classes, meals, lodging, and even entertainment. (The overseas programs cost more, since they include round-trip airfare, sightseeing, transfers, and all other costs.) Even the RV hostelers are bused to the campus or course site, where they receive all their meals. Please note that you, or your spouse, must be at least 60 to participate, but there is no membership fee. Elderhostel's programs provide a wonderful avenue to new interests, friends, and travels, at a very reasonable price. For information, write to Elderhostel, 75 Federal St., 3rd Fl., Boston, MA 02110.

Imagine taking up painting on the coast of Cornwall, or embarking on a safari by jeep in New Mexico. These are two of hundreds of educational opportunities that have been enjoyed through *Learning Vacations* (Peterson's Guides, 1986), by Gerson G. Eisenberg. Although some of the programs are limited to enrolled students, most are extension courses taught on campuses in the United States, Canada, Europe, and as far afield as Tanzania. Prices for the courses vary considerably from program to program, usually depending on the type of accommodations. *Learning Vacations* is available from The Complete Traveller Bookstore, listed in the "Other Resources" section at the end of this chapter.

STUDENT TRAVEL

Like seniors, students can benefit from a variety of travel opportunities and savings. One of the best-known names in this field is the *Council on International Educational Exchange (CIEE),* which also runs Council Charter (see the previous section, "Consolidators/Bucket Shops"). If you're a high school or college student working toward a degree, CIEE can issue you an International Student Identity Card (ISIS), which you'll need to qualify for discounts on train and plane travel, admission to cultural and entertainment centers, and CIEE's own travel programs. The card costs $14, and comes with the *Student Travel Guide.* CIEE also publishes the highly recommended *Work, Study, Travel Abroad: The Whole World Handbook,* by Marjorie Cohen and Margaret Sherman ($10.95). For the *Student Travel Catalog* with details on the card and the program, write to Council on International Educational Exchange, 205 E. 42nd St., New York, NY 10017, or call 212-661-1414.

CAMPUS ACCOMMODATIONS

Staying on campus *sans* academics is often the cheapest alternative to everything but budget hotels. Rooms are usually available during college vacation periods, at prices as low as $19 a night. Amenities vary widely, but the rates are so good that it makes sense to consider this alternative when you're planning a trip.

Campus Holidays USA, Inc. has been arranging campus accommodations and other travel services since 1975. You can call or write for a list of the United States and British accommodations currently on offer, and purchase a book of coupons that can be used to pay for your stay. Campus Holidays can provide "lower-cost youth/student and teacher airfares," and tours of Europe, Asia, Africa, South America, and Australia for travelers who are 18 to 35 years old. Among these trips, its "Top Deck" tours are quite popular: British double-decker buses, which have been converted to hotels (sleeping quarters on top, dining and kitchen facilities below), take intrepid travelers on jaunts of 2 to 20 weeks. (The overland trek from London to Katmandu is a standout.) For information on what's currently available, write to Campus Holidays USA, Inc., 242 Bellevue Ave., Upper Montclair, NJ 07043; you can also call 201-744-8724, or fax 201-744-0531.

If you're interested in exploring the university option, don't miss the directory published by *Campus Travel Service,* "U.S. and Worldwide Travel Accommodations Guide." This 76-page book lists 600 universities in the United States, and others in Canada, Australia, Ireland, England, Wales, Scotland, Scandinavia, Europe, Israel, Japan, Mexico, New Zealand, Africa, Asia, and Yugoslavia. The name, address, and phone number of each institution are given, as well as rates for singles and doubles, open dates, food service availability, nearby cultural and entertainment opportunities, whether children are accommodated, etc. The guide features listings of YMCA residences (51 in the United States, 67 in Canada, and 23 overseas), including prices, amenities, restrictions, and booking policies. There are also several pages of valuable tips and references—on travel overseas, information on youth hostels, bargains for those under 30, travel opportunities for educators, toll-free airline numbers, bed-and-breakfast reservation services worldwide, home-exchange services, addresses of United States and foreign tourist offices, and some excellent health advice for travelers. All of this costs $13 ($11.95 plus $1.05 shipping); send a check or money order for the "Travel Accommodations Guide" to Campus Travel Service, P.O. Box 5007, Laguna Beach, CA 92652.

HOME EXCHANGES

One of the cheapest ways to save on hotel bills, especially if you're quartering a family, is to billet in someone else's home. There are a number of organizations that can help you effect a trade, either by arranging it or by providing a directory of like-minded parties with whom you negotiate.

Home Exchange International arranges the trades of homes of persons in the United States, France, Italy, England, and other locations. To register, you pay a one-time fee of $50 and supply photographs of your home. When you've planned your vacation or narrowed your choices, contact the agency with details. Once a trade is arranged, you also pay a "closing fee" that runs from about $150 to $500, depending on the length of stay planned, type of home, etc. For more information, request a brochure from the Home Exchange International office nearer you: 185 Park Row, P.O. Box 878, New York, NY 10038 (212-349-5340); or 22458 Ventura Blvd., Suite E, Woodland Hills, CA 91364-1581 (818-992-8990).

Do-it-yourselfers may prefer dealing with *International Home Exchange Service/Intervac,* an organization that compiles three directories a year listing over 9,000 homes worldwide (most are outside the United States). A year's subscription costs $44 ($35 plus $9 for postage), and entitles you to one free listing. The apartments and houses in this directory are available for exchange *and* rent, so you don't necessarily have to exchange your own home to take advantage of a good deal. For more information, write to International Home Exchange Service/Intervac, P.O. Box 190070, San Francisco, CA 94119, or call 415-435-3497.

THE TRAVELER WITH DISABILITIES

Travel can be especially trying for persons with disabilities, which is why *Access to the World* (Henry Holt and Company, 1986), by Louise Weiss, is such an important book. It lists hotels with accommodations for the handicapped, covers all aspects of travel by plane, bus, train, ship, car, and RV, and gives hundreds of references to *other* access guides, travel services for the disabled, and travel tips. *Access to the World* is available from The Complete Traveller Bookstore, listed in the "Other Resources" section at the end of this chapter.

Whole Person Tours, an enterprise providing tours for the disabled in Europe and the United States, also publishes *The Itinerary,* a bimonthly magazine for the disabled traveler. The cost is $10 for one year, or $18 for two, from The Itinerary, P.O. Box 1084, Bayonne, NJ 07002.

DEALING WITH PROBLEMS ABROAD

No one plans to fall ill while traveling, but it happens. If you go abroad frequently or want to play it safe on your vacation, consider becoming a member of the *International Association for Medical Assistance to Travelers (IAMAT).* Your $10 contribution to this not-for-profit organization nets you membership and a 70-plus-page roster of English-speaking doctors in hundreds of foreign cities, as well as tips on staying healthy during your trip. For more information, write to IAMAT, 417 Center St., Lewiston, NY 14092, or call 716-754-4883.

A physician-run firm, *Intercontinental Medical Limited,* maintains a data base of health-care providers worldwide, and run checks on the credentials of some, but not all, of the doctors. You can get current listings for three countries for $28.50 at this writing, and $3 for each country in addition to the first three. Write to Intercontinental Medical Limited, 2720 Enterprise Parkway, Suite 106, Richmond, VA 23294, or call 800-426-8828.

The State Department "assists Americans in distress abroad," and may be able to provide information about the arrest, welfare, or whereabouts of a traveler through its Overseas Citizens Emergency Center. The State Department also issues travel advisories for countries afflicted by civil unrest, natural disasters, or outbreaks of serious diseases. All of this information, as well as visa requirements for travel to specific countries, may be obtained by calling 202-647-5225.

Planning the problems *out* of your trip is the best way to avoid them. Here are some pamphlets that can help ensure a pleasant experience: "Your Trip Abroad," "Travel Tips for Senior Citizens," "A Safe Trip Abroad," and "Tips for Americans Residing Abroad." Each booklet costs $1; request them by title from The Superintendent of Documents, U.S. Government Printing Office, Washington, DC 20402.

NEWSLETTERS

If you travel frequently or would like to be able to afford to, you'll find the following newsletters of interest:

Consumer Reports Travel Letter, produced by Consumers Union, is a well-regarded "consumerist" publication for both business and recreational travelers. *CRTL* conducts in-depth comparisons of accommodations and prices in the United States and abroad, scrutinizes airline food, investigates travel scams, recommends methods of screening travel agents, and has probed the mare's nest of airline booking systems. Each monthly issue of *CRTL* runs around 12 pages; a year's subscription costs $37 at this writing. See the current *Consumer Reports* for an order form, or write to Circulation Department, Consumer Reports Travel Letter, 256 Washington St., Mount Vernon, NY 10553, for information. Single copies of back issues are available for $5 each.

Travel Smart is another newsletter that stays current with travel opportunities of all types, including discount fares and rates (including specials for seniors). Subscribers are offered deals on car rentals, cruises, accommodations, and air travel. And Travel Smart is full of great tips especially valuable to frequent travelers: A recent issue cited the end of an encephalitis alert in Florida, listed a number of short-term hotel bargains that were linked with bonus mileage offers, recommended restaurants in several cities for their moderately priced meals, and featured a two-season guide to cruises—along with the 800 numbers of dozens of cruise lines. A year of monthly issues costs $37; for more information, write to Travel Smart, 40 Beechdale Rd., Dobbs Ferry, NY 10522-9989.

OTHER RESOURCES

Whether your travels are confined to your armchair or you actually get up and go, you'll find travel guides a great help in planning your trip. The best-known series are *Fodor's, Fielding's, Frommer's, Baedeker's,* and *Birnbaum's.* These are reliable, general-purpose guide books to whole countries and major cities. The Frommer "$-A-Day" series is especially helpful if you're pinching pennies, but don't overlook the other books. If you're traveling abroad and want an informed guide to culturally and historically significant sites, see the *Blue Guide* series, which is highly recommended. The Zagats have entered the fray stateside with *Zagat's United States Hotel Survey,* a compilation on accommodations nationwide that have been rated by the Zagats' corps of paying guests and diners.

Many of the firms listed in "Books" sell travel guides and related literature, but specialty bookstores have far better stock and selection, and the staff can usually provide personal assistance in selecting the right book for your needs, even by mail.

The Complete Traveller Bookstore does a brisk mail-order trade through its 48-page catalog, which lists all the major guides, as well as *Insider's Guides,* the *Michelin* green and red guides, *Crown Insider's Guides* (written by expatriate Americans), the fascinating *Lonely Planet* books, which take you to the Cook Islands as well as Canada, and scores of specialty guides that cover everything from Alaskan hideaways to shopping in Seoul. Maps, foreign language tapes, and travel accessories are sold through the catalog as well. Store shoppers can peruse the collection of antiquarian travel books, including some early Baedekers, which are perched at the tops of the bookcases. For a copy of the catalog, send $1 to The Complete Traveller Bookstore, 199 Madison Ave., New York, NY 10016. Please note: This is *not* a discount bookseller.

The Forsyth Travel Library has an extensive selection of popular guides, road maps to cities and countries around the world, Berlitz phrase books, Audio-Forum language tapes, and Thomas Cook surface transit timetables. Through Forsyth, you can order rail passes to Europe and Britain (including "The Britainshrinkers" sightseeing tours), join American Youth Hostels (an application form is provided in Forsyth's brochure), and even subscribe to over a dozen travel publications, including *Consumer Reports Travel Letter.* Voltage converters and plug adapters, money belts, and other travel accessories are also available.

Send 50¢ for the current brochure to Forsyth Travel Library, Inc., 9154 W. 57th St., Shawnee Mission, KS 66201-1375. Forsyth does *not* sell at a discount.

Book Passage publishes a 44-page catalog full of tantalizing reads: *Underwater Paradise: The World's Best Diving Sites, Muddling Through in Madagascar,* and *Doing Children's Museums* were just a few of the hundreds that caught our attention. In addition to the major travel guides and several language courses on tape, Book Passage offers titles on family travel, menu converters, railway timetables, shopping guides, maps, a number of guides to doing business abroad, and accessories— overnight bags, pocket-sized computer translators, fanny packs, etc. Request the catalog from Book Passage, 51 Tamal Vista Blvd., Corte Madera, CA 94925. Book Passage does *not* sell at a discount.

TravelBooks bills itself as "the compleat travel bookstore for domestic or international travel literature," and offers publications on adventure travel, trekking, hiking, student opportunities, and hundreds of maps. Write for the free catalog from TravelBooks, 113 Corporation Rd., Hyannis, MA 02601-2204, or call 800-869-3535.

Traveler's Checklist specializes in travel accessories, including money converters, adaptors and plugs, personal-care items, and related goods. Request a catalog from Traveler's Checklist, Cornwall Bridge Rd., Sharon, CT 06069. Please note that Traveler's Checklist does *not* sell at a discount.

Travel Accessories & Things has just that—those little items that can make life away from home a little easier. Inflatable pillows, personal "safes" of several types, eye masks, a folding cane, world-time alarm clocks, currency converters, and other useful travel aids have been offered in the past. Write to Travel Accessories & Things, P.O. Box 1178, Agoura Hills, CA 91301 for the current catalog.

SEE ALSO

Ace Luggage and Gifts • *travel clocks, gift items* • **LEATHER**
American Association of Retired Persons • *car rental and lodging discounts* • **GENERAL MERCHANDISE**
Consumer Information Center • *travel tips and related information* • **BOOKS**
Grandma's Spice Shop • *Melitta coffee travel kit* • **FOOD: BEVERAGES AND FLAVORINGS**
Jobson's Luggage Warehouse • *travel accessories* • **LEATHER**
The Kennel Vet Corp. • *airline animal carriers* • **ANIMAL**
The Luggage Center • *travel accessories* • **LEATHER**
Superintendent of Documents • *travel tips and related information* • **BOOKS**

THE COMPLETE GUIDE TO BUYING BY MAIL

CATALOGS AND PRICE QUOTES

CATALOGS

Most of the companies in this book publish catalogs, which usually cost between $1 and $5. Firms sometimes ask for a SASE, which is a long (#10), self-addressed with one first-class stamp. If a SASE is requested and you don't send one, don't expect a response.

You can order the stamps to mail all those catalog requests by mail, directly from the U.S. Postal Service. Both stamps and stamped envelopes are available; ask your postmaster or carrier for PS Form 3227, "Stamps by Mail," or request it from the Consumer Advocate, U.S. Postal Service, Washington, DC 20260. You can also call 800-STAMP-24 (MasterCard and VISA are accepted). The stamps are usually delivered within a few days.

"Refundable" Catalogs. Catalog fees that are "refundable" can be recouped when you place an order. Please note: If you don't place an order, you won't get the refund. Procedures for reimbursement vary; some firms send a coupon with instructions to enclose it with your order and deduct the amount from the total. (The coupon may be dated, forcing you to order within a limited time to recoup the fee.) If there's no coupon in the catalog, deduct the amount from the order total after adding tax, shipping, and other surcharges, and note the reason for the deduction on the order form.

Sending for Catalogs. Write a letter or postcard requesting the catalog you want (some firms have several), mention enclosures, include your return address in the letter, and refer to WBMC as your source. If the catalog costs up to $1, you can send a dollar bill or coins taped between thick pieces of cardboard. For catalogs costing over a dollar, send a check or money order. Don't send stamps unless they're requested, and don't use a credit card to pay for a catalog or a subscription unless the listing advises it.

Catalogs from Foreign Firms. When ordering a catalog from a foreign firm, use an international money order (IMO) or personal check if the catalog costs $5 or more, and cash or International Reply Coupons (see below) if it costs less than that. Money orders can be purchased at a bank or post office.

International Reply Coupons (IRCs) are certificates that can be exchanged for units of surface postage in foreign countries. They're available at the post office for 95¢ each, and are recommended when the catalog costs 75¢ or less.

You can save handling charges if the catalog costs $5 or less by sending cash through the mail. (In fact, several firms have requested it.) Technically it's risky and should be used only when you're dealing with currency. To conceal money and enclosures and remain within the half-ounce weight limit of a 50¢ stamp, slip the currency inside a piece of lacquered wrapping paper, or other kind of lightweight, opaque paper. This will camouflage the enclosure completely. Remember to mention enclosures in your letter.

Receiving Catalogs. Catalog publication schedules vary, and when firms run out of catalogs, are between printings, or issue catalogs seasonally, there can be a delay of weeks or months before you receive one. Some firms notify customers of delays; most don't. Consequently, please allow six to eight weeks to receive your catalog.

PRICE QUOTES

Some mail-order firms don't publish catalogs, but sell their goods on a price-quote basis. Their name-brand goods can be identified by manufacturer's name, stock or model number, and color or pattern name or code. Cameras, appliances, audio and TV/video components, tableware, furniture, and sporting goods are commonly sold by discounters on a price-quote basis.

A price quote is simply the statement of the cost of that item from that firm. The company may guarantee that price for a limited period of time, or until stock is depleted. Some firms include tax, shipping charges, insurance, and handling in their price quotes, giving you one figure for the final cost.

Finding the Information. Before writing or calling for a price quote, have the manufacturer's name, product code (model or style number or pattern name), and size and color information, if applicable. You'll find this information on the factory cartons or tags of goods in stores and in manufacturers' brochures. If you're pricing an item you found in a catalog, remember to look for the manufacturer's data, not the vendor's catalog code numbers. If you're using a buying guide or magazine as a source for information, verify the information before requesting a price quote—the reference may be out of date or contain typos.

Price Quotes by Letter. Most of the firms listed in this book will give quotes over the phone—in fact, many prefer it. When you write requesting price quotes, include all of the available information about the item or items. Leave blanks next to each item so the person giving the quote can enter the price, shipping cost or estimate, and related charges. Ask the firm to note how long it will honor the given prices, and ask for prices of no more than three items at a time. Note: You must include a SASE with your request if you want a response.

Price Quotes by Phone. Have all of the information in front of you when you call. Don't make collect calls, and to avoid problems later, ask to speak to the manager, take down his or her name, and make notes of the conversation.

HOW TO ORDER

Before ordering, make sure you're getting the best deal:

COST COMPARISONS

Your chief consideration is the delivered price of the product. Compute this from your price quotes and/or catalogs, then compare the figure to the delivered cost of the item if purchased from a local supplier. Consider mileage costs if you must drive to the local source, parking fees, sales and use tax, shipping and trucking, installation, etc. If you're buying a gift, compare the costs of having the mail-order firm wrap and send the item to the value of your own time, and materials and mailing costs. Finally, weigh the intangibles—return policies, the prospect of waiting for a mail delivery versus getting the item immediately, the guarantees offered by the retailer and mail-order firm, etc. After contemplating costs and variables, you'll reach the bottom line and best buying option.

Before ordering any large item, measure all of the doorways through which the article must pass, allowing for narrow hallways, stairs, and the like. Some savvy shoppers even construct a carton dummy of the item by taping boxes together, and maneuver that through a dry-run delivery before ordering.

ORDERING

If the catalog is more than six months old and unless it's an annual, verify stock availability and prices by phone, or request a new edition and order from that. (You may find yourself billed for the difference between the old price and the new if you order from an out-of-date catalog.) Use the catalog order form, along with the self-sticking address label on the catalog. If there's no order blank, use one from another catalog as a guide. Transcribe the code numbers, names of items, number of items ordered, units, prices, tax, and shipping charges—onto a separate piece of paper. Include your name, address, and phone number, the firm's name and address, and appropriate information if you're having the order sent to another address. Note any minimum-order requirements. Make a copy of the order, and file it with the catalog.

Second Choices and Substitutions. When the firm advises it and you're willing to accept them, give second choices. These usually refer to differences in color, not product. If you'll accept substitutions, which may be different products that the firm considers comparable to what you ordered, you must give permission in writing on the order form. It's unlawful for a firm to make substitutions without written authorization from the buyer. If you don't want second choices and want to be sure the firm knows this, write "NO SECOND CHOICES OR SUBSTITUTIONS ACCEPTED" in red on the order form.

WBMC Reader Offers. If you want to take advantage of a WBMC reader discount, rebate, bonus, or other special, be sure to comply with the conditions stated in the listing. Unless otherwise indicated, calculate discounts on the total cost of the goods only, not from the total that includes shipping, handling, insurance, and tax.

PHONE ORDERS

Phone orders have certain advantages over mail orders. They're usually processed more quickly and, when the phone operator has stock information, you'll know right away whether an item is available.

ORDERING

Before picking up the phone to place your order, follow this procedure:

1. Have your credit card ready.
2. Make sure the card is one that's accepted by the firm, has not expired, and has a credit line sufficient for the purchase.
3. Have the delivery name, address, and ZIP code available.
4. Fill out the order form to use as a guide, and a record of the transaction. Include the catalog code numbers, units, colors, sizes, etc.
5. Have the catalog from which you're ordering at hand—the operator may ask for encoded information on the address label.

When you place the call, ask the operator the following:

1. What is your name or operator number?
2. What are the terms of the return policy (unless they're clearly stated in the catalog)?
3. Are any of the items you're ordering out of stock? If yes, when is new stock expected?
4. When will the order be shipped?
5. Will any of the items be shipped separately?
6. What is the total, including shipping and tax, that will be charged to my account?
7. What is my order number?

Many operators are required to ask for your home phone number, and sometimes your office number as well. This is done so they can verify that you are the person placing the order, not a criminal who's obtained your card information illegally. Since the firm may be stuck with the bill if the charge is fraudulent, it may refuse your order if you won't divulge your number, especially if you're buying certain types of goods and your order total is high.

While you're on the phone, the operator may try to "upsell" you, or get you to buy more goods. Beware of such unplanned purchases if you're trying to stick to a budget, but listen—you may be offered a real bargain on goods the firm wants to clear out. When this happens, the company's loss is your gain. Just make sure you really want the item, since a bargain you'll never use is no bargain at all.

Once the transaction is completed and you've noted the operator's name or number, recorded the order number, checked off the items you ordered, struck off those you didn't, entered the billing amount, and noted the date of the call, put this record in your file with the catalog. They may prove valuable later, if you have problems with your order.

ORDERING FROM FOREIGN FIRMS

Despite the fact that the world was supposed to be switching to the metric scale, many of the catalogs from Europe and elsewhere use the U.S. system—inches and pounds—in measurements. Converting metric measurements to U.S. equivalents is easy, though. Use the chart you'll find in any good dictionary.

There are confusing differences in sizing systems, color descriptions, and generic terms from one country to another. Sizes fall into three categories: U.S., British, and Continental, and the sizing chart on page 620 can be used as a general guide to equivalents. Always measure yourself before ordering clothing, and list the measurements on the order form if you're unsure of the proper size.

Color descriptions and terms are usually more poetic than precise, in both U.S. and foreign catalogs. Remember that color charts can resolve these questions, but you must allow for variations between photographic reproductions and the product itself. For a true match, write to the firm and ask for samples before you order, or at least make sure the firm will make refunds on returns.

The majority of foreign firms listed in this book give their prices in U.S. dollars. If they don't, you'll have to convert the firm's currency when you order. First, compute the total, including shipping, insurance, and other charges (but do not include duty). Next, convert this figure to dollars using the rate of exchange prevailing on the day you send the order. Get the rate from a bank, business newspaper, or the American Express office nearest you.

Before ordering, determine the rate of duty you'll be charged when the goods arrive and any shipping or transportation costs not included in the order total. See these sections for more information: "Paying for Goods from Foreign Firms," page 592; "Shipments from Foreign Countries," page 596; "Duty," page 599; and "Deliveries from Foreign Firms," page 605.

BUYING AT WHOLESALE

Buying at true wholesale assumes that you're operating as a business, which intends to resell what you're buying, whether in its purchased state or in another form. You can buy at wholesale from those firms listed in this book that have a star in the row of symbols—but only if you and/or your order qualify. At least one of the following special sales terms will apply to your order:

Letterhead or Business Card Required. This provides evidence that you're doing business as a company, not as an individual.

Resale Number or Business Certificate Required. This proves that you're registered with local authorities as a business entity. Resale numbers are usually required for sales tax exemption.

Bank and Credit References Required. These are not usually necessary unless you want to open an account or have the order invoiced instead of paying when you place it.

Limitation of Payment Methods. Some firms allow you to charge a wholesale order to a credit card, and some require a check or money order—especially with the first order.

Minimum Order Requirements. Minimums almost invariably apply to wholesale orders; they're usually stated in dollars, although they may be in number of items or multiples, and sometimes a combination of the two.

Many of the firms listed in this book that sell at wholesale will send you the same catalog that consumers receive, with a discount schedule or a separate price list. Some have completely separate retail and wholesale catalogs, with different product lines. Wholesale catalogs often have much less descriptive information than their consumer equivalents, making "sample orders" quite valuable. Because return policies are traditionally very strict—restocking fees of 10% to 25% are often charged—be sure you know what you're buying before you order. (It's not wise to buy anything that's marked "final sale, no returns accepted.") On the positive side, the shipping costs are usually charged as a fraction of the order value, or are the actual shipping costs, paid C.O.D. to the carrier. In several comparisons to the rates charged to consumers, they worked out to much less—which should surprise no one who's bought by mail recently.

Be sure to check the listing before contacting the company as a wholesale buyer, since wholesale sales terms may be noted in the text. And please don't ask the company to accept your order if you won't meet their terms.

PAYMENT

There are two basic ways to pay for your order: now or later. You can prepay, using a check, money order, or debit card, or buy on credit. The distinction between these types of payments is based on the rules that apply to refunds under the FTC Mail or Telephone Order Rule, but some methods have characteristics of both categories.

Prepaid Orders. Payments made by check or money order are sometimes called "cash" by catalogers, since the firm receives dollars instead of extending credit on the basis of a promise to pay.

Personal checks, accepted by most firms, are inexpensive and can be sent without going to the bank or post office. Since some firms wait until your check has cleared before sending your order, shipment may be delayed by as much as two weeks. Checks do provide you with a receipt (the canceled check), which is returned with your monthly statement. Use the "memo" space on your checks to jot down the firm's address, so if you lose track of the company in the future, you'll have a way to find it again.

Certified checks are guaranteed personal checks. You bring your check to the bank on which it's drawn, and pay a fee of about $5 to $9. The bank marks the check "certified" and freezes that sum in your account. Every company that accepts personal checks will accept a certified check, and the guarantee of funds should obviate the delay for clearance. The canceled certified check is returned with the other canceled checks in your statement. Firms that request certified checks for payment will usually accept a bank check, a teller's check, or a cashier's check as well.

Bank money orders are issued by banks for a fee, usually $1 to $3. Ask the teller for a money order in the desired amount and fill in the firm's name and your name and address. If the order isn't dated mechanically, insert the date. Most come with a carbon receipt; some have stubs that should be filled in on the spot before you forget the information.

Bank money orders are generally treated as certified checks (i.e., no waiting for clearance). If necessary, you can have the order traced, payment stopped, and a refund issued. You'll find this vital if your order is lost in the mail, since there's always a chance it's been intercepted.

Postal money orders, sold at the post office, are available in amounts up to $700 and cost 75¢. They're self-receipting and dated, and can be replaced if the order is lost or stolen. Copies of the cashed money order can be obtained through the post office for up to two years after it's paid. This can prove helpful in settling disputes with firms that claim nonreceipt of payment. And, like stamped envelopes and stamps, money orders can be bought from postal carriers by customers who live on rural routes, or have limited access to the post office.

Bank international money orders, issued by banks, are used to pay foreign firms. You complete a form at the bank and, if the catalog prices are listed in foreign currency, the bank computes the amount in dollars based on the day's exchange rate. These orders cost a few dollars or more, and they are receipted. Like domestic money orders, you send them to the firm yourself with the order. They are usually treated as immediate payment.

Postal international money orders are used to pay foreign firms; their cost varies, depending on the amount of the order. (For example, the service charge on a $200 postal IMO sent to Britain is $3 at this writing.) They're not for every transaction: ceilings on amounts to different nations vary from $200 to $500, they can't be sent to every country, and amounts of $400 or more must be registered. When you buy a postal IMO, you fill out a form with your name and address and the name and address of the firm, and you pay the order amount and surcharge. The post office forwards the information to the International Exchange Office in St. Louis, Missouri, which sends a receipt to you and forwards the money order, in native currency, directly to the firm (or to the post office nearest it, which sends it on). The entire procedure takes few weeks; if you use postal IMOs, allow for this delay.

Bank drafts, or transfer checks, are the closest you can come to sending cash to a foreign firm through the mail. You pay the order amount, a mailing fee, and a service charge to your bank, then send one copy of the draft form to the firm and another to the firm's bank. You must have the name and address of the company's bank to do this. When the firm receives the form, it takes it to the bank, matches it to the other copy, and collects the funds. The forms will take five to ten days to reach the foreign country, provided they're sent airmail. Most banks charge $5 or more for bank drafts, depending on the amount of the check, but all foreign firms accept them.

Debit cards, which look like credit cards, are actually more like remote-control cash cards that are hooked into your checking account. See the following section for special caveats that apply to the use of debit cards when buying by mail.

Credit, Charge, and Debit Cards. Those wafers of plastic in your wallet have been important factors in the mail-order boom, and the pairing of 800 lines and credit cards has proven an irresistible combination for millions of consumers, creating phenomenal growth in phone orders.

Paying for an order with a credit card is simplicity itself—use a card accepted by the firm, make out the order form, and provide your account number, card expiration date, phone number, and signature in the blanks. If you're ordering from a catalog without a form, supply the same information on a sheet of paper. Using credit cards can make life easier if the shipping costs aren't given or are difficult to calculate—they'll be added to the order total, and the order won't be held up as it might be if you paid by check or with a money order. Always check the minimum-order requirements when using a card, since they're often higher than those imposed on prepaid orders.

If you're low on cash but determined to order from a firm that doesn't accept cards, you can have Western Union send the company a money order and charge it to your MasterCard or VISA account. The surcharge is high—$14 to $37, and higher if you call in the order instead of placing it in person at a Western Union office. But it can be worth the expense if you might otherwise miss the buy of a lifetime.

The card companies, banks, and financial institutions that issue credit cards consider your past credit history, your current salary, and the length of time you've been at your current job when reviewing your application for a card. Minimums are raised when the interest rate climbs, but at this writing, a salary of about $20,000 and two years' employment with the same firm should net you a MasterCard or VISA account, provided you're credit-worthy in other respects. Getting an American Express, Diners Club, or debit card usually requires a higher salary and an excellent credit rating, and the issuers of "gold" accounts that offer larger credit lines and special programs geared for business and travel use usually look for an income of at least $40,000 and an excellent credit history.

Since there are thousands of card issuers and the market is considered saturated, the consumer is being wooed with reduced yearly fees and APRs, extended warranties, tie-ins with frequent-flyer programs, personal and auto insurance, discounts on lodging, charitable contributions, and other benefits. If you need help comparing cards, Bankcard Holders of America (BHA), a not-for-profit consumer advocacy organization, can help you compare cards and find the one that best suits your buying habits. BHA publishes a list of banks with low APRs, and its bimonthly newsletters have useful information and updates on pending legislation that will affect bank card holders. For membership information and a publications list, write to Bankcard Holders of America, 560 Herndon Parkway, Suite 120, Herndon, VA 22070.

"Debit" cards deserve a special mention because they look like regular credit cards, but when the issuing bank receives the invoices for purchases, it deducts those amounts from your checking, savings, or money management account. This makes the debit card an electronic, instantly debited check, not a credit card, and it's important to know that the FTC views debit-card payments as cash payments. See the discussion of the FTC Mail or Telephone Order Rule for more information on the debit-card issue.

Paying for Goods from Foreign Firms. You can usually pay for goods from foreign firms with a personal check, bank draft, or credit card. Using a credit card is advisable (see "The Fair Credit Billing Act, page 617, for an explanation), but keep the following caution in mind:

If you use a credit card, the card issuer will charge you for the currency-conversion expense—a surcharge of 0.25% to 1%. The methods used to determine the rate of exchange vary widely, and are subject to the regulations existing in each foreign country. Your credit card statement should tell you the date the conversion was made and the surcharge. Check it carefully; the foreign currency total should be the same as your original order total, unless there was a price increase, short shipment, or shipping costs were higher than originally calculated. Check the interbank rate of exchange valid on the day the money was converted or the invoice was processed by the card company (your bank should be able to quote this). If there's a significant discrepancy between the interbank rate and the one the card firm used, write or call the customer-service department for an explanation.

Please read "Ordering from Foreign Firms," page 587, before ordering.

RETURN POLICIES

Most catalog firms guarantee satisfaction and will accept returns within 10, 14, or 30 days after you've received the order. Firms selling on a price-quote basis usually accept returns only if the product is defective. There are companies that don't accept any returns under any circumstances, but they're not listed in this book.

Some goods—personalized or monogrammed, custom-made, surplus, and sale items—are routinely exempted from full return policies. (If a firm has to special order an item for you, it may refuse to accept returns on that item—and may require you to buy a minimum number or amount.) Health regulations usually prohibit returns of intimate apparel and bathing suits, but some companies will accept them. For more information, see "Returns," page 607.

Check the company's return policy before ordering. If you're shopping for a big-ticket item that carries a manufacturer's warranty, ask the mail-order firm for a copy before you buy, and see "Evaluating Warranties," page 611, for determining its value.

For more information, see "Returns," page 607.

CANCELING YOUR ORDER

When you order goods or services from a firm, whether by phone or mail, you enter into a contract of sale. You don't have the right to call the firm and rescind an order, nor do you have the right to stop payment on a check or money order on the basis of what an FTC staffer described as "buyer's remorse." (This term seems almost poetic in an industry that thrives on impulse purchases.) State laws vary on matters of contract, but, strictly speaking, your second thoughts might give the firm cause to bring legal action against you. This is especially true if the company has undertaken action on an order, in what is termed "constructive acceptance of payment."

But if, after placing an order, you learn that the firm is in financial trouble or has a bad business record, stopping payment might be worth the risk. If you try to cancel, check the terms of the offer first. Magazine and book subscriptions are often sent on an approval basis, giving you a cancellation option. Goods offered with an unconditional guarantee of satisfaction can be sent back when they arrive. If these terms aren't offered and you're determined to cancel, contact the firm to discuss the matter.

SHIPPING, HANDLING, INSURANCE, SALES TAX, DUTY, AND SHIPMENTS ABROAD

When comparison shopping, consider shipping, insurance, tax, and handling as part of the total. (See "Cost Comparisons," page 585, for more information.) If you're having goods sent to Canada, an APO or FPO address, or another country, see "Shipments Abroad," page 600, for more information.

SHIPPING

This section addresses the concerns of consumers buying from U.S. firms who are having goods delivered to addresses in the United States.

Shipping Computations. The largest ancillary cost of an order is usually shipping, which is calculated in a variety of methods described below:

Postpaid item prices, which include shipping charges, are popular because there's no math for customers to do. The shipping and packing costs are passed along in the item price, however.

Itemized shipping costs are often seen as amounts in parentheses after the product price or code number. If you compare the UPS or USPS tape on the delivered parcel, you may find that the shipping fee you paid the firm is higher than what it really cost. But your fee may include the cost of packing and materials, or it may be prorated. (A California firm might compute all shipping charges based on the price of sending goods to Kansas, midway across the country, making up on local deliveries what it loses on shipments to the East Coast.) And there are some firms that, quite simply, seem to be gouging the consumer with shipping charges that are far higher than their real costs. If you feel charges are exorbitant, contact the company and protest—or take your business elsewhere.

Numeric charges are based on the number of items you're ordering, as in "$2.50 for the first item; 75¢ each additional item." Companies often limit these kinds of charges, so additional purchases made after you reach a certain number of items are exempted from shipping charges entirely.

Flat order fees are simple dollar amounts charged on all orders, usually regardless of the number of items or weight. (Extra charges may apply if part of the order is shipped to another address.) A flat fee may represent a bargain if you're placing a large order, but note that some firms selling this way will charge extra for heavy, outsized, or fragile items. Check the catalog carefully before ordering.

Free shipping is offered, often by smaller companies, on large orders. Customarily, orders under a certain dollar or item amount are charged shipping on some basis, but if your order exceeds a certain amount, no shipping is charged. The fact is often noted on the order blank—"on orders $100 and over, WE pay postage," or "free shipping on three dozen pairs or more same size, style, and color"—usually with the proviso that the order must be sent to one address.

Sliding scales, tied to the cost of the order, are used by many companies. For example, if the goods total $15.00, you pay $2.75 for shipping; from $15.01 to $30.00, the charge is $3.50, etc. This is great if you're ordering many inexpensive, heavy items, but seems unfair when you're buying one, expensive thing. Some firms remedy this by using itemized shipping charges for small, high-ticket goods, and most limit the shipping charges to a maximum dollar amount, usually $7 to $12.

Tables, based on the weight and sometimes delivery distance of the order, require the most work on your part: You must tally the shipping weights given with the item prices, find your zone or area on the rate chart, and then compute the shipping charges. Outsized goods will have to be shipped by truck; their catalog code numbers often have a suffix letter indicating this. Some firms include in their catalogs all the rate charts you'll need to figure exact costs; others state at the bottom of the order form, "Add enough for postage and insurance. We will refund overpayment." In this case, the best solution is to pay by credit card, or call the firm itself and ask the shipping department to give you a quick calculation over the phone. If you're paying by check, you could send in the order without adding anything for shipping and ask the firm to bill you, but this may delay delivery.

Saving on Shipping Costs. When you have a chance to save on shipping by placing a large order, consult friends and coworkers to see if they want to combine orders with you. But count the time spent conferring, consolidating orders, and distributing the goods as part of the cost of the order.

Carriers. No matter which method a firm uses to calculate shipping, it will usually send your goods by USPS, UPS, truck, or an overnight delivery service.

United Parcel Service (UPS): UPS is the delivery system many businesses prefer for mail order. UPS is cheaper, all costs considered, than USPS; it automatically insures each package for up to $100; it also picks up the packages at the firm's office or warehouse.

Under its Common Carrier Service, UPS handles packages weighing up to 70 pounds with a combined girth and length measurement of up to 108", with some qualifications. (A 150-pound limit is being negotiated at this writing.) If your package exceeds the size/weight restrictions, it will be transported by a private trucking firm. UPS offers overnight delivery to certain states and ZIP codes through its Next Day Air service, and 2nd Day Air delivery to the contiguous United States and some parts of Hawaii. The delivery fee charged by UPS is determined by the delivery address, pickup location, the dimensions and weight of the package, and the service used.

United States Postal Service (USPS)—Parcel Post (PP): The costs for Parcel Post, or fourth-class mail, are somewhat higher than UPS charges, but Parcel Post offers one distinct advantage: only packages sent by the U.S. Postal Service can be delivered to a post-office box. (UPS must have a street address to deliver goods, although carriers will usually deliver to rural routes.) If you're having a package sent to a post-office box, write "DELIVERY BY PARCEL POST ONLY; UPS NOT ACCEPTABLE" in bold red letters on the order form, unless there's a box to check to indicate your preference. On the check, write "GOODS TO BE DELIVERED BY PARCEL POST ONLY." When the firm cashes the check, it's agreeing implicitly to this arrangement and should send the goods by Parcel Post.

While postal rates escalate by leaps and bounds, the size/weight restrictions remain relatively constant. USPS accepts parcels with a combined girth and length measurement of up to 84" that weigh up to 70 pounds. Packages weighing under 15 pounds, with a combined girth/length measurement over 84", are accepted at rates for 15-pound packages.

Truck: When the firm specifies that an item must be sent by truck, or if you've ordered both mailable and nonmailable (outsized) goods, the entire order may be sent by truck. Sometimes firms indicate that goods are to be trucked with the term "FOB" or "freight," followed by the word "warehouse," "manufacturer," or the name of the city from which the goods are trucked. "FOB" stands for "free on board," and it means that the trucking charges will be billed from that point. When "manufacturer" follows FOB in the catalog, it means that the mail-order firm is probably having that item "drop-shipped," or sent from the manufacturer, instead of maintaining its own warehouse inventories of the product. If you're ordering nonmailable goods that you think will be drop-shipped, ask for the location of the manufacturer's warehouse so you can estimate the trucking costs. If you want the item quickly, ask the mail-order company to verify that the manufacturer has the product in stock before placing the order, and whether the manufacturer can ship it by an overnight service.

Truck charges are usually collected in cash or certified check upon delivery, and the additional expense is a real factor to consider when ordering very heavy items from a firm that's located far away. Truckers usually make "dump deliveries," meaning they unload the goods on the sidewalk in front of your home or business. For an additional fee (usually $10 to $20), you can usually have the goods delivered inside your house or apartment. Additional fees may be incurred if your order happens to be the only one the trucker is picking up from the firm that day or if the driver has to notify you of delivery. Before ordering an item you know will have to be trucked, get the price plus trucking charges and compare it to the cost of the same item if bought locally and delivered.

SHIPMENTS FROM FOREIGN COUNTRIES

After your payment has been authorized or has cleared the bank, the firm should ship your order. Depending on the dimensions and weight of the package, it may be shipped by mail or sent by sea or air freight.

Mailable Orders. If the package weighs up to 20kg (about 44 pounds) and has a length of up to 1.5m (about 59") and a length/girth measurement of up to 3m (about 118") for surface mail or up to 2m (about 79") for airmail, it can be mailed. Almost everything you can buy from the non-U.S. firms listed in this book will be mailable, but you may have a choice of air or surface shipment. Mailed packages will be delivered by your postal carrier, regardless of the service used by the company, and duty will be collected on delivery.

Airmail is the most expensive service; airmailed packages generally take a week to ten days to arrive after they're dispatched, although some firms ask you to allow three weeks for delivery.

Surface mail, which includes both overland and boat shipment, is the cheapest service, but orders can take up to two months.

Nonmailable Orders. In the unlikely event your order exceeds mail weight and/or size restrictions, it will have to be sent by an air or ship carrier.

Air freight is the best choice when the item or order just exceeds mail restrictions. Charges are based on the weight and size of the order, as well as the flight distance. The firm arranges to have the order sent to the airport with a U.S. Customs office that's closest to your delivery address. You pay the firm for air-freight charges, it sees the order to the airport and sends you a Customs declaration form and invoice. When the airport apprises you of arrival, get right over with the forms, since most airports will charge a holding fee on goods still unclaimed five to ten days after delivery. In addition, you should make arrangements to have the package trucked to your home if it's too large to transport yourself. Once you clear Customs, you can take the goods home or release them to the truckers you've hired and they'll make the delivery.

Sea freight is much less expensive than air, but it can take months for an order to reach you. If you live near a port, you may want to handle Customs clearance yourself and hire a trucker to deliver the goods to your home. You can also hire an agent (customs broker) to clear Customs and arrange inland trucking. This service will cost from $75 to $125, but it's the only practical way to deal with the process if you live far from the docking site and the foreign firm that sent the goods doesn't have arrangements with a U.S. agent who could take care of these details for you.

The procedure is similar to that of clearing an air shipment: You present the forms the firm has provided to the shipper and Customs officer, pay duty charges, and transport the goods home or release them to the truckers you've hired.

For information on duty rates, trademark regulations, and shipment of problematical or prohibited goods, see "Duty," page 599. For information on payment of duty on mailed goods, see "Deliveries from Foreign Firms," page 605.

HANDLING

Some firms charge an extra fee for processing or packing your order (usually $1 to $5), which is often waived on orders over a certain dollar amount. The handling fee helps to cover the costs of labor and materials used in processing your order, and it, like the shipping fee, may be taxed in certain states.

INSURANCE

Packages shipped by UPS are automatically insured for up to $100; you shouldn't have to pay extra insurance on those orders. (If you're buying from a firm that delivers via UPS but has a preprinted charge for insurance on the order form, don't pay it.) UPS charges an additional fee for each additional $100 in value on the same package, the cost of which is usually covered in the shipping charge. The USPS doesn't insure automatically, so if you're having your package delivered by mail, not UPS, be sure to request insurance. Charges for postal insurance range from 70¢ for goods worth up to $50, to $5.00 for package contents worth from $400.01 to $500.00. Goods valued at more than $500 but under $25,000 must be registered as well as insured, and some goods can't be insured. If the item you're buying is uninsurable, have the firm arrange shipping with a carrier that will insure it. If you're not sure whether the firm will insure your goods, ask—before you order. The small fee is a worthwhile expense, something you know if you've ever had an uninsured order go awry. (See "Accepting Deliveries" for more information.)

Most insurance claims arise as a result of damage to or loss of goods. Procedures for claiming and reimbursement vary according to the carrier's rules and the firm's policy, but contact the firm as soon as you discover any damage to your shipment and ask the customer service department what to do. If there is documentation (signature of receipt on the UPS carrier's log or USPS insurance receipt), the claim can be verified and processed, and eventually you should be reimbursed or receive replacement goods. If there is no documentation and the worst happens—the goods never arrive—the firm may absorb the loss and send a replacement order. It may also refuse to do so, especially if its records indicate that the order was shipped. In such cases, it might be nearly impossible to prove that you didn't receive the order. (If you paid with a credit card, you may be able to get a chargeback. See "The Fair Credit Billing Act," page 617, for more information.) But if repeated entreaties for a refund or duplicate order meet resistance, state your case to the agencies listed in "Obtaining Help," page 615. And be sure to tell us—see "Feedback, " page 619, for more information.

SALES TAX

You're supposed to pay sales tax on an order if you're having goods delivered to an address in the same state in which the mail-order firm, a branch office, or representative is located, and when the goods ordered are taxable under the laws prevailing in the area. Most states require payment of sales tax on handling, packing, and shipping charges.

Those are the general rules. The right of a state to create its own definition of "doing business" in that state, or "establishing nexus," rankles consumers who have to pay tax on what they perceive as out-of-state orders, and businesses that have to be tax collectors for 50 states. The issue of nexus is no stranger to the Supreme Court; one energetic individual took on both Sears and Montgomery Ward over 40 years ago and lost, and other mail-order firms have done battle with state governments and lost as well.

State governments are trying to collect tax on all mail-order purchases delivered to residents of their states, calling such a tax a "use" tax (the actual sale takes place out of state, at the seller's place of business). Mail-order companies envision an accounting nightmare, and consumers stand to lose one of the benefits of shopping out-of-state: no sales tax on their purchases (unless nexus exists). The court cases being decided now are running in favor of the tax department, which means you could see changes—and start paying more—quite soon. But until the issue is resolved, keep paying sales taxes according to previously established guidelines.

DUTY

Orders from foreign firms are usually charged duty, which can't be prepaid. Duty is paid to the postal carrier who delivers your package or the Customs agent if the order is delivered by air or sea freight.

Assessment of Duty. U.S. duty is calculated on the transaction value, or actual price, of the goods being imported, on an ad valorem (percentage) or specific (per-unit) basis, and sometimes a combination of the two. Some goods—such as certified antiques, postage stamps, truffles, and original paintings—are imported duty-free. Check your local U.S. Customs office for current regulations, since rates and classifications are subject to change.

Prohibitions and Restrictions. Some goods can be imported only under certain conditions, and others are prohibited outright. You can't import narcotics, pornography, fireworks, switchblade knives, absinthe, poison, or dangerous toys. If you wish to import animals, animal products, biologicals, petroleum products, plants, or seeds, you must make prior arrangements with certain agencies for the necessary permits. And if you want to buy name-brand goods, be sure to check trademark restrictions. The manufacturers of certain goods register the trademarks with Customs, limiting the number of those items that an individual may import. Sometimes the manufacturer requires removal of the trademarked symbols or names, which is done by the Customs agent or the firm selling the goods. Goods that often fall under trademark restrictions include cameras, lenses, optics, tape recorders, perfumes, cosmetics, musical instruments, jewelry, flatware, and timepieces. Many foreign firms offer trademark-restricted goods in their catalogs, but don't inform you of U.S. regulations—find out before you buy.

Obtaining Information. If you want to know more about duty rates and classifications, import restrictions, permits, and prohibitions, request the free booklet "Rates of Duty for Popular Tourist Items" from the Office of Information and Publications, Bureau of Customs, 1301 Constitution Ave., N.W., Rm. 6303, Washington, DC 20226. Use it as a general guide only—contact your local Customs office for the latest rates. Provide a description of the goods you're ordering (materials, composition, and decoration or ornamentation), since the classification of goods is more specific than is indicated by the brochure.

If you want to import fruits, vegetables, or plants from abroad, write to Quarantines, Department of Agriculture, Federal Center Building, Hyattsville, MD 20782, and ask for an import permit application.

For more information on related matters, see "Ordering from Foreign Firms," page 587; "Paying for Goods from Foreign Firms," page 592; "Shipments from Foreign Countries," page 596; and "Deliveries from Foreign Firms," page 605.

SHIPMENTS ABROAD

Shipments to and from Canada: The U.S.–Canada Free Trade Agreement. The Free Trade Agreement (FTA) is a pact between the U.S. and Canada intended to promote trade and expand and enhance markets in both countries by removing some restrictions. The linchpin of the FTA is the mutual elimination of duties by 1998. Duties are being reduced in three ways: Some were eliminated when the FTA went into effect January 1, 1989; others are being reduced 20% a year over five years; and all others are being phased out over ten years. This tripartite formula allowed industries that were ready for the increased competition to benefit from the new policy immediately, while protecting others that might be destabilized by the rapid abatement of tariffs.

The FTA affects an enormous range of raw materials and consumer goods—from fish and computers to ferrous alloys and plywood—but only those goods that are produced in the United States or Canada are entitled to free-trade treatment. (Tariffs on products of other countries are unaffected by the FTA, which is intended to benefit the U.S.–Canadian market.) The pact permits restrictions and quotas on products of certain industries and includes provisions dealing with "dumping" of goods at below-market prices and special considerations for government-subsidized products of both countries.

Despite the scope of the Free Trade Agreement, it's worth noting that prior to its enactment, more than 75% of the goods traded between the United States and Canada were exempt from tariffs. It may take a number of years for the effects of economies of scale and specialization to be discerned in the marketplace. Since only domestically produced goods are covered and phase-in periods may apply, mail-order shoppers must consult the nearest office of U.S. Customs or the Customs and Excise Office in Canada for rates and current information.

Shipments to APO/FPO Addresses. Most of the firms listed in this book will send goods to APO and FPO addresses. Finding out which is easy: Look for the stars and stripes next to the maple leaf on the line with the dollar signs and phone symbol.

Mail-order firms generally ship orders via the USPS's PAL (parcel airlift) to the military mail dispatch center, where they are shipped overseas via SAM (space available mail). The size restrictions are 60" in combined girth and length, and 30 pounds in weight. Firms sometimes charge additional handling fees for shipping to APO/FPO addresses, so read the catalog carefully and write for a shipping estimate before ordering if instructions aren't clear. Please note that neither UPS nor Federal Express makes APO/FPO deliveries, and that the USPS does not offer C.O.D. service to APO/FPO addresses.

Shipments Worldwide. Many of the companies that ship to Canada and U.S. military personnel also ship orders worldwide. (This is noted in the "Special Factors" section at the end of each listing.) If you're planning to have goods delivered to Japan, Israel, Europe, or any other address not in the United States or Canada, see the catalog (if available) for details on the firm's shipping policy. If it's not clear, or if the firm sells on a price-quote basis, write or call the company before sending any funds and request a shipping quote. Since the employees of firms listed in this book are unlikely to be familiar with import restrictions and duty rates in other countries, check before placing your order to avoid unpleasant surprises. Most firms request payment in U.S. funds; this may be most easily handled by charging your purchase to your credit card, but before ordering check with your issuing bank for rates and charges that may apply to converting funds. Note that "The Complete Guide to Buying by Mail" has been compiled for readers who are having goods delivered to U.S. addresses and will not apply in all parts to non-U.S. deliveries.

RECEIVING YOUR ORDER

What do you do when your order arrives? And if it doesn't? The following section details your basic rights and responsibilities:

ACCEPTING DELIVERIES

When the postal or UPS carrier or trucker delivers your order, inspect the carton, bag, or crate before signing for it. If you're having someone else accept the package, ask that person to do the same. If the packaging is extensively damaged, you can refuse to sign for or accept the goods. See "Returns," in this section, for caveats on this practice.

If the box, bag, or carton is in good condition, accept it and open it as soon as possible. Unpack the goods carefully, putting aside the packing materials and any inserts until you've examined the contents. Most firms include a copy of your order form or a computerized invoice itemizing the order. If it's a printout or there's no invoice at all, get your copy of the order and check to make sure you got what you requested. Check the outside of the box, since some firms insert the invoice with the packing slip in a plastic envelope affixed to the top or side of the carton.

Check your order for the following: damaged goods, short shipments, unauthorized substitutions, wrong sizes, colors, styles, or models; warranty forms if the products carry manufacturers' warranties; missing parts; and instruction sheets if a product requires assembly. Make sure ensembles are complete—that scarves, belts, hats, vests, ties, ascots, and other components have been included. Test electronic goods as soon as possible to make sure they function properly, and do not fill out the warranty card until you've tried the product and are satisfied that it's not defective. (Check the product itself for signs that it's been used. If you've been sold a demonstration model, reconditioned unit, or someone else's return as new and unused goods, you should seriously consider returning it—or negotiating a lower price.) Try on clothing and shoes to make sure they fit. Check printed, engraved, or monogrammed goods for accuracy. If you decide to return a product, see "Returns" for more information.

If the goods are damaged, contact the seller immediately. Describe the condition of the goods and what you'd like done to correct the problem. If the firm asks you to file a complaint with the delivery service, request shipping information from the seller (the seller's shipping address, day of shipment, seller's account number, applicable shipment codes, and other relevant data). File the complaint with the delivery service, documenting your claim with photographs, if it seems necessary, and send a copy of the complaint to the seller. If you charged the purchase on a card with an extended warranty program, contact the issuer about the matter. Be persistent but reasonable.

If you receive a short shipment (one or more items you ordered are not included in the package), the firm may have inserted a notice that the item is being shipped separately or an option notice if it's out of stock. (See "The Option Notice," page 604, for more information.) Some companies don't back order, and will include a refund check with the order or under separate cover when a product is out of stock, or bill your account with the adjusted total if you used a credit card. If your shipment is short and there's no explanation, first check the catalog from which you ordered to see whether that item is shipped from the manufacturer or shipped separately by the firm. If there's no mention of special shipping conditions or delays in shipment in the catalog, contact the firm immediately.

DELAYED SHIPMENTS

What constitutes a real delay in receiving an order? What should you expect from the company if it has to delay shipping your order? The following section details your basic rights and responsibilities in this event:

The FTC Mail or Telephone Order Rule. The Federal Trade Commission's "Mail or Telephone Order Rule" addresses one of the biggest problems in the mail-order industry: late delivery. Mail-order shoppers should understand principles of the Rule, know what types of transactions are exempt from its protection, and understand what actions they're obliged to take to ensure protection under the regulations.

Please note: When a state or county has enacted laws similar in purpose to the functions of the FTC Mail or Telephone Order Rule, the law that gives the consumer the most protection takes precedence.

General terms of the Rule: The Rule specifies that a firm, or "seller," must ship goods within 30 days of receipt of a properly completed order, unless the firm asks for more time in its catalog, advertisement, or promotional literature. The operative term here is "ship"—the firm does not have to have delivered the goods within 30 days under the terms of the Rule. And it must have received a properly completed order: Your check or money order must be good, your credit must be good if you're charging the order, and the firm must have all the information necessary to process the order. The 30-day clock begins ticking when the firm gets your check or money order made out in the proper amount, but stops if it's dishonored. If you're paying with a credit card, it begins when the firm receives valid account data.

If your check or money order is insufficient to cover the order total or is dishonored by the bank, if your credit card payment is refused authorization, or if you neglect to include data necessary to the processing of your order (which could include size or color information, your address, etc.), the 30-day clock will not start until the problems are remedied—the firm receives complete payment, payment is honored by the bank, the credit card purchase is authorized, or you supply the missing data.

Exceptions to the Rule: The 30-day limit applies only when a firm does not ask you to allow more time for shipment. (Most qualifiers request extra time for delivery, which only confuses the issue.) Certain kinds of goods and purchases are not protected by the Rule. These include: seeds and growing plants; C.O.D. orders; purchases made under negative-option plans (such as book and record clubs); and magazine subscriptions and other "serial deliveries," except for the first issue. Genuinely "free" items don't fall under the Rule, but catalogs for which payment or compensation is requested are protected.

Assuming your order is covered under the Rule, the firm from which you're ordering must follow a specific procedure if it's unable to ship your order within 30 days. You must respond under the terms of the Rule if you want to retain all of your rights. Read on.

The Option Notice: If a firm is unable to ship within 30 days of receiving your properly completed order, or by the deadline it's given in its literature, it must send you an option notice. An option notice written in compliance with the Rule will tell you that there is a delay in shipping the item and may include a revised shipping date. If it does, and that date is up to 30 days later than the original deadline (either 30 days or a date specified by the firm), it should offer you the option of consenting to the delay or canceling the order and receiving a refund. The option notice must also state that lack of response on your part is implied consent to the delay. If you decide to cancel the order, the firm must receive the cancellation before it ships the order.

If the new shipping deadline is over 30 days after the original date, or the firm can't provide a revised shipping date, the option notice must say so. The notice should also state that your order will be automatically canceled unless the firm receives consent to the delay from you within 30 days of the original shipping date, and unless it's able to ship the order within 30 days after the original deadline and has not received an order cancellation from you as of the time of shipping.

The firm is required to send notices by first-class mail and to provide you with a cost-free means of response—a prepaid business-reply envelope or postcard. Accepting collect calls or cancellations over WATS lines is acceptable as long as the operators are trained to take them. If you want to cancel an order, get the response back to the firm as quickly as possible after you receive the option notice. Photocopy the card, form, or letter, and send it "return receipt requested" if you want absolute proof of the date it was received. (If the firm ships your order the day after it received your cancellation, and you can prove it, you have the right to refuse delivery, have the order returned to the firm at its expense, and claim a prompt refund or credit.)

The renewed option notice: When a firm is unable to meet its revised shipping deadline, it must send you a renewed option notice in advance of the revised deadline. Unlike the first notice, second and subsequent notices must state that if you don't agree in writing to a new shipping date or indefinite delay, the order will be canceled. And the consent to a second delay must be received before the first delay period ends, or the order must be canceled, according to the Rule.

If you consent to an indefinite delay, you retain the right to cancel the order at any time before the goods are shipped. And the firm itself may cancel the order if it's unable to ship the goods within the delay period, and must cancel the order under a variety of circumstances.

The Rule and refunds: Under the terms of the Rule, when you or the firm cancel the order, you're entitled to a prompt refund. If your order was prepaid, the firm must send you a refund check or money order by first-class mail within seven working days after the cancellation. If you paid with a debit card, inform the firm when you cancel or when it notifies you that it's canceling the order that it must treat the payment as if it were cash, a check, or a money order, and reimburse your account within seven working days or send you a refund check. If you used a credit card, the Rule states that refunds must be made within one billing cycle. (We assume that these "refunds" are credits to your account, which will void the charge made for the goods.) The firm is not permitted to substitute credit vouchers for its own goods instead of making a reimbursement.

DELIVERIES FROM FOREIGN FIRMS

The general guidelines outlined in "Accepting Deliveries," page 602, apply to deliveries from foreign firms. Please note that most FTC regulations do not apply to shipments from non-U.S. firms.

The delivery procedure for foreign orders is determined by the shipping method the firm has used. For a complete discussion of carriers, see "Shipments from Foreign Countries," page 596.

You usually pay duty, or Customs charges, when you receive your order. The amount you pay is based on the value, type, and origin of the goods. See "Duty," page 599, for more information.

Most orders from foreign firms are mailable and are delivered by your postal carrier. Before your order reaches you, it's sent through Customs. Orders processed with the least delay are those with goods designated as duty-free because they qualify under certain provisions of Customs laws, or those worth under $50 that are marked "unsolicited gift." Some firms mark orders as gifts to save you money; this is not in keeping with Customs regulations, unless the order originates outside the United States. Please don't ask a firm to send your order as an unsolicited gift, which can create problems.

The clearance procedure on dutiable goods includes entry, inspection, valuation, appraisal, and "liquidation," another term for determination of duty. Provided the necessary permits and entry papers have been filed with U.S. Customs and shipment of the goods violates no regulations, the Customs department will attach an entry form listing a tariff item number, rate of duty, and the amount of duty owed on the goods to the package. It will be sent to the post office and delivered to you by your postal carrier. He or she will collect the amount of duty and a "Customs Clearance and Delivery Fee," currently $3.25, as "postage due." Some foreign firms are annoyed by this term, since customers assume that the charge is for insufficient postage and complain to the company. Postal authorities have told us that the handling fee is not charged unless the order is assessed duty. But even if your order has dutiable goods, you may not have to pay any Customs charges—a high proportion of small orders are delivered fee-free.

If your parcel is held at the post office and you don't collect it within 30 days, it will be returned to the firm. If you disagree with the duty charge, you can challenge it within 90 days of receiving the order by sending the yellow copy of the mail-entry form to the Customs office named on the form, along with a statement explaining your reasons for contesting the charge.

DELAYED SHIPMENTS FROM FOREIGN FIRMS

You can reasonably expect your goods to arrive within six to eight weeks, provided you sent the order by air, are having it shipped by airmail or air freight, didn't order custom-made goods, and paid the correct amount—and as long as the country concerned is not at war. If you sent the order via surface mail and/or are having the goods shipped that way, are having any custom work done, or the country is in turmoil, don't hold your breath. We've been told that the delay for orders sent by surface mail averages three to six months.

Transactions with foreign firms generally come under the jurisdiction of international law. If your order doesn't arrive, write to the company, including photocopies of your order and proof of payment, and send the letter by registered airmail. Allow at least one month for a response, then try again. Put a stop on your check, or a tracer and a stop on a money order, if you paid with one. If the check or money order has been cashed, go to the post office and fill out an "International Inquiry" form. It will be sent to the postal service in the country concerned, which should investigate the matter. Notify the firm of your actions, and keep copies of all correspondence related to the affair, since you may need them at a later date.

If you paid with a credit card and you have not received your order, follow the querying procedure outlined above. If you don't hear from the company, but find that your credit card has been charged for the order, dispute the charge immediately under the provisions of the Fair Credit Billing Act. You may do this only if you have not received the goods at all and if the bank issuing the credit card is a U.S. bank. For more information, see "The Fair Credit Billing Act," page 617.

For more information on resolving problems with foreign companies, see "Complaints About Foreign Firms," page 618.

RETURNS, GUARANTEES, AND WARRANTIES

Your right to return goods is determined by the policy of the firm, the problem with the order, the conditions under which you make the return, and state and federal laws. See "Return Policies" and "Accepting Deliveries" for general information. Product warranties, whether written or implied, apply to many goods bought by mail. "Guarantees and Warranties," following, provides a comprehensive discussion of all types of warranties.

RETURNS

Return policies are often extensions of a firm's pledge of satisfaction. The policy determines how quickly you must return the product after receipt (if there's a time limit), acceptable causes for return, and what the firm will do to remedy the problem. Some companies will take anything back, but most exclude custom-made goods, personalized items, special orders, intimate apparel, bathing suits, and hats. Some also exempt sale items. Even a no-frills policy usually makes provisions for exchanges when the firm has erred or if the product is defective. It's important to read "Implied Warranties" for information on laws concerning product performance and rights you may have that are not stated in the catalog.

Obtaining Authorization. Before returning a product for any reason, check the inserts that may have been packed with the order, as well as the catalog, for instructions on return procedures. If there are no instructions, contact the firm for authorization to return the item. This is easiest handled by phone; you'll usually receive an "RMA," or authorization number, which you must use on all correspondence concerning that return, and on the package when you send it back. The reverse side of the statement that was enclosed with your order may be printed as a return form; if so, complete it. If it's not, write a letter: State the reason for the return, the item price and order number, date of delivery, and what you'd like done. Depending on the firm's policy, you may request repairs or replacement of the item, an exchange, a refund check, credit to your charge account, or store credit for future purchases from the firm. Keep a photocopy of the letter for your files, or notes of your phone conversation.

Restocking Fees. Some firms impose a charge on returned goods, to offset the labor and incidental costs of returning the item to inventory. Restocking fees, usually 10% to 15% of the price of the item, are most commonly charged by firms selling furniture, appliances, and electronics. Restocking fees are not usually charged when you're returning defective goods, or if the item was shipped incorrectly.

Sending the Item. Follow the mailing procedure outlined in the catalog, order insert, or authorization notice from the firm. When you send the goods back, include the return form or a dated letter with your name and address, the order number, authorization number or name of the person approving the return (if applicable), and a statement of what you want—repair, exchange, refund, or credit. Keep file copies of your letter and invoices.

Pack the item in the original box and padding materials if requested, and insure it for the full value. Allow the firm at least 30 days to process the return or respond before writing or calling again, unless you were promised a more speedy resolution.

Refunds and Credits. If you want your charge account credited for the return, provide the relevant data. Not every firm will issue a refund check or credit your account; some offer replacement or repair of the product, an exchange, or catalog credit only.

Exchanges. If you're exchanging the product for something entirely different, state the catalog code number, size, color, price, unit, etc. of the item you want in the letter you enclose with the return or on the authorization form.

Postage Reimbursement. Some firms send UPS to pick up a return free, or accept returns sent postage-collect, or will reimburse you for the shipping and insurance charges on a return. Lots will not. Businesses are not required by federal law to refund the cost of returning goods, even when the return is a result of the firm's error. State and local laws, however, may make provisions for this; check to see whether they do.

GUARANTEES AND WARRANTIES

Although the terms "guarantee" and "warranty" are virtually synonymous, they're distinguished here for the sake of clarity. In this book, a "guarantee" is the general pledge of satisfaction or service a firm offers on the sales it makes. Guarantees and related matters are discussed in "Return Policies," "Returns," and "Implied Warranties." A "warranty" is used to mean the written policy covering the performance of a particular product. Both guarantees and warranties are free; paid policies (including "extended warranties") are service contracts.

Warranties are regulated by state and federal law. Understanding policy terms will help you shop for the best product/warranty value; knowing your rights may mean the difference between paying for repairs or a replacement and having the firm or manufacturer do it.

The Magnuson-Moss Warranty—Federal Trade Commission Improvement Act. Also known as the Warranty Act, this 1975 law regulates warranties that are in print. Oral "warranties"—the salesperson's assurance of product performance and pledge of satisfaction—are worthless unless they're in writing.

The Warranty Act requires that warranties be written in "simple and readily understood language" that states all terms and conditions. If the product costs more than $15, a copy of the warranty must be available before purchase. In a store, it should be posted on or near the product, or filed in a catalog of warranties kept on the premises with a notice posted concerning its location. Mail-order firms comply with the law by making copies of warranties available upon request.

The Warranty Act requires the warrantor to use the term "full" or "limited" in describing the policy. A single product can have several warranties covering different parts, and each can be labeled separately as "full" or "limited." For example, a TV set may have a full one-year policy on the set and a limited 90-day policy on the picture tube. Generally speaking, the conditions stated here apply to warranties on goods costing over $15.

Full warranties provide for repair or replacement of the product at no cost to you, including the removal and reinstallation of the item, if necessary. The warranty may be limited to a certain length of time, and must state the period of coverage. Full warranties can't be limited to the original purchaser—the warrantor must honor the policy for the full term even if the item has changed hands. Implied warranties (see page 610) may not be limited in duration by the terms of the full warranty, and in some states may last up to four years.

The item should be repaired within a "reasonable" length of time after you've notified the firm of the problem. If, after a "reasonable" number of attempts to repair, the product is still not functioning properly, you may invoke the "lemon provision." This entitles you to a replacement or refund for the product.

Registering your product with the warrantor under a full warranty is voluntary, a fact that must be stated clearly in the terms. You can send the registration card to the firm, but this is at your discretion and not necessary to maintain the protection of the warranty.

Limited warranties provide less coverage than full warranties. Under them, you can be required to remove, transport, and reinstall a product; to pay for labor if repairs are made; and to return the warranty card to the firm in order to validate the policy. The warrantor can also limit the warranty to the original purchaser and give you prorated refunds or credits for the product. (The "lemon provision" doesn't apply to a limited warranty.)

Warrantors may also limit implied warranties (see the following section) to the length of time their policies run, but no less. If they limit the implied-warranty time, they must also state: "Some states do not allow limitations on how long an implied warranty lasts, so the above limitation may not apply to you." The warrantor may not limit the extent of protection you have under implied warranties, however.

Other provisions of the Warranty Act include the following:

- If you complain within the warranty period, the firm must act to remedy the problem within the terms of the warranty.
- If a written warranty is provided with the product, the warrantor can't exclude it from protection under implied warranties.
- A warrantor can exclude or limit consequential damages (see the following section) from coverage under both full and limited policies as long as the warranty states: "Some states do not allow the exclusion or limitation of incidental or consequential damages, so the above limitation or exclusion may not apply to you."
- All warranties must include information on whom to contact, where to bring or mail the product, and the name, address, or toll-free phone number of the warrantor.
- All warranties, full and limited, must state: "This warranty gives you specific legal rights, and you may have other rights that vary from state to state."

Implied Warranties. Implied warranties are state laws that offer protection against major hidden defects in products. Every state has these laws, which cover every sale unless the seller states that no warranties or guarantees are offered—that goods are sold "as is." But if a particular product sold by a firm with a no-guarantee policy carries a written warranty, the implied warranty of the state is also valid on that item. The terms of implied warranties differ from state to state, but many have similar sorts of provisions.

The warranty of merchantability is a common implied warranty. It means that the product must function properly for conventional use—a freezer must freeze, a knife must cut, etc. If the product does not function properly and your state has a warranty of merchantability, you're probably entitled to a refund for that item.

The warranty of fitness for a particular purpose covers cases in which the seller cites or recommends special uses for the product. For example, if a seller says that a coat is "all-weather," it should offer protection in rain and snow. If it claims that a glue will "bond any two materials together," the glue should be able to do that. When a salesperson makes these assurances, check the printed product information to verify the recommendation or call the manufacturer. While the salesperson may have a direct incentive—commissions—to inveigle you into buying a product, the manufacturer should be more committed to your satisfaction and return business.

Consequential Damages. Incidental or consequential damages occur when a product malfunction causes damage to or loss of other property. The FTC uses the example of an engine block cracking when the antifreeze is faulty. Less extreme is the food spoilage caused by a refrigerator breakdown or the damage resulting from a leaky waterbed mattress.

Written warranties usually entitle you to consequential damages, but warrantors are allowed to exempt this coverage under both full and limited warranties. If the warrantor excludes consequential damages from coverage, the warranty must state: "Some states do not allow exclusion or limitation of incidental or consequential damages, so the above limitation or exclusion may not apply to you."

Provisions for consequential damages entitle you to compensation for the property damage or loss, as well as repair or replacement of the defective product. In the engine block example, the exemption of damages must be considered as a definite disadvantage when evaluating the product/warranty value.

Evaluating Warranties. Appraise the written warranty as thoroughly as you do the product's other features before you buy. In reading the warranty, bear in mind past experiences with products and warranty service from that manufacturer or seller, experiences with similar products, and your actual needs. Don't rush to buy the first model of a new product if you can wait. Later models are sure to be cheaper and better—just consider VCRs, CD players, and computers.

In evaluating a warranty, ask yourself the following questions:

- Is the warranty full or limited?
- Does it cover the whole product, or specific parts?
- How long is the warranty period?
- Do you contact the manufacturer, seller, or a service center for repairs?
- Will you have to remove, deliver, and reinstall the product yourself?
- Do you have to have repairs done by an authorized service center or representative? If so, how close is the nearest facility?
- Will the warrantor provide a temporary replacement for use while your product is being serviced?
- Are consequential damages excluded? If the product turns out to be defective, could the consequential damages result in a significant loss?
- If reimbursement is offered on a pro-rata basis, is it computed on a time, use, or price schedule?
- Do you have the choice of a refund or replacement if the item can't be repaired?

Envision a worst-case scenario in which the product breaks down or malfunctions completely. What expenses could be incurred in consequential damages, supplying a substitute product or service, transporting the product to the service center or seller, and repair bills? Will returning the product be troublesome, and living without it while it's being repaired inconvenient? Your answers determine the value the warranty has for you. Consider that quotient along with the price and features of the product when comparison shopping to find your best buy.

Complying with Warranty Terms. Understanding and fulfilling the conditions of a warranty should be simple, but we've outlined a few tips that may make it easier:

- Read the warranty card as requested.
- Read the instructions or operations manual before using the product, and follow directions for use.
- Keep the warranty and dated receipt or proof of payment in a designated place.
- If the manufacturer offers a rebate on the product that requires sending the proof of payment, photocopy the receipt and keep the copy with the warranty.
- Abuse, neglect, and mishandling usually void the warranty. Other practices that may invalidate the policy include improper installation, repair or service by an unauthorized person or agency, use of the product on the wrong voltage, and commercial use. If others

will be using the product, be sure they know how to operate it.

- Perform routine maintenance (cleaning, oiling, dusting, replacement of worn components, etc.) as required by the manual, but don't attempt repairs or maintenance that isn't required or permitted in the warranty or guide.

If you have a question about maintenance or use, contact the manufacturer or service center. If you void the warranty by violating its terms, you'll probably have to absorb the costs of repairs or replacement.

Obtaining Service. If the product breaks down or malfunctions, you'll find that you can expedite resolution if you follow these guidelines:

- Read the operating manual or instructions. The problem may be covered in a troubleshooting section, or you may find that you expected the product to do something for which it wasn't designed.
- Contact the warrantor, whose name, address, and/or phone number appear on the warranty, unless the seller offers service under warranty.
- Call, write, or visit as appropriate. State the nature of the problem, the date it occurred, and whether you want a repair, replacement, refund, and/or consequential damages. Bring a copy of the warranty and proof of payment when you visit, and include copies if you write. (Remember that your rights in respect to the nature and extent of compensation depend upon the terms of the warranty and laws prevailing in your area.)
- If you leave the product for repairs or have it picked up, get a signed receipt that includes the date on which it should be ready, an estimate of the bill if you have to pay for repairs, and the serial number of the product, if one is given.
- If you send the product, insure it for the full value. Include a letter describing the problem, the date on which it occurred, and how you'd like it resolved.
- After a call or visit, the FTC recommends sending a follow-up letter reiterating the conversation. Keep a photocopy, and send it by certified mail to the person or agency with which you spoke.
- Keep a log of all actions you take in having the warranty honored, including dates on which actions, visits, and calls were made, and keep a record of the expenses you incur in the process.
- If you've written to the seller or manufacturer concerning the problem and received no response after three to four weeks, write again. Include a photocopy of the first letter, ask for an answer within four weeks, and send the second letter by certified mail (keep a photocopy). Direct the letter to the head of customer rela-

tions or the warranty department, unless you've been dealing with an individual.

- If you've written to the manufacturer, it may help to contact the seller (or vice versa). A reputable firm doesn't want to merchandise through a seller who won't maintain good customer relations, and a responsible seller knows that marketing shoddy goods is bad for business. Bilateral appeals should be made after you've given the responsible party an opportunity to resolve the problem.

- If you have repairs done, ask to see the product demonstrated before you accept it, especially if you're paying for repairs. If there are indications that the problem may recur (e.g., it exhibits the same "symptoms" it had before it broke or malfunctioned), tell the service representative—it may be due to something that wasn't noticed during the repair.

- If you're paying for repairs, ask for a guarantee on parts and/or labor so you won't face another bill if the product breaks down shortly after you begin using it again.

- If the product keeps malfunctioning after it's repaired and it's under full warranty, you can probably get a replacement or refund under the "lemon provision." Write to the manufacturer or seller, provide a history of the problems and repairs, plus a copy of the warranty, and ask for a replacement or refund. If the warranty is limited, the terms may entitle you to a replacement or refund. Write to the manufacturer or seller with the product history and a copy of the warranty, and ask for a new product or compensation.

- Explore your rights under your state's implied-warranty and consequential-damages laws. They may offer you protections not given in the product warranty.

- If you've been injured by a malfunctioning product, contact an attorney.

- If, after acting in good faith and allowing the manufacturer or seller time to resolve the problem, you are still dissatisfied, contact your local consumer-protection agency for advice.

You may also report problems to other agencies and organizations. For more information, see "Obtaining Help," following.

COMPLAINTS

COMPLAINT PROCEDURES

A formal complaint is justified if you've notified the firm of a problem and asked for resolution, following procedures outlined in the catalog, warranty, or this guide, with unsatisfactory results. Give the firm one last chance to remedy the situation before asking for help from outside agencies. If your problem concerns nondelivery or dissatisfaction with a product and you paid with a credit card, you may be able to withhold payment or ask for a chargeback under the Fair Credit Billing Act. See "The Federal Trade Commission," following, for more information.

The Complaint Letter. State your complaint clearly and concisely with a history of the problem and all the appropriate documentation: photocopies of previous letters, proof of payment, the warranty, repair receipts, etc. Don't send original documents—use photocopies and keep the originals in your file. Make sure your letter includes your name and address, the order or product number or code and descriptive information about the product, and the method of payment you used. Type or print the letter, and please don't be abusive. Tell the firm exactly what you want done. Give a deadline of 30 days for a reply or resolution, and note that if you don't receive a response by that time, you'll report the firm to the U.S. Postal Service, Better Business Bureau, Direct Marketing Association, Federal Trade Commission, or other appropriate agency. (See "Obtaining Help," following, for information.)

If the firm doesn't acknowledge the request or you're not satisfied by the response, take action.

OBTAINING HELP

There are several agencies and organizations that can help you with different types of problems. Some undertake investigations on a case-by-case basis, and others compile files on firms and act when the volume of complaints reaches a certain level.

When you seek help, provide a copy of your final complaint letter to the firm, as well as the documentation described in "The Complaint Letter."

Consumer Action Panels (CAPs). CAPs are third-party dispute resolution programs established by the industries they represent. They investigate consumer complaints, provide service information to consumers, and give their members suggestions on improving service to consumers.

MACAP helps with problems concerning major appliances. Write to Major Appliance Consumer Action Panel, 20 N. Wacker Dr., Chicago, IL 60606, or call 800-621-0477 for information.

Better Business Bureaus (BBBs). Better Business Bureaus are self-regulatory agencies, funded by businesses and professional firms, that monitor advertising and selling practices, maintain files on firms, help resolve consumer complaints, and disseminate service information to consumers. BBBs also perform the vital service of responding to inquiries about a firm's selling history, although they can't make recommendations. Most BBBs have mediation and arbitration programs, and are empowered to make awards (binding arbitration).

Whether you want to check a firm's record before ordering or file a complaint, you must contact the BBB nearest the company, not the office in your area. You can obtain a directory of BBB offices by sending your request and a SASE to the Council of Better Business Bureaus, Inc., 4200 Wilson Blvd., Suite 800, Arlington, VA 22203. Write to the appropriate office, and ask for a "consumer complaint" or "consumer inquiry" form, depending on your purpose.

Direct Marketing Association (DMA). The DMA is the largest and oldest trade organization of direct marketers and mail-order companies in existence. Over half of its members are non-U.S. firms; this gives it some clout in dealing with problematical foreign orders placed with member firms.

The DMA's Mail Order Action Line (MOAL) helps to resolve nondelivery problems with any direct-marketing firm, not just members. Upon receiving your written complaint, the DMA contacts the firm, attempts to resolve the problem, notifies you that it's involved, and asks you to allow 30 days for the firm to solve or act on the problem. To get help, send a copy of your complaint letter and documentation to Mail Order Action Line, DMA, 1101 17th St. NW, Washington, DC 20036.

Consumers may also use the DMA's "Telephone Preference Service" and "Mail Preference Service" to reduce the number of solicitation calls and/or mailings they receive. The DMA will keep your name on a list for five years; marketers who want to avoid mailing or calling unreceptive consumers can consult the list before launching a sales campaign. To reduce mail, request an "MPS" form from Mail Preference Service, Direct Marketing Association, P.O. Box 9008, Farmingdale, NY 11735-9008. To reduce the number of solicitation calls you receive, request a "TPS" form from Telephone Preference Service, Direct Marketing Association, P.O. Box 9014, Farmingdale, NY 11735-9014. If, after a few months, you're still receiving calls and/or mail, try dealing with the marketer directly.

The Federal Trade Commission (FTC). The FTC is a law-enforcement agency that protects the public against anticompetitive, unfair, and deceptive business practices. While it doesn't act on "individual" complaints, it does use your complaint letters to build files on firms. When the volume or nature of problems indicates an investigation is justified, the FTC will act. Several levels of action are possible, including court injunctions and fines of up to $10,000 for each day the violation is occurring. Report deviations from FTC regulations; your letter may be the one that prompts an investigation.

The Fair Credit Billing Act (FCBA), passed in 1975 under the FTC's Consumer Credit Protection Act, offers mail-order shoppers who use credit cards as payment some real leverage if they have a problem with nondelivery. The Act established a settlement procedure for billing errors that include, among other discrepancies, charges for goods or services not accepted or not delivered as agreed. The procedure works as follows:

- You must write to the creditor (phoning will not trigger FCBA protection) at the "billing error" address given on the bill.
- The letter must include your name and account number, the dollar amount of the error, and a statement of why you believe the error exists.
- The letter must be received by the creditor within 60 days after the first bill with the error was mailed to you. The FTC recommends sending it by certified mail, return receipt requested.
- The creditor has to acknowledge your letter, in writing, within 30 days of receipt, unless the problem is resolved within that time.
- You do not have to pay the disputed amount, the related portion of the minimum payment, or the related finance charges while it's being disputed.
- If an error is found, the creditor must write to you, explaining the correction. The disputed amount must be credited to your account and related finance charges must be removed. If the creditor finds that you owe part of the amount, it must be explained in writing.
- If the creditor finds that the bill is correct, the reasons must be explained in writing and the amount owed stated. You will be liable for finance charges accrued during the dispute and missed minimum payments.
- You may continue to dispute at this point, but only if your state's laws give you the right to take action against the seller rather than the creditor. Write to the creditor within ten days of receiving the justification of the charge and state that you still refuse to pay the disputed amount. If you continue to challenge, contact your local consumer protection agency, since the creditor can begin collection proceedings against you and the agency may be able to recommend other means of handling the problem that don't jeopardize your credit rating.

Disputes over the quality of goods or services are covered under the FCBA if state law permits you to withhold payment from a seller. This applies to credit-card purchases over $50 that are made in your home state or within 100 miles of your mailing address. (The limits do not apply if the seller is also the card issuer, as is often the case with department stores.) Contact your local consumer protection agency for advice before taking action.

The United States Postal Service (USPS). The USPS takes action on complaints and resolves about 85% of the problems. This may be because, under provisions of the U.S. Code, it can go to court, get a restraining order, and withhold mail delivery to a company. (This is a very serious action and is never undertaken simply at a private citizen's request.) A number of readers have reported that the USPS acts more swiftly, with better results, than do any of the other agencies we've cited here. You can send a copy of your final complaint letter and documentation to the Chief Postal Inspector, U.S. Postal Service, Washington, DC 20260—but readers have told us that writing directly to the Postmaster of the post office nearest the firm is what does the trick.

Bankruptcy Courts. Bankruptcy courts may offer information, if no actual compensation, on errant orders and refunds. If you've written to the company and received no response and its phone has been disconnected, contact the U.S. Bankruptcy Court nearest the firm. Tell the clerk why you're calling, and ask whether the company has filed for reorganization under Chapter 11. If it has, get the case number and information on filing a claim. Chapter 11 protects a business against the claims of its creditors; all you can do is file as one of them, and hope. As a customer, your claim comes after those of the firm's suppliers, utilities, banks, etc. The "take a ticket" approach is no guarantee that you'll get anything back, but if it's your only shot, take the trouble to file.

COMPLAINTS ABOUT FOREIGN FIRMS

For general information on dealing with complaints about foreign firms, see "Delayed Shipments from Foreign Firms," page 605.

The DMA may be able to undertake an investigation on your behalf. See page 616 for more information on the organization and its address.

The Council of Better Business Bureaus has affiliates in Canada, Mexico, Israel, and Venezuela. If the firm is located in any of those countries, write to the Council for the address of the office nearest the company, and contact that office with the complaint. See page 616 for more information and the Council's address.

The foreign trade council representing the firm's country may be able to provide information that could prove helpful. Contact the council and briefly describe your problem. Ask whether the organization can supply the name of a regulatory agency or trade organization in that country that might be of help. The councils have offices in New York City, and directory assistance can provide you with their phone numbers.

We'll try to help resolve problems with firms listed in this book. See "Feedback," following, for more information.

FEEDBACK

Your suggestions, complaints, and comments help to shape each edition of *The Wholesale-by-Mail Catalog*®. When you write, please use the guidelines that follow.

Firms: If you'd like your company considered for inclusion in the next edition of WBMC, have your marketing director send me a copy of your current catalog or literature with background information. Firms are listed at my discretion and must meet the established criteria to qualify for inclusion.

Consumers: If you're writing a letter of complaint, please read the sections of "The Complete Guide to Buying by Mail" that may apply to your problem, and try to work it out yourself. If you can't remedy the situation on your own, write to me, and please include:

- a brief history of the transaction
- copies (not originals) of all letters and documents related to the problem
- a list of the dates on which events occurred, if applicable (the date a phone order was placed, goods were received, account charged, etc.)
- a description of what you want done (goods delivered, warranty honored, return accepted, money refunded or credited, etc.)

Include your name, address, and day phone number in your cover letter. I'll look into the matter, and while I can't guarantee resolution, I may be able to help you.

If you just want to sound off, feel free. And suggestions for the next edition of WBMC are welcomed. Send your postcard or letter to:

P. McCullough, Executive Editor
WBMC 1996
P.O. Box 150522
Brooklyn, NY 11215-0522

SIZE CHART

CLOTHING SIZES

Women's Garments

U.S.A.	6	8	10	12	14	16	18	20
Great Britain	8	10	12	14	16	18	20	22
Europe	36	38	40	42	44	46	48	50

Women's Sweaters

U.S.A.	XS	S	M	M	L	L
Great Britain	34	36	38	40	42	44
Europe	40	42	44	46	48	50

Women's Shoes

U.S.A.	5	5½	6	6½	7	7½	8	8½	9	9½	10
Great Britain	3½	4	4½	5	5½	6	6½	7	7½	8	8½
Europe	36		37		38		39		40		41

Men's Suits and Sweaters

	S	S	M	M	L	XL
U.S.A.	34	36	38	40	42	44
Great Britain	34	36	38	40	42	44
Europe	44	46	48	50	52	54

Men's Shirts

U.S.A./Great Britain	14	14½	15	15½	15¾	16	16½	17	17½	18
Europe	36	37	38	39	40	41	42	43	44	46

Men's Shoes

U.S.A.	7½	8	8½	9	9½	10	10½	11	11½	12	12½
Great Britain	6	6½	7	7½	8	8½	9	9½	10	10½	11
Europe	39½	40	40½	41	42	42½	43	44	44½	45	45½

COMPANY INDEX

PRODUCT INDEX

Editor's Note: To avoid duplication of information found elsewhere, this index has been designed as a *supplement* to other features of this book, including the organization of the company listings within chapters; the "Find It Fast" section (found right before the first company listing in most chapters); and the "See Also" cross-references at the end of each chapter. See "Using This Book," page ix, for more information.

clock parts, 53, 173, 177, 215, 216, 217, 425
closed-caption decoders, 34
clothing, auto racing, 83, 84
combine parts, 74
commercial food-preparation equipment, 382–383, 384, 387
concrete-handling equipment, 556
cookware, copper, 389
Corvair parts, 76
cruises, discount, 574
cuff links, 141
cutlery, professional, 382, 388

dance studio equipment, 518
decoupage supplies, 52, 185
dining, discount, 575
disk jockey equipment, 459
dolls, collector, 225
doors, 371, 375
dry-mounting presses, 56
drywall hardware, 546

embossing powder, 203
evergreens, seedling, 226, 232
exercise equipment, 308, 518

fabric, crewel, 331
fabric, extra-wide, 327
fat calipers, 308
feathers, 145, 180
ferret supplies, 8, 10, 11, 17
first aid kits, 525
fish supplies, freshwater and saltwater, 4, 5, 10, 11, 13, 14, 15
fish supplies, tropical, 5
flowers, dried, 174, 184
flowers, silk, 145, 174
forklifts, 560
fruit crate labels, 45
fruitcake mix, 248

garbage disposals, 33
gas engines, 552

gemstones, 425–427
gift wrap, 96, 296
go-carts and parts, 552
goat supplies, 10
grasses, 233, 238, 239
ground cover plants, 236, 239, 241
guinea pig supplies, 11, 13, 17

hamster supplies, 11, 13, 17
handbags, designer copies, 436
hat-making supplies, 145
hatboxes, 175–176
heat sinks, 543
hemostats, 543
herb plants, 225, 230, 232
hermit crabs, 13
home exchanges, 578–579
homeopathic remedies, 166, 314
horse supplies, 5, 7, 8, 12, 14, 17

ikats, 198
Indian food ingredients, 263
inline skates, 531
insoles, 538
ironing equipment, professional, 189, 206

jewelry findings, 425
jewelry, antique, 41
jewelry, diamond, 424, 429
jewelry, diamond, custom made, 385
jewelry, fashion, 427, 428
jewelry, religious, 282

labels, personalized, 294, 295–296, 297
lamp parts, 53, 177, 186, 217
lawnmower parts, 551, 562
leather balm, 5
livestock supplies, 5, 10, 12
lock sets, 546
luggage, rolling, 432
lumber, cabinet-grade, 373–374

machine shop equipment, 548
mailing and storage tubes, 66
meats, organic, 250
mechanics' cabinets, 557
Mercedes-Benz auto parts, 81
metronomes, 470, 473, 474
microscopes, 123
Middle Eastern food ingredients, 258
moisture meters, 557
mosquito netting, 142
movie memorabilia, 42, 44, 46
moving pads, 559
mushrooms, 247, 252, 254, 257
music box parts, 53, 173, 215

novelty items, 287, 568, 569, 571
nurses' uniforms, 150
nutritional supplements, 311, 312, 314, 446

old advertising reproductions, 42–43

painting supplies, house, 550, 552
park benches, 476
party supplies, 287, 568, 569, 571
pet food, 11
petites, clothing for, 153
pews, 476
phone wiring supplies, 547, 549
photostat equipment, 56
piñatas, 569–570
piezoelectric elements, 543
pillow inserts, 190, 324
pillows, leather, 330
plasma-cutting tools, 550
pond supplies, 11, 13
posters, movie, 42, 44, 46
posters, vintage, 42, 44, 46
potentiometers, 543
potpourri ingredients, 174, 184, 207, 225, 265, 273
poultry supplies, 10
printers' equipment, 488
pulpits, 476

rabbit supplies, 10, 11, 13, 17
radar detectors, 30, 31, 33
raku supplies, 53
reading glasses, 444
record-care products, 32
recording equipment, 459
reforestation supplies, 544
reptile supplies, 11, 13, 17
riding clothing, 14
rugs, sheepskin, 133, 434

salad bowls, wooden, 290
scaffolding, 556, 557
scuba-diving equipment, 517–518, 522, 530
seat-reweaving supplies, 176, 179, 217
seeds, open-pollinated, 224
sewing equipment, commercial, 189, 206
sheep supplies, 10
sheeting, 142
shoe repairs by mail, 157
shower curtains, 283, 393–397
shutters, 379
silver cloth, 203
silver, estate, 400, 401, 404, 408
ski machines, 518
skylights, 371
snorkeling gear, 528
snowboarding gear, 531
snowmobile parts, 551
soaps, 137, 313
soil test kits, 219
sphygmomanometers: *see* blood pressure gauges
stair climbers, 308
stair rods, brass, 341
stationary bicycles, 308
stencils, 215
stethoscopes, 150, 308, 450
stickers, novelty, 570
stuffed toys, 565, 568, 571
surplus goods, 288, 549, 554, 555
survivalist products, 536
suspenders, 143
sweet potato plants, 229
swimming pool supplies, 374

tailoring equipment, 189, 206
tarps, 521–522, 524, 556
tents, 521–522, 524, 525, 539
Thai food ingredients, 263
theater glasses, 123
toys, educational, 567
tractor parts, 74
trail mix, 248, 255
trailers, 556
transducers, 543
travel accessories, 582
travel advisories, State Dept., 580
travel agents, discount, 574
travel alarms, 432
travel guides, 581–582
travel newsletters, 580
travel, and medical care, 579–580
travel, consolidators, 573
travel, educational, 576–577
travel, in Europe, discount, 575–576
travel, standby, 575
travel, student, 577
travel, with disabilities, 579
treadmills, 308, 518
turntable cartridges and styli, 32
tuxedos, 134

umbrellas, 137
uniforms, 150, 151

veils, 145
ventilation equipment, 387
video duplicating, 38

weathervanes, 282
wedding invitations, 293
welding equipment, 552, 555
Western boots, 158
wheelbarrows, 233
wildflowers, 235
windows, 371
windsurfing gear, 531
wood-burning furnaces, 551
woodpile covers, 283

zippers, 189, 191, 195, 199, 202, 206,
    521–522